The Inform Designer's Manual

Graham Nelson

Fourth Edition 2001

The Inform Designer's Manual, Fourth Edition

Author: Graham Nelson
Editor: Gareth Rees
Proofreaders: Torbjörn Andersson, Toby Nelson, Andrew Plotkin
Printed edition managed by: David Cornelson

Cover: *Wing of a Roller* (watercolour and gouache on vellum, 1512), Albrecht Dürer (1471–1528)

First edition September 1994
Second expanded edition October 1995
Third edition September 1996
Web edition with minor revisions May 1997
Fourth expanded edition May 2001: Release 4/2 (July 2001)

Published by The Interactive Fiction Library (IFLibrary.Org)
P.O. Box 3304, St. Charles, Illinois 60174
Printed in the United States of America
ISBN 0-9713119-0-0

Contents

Chapter II: Introduction to Designing

Chapter III: The Model World

Chapter IV: Describing and Parsing

Chapter V: Natural Language

Chapter VI: Using the Compiler

Chapter VII: The Z-Machine

Chapter VIII: The Craft of Adventure

TABLES

INDEX

Introduction

 Inform is a system for creating adventure games, and this is the book to read about it. It translates an author's textual description into a simulated world which can be explored by readers using almost any computer, with the aid of an "interpreter" program.

Inform is a suite of software, called the "library", as well as a compiler. Without the library, it would be a major undertaking to design even the smallest game. The library has two ingredients: the "parser", which tries to make sense of the player's typed commands, and the "world model", a complex web of standard rules, such as that people can't see without a source of light. Given these, the designer only needs to describe places and items, mentioning any exceptional rules that apply. ("There is a bird here, which is a normal item except that you can't pick it up.") This manual describes Inform 6.21 (or later), with library 6/9 (or later), but earlier Inform 6 releases are similar.

Since its invention in 1993, Inform has been used to design some hundreds of works of interactive fiction, in eight languages, reviewed in periodicals ranging in specialisation from *XYZZYnews* (www.xyzzynews.com) to *The New York Times* (see Edward Rothstein's 'Connections' column for 6 April 1998). It accounts for around ten thousand postings per year to Internet newsgroups. Commercially, Inform has been used as a multimedia games prototyping tool. Academically, it has turned up in syllabuses and seminars from computer science to theoretical architecture, and appears in books such as *Cybertext: Perspectives on Ergodic Literature* (E. J. Aarseth, Johns Hopkins Press, 1997). Having started as a revival of the then-disused Infocom adventure game format, the "Z-Machine", Inform came full circle when it produced Infocom's only text game of the 1990s: 'Zork: The Undiscovered Underground', by Mike Berlyn and Marc Blank.

Nevertheless, Inform is not the only system available, and the intending game designer should shop around. This author at least has long admired the elegance of Mike Roberts's Text Adventure Development System (TADS).

. . . . .

In trying to be both a tutorial and reference work, this book aims itself in style halfway between the two extremes of manual, Tedium and Gnawfinger's *Elements of Batch Processing in COBOL-66*, third edition, and Mr Blobby's *Blobby Book of Computer Fun*. (This makes some sections both leaden *and* patronising.) Diversionary or seldom-needed passages are marked with a warning triangle △ or two. Examples of program are set in typewriter font.

I

Mundane or irrelevant passages in longer examples are sometimes replaced with a line reading just "...". Further examples are couched instead as exercises, with answers given in §A6. Many are intended not for first readers but to help those returning for some variation on the usual rules.

Chapter I introduces the language used to describe games without doing any actual game design. The real flavour of Inform begins in Chapter II, so that readers may want to begin there, turning back to Chapter I only as needed. Equally, the essential material designers need is mostly done by halfway through Chapter IV, so the book is not as epic as it looks.

One way to get a feeling for Inform is to design a simple game and to add an example of each new feature as it turns up. This book does just that with an eleven-location short story of 1930s archaeology, called 'Ruins', taking it from opening lines in §4 to a completed work with a step-by-step solution by the end of §23. Other example games for Inform include 'Advent', 'Adventureland', 'Balances', 'Toyshop' and 'Museum of Inform'.

· · · · ·

The Alexandrian Library of the interactive fiction world is an anonymous FTP site at the German National Research Centre for Computer Science, where Volker Blasius and David Kinder maintain the archive:

```
ftp://ftp.gmd.de/if-archive/
```

Its unrivalled collection of early and modern interactive fiction (IF), including two dozen rival design systems, makes `ftp.gmd.de` the essential port of call for the IF tourist.† Also archived are "library extensions" and translations of Inform, and the source code of around fifty Inform-written games. Inform's home on the World Wide Web, which includes Gareth Rees's 'Alice Through the Looking-Glass' tutorial, is located at:

```
http://www.gnelson.demon.co.uk/inform.html
```

Here you can find a PDF ("Acrobat") copy of this book; *The Inform Technical Manual,* a dry account of internal workings for the benefit of those working on the compiler; and *The Z-Machine Standards Document,* which minutely defines the run-time format.

· · · · ·

---

† Stop press: as this book goes to the printers, the archive is in the early stages of migrating to `ftp.ifarchive.org`, a process likely to be complete by end 2001.

Much of this book is given over to syntax and implementation, but the world model and its underlying rules are at the heart of Inform, and they owe much to earlier work in the field. Ideas of how to represent places and the location of items are owed to Will Crowther (c. 1975), while the use of a tree to represent containment derives from work towards 'Zork' (c. 1978) by students at MIT, whose artificial intelligence lab promoted the doctrine that such structures occur "naturally". (Terry Winograd's 'SHRDLU' (1972) had provided an adventure-like parser for a world of blocks supporting pyramids: it recognised pronouns, and allowed the "game" state to be saved.) The completion of today's standard model of space, objects, lighting and the passage of time can conveniently be dated to April 1979, the publication date of the influential *IEEE Computer* article 'Zork: A Computerized Fantasy Simulation Game' by P. David Lebling, Marc Blank and Tim Anderson. The question of how best to model supplementary world rules, of the "you can't pick up the slippery eel" variety, is less settled. Influenced by post-'Zork' Infocom, TADS (c. 1987) has a "verification stage" in processing actions, for instance, which may well be a better scheme than Inform's before and after. The latter derive from a second tradition, based in Cambridge, England, not Cambridge, Massachusetts: in the first instance from an incremental multi-player game called 'Tera' for the Cambridge University mainframe Phoenix, written by Dilip Sequeira and the author in 1990. (The compiler was called Teraform, a pun of Dr Sequeira's. 'Tera' was the sequel to 'Giga' and before that 'Mega' – anagram of 'game' – by Mark Owen and Matthew Richards.) This stole from the vastly more significant Phoenix game assembler by David Seal and Jonathan Thackray which in turn dates back to their creation, with Jonathan Partington, of 'Acheton' (c. 1979), the first substantial game written outside America.

.   .   .   .   .

In the defensive words of its first, makeshift documentation, "Inform is an easel, not a painting". Though I am no longer so sure that the two can be divided. While revising this book, I have been ruefully reminded of Coleridge's notebooks, that vaulted miscellany of staircases and hidden doors, connections found and lost, plans abandoned and made again. Slipping away from my attempts to index and organise it, this book, too, remains for me a maze of twisty little passages, all different, a kind of interactive fiction in itself.

Over the last seven years, more than a thousand people have trodden these passages, repairing or ramifying by turns with amendments and suggestions: far too many to name but I would like to thank them all, and especially Volker Blasius, Kevin Bracey, Mark Howell, Stefan Jokisch, Kirk Klobe, the ever avuncular Bob Newell, Robert Pelak, Jørund Rian, Dilip Sequeira, Richard Tucker, Christopher Wichura, John Wood and the games designers of Activision. Particular thanks go to Mike Berlyn, who besides being one of the subjects of Chapter VIII was also instrumental in the reshaping of this text as an unabashed book. His enthusiasm was greatly valued.

Few books can have been so fortunate in receiving the generous attention of others as this new edition. First and foremost its every paragraph was reshaped by Gareth Rees's skilled, tactful and invariably wise editing. The stack of proofs of draft chapters, meticulously annotated in his calligraphic handwriting, is now five and a half inches high; his contribution to the ideas in this book was equally substantial, and especially in Chapter VIII. Toby Nelson and Andrew Plotkin each proof-read the text, making helpful comments such as "Had a bad day at the office?" next to one of the paragraphs, and "Inform is curled up in my head, like a parasitic alien that doesn't spring out and eat the host for a surprisingly long time." Torbjörn Andersson checked the solutions to the exercises: no mean feat, and it resulted in no less than 242 specific suggestions, only four of them pointing out that I'd got the accent in his name wrong again. Later on he proofed the whole book again, so that at times it seemed it would never be finished (delays, however, being solely my own fault). Michael Baum's census of known Z-machine story files greatly assisted the bibliography of cited works. Paul David Doherty, interactive fiction's most careful and dedicated historian, was tireless in tracking down early games designers and in vetting §46 for factual accuracy, and interviews by Dennis G. Jerz further clarified the mid-1970s picture: opinions and errors remain, of course, my own. David Cornelson's enthusiasm and capability made this printed edition possible, assisted by Roger Firth and Florian Edlbauer as English and German agents, and by Ryan Freebern, Duncan Stevens, Nick Montfort and Duncan Cross who proofed pages yet again. Inform designers too numerous to name participated in a survey of what they would like to see appearing in this book, and in a trawling exercise for misprints in the first PDF edition. A generous award from the Society of Authors in 1997 allowed me more time for writing.

One final word. I should like to dedicate this book, impertinently perhaps, to our illustrious predecessors: Will Crowther, Don Woods and the authors of Infocom, Inc.; among them Douglas Adams, whose sudden death only weeks ago robs us of one of our most inventive and maddening writers.

Graham Nelson
University of Oxford
April 1993 – July 2001

Chapter I: The Inform Language

Language is a cracked kettle on which we beat out tunes for bears to dance to, while all the time we long to move the stars to pity.

— from the letters of Gustave Flaubert (1821–1880)

§1   Routines

 If you have already dipped into Chapter II and looked at how some simple games and puzzles are designed, you'll have seen that any really interesting item needs to be given instructions on how to behave, and that these instructions are written in a language of their own. Chapter I is about that language, and its examples are mostly short programs to carry out mundane tasks, undistracted by the lure of adventure.

§1.1   Getting started

Inform turns your description of a game (or other program), called the "source code", into a "story file" which can be played (or run through) using an "interpreter". Interpreter programs are available for very many models of computer, and if you can already play Infocom's games or other people's Inform games on your machine then you already have an interpreter. There are several interpreter programs available, in a sort of friendly rivalry. You should be able to use whichever you prefer and even the oldest, most rickety interpreter will probably not give serious trouble. A good sign to look out for is compliance with the exacting *Z-Machine Standards Document*, agreed by an informal committee of interested parties between 1995 and 1997. At time of writing, the current version is Standard 1.0, dating from June 1997.

Turning source code into a story file is called "compilation", and Inform itself is the compiler. It's also supplied with a whole slew of ready-made source code called the "library" and giving all the rules for adventure games. The story of what the library does and how to work with it occupies most of this manual, but not this chapter.

It isn't practicable to give installation instructions here, because they vary so much from machine to machine, but before you can go any further you'll need to install Inform: try downloading the software for your own machine from ftp.gmd.de, which should either install itself or give instructions. A useful test exercise would be to try to create the "Hello World" source code given below, then to compile it with Inform, and finally "play" it on your interpreter. (You can type up source code with any text editor or even with a word-processor, provided you save its documents as "text only".)

Inform can run in a number of slightly different ways, controlled by "switches". The way to set these varies from one installation to another. Note that this chapter assumes that you're running Inform in "Strict mode", controlled by the -S switch, which is normally set and ensures that helpful error messages will be printed if a story file you have compiled does something it shouldn't.

§1.2   Hello World

Traditionally, all programming language tutorials begin by giving a program which does nothing but print "Hello world" and stop. Here it is in Inform:

```
!  "Hello world" example program
[ Main;
   print "Hello world^";
];
```

The text after the exclamation mark is a "comment", that is, it is text written in the margin by the author to remind himself of what is going on here. Such text means nothing to Inform, which ignores anything on the same line and to the right of an exclamation mark. In addition, any gaps made up of line and page breaks, tab characters and spaces are treated the same and called "white space", so the layout of the source code doesn't much matter. Exactly the same story file would be produced by:

```
    [
        Main   ;
   print
            "Hello world^"              ;
        ]
   ;
```

or, at the other extreme, by:

```
[Main;print"Hello world^";];
```

Laying out programs legibly is a matter of personal taste.

△   The exception to the rule about ignoring white space is inside quoted text, where `"Hello    world^"` and `"Hello world^"` are genuinely different pieces of text and are treated as such. Inform treats text inside quotation marks with much more care than its ordinary program material: for instance, an exclamation mark inside quotation marks will not cause the rest of its line to be thrown away as a comment.

Inform regards its source code as a list of things to look at, divided up by semicolons ;. These things are generally objects, of which more later. In this case there is only one, called Main, and it's of a special kind called a "routine".

Every program has to contain a routine called Main. When a story file is set running the interpreter follows the first instruction in Main, and it carries on line by line from there. This process is called "execution". Once the Main routine is finished, the interpreter stops.

These instructions are called "statements", a traditional term in computing albeit an ungrammatical one. In this case there is only one statement:

```
print "Hello world^";
```

Printing is the process of writing text onto the computer screen. This statement prints the two words "Hello world" and then skips the rest of the line (or "prints a new-line"), because the ^ character, in quoted text, means "new-line". For example, the statement

```
print "Blue^Red^Green^";
```

prints up:

Blue
Red
Green

print is one of 28 different statements in the Inform language. Only about 20 of these are commonly used, but the full list is as follows:

box	break	continue	do	font	for
give	if	inversion	jump	move	new_line
objectloop	print	print_ret	quit	read	remove
restore	return	rfalse	rtrue	save	spaces
string	style	switch	while		

§1.3   *Routine calls, errors and warnings*

The following source code has three routines, Main, Rosencrantz and Hamlet:

```
[ Main;
  print "Hello from Elsinore.^";
  Rosencrantz();
];
[ Rosencrantz;
  print "Greetings from Rosencrantz.^";
];
[ Hamlet;
  print "The rest is silence.^";
];
```

The resulting program prints up

> Hello from Elsinore.
> Greetings from Rosencrantz.

but the text "The rest is silence." is never printed. Execution begins at Main, and "Hello from Elsinore" is printed; next, the statement Rosencrantz() causes the Rosencrantz routine to be executed. That continues until it ends with the close-routine marker], whereupon execution goes back to Main just after the point where it left off: since there is nothing more to do in Main, the interpreter stops. Thus, Rosencrantz is executed but Hamlet is not.

In fact, when the above source code is compiled, Inform notices that Hamlet is never needed and prints out a warning to that effect. The exact text produced by Inform varies from machine to machine, but will be something like this:

```
RISC OS Inform 6.20 (10th December 1998)
line 8: Warning: Routine "Hamlet" declared but not used
Compiled with 1 warning
```

Errors are mistakes in the source which cause Inform to refuse to compile it, but this is only a warning. It alerts the programmer that a mistake may have been made (because presumably the programmer has simply forgotten to put in a statement calling Hamlet) but it doesn't prevent the compilation from taking place. Note that the opening line of the routine Hamlet occurs on the 8th line of the program above.

There are usually mistakes in a newly-written program and one goes through a cycle of running a first draft through Inform, receiving a batch of error messages, correcting the draft according to these messages, and trying again. A typical error message would occur if, on line 3, we had mistyped Rosncrantz() for Rosencrantz(). Inform would then have produced:

```
RISC OS Inform 6.20 (10th December 1998)
line 5: Warning: Routine "Rosencrantz" declared but not used
line 8: Warning: Routine "Hamlet" declared but not used
line 3: Error: No such constant as "Rosncrantz"
Compiled with 1 error and 2 warnings (no output)
```

The error message means that on line 3 Inform ran into a name which did not correspond to any known quantity: it's not the name of any routine, in particular. A human reader would immediately realise what was intended, but Inform doesn't, so that it goes on to warn that the routine Rosencrantz is never used. Warnings (and errors) are quite often produced as knock-on effects of other mistakes, so it is generally a good idea to worry about fixing errors first and warnings afterward.

Notice that Inform normally doesn't produce the final story file if errors occurred during compilation: this prevents it from producing damaged story files.

§1.4   Numbers and other constants

Inform numbers are normally whole numbers in the range −32,768 to 32,767. (Special programming is needed to represent larger numbers or fractions, as we shall see when parsing phone numbers in Chapter IV.) There are three notations for writing numbers in source code: here is an example of each.

```
-4205
$3f08
$$1000111010110
```

The difference is the radix, or number base, in which they are expressed. The first is in decimal (base 10), the second hexadecimal (base 16, where the digits after 9 are written a to f or A to F) and the third binary (base 2). Once Inform has read in a number, it forgets which notation was used: for instance, if the source code is altered so that $$10110 is replaced by 22, this makes no difference to the story file produced.

A print statement can print numbers as well as text, though it always prints them back in ordinary decimal notation. For example, the program

```
[ Main;
  print "Today's number is ", $3f08, ".^";
];
```

prints up

Today's number is 16136.

since 16,136 in base 10 is the same number as 3f08 in hexadecimal.

Literal quantities written down in the source code are called "constants". Numbers are one kind; strings of text like "Today's number is " are another. A third kind are characters, given between single quotation marks. For instance, 'x' means "the letter lower-case x". A "character" is a single letter or typewriter-symbol.

△   Just as $3f08 is a fancy way of writing the number 16,136, so 'x' is a fancy way of writing the number 120. The way characters correspond to numeric values is given by a code called ZSCII, itself quite close to the traditional computing standard called ASCII. 120 means "lower-case x" in ASCII, too, but ZSCII does its own thing with non-English characters like "é". (You can type accented letters directly into source code: see §1.11.) The available characters and their ZSCII values are laid out in Table 2.

Inform also provides a few constants named for convenience, the most commonly used of which are true and false. A condition such as "the jewelled box is unlocked" will always have either the value true or the value false.

△   Once again these are numbers in disguise. true is 1, false 0.

△   Inform is a language designed with adventure games in mind, where a player regularly types in commands like "unlock the box", using a fairly limited vocabulary. Writing a word like 'box' in the source code, in single-quotation marks, adds it to the "dictionary" or vocabulary of the story file to be compiled. This is a kind of constant, too: you can use it for writing code like "if the second word typed by the player is 'box', then...".

△   If you need to lodge a single-letter word (say "h") into the dictionary, you can't put it in single quotes because then it would look like a character constant ('h'). Instead, the best you can write is 'h//'. (The two slashes are sometimes used to tack a little linguistic information onto the end of a dictionary word, so that in some circumstances, see §29, you might want to write 'pears//p' to indicate that "pears" must go into the dictionary marked as a plural. In this case the two slashes only serve to clarify that it isn't a character.)

△   You can put an apostrophe ' into a dictionary word by writing it as ^: for instance 'helen^s'.

△△ In two places where dictionary words often appear, the name slot of an object definition and in grammar laid out with Verb and Extend, you're allowed to use single or double quotes interchangeably, and people sometimes do. For clarity's sake, this book tries to stick to using single quotes around dictionary words at all times. The handling of dictionary words is probably the single worst-designed bit of syntax in Inform, but you're past it now.

§1.5   Variables

Unlike a literal number, a variable is able to vary. It is referred to by its name and, like the "memory" key on some pocket calculators, remembers the last value placed in it. For instance, if oil_left has been declared as a variable (see below), then the statement

```
print "There are ", oil_left, " gallons remaining.^";
```

would cause the interpreter to print "There are 4 gallons remaining." if oil_left happened to be 4, and so on. It's possible for the statement to be executed many times and produce different text at different times.

Inform can only know the named quantity oil_left is to be a variable if the source code has "declared" that it is. Each routine can declare its own selection of up to 15 variables on its opening line. For example, in the program

```
[ Main alpha b;
  alpha = 2200;
  b = 201;
  print "Alpha is ", alpha, " while b is ", b, "^";
];
```

the Main routine has two variables, alpha and b.

Going back to the Main routine above, the = sign which occurs twice is an example of an "operator": a notation usually made up of the symbols on the non-alphabetic keys on a typewriter and which means something is to be done with or calculated from the items it is written next to. Here = means "set equal to". When the statement alpha = 2200; is interpreted, the current value of the variable alpha is changed to 2,200. It then keeps that value until another such statement changes it. All variables have the value 0 until they are first set.

The variables alpha and b are called "local variables" because they are local to Main and are its private property. The source code

```
[ Main alpha;
  alpha = 2200;
  Rival();
];
[ Rival;
  print alpha;
];
```

causes an error on the print statement in Rival, since alpha does not exist there. Indeed, Rival could even have defined a variable of its own also called alpha and this would have been an entirely separate variable.

. . . . .

That's now two kinds of name: routines have names and so have variables. Such names, for instance Rival and alpha, are called "identifiers" and can be up to 32 characters long. They may contain letters of the alphabet, decimal digits or the underscore _ character (often used to impersonate a space). To prevent them looking too much like numbers, though, they cannot start with a decimal digit. The following are examples of legal identifiers:

```
turns_still_to_play      room101      X
```

Inform ignores any difference between upper and lower case letters in such names, so for instance room101 is the same name as Room101.

§1.6   *Arithmetic, assignment and bitwise operators*

The Inform language is rich with operators, as Table 1 shows. This section introduces a first batch of them.

A general mixture of quantities and operators, designed to end up with a single resulting quantity, is called an "expression". For example: the statement

```
seconds = 60*minutes + 3600*hours;
```

sets the variable seconds equal to 60 times the variable minutes plus 3600 times the variable hours. White space is not needed between operators and "operands" (the quantities they operate on, such as 3600 and hours). The spaces on either side of the + sign were written in just for legibility.

The arithmetic operators are the simplest ones. To begin with, there are + (plus), - (minus), * (times) and / (divide by). Dividing one whole number by another usually leaves a remainder: for example, 3 goes into 7 twice, with remainder 1. In Inform notation,

7/3 evaluates to 2 and 7%3 evaluates to 1

the % operator meaning "remainder after division", usually called just "remainder".

△   The basic rule is that a == (a/b)*b + (a%b), so that for instance:

```
13/5 == 2     13/-5 == -2     -13/5 == -2     -13/-5 == 2
13%5 == 3     13%-5 == 3      -13%5 == -3     -13%-5 == -3
```

• **WARNING**
Dividing by zero, and taking remainder after dividing by zero, are impossible. You must write your program so that it never tries to. It's worth a brief aside here on errors, because dividing by zero offers an example of how and when Inform can help the programmer to spot mistakes. The following source code:

```
[ Main; print 73/0; ];
```

won't compile, because Inform can see that it definitely involves something illegal:

```
line 2: Error: Division of constant by zero
>    print 73/0;
```

However, Inform fails to notice anything amiss when compiling this:

```
[ Main x; x = 0; print 73/x; ];
```

and this source code compiles correctly. When the resulting story file is interpreted, however, the following will be printed:

[** Programming error: tried to divide by zero **]

This is only one of about fifty different programming errors which can turn up when a story file is interpreted. As in this case, they arise when the interpreter has accidentally been asked to do something impossible. The moral is that just because Inform compiles source code without errors, it does not follow that the story file does what the programmer intended.

△   Since an Inform number has to be between −32,768 and 32,767, some arithmetic operations overflow. For instance, multiplying 8 by 5,040 ought to give 40,320, but this is over the top and the answer is instead −25,216. Unlike dividing by zero, causing arithmetic overflows is perfectly legal. Some programmers make deliberate use of overflows, for instance to generate apparently random numbers.

△△ Only *apparently* random, because overflows are perfectly predictable. Inform story files store numbers in sixteen binary digits, so that when a number reaches $2^{16} = 65,536$ it clocks back round to zero (much as a car's odometer clocks over from 999999 miles to 000000). Now, since 65,535 is the value that comes before 0, it represents −1, and 65,534 represents −2 and so on. The result is that if you start with zero and keep adding 1 to it, you get $1, 2, 3, \ldots, 32,767$ and then $−32,768, −32,767, −32,766, \ldots,$ −1 and at last zero again. Here's how to predict an overflowing multiplication, say: first, multiply the two numbers as they stand, then keep adding or subtracting 65,536 from the result until it lies in the range −32,768 to 32,767. For example, 8 multiplied by 5,040 is 40,320, which is too big, but we only need to subtract 65,536 once to bring it into range, and the result is −25,216.

·   ·   ·   ·   ·

In a complicated expression the order in which the operators work may affect the result. As most human readers would, Inform works out both of

```
3 + 2 * 6
2 * 6 + 3
```

as 15, because the operator * has "precedence" over + and so is acted on first. Brackets may be used to overcome this:

```
(3 + 2) * 6
2 * (6 + 3)
```

evaluate to 30 and 18 respectively. Each operator has such a "precedence level". When two operators have the same precedence level (for example, + and − are of equal precedence) calculation is (almost always) "left associative", that is, carried out left to right. So the notation a-b-c means (a-b)-c and not a-(b-c). The standard way to write formulae in maths is to give + and − equal precedence, but lower than that of * and / (which are also equal). Inform agrees and also pegs % equal to * and /.

The last purely arithmetic operator is "unary minus". This is also written as a minus sign − but is not quite the same as subtraction. The expression:

```
-credit
```

means the same thing as 0-credit. The operator - is different from all those mentioned so far because it operates only on one value. It has higher precedence than any of the five other arithmetic operators. For example,

```
-credit - 5
```

means (-credit) - 5 and not -(credit - 5).

One way to imagine precedence is to think of it as glue attached to the operator. A higher level means stronger glue. Thus, in

```
3 + 2 * 6
```

the glue around the * is stronger than that around the +, so that 2 and 6 belong bound to the *.

△   Some languages have a "unary plus" too, but Inform hasn't.

·   ·   ·   ·   ·

Some operators don't just work out values but actually change the current settings of variables: expressions containing these are called "assignments". One such is "set equals":

```
alpha = 72
```

sets the variable alpha equal to 72. Like + and the others, it also comes up with an answer: which is the value it has set, in this case 72.

The other two assignment operators are ++ and --, which will be familiar to any C programmer. They are unary operators, and mean "increase (or decrease) the value of this variable by one". If the ++ or -- goes before the variable, then the increase (or decrease) happens before the value is read off; if after, then after. For instance, if variable currently has the value 12 then:

> variable++ evaluates to 12 and leaves variable set to 13;
> ++variable evaluates to 13 and leaves variable set to 13;
> variable-- evaluates to 12 and leaves variable set to 11;
> --variable evaluates to 11 and leaves variable set to 11.

These operators are provided as convenient shorthand forms, since their effect could usually be achieved in other ways. Note that expressions like

```
500++        (4*alpha)--      34 = beta
```

are quite meaningless: the values of 500 and 34 cannot be altered, and Inform knows no way to adjust alpha so as to make 4*alpha decrease by 1. All three will cause compilation errors.

· · · · ·

The "bitwise operators" are provided for manipulating binary numbers on a digit-by-digit basis, something which is only done in programs which are working with low-level data or data which has to be stored very compactly. Inform provides &, bitwise AND, |, bitwise OR and ~, bitwise NOT. For each digit, such an operator works out the value in the answer from the values in the operands. Bitwise NOT acts on a single operand and results in the number whose i-th binary digit is the opposite of that in the operand (a 1 for a 0, a 0 for a 1). Bitwise AND (and OR) acts on two numbers and sets the i-th digit to 1 if both operands have (either operand has) i-th digit set. All Inform numbers are sixteen bits wide. So:

```
$$10111100 & $$01010001   ==   $$0000000000010000
$$10111100 | $$01010001   ==   $$0000000011111101
           ~ $$01010001   ==   $$1111111110101110
```

§1.7   Arguments and Return Values

Here is one way to imagine how an Inform routine works: you feed some values into it, it then goes away and works on them, possibly printing some text out or doing other interesting things, and it then returns with a single value which it gives back to you. As far as you're concerned, the transaction consists of turning a group of starting values, called "arguments", into a single "return value":

$$A_1, A_2, A_3, \ldots \longrightarrow \text{Routine} \longrightarrow R$$

The number of arguments needed varies with the routine: some, like Main and the other routines in this chapter so far, need none at all. (Others need anything up to seven, which is the maximum number allowed by Inform.) On the other hand, every routine without exception produces a return value. Even when it looks as if there isn't one, there is. For example:

```
[ Main;
  Sonnet();
];
[ Sonnet;
  print "When to the sessions of sweet silent thought^";
  print "I summon up remembrance of things past^";
];
```

Main and Sonnet both take no arguments, but they both return a value: as it
happens this value is true, in the absence of any instruction to the contrary.
(As was mentioned earlier, true is the same as the number 1.) The statement
Sonnet(); calls Sonnet but does nothing with the return value, which is just
thrown away. But if Main had instead been written like so:

```
[ Main;
  print Sonnet();
];
```

then the output would be

> When to the sessions of sweet silent thought
> I summon up remembrance of things past
> 1

because now the return value, 1, is not thrown away: it is printed out.

You can call it a routine with arguments by writing them in a list,
separated by commas, in between the round brackets. For instance, here is a
call supplying two arguments:

```
Weather("hurricane", 12);
```

When the routine begins, the value "hurricane" is written into its first local
variable, and the value 12 into its second. For example, suppose:

```
[ Weather called force;
  print "I forecast a ", (string) called, " measuring force ",
    force, " on the Beaufort scale.^";
];
```

Leaving the details of the print statement aside for the moment, the call to
this routine produces the text:

> I forecast a hurricane measuring force 12 on the Beaufort scale.

The Weather routine finishes when its] end-marker is reached, whereupon
it returns true, but any of the following statements will finish a routine the
moment they are reached:

rfalse;	which returns false,
rtrue;	which returns true,

```
    return;              which also returns true,
    return ⟨value⟩;     which returns ⟨value⟩.
```

For example, here is a routine to print out the cubes of the numbers 1 to 5:

```
[ Main;
  print Cube(1), " ";
  print Cube(2), " ";
  print Cube(3), " ";
  print Cube(4), " ";
  print Cube(5), "^";
];
[ Cube x;
  return x*x*x;
];
```

When interpreted, the resulting story file prints up the text:

1 8 27 64 125

△   Any "missing arguments" in a routine call are set equal to zero, so the call Cube() is legal and does the same as Cube(0). What you mustn't do is to give too many arguments: Cube(1,2) isn't possible because there is no variable to put the 2 into.

△   A hazardous, but legal and sometimes useful practice is for a routine to call itself. This is called recursion. The hazard is that the following mistake can be made, probably in some much better disguised way:

```
[ Disaster; return Disaster(); ];
```

Despite the reassuring presence of the word return, execution is tied up forever, unable to finish evaluating the return value. The first call to Disaster needs to make a second before it can finish, the second needs to make a third, the third... and so on. (Actually, for "forever" read "until the interpreter runs out of stack space and halts", but that's little comfort.)

§1.8   Conditions: if, true and false

The facilities described so far make Inform about as powerful as the average small programmable calculator. To make it a proper programming language, it needs much greater flexibility of action. This is provided by special statements which control whether or not, and if so how many times or in what order, other statements are executed. The simplest is if:

```
if (⟨condition⟩) ⟨statement⟩
```

which executes the ⟨statement⟩ only if the ⟨condition⟩, when it is tested, turns out to be true. For example, when the statement

```
if (alpha == 3) print "Hello";
```

is executed, the word "Hello" is printed only if the variable alpha currently has value 3. It's important not to confuse the == (test whether or not equal to) with the = operator (set equal to). But because it's easy to write something plausible like

```
if (alpha = 3) print "Hello";
```

by accident, which always prints "Hello" because the condition evaluates to 3 which is considered non-zero and therefore true (see below), Inform will issue a warning if you try to compile something like this. ('=' used as condition: '==' intended?)

. . . . .

Conditions are always given in brackets. There are 12 different conditions in Inform (see Table 1), six arithmetic and half a dozen to do with objects. Here are the arithmetic ones:

```
(a == b)   a equals b
(a ~= b)   a doesn't equal b
(a >= b)   a is greater than or equal to b
(a <= b)   a is less than or equal to b
(a > b)    a is greater than b
(a < b)    a is less than b
```

A useful extension to this set is provided by the special operator or, which gives alternative possibilities. For example,

```
if (alpha == 3 or 4) print "Scott";
if (alpha ~= 5 or 7 or 9) print "Amundsen";
```

where two or more values are given with the word or between. "Scott" is printed if alpha has value either 3 or 4, and "Amundsen" if the value of alpha is not 5, is not 7 and is not 9. or can be used with any condition, and any number of alternatives can be given. For example

```
if (player in Forest or Village or Building) ...
```

often makes code much clearer than writing three separate conditions out. Or you might want to use

```
if (x > 100 or y) ...
```

to test whether x is bigger than the minimum of 100 and y.

Conditions can also be built up from simpler ones using the three logical operators &&, || and ~~, pronounced "and", "or" and "not". For example,

```
if (alpha == 1 && (beta > 10 || beta < -10)) print "Lewis";
if (~~(alpha > 6)) print "Clark";
```

"Lewis" is printed if alpha equals 1 and beta is outside the range -10 to 10; "Clark" is printed if alpha is less than or equal to 6.

△   && and || work left to right and stop evaluating conditions as soon as the final outcome is known. So for instance if (A && B) ... will work out A first. If this is false, there's no need to work out B. This is sometimes called short-cut evaluation and can be convenient when working out conditions like

```
if (x~=nothing && TreasureDeposited(x)==true) ...
```

where you don't want TreasureDeposited to be called with the argument nothing.

· · · · ·

Conditions are expressions like any other, except that their values are always either true or false. You can write a condition as a value, say by copying it into a variable like so:

```
lower_caves_explored = (Y2_Rock_Room has visited);
```

This kind of variable, storing a logical state, is traditionally called a "flag". Flags are always either true or false: they are like the red flag over the beach at Lee-on-Solent in Hampshire, which is either flying, meaning that the army is using the firing range, or not flying, when it is safe to walk along the shore. Flags allow you to write natural-looking code like:

```
if (lower_caves_explored) print "You've already been that way.";
```

The actual test performed by if (x) ... is x~=0, not that x==true, because all non-zero quantities are considered to represent truth whereas only zero represents falsity.

. . . . .

△   Now that the `if` statement is available, it's possible to give an example of a recursion that does work:

```
[ GreenBottles n;
   print n, " green bottles, standing on a wall.^";
   if (n == 0) print "(And an awful lot of broken glass.)^";
   else {
       print "And if one green bottle should accidentally fall^";
       print "There'd be ", n-1, " green bottles.^";
       return GreenBottles(n-1);
   }
];
```

Try calling `GreenBottles(10)`. It prints the first verse of the song, then before returning it calls `GreenBottles(9)` to print the rest. So it goes on, until `GreenBottles(0)`. At this point n is zero, so the text "(And an awful lot of broken glass.)" is printed for the first and only time. `GreenBottles(0)` then returns back to `GreenBottles(1)`, which returns to `GreenBottles(2)`, which... and so on until `GreenBottles(10)` finally returns and the song is completed.

△△ Thus execution reached "ten routines deep" before starting to return back up, and each of these copies of `GreenBottles` had its own private copy of the variable n. The limit to how deep you are allowed to go varies from one player's machine to another, but here is a rule of thumb, erring on the low side for safety's sake. (On a standard interpreter it will certainly be safe.) Total up 4 plus the number of its variables for each routine that needs to be running at the same time, and keep the total beneath 1,000. Ten green bottles amounts only to a total of $10 \times 5 = 50$, and as it seems unlikely that anyone will wish to read the lyrics to "two hundred and one green bottles" the above recursion is safe.

§1.9   Code blocks, `else` and `switch`

A feature of all statements choosing what to do next is that instead of just giving a single ⟨statement⟩, one can give a list of statements grouped together into a unit called a "code block". Such a group begins with an open brace { and ends with a close brace }. For example,

```
if (alpha > 5) {
    v = alpha*alpha;
    print "The square of alpha is ", v, ".^";
}
```

If alpha is 3, nothing is printed; if alpha is 9,

>   The square of alpha is 81.

is printed. (The indentation used in the source code, like all points of source code layout, is a matter of personal taste.†) In some ways, code blocks are like routines, and at first it may seem inconsistent to write routines between [and] brackets and code blocks between braces { and }. However, code blocks cannot have private variables of their own and do not return values; and it is possible for execution to break out of code blocks again, or to jump from block to block, which cannot happen with routines.

.   .   .   .   .

An if statement can optionally have the form

>   if (⟨condition⟩) ⟨statement1⟩ else ⟨statement2⟩

whereupon ⟨statement1⟩ is executed if the condition is true, and ⟨statement2⟩ if it is false. For example,

```
if (alpha == 5) print "Five."; else print "Not five.";
```

Note that the condition is only checked once, so that the statement

```
if (alpha == 5) {
    print "Five.";
    alpha = 10;
}
else print "Not five.";
```

cannot ever print both "Five" and then "Not five".

△   The else clause has a snag attached: the problem of "hanging elses". In the following, which if statement does the else attach to?

```
if (alpha == 1) if (beta == 2)
    print "Clearly if alpha=1 and beta=2.^";
else
    print "Ambiguous.^";
```

---

† Almost everybody indents each code block as shown, but the position of the open brace is a point of schism. This book adopts the "One True Brace Style", as handed down in such sacred texts as the original Unix source code and Kernighan and Ritchie's textbook of C. Other conventions place the open brace vertically above its matching closure, perhaps on its own otherwise blank line of source code.

Without clarifying braces, Inform pairs an else to the most recent if. (Much as the U.S. Supreme Court rigorously interprets muddled laws like "all animals must be licensed, except cats, other than those under six months old" by applying a so-called Last Antecedent Rule to ambiguous qualifications like this "other than....".) The following version is much better style:

```
if (alpha == 1) {
    if (beta == 2)
        print "Clearly if alpha=1 and beta=2.^";
    else
        print "Clearly if alpha=1 but beta not 2.^";
}
```

.   .   .   .   .

The if ... else ... construction is ideal for switching execution between two possible "tracks", like railway signals, but it is a nuisance trying to divide between many different outcomes this way. To follow the analogy, the switch construction is like a railway turntable.

```
print "The train on platform 1 is going to ";
switch (DestinationOnPlatform(1)) {
    1: print "Dover Priory.";
    2: print "Bristol Parkway.";
    3: print "Edinburgh Waverley.";
    default: print "a siding.";
}
```

The default clause is optional but must be placed last if at all: it is executed when the original expression matches none of the other values. Otherwise there's no obligation for these clauses to be given in numerical or any other order. Each possible alternative value must be a constant, so

```
switch (alpha) {
    beta: print "The variables alpha and beta are equal!";
}
```

will produce a compilation error. (But note that in a typical game, the name of an object or a location, such as First_Court, is a constant, so there is no problem in quoting this as a switch value.)

Any number of outcomes can be specified, and values can be grouped together in lists separated by commas, or in ranges like 3 to 6. For example:

```
print "The mission Apollo ", num, " made ";
switch (num) {
    7, 9: print "a test-flight in Earth orbit.";
    8, 10: print "a test-flight in lunar orbit.";
    11, 12, 14 to 17: print "a landing on the Moon.";
    13: print "it back safely after a catastrophic explosion.";
}
```

Each clause is automatically a code block, so a whole run of statements can be given without the need for any braces { and } around them.

△   If you're used to the C language, you might want to note a major difference: Inform doesn't have "case fall-through", with execution running from one case to the next, so there's no need to use break statements.

△△ A good default clause for the above example would be a little complicated: Apollo 1 was lost in a ground fire, causing a shuffle so that 2 and 3 never happened, while automatic test-flights of the Saturn rocket were unofficially numbered 4 to 6. Apollo 20 was cancelled to free up a heavy launcher for the Skylab station, and 18 and 19 through budget cuts, though the Apollo/Soyuz Test Project (1975) is sometimes unhistorically called Apollo 18. The three Apollo flights to Skylab were called Skylab 2, 3 and 4. All six Mercury capsules were numbered 7, while at time of writing the Space Shuttle mission STS-88 has just landed and the next to launch, in order, are projected to be 96, 93, 99, 103, 101 and 92. NASA has proud traditions.

§1.10   while, do ... until, for, break, continue

The other four Inform control constructions are all "loops", that is, ways to repeat the execution of a given statement or code block. Discussion of one of them, called objectloop, is deferred until §3.4.

The two basic forms of loop are while and do ... until:

while (⟨condition⟩) ⟨statement⟩
do ⟨statement⟩ until (⟨condition⟩)

The first repeatedly tests the condition and, provided it is still true, executes the statement. If the condition is not even true the first time, the statement is never executed even once. For example:

```
[ SquareRoot n x;
   while (x*x < n) x = x + 1;
   if (x*x == n) return x;
   return x - 1;
];
```

which is a simple if rather inefficient way to find square roots, rounded down to the nearest whole number. If SquareRoot(200) is called, then x runs up through the values $0, 1, 2, \ldots, 14, 15$, at which point x*x is 225: so 14 is returned. If SquareRoot(0) is called, the while condition never holds at all and so the return value is 0, made by the if statement.

The do ... until loop repeats the given statement until the condition is found to be true. Even if the condition is already satisfied, like (true), the statement is always executed the first time through.

·   ·   ·   ·   ·

One particular kind of while loop is needed so often that there is an abbreviation for it, called for. This can produce any loop in the form

```
⟨start⟩
while (⟨condition⟩) {
    ...
    ⟨update⟩
}
```

where ⟨start⟩ and ⟨update⟩ are expressions which actually do something, such as setting a variable. The notation to achieve this is:

```
for (⟨start⟩ : ⟨condition⟩ : ⟨update⟩) ...
```

Note that if the condition is false the very first time, the loop is never executed. For instance, this prints nothing:

```
for (counter=1 : counter<0 : counter++) print "Banana";
```

Any of the three parts of a for statement can be omitted. If the condition is missed out, it is assumed always true, so that the loop will continue forever, unless escaped by other means (see below).

For example, here is the while version of a common kind of loop:

```
counter = 1;
while (counter <= 10) {
    print counter, " ";
    counter++;
}
```

which produces the output "1 2 3 4 5 6 7 8 9 10". (Recall that `counter++` adds 1 to the variable `counter`.) The abbreviated version is:

```
for (counter=1 : counter<=10 : counter++)
    print counter, " ";
```

△   Using commas, several assignments can be joined into one. For instance:

```
i++, score=50, j++
```

is a single expression. This is never useful in ordinary code, where the assignments can be divided up by semicolons in the usual way. But in `for` loops it can be a convenience:

```
for (i=1, j=5: i<=5: i++, j--) print i, " ", j, ", ";
```

produces the output "1 5, 2 4, 3 3, 4 2, 5 1,".

△△ Comma , is an operator, and moreover is the one with the lowest precedence level. The result of `a,b` is always b, but a and b are both evaluated and in that order.

. . . . .

On the face of it, the following loops all repeat forever:

```
while (true) ⟨statement⟩
do ⟨statement⟩ until (false)
for (::) ⟨statement⟩
```

But there is always an escape. One way is to `return` from the current routine. Another is to `jump` to a label outside the loop (see below), though if one only wants to escape the current loop then this is seldom good style. It's neatest to use the statement `break`, which means "break out of" the current innermost loop or `switch` statement: it can be read as "finish early". All these ways out are entirely safe, and there is no harm in leaving a loop only half-done.

The other simple statement used inside loops is `continue`. This causes the current iteration to end immediately, but the loop then continues. In particular, inside a `for` loop, `continue` skips the rest of the body of the loop and goes straight to the ⟨update⟩ part. For example,

```
for (i=1: i<=5: i++) {
    if (i==3) continue;
    print i, " ";
}
```

will output "1 2 4 5".

·   ·   ·   ·   ·

△   The following routine is a curious example of a loop which, though apparently simple enough, contains a trap for the unwary.

```
[ RunPuzzle n count;
  do {
      print n, " ";
      n = NextNumber(n);
      count++;
  }
  until (n==1);
  print "1^(taking ", count, " steps to reach 1)^";
];
[ NextNumber n;
  if (n%2 == 0) return n/2;      ! If n is even, halve it
  return 3*n + 1;                ! If n is odd, triple and add 1
];
```

The call RunPuzzle(10), for example, results in the output

10 5 16 8 4 2 1
(taking 6 steps to reach 1)

The definition of RunPuzzle assumes that, no matter what the initial value of n, enough iteration will end up back at 1. If this did not happen, the interpreter would lock up into an infinite loop, printing numbers forever. The routine is apparently very simple, so it would seem reasonable that by thinking carefully enough about it, we ought to be able to decide whether or not it will ever finish. But this is not so easy as it looks. RunPuzzle(26) takes ten steps, but there again, RunPuzzle(27) takes 111. Can this routine ever lock up into an infinite loop, or not?

△△ The answer, which caught the author by surprise, is: yes. Because of Inform's limited number range, eventually the numbers reached overflow 32,767 and Inform interprets them as negative – and quickly homes in on the cycle $-1, -2, -1, -2, \ldots$ This first happens to RunPuzzle(447). Using proper arithmetic, unhindered by a limited number range, the answer is unknown. As a student in Hamburg in the 1930s, Lothar Collatz conjectured that every positive n eventually reaches 1. Little progress has been made (though it is known to be true if n is less than 2^{40}), and even Paul Erdös said of it that "Mathematics is not yet ready for such problems." See Jeffrey Lagarias's bibliography *The 3x + 1 Problem and its Generalisations* (1996).

§1.11 How text is printed

Adventure games take a lot of trouble over printing, so Inform is rich in features to make printing elegant output more easy. During story-file interpretation, your text will automatically be broken properly at line-endings. Inform story files are interpreted on screen displays of all shapes and sizes, but as a programmer you can largely ignore this. Moreover, Inform itself will compile a block of text spilling over several source-code lines into normally-spaced prose, so:

```
print "Here in her hairs
        the painter plays the spider, and hath woven
        a golden mesh t'untrap the hearts of men
        faster than gnats in cobwebs";
```

results in the line divisions being replaced by a single space each. The text printed is: "Here in her hairs the painter plays the spider, and hath woven a golden mesh..." and so on. There is one exception to this: if a line finishes with a ^ (new-line) character, then no space is added.

△   You shouldn't type double-spaces after full stops or other punctuation, as this can spoil the look of the final text on screen. In particular, if a line break ends up after the first space of a double-space, the next line will begin with the second space. Since many typists habitually double-space, Inform has a switch -d1 which contracts ".   " to ". " wherever it occurs, and then a further setting -d2 which also contracts "!   " to "! " and "?   " to "? ". A modest warning, though: this can sometimes make a mess of diagrams. Try examining the 1851 Convention on Telegraphy Morse Code chart in 'Jigsaw', for instance, where the present author inadvertently jumbled the spacing because -d treated the Morse dots as full stops.

> . . . . .

When a string of text is printed up with print, the characters in the string normally appear exactly as given in the source code. However, four characters have special meanings. ^ means "print a new-line". The tilde character ~, meaning "print a quotation mark", is needed since quotation marks otherwise finish strings. Thus,

```
print "~Look,~ says Peter. ~Socks can jump.~^Jane agrees.^";
```

is printed as

> "Look," says Peter. "Socks can jump."
> Jane agrees.

The third remaining special character is @, occasionally used for accented characters and other unusual effects, as described below. Finally, \ is reserved for "folding lines", and is no longer needed but is retained so that old programs continue to work.

△ If you want to print an actual ~, ^, @ or \, you may need one of the following "escape sequences". A double @ sign followed by a decimal number means the character with the given ZSCII value, so in particular

@@92	comes out as "\"	@@64	comes out as "@"
@@94	comes out as "^"	@@126	comes out as "~"

· · · · ·

A number of Inform games have been written in European languages other than English, and even English-language games need accented letters from time to time. Inform can be told via command-line switches to assume that quoted text in the source code uses any of the ISO 8859-1 to -9 character sets, which include West and Central European forms, Greek, Arabic, Cyrillic and Hebrew. The default is ISO Latin-1, which means that you should be able to type most standard West European letters straight into the source code.

△ If you can't conveniently type foreign accents on your keyboard, or you want to make a source code file which could be safely taken from a PC to a Macintosh or vice versa, you can instead type accented characters using @. (The PC operating system Windows and Mac OS use incompatible character sets, but this incompatibility would only affect your source code. A story file, once compiled, behaves identically on PC and Macintosh regardless of what accented letters it may contain.) Many accented characters can be written as @, followed by an accent marker, then the letter on which the accent appears:

@^   put a circumflex on the next letter: a e i o u A E I O or U
@'   put an acute on the next letter: a e i o u y A E I O U or Y
@`   put a grave on the next letter: a e i o u A E I O or U
@:   put a diaeresis on the next letter: a e i o u A E I O or U
@c   put a cedilla on the next letter: c or C
@~   put a tilde on the next letter: a n o A N or O
@\   put a slash on the next letter: o or O
@o   put a ring on the next letter: a or A

A few other letter-forms are available: German ß (@ss), ligatures (@oe, @ae, @OE, @AE), Icelandic "thorn" @th and "eth" @et, a pounds-sterling sign (@LL), Spanish inverted punctuation (@!! and @??) and continental European quotation marks (@<< and @>>): see Table 2. For instance,

```
print "Les @oeuvres d'@AEsop en fran@ccais, mon @'el@`eve!";
print "Na@:ive readers of the New Yorker re@:elected Mr Clinton.";
print "Gau@ss first proved the Fundamental Theorem of Algebra.";
```

Accented characters can also be referred to as constants, like other characters. Just as 'x' represents the character lower-case-X, so '@^A' represents capital-A-circumflex.

△△ It takes a really, really good interpreter with support built in for Unicode and access to the proper fonts to use such a story file, but in principle you can place any Unicode character into text by quoting its Unicode value in hexadecimal. For instance, @{a9} produces a copyright sign (Unicode values between $0000 and $00ff are equal to ISO Latin1 values); @{2657} is a White bishop chess symbol; @{274b} is a "heavy eight teardrop-spoked propeller asterisk"; @{621} is the Arabic letter Hamza, and so on for around 30,000 more, including vast sets for Pacific Rim scripts and even for invented ones like Klingon or Tolkien's Elvish. Of course none of these new characters are in the regular ZSCII set, but ZSCII is configurable using Inform's Zcharacter directive. See §36 for more.

·   ·   ·   ·   ·

△   The remaining usage of @ is hacky but powerful. Suppose you are trying to implement some scenes from Infocom's spoof of 1930s sci-fi, 'Leather Goddesses of Phobos', where one of the player's companions has to be called Tiffany if the player is female, and Trent if male. The name turns up in numerous messages and it would be tiresome to keep writing

```
if (female_flag) print "Tiffany"; else print "Trent";
```

Instead you can use one of Inform's 32 "printing-variables" @00 to @31. When the text @14 is printed, for instance, the contents of string 14 are substituted in. The contents of string 14 can be set using the string statement, so:

```
if (female_flag) string 14 "Tiffany"; else string 14 "Trent";
...
print "You offer the untangling cream to @14, who whistles.^";
```

The value specified by a string statement has to be a literal, constant bit of text. There are *really* hacky ways to get around this, but if you needed to then you'd probably be better off with a different solution anyway.

§1.12   *The* print *and* print_ret *statements*

The print and print_ret statements are almost identical. The difference is that the second prints out a final and extra new-line character, and then causes a return from the current routine with the value true. Thus, print_ret should be read as "print this, print a new-line and then return true", and so

```
print_ret "That's enough of that.";
```

is equivalent to

```
print "That's enough of that.^"; rtrue;
```

As an abbreviation, it can even be shortened to:

```
"That's enough of that.";
```

Although Inform newcomers are often confused by the fact that this innocently free-standing bit of text actually causes a return from the current routine, it's an abbreviation which pays dividends in adventure-writing situations:

```
if (fuse_is_lit) { deadflag = true; "The bomb explodes!"; }
"Nothing happens.";
```

Note that if the source code:

```
[ Main;
  "Hello, and now for a number...";
  print 21*764;
];
```

is compiled, Inform will produce the warning message:

```
line 3: Warning: This statement can never be reached.
>     print 21*764;
```

because the bare string on line 2 is printed using print_ret: so the text is printed, then a new-line is printed, and then a return takes place immediately. As the warning message indicates, there is no way the statement on line 3 can ever be executed.

So what can be printed? The answer is a list of terms, separated by commas. For example,

```
print "The value is ", value, ".";
```

contains three terms. A term can take the following forms:

⟨a value⟩   printed as a (signed, decimal) number
⟨text in double-quotes⟩ printed as text
(⟨rule⟩) ⟨value⟩   printed according to some special rule

Inform provides a stock of special printing rules built-in, and also allows the programmer to create new ones. The most important rules are:

(char)   print out the character which this is the ZSCII code for
(string)   print out this string
(address) print out the text of this dictionary word
(name)   print out the name of this object (see §3)

Games compiled with the Inform library have several other printing rules built-in (like print (The) ...), but as these aren't part of the Inform language as such they will be left until §26.

△   print (string) ... requires a little explanation. Of the following lines, the first two print out "Hello!" but the third prints only a mysterious number:

```
print (string) "Hello!";
x = "Hello!"; print (string) x;
x = "Hello!"; print x;
```

This is because strings are internally represented by mysterious numbers. print (string) means "interpret this value as the mysterious number of a string, and print out that string": it is liable to give an error, or in some cases print gibberish, if applied to a value which isn't the mysterious number of any string.

.   .   .   .   .

Any Inform program can define its own printing rules simply by providing a routine whose name is the same as that of the rule. For example, the following pair of routines provides for printing out a value as a four-digit, unsigned hexadecimal number:

```
[ hex x y;
  y = (x & $7f00) / $100;
  if (x<0) y = y + $80;
  x = x & $ff;
  print (hexdigit) y/$10, (hexdigit) y,
        (hexdigit) x/$10, (hexdigit) x;
];
[ hexdigit x;
  x = x % $10;
  switch (x) {
     0 to 9: print x;
     10: print "a";   11: print "b";   12: print "c";
     13: print "d";   14: print "e";   15: print "f";
  }
];
```

You can paste these two routines into any Inform source code to make these new printing rules hex and hexdigit available to that code. For example, print (hex) 16339; will then print up "3fd3", and print (hex) -2; will print "fffe". Something to look out for is that if you inadvertently write

```
print hex(16339);
```

then the text printed will be "3fd31", with a spurious 1 on the end: because you've printed out the return value of the routine hex, which was true, or in other words 1.

§1.13   Other printing statements

Besides `print` and `print_ret`, several other statements can also be used for printing.

```
new_line
```

prints a new-line, otherwise known as a carriage return (named for the carriage which used to move paper across a typewriter). This is equivalent to

```
print "^"
```

but is a convenient abbreviation. Similarly,

```
spaces ⟨number⟩
```

prints a sequence of the given number of spaces.

```
box ⟨string1⟩ …⟨stringn⟩
```

displays a reverse-video panel in the centre of the screen, containing each string on its own line. For example, the statement

```
box "Passio domini nostri" "Jesu Christi Secundum" "Joannem";
```

displays the opening line of the libretto to Arvo Pärt's 'St John Passion':

```
Passio domini nostri
Jesu Christi Secundum
Joannem
```

. . . . .

Text is normally displayed in an unembellished but legible type intended to make reading paragraphs comfortable. Its actual appearance will vary from machine to machine running the story file. On most machines, it will be displayed using a "font" which is variably-pitched, so that for example a "w" will be wider on-screen than an "i". Such text is much easier to read, but makes it difficult to print out diagrams. The statement

```
print "+------------+
      ^+   Hello    +
      ^+------------+^";
```

will print something irregular if the letters in "Hello" and the characters "-",
"+" and " " (space) do not all have the same width on-screen:

```
+------------+
+   Hello   +
+------------+
```

Because one sometimes does want to print such a diagram, to represent a
sketch-map, say, or to print out a table, the statement font is provided:

```
font on
font off
```

font off switches into a fixed-pitch display style. It is now guaranteed that
the interpreter will print all characters at the same width. font on restores the
usual state of affairs.

   In addition, you can choose the type style from a small set of possibilities:
roman (the default), boldface, underlined or otherwise emphasized (some
interpreters will use italic for this), reverse-colour:

```
style roman
style bold
style underline
style reverse
```

"Reverse colour" would mean, for instance, yellow on blue if the normal
text appearance happened to be blue on yellow. An attempt will be made to
approximate these effects whatever kind of machine is running the story file.

△   Changes of foreground and background colours, so memorably used in games
like Adam Cadre's 'Photopia', can be achieved with care using Z-machine assembly
language. See §42.

§1.14   *Generating random numbers*

Inform provides a small stock of functions ready-defined, but which are used
much as other routines are. As most of these concern objects, only one will be
give here: random, which has two forms:

```
random(N)
```

returns a random number in the range $1, 2, \ldots, $ N, each of these outcomes being (in theory) equally likely. N should be a positive number, between 1 and 32,767, for this to work properly.

    random(⟨two or more constant quantities, separated by commas⟩)

returns a random choice from the given selection of constant values. Thus,

```
print (string) random("red", "blue", "green", "violet");
```

prints the name of one of these four colours at random. Likewise,

```
print random(13, 17);
```

has a 50% chance of printing "13", and a 50% chance of printing "17".

△   Random numbers are produced inside the interpreter by a "generator" which is not truly random in its behaviour. Instead, the sequence of numbers it produces depend on a value inside the generator called the "seed". Setting this value is called "seeding the random-number generator". Whenever it has the same seed value, the same sequence of random values will be harvested. This is called "pseudo-randomness". An interpreter normally goes to some effort to start up with a seed value which is unpredictable: say, the current time of day in milliseconds. Because you just might want to make it predictable, though, you can change the seed value within the story file by calling random(N) for a negative number N of your own choosing. (This returns zero.) Seeding is sometimes useful to test a game which contains random events or delays. For example if you have release 29 of Infocom's game 'Enchanter', you may be surprised to know that you can type "#random 14" into it, after which its random events will be repeatable and predictable. Internally, 'Enchanter' does this by calling random(-14).

§1.15   Deprecated ways to jump around

There are four statements left which control the flow of execution, but one should try to avoid using any of them if, for instance, a while loop would do the job more tidily. Please stop reading this section now.

△   Oh very well. 'Deprecated' is too strong a word, anyway, as there are circumstances where jumping is justified and even elegant: to break out of several loops at once, for instance, or to construct a finite state machine. It's the *gratuitous* use of jumping which is unfortunate, as this rapidly decreases the legibility of the source code.

△   The jump statement transfers execution to some named place in the same routine. (Some programming languages call this goto.) To use jump a notation is needed to mark particular places in the source code. Such markers are called "labels". For example, here is a never-ending loop made by hand:

```
[ Main i;
  i=1;
  .Marker;
  print "I have now printed this ", i++, " times.^";
  jump Marker;
];
```

This routine has one label, Marker. A statement consisting only of a full stop and then an identifier means "put a label here and call it this". Like local variables, labels belong to the routines defining them and cannot be used by other routines.

△   The quit statement ends interpretation of the story file immediately, as if a return had taken place from the Main routine. This is a drastic measure, best reserved for error conditions so awful that there is no point carrying on.

△△ An Inform story file has the ability to save a snapshot of its entire state and to restore back to that previous state. This snapshot includes values of variables, the point where code is currently being executed, and so on. Just as we cannot know if the universe is only six thousand years old, as creationists claim, having been endowed by God with a carefully faked fossil record, so an Inform story file cannot know if it has been executing all along or if it was only recently restarted. The statements required are save and restore:

save ⟨label⟩
restore ⟨label⟩

This is a rare example of an Inform feature which may depend on the host machine's state of health: for example, if all disc storage is full, then save will fail. It should always be assumed that these statements may well fail. A jump to the label provided occurs if the operation has been a success. This is irrelevant in the case of a restore since, if all has gone well, execution is now resuming from the successful branch of the save statement: because that is where execution was when the state was saved.

△△ If you don't mind using assembly language (see §42), you can imitate exceptions, in the sense of programming languages like Java. The opcodes you would need are @throw and @catch.

● REFERENCES
If you need to calculate with integers of any size then the restriction of Inform numbers to the range −32,768 to 32,767 is a nuisance. The function library "longint.h", by Chris Hall and Francis Irving, provides routines to calculate with signed and unsigned

36

4-byte integers, increasing the range to about $\pm 2,147,000,000$.   ●L. Ross Raszewski's function library `"ictype.h"` is an Inform version of the ANSI C routines `"ctype.h"`, which means that it contains routines to test whether a given character is lower or upper case, or is a punctuation symbol, and so forth. (See also the same author's `"istring.h"`.)

§2　The state of play

§2.1　Directives construct things

 Every example program so far has consisted only of a sequence of routines, each within beginning and end markers [and]. Such routines have no way of communicating with each other, and therefore of sharing information with each other, except by calling each other back and forth. This arrangement is not really suited to a large program whose task may be to simulate something complicated, such as the world of an adventure game: instead, some central registry of information is needed, to which all routines can have access. In the author's game 'Curses', centrally-held information ranges from the current score, held in a single variable called score, to Madame Sosostris's tarot pack, which uses an array of variables representing the cards on the pack, to a slide-projector held as an "object": a bundle of variables and routines encoding the relevant rules of the game, such as that the whitewashed wall is only lit up when the slide projector is switched on.

Every Inform source program is a list of constructions, made using commands called "directives". These are quite different from the statements inside routines, because directives create something at compilation time, whereas statements are only instructions for the interpreter to follow later, when the story file is being played.

In all there are 38 Inform directives, but most of them are seldom used, or else are just conveniences to help you organise your source code: for instance Include means "now include another whole file of source code here", and there are directives for "if I've set some constant at the start of the code, then don't compile this next bit" and so on. The 10 directives that matter are the ones creating data structures, and here they are:

```
[           Array       Attribute   Class      Constant
Extend      Global      Object      Property   Verb
```

The directive written [, meaning "construct a routine containing the following statements, up to the next]", was the subject of §1. The four directives to do with objects, Attribute, Class, Object and Property, will be the subject of

§3. The two directives to do with laying out grammar, Verb and Extend, are intimately tied up with the needs of adventure games using the Inform library, and are useless for any other purpose, so these are left until §30. That leaves just Array, Constant and Global.

§2.2   Constants

The simplest construction you can make is of a Constant. The following program, an unsatisfying game of chance, shows a typical usage:

```
Constant MAXIMUM_SCORE = 100;
[ Main;
  print "You have scored ", random(MAXIMUM_SCORE),
      " points out of ", MAXIMUM_SCORE, ".^";
];
```

The maximum score value is used twice in the routine Main. The resulting story file is exactly the same as it would have been if the constant definition were not present, and MAXIMUM_SCORE were replaced by 100 in both places where it occurs. But the advantage of using Constant is that it makes it possible to change this value from 100 to, say, 50 with only a single change to the source code, and it makes the source code more legible.

People often write the names of constants in full capitals, but this is not compulsory. Another convention is that the = sign, which is optional, is often left out if the value is a piece of text rather than a number. If no value is specified for a constant, as in the line

```
Constant BETA_TEST_VERSION;
```

then the constant is created with value 0.

A constant can be used from anywhere in the source code *after* the line on which it is declared. Its value cannot be altered.

§2.3   Global variables

The variables in §1 were all "local variables", each owned privately by its own routine, inaccessible to the rest of the program and destroyed as soon as the routine stops. A "global variable" is permanent and its value can be used or altered from every routine.

The directive for declaring a global variable is `Global`. For example:

```
Global score = 36;
```

This creates a variable called `score`, which at the start of the program has the value 36. (If no initial value is given, it starts with the value 0.)

A global variable can be altered or used from anywhere in the source code *after* the line on which it is declared.

§2.4 *Arrays*

An "array" is an indexed collection of variables, holding a set of numbers organised into a sequence. To see why this useful, suppose that a pack of cards is to be simulated. You could define 52 different variables with `Global`, with names like `Ace_of_Hearts`, to hold the position of each card in the pack: but then it would be very tiresome to write a routine to shuffle them around.

Instead, you can declare an array:

```
Array pack_of_cards --> 52;
```

which creates a stock of 52 variables, called the "entries" of the array, and referred to in the source code as

```
pack_of_cards-->0   pack_of_cards-->1   ...   pack_of_cards-->51
```

and the point of this is that you can read or alter the variable for card number i by calling it `pack_of_cards-->i`. Here is an example program, in full, for shuffling the pack:

```
Constant SHUFFLES = 100;
Array pack_of_cards --> 52;
[ ExchangeTwo x y z;
  !   Randomly choose two different numbers between 0 and 51:
  while (x==y) {
      x = random(52) - 1; y = random(52) - 1;
  }
  z = pack_of_cards-->x; pack_of_cards-->x = pack_of_cards-->y;
  pack_of_cards-->y = z;
];
[ Card n;
  switch(n%13) {
```

```
        0: print "Ace";
        1 to 9: print n%13 + 1;
        10: print "Jack";  11: print "Queen";  12: print "King";
    }
    print " of ";
    switch(n/13) {
        0: print "Hearts"; 1: print "Clubs";
        2: print "Diamonds"; 3: print "Spades";
    }
];
[ Main i;
    !   Create the pack in "factory order":
    for (i=0:i<52:i++) pack_of_cards-->i = i;
    !   Exchange random pairs of cards for a while:
    for (i=1:i<=SHUFFLES:i++) ExchangeTwo();
    print "The pack has been shuffled into the following order:^";
    for (i=0:i<52:i++)
        print (Card) pack_of_cards-->i, "^";
];
```

The cards are represented by numbers in the range 0 (the Ace of Hearts) to 51 (the King of Spades). The pack itself has 52 positions, from position 0 (top) to position 51 (bottom). The entry pack_of_cards-->i holds the number of the card in position i. A new pack as produced by the factory would come with Ace of Hearts on top (card 0 in position 0), running down to the King of Spades on the bottom (card 51 in position 51).

△   A hundred exchanges is only just enough. Redefining SHUFFLES as 10,000 takes a lot longer, while redefining it as 10 makes for a highly suspect result. Here is a more efficient method of shuffling (contributed by Dylan Thurston), perfectly random in just 51 exchanges.

```
pack_of_cards-->0 = 0;
for (i=1:i<52:i++) {
    j = random(i+1) - 1;
    pack_of_cards-->i = pack_of_cards-->j; pack_of_cards-->j = i;
}
```

· · · · ·

In the above example, the array entries are all created containing 0. Instead, you can give a list of constant values. For example,

```
Array small_primes --> 2 3 5 7 11 13;
```

is an array with six entries, `small_primes-->0` to `small_primes-->5`, initially holding 2, 3, 5, 7, 11 and 13.

The third way to create an array gives some text as an initial value, occasionally useful because one popular use for arrays is as "strings of characters" or "text buffers". For instance:

```
Array players_name --> "Frank Booth";
```

is equivalent to the directive:

```
Array players_name --> 'F' 'r' 'a' 'n' 'k' ' ' 'B' 'o' 'o' 't' 'h';
```

Literal text like `"Frank Booth"` is a constant, not an array, and you can no more alter its lettering than you could alter the digits of the number 124. The array `players_name` is quite different: its entries can be altered. But this means it cannot be treated as if it were a string constant, and in particular can't be printed out with `print (string)`. See below for the right way to do this.

• **WARNING**

In the pack of cards example, the entries are indexed 0 to 51. It's therefore impossible for an interpreter to obey the following statement:

```
pack_of_cards-->52 = 0;
```

because there is no entry 52. Instead, the following message will be printed when it plays:

[** Programming error: tried to write to -->52 in the array "pack_of_cards", which has entries 0 up to 51 **]

Such a mistake is sometimes called breaking the bounds of the array.

.   .   .   .   .

The kind of array constructed above is sometimes called a "word array". This is the most useful kind and many game designers never use the other three varieties at all.

△   The first alternative is a "byte array", which is identical except that its entries can only hold numbers in the range 0 to 255, and that it uses the notation `->` instead of `-->`. This is only really useful to economise on memory usage in special circumstances, usually when the entries are known to be characters, because ZSCII character codes are all between 0 and 255. The "Frank Booth" array above could safely have been a byte array.

△ In addition to this, Inform provides arrays which have a little extra structure: they are created with the 0th entry holding the number of entries. A word array with this property is called a `table`; a byte array with this property is a `string`. For example, the table

```
Array continents table 5;
```

has six entries: `continents-->0`, which holds the number 5, and further entries `continents-->1` to `continents-->5`. If the program changed `continents-->0` this would *not* magically change the number of array entries, or indeed the number of continents.

△△ One main reason you might want some arrangement like this is to write a general routine which can be applied to any array. Here is an example using `string` arrays:

```
Array password string "danger";
Array phone_number string "0171-930-9000";
...
print "Please give the password ", (PrintStringArray) password,
    " whenever telephoning Universal Exports at ",
    (PrintStringArray) phone_number, ".";
...
[ PrintStringArray the_array i;
  for (i=1: i<=the_array->0: i++) print (char) the_array->i;
];
```

Such routines should be written with care, as the normal checking of array bounds isn't performed when arrays are accessed in this indirect sort of fashion, so any mistake you make may cause trouble elsewhere and be difficult to diagnose.

△△ With all data structures (i.e., with objects, strings, routines and arrays) Inform calls by reference, not by value. So, for instance:

```
[ DamageStringArray the_array i;
  for (i=1: i<=the_array->0: i++) {
      if (the_array->i == 'a' or 'e' or 'i' or 'o' or 'u')
          the_array->i = random('a', 'e', 'i', 'o', 'u');
      print (char) the_array->i;
  }
];
```

means that the call `DamageStringArray(password_string)` will not just print (say) "dungor" but also alter the one and only copy of `password_string` in the story file.

§2.5   *Reading into arrays from the keyboard*

Surprisingly, perhaps, given that Inform is a language for text adventure games, support for reading from the keyboard is fairly limited. A significant difference of approach between Inform and many other systems for interactive fiction is that mechanisms for parsing textual commands don't come built into the language itself. Instead, game designers use a standard Inform parser program which occupies four and a half thousand lines of Inform code.

Reading single key-presses, perhaps with time-limits, or for that matter reading the mouse position and state (in a Version 6 game) requires the use of Inform assembly language: see §42.

A statement called read does however exist for reading in a single line of text and storing it into a byte array:

```
read text_array 0;
```

You must already have set text_array->0 to the maximum number of characters you will allow to be read. (If this is N, then the array must be defined with at least $N + 3$ entries, the last of which guards against overruns.) The number of characters actually read, not counting the carriage return, will be placed into text_array->1 and the characters themselves into entries from text_array->2 onwards. For example, if the player typed "GET IN":

->0	1	2	3	4	5	6	7
max	*characters*	*text typed by player, reduced to lower case*					
60	6	'g'	'e'	't'	' '	'i'	'n'

The following echo chamber demonstrates how to read from this array:

```
Array text_array -> 63;
[ Main c x;
  for (::) {
      print "^> ";
      text_array->0 = 60;
      read text_array 0;
      for (x=0:x<text_array->1:x++) {
          c = text_array->(2+x);
          print (char) c; if (c == 'o') print "h";
      }
  }
];
```

△   read can go further than simply reading in the text: it can work out where the words start and end, and if they are words registered in the story file's built-in vocabulary, known as the "dictionary". To produce all this information, read needs to be supplied with a second array:

```
read text_array parse_array;
```

read not only stores the text (just as above) but breaks down the line into a sequence of words, in which commas and full stops count as separate words in their own right. (An example is given in Chapter IV, §30.) In advance of this parse_array->0 must have been set to W, the maximum number of words you want to parse. Any further text will be ignored. parse_array should have at least $4W + 2$ entries, because parse_array->1 is set to the actual number of words parsed, and then a four-entry block is written into the array for each word parsed. Numbering the words as 1, 2, 3, ..., the number of letters in word n is written into parse_array->(n*4), and the position of the start of the word in text_array. The dictionary value of the word, or zero if it isn't recognised, is stored as parse_array-->(n*2-1). The corresponding parsing array to the previous text array, for the command "GET IN", looks like so:

->0	1	2	3	4	5	6	7	8	9
max	*words*	*first word*				*second word*			
10	2	'get'	2	3		'in'	5	2	

In this example both words were recognised. The word "get" began at position ->2 in the text array, and was 3 characters long; the word "in" began at ->5 and was 2 characters long. The following program reads in text and prints back an analysis:

```
Array text_array -> 63;
Array parse_array -> 42;
[ Main w x length position dict;
    w = 'mary'; w = 'had'; w = 'a//'; w = 'little'; w = 'lamb';
    for (::) {
        print "^> ";
        text_array->0 = 60; parse_array->0 = 10;
        read text_array parse_array;
        for (w=1:w<=parse_array->1:w++) {
            print "Word ", w, ": ";
            length = parse_array->(4*w);
            position = parse_array->(4*w + 1);
            dict = parse_array-->(w*2-1);
            for (x=0:x<length:x++)
                print (char) text_array->(position+x);
```

```
                    print " (length ", length, ")";
                    if (dict) print " equals '", (address) dict, "'^";
                        else print " is not in the dictionary^";
            }
        }
    ];
```

Note that the pointless-looking first line of Main adds five words to the dictionary. The result is:

>MARY, hello
Word 1: mary (length 4) equals 'mary'
Word 2: , (length 1) is not in the dictionary
Word 3: hello (length 5) is not in the dictionary

△   What goes into the dictionary? The answer is: any of the words given in the name of an object (see §3), any of the verbs and prepositions given in grammar by Verb and Extend directives (see §26), and anything given as a dictionary-word constant. The last is convenient because it means that code like

```
    if (parse_array -->(n*2-1)) == 'purple';
```

does what it looks as if it should. When compiling this line, Inform automatically adds the word "purple" to the story file's dictionary, so that any read statement will recognise it.

● **REFERENCES**
Evin Robertson's function library "array.h" provides some simple array-handling utilities.   ●L. Ross Raszewski's function library "istring.h" offers Inform versions of the ANSI C string-handling routines, including strcmp(), strcpy() and strcat(). The further extension "znsi.h" allows the printing out of string arrays with special escape sequences like [B interpreted as "bold face." (See also the same author's "ictype.h".)   ●Adam Cadre's function library "flags.h" manages an array of boolean values (that is, values which can only be true or false) so as to use only one-sixteenth as much memory as a conventional array, though at some cost to speed of access.

§3 Objects and classes

> Objects make up the substance of the world.
> —Ludwig Wittgenstein (1889–1951), *Tractatus*

§3.1 *Objects, classes, metaclasses and* nothing

In Inform, objects are little bundles of routines and variables tied up together. Dividing up the source code into objects is a good way to organise any large, complicated program, and makes particular sense for an adventure game, based as it usually is on simulated items and places. One item in the simulated world corresponds to one "object" in the source code. Each of these pieces of the story file should take responsibility for its own behaviour, so for instance a brass lamp in an adventure game might be coded with an Inform object called brass_lamp, containing all of the game rules which affect the lamp. Then again, objects *do* have to interact.

> *In West Pit*
> You are at the bottom of the western pit in the twopit room. There is a large hole in the wall about 25 feet above you.
> There is a tiny little plant in the pit, murmuring "Water, water, …"

In this moment from 'Advent', the player is more or less openly invited to water the plant. There might be many ways to bring water to it, or indeed to bring liquids other than water, and the rules for what happens will obviously affect the bottle carrying the water, the water itself and the plant. Where should the rules appear in the source code? Ideally, the plant object should know about growing and the bottle about being filled up and emptied. Many people feel that the most elegant approach is for the bottle, or any other flask, not to interfere with the plant directly but instead to send a "message" to the plant to say "you have been watered". It's then easy to add other solutions to the same puzzle: a successful rain dance, for instance, could also result in a "you have been watered" message being sent to plant. The whole behaviour of the plant could be altered without needing even to look at the rain-dance or the bottle source code. Objects like this can frequently be cut out of the source code for one game and placed into another, still working.

This traffic of messages between objects goes on continuously in Inform-compiled adventure games. When the player tries to pick up a wicker cage, the Inform library sends a message to the cage object asking if it minds being picked up. When the player tries to go north from the Hall of Mists, the library sends a message to an object called Hall_of_Mists asking where that would lead, and so on.

. . . . .

Typical large story files have so many objects ('Curses', for instance, has 550) that it is convenient to group similar objects together into "classes". For instance, 'Advent' began life as a simulation of part of the Mammoth and Flint Ridge cave system of Kentucky, caves which contain many, many dead ends. The Inform source code could become very repetitive without a class like so:

```
Class DeadEndRoom
  with short_name "Dead End",
       description "You have reached a dead end.",
       cant_go "You'll have to go back the way you came.";
```

Leaving the exact syntax for later, this code lays out some common features of dead ends. All kinds of elegant things can be done with classes if you like, or not if you don't.

Objects can belong to several different classes at once, and it is sometimes convenient to be able to check whether or not a given object belongs to a given class. For instance, in adventures compiled with the Inform library, a variable called location always holds the player's current position, so it might be useful to do this:

```
if (location ofclass DeadEndRoom) "Perhaps you should go back.";
```

. . . . .

Items and places in an Inform game always belong to at least one class, whatever you define, because they always belong to the "metaclass" Object. ("Meta" from the Greek for "beyond".) As we shall see, all of the objects explicitly written out in Inform source code always belong to Object. Though you seldom need to know this, there are three other metaclasses. Classes turn out to be a kind of object in themselves, and belong to Class. (So that Class belongs to itself. If you enjoy object-oriented programming, this will give you a warm glow inside). And although you almost never need to know or care, routines as in §1 are internally considered as a kind of object, of class Routine; while strings in double-quotes are likewise of class String. That's all, though. If in doubt, you can always find out what kind of object obj is, using the built-in function metaclass(obj). Here are some example values:

```
metaclass("Violin Concerto no. 1") == String
metaclass(Main) == Routine
metaclass(DeadEndRoom) == Class
metaclass(silver_bars) == Object
```

Classes are useful and important, but for most game-designing purposes it's now safe to forget all about metaclasses.

It turns out to be useful to have a constant called nothing and meaning "no object at all". It really does mean that: nothing *is not an object*. If you try to treat it as one, many programming errors will be printed up when the story file is played.

△   If X is not an object at all, then metaclass(X) is nothing, and in particular metaclass(nothing) is nothing.

§3.2   *The object tree*

Objects declared in the source code are joined together in an "object tree" which grows through every Inform story file. Adventure games use this to represent which items are contained inside which other items.

It's conventional to think of this as a sort of family tree without marriages. Each object has a parent, a child and a sibling. Such a relation is always either another object in the tree, or else nothing, so for instance the parent of an orphan would be nothing. Here is a sample object tree:

```
Meadow
  │ child
  │        sibling
  Mailbox  ⟶      Player
  │ child          │ child
  Note             Sceptre  sibling  Bottle  sibling  Torch  sibling  Stone
                            ⟶               ⟶               ⟶
                                                     │ child
                                                     Battery
```

The Mailbox and Player are both children of the Meadow, which is their parent, but only the Mailbox is *the* child of the Meadow. The Stone is the sibling of the Torch, which is the sibling of the Bottle, and so on.

Inform provides special functions for reading off positions in the tree: parent, sibling do the obvious things, and child gives the first child: in addition there's a function called children which counts up how many children an object has (note that grandchildren don't count as children). Here are some sample values:

```
parent ( Mailbox )  == Meadow
children ( Player ) == 4
child ( Player )    == Sceptre
child ( Sceptre )   == nothing
sibling ( Torch )   == Stone
```

● **WARNING**

It is incorrect to apply these functions to the value nothing, since it is *not an object*. If you write a statement like print children(x) ; when the value of x happens to be nothing, the interpreter will print up the message:

[** Programming error: tried to find the "children" of nothing **]

You get a similar error message if you try to apply these tree functions to a routine, string or class.

§3.3   *Declaring objects 1: setting up the tree*

Objects are made with the directive Object. Here is a portion of source code, with the bulk of the definitions abbreviated to "...":

```
Object Bucket ...
Object -> Starfish ...
Object -> Oyster ...
Object -> -> Pearl ...
Object -> Sand ...
```

The resulting tree looks a little like the source code turned on its side:

The idea is that if no arrows -> are given in the Object definition, then the object has no parent. If one -> is given, then the object is made a child of the last object defined with no arrows; if two are given, it's made a child of the last object defined with only one arrow; and so on.

An object definition consists of a "head" followed by a "body", itself divided into "segments", though there the similarity with caterpillars ends. The head takes the form:

```
Object ⟨arrows⟩ ⟨identifier⟩ "textual name" ⟨parent⟩
```

(1) The ⟨arrows⟩ are as described above. Note that if one or more arrows are given, that automatically specifies what object this is the child of, so a ⟨parent⟩ cannot be given as well.
(2) The ⟨identifier⟩ is what the object can be called inside the program, in the same way that a variable or a routine has a name.
(3) The "textual name" can be given if the object's name ever needs to be printed by the program when it is running.
(4) The ⟨parent⟩ is an object which this new object is to be a child of. This is an alternative to supplying arrows.

All four parts are optional, so that even this bare directive is legal:

```
Object;
```

though it makes a nameless and featureless object which is unlikely to be useful.

§3.4   Tree statements: move, remove, objectloop

The positions of objects in the tree are by no means fixed: objects are created in a particular formation but then shuffled around extensively during the story file's execution. (In an adventure game, where the objects represent items and rooms, objects are moved across the tree whenever the player picks something up or moves around.) The statement

```
move ⟨object⟩ to ⟨object⟩
```

moves the first-named object to become a child of the second-named one. All of the first object's own children "move along with it", i.e., remain its own children.

For instance, starting from the tree as shown in the diagram of §3.2 above,

```
move Bottle to Mailbox;
```

results in the tree

```
Meadow
  ↓ child
Mailbox         sibling        Player
  ↓ child        ⟶               ↓ child
Bottle  sibling  Note    Sceptre  sibling   Torch  sibling   Stone
        ⟶                         ⟶                ⟶
                                           ↓ child
                                          Battery
```

When an object becomes the child of another in this way, it always becomes
the "eldest" child: that is, it is the new child() of its parent, pushing the
previous children over into being its siblings. In the tree above, Bottle has
displaced Note just so.

You can only move one object in the tree to another: you can't

```
move Torch to nothing;
```

because nothing *is not an object*. Instead, you can detach the Torch branch
from the tree with

```
remove Torch;
```

and this would result in:

```
Meadow                                              Torch
  ↓ child                                             ↓ child
Mailbox         sibling                              Battery
  ↓ child        ⟶          Player
Bottle  sibling  Note        ↓ child
        ⟶                  Sceptre  sibling  Stone
                                    ⟶
```

The "object tree" is often fragmented like this into many little trees, and is not
so much a tree as a forest.

• WARNING

It would make no sense to have a circle of objects each containing the next, so
if you try to move Meadow to Note; then you'll only move the interpreter to
print up:

> [** Programming error: tried to move the Meadow to the note, which would
> make a loop: Meadow in note in mailbox in Meadow **]

· · · · ·

Since objects move around a good deal, it's useful to be able to test where an object currently is, and the condition in is provided for this. For example,

```
Bottle in Mailbox
```

is true if and only if the Bottle is one of the *direct* children of the Mailbox. (Bottle in Mailbox is true, but Bottle in Meadow is false.) Note that

```
X in Y
```

is only an abbreviation for parent(X)==Y but it occurs so often that it's worth having. Similarly, X notin Y means parent(X)~=Y. X has to be a bona-fide member of the object tree, but Y is allowed to be nothing, and testing X in nothing reveals whether or not X has been removed from the rest of the tree.

· · · · ·

The remaining loop statement left over from §1 is objectloop.

```
objectloop(⟨variable-name⟩) ⟨statement⟩
```

runs through the ⟨statement⟩ once for each object in the game, putting each object in turn into the variable. For example,

```
objectloop(x) print (name) x, "^";
```

prints out a list of the textual names of every object in the game. More powerfully, any condition can be written in the brackets, as long as it begins with a variable name.

```
objectloop (x in Mailbox) print (name) x, "^";
```

prints the names only of those objects which are direct children of the Mailbox object.

The simple case where the condition reads "⟨variable⟩ in ⟨object⟩" is handled in a faster and more predictable way than other kinds of objectloop: the loop variable is guaranteed to run through the children of the object in sibling order, eldest down to youngest. (This is faster because it doesn't waste time considering every object in the game, only the children.) If the condition is not in this form then no guarantee is made as to the order in which the objects are considered.

• **WARNING**

When looping over objects with in, it's not safe to move these same objects around: this is like trying to cut a branch off an elm tree while sitting on it. Code like this:

```
objectloop(x in Meadow) move x to Sandy_Beach;
```

looks plausible but is not a safe way to move everything in the Meadow, and will instead cause the interpreter to print up

[** Programming error: objectloop broken because the object mailbox was moved while the loop passed through it **]

Here is a safer way to move the meadow's contents to the beach:

```
while (child(Meadow)) move child(Meadow) to Sandy_Beach;
```

This works because when the Meadow has no more children, its child is then nothing, which is the same as false.

△   But it moves the eldest child first, with the possibly undesirable result that the children arrive in reverse order (Mailbox and then Player, say, become Player and then Mailbox). Here is an alternative, moving the youngest instead of the eldest child each time, which keeps them in the same order:

```
while (child(Meadow)) {
    x = child(Meadow); while (sibling(x)) x = sibling(x);
    move x to Sandy_Beach;
}
```

Keeping children in order can be worth some thought when game designing. For instance, suppose a tractor is to be moved to a farmyard in which there is already a barn. The experienced game designer might do this like so:

```
move tractor to Farmyard;
move barn to Farmyard;
```

Although the barn was in the farmyard already, the second statement wasn't redundant: because a moved object becomes the eldest child, the statement does this:

$$
\begin{array}{ccc}
\text{Farmyard} & & \text{Farmyard} \\
\downarrow child & \Longrightarrow & \downarrow child \\
\text{tractor} \xrightarrow{\;sibling\;} \text{barn} & & \text{barn} \xrightarrow{\;sibling\;} \text{tractor}
\end{array}
$$

And this is desirable because the ordering of paragraphs in room descriptions tends to follow the ordering of items in the object tree, and the designer wants the barn mentioned before the tractor.

54

△   An `objectloop` range can be any condition so long as a named local or global variable appears immediately after the open bracket. This means that

```
objectloop (child(x) == nothing) ...
```

isn't allowed, because the first thing after the bracket is `child`, but a dodge to get around this is:

```
objectloop (x && child(x) == nothing) ...
```

The loop variable of an `objectloop` can never equal `false`, because that's the same as `nothing`, which isn't an object.

△△ The `objectloop` statement runs through all objects of metaclass `Object` or `Class`, but skips any `Routine` or `String`.

§3.5   *Declaring objects 2:* `with` *and* `provides`

So far `Objects` are just tokens with names attached which can be shuffled around in a tree. They become interesting when data and routines are attached to them, and this is what the body of an object definition is for. The body contains four different kinds of segments, introduced by the keywords:

```
with     has     class     private
```

These are all optional and can be given in any order.

△   They can even be given more than once: that is, there can be two or more of a given kind, which Inform will combine together as if they had been defined in one go. (This is only likely to be useful for automated Inform-writing programs.)

· · · · ·

The most important segment is `with`, which specifies variables and, as we shall see, routines and even arrays, to be attached to the object. For example,

```
Object magpie "black-striped bird"
  with wingspan, worms_eaten;
```

attaches two variables to the bird, one called `wingspan`, the other called `worms_eaten`. Commas are used to separate them and the object definition as a whole ends with a semicolon, as always. Variables of this kind are called properties, and are referred to in the source code thus:

```
magpie.wingspan
magpie.worms_eaten
```

Properties are just like global variables: any value you can store in a variable can be stored in a property. But note that

```
crested_grebe.wingspan
magpie.wingspan
```

are different and may well have different values, which is why the object whose wingspan it is (the magpie or the grebe) has to be named.

The property wingspan is said to be provided by both the magpie and crested_grebe objects, whereas an object whose with segment didn't name wingspan would not provide it. The dot . operator can only be used to set the value of a property which is provided by the object on the left of the dot: if not a programming error will be printed up when the story file is played.

The presence of a property can be tested using the provides condition. For example,

```
objectloop (x provides wingspan) ...
```

executes the code ... for each object x in the program which is defined with a wingspan property.

△   Although the provision of a property can be tested, it can't be changed while the program is running. The *value* of magpie.wingspan may change, but not the *fact* that the magpie provides a wingspan.

△△ Some special properties, known as "common properties", can have their values *read* (but not changed) even for an object which doesn't provide them. All of the properties built into the Inform library are common properties. See §3.14.

.   .   .   .   .

When the magpie is created as above, the initial values of

```
magpie.wingspan
magpie.worms_eaten
```

are both 0. To create the magpie with a given wingspan, we have to specify an initial value, which we do by giving it after the name, e.g.:

```
Object magpie "black-striped bird"
    with wingspan 5, worms_eaten;
```

The story file now begins with magpie.wingspan equal to 5, though magpie.worms_eaten still equal to 0.

. . . . .

A property can contain a routine instead of a value. In the definition

```
Object magpie "black-striped bird"
    with name 'magpie' 'bird' 'black-striped' 'black' 'striped',
        wingspan 5,
        flying_strength [;
            return magpie.wingspan + magpie.worms_eaten;
        ],
        worms_eaten;
```

The value of magpie.flying_strength is given as a routine, in square brackets as usual. Note that the Object continues where it left off after the routine-end marker,]. Routines which are written in as property values are called "embedded" and are the way objects receive messages, as we shall see.

△   If, during play, you want to change the way a magpie's flying strength is calculated, you can simply change the value of its property:

```
magpie.flying_strength = ExhaustedBirdFS;
```

where ExhaustedBirdFS is the name of a routine to perform the new calculation.

△   Embedded routines are just like ordinary ones, with two exceptions:

(1) An embedded routine has no name of its own, since it is referred to as a property such as magpie.flying_strength instead.

(2) If execution reaches the] end-marker of an embedded routine, then it returns false, not true (as a non-embedded routine would).

△△ Properties can be arrays instead of variables. If two or more consecutive values are given for the same property, it becomes an array. Thus,

```
Object magpie "black-striped bird"
    with name 'magpie' 'bird' 'black-striped' 'black' 'striped',
        wingspan 5, worms_eaten;
```

You can't write magpie.name because there is no single value: rather, there is an --> array (see §2.4). This array must be accessed using two special operators, .& and .#, for the array and its length, as follows.

```
magpie.&name
```

means "the array held in magpie's name property", so that the actual name values are in the entries

```
magpie.&name-->0, magpie.&name-->1, ..., magpie.&name-->4
```

The size of this array can be discovered with

```
magpie.#name
```

which evaluates to the twice the number of entries, in this case, to 10. Twice the number of entries because that is the number of bytes in the array: people fairly often use property arrays as byte arrays to save on memory.

△   name is a special property created by Inform, intended to hold dictionary words which can refer to an object.

§3.6   Declaring objects 3: private properties

△   A system is provided for "encapsulating" certain properties so that only the object itself has access to them. These are defined by giving them in a segment of the object declaration called private. For instance,

```
Object sentry "sentry"
  private pass_number 16339,
  with challenge [ attempt;
            if (attempt == sentry.pass_number)
                "Approach, friend!";
            "Stand off, stranger.";
        ];
```

provides for two properties: challenge, which is public, and pass_number, which can be used only by the sentry's own embedded routines.

△△ This makes the provides condition slightly more interesting than it appeared in the previous section. The answer to the question of whether or not

```
sentry provides pass_number
```

depends on who's asking: this condition is true if it is tested in one of the sentry's own routines, and elsewhere false. A private property is so well hidden that nobody else can even know whether or not it exists.

§3.7   Declaring objects 4: has and give

In addition to properties, objects have flags attached, called "attributes". (Recall that flags are a limited form of variable which can only have two values, sometimes called set and clear.) Unlike property names, attribute names have to be declared before use with a directive like:

```
Attribute hungry;
```

Once this declaration is made, every object in the tree has a hungry flag attached, which is either true or false at any given time. The state can be tested with the has condition:

```
magpie has hungry
```

is true if and only if the magpie's hungry flag is currently set. You can also test if magpie hasnt hungry. There's no apostrophe in hasnt.

The magpie can now be born hungry, using the has segment in its declaration:

```
Object magpie "black-striped bird"
  with wingspan, worms_eaten
  has  hungry;
```

The has segment contains a list (without commas in between) of the attributes which are initially set: for instance, the steel grate in the Inform example game 'Advent' includes the line

```
has   static door openable lockable locked;
```

The state of an attribute can be changed during play using the give statement:

```
give magpie hungry;
```

sets the magpie's hungry attribute, and

```
give magpie ~hungry;
```

clears it again. The give statement can take more than one attribute at a time, too:

```
give double_doors_of_the_horizon ~locked openable open;
```

means "clear locked and set openable and open".†

---

† The refrain from the prelude to Act I of Philip Glass's opera *Akhnaten* is "Open are the double doors of the horizon/ Unlocked are its bolts".

△△ An attribute can also have a tilde ˜ placed in front in the has part of an object declaration, indicating "this is definitely not held". This is usually what would have happened anyway, except that class inheritance (see below) might have passed on an attribute: if so, this is how to get rid of it again. Suppose there is a whole class of steel grates like the one in 'Advent' mentioned above, providing for a dozen grates scattered through a game, but you also want a loose grate L whose lock has been smashed. If L belongs to the class, it will start the game with attributes making it locked like the others, because the class sets these automatically: but if you include has ˜lockable ˜locked; in its declaration, these two attributes go away again.

§3.8 *Declaring objects 5:* class *inheritance*

A class is a prototype design from which other objects are manufactured. These resulting objects are sometimes called instances or members of the class, and are said to inherit from it.

Classes are useful when a group of objects are to have common features. In the definition of the magpie above, a zoologically doubtful formula was laid out for flying strength:

```
flying_strength [;
    return magpie.wingspan + magpie.worms_eaten;
],
```

This formula ought to apply to birds in general, not just to magpies, and in the following definition it does:

```
Attribute flightless;
Class Bird
 with wingspan 7,
      flying_strength [;
          if (self has flightless) return 0;
          return self.wingspan + self.worms_eaten;
      ],
      worms_eaten;
Bird "ostrich" with wingspan 3, has flightless;
Bird "magpie" with wingspan 5;
Bird "crested grebe";
Bird "Great Auk" with wingspan 15;
Bird "early bird" with worms_eaten 1;
```

Facts about birds in general are now located in a class called Bird. Every example of a Bird automatically provides wingspan, a flying_strength routine and a count of `worms_eaten`. Notice that the Great Auk is not content with the average avian wingspan of 7, and insists on measuring 15 across. This is an example of inheritance from a class being over-ridden by a definition inside the object. The actual values set up are as follows:

B	B.wingspan	B.worms_eaten
ostrich	3	0
magpie	5	0
crested grebe	7	0
Great Auk	15	0
early bird	7	1

Note also the use of the special value `self` in the definition of `Bird`. It means "whatever bird I am": if the `flying_strength` routine is being run for the ostrich, then `self` means the ostrich, and so on.

The example also demonstrates a general rule: to create something, begin its declaration with the name of the class you want it to belong to: a plain `Object`, a `Class` or now a `Bird`.

△   Sometimes you need to specify that an object belongs to many classes, not just one. You can do this with the `class` segment of the definition, like so:

```
Object "goose that lays the golden eggs"
  class Bird Treasure;
```

This goose belongs to three classes: `Object` of course, as all declared objects do, but also `Bird` and `Treasure`. (It inherits from `Object` first and then `Bird` and then `Treasure`, attribute settings and property values from later-mentioned classes overriding earlier ones, so if these classes should give contradictory instructions then `Treasure` gets the last word.) You can also make class definitions have classes, or rather, pass on membership of other classes:

```
Class BirdOfPrey
  class Bird
  with wingspan 15,
       people_eaten;
BirdOfPrey kestrel;
```

makes `kestrel` a member of both `BirdOfPrey` and of `Bird`. Dutiful apostles of object-oriented programming may want to call `BirdOfPrey` a "subclass" of `Bird`. Indeed, they may want to call Inform a "weakly-typed language with multiple-inheritance", or more probably a "shambles".

△△ For certain "additive" common properties, clashes between what classes say and what an instance says are resolved differently: see §5. Inform's built-in property name is one of these.

§3.9 Messages

Objects communicate with each other by means of messages. A message has a sender, a receiver and some parameter values attached, and it always produces a reply, which is just a single value. For instance,

```
x = plant.pour_over(cold_spring_water);
```

sends the message pour_over with a single parameter, cold_spring_water, to the object plant, and puts the reply value into x.

In order to receive this message, plant has to provide a pour_over property. If it doesn't, then the interpreter will print something like

[** Programming error: the plant (object number 21) has no property pour_over to send message **]

when the story file is played. The pour_over property will normally be a routine, perhaps this one:

```
pour_over [ liquid;
    remove liquid;
    switch(liquid) {
        oil: "The plant indignantly shakes the oil off its
            leaves and asks, ~Water?~";
        ...
    }
];
```

Inside such a routine, self means the object receiving the message and sender means the object which sent it. In a typical Inform game situation, sender will often be the object InformLibrary, which organises play and sends out many messages to items and places in the game, consulting them about what should happen next. Much of any Inform game designer's time is spent writing properties which receive messages from InformLibrary: before, after, each_turn and n_to among many others.

You can see all the messages being sent in a game as it runs using the debugging verb "messages": see §7 for details. This is the Inform version of listening in on police-radio traffic.

△ It was assumed above that the receiving property value would be a routine. But this needn't always be true. It can instead be: nothing, in which case the reply value is also nothing (which is the same as zero and the same as false). Or it can be an Object or a Class, in which case nothing happens and the object or class is sent back as the reply value. Or it can be a string in double-quotes, in which case the string is printed out, then a new-line is printed, and the reply value is true.

△ This can be useful. Here is approximately what happens when the Inform library tries to move the player northeast from the current room (the location) in an adventure game (leaving out some complications to do with doors):

```
if (location provides ne_to) {
    x = location.ne_to();
    if (x == nothing) "You can't go that way.";
    if (x ofclass Object) move player to x;
} else "You can't go that way.";
```

This neatly deals with all of the following cases:

```
Object Octagonal_Room "Octagonal Room"
    with ...
            ne_to "The way north-east is barred by an invisible wall!",
            w_to Courtyard,
            e_to [;
                if (Amulet has worn) {
                    print "A section of the eastern wall suddenly parts
                            before you, allowing you into...^";
                    return HiddenShrine;
                }
            ],
            s_to [;
                if (random(5) ~= 1) return Gateway;
                print "The floor unexpectedly gives way, dropping you
                        through an open hole in the plaster...^";
                return random(Maze1, Maze2, Maze3, Maze4);
            ];
```

Noteworthy here is that the e_to routine, being an embedded routine, returns false which is the same as nothing if the] end-marker is reached, so if the Amulet isn't being worn then there is no map connection east.

△△ The receiving property can even hold an array of values, in which case the message is sent to each entry in the array in turn. The process stops as soon as one of these entries replies with a value other than nothing or false. If every entry is tried and they all replied nothing, then the reply value sent back is nothing. (This is useful to the Inform library because it allows before rules to be accumulated from the different classes an object belongs to.)

§3.10   *Passing messages up to the superclass*

△   It fairly often happens that an instance of a class needs to behave almost, but not quite, as the class would suggest. For instance, suppose the following Treasure class:

```
Class Treasure
 with deposit [;
            if (self provides deposit_points)
                score = score + self.deposit_points;
            else score = score + 5;
            move self to trophy_case;
            "You feel a sense of increased esteem and worth.";
        ];
```

and we want to create an instance called Bat_Idol which flutters away, resisting deposition, but only if the room is dark:

```
Treasure Bat_Idol "jewelled bat idol"
    with deposit [;
            if (location == thedark) {
                remove self;
                "There is a clinking, fluttering sound!";
            }
            ...
        ];
```

In place of ..., what we want is all of the previous source code about depositing treasures. We could just copy it out again, but a much neater trick is to write:

```
self.Treasure::deposit();
```

Instead of sending the message deposit, we send the message Treasure::deposit, which means "what deposit would do if it used the value defined by Treasure". The double-colon :: is called the "superclass operator". (The word "superclass", in this context, is borrowed from the Smalltalk-80 language.)

△△ object.class::property is the value of property which the given object would normally inherit from the given class. (Or it gives an error if the class doesn't provide that property or if the object isn't a member of that class).

△△ It's perfectly legal to write something like x = Treasure::deposit; and then to send Bat_Idol.x();.

§3.11 Creating and deleting objects during play

In an adventure-game setting, object creation is useful for something like a beach full of stones: if the player wants to pick up more and more stones, the game needs to create a new object for each stone brought into play.

Besides that, it is often elegant to grow structures organically. A maze of caves being generated during play, for example, should have new caves gradually added onto the map as and when needed.

The trouble with this is that since resources cannot be infinite, the cave-objects have to come from somewhere, and at last they come no more. The program must be able to cope with this, and it can present the programmer with real difficulties, especially if the conditions that will prevail when the supply runs out are hard to predict.

Inform does allow object creation during play, but it insists that the programmer must specify in advance the maximum resources which will ever be needed. (For example, the maximum number of beach stones which can ever be in play.) This is a nuisance, but means that the resulting story file will always work, or always fail, identically on every machine running it. It won't do one thing on the designer's 256-megabyte Sun workstation in Venice and then quite another on a player's personal organiser in a commuter train in New Jersey.

· · · · ·

If you want to create objects, you need to define a class for them and to specify N, the maximum number ever needed at once. Objects can be deleted once created, so if all N are in play then deleting one will allow another to be created.

Suppose the beach is to contain up to fifty pebbles. Then:

```
Class Pebble(50)
  with name 'smooth' 'pebble',
       short_name "smooth pebble from the beach";
```

Pebble is an ordinary class in every respect, except that it has the ability to create up to $N = 50$ instances of itself.

Creating and destroying objects is done by sending messages to the class Pebble itself, so for instance sending the message Pebble.create() will bring another pebble into existence. Classes can receive five different messages, as follows:

`remaining()`
How many more instances of this class can be created?

`create(⟨parameters⟩)`
Replies with a newly created object of this class, or else with nothing if no more can be created. If given, the parameters are passed on to the object so that it can use them to configure itself (see below).

`destroy(I)`
Destroys the instance I, which must previously have been created. You can't destroy an object which you defined by hand in the source code. (This is quite unlike remove, which only takes an object out of the tree for a while but keeps it in existence, ready to be moved back again later.)

`recreate(I, ⟨parameters⟩)`
Re-initialises the instance I, as if it had been destroyed and then created again.

`copy(I, J)`
Copies the property and attribute values from I to be equal to those of J, where both have to be instances of the class. (If a property holds an array, this is copied over as well.)

△   It's rather useful that `recreate` and copy can be sent for any instances, not just instances which have previously been created. For example,

```
Plant.copy(Gilded_Branch, Poison_Ivy)
```

copies over all the features of a `Plant` from `Poison_Ivy` to `Gilded_Branch`, but leaves any other properties and attributes of the gilded branch alone. Likewise,

```
Treasure.recreate(Gilded_Branch)
```

only resets the properties to do with `Treasure`, leaving the `Plant` properties alone.

△   If you didn't give a number like (50) in the class definition, then you'll find that N is zero. copy will work as normal, but remaining will return zero and create will always return nothing. There is nothing to destroy and since this isn't a class which can create objects, recreate will not work either. (Oh, and don't try to send these messages to the class `Class`: creating and destroying classes is called "programming", and it's far too late when the game is already being played.)

△△ You can even give the number as (0). You might do this either so that Class Gadget(MAX_GADGETS) in some library file will work even if the constant MAX_GADGETS happens to be zero. Or so that you can at least recreate existing members of the class even if you cannot create new ones.

66

.   .   .   .   .

The following example shows object creation used in a tiny game, dramatising a remark attributed to Isaac Newton (though it appears only in Brewster's *Memoirs of Newton*).

```
Constant Story "ISAAC NEWTON'S BEACH";
Constant Headline "^An Interactive Metaphor^";
Include "Parser";
Include "VerbLib";
Class Pebble(50)
 with name 'smooth' 'pebble' 'stone' 'pebbles//p' 'stones//p',
      short_name "smooth pebble from the beach",
      plural "smooth pebbles from the beach";
Object Shingle "Shingle"
  with description
          "You seem to be only a boy playing on a sea-shore, and
             diverting yourself in finding a smoother pebble or a
             prettier shell than ordinary, whilst the great ocean of
             truth lies all undiscovered before you.",
  has  light;
Object -> "pebble"
  with name 'smoother' 'pebble' 'stone' 'stones' 'shingle',
      initial "The breakers drain ceaselessly through the shingle,
             spilling momentary rock-pools.",
      before [ new_stone;
          Take:
              new_stone = Pebble.create();
              if (new_stone == nothing)
                "You look in vain for a stone smoother than
                   the fifty ever-smoother stones you have
                   gathered so far.";
              move new_stone to Shingle;
              <<Take new_stone>>;
          ],
  has  static;
[ Initialise;
  location = Shingle; "^^^^^^Welcome to...^";
];
Include "Grammar";
```

In this very small adventure game, if the player types "take a pebble", he will get one: more surprisingly, if he types "take a smoother pebble" he will get another one, and so on until his inventory listing reads "fifty smooth pebbles from the beach". (See §29 for how to make sure identical objects are described well in Inform adventure games.)   Notice that a newly-created object is in nothing, that is, is outside the object tree, so it must be moved to Shingle in order to come to the player's hand.

. . . . .

However smooth, one pebble is much like another. More complicated objects sometimes need some setting-up when they are created, and of course in good object-oriented style they ought to do this setting-up for themselves. Here is a class which does:

```
Class Ghost(7)
  with haunting,
       create [;
            self.haunting = random(Library, Ballroom, Summer_House);
            move self to self.haunting;
            if (self in location)
                "^The air ripples as if parted like curtains.";
       ];
```

What happens is that when the program sends the message

```
Ghost.create();
```

the class Ghost creates a new ghost G, if there aren't already seven, and then sends a further message

```
G.create();
```

This new object G chooses its own place to haunt and moves itself into place. Only then does the class Ghost reply to the outside program. A class can also give a destroy routine to take care of the consequences of destruction, as in the following example:

```
Class Axe(30);
Class Dwarf(7)
  with create [ x;
            x = Axe.create(); if (x ~= nothing) move x to self;
       ],
       destroy [ x;
            objectloop (x in self && x ofclass Axe) Axe.destroy(x);
       ];
```

A new axe is created whenever a new dwarf is created, while stocks last, and when a dwarf is destroyed, any axes it carries are also destroyed.

Finally, you can supply create with up to 3 parameters. Here is a case with only one:

```
Class GoldIngot (10)
  with weight, value,
      create [ carats;
          self.value = 10*carats;
          self.weight = 20 + carats;
      ];
```

and now GoldIngot.create(24) will create a 24-carat gold ingot.

§3.12   Sending messages to routines and strings

△   §3.9 was about sending messages to Objects, and then in §3.11 it turned out that there are five messages which can be sent to a Class. That's two of the four metaclasses, and it turns out that you can send messages to a Routine and a String too.

The only message you can send to a Routine is call, and all this does is to call it. So if Explore is the name of a routine,

```
Explore.call(2, 4);    and    Explore(2, 4);
```

do exactly the same as each other. This looks redundant, except that it allows a little more flexibility: for instance

```
(random(Hello, Goodbye)).call(7);
```

has a 50% chance of calling Hello(7) and a 50% chance of calling Goodbye(7). As you might expect, the call message replies with whatever value was returned by the routine.

Two different messages can be sent to a String. The first is print, which is provided because it logically ought to be, rather than because it's useful. So, for example,

```
("You can see an advancing tide of bison!").print();
```

prints out the string, followed by a new-line, and evaluates as true.

The second is print_to_array. This copies out the text of the string into entries 2, 3, 4, . . . of the supplied byte array, and writes the number of characters as a word

69

into entries 0 and 1. (Make sure that the byte array is large enough to hold the text of the string.) For instance:

```
Array Petals->30;
...
    ("A rose is a rose is a rose").print_to_array(Petals);
```

will leave Petals-->0 set to 26 and place the letters 'A', ' ', 'r', 'o', ..., 'e' into the entries Petals->2, Petals->3, ..., Petals->27. For convenience, the reply value of the message print_to_array is also 26. You can use this message to find the length of a string, copying the text into some temporary array and only making use of this return value.

§3.13   Common properties and Property

△△ Many classes, the Bird class for example, pass on properties to their members. Properties coming from the class Object are called "common properties". Every item and place in an adventure game belongs to class Object, so a property inherited from Object will be not just common but well-nigh universal. Properties which aren't common are sometimes called "individual".

The Inform library sets up the class Object with about fifty common properties. Story files would be huge if all of the objects in a game actually used all of these common properties, so a special rule applies: *you can read a common property for any* Object, *but you can only write to it if you've written it into the object's declaration yourself.* For instance, the library contains the directive

```
Property cant_go "You can't go that way.";
```

This tells Inform to add cant_go to the class definition for Object. The practical upshot is that you can perform

```
print_ret (string) location.cant_go;
```

whatever the location is, and the resulting text will be "You can't go that way." if the location doesn't define a cant_go value of its own. On the other hand

```
location.cant_go = "Please stop trying these blank walls.";
```

will only work if location actually provides a cant_go value of its own, which you can test with the condition location provides cant_go.

△△ Using the superclass operator you can read and even alter the default values of common properties at run-time: for instance,

```
location.Object::cant_go = "Another blank wall. Tsk!";
```

will substitute for "You can't go that way."

△△ The Inform library uses common properties because they're marginally faster to access and marginally cheaper on memory. Only 62 are available, of which the compiler uses 3 and the library a further 47. On the other hand, you can have up to 16,320 individual properties, which in practical terms is as good as saying they are unlimited.

§3.14 *Philosophy*

△△ "Socialism is all very well in practice, but does it work in theory?" (Stephen Fry). While the chapter is drizzling out into small type, this last section is aimed at those readers who might feel happier with Inform's ideas about classes and objects if only there were some *logic* to it all. Other readers may feel that it's about as relevant to actual Inform programming as socialist dialectic is to shopping for groceries. Here are the rules anyway:

(1) Story files are made up of objects, which may have variables attached of various different kinds, which we shall here call "properties".
(2) Source code contains definitions of both objects and classes. Classes are abstract descriptions of common features which might be held by groups of objects.
(3) Any given object in the program either is, or is not, a member of any given class.
(4) For every object definition in the source code, an object is made in the story file. The definition specifies which classes this object is a member of.
(5) If an object X is declared as a member of class C, then X "inherits" property values as given in the class definition of C.

Exact rules of inheritance aren't relevant here, except perhaps to note that one of the things inherited from class C might be the membership of some other class, D.

(6) For every class definition, an object is made in the story file to represent it, called its "class-object".

For example, suppose we have a class definition like:

```
Class Shrub
  with species;
```

The class Shrub will generate a class-object in the final program, also called Shrub. This class-object exists to receive messages like create and destroy and, more philosophically, to represent the concept of "being a shrub" within the simulated world.

The class-object of a class is not normally a member of that class. The concept of being a shrub is not itself a shrub, and the condition Shrub ofclass Shrub is false. Individual shrubs provide a property called species, but the class-object of Shrub does not: the concept of being a shrub has no single species.

(7) Classes which are automatically defined by Inform are called "metaclasses". There are four of these: Class, Object, Routine and String.

It follows by rule (6) that every Inform program contains the class-objects of these four, also called Class, Object, Routine and String.

(8) Every object is a member of one, and only one, metaclass:
  (8.1) The class-objects are members of Class, and no other class.
  (8.2) Routines in the program, including those given as property values, are members of Routine and no other class.
  (8.3) Constant strings in the program, including those given as property values, are members of String, and of no other class.
  (8.4) The objects defined in the source code are members of Object, and possibly also of other classes defined in the source code.

It follows from (8.1) that Class is the unique class whose class-object is one of its own members: so Class ofclass Class is true.

(9) Contrary to rules (5) and (8.1), the class-objects of the four metaclasses do not inherit from Class.
(10) Properties inherited from the class-object of the metaclass Object are read-only and cannot be set.

.   .   .   .   .   .

To see what the rules entail means knowing the definitions of the four metaclasses. These definitions are never written out in any textual form inside Inform, as it happens, but this is what they would look like if they were. (Metaclass is an imaginary directive, as the programmer isn't allowed to create new metaclasses.)

```
Metaclass Object
with name,
     ...;
```

A class from which the common properties defined by Property are inherited, albeit (by rule (10), an economy measure) in read-only form.

```
Metaclass Class
with create    [ ...; ... ],
     recreate  [ instance ...; ... ],
     destroy   [ instance; ... ],
     copy      [ instance1 instance2; ... ],
     remaining [; ... ];
```

So class-objects respond only to these five messages and provide no other properties: except that by rule (9), the class-objects Class, Object, Routine and String provide no properties at all. The point is that these five messages are concerned with object creation and deletion at run time. But Inform is a compiler and not, like Smalltalk-80 or other highly object-oriented languages, an interpreter. Rule (9) expresses our inability to create the program while it is actually running.

```
Metaclass Routine
with call [ parameters...; ... ];
```

Routines therefore provide only call.

```
Metaclass String
with print           [; print_ret (string) self; ],
     print_to_array [ array; ... ];
```

Strings therefore provide only print and print_to_array.

● REFERENCES

L. Ross Raszewski's library extension "imem.h" manages genuinely dynamic memory allocation for objects, and is most often used when memory is running terribly short.

Chapter II: Introduction to Designing

But 'why then publish?' There are no rewards
   Of fame or profit when the world grows weary.
I ask in turn why do you play at cards?
   Why drink? Why read? To make some hour less dreary.
It occupies me to turn back regards
   On what I've seen or pondered, sad or cheery,
And what I write I cast upon the stream
To swim or sink. I have had at least my dream.

— Lord Byron (1788–1824), *Don Juan, canto XIV*

§4 'Ruins' begun

This chapter introduces five fundamentals of Inform: how to construct games; messages, classes and actions; and how to debug games. Chapter III then makes a systematic exploration of the model world available to Inform games. Throughout both chapters, examples gradually build up a modest game called 'Ruins', a tale of Central American archaeology in the 1930s. Here is its first state:

```
Constant Story "RUINS";
Constant Headline "^An Interactive Worked Example^
           Copyright (c) 1999 by Angela M. Horns.^";
Include "Parser";
Include "VerbLib";
Object Forest "~Great Plaza~"
  with description
          "Or so your notes call this low escarpment of limestone,
          but the rainforest has claimed it back. Dark olive
          trees crowd in on all sides, the air steams with the
          mist of a warm recent rain, midges hang in the air.
          ~Structure 10~ is a shambles of masonry which might
          once have been a burial pyramid, and little survives
          except stone-cut steps leading down into darkness below.",
```

```
has  light;
[ Initialise;
  location = Forest;
  "^^^Days of searching, days of thirsty hacking through the briars of
  the forest, but at last your patience was rewarded. A discovery!^";
];
Include "Grammar";
```

If you can compile this tiny beginning successfully, Inform is probably set up
and working properly on your computer. Compilation may take a few seconds,
because although you have only written twenty lines or so, the Include
directives paste in another seven and a half thousand. This is "the Library",
a computer program which acts as umpire during play. The library is divided
into three parts:

Parser   which decodes what the player types;
VerbLib   how actions, like "take" or "go north", work;
Grammar   the verbs and phrases which the game understands.

It does matter what order the three lines beginning with Include come in, and
it sometimes matters where your own code goes with respect to them: objects
shouldn't be declared until after the inclusion of the parser, for instance. For
now, follow the structure above, with everything interesting placed between
the inclusions of VerbLib and Grammar.

△   Chapter I above said that every Inform program had to contain a routine called
Main. Games like 'Ruins' are no exception, but their Main routine is part of the library,
so that game designers do not need to write a Main.

· · · · ·

The two constants at the beginning are text giving the game's name and
copyright message, which the library needs in order to print out the "banner"
announcing the game. Similarly, the library expects to find a routine named
Initialise somewhere in your source code. This routine is called when the
game starts up, and is expected to carry out any last setting-up operations
before play begins. In most games, it also prints up a 'welcome' message, but
the one thing it *has* to do is to set the location variable to the place where
the player begins. And this means that every game has to declare at least one
object, too: the room where the player begins.

△   In this book places are often called "rooms" even when outdoors (like Forest) or
underground. This goes back at least to Stephen Bishop's 1842 map of the Mammoth
and Flint Ridge cave system of Kentucky, which was the setting of the first adventure
game, 'Advent', also called 'Colossal Cave' (c.1975). The author, Will Crowther, was a

caver and used the word "room" in its caving sense. Don Woods, who recast the game in 1976–7, confused the word further with its everyday sense. Players of adventure games continue to call locations "rooms" to this day.

. . . . .

'Ruins' is at this stage an exceedingly dull game:

> Days of searching, days of thirsty hacking through the briars of the forest, but at last your patience was rewarded. A discovery!
>
> *RUINS*
> An Interactive Worked Example
> Copyright (c) 1998 by Angela M. Horns.
> Release 1 / Serial number 990220 / Inform v6.20 Library 6/8
>
> *"Great Plaza"*
> Or so your notes call this low escarpment of limestone, but the rainforest has claimed it back. Dark olive trees crowd in on all sides, the air steams with the mist of a warm recent rain, midges hang in the air. "Structure 10" is a shambles of masonry which might once have been a burial pyramid, and little survives except stone-cut steps leading down into darkness below.
> >inventory
> You are carrying nothing.
> >north
> You can't go that way.
> >wait
> Time passes.
> >quit
> Are you sure you want to quit? yes

. . . . .

In an Inform game, objects are used to simulate everything: rooms and items to be picked up, scenery, the player, intangible things like mist and even some abstract ideas, like the direction "north" or the idea of "darkness". The library itself is present as an object, called InformLibrary, though like the concept of "north" it cannot be picked up or visited during play. All told, 'Ruins' already contains twenty-four objects.

It is time to add something tangible, by writing the following just after the definition of Forest:

```
Object -> mushroom "speckled mushroom"
  with name 'speckled' 'mushroom' 'fungus' 'toadstool';
```

The arrow -> means that the mushroom begins inside the previous object, which is to say, the Forest. If the game is recompiled, the mushroom is now in play: the player can call it "speckled mushroom", "mushroom", "toadstool" and so on. It can be taken, dropped, looked at, looked under and so on. However, it only adds the rather plain line "There is a speckled mushroom here." to the Forest's description. Here is a more decorative species:

```
Object -> mushroom "speckled mushroom"
  with name 'speckled' 'mushroom' 'fungus' 'toadstool',
       initial
          "A speckled mushroom grows out of the sodden earth, on
          a long stalk.";
```

The initial message is used to tell the player about the mushroom when the Forest is described. (Once the mushroom has been picked or moved, the message is no longer used: hence the name 'initial'.) The mushroom is, however, still "nothing special" when the player asks to "look at" or "examine" it. To provide a more interesting close-up view, we must give the mushroom its own description:

```
Object -> mushroom "speckled mushroom"
  with name 'speckled' 'mushroom' 'fungus' 'toadstool',
       initial
          "A speckled mushroom grows out of the sodden earth, on
          a long stalk.",
       description
          "The mushroom is capped with blotches, and you aren't
          at all sure it's not a toadstool.",
  has  edible;
```

Now if we examine the mushroom, as is always wise, we get a cautionary hint. But the edible notation means that it *can* be eaten, so that for the first time the player can change the game state irrevocably: from a game with a forest and a mushroom into a game with just a forest.

The mushroom shows the two kinds of feature something can have: a "property" with some definite value or list of values and an "attribute", which is either present or not but has no particular value. name, initial and description are all properties, while light and edible are attributes. The current state of these properties changes during play: for instance, it can be changed by code like the following.

```
mushroom.description = "You're sure it's a toadstool now.";
give mushroom light;
if (mushroom has edible) print "It's definitely edible.^";
```

light is the attribute for "giving off light". The Forest was defined as having light on account of daylight, so it doesn't much matter whether or not the mushroom has light, but for the sake of botanical verisimilitude it won't have light in the final game.

. . . . .

Declaring objects has so far been a matter of filling in forms: fill some text into the box marked description, and so on. We could go much further like this, but for the sake of example it's time to add some rules:

```
after [;
    Take: "You pick the mushroom, neatly cleaving its thin stalk.";
    Drop: "The mushroom drops to the ground, battered slightly.";
],
```

The property after doesn't just have a string for a value: it has a routine of its own. What happens is that after something happens to the mushroom, the library asks the mushroom if it would like to react in some way. In this case, it reacts only to Take and Drop, and the only effect is that the usual messages ("Taken." "Dropped.") are replaced by new ones. (It doesn't react to Eat, so nothing out of the ordinary happens when it's eaten.) 'Ruins' can now manage a briefly plausible dialogue:

"Great Plaza"
Or so your notes call this low escarpment of limestone, but the rainforest has claimed it back. Dark olive trees crowd in on all sides, the air steams with the mist of a warm recent rain, midges hang in the air. "Structure 10" is a shambles of masonry which might once have been a burial pyramid, and little survives except stone-cut steps leading down into darkness below.
A speckled mushroom grows out of the sodden earth, on a long stalk.
>get mushroom
You pick the mushroom, neatly cleaving its thin stalk.
>look at it
The mushroom is capped with blotches, and you aren't at all sure it's not a toadstool.
>drop it
The mushroom drops to the ground, battered slightly.

△ Gareth Rees persuasively advocates writing this sort of transcript, of an ideal sequence of play, first, and worrying about how to code up the design afterwards. Other designers prefer to build from the bottom up, crafting the objects one at a time and finally bringing them together into the narrative.

. . . . .

The mushroom is a little more convincing now, but still does nothing. Here is a more substantial new rule:

```
before [;
    Eat: if (random(100) <= 30) {
            deadflag = true;
            "The tiniest nibble is enough. It was a toadstool,
            and a poisoned one at that!";
        }
        "You nibble at one corner, but the curious taste
        repels you.";
    ],
```

The library consults before just before the player's intended action would take place. So when the player tries typing, say, "eat the mushroom", what happens is: in 30% of cases, death by toadstool poisoning; and in the other 70%, a nibble of a corner of fungus, without consuming it completely.

Like location, deadflag is a variable belonging to the library. It's normally false, meaning that the player is still alive and playing. Setting it to true thus kills the player. (Setting it to 2 causes the player to win the game and there are other uses: see §21.)

If the "tiniest nibble" text is printed, the rule ends there, and does not flow on into the second "You nibble at" text. So one and only one message is printed. Here is how this is achieved: although it's not obvious from the look of the program, the before routine is being asked the question "Do you want to interfere with the usual rules?". It must reply, that is, return, either true or false meaning yes or no. Because this question is asked and answered many times in a large Inform game, there are several abbreviations for how to reply. For example,

```
return true;   and   rtrue;
```

both do the same thing. Moreover,

```
print_ret "The tiniest nibble... ...at that!";
```

performs three useful tasks: prints the message, then prints a carriage return, and then returns true. And this is so useful that a bare string

```
"The tiniest nibble... ...at that!";
```

is understood to mean the same thing. To print the text without returning, the statement print has to be written out in full. Here is an example:

```
before [;
    Taste: print "You extend your tongue nervously.^";
        rfalse;
];
```

In this rule, the text is printed, but the answer to "Do you want to interfere?" is no, so the game will then go on to print something anodyne like "You taste nothing unexpected." (In fact the rfalse was unnecessary, because if a rule like this never makes any decision, then the answer is assumed to be false.)

●**EXERCISE 1**
The present after routine for the mushroom is misleading, because it says the mushroom has been picked every time it's taken (which will be odd if it's taken, dropped then taken again). Correct this.

· · · · ·

The following example of "form-filling" is typical of the way that the library provides for several standard kinds of object. This one is a kind of door, which will be gone into properly in §13, but for now suffice to say that a door doesn't literally have to be a door: it can be any object which comes in between where the player is and where the player can go. Because the object is also marked as scenery (see §8), it isn't given any special paragraph of description when the Forest is described. Finally, it is marked as static to prevent the player from being able to pick it up and walk off with it.

```
Object -> steps "stone-cut steps"
  with name 'steps' 'stone' 'stairs' 'stone-cut' 'pyramid' 'burial'
            'structure' 'ten' '10',
       description
           "The cracked and worn steps descend into a dim chamber.
           Yours might be the first feet to tread them for five
           hundred years.",
       door_to Square_Chamber,
       door_dir d_to
  has  scenery static door open;
```

We also need to add a new line to the Forest's definition to tell it that the way down is by these steps:

```
Object Forest "^Great Plaza^"
     ...
       d_to steps,
```

Now "examine structure 10", "enter stone-cut pyramid" and so forth will all work.

• **EXERCISE 2**
Except of course that now 'Ruins' won't compile, because Inform expects to find a room called Square_Chamber which the steps lead to. Design one.

§5 Introducing messages and classes

On a round ball
A workman that hath copies by, can lay
An Europe, Afrique and an Asia,
And quickly make that, which was nothing, All.

— John Donne (1571?–1631), *Valediction: Of Weeping*

 Though §4 was a little vague in saying "the library asks the mushroom if it would like to react", something basic was happening in Inform terms: the object `InformLibrary` was sending the message `before` to the object `mushroom`. Much more on how actions take place in §6, but here is roughly what the library does if the player types "eat mushroom":

```
if (mushroom.before() == false) {
    remove mushroom;
    if (mushroom.after() == false)
        print "You eat the mushroom. Not bad.^";
}
```

The library sends the message `before` to ask the mushroom if it minds being eaten; then, if not, it consumes the mushroom; then it sends the message `after` to ask if the mushroom wishes to react in some way; then, if not, it prints the usual eating-something text. In response to the messages `before` and `after`, the mushroom is expected to reply either `true`, meaning "I'll take over from here", or `false`, meaning "carry on".

Most of the other properties in §4 are also receiving messages. For example, the message

```
mushroom.description();
```

is sent when the player tries to examine the mushroom: if the reply is `false` then the library prints "You see nothing special about the speckled mushroom." Now the mushroom was set up with

```
description
    "The mushroom is capped with blotches, and you aren't at all
    sure it's not a toadstool.",
```

which doesn't look like a rule for receiving a message, but it is one all the same: it means "print this text out, print a new-line and reply true". A more complicated rule could have been given instead, as in the following elaboration of the stone-cut steps in 'Ruins':

```
description [;
    print "The cracked and worn steps descend into a dim chamber.
        Yours might ";
    if (Square_Chamber hasnt visited)
        print "be the first feet to tread";
    else print "have been the first feet to have trodden";
    " them for five hundred years. On the top step is inscribed
    the glyph Q1.";
],
```

visited is an attribute which is currently held only by rooms which the player has been to. The glyphs will come into the game later on.

The library can send out about 40 different kinds of message, before and description being two of these. The more interesting an object is, the more ingeniously it will respond to these messages. An object which ignores all incoming messages will be lifeless and inert in play, like a small stone.

△ Some properties are just properties, and don't receive messages. Nobody ever sends a name message, for instance: the name property is just what it seems to be, a list of words.

·　·　·　·　·

So the library is sending out messages to your objects all the time during play. Your objects can also send each other messages, including "new" ones that the library would never send. It's sometimes convenient to use these to trigger off happenings in the game. For example, one way to provide hints in 'Ruins' might be to include a macaw which squawks from time to time, for a variety of reasons:

```
Object -> macaw "red-tailed macaw"
  with name 'red' 'tailed' 'red-tailed' 'macaw' 'bird',
       initial "A red-tailed macaw eyes you from an upper branch.",
       description "Beautiful plumage.",
       before [;
           Take: "The macaw flutters effortlessly out of reach.";
       ],
       squawk [ utterance;
           if (self in location)
```

```
           print "The macaw squawks, ~", (string) utterance,
                 "! ", (string) utterance, "!~^^";
     ],
  has  animate;
```

(For the final version of 'Ruins' the designer thought better of the macaw and removed it, but it still makes a good example.) We might then, for instance, change the after rule for dropping the mushroom to read:

```
Drop: macaw.squawk("Drop the mushroom");
      "The mushroom drops to the ground, battered slightly.";
```

so that the maddening creature would squawk "Drop the mushroom! Drop the mushroom!" each time this was done. At present it would be an error to send a squawk message to any object other than the macaw, since only the macaw has been given a rule telling it what to do if it receives one.

. . . . .

In most games there are groups of objects with certain rules in common, which it would be tiresome to have to write out many times. For making such a group, a class definition is simpler and more elegant. These closely resemble object definitions, but since they define prototypes rather than actual things, they have no initial location. (An individual tree may be somewhere, but the concept of being a tree has no particular place.) So the 'header' part of the definition is simpler.

For example, the scoring system in 'Ruins' works as follows: the player, an archaeologist of the old school, gets a certain number of points for each 'treasure' (i.e., cultural artifact) he can filch and put away into his packing case. Treasures clearly have rules in common, and the following class defines them:

```
Class Treasure
  with cultural_value 5, photographed_in_situ false,
       before [;
           Take, Remove:
               if (self in packing_case)
                   "Unpacking such a priceless artifact had best wait
                   until the Carnegie Institution can do it.";
               if (self.photographed_in_situ == false)
                   "This is the 1930s, not the bad old days. Taking an
                   artifact without recording its context is simply
                   looting.";
           Photograph:
```

```
            if (self has moved)
                "What, and fake the archaeological record?";
            if (self.photographed_in_situ) "Not again.";
    ],
    after [;
        Insert:
            if (second == packing_case)
            {   score = score + self.cultural_value;
                "Safely packed away.";
            }
        Photograph: self.photographed_in_situ = true;
    ];
```

(The packing case won't be defined until §12, which is about containers.) Note that self is a variable, which always means "whatever object I am". If we used it in the definition of the mushroom it would mean the mushroom: used here, it means whatever treasure happens to be being dealt with. Explanations about Insert and Remove will come later (in §12). The action Photograph is not one of the standard actions built in to the library, and will be added to 'Ruins' in the next section.

An object of the class Treasure automatically inherits the properties and attributes given in the class definition. Here for instance is an artifact which will eventually be found in the Stooped Corridor of 'Ruins':

```
Treasure -> statuette "pygmy statuette"
  with name 'snake' 'mayan' 'pygmy' 'spirit' 'precious' 'statuette',
       description
           "A menacing, almost cartoon-like statuette of a pygmy spirit
            with a snake around its neck.",
       initial "A precious Mayan statuette rests here!";
```

From Treasure, this statuette inherits a cultural_value score of 5 and the rules about taking and dropping treasures. If it had itself set cultural_value to 15, say, then the value would be 15, because the object's actual definition always takes priority over anything the class might have specified. Another of the five 'Ruins' treasures, which will be found in the Burial Shaft, has a subtlety in its definition:

```
Treasure -> honeycomb "ancient honeycomb"
  with article "an",
       name 'ancient' 'old' 'honey' 'honeycomb',
       description "Perhaps some kind of funerary votive offering.",
       initial
           "An exquisitely preserved, ancient honeycomb rests here!",
```

```
    after [;
        Eat: "Perhaps the most expensive meal of your life.  The
             honey tastes odd, perhaps because it was used to
             store the entrails of the Lord buried here, but still
             like honey.";
    ],
  has  edible;
```

The subtlety is that the honeycomb now has two after rules: a new one of its own, plus the existing one that all treasures have. Both apply, but the new one happens first.

△△ So comparing cultural_value and after, there seems to be an inconsistency. In the case of cultural_value, an object's own given value wiped out the value from the class, but in the case of after, the two values were joined up into a list. Why? The reason is that some of the library's properties are "additive", so that their values accumulate into a list when class inheritance takes place. Three useful examples are before, after and name.

△△ Non-library properties you invent (like squawk or cultural_value) will never be additive, unless you declare them so with a directive like

```
    Property additive squawk;
```

before squawk is otherwise mentioned. (Or you could imitate similar kinds of inheritance using the superclass operator.)

● REFERENCES

See 'Balances' for an extensive use of message-sending. The game defines several complicated classes, among them the white cube, spell and scroll classes.   ●'Advent' has a treasure-class similar to this one, and uses class definitions for the many similar maze and dead-end rooms, as well as the sides of the fissure.   ●'Toyshop' contains one easy class (the wax candles) and one unusually hard one (the building blocks). ●Class definitions can be worthwhile even when as few as two objects use them, as can be seen from the two kittens in 'Alice Through the Looking-Glass'.

§6   Actions and reactions

Only the actions of the just
Smell sweet and blossom in their dust.

— James Shirley (1594–1666),
The Contention of Ajax and Ulysses

[Greek is] a language obsessed with action, and with the joy of seeing action multiply from action, action marching relentlessly ahead and with yet more actions filing in from either side to fall into neat step at the rear, in a long straight rank of cause and effect, to what will be inevitable, the only possible end.

— Donna Tartt, *The Secret History*

 Inform is a language obsessed with actions. An 'action' is an attempt to perform one simple task: for instance,

> Inv   Take sword   Insert gold_coin cloth_bag

are all examples. Here the actual actions are Inv (inventory), Take and Insert. An action has none, one or two objects supplied with it (or, in a few special cases, some numerical information rather than objects). It also has an "actor", the person who is to perform the action, usually the player. Most actions are triggered off by the game's parser, whose job can be summed up as reducing the player's keyboard commands to actions: "take my hat off", "remove bowler" or "togli il cappello" (if in an Italian game) might all cause the same action. Some keyboard commands, like "drop all", cause the parser to fire off whole sequences of actions: others, like "empty the sack into the umbrella stand", cause only a single action but one which may trigger off an avalanche of other actions as it takes place.

An action is only an attempt to do something: it may not succeed. Firstly, a before rule might interfere, as we have seen already. Secondly, the action might not even be very sensible. The parser will happily generate the action Eat iron_girder if the player asked to do so in good English. In this case, even if no before rule interferes, the normal game rules will ensure that the girder is not consumed.

Actions can also be generated by your own code, and this perfectly simulates the effect of a player typing something. For example, generating a Look action makes the game produce a room description as if the player had typed "look". More subtly, suppose the air in the Pepper Room causes the player to sneeze each turn and drop something at random. This could be programmed directly, with objects being moved onto the floor by explicit move statements. But then suppose the game also contains a toffee apple, which sticks to the player's hands. Suddenly the toffee apple problem has an unintended solution. So rather than moving the objects directly to the floor, the game should generate Drop actions, allowing the game's rules to be applied. The result might read:

> You sneeze convulsively, and lose your grip on the toffee apple...
> The toffee apple sticks to your hand!

which is at least consistent.

As an example of causing actions, an odorous low_mist will soon settle over 'Ruins'. It will have the description "The mist carries an aroma reminisicent of tortilla." The alert player who reads this will immediately type "smell mist", and we want to provide a better response than the game's stock reply "You smell nothing unexpected." An economical way of doing this is to somehow deflect the action Smell low_mist into the action Examine low_mist instead, so that the "aroma of tortilla" message is printed in this case too. Here is a suitable before rule to do that:

```
Smell: <Examine self>; rtrue;
```

The statement <Examine self> causes the action Examine low_mist to be triggered off immediately, after which whatever was going on at the time resumes. In this case, the action Smell low_mist resumes, but since we immediately return true the action is stopped dead.

Causing an action and then returning true is so useful that it has an abbreviation, putting the action in double angle-brackets. For example, the following could be added to 'Ruins' if the designer wanted to make the stone-cut steps more enticing:

```
before [;
    Search: <<Enter self>>;
],
```

If a player types "search steps", the parser will produce the action Search steps and this rule will come into play: it will generate the action Enter steps instead, and return true to stop the original Search action from going any further. The net effect is that one action has been diverted into another.

. . . . .

At any given time, just one action is under way, though others may be waiting to resume when the current one has finished. The current action is always stored in the four variables

```
actor        action       noun        second
```

actor, noun and second hold the objects involved, or the special value nothing if they aren't involved at all. (There's always an actor, and for the time being it will always be equal to player.) action holds the kind of action. Its possible values can be referred to in the program using the ## notation: for example

```
if (action == ##Look) ...
```

tests to see if the current action is a Look.

△   Why have ## at all, why not just write Look? Partly because this way the reader of the source code can see at a glance that an action type is being referred to, but also because the name might be used for something else. For instance there's a variable called score (holding the current game score), quite different from the action type ##Score.

△△ For a few actions, the 'noun' (or the 'second noun') is actually a number (for instance, "set timer to 20" would probably end up with noun being timer and second being 20). Occasionally one needs to be sure of the difference, e.g., to tell if second is holding a number or an object. It's then useful to know that there are two more primitive variables, inp1 and inp2, parallel to noun and second and usually equal to them – but equal to 1 to indicate "some numerical value, not an object".

. . . . .

The library supports about 120 different actions and most large games will add some more of their own. The full list, given in Table 6, is initially daunting, but for any given object most of the actions are irrelevant. For instance, if you only want to prevent an object from entering the player's possession, you need only block the Take action, unless the object is initially in something or on something, in which case you need to block Remove as well. In the author's game 'Curses', one exceptional object (Austin, the cat) contains rules concerning 15 different actions, but the average is more like two or three action-rules per object.

The list of actions is divided into three groups, called Group 1, Group 2 and Group 3:

1. Group 1 contains 'meta' actions for controlling the game, like Score and Save, which are treated quite differently from other actions as they do not happen in the "model world".

2. Actions in group 2 normally do something to change the state of the model world, or else to print important information about it. Take ("pick up") and Inv ("inventory") are examples of each. Such actions will affect any object which doesn't block them with a before rule.

3. Finally, group 3 actions are the ones which normally do nothing but print a polite refusal, like Pull ("it is fixed in place"), or a bland response, like Listen ("you hear nothing unexpected"). Such actions will never affect any object which doesn't positively react with a before rule.

△ Some of the group 2 actions can be ignored by the programmer because they are really only keyboard shorthands for the player. For example, <Empty rucksack table> means "empty the contents of the rucksack onto the table" and is automatically broken down into a stream of actions like <Remove fish rucksack> and <PutOn fish table>. You needn't write rules concerning Empty, only Remove and PutOn.

△ Most of the library's group 2 actions are able to "run silently". This means that if the variable keep_silent is set to true, then the actions print nothing in the event of success. The group 2 actions which can't run silently are exactly those ones whose successful operation does nothing but print: Wait, Inv, Look, Examine, Search.

● △EXERCISE 3
"The door-handle of my room. . . was different from all other door-handles in the world, inasmuch as it seemed to open of its own accord and without my having to turn it, so unconscious had its manipulation become. . ." (Marcel Proust). Use silent-running actions to make an unconsciously manipulated door: if the player tries to pass through when it's closed, print "(first opening the door)" and do so. (You need to know some of §13, the section on doors, to answer this.)

● △△EXERCISE 4
Now add "(first unlocking the door with . . .)", automatically trying to unlock it using either a key already known to work, or failing that, any key carried by the player which hasn't been tried in the lock before.

· · · · ·

△ Some actions happen even though they don't arise *directly* from anything the player has typed. For instance, an action called ThrownAt is listed under group 3 in Table 6. It's a side-effect of the ordinary ThrowAt action: if the player types "throw rock at dalek", the parser generates the action ThrowAt rock dalek. As usual the rock is sent a before message asking if it objects to being thrown at a Dalek. Since the Dalek may also have an opinion on the matter, another before message is sent to the Dalek, but this time with the action ThrownAt. A dartboard can thus distinguish between being thrown, and having things thrown at it:

```
before [;
    ThrowAt: "Haven't you got that the wrong way round?";
    ThrownAt:
        if (noun==dart) {
            move dart to self;
            if (random(31)==1)
                print (string) random("Outer bull", "Bullseye");
            else {
                print (string) random("Single", "Double", "Triple");
                print " ", (number) random(20);
            }
            "!";
        }
        move noun to location;
        print_ret (The) noun, " bounces back off the board.";
],
```

Such an imaginary action – usually, as in this case, a perfectly sensible action seen from the point of view of the second object involved, rather than the first – is sometimes called a "fake action". Two things about it are fake: there's no grammar that produces ThrownAt, and there's no routine called ThrownAtSub. The important fake actions are ThrownAt, Receive and LetGo, the latter two being used for containers: see §12.

△△ If you really need to, you can declare a new fake action with the directive Fake_action ⟨Action-name⟩;. You can then cause this action with < and > as usual.

● △△EXERCISE 5
ThrownAt would be unnecessary if Inform had an idea of before and after routines which an object could provide if it were the second noun of an action. How might this be implemented?

△△ Very occasionally, in the darker recesses of §18 for instance, you want "fake fake actions", actions which are only halfway faked in that they still have action routines. Actually, these are perfectly genuine actions, but with the parser's grammar jinxed so that they can never be produced whatever the player types.

. . . . .

The standard stock of actions is easily added to. Two things are necessary to create a new action: first one must provide a routine to make it happen. For instance:

```
[ BlorpleSub;
    "You speak the magic word ~Blorple~. Nothing happens.";
];
```

Every action has to have a "subroutine" like this, the name of which is always the name of the action with Sub appended. Secondly, one must add grammar so that Blorple can actually be called for. Far more about grammar in Chapter IV: for now we add the simplest of all grammar lines, a directive

```
Verb 'blorple' * -> Blorple;
```

placed after the inclusion of the Grammar file. The word "blorple" can now be used as a verb. It can't take any nouns, so the parser will complain if the player types "blorple daisy".

Blorple is now a typical Group 3 action. before rules can be written for it, and it can be triggered off by a statement like

```
<Blorple>;
```

The unusual action in 'Ruins', Photograph, needs to be a Group 2 action, since it actually does something, and objects need to be able to react with after rules. (Indeed, the definition of the Treasure class in the previous section contains just such an after rule.) A photographer needs a camera:

```
Object -> -> camera "wet-plate camera"
   with name 'wet-plate' 'plate' 'wet' 'camera',
        description
            "A cumbersome, sturdy, stubborn wooden-framed wet plate
            model: like all archaeologists, you have a love-hate
            relationship with your camera.";
```

(This is going to be inside a packing case which is inside the Forest, hence the two arrows ->.) And now the action subroutine. The sodium lamp referred to will be constructed in §14.

```
[ PhotographSub;
   if (camera notin player) "Not without the use of your camera.";
   if (noun == player) "Best not. You haven't shaved since Mexico.";
   if (children(player) > 1)
      "Photography is a cumbersome business, needing the use of both
       hands. You'll have to put everything else down.";
   if (location == Forest) "In this rain-soaked forest, best not.";
   if (location == thedark) "It is far too dark.";
   if (AfterRoutines()) return;
  "You set up the elephantine, large-format, wet-plate camera, adjust
   the sodium lamp and make a patient exposure of ", (the) noun, ".";
];
```

What makes this a Group 2 action is that, if the action successfully takes place, then the library routine AfterRoutines is called. This routine takes care of all the standard rules to do with after (see below), and returns true if any object involved has dealt with the action and printed something already. (Failing that, the message "You set up..." will be printed.) Finally, some grammar for the parser:

```
Verb 'photograph' * noun -> Photograph;
```

This matches input like "photograph statuette", because the grammar token noun tells the parser to expect the name of a visible object. See §30 and §31 for much more on grammar.

△   To make a Group 1 action, define the verb as meta (see §30).

· · · · ·

Actions are processed in a simple way, but one which involves many little stages. There are three main stages:

(1) 'Before', for group 2 and 3 actions. An opportunity for your code to interfere with or block altogether what might soon happen.

(2) 'During', for all actions. The library takes control and decides if the action makes sense according to its normal world model: for example, only an edible object may be eaten; only an object in the player's possession can be thrown at somebody, and so on. If the action is impossible, a complaint is printed and that's all. Otherwise the action is now carried out.

(3) 'After', for group 2 actions. An opportunity for your code to react to what has happened, after it has happened but before any text announcing it has been printed. If it chooses, your code can print and cause an entirely different outcome. If your code doesn't interfere, the library reports back to the player (with such choice phrases as "Dropped.").

△   Group 1 actions, like Score, have no 'Before' or 'After' stages: you can't (easily) stop them from taking place. They aren't happening in the game's world, but in the player's.

△   The 'Before' stage consults your code in five ways, and occasionally it's useful to know in what order:

(1a) The GamePreRoutine is called, if you have written one. If it returns true, nothing else happens and the action is stopped.

(1b) The orders property of the player is called on the same terms. For more details, see §18.

(1c) And the react_before of every object in scope, which roughly means 'in the vicinity'. For more details, see §32.

(1d) And the `before` of the current room.

(1e) If the action has a first noun, its `before` is called on the same terms.

△   The library processes the 'During' stage by calling the action's subroutine: for instance, by calling `TakeSub`.

△   The 'After' stage only applies to Group 2 actions, as all Group 3 actions have been wound up with a complaint or a bland response at the 'During' stage. During 'After' the sequence is as follows: (3a) `react_after` rules for every object in scope (including the player object); (3b) the room's `after`; (3c) the first noun's `after` and (3d) finally `GamePostRoutine`.

△△ To some extent you can even meddle with the 'During' stage, and thus even interfere with Group 1 actions, by unscrupulous use of the `LibraryMessages` system. See §25.

· · · · ·

As mentioned above, the parser can generate decidedly odd actions, such as `Insert camel eye_of_needle`. The parser's policy is to allow any action which the player has clearly asked for at the keyboard, and it never uses knowledge about the current game position except to resolve ambiguities. For instance, "take house" in the presence of the Sydney Opera House and also a souvenir model of the same will be resolved in favour of the model. But if there is no model to cloud the issue, the parser will cheerfully generate Take `Sydney_Opera_House`.

Actions are only checked for sensibleness *after* the `before` stage. In many ways this is a good thing, because in adventure games the very unlikely is sometimes correct. But sometimes it needs to be remembered when writing `before` rules. Suppose a `before` rule intercepts the action of putting the mushroom in the crate, and exciting things happen as a result. Now even if the mushroom is, say, sealed up inside a glass jar, the parser will still generate the action `Insert mushroom crate`, and the `before` rule will still cut in, because the impossibility of the action hasn't yet been realised.

The upshot of this is that the exciting happening should be written not as a `before` but as an `after` rule, when it's known that the attempt to put the mushroom in the crate has already succeeded.

△   That's fine if it's a Group 2 action you're working with. But consider the following scenario: a siren has a cord which needs to be pulled to sound the alarm. But the siren can be behind glass, and is on the other side of a barred cage in which the player is imprisoned. You need to write a rule for `Pull cord`, but you can't place this among the cord's `after` rules because `Pull` is a group 3 action and there isn't any "after": so it has to be a `before` rule. Probably it's best to write your own code by hand to check that the cord is reachable. But an alternative is to call the library's routine:

```
ObjectIsUntouchable(item, silent_flag, take_flag)
```

This determines whether or not the player can touch item, returning true if there is some obstruction. If silent_flag is true, or if there's no obstruction anyway, nothing will be printed. Otherwise a suitable message will be printed up, such as "The barred cage isn't open." So a safe way to write the cord's before rule would be:

```
before [;
    Pull: if (ObjectIsUntouchable(self)) rtrue;
          "~Vwoorp! Vwoorp!~";
],
```

ObjectIsUntouchable can also be a convenience when writing action subroutines for new actions of your own.

△△ If you set take_flag, then a further restriction will be imposed: the item must not belong to something or someone already: specifically, it must not be in the possession of an animate or a transparent object that isn't a container or supporter. For instance, the off button on a television set can certainly be touched, but if take_flag is true, then ObjectIsUntouchable will print up "That seems to be a part of the television set." and return true to report an obstacle.

● **REFERENCES**
In a game compiled with the -D for "Debugging" switch set, the "actions" verb will result in trace information being printed each time any action is generated. Try putting many things into a rucksack and asking to "empty" it for an extravagant list.
●Diverted actions (using << and >>) are commonplace. They're used in about 20 places in 'Advent': a good example is the way "take water" is translated into a Fill bottle action.   ●L. Ross Raszewski's library extension "yesno.h" makes an interesting use of react_before to handle semi-rhetorical questions. For instance, suppose the player types "eat whale", an absurd command to which the game replies "You can fit a blue whale in your mouth?" Should the player take this as a literal question and type "yes", the designer might want to be able to reply "Oh. I should never have let you go through all those doors." How might this be done? The trick is that, when the game's first reply is made, an invisible object is moved into play which does nothing except to react to a Yes action by making the second reply.

> If builders built buildings the way programmers write programs,
> the first woodpecker that came along would destroy civilisation.
>
> — old computing adage

Infocom fixed 1,695 documented bugs in the course of getting 'Sorcerer' from rough draft to first released product. Alpha testing of 'A Mind Forever Voyaging' turned up one bug report every three minutes. Adventure games are exhausting programs to test and debug because of the number of states they can get into, many of them unanticipated. (For instance, if the player solves the "last" puzzle first, do the other puzzles still work properly? Are they still fair?) The main source of error is simply the designer not noticing that some states are possible. The Inform library can't help with this, but it does contain some useful features designed to help the tester. These are worth finding out about, because if you're going to code up a game, you'll be spending a lot of time testing one thing or another.

Inform has three main debugging features, each making the story file larger and slower than it needs to be: each can be turned on or off with compiler switches. One feature is "strict mode" (switch -S), which checks that the story file isn't committing sins such as over-running arrays or treating nothing as if it were an object: trying to calculate child(nothing), for instance. Strict mode is on by default, and automatically sets Debug mode whenever it is on. To get rid of strict mode, compile with -~S to turn switch S off.

Over and above this is the extensive "Infix" (switch -X), a far more potent set of debugging verbs, which significantly adds to the size of a story file (so that a really large story file might not be able to fit it in). Infix allows you to watch changes happening to objects and monitor routines of your choice, to send messages, call routines, set variables and so forth. Like Strict mode, Infix automatically switches Debug mode on.

Debug mode (switch -D) adds only a small suite of commands, the "debugging verbs", to any game. For instance, typing "purloin mousetrap" allows you to take the mousetrap wherever it happens to be in the game. The debugging verbs do take up extra space, but very little, and note that even if Strict mode and Infix are both off, you can still have Debug on its own.

The Infix and Debug modes give the player of a story file what amount to god-like powers, which is fine for testing but not for final release versions. As a precaution against accidents, the end of a game's printed banner indicates Infix mode with a capital letter 'X', Debug with 'D', and Strict with 'S'. Your source code can also detect which are set: in Strict mode the constant STRICT_MODE is defined; in Debug mode the constant DEBUG; with Infix the constant INFIX.

§7.1 *Debugging verbs for command sequences*

The basic testing technique used by most designers is to keep a master-list of commands side by side with the growing game: a sequence which takes the player from the beginning, explores everywhere, thoroughly tests every blind alley, sudden death and textual response and finally wins the game.

"recording" *or* "recording on" *or* "recording off"

Records all the commands you type into a file on your machine (your interpreter will probably ask you for a filename). When a new region of game is written, you may want to turn recording on and play through it: you can then add the resulting file to the master-list which plays the entire game.

"replay"

This immensely useful verb plays the game taking commands from a file on your machine, rather than from the keyboard. This means you can test every part of the entire game with minimal effort by replaying the master-list of commands through it.

"random"

If you're going to replay such recordings, you need the game to behave predictably: so that chance events always unfold in the same way. This means nobbling the random number generator, and the "random" verb does just that: i.e., after any two uses of "random", the same stream of random numbers results. So you want the first command in your master-list to be "random" if your game has any chance events in it.

△ If you have written a large and complicated game, you may well want to release occasional updates to correct mistakes found by players. But tampering with the code always runs the risk that you may fix one thing only to upset another. A useful insurance policy is to keep not only the master list of commands, but also the transcript of the text it should produce. Then when you amend something, you can replay the master list again and compare the new transcript with the old, ideally with a program like the Unix utility "diff". Any deviations mean a (possibly unintended) side effect of something you've done.

§7.2 *Undo*

Every Inform game provides the "undo" verb, which exactly restores the position before the last turn took place. Though this is not advertised, "undo" can even be used after death or victory, typed in at the "Would you like to RESTART, RESTORE a saved game..." prompt. It can be useful to include fatal moves, followed by "undo", in the master-list of commands, so testing death as well as life.

§7.3 *Debugging verbs which print useful information*

"showobj" ⟨anything⟩

"showobj" is very informative about the current state of an object, revealing which attributes it presently has and the values of its properties. ⟨anything⟩ can be the name of any object anywhere in the game (not necessarily in sight), or even the number of an object, which you might need if the object doesn't have a name.

"tree" *or* "tree" ⟨anything⟩

To see a listing of the objects in the game and how they contain each other, type "tree", and to see the possessions of one of them alone, use "tree ⟨that⟩". So "tree me" is quite like "inventory".

"showverb" ⟨verb⟩

For instance, "showverb unlock". This prints out what the parser thinks is the grammar for the named verb, in the form of an Inform Verb directive. This is useful if you're using the Extend directive to alter the library's grammar and want to check the result.

"scope" *or* "scope" ⟨anything⟩

Prints a list of all the objects currently in scope, and can optionally be given the name of someone else you want a list of the scope for ("scope pirate"). Roughly speaking, something is in your scope if you can see it from where you are: see §32.

§7.4   *Debugging verbs which trace activity behind the scenes*

Tracing is the process of printing up informative text which describes changes as they happen. Each of the following verbs can be given on its own, which sets tracing on; or followed by the word "on", which does the same; or followed by "off", which turns it off again.

"actions" *or* "actions on" *or* "actions off"

Traces all the actions generated in the game. For instance, here's what happens if you unlock and then enter the steel grate in 'Advent':

```
>enter grate
[ Action Enter with noun 51 (steel grate) ]
[ Action Go with noun 51 (steel grate) (from < > statement) ]
...
```

Which reveals that the Enter action has handed over to Go.

"messages" *or* "messages on" *or* "messages off"

Traces all messages sent between objects in the game. (Except for short_name messages, because this would look chaotic, especially when printing the status line.)

"timers" *or* "timers on" *or* "timers off"

Turning on "timers" shows the state of all active timers and daemons at the end of each turn. Typing this in the start of 'Advent' reveals that three daemons are at work: two controlling the threatening little dwarves and the pirate, and one which monitors the caves to see if every treasure has been found yet.

"changes" *or* "changes on" *or* "changes off"

Traces all movements of any object and all changes of attribute or property state.

```
>switch lamp on
[Giving brass lantern on]
[Giving brass lantern light]
You switch the brass lantern on.
[Setting brass lantern.power_remaining to 329]
```
In Debris Room

> You are in a debris room filled with stuff washed in from the surface. A low wide passage with cobbles becomes plugged with mud and debris here, but an awkward canyon leads upward and west.
> A note on the wall says, "Magic word XYZZY."
> A three foot black rod with a rusty star on one end lies nearby.
> [Giving In Debris Room visited]

Warning: this verb has effect only if the story file was compiled with the -S switch set, which it is by default.

△   Two things "changes" will not notice: (i) changes in the workflag attribute, because this flickers rapidly on and off with only temporary significance as the parser works, and (ii) changes to the entries in an array which is held in a property.

"trace" *or* "trace" ⟨number⟩ *or* "trace off"

There are times when it's hard to work out what the parser is up to and why (actually, most times are like this: but sometimes it matters). The parser is written in levels, the lower levels of which are murky indeed. Most of the interesting things happen in the middle levels, and these are the ones for which tracing is available. The levels which can be traced are:

Level 1   Parsing a ⟨grammar line⟩
Level 2   Individual tokens of a ⟨grammar line⟩
Level 3   Parsing a ⟨noun phrase⟩
Level 4   Resolving ambiguities and making choices of object(s)
Level 5   Comparing text against an individual object

"trace" or "trace on" give only level 1 tracing. Be warned: "trace 5" can produce reams and reams of text. There is a level lower even than that, but it's too busy doing dull spade-work to waste time printing. There's also a level 0, but it consists mostly of making arrangements for level 1 and doesn't need much debugging attention.

§7.5   *Debugging verbs which alter the game state in supernatural ways*

"purloin" ⟨anything⟩

You can "purloin" any item or items in your game at any time, wherever you are, even if they wouldn't normally be takeable. A typical use: "purloin all keys". Purloining something automatically takes away the concealed attribute, if necessary.

"abstract" ⟨anything⟩ "to" ⟨anything⟩

You can likewise "abstract" any item to any other item, meaning: move it to the other item. This is unlikely to make sense unless the other item is a container, supporter or animate object.

"goto" ⟨room number⟩

Teleports you to the numbered room. Because rooms don't usually have names, referring to them by number (as printed in the "tree" output) is the best that can be done...

"gonear" ⟨anything⟩

... unless you can instead name something which is in that room. So for instance "gonear trident" teleports to the room containing the trident.

§7.6   *The Infix verbs*

Although Infix adds relatively few additional verbs to the stock, they are immeasurably stronger. All of them begin with a semicolon ; and the convention is that anything you type beginning with a semicolon is addressed to Infix.

";" ⟨expression⟩

This calculates the value of the expression and prints it out. At first sight, this is no more than a pocket calculator, and indeed you can use it that way:

```
>; 1*2*3*4*5*6*7
; == 5040
```

But the ⟨expression⟩ can be *almost any Inform expression*, including variables, constants, action, array, object and class names, routine calls, message-sending and so on. It can be a condition, in which case the answer is 0 for false and 1 for true. It can even be an assignment.

```
>; score
; == 36
>; score = 1000
; == 1000
```

[Your score has just gone up by nine hundred and sixty-four points.]
```
>; brass_lantern has light
```
; false
```
>; lamp.power_remaining = 330
```
(brass lantern (39))
; == 330
```
>; child(wicker cage)
```
(wicker cage (55))
; == "nothing" (0)
```
>; children(me)
```
(yourself (20))
; == 4

In the dialogue above, from 'Advent' compiled with -X, the player called the
same item both `brass_lantern`, the name it has in the source code, and
"lamp", the name it normally has in the game. When Infix is unable to
understand a term like "lamp" as referring to the source code, it tries to match
it to an object somewhere in the game, and prints up any guess it makes. This
is why it printed "(brass lantern (39))". (39 happens to be the object number
of the brass lantern.) Pronouns like "me" and "it" can also be used to refer to
objects.

```
>; StopDaemon(pirate)
```
; == 1
```
>; InformLibrary.begin_action(##Take, black_rod)
```
black rod with a rusty star on the end: Taken.
; == 0

The routine `StopDaemon` will appear later in §20: roughly speaking, "daemons"
control random interventions, and stopping them is useful to keep (say) the
bearded pirate from appearing and disrupting the replay of a sequence of
commands. The second example shows a message being sent, though there is
a simpler way to cause actions:

";<" ⟨action⟩ ⟨noun⟩ ⟨second⟩

which generates any action of your choice, whether or not the given ⟨noun⟩
and ⟨second⟩ (which are optional) are in your scope. Once generated, the
action is subject to all the usual rules:

```
>;< Take black_rod
```
; <Take (the black rod with a rusty iron star on the end)
That isn't available.

Three Inform statements for changing objects are also available from Infix:

";give" ⟨expression⟩ ⟨attribute⟩
";move" ⟨expression⟩ "to" ⟨expression⟩
";remove" ⟨expression⟩

These do just what you'd expect. ";give" is especially useful if, as often happens, you find that you can't test some complicated new area of a game because you've forgotten to do something basic, such as to make a door a door, or to set up an outdoor afternoon location as having light. Using ";give" you can illuminate any dark place you stumble into:

> *Darkness*
> It is pitch dark, and you can't see a thing.
> >;give real_location light
> ; give (the At "Y2") light
> >wait
> Time passes.
> *At "Y2"*
> You are in a large room, with a passage to the south, a passage to the west, and a wall of broken rock to the east. There is a large "Y2" on a rock in the room's center.

(The waiting was because Inform only checks light at the end of each turn, but ";give" and the other debugging verbs are set up to occupy no game time at all -- which is often useful, even if it's a slight nuisance here.) Infix also extends the facilities for watching the changing state of the game:

";watch" *or* ";w" ⟨named routine⟩
";watch" *or* ";w" ⟨named routine⟩ "off"
";watch" *or* ";w" ⟨object⟩
";watch" *or* ";w" ⟨object⟩ "off"

When a named routine is being watched, text is printed each time it is called, giving its name and the values of the arguments it started up with. For instance, ";watch StartTimer" will ensure that you're told of any StartTimer(object, time_to_run) call, and so of any timer that begins working. Watching an object, say ";watch lamp", will notify you when:

(1) any attribute of the lamp is given or taken away;
(2) any property of the lamp is set;
(3) any message is sent to a routine attached to the lamp;
(4) the lamp is moved;

(5) anything is moved to the lamp.

You can also watch things in general:

";watch objects"	watches every object
";watch timers"	watches timers and daemons each turn
";watch messages"	watches every message sent
";watch actions"	watches all actions generated

The final two Infix verbs extend the facilities for looking at things.

";examine" *or* ";x" ⟨something⟩
";inventory" *or* ";i"

";inventory" tells you the names known to Infix, which is a practical way to find out which classes, routines, objects and so on are inside the story file. ";examine" looks at the ⟨something⟩ and tells you whatever Infix knows about it: (a) numbers are translated to hexadecimal and to ZSCII values, where possible; (b) objects are "shown"; (c) classes are listed; (d) constants have their values given; (e) attributes produce a list of all objects currently having them; (f) properties produce a list of all objects currently providing them; (g) dictionary words are described; (h) verbs have their grammars listed; (i) arrays have their definitions shown and their contents listed; (j) global variables have their values given; (k) actions produce a list of all grammar known to the parser which can produce them. For instance:

```
>;x 'silver'
; Dictionary word 'silver' (address 27118): noun
>;x buffer
; Array buffer -> 120
; == 120 9 59 120 32 98 117 102 102 101 114 0 101 114 32 (then 105 zero
entries)
```

△ You can watch routines even without Infix, and the Inform language provides two features for this. Firstly, you can declare a routine with an asterisk * immediately after the name, which marks it for watching. For example, declaring a routine as follows

```
[ AnalyseObject * obj n m;
```

results in the game printing out lines like

[AnalyseObject, obj=26, n=0, m=0]

every time the routine is called. A more drastic measure is to compile the story file with the –g set. The ordinary setting –g or –g1 marks every routine in your own source code to be watched, but not routines in the library (more accurately, not to routines defined in any "system file"). The setting –g2 marks every routine from anywhere, but be warned, this produces an enormous melée of output.

△   If you do have Infix present, then you can always type ";watch ... off" to stop watching any routine marked with a * in the source code. Without Infix, there's no stopping it.

△△ At present, there is no source-level debugger for Inform. However, for the benefit of any such tool which somebody might like to write, Inform has a switch -k which makes it produce a file of "debugging information" to go with the story file. This file mostly contains cross-references between positions in the game and lines of source code. The details of its format are left to the *Technical Manual*.

● **REFERENCES**
Several exercises in this book are about defining new debugging verbs to test one thing or another, and most games have invented a few of their own. Early versions of 'Curses', for instance, allowed various supernatural actions beginning with "x" once the player had typed the command "xallow 57" (the author was then living above a carpet shop at 57 High Street, Oxford). But Paul David Doherty eventually disassembled the story file and found the secret. Moral: place any new debugging verbs inside an Ifdef DEBUG; directive, unless you plan on leaving them in as "Easter eggs" for people to find.   ●A simple debugging verb called "xdeterm" is defined in the DEBUG version of 'Advent': it takes random events out of the game.   ●Marnie Parker's library extension "objlstr.h", which has contributions from Tony Lewis, provides a useful debugging verb "list", allowing for instance "list has door lockable locked", which lists all objects having that combination of attributes.

Chapter III: The Model World

A Model must be built which will get everything in without a clash; and it can do this only by becoming intricate, by mediating its unity through a great, and finely ordered, multiplicity.

— C. S. Lewis (1898–1963), *The Discarded Image*

§8   Places and scenery

In this longer chapter the model world of an Inform game will be explored and examples will gradually complete the 'Ruins' begun in Chapter II. So far, 'Ruins' contains just a location of rainforest together with some rules about photography. The immediate need is for a more substantial map, beginning with a sunken chamber. Like the Forest, this too has light, however dim. If it didn't, the player would never see it: in Inform's world darkness prevails unless the designer provides some kind of lamp or, as in this case, ambient light.

```
Object Square_Chamber "Square Chamber"
  with name 'lintelled' 'lintel' 'lintels' 'east' 'south' 'doorways',
       description
          "A sunken, gloomy stone chamber, ten yards across. A shaft
          of sunlight cuts in from the steps above, giving the
          chamber a diffuse light, but in the shadows low lintelled
          doorways to east and south lead into the deeper darkness
          of the Temple.",
  has  light;
```

This room has a name property even though rooms are not usually referred to by players. The nouns given are words which Inform knows "you don't need to refer to", and it's a convention of the genre that the designer should signpost the game in this way. For the game to talk about something and later deny all knowledge – "I can't see any such thing" – is not merely rude but harmful to the player's illusion of holding a conversation about a real world. Better to parry with:

```
>examine lintel
```

That's not something you need to refer to in the course of this game.

.   .   .   .   .

Not all of the Square Chamber's décor is so irrelevant:

```
Object -> "carved inscriptions"
  with name 'carved' 'inscriptions' 'carvings' 'marks' 'markings'
        'symbols' 'moving' 'scuttling' 'crowd' 'of',
      initial
        "Carved inscriptions crowd the walls, floor and ceiling.",
      description
        "Each time you look at the carvings closely, they seem
        to be still. But you have the uneasy feeling when you
        look away that they're scuttling, moving about. Two
        glyphs are prominent: Arrow and Circle.",
  has   static pluralname;
```

The static attribute means that the inscriptions can't be taken or moved. As we went out of our way to describe a shaft of sunlight, we'll include that as well:

```
Object -> sunlight "shaft of sunlight"
  with name 'shaft' 'of' 'sunlight' 'sun' 'light' 'beam' 'sunbeam'
        'ray' 'rays' 'sun^s' 'sunlit' 'air' 'motes' 'dust',
      description
        "Motes of dust glimmer in the shaft of sunlit air, so
        that it seems almost solid.",
  has   scenery;
```

The ^ symbol in "sun^s" means an apostrophe, so the word is "sun's". This object has been given the constant name sunlight because other parts of the 'Ruins' source code will need to refer to it later on. Being scenery means that the object is not only static but also not described by the game unless actually examined by the player. A perfectionist might add a before rule:

```
        before [;
            Examine, Search: ;
            default: "It's only an insubstantial shaft of sunlight.";
        ],
```

so that the player can look at or through the sunlight, but any other request involving them will be turned down. Note that a default rule, if given, means "any action except those already mentioned".

△   Objects having `scenery` are assumed to be mentioned in the `description` text of the room, just as the "shaft of sunlight" is mentioned in that of the Square Chamber. Giving an object `concealed` marks it as something which is present to a player who knows about it, but hidden from the casual eye. It will not be cited in lists of objects present in the room, and "take all" will not take it, but "take secret dossier", or whatever, will work. (Designers seldom need `concealed`, but the library uses it all the time, because the player-object is `concealed`.)

. . . . .

Some scenery must spread across several rooms. The 'Ruins', for instance, are misty, and although we *could* design them with a different "mist" object in every misty location, this would become tiresome. In 'Advent', for instance, a stream runs through seven locations, while mist which (we are told) is "frequently a sign of a deep pit leading down to water" can be found in ten different caves. Here is a better solution:

```
Object low_mist "low mist"
  with name 'low' 'swirling' 'mist',
       description "The mist has an aroma reminiscent of tortilla.",
       found_in  Square_Chamber  Forest,
       before [;
           Examine, Search: ;
           Smell: <<Examine self>>;
           default: "The mist is too insubstantial.";
       ],
  has  scenery;
```

The `found_in` property gives a list of places in which the mist is found: so far, just the Square Chamber and the Forest.

△   This allows for up to 32 misty locations. If scenery has to be visible even more widely than that, or if it has to change with circumstances (for instance, if the mist drifts) then it is simpler to give a routine instead of a list. This can look at the current `location` and say whether or not the object should be present, as in the following example from a game taking place at night:

```
Object Procyon "Procyon",
  with name 'procyon' 'alpha' 'canis' 'minoris' 'star',
       description "A double-star eleven light years distant.",
       found_in [;
           return (location ofclass OutsideRoom);
       ],
  has  scenery;
```

found_in is only consulted when the player's location changes, and works by moving objects around to give the illusion that they are in several places at once: thus, if the player walks from a dark field to a hilltop, Procyon will be moved ahead to the hilltop just in advance of the player's move. This illusion is good enough for most practical purposes, but sometimes needs a little extra work to maintain, for instance if the sky must suddenly cloud over, concealing the stars. Since it often happens that an object must be removed from all the places in which it would otherwise appear, an attribute called absent is provided which overrides found_in and declares that the object is found nowhere. Whatever change is made to found_in, or in giving or removing absent, the Inform library needs also to be notified that changes have taken place. For instance, if you need to occult Procyon behind the moon for a while, then:

```
give Procyon absent; MoveFloatingObjects();
```

The library routine MoveFloatingObjects keeps the books straight after a change of state of found_in or absent.

. . . . .

Whereas Procyon is entirely visual, some scenery items may afflict the other four senses. In 'Ruins', the Forest contains the rule:

```
before [;
    Listen: "Howler monkeys, bats, parrots, macaw.";
],
```

Besides which, we have already said that the mist smells of tortilla, which means that if the player types "smell" in a place where the mist is, there should clearly be some reaction. For this, a react_before rule attached to the mist is ideal:

```
react_before [;
    Smell: if (noun == nothing) <<Smell self>>;
],
```

This is called a "react" rule because the mist is reacting to the fact that a Smell action is taking place nearby. noun is compared with nothing to see if the player has indeed just typed "smell" and not, say, "smell crocus". Thus, when the action Smell takes place near the mist, it is converted into Smell low_mist, whereas the action Smell crocus would be left alone.

The five senses all have actions in Inform: Look, Listen, Smell, Taste and Touch. Of these, Look never has a noun attached (because Examine, LookUnder and Search are provided for close-up views), Smell and Listen may or may not have while Taste and Touch always have.

• **EXERCISE 6**

(Cf. 'Spellbreaker'.) Make an orange cloud descend on the player, which can't be seen through or walked out of.

. . . . .

Rooms also react to actions that might occur in them and have their own before and after rules. Here's one for the Square Chamber:

```
before [;
    Insert:
        if (noun == eggsac && second == sunlight) {
            remove eggsac; move stone_key to self;
            "You drop the eggsac into the glare of the shaft of
            sunlight. It bubbles obscenely, distends and then
            bursts into a hundred tiny insects which run in all
            directions into the darkness. Only spatters of slime
            and a curious yellow-stone key remain on the chamber
            floor.";
        }
],
```

(The variables noun and second hold the first and second nouns supplied with an action.) As it happens this rule could as easily have been part of the definition of the eggsac or the sunlight, but before and after rules for rooms are invaluable to code up geographical oddities.

• **EXERCISE 7**

Create a room for 'Ruins' called the Wormcast, which has the oddity that anything dropped there ends up back in the Square Chamber.

△   Sometimes the room may be a different one after the action has taken place. The Go action, for instance, is offered to the before routine of the room which is being left, and the after routine of the room being arrived in. For example:

```
after [;
    Go: if (noun == w_obj)
        print "You feel an overwhelming sense of relief.^";
],
```

will print the message when its room is entered from the "west" direction. Note that this routine returns false, in the absence of any code telling it to do otherwise, which means that the usual game rules resume after the printing of the message.

● **REFERENCES**
'A Scenic View' by Richard Barnett demonstrates a system for providing examinable scenery much more concisely (without defining so many objects).   ●found_in can allow a single object to represent many different but similar objects across a game, and a good example is found in Martin Braun's "elevator.inf" example game, where every floor of a building has an up-arrow and a down-arrow button to summon an elevator.

§9   Directions and the map

I wisely started with a map, and made the story fit (generally with meticulous care for distances). The other way about lands one in confusions and impossibilities, and in any case it is weary work to compose a map from a story – as I fear you have found.

—J. R. R. Tolkien (1892–1973), *to Naomi Mitchison, 25 April 1954*

 'Ruins' so far contains two disconnected rooms. It is time to extend it into a modest map in which, as promised, the Square Chamber lies underneath the original Forest location. For the map of the finished game, see §23 below, but here is the beginning of the first level beneath ground, showing the Square Chamber and its two main side-chambers:

```
        Square Chamber  ↔  Wormcast
                ↕
            Corridor
                ↕
             Shrine
```

To make these map connections, we need to add:

```
u_to Forest, e_to Wormcast, s_to Corridor,
```

to the Square Chamber. This seems a good point to add two more map connections, or rather non-connections, to the Forest as well:

```
u_to "The trees are spiny and you'd cut your hands to ribbons
    trying to climb them.",
cant_go "The rainforest is dense, and you haven't hacked
    through it for days to abandon your discovery now. Really,
    you need a good few artifacts to take back to civilization
    before you can justify giving up the expedition.",
```

The property cant_go contains what is printed when the player tries to go in a nonexistent direction, and replaces "You can't go that way". Instead of giving an actual message you can give a routine to print one out, to vary what's printed with the circumstances. The Forest needs a cant_go because in real life one could go in every direction from there: what we're doing is explaining the game rules to the player: go underground, find some ancient treasure, then get out to win. The Forest's u_to property is a string of text, not a room, and this means that attempts to go up result only in that string being printed.

△ Here's how this is done. When the library wants to go in a certain direction, let's say "north", it sends the message location.n_to() and looks at the reply: it takes false to mean "Player can't go that way" and says so; true means "Player can't go that way, and I've already said why"; and any other value is taken as the destination.

• **EXERCISE 8**
Many early games have rooms with confused exits: 'Advent' has Bedquilt, 'Acheton' has a magnetic lodestone which throws the compass into confusion, 'Zork II' has a spinning carousel room and so on. Make the Wormcast room in 'Ruins' similarly bewildering.

. . . . .

For each of the twelve standard Inform directions there is a "direction property":

```
n_to     s_to     e_to     w_to     d_to     u_to
ne_to    nw_to    se_to    sw_to    in_to    out_to
```

Each direction also has a "direction object" to represent it in the game. For instance, n_obj is the object whose name is "north" and which the player invokes by typing "go north" or just "n". So there are normally twelve of these, too:

```
n_obj    s_obj    e_obj    w_obj    d_obj    u_obj
ne_obj   nw_obj   se_obj   sw_obj   in_obj   out_obj
```

Confusing the direction objects with the direction properties is easily done, but they are quite different. When the player types "go north", the action is Go n_obj, with noun being n_obj: only when this action has survived all possible before rules is the n_to value of the current location looked at.

△ The set of direction objects is not fixed: the current direction objects are the children of a special object called compass, and the game designer is free to add to or take from the current stock. Here for instance is the definition of "north" made by the library:

```
CompassDirection n_obj "north wall" compass
    with name 'n' 'north' 'wall', door_dir n_to;
```

CompassDirection is a class defined by the library for direction objects. door_dir is a property more usually seen in the context of doors (see §13) and here tells Inform which direction property corresponds to which direction object.

• △EXERCISE 9

In the first millennium A.D., the Maya peoples of the Yucatán Peninsula had 'world colours' white (*sac*), red (*chac*), yellow (*kan*) and black (*chikin*) for what we call the compass bearings north, east, south, west (for instance west is associated with 'sunset', hence black, the colour of night). Implement this.

• △EXERCISE 10

In Level 9's version of 'Advent', the magic word "xyzzy" was implemented as a thirteenth direction. How can this be done?

• △EXERCISE 11

(Cf. 'Trinity'.) How can the entire game map be suddenly east–west reflected?

• △△EXERCISE 12

Even when the map is reflected, there may be many room descriptions referring to "east" and "west" by name. Reflect these too.

• △△EXERCISE 13

Some designers find it a nuisance to have to keep specifying all map connections twice: once east from *A* to *B*, then a second time west from *B* to *A*, for instance. Write some code to go in the Initialise routine making all connections automatically two-way.

• **REFERENCES**

'Advent' has a very tangled-up map in places (see the mazes) and a well-constructed exterior of forest and valley giving an impression of space with remarkably few rooms. The mist object uses found_in to the full, and see also the stream (a single object representing every watercourse in the game). Bedquilt and the Swiss Cheese room offer classic confused-exit puzzles. •For a simple movement rule using e_to, see the Office in 'Toyshop'. •The opening location of Infocom's 'Moonmist' provides a good example of cant_go used to guide the player in a tactful way: "(The castle is south of here.)" •The library extension "smartcantgo.h" by David Wagner provides a system for automatically printing out "You can only go east and north."-style messages. •Ricardo Dague's "cmap.h" constructs maps of American-style cities. The same author's "makemaze.inf" prints out Inform source code for random rectangular mazes. •Nicholas Daley and Gunther Schmidl have each independently written a "dirs.h" providing a "dirs" or "exits" verb which lists available exits. Marnie Parker's "dirsmap.h" goes further by plotting up exits in map style or writing them out in English, at the player's discretion. •Brian D. Smith's example program "spin.inf" abolishes the convention that a player has an in-built ability to know which way is north: it replaces conventional compass directions with "left", "right", "ahead" and "back".

§10 Food and drink

 Any object with the attribute edible can be eaten by the player, and the library provides the action Eat for this. If it succeeds, the library removes whatever was eaten from the object tree, so that it disappears from play (unless the designer has written any code which later moves it back again). Two edible objects have already appeared in 'Ruins': the mushroom, §4, and the honeycomb, §5.

Because drinking is a less clear-cut matter than eating, there is no attribute called drinkable. Although the library does provide the action Drink, you have to write your own code to show what happens when the object has been drunk. Here is an example where the object is entirely consumed:

```
Object -> "glass of milk"
  with name 'glass' 'of' 'milk',
       before [;
           Drink: remove self;
               "Well, that's the sixth stomach that hillside
               of grass has been in.";
       ];
```

Other rules which might be needed, instead of simply removing the object, would be to replace it with an "empty glass" object, or to change some counter which records how many sips have been taken from a large supply of drink.

● **REFERENCES**
Players discover almost at once that 'Advent' contains "tasty food", actually tripe although the text is too delicate to say so. (Type "get tripe ration" if you don't believe this.) Less well known is that the moss growing on the Soft Room's walls is also edible. ●The product-placement parody 'Coke Is It' contains the occasional beverage. ("You are standing at the end of a road before a small brick building. Coca-Cola... Along The Highway To Anywhere, Around The Corner From Everywhere, Coca-Cola is The Best Friend Thirst Ever Had. A small stream flows out of the building and down a gully.") ●Inform doesn't provide an automatic system for handling liquids because it is difficult to find one that would satisfy enough people for enough of the time: for more on the issues that liquids raise, see §50. In its handling of liquids the source code for the alchemical mystery 'Christminster' is much borrowed from.

§11 Clothing

The player's possessions are normally thought of as being held in the hands, but there are two alternative possibilities: some items might be being carried indirectly in a bag or other container (see §12 next), while others might be worn as clothing. Wearing a hat is evidently different from carrying it. Some consequences are left to the designer to sort out, such as taking account of the hat keeping the rain off, but others are automatically provided: for instance, a request to "drop all" will not be taken as including the hat, and the hat will not count towards any maximum number of items allowed to be held in the player's hands. The library provides two actions for clothing: Wear and Disrobe. There is already an action called Remove for taking items out of containers, which is why the name Remove is not used for taking clothes off.

'Ruins' contains only one item of clothing, found resting on an altar in the Shrine: it summons a priest.

```
Treasure -> -> mask "jade mosaic face-mask"
  with description "How exquisite it would look in the Museum.",
      initial "Resting on the altar is a jade mosaic face-mask.",
      name 'jade' 'mosaic' 'face-mask' 'mask' 'face',
      cultural_value 10,
      after [;
          Wear: move priest to Shrine;
              if (location == Shrine)
                  "Looking through the obsidian eyeslits of the
                  mosaic mask, a ghostly presence reveals itself:
                  a mummified calendrical priest, attending your
                  word.";
          Disrobe: remove priest;
          ],
  has   clothing;
```

The attribute clothing signifies that the mask can be worn. During the time something is worn, it has the attribute worn. The library's standard rules ensure that:

> An object can only have worn if it is in player, that is, if it is an immediate possession of the player.

If you use move or remove to shift items of clothing in your own code, or give or take away the worn attribute, then you too should follow this principle.

△   A risk of providing clothing for the player is that it's hard to resist the lure of realism. A tweed jacket would add some colour to 'Ruins'. But if a jacket, why not plus-four trousers, an old pair of army boots and a hat with a mosquito net? And if trousers, why not underwear? What are the consequences if the player strips off? Too much of this kind of realism can throw a game off balance, so: no tweed.

● △△EXERCISE 14
Design a pair of white silk gloves, left and right, which are a single object called "pair of white gloves" until the player asks to do something which implies dividing them (typing "wear left glove", say, or "put right glove in drawer"). They should automatically rejoin into the pair as soon as they are together again. (By Richard Tucker. Hint: react_before and before rules are all you need.)

● REFERENCES
For designers who do want to go down the "if trousers, why not underwear?" road, Denis Moskowitz's library extension "clothing.h" models clothing by layer and by area of body covered.   ●For players who also want to, the road to take is 'I-0', by Adam Cadre.

§12 Containers, supporters and sub-objects

The year has been a good one for the Society *(hear, hear)*. This year our members have put more things on top of other things than ever before. But, I should warn you, this is no time for complacency. No, there are still many things, and I cannot emphasize this too strongly, *not* on top of other things.

— 'The Royal Society For Putting Things On Top Of Other Things' sketch, *Monty Python's Flying Circus*, programme 18 (1970)

In almost every game, certain objects need to be thought of as on top of or inside other objects. The library provides actions Insert and PutOn for placing things inside or on top of something, and Remove for taking things out of or off the top of something. Many objects, such as house-bricks, cannot sensibly contain things, and a designer usually only wants certain specific items ever to have other things on top of them. In the model world, then, only objects which the designer has given the container attribute can contain things, and only those given the supporter attribute can have items on top.

The packing case brought by our archaeologist hero to the scene of the 'Ruins' (found in the opening location, the Forest) is a thoroughly typical container:

```
Object -> packing_case "packing case"
  with name 'packing' 'case' 'box' 'strongbox',
       initial
           "Your packing case rests here, ready to hold any important
           cultural finds you might make, for shipping back to
           civilisation.",
       before [;
           Take, Remove, PushDir:
               "The case is too heavy to bother moving, as long as
               your expedition is still incomplete.";
           ],
  has   static container open openable;
```

A container can hold anything up to 100 items, but this limit can be modified by giving the container a capacity property.

Note that the packing case is defined having an attribute called open. This is essential, because the library will only allow the player to put things in a container if it is currently open. (There is no attribute called closed, as any container lacking open is considered closed.) If a container has openable, the player can open and close it at will, unless it also has locked. A locked object, whether it be a door or a container, cannot be opened. But if it has lockable then it can be locked or unlocked with the key object given in its with_key property. If with_key is undeclared or equal to nothing, then no key will fit, but this will not be told to the player. The actions Open, Close, Lock and Unlock handle all of this.

● **EXERCISE 15**
Construct a musical box with a silver key.

. . . . .

An object having supporter can have up to 100 items put on top of it, or, once again, its capacity value if one is given. An object cannot be both a container and a supporter at once, and there's no concept of being "open" or "locked" for supporters. Here is an example from the Shrine:

```
Object -> stone_table "slab altar"
  with name 'stone' 'table' 'slab' 'altar' 'great',
       initial "A great stone slab of a table, or altar, dominates
           the Shrine.",
  has   enterable supporter static;
```

See §15 for enterable and its consequences.

. . . . .

Containers and supporters are able to react to things being put inside them, or removed from them, by acting on the signal to Receive or LetGo. For example, further down in the 'Ruins' is a chasm which, perhaps surprisingly, is implemented as a container:

```
Object -> chasm "horrifying chasm"
  with name 'blackness' 'chasm' 'pit' 'horrifying' 'bottomless',
       react_before [;
           Jump: <<Enter self>>;
           Go: if (noun == d_obj) <<Enter self>>;
       ],
       before [;
           Enter: deadflag = true;
               "You plummet through the silent void of darkness!";
           JumpOver: "It's far too wide.";
       ],
       after [;
           Receive: remove noun;
```

```
            print_ret (The) noun, " tumbles silently into the
                darkness of the chasm.";
        Search: "The chasm is deep and murky.";
    ],
 has  scenery open container;
```

(Actually the definition will grow in §23, so that the chasm reacts to an eight-foot pumice-stone ball being rolled into it.) Note the use of an after rule for the Search action: this is because an attempt to "examine" or "look inside" the chasm will cause this action. Search means, in effect, "tell me what is inside the container" and the after rule prevents a message like "There is nothing inside the chasm." from misleading the player. Note also that the chasm 'steals' any stray Jump action in the vicinity using react_before and converts it into an early death.

● **EXERCISE 16**
Make an acquisitive bag which will swallow things up but refuses to disgorge them.

△   Receive is sent to an object *O* when a player tries to put something in *O*, or on *O*. In the rare event that *O* needs to react differently to these two attempts, it may consult the library's variable receive_action to find out whether ##PutOn or ##Insert is the cause.

.   .   .   .   .

Not all containment is about carrying or supporting things. For instance, suppose a machine has four levers. If the machine is fixed in place somewhere, like a printing press, the levers could be provided as four further static objects. But if it is portable, like a sewing machine, we need to make sure that the levers always move whenever it moves, and vice versa. The natural solution is to make the lever-objects children of the machine-object, as though the machine were a container and the levers were its contents.

However, members of an object which isn't a container or supporter are normally assumed by the library to be hidden invisibly inside. In the case of the levers, this would defeat the point. We can get around this by giving the machine the transparent attribute, making the levers visible but not removable.

Containers can also be transparent, making their contents visible even when closed. The items on top of a supporter are of course always visible, and it makes no sense for a supporter to be transparent. See §26 for further details on when contents are listed in inventories and room descriptions.

● **EXERCISE 17**

Make a glass box and a steel box, which behave differently when a lamp is shut up inside them.

● **EXERCISE 18**

Make a television set with attached power button and screen.

● △**EXERCISE 19**

Implement a macramé bag hanging from the ceiling, inside which objects are visible, audible and so forth, but cannot be touched or manipulated in any way.

△   The most difficult case to handle is when an object needs to be portable, and to have sub-objects like lamps and buttons, *and* also to be a container in its own right. The solution to this will have to be left until the "scope addition" rules in §32, but briefly: an object's add_to_scope property may contain a list of sub-objects to be kept attached to it but which are not its children.

● **REFERENCES**

Containers and supporters abound in the example games (except 'Advent', which is too simple, though see the water-and-oil carrying bottle). Interesting containers include the lottery-board and the podium sockets from 'Balances' and the 'Adventureland' bottle.   ●For supporters, the hearth-rug, chessboard, armchair and mantelpiece of 'Alice Through the Looking-Glass' are typical examples; the mantelpiece and spirit level of 'Toyshop' make a simple puzzle, and the pile of building blocks a complicated one; see also the scales in 'Balances'.

§13 Doors

> The happiness of seizing one of these tall barriers to a room by the porcelain knob of its belly; this quick hand-to-hand, during which progress slows for a moment, your eye opens up and your whole body adapts to its new apartment.
>
> — Francis Ponge (1899–1988), *Les plaisirs de la porte*

 When is a door not a door? It might be a rope-bridge or a ladder, for instance. Inform provides doors for any situation in which some game object is intermediate between one place and another, and might on occasion become a barrier. Doors have a good deal in common with containers, in that they need to be open to allow access and to this end can also have openable, lockable or locked. Just as with containers, any key they have should be stored in the with_key property. The same actions Open, Close, Lock and Unlock all apply to doors just as they apply to containers. There are four steps in creating a new door:

(1) give the object the door attribute;
(2) set its door_to property to the location on the other side;
(3) set its door_dir property to the direction which that would be, such as n_to;
(4) make the location's map connection in that direction point to the door itself.

For example, here is a closed and locked door, blocking the way into the 'Ruins' Shrine:

```
Object Corridor "Stooped Corridor"
  with description "A low, square-cut corridor, running north to south,
          stooping you over.",
       n_to Square_Chamber,
       s_to StoneDoor;
Object -> StoneDoor "stone door"
  with description "It's just a big stone door.",
       name 'door' 'massive' 'big' 'stone' 'yellow',
       when_closed "Passage south is barred by a massive door of
          yellow stone.",
       when_open "The great yellow stone door to the south is open.",
       door_to Shrine,
       door_dir s_to,
```

```
      with_key stone_key
  has  static door openable lockable locked;
```

Note that the door is static – otherwise the player could pick it up and walk away with it. (Experienced play-testers of Inform games try this every time, and usually come away with a door or two.) The properties when_closed and when_open give descriptions appropriate for the door in these two states.

A door is ordinarily only present on one side of a map connection. If a door needs to be accessible, say openable or lockable, from either side, then the standard trick is to make it present in both locations using found_in and to fix the door_to and door_dir to be the right way round for whichever side the player is on. Here, then, is a two-way door:

```
Object -> StoneDoor "stone door"
  with description "It's just a big stone door.",
       name 'door' 'massive' 'big' 'stone' 'yellow',
       when_closed "The passage is barred by a massive door
           of yellow stone.",
       when_open "The great yellow stone door is open.",
       door_to [;
           if (self in Corridor) return Shrine; return Corridor;
       ],
       door_dir [;
           if (self in Shrine) return n_to; return s_to;
       ],
       with_key stone_key,
       found_in Corridor Shrine,
  has  static door openable lockable locked;
```

where Corridor has s_to set to StoneDoor, and Shrine has n_to set to StoneDoor. The door can now be opened, closed, entered, locked or unlocked from either side. We could also make when_open and when_closed into routines to print different descriptions of the door on each side.

·   ·   ·   ·   ·

Puzzles more interesting than lock-and-key involve writing some code to intervene when the player tries to pass through. The interactive fiction literature has no shortage of doors which only a player with no possessions can pass through, for instance.

Care is required here because two different actions can make the player pass through the door. In the Corridor above, the player might type "s" or "go south", causing the action Go s_obj. Or might "enter stone door" or "go through door", causing Enter StoneDoor. Provided the door is actually open, the Enter action then looks at the door's door_dir property, finds that the door faces south and generates the action Go s_obj. Thus, *provided that the door is open,* the outcome is the same and you need only write code to trap the Go action.

A neater alternative is to make the door_to property a routine. If a door_to routine returns false instead of a room, then the player is told that the door "leads nowhere", like the broken bridge of Avignon. If door_to returns true, then the library stops the action on the assumption that something has happened and the player has been told already.

● **EXERCISE 20**
Create a plank bridge across a chasm, which collapses if the player walks across it while carrying anything.

● **EXERCISE 21**
Create a locked door which turns out to be an immaterial illusion only when the player tries to walk through it in blind faith.

● **REFERENCES**
'Advent' is especially rich in two-way doors: the steel grate in the streambed, two bridges (one of crystal, the other of rickety wood) and a door with rusty hinges. See also the iron gate in 'Balances'.   ●The library extension "doors.h" by L. Ross Raszewski defines a class called Connector of two-way doors, which are slotted automatically into the map for convenience. Max Kalus's further extension "doors2.h" enables such doors to respond to, say, "the north door" from one side and "the south door" from the other.

§14   Switchable objects

 A switchable object is one which can be switched off or on, usually
because it has some obvious button, lever or switch on it. The object
has the attribute on if it's on, and doesn't have it if it's off. (So
there's no attribute called off, just as there's no attribute called
closed.) The actions SwitchOn and SwitchOff allow the player to manipulate
anything which is switchable. For example:

```
Object searchlight "Gotham City searchlight" skyscraper
  with name 'search' 'light' 'searchlight' 'template',
       article "the",
       description "It has some kind of template on it.",
       when_on "The old city searchlight shines out a bat against
           the feather-clouds of the darkening sky.",
       when_off "The old city searchlight, neglected but still
           functional, sits here."
  has  switchable static;
```

Something more portable would come in handy for the explorer of 'Ruins',
who would hardly have embarked on his expedition without a decent lamp:

```
Object sodium_lamp "sodium lamp"
  with name 'sodium' 'lamp' 'heavy',
       describe [;
           if (self has on)
               "^The sodium lamp squats on the ground, burning away.";
           "^The sodium lamp squats heavily on the ground.";
       ],
       battery_power 100,
       before [;
           Examine: print "It is a heavy-duty archaeologist's lamp, ";
               if (self hasnt on) "currently off.";
               if (self.battery_power < 10) "glowing a dim yellow.";
               "blazing with brilliant yellow light.";
           Burn: <<SwitchOn self>>;
```

```
      SwitchOn:
          if (self.battery_power <= 0)
              "Unfortunately, the battery seems to be dead.";
          if (parent(self) hasnt supporter
              && self notin location)
              "The lamp must be securely placed before being
              lit.";
      Take, Remove:
          if (self has on)
              "The bulb's too delicate and the metal handle's too
              hot to lift the lamp while it's switched on.";
  ],
  after [;
      SwitchOn: give self light;
      SwitchOff: give self ~light;
  ],
has  switchable;
```

The 'Ruins' lamp will eventually be a little more complicated, with a daemon
to make the battery power run down and to extinguish the lamp when it runs
out; and it will be pushable from place to place, making it not quite as useless
as the player will hopefully think at first.

△   The reader may be wondering why the lamp needs to use a describe routine to
give itself a description varying with its condition: why not simply write the following?

```
when_off "The sodium lamp squats heavily on the ground.",
when_on "The sodium lamp squats on the ground, burning away.",
```

The answer is that when_on and when_off properties, like initial, only apply until an
object has been held by the player, after which it is normally given only a perfunctory
mention in room descriptions. "You can also see a sodium lamp here." As the
describe property has priority over the whole business of how objects are described in
room descriptions, the above ensures that the full message always appears even if the
object has become old and familiar. For much more on room descriptions, see §26.

●REFERENCES
The original switchable object was the brass lamp from 'Advent', which even provides
verbs "on" and "off" to switch it.   ●Jayson Smith's library extension "links.h"
imitates a set of gadgets found in Andrew Plotkin's game 'Spider and Web'. In this
scheme, "linkable" machines only work when linked to "actuators", which are switches
of different kinds (remote controls, attachable push-buttons and so on).

§15 Things to enter, travel in and push around

> Vehicles were objects that became, in effect, mobile rooms... The code for the boat itself was not designed to function outside the river section, but nothing kept the player from carrying the deflated boat to the reservoir and trying to sail across...
>
> — Tim Anderson, *The History of Zork*

 Quite so. Even the case of an entirely static object which can be climbed into or onto poses problems of realism. Sitting on a garden roller, is one in the gardens, or not? Can one reasonably reach to pick up a leaf on the ground? The Inform library leaves most of these subtleties to the designer but has at least a general concept of "enterable object". These have enterable and the Enter and Exit actions allow the player to get in (or on) and out (or off) of them.

Enterable items might include, say, an open-topped car, a psychiatrist's couch or even a set of manacles attached to a dungeon wall. In practice, though, manacles are an exceptional case, and one usually wants to make an enterable thing also a container, or – as in the case of the altar from 'Ruins' which appeared in the previous section – a supporter:

```
Object -> stone_table "slab altar"
  with name 'stone' 'table' 'slab' 'altar' 'great',
       initial "A great stone slab of a table, or altar, dominates the
          Shrine.",
  has  enterable supporter static;
```

A chair to sit on, or a bed to lie down on, should also be a supporter.

Sitting on furniture, one is hardly in a different location altogether. But suppose the player climbs into a container which is not transparent and then closes it from the inside? To all intents and purposes this has become another room. The interior may be dark, but if there's light to see by, the player will want to see some kind of room description. In any case, many enterable objects ought to look different from inside or on top. Inside a vehicle, a player might be able to see a steering wheel and a dashboard, for instance. On top of a cupboard, it might be possible to see through a skylight window.

For this purpose, any enterable object can provide a property called inside_description, which can hold a string of text or else a routine to print some text, as usual. If the exterior location is still visible, then the "inside description" is appended to the normal room description; if not, it replaces the room description altogether. As an extreme example, suppose that the player gets into a huge cupboard, closes the door and then gets into a plastic cabinet inside that. The resulting room description might read like so:

> *The huge cupboard (in the plastic cabinet)*
> It's a snug little cupboard in here, almost a room in itself.
> In the huge cupboard you can see a pile of clothes.
> The plastic walls of the cabinet distort the view.

The second line is the inside_description for the huge cupboard, and the fourth is that for the plastic cabinet.

• **EXERCISE 22**
(Also from 'Ruins'.) Implement a cage which can be opened, closed and entered.

· · · · ·

All the classic games have vehicles (like boats, or fork lift trucks, or hot air balloons) which the player can journey in, and Inform makes this easy. Here is a simple case:

```
Object car "little red car" cave
  with name 'little' 'red' 'car',
       description "Large enough to sit inside. Among the controls is a
           prominent on/off switch. The numberplate is KAR 1.",
       when_on  "The red car sits here, its engine still running.",
       when_off "A little red car is parked here.",
       before [;
           Go: if (car has on) "Brmm! Brmm!";
               print "(The ignition is off at the moment.)^";
       ],
  has  switchable enterable static container open;
```

Actually, this demonstrates a special rule. If a player is inside an enterable object and tries to move, say "north", the before routine for the object is called with the action Go n_obj. It may then return:

> 0   to disallow the movement, printing a refusal;
> 1   to allow the movement, moving vehicle and player;
> 2   to disallow but print and do nothing; or
> 3   to allow but print and do nothing.

If you want to move the vehicle in your own code, return 3, not 2: otherwise the old location may be restored by subsequent workings. Notice that if you write no code, the default value false will always be returned, so enterable objects won't become vehicular unless you write them that way.

△ Because you might want to drive the car "out" of a garage, the "out" verb does not make the player get out of the car. Instead the player generally has to type something like "get out" or "exit" to make this happen.

● **EXERCISE 23**
Alter the car so that it will only drive along roads, and not through all map connections.

. . . . .

Objects like the car or, say, an antiquated wireless on casters, are too heavy to pick up but the player should at least be able to push them from place to place. When the player tries to do this, an action like PushDir wireless is generated.

Now, if the before routine for the wireless returns false, the game will just say that the player can't move the wireless; and if it returns true, the game will do nothing at all, assuming that the before routine has already printed something more interesting. So how does one actually tell Inform that the push should be allowed? The answer is: first call the AllowPushDir routine (a library routine), and then return true. For example ('Ruins' again), here is a ball on a north-south corridor which slopes upward at the northern end:

```
Object -> huge_ball "huge pumice-stone ball"
  with name 'huge' 'pumice' 'pumice-stone' 'stone' 'ball',
       description
           "A good eight feet across, though fairly lightweight.",
       initial
           "A huge pumice-stone ball rests here, eight feet wide.",
       before [;
           PushDir:
               if (location == Junction && second == ne_obj)
                   "The Shrine entrance is far less than eight feet
                   wide.";
               AllowPushDir(); rtrue;
           Pull, Push, Turn:
               "It wouldn't be so very hard to get rolling.";
           Take, Remove:
               "There's a lot of stone in an eight-foot sphere.";
       ],
       after [;
           PushDir:
               if (second == s_obj)
                   "The ball is hard to stop once underway.";
               if (second == n_obj)
                   "You strain to push the ball uphill.";
```

```
      ],
  has   static;
```

• △EXERCISE 24

The library does not normally allow pushing objects up or down. How can the pumice ball allow this?

• REFERENCES

For an enterable supporter puzzle, see the magic carpet in 'Balances' (and several items in 'Alice Through the Looking-Glass').   •When a vehicle has a sealed interior large enough to be a location, it is probably best handled as a location with changing map connections and not as a vehicle object moved from room to room. See for instance Martin Braun's "elevator.inf" example game, providing an elevator which serves eight floors of a building.

§16 Reading matter and consultation

> Making books is a skilled trade, like making clocks.
>
> — Jean de la Bruyère (1645-1696)

 "Look up figure 18 in the engineering textbook" is a difficult line for Inform to understand, because almost anything could appear in the first part: even its format depends on what the second part is. This kind of request, and more generally

```
>look up ⟨any words here⟩ in ⟨the object⟩
>read about ⟨any words here⟩ in ⟨the object⟩
>consult ⟨the object⟩ about ⟨any words here⟩
```

cause the Consult action. In such cases, the noun is the book and there is no second object. Instead, the object has to parse the ⟨any words here⟩ part itself. The following variables are set up to make this possible:

consult_from holds the number of the first word in the ⟨any...⟩ clause;

consult_words holds the number of words in the ⟨any...⟩ clause.

The ⟨any words here⟩ clause must contain at least one word. The words given can be parsed using library routines like NextWord(), TryNumber(word-number) and so on: see §28 for full details. As usual, the before routine should return true if it has managed to deal with the action; returning false will make the library print "You discover nothing of interest in...".

Little hints are placed here and there in the 'Ruins', written in the glyphs of a not altogether authentic dialect of Mayan. Our explorer has, naturally, come equipped with the latest and finest scholarship on the subject:

```
Object dictionary "Waldeck's Mayan dictionary"
  with name 'dictionary' 'local' 'guide' 'book' 'mayan'
         'waldeck' 'waldeck^s',
       description "Compiled from the unreliable lithographs of the
           legendary raconteur and explorer ~Count~ Jean Frederic
           Maximilien Waldeck (1766??-1875), this guide contains
           what little is known of the glyphs used in the local
           ancient dialect.",
       correct false,
       before [ w1 w2 glyph;
         Consult:
```

```
        wn = consult_from;
        w1 = NextWord(); ! First word of subject
        w2 = NextWord(); ! Second word (if any) of subject
        if (consult_words==1 && w1~='glyph' or 'glyphs') glyph = w1;
        else if (consult_words==2 && w1=='glyph') glyph = w2;
        else if (consult_words==2 && w2=='glyph') glyph = w1;
        else "Try ~look up <name of glyph> in book~.";
        switch (glyph) {
            'q1': "(This is one glyph you have memorised!)^^
                    Q1: ~sacred site~.";
            'crescent': "Crescent: believed pronounced ~xibalba~,
                though its meaning is unknown.";
            'arrow': "Arrow: ~journey; becoming~.";
            'skull': "Skull: ~death, doom; fate (not nec. bad)~.";
            'circle': "Circle: ~the Sun; also life, lifetime~.";
            'jaguar': "Jaguar: ~lord~.";
            'monkey': "Monkey: ~priest?~.";
            'bird': if (self.correct) "Bird: ~dead as a stone~.";
                "Bird: ~rich, affluent?~.";
            default: "That glyph is so far unrecorded.";
        }
    ],
  has proper;
```

Note that this understands any of the forms "q1", "glyph q1" or "q1 glyph". (These aren't genuine Maya glyphs, but some of the real ones once had similar names, dating from when their syllabic equivalents weren't known.)

● △△EXERCISE 25
To mark the 505th anniversary of William Tyndale, the first English translator of the New Testament (who was born some time around 1495 and burned as a heretic in Vilvorde, Denmark, in 1535), prepare an Inform edition.

· · · · ·

△△ Ordinarily, a request by the player to "read" something is translated into an Examine action. But the "read" verb is defined independently of the "examine" verb in order to make it easy to separate the two requests. For instance:

```
Attribute legible;
...
Object textbook "textbook"
  with name 'engineering' 'textbook' 'text' 'book',
       description "What beautiful covers and spine!",
```

```
    before [;
        Consult, Read:
            "The pages are full of senseless equations.";
    ],
    has   legible;
...
[ ReadSub; <<Examine noun>>; ];
Extend 'read' first * legible -> Read;
```

Note that "read" causes a Read action only for legible objects, and otherwise causes Examine in the usual way. ReadSub is coded as a translation to Examine as well, so that if a legible object doesn't provide a Read rule then an Examine happens after all.

● **REFERENCES**
Another possibility for parsing commands like "look up ⟨something⟩ in the catalogue", where any object name might appear as the ⟨something⟩, would be to extend the grammar for "look". See §30.

§17   People and animals

To know how to live is my trade and my art.

— Michel de Montaigne (1533–1592), *Essays*

 Living creatures should be given the attribute animate so that the library knows such an object can be talked to, given things, woken from sleep and so on. When the player treats an animate object as living in this way, the library calls upon that object's life property. This looks like before or after, but only applies to the following actions:

Attack   The player is making hostile advances. . .

Kiss   . . . or amorous ones. . .

WakeOther   . . . or simply trying to rouse the creature from sleep.

ThrowAt   The player asked to throw noun at the creature.

Give   The player asked to give noun to the creature. . .

Show   . . . or, tantalisingly, just to show it.

Ask   The player asked about something. Just as with a "consult" topic (see §16 above), the variables consult_from and consult_words are set up to indicate which words the object might like to think about. (In addition, second holds the dictionary value for the first word which isn't 'the', but this is much cruder.)

Tell   The player is trying to tell the creature about something. The topic is set up just as for Ask (that is, consult_from and consult_words are set, and second also holds the first interesting word).

Answer   This can happen in two ways. One is if the player types "answer ⟨some text⟩ to troll" or "say ⟨some text⟩ to troll"; the other is if an order is given which the parser can't sort out, such as "troll, og south", and which the orders property hasn't handled already. Once again, variables are set as if it were a "consult" topic. (In addition, noun is set to the first word, and an attempt to read the text as a number is stored in the variable special_number: for instance, "computer, 143" will cause special_number to be set to 143.)

Order   This catches any 'orders' which aren't handled by the orders
             property (see the next section); action, noun and second are set
             up as usual.

If the life rule isn't given, or returns false, events take their usual course.
life rules vary dramatically in size. The coiled snake from 'Balances' shows
that even the tiniest life routine can be adequate for an animal:

```
Object -> snake "hissing snake"
  with name 'hissing' 'snake',
       initial "Tightly coiled at the edge of the chasm is a
           hissing snake.",
       life "The snake hisses angrily!",
  has  animate;
```

It's far from unknown for people in interactive fiction to be almost as simplistic
as that, but in most games even relatively passive characters have some ability
to speak or react. Here is the funerary priest standing in the 'Ruins' Shrine:

```
Object priest "mummified priest"
  with name 'mummified' 'priest',
       description
           "He is desiccated and hangs together only by will-power.
           Though his first language is presumably local Mayan,
           you have the curious instinct that he will understand
           your speech.",
       initial "Behind the slab, a mummified priest stands waiting,
           barely alive at best, impossibly venerable.",
       life [;
           Answer: "The priest coughs, and almost falls apart.";
           Ask: switch (second) {
                   'dictionary', 'book':
                       if (dictionary.correct == false)
                           "~The ~bird~ glyph... very funny.~";
                       "~A dictionary? Really?~";
                   'glyph', 'glyphs', 'mayan', 'dialect':
                       "~In our culture, the Priests are ever
                       literate.~";
                   'lord', 'tomb', 'shrine', 'temple':
                       "~This is a private matter.~";
                   'ruins': "~The ruins will ever defeat thieves.
                       In the underworld, looters are tortured
                       throughout eternity.~ A pause. ~As are
                       archaeologists.~";
```

```
                    'web', 'wormcast':
                         "~No man can pass the Wormcast.~";
                    'xibalba': if (Shrine.sw_to == Junction)
                             "The priest shakes his bony finger.";
                         Shrine.sw_to = Junction;
                         "The priest extends one bony finger
                         southwest toward the icicles, which
                         vanish like frost as he speaks.
                         ~Xibalb@'a, the Underworld.~";
               }
               "~You must find your own answer.~";
          Tell: "The priest has no interest in your sordid life.";
          Attack, Kiss:  remove self;
               "The priest desiccates away into dust until nothing
               remains, not a breeze nor a bone.";
          ThrowAt: move noun to location; <<Attack self>>;
          Show, Give:
               if (noun == dictionary && dictionary.correct == false) {
                    dictionary.correct = true;
                    "The priest reads a little of the book, laughing
                    in a hollow, whispering way. Unable to restrain
                    his mirth, he scratches in a correction somewhere
                    before returning the book.";
               }
               "The priest is not interested in earthly things.";
          ],
     has  animate;
```

The Priest only stands and waits, but some characters need to move around,
or to appear and reappear throughout a game, changing in their responses
and what they know. This makes for a verbose object definition full of cross-
references to items and places scattered across the source code. An alternative
is to use different objects to represent the character at different times or places:
in 'Jigsaw', for instance, the person called "Black" is seven different objects.

. . . . .

Animate objects representing people with proper names, like "Mark Antony",
need to be given the proper attribute, and those with feminine names, such
as "Cleopatra", need to be both female and proper, though of course history
would have been very different if... Inanimate objects sometimes have proper
names, too: Waldeck's Mayan dictionary in §16 was given proper. See §26 for
more on naming.

. . . . .

Some objects are not alive as such, but can still be spoken to: microphones, tape recorders and so on. It would be a nuisance to implement these as animate, since they have none of the other characteristics of life. Instead, they can be given just the attribute talkable, making them responsive only to conversation. They have a life property to handle Answer and so on, but it will never be asked to deal with, for instance, Kiss. Talkable objects can also receive orders: see the next section.

. . . . .

Designers often imagine animate objects as being altogether different from things, so it's worth noting that all the usual Inform rules apply equally well to the living. An animate object still has before and after routines like any other, so the short list of possible life rules is not as restrictive as it appears. Animate objects can also react_before and react_after, and it's here that these properties really come into their own:

```
react_before [;
    Drop: if (noun == satellite_gadget)
        print "~I wouldn't do that, Mr Bond,~ says Blofeld.^^";
    Shoot: remove beretta;
        "As you draw, Blofeld snaps his fingers and a giant
        magnet snatches the gun from your hand. It hits the
        ceiling with a clang. Blofeld silkily strokes his cat.";
];
```

If Blofeld moves from place to place, these rules usefully move with him.

Animate objects often have possessions as part of the game design. Two examples, both from 'The Lurking Horror':

- an urchin with something bulging inside his jacket pocket;
- a hacker who has a bunch of keys hanging off his belt.

Recall from §12 that the child-objects of an object which isn't a container or supporter are outwardly visible only if the object has the transparent attribute. Here, the hacker should have transparent and the urchin not. The parser then prevents the player from referring to whatever the urchin is hiding, even if the player has played the game before and knows what is in there.

● **EXERCISE 26**
Arrange for a bearded psychiatrist to place the player under observation, occasionally mumbling insights such as "Subject puts green cone on table. Interesting."

§18   Making conversation

To listen is far harder than to speak. This section overlaps with Chapter IV, the chapter on parsing text, and the later exercises are among the hardest in the book. As the following summary table shows, the simpler ways for the player to speak to people were covered in the previous section: this section is about "orders".

Example command	*Rule*	action	noun	second	*consult*	
"say troll to orc"	life	Answer	'troll'	orc	2	1
"answer troll to orc"	life	Answer	'troll'	orc	2	1
"orc, tell me about coins"	life	Ask	orc	'coins'	6	1
"ask orc about the big troll"	life	Ask	orc	'big'	4	3
"ask orc about wyvern"	life	Ask	orc	0	4	1
"tell orc about lost troll"	life	Tell	orc	'lost'	4	2
"orc, take axe"	order	Take	axe	0		
"orc, yes"	order	Yes	0	0		
"ask orc for the shield"	order	Give	shield	player		
"orc, troll"	order	NotU...	'troll'	orc	3	1

Here we're supposing that the game's dictionary includes "troll", "orc" and so forth, but not "wyvern", which is why "ask orc about wyvern" results in the action Ask orc 0. The notation NotU... is an abbreviation for NotUnderstood, of which more later. The two numbers in the "consult" column are the values of consult_from and consult_words, in cases where they are set.

. . . . .

When the player types in something like "pilot, fly south", addressing an object which has animate or at least talkable, the result is called an 'order'.

The order is sent to the pilot's orders property, which may if it wishes comply or react in some other way. Otherwise, the standard game rules will simply print something like "The pilot has better things to do." The 'Ruins' priest is especially unhelpful:

```
orders [;
    Go: "~I must not leave the Shrine.~";
    NotUnderstood: "~You speak in riddles.~";
    default: "~It is not your orders I serve.~";
],
```

The NotUnderstood clause of an orders rule is run when the parser couldn't understand what the player typed: e.g., "pilot, fly somersaults".

△ The Inform library regards the words "yes" and "no" as being verbs, so it parses "delores, yes" into a Yes order. This can be a slight nuisance, as "say yes to delores" is treated differently: it gets routed through the life routine as an Answer.

△ When a NotUnderstood order is being passed to orders, the library sets up some variables to help you parse by hand if you need to. The actual order, say "fly somersaults", becomes a sort of consultation topic, with consult_from and consult_words set to the first word number and the number of words. The variable etype holds the parser error that would have been printed out, had it been a command by the player himself. See §33: for instance, the value CANTSEE_PE would mean "the pilot can't see any such object".

△ If the orders property returns false or if there wasn't an orders property in the first place, the order is sent on either to the Order: part of the life property, if it was understood, or to the Answer: part, if it wasn't. (This is how all orders used to be processed, and it's retained to avoid making old Inform code go wrong.) If these also return false, a message like "X has better things to do" (if understood) or "There is no reply" (if not) is finally printed.

● EXERCISE 27
(Cf. 'Starcross'.) Construct a computer responding to "computer, theta is 180".

● EXERCISE 28
For many designers, Answer and Tell are just too much trouble. How can you make attempts to use these produce a message saying "To talk to someone, try 'someone, something'."?

· · · · ·

When the player issues a request to an animate or talkable object, they're normally parsed in the standard way. "avon, take the bracelet" results in the order Take bracelet being sent to Kerr Avon, just as typing "take the bracelet" results in the action Take bracelet passing to the player. The range of text understood is the same, whether or not the person addressed is Avon. Sometimes, though, one would rather that different people understood entirely different grammars.

For instance, consider Zen, the flight computer of an alien spacecraft. It's inappropriate to tell Zen to pick up a teleport bracelet and the crew tend to give commands more like:

"Zen, set course for Centauro"
"Zen, speed standard by six"
"Zen, scan 360 orbital"
"Zen, raise the force wall"

"Zen, clear the neutron blasters for firing"

For such commands, an `animate` or `talkable` object can if it likes provide a `grammar` property. This is called at a time when the parser has worked out the object being addressed and has set the variables `verb_wordnum` and `verb_word` to the word number of the 'verb' and its dictionary entry, respectively. For example, in "orac, operate the teleport" `verb_wordnum` would be 3, because the comma counts as a word on its own, and `verb_word` would be `'operate'`.

Once called, the `grammar` routine can reply to the parser by returning:

 `false` Meaning "carry on as usual".
  `true` Meaning "you can stop parsing now because I have done it all, and put the resulting order into the variables `action`, `noun` and `second`".
 `'verb'` Meaning "don't use the standard game grammar: use the grammar lines for this verb instead".
`-'verb'` Meaning "use the grammar lines for this verb, and if none of them match, use the standard game grammar as usual".

In addition, the `grammar` routine is free to do some partial parsing of the early words provided it moves on `verb_wordnum` accordingly to show how much it's got through.

● △**EXERCISE 29**
Implement Charlotte, a little girl who's playing Simon Says (a game in which she only follows your instructions if you remember to say "Simon says" in front of them: so she'll disobey "charlotte, wave" but obey "charlotte, simon says wave").

● △**EXERCISE 30**
Another of Charlotte's rules is that if you say a number, she has to clap that many times. Can you play?

● △**EXERCISE 31**
Regrettably, Dyslexic Dan has always mixed up the words "take" and "drop". Implement him anyway.

·   ·   ·   ·   ·

△   When devising unusual grammars, you sometimes want to define grammar lines that the player can only use when talking to other people. The vile trick to achieve this is to attach these grammar lines to an "untypeable verb", such as `'comp,'`. This can never match what the player typed because the parser automatically separates the text "comp," into two words, "comp" and ",", with a space between them. The same will happen with any word of up to 7 letters followed by a comma or full stop. For instance, here's one way to solve the 'Starcross' computer exercise, using an untypeable verb:

```
[ Control;
  switch (NextWord()) {
      'theta': parsed_number = 1; return GPR_NUMBER;
      'phi':   parsed_number = 2; return GPR_NUMBER;
      'range': parsed_number = 3; return GPR_NUMBER;
      default: return GPR_FAIL;
  }
];
Verb 'comp,' * Control 'is' number -> SetTo;
```

(Here, Control is a "general parsing routine": see §31.) The computer itself then needs these properties:

```
grammar [; return 'comp,'; ],
orders [;
    SetTo:
        switch (noun) {
            1: print "~Theta"; 2: print "~Phi"; 3: print "~Range";
        }
        " set to ", second, ".~";
    default: "~Does not compute!~";
];
```

This may not look easier, but it's much more flexible, as the exercises below may demonstrate.

● △△EXERCISE 32
How can you make a grammar extension to an ordinary verb that will apply only to Dan?

● △EXERCISE 33
Make an alarm clock responding to "alarm, off", "alarm, on" and "alarm, half past seven" (the latter to set its alarm time).

● △EXERCISE 34
Implement a tricorder (from Star Trek) which analyses nearby objects on a request like "tricorder, the quartz stratum".

● △EXERCISE 35
And, for good measure, a replicator responding to commands like "replicator, tea earl grey" and "replicator, aldebaran brandy".

● △△EXERCISE 36
And a communications badge in contact with the ship's computer, which answers questions like "computer, where is Admiral Blank". (This is best done with "scope hacking", for which see §32.)

• △△**EXERCISE 37**
Finally, construct the formidable flight computer Zen. (Likewise.)

△△ To trump one vile trick with another, untypeable verbs are also sometimes used to create what might be called 'fake fake actions'. Recall that a fake action is one which is never generated by the parser, and has no action routine. For instance, there's no ThrownAtSub, because ThrownAt is a fake. A fake fake action is a half-measure: it's a full action in every respect, including having an action routine, except that it can never be generated by the parser. The following grammar line creates three of them, called Prepare, Simmer and Cook:

```
Verb 'fakes.' * -> Prepare * -> Simmer * -> Cook;
```

The author is indebted for this terminology to an algebraic geometry seminar by Peter Kronheimer on fake and fake fake K3 surfaces.

. . . . .

△ Difficult "someone on the other end of a phone" situations turn up quite often in one form or another (see, for instance, the opening scene of 'Seastalker') and often a quite simple solution is fine. If you just want to make something like "michael, tell me about the crystals" work, when Michael is at the other end of the line, give the phone the talkable attribute and make the word 'michael' one of its names. If several people are on the phone at different times, you can always give the phone a parse_name property (see §28) to respond to different names at different times.

• △**EXERCISE 38**
Via the main screen of the Starship Enterprise, Captain Jean-Luc Picard wants to see and talk to Noslen Maharg, the notorious tyrant, who is down on the planet Mrofni. Make it so.

• △△**EXERCISE 39**
Put the player in telepathic contact with Martha, who is in a sealed room some distance away, but who has a talent for telekinesis. Martha should respond to "martha, look", "ask martha about...", "say yes to martha", "martha, give me the red ball" and the like.

• **REFERENCES**
A much fuller example of a 'non-player character' is given in the example game 'The Thief', by Gareth Rees (though it's really an implementation of the gentleman in 'Zork I', himself an imitation of the pirate in 'Advent'). The thief is capable of walking around, being followed, stealing things, picking locks, opening doors and so on.   •Other good definitions of animate objects to look at are Christopher in 'Toyshop', who will stack up building blocks on request; the kittens in 'Alice Through the Looking-Glass'; the barker in 'Balances', and the animals and dwarves of 'Advent'.   •Following

people means being able to refer to them after they've left the room: see the library extension "follower.h" by Gareth Rees, Andrew Clover and Neil James Brown.   •A wandering character with a destination to aim for needs to be able to navigate from room to room, and possibly through doors. Ideally, a designer should be able to make a simple instruction like "head for the West Ballroom" without specifying any route. Two independent library extensions allow this: "MoveClass.h", by Neil James Brown and Alan Trewartha, is compatible with "follower.h" and is especially strong on handling doors. Volker Lanz's "NPCEngine" is designed for what might be called detective-mystery situations, in which the people inside a country house are behaving independently in ways which must frequently be described to the player.   •Irene Callaci's "AskTellOrder.h" library extension file automatically handles commands in the form "ask/tell someone to do something".

§19 The light and the dark

```
>examine darkness
```
You can't see the darkness without a light!
```
>let there be light
```
Okay, there is light.
```
>examine the light
```
It is good.
```
>divide the light from the darkness
```
It is so.
```
>call the light "day" then call the darkness "night"
```
Called.
Called.
– from a transcript of 'The Creation', a game never written but proposed in some of Infocom's surviving documents. ("Estimated development time 8-10 months... shalts and begats and haths.")

 Sighted people observe whether it's light or dark so instantly that the matter seems self-evident. The Inform library has to use reason instead, and it rechecks this reasoning very frequently, because almost any change in the world model can affect the light:

a total eclipse of the sun;
fusing all the lights in the house;
your lamp going out;
a dwarf stealing it and running away;
dropping a lit match which you were seeing by;
putting your lamp into an opaque box and shutting the lid;
black smoke filling up the glass jar that the lamp is in;
the dwarf with your lamp running back into your now-dark room.

The designer of an Inform game isn't allowed to tell the library "the player is now in darkness", because this would soon lead to inconsistencies. (If you want it to be dark, ensure that there are no light sources nearby.) Because light is automatically calculated, you can write statements like the following, and leave the library to sort out the consequences:

```
give lamp light;
remove match;
give glass_jar ~transparent;
move dwarf to Dark_Room;
```

The `light` attribute means that an object is giving off light, or that a room is currently lit, for instance because it is outdoors in day-time.

Abolish darkness altogether, without having to give every location `light`.

· · · · ·

When the player is in darkness, the current `location` becomes `thedark`, a special object which behaves like a room and has the short name "Darkness". Instead, the variable `real_location` always contains the actual room occupied, regardless of the light level.

The designer can "customise" the darkness in a game by altering its initial, `description` or `short_name` properties. For example, the `Initialise` routine of the game might include:

```
thedark.short_name = "Creepy, nasty darkness";
```

See §20 for how 'Ruins' makes darkness menacing.

· · · · ·

Light is reconsidered at the start of the game, after any movement of the player, after any change of player, and at the end of each turn regardless. The presence or absence of light affects the Look, Search, LookUnder and Examine actions, and, since this is a common puzzle, also the Go action: you can provide a routine called

```
DarkToDark()
```

and if you do then it will be called when the player goes from one dark place to another. (It's called just before the room description for the new dark room, normally "Darkness", is printed). You could then take the opportunity to kill the player off or extract some other forfeit. If you provide no such routine, then the player can move about as freely in the darkness as in the light.

· · · · ·

△△ *Darkness rules.*   Here is the full definition of "when there is light". Remember that the parent of the player object may not be a room: it may be, say, a red car whose parent is a large closed cardboard box whose parent is a room.

(1) There is light exactly when the parent of the player 'offers light'.

(2) An object is see-through if:
    (a) it is transparent, *or*
    (b) it is a supporter, *or*
    (c) it is a container which is open, *or*
    (d) it is enterable but not a container.

(3) An object offers light if:
    (a) it itself has the light attribute set, *or*
    (b) any of its immediate possessions have light, *or*
    (c) it is see-through and its parent offers light.

(4) An object has light if:
    (a) it itself has the light attribute set, *or*
    (b) it is see-through and any of its immediate possessions have light, *or*
    (c) any object it places in scope using the property add_to_scope has light.

It may help to note that to "offer light" is to cast light inward, that is, down the object tree, whereas to "have light" is to cast light outward, that is, up the object tree. The library routines IsSeeThrough(obj), OffersLight(obj) and HasLightSource(obj) check conditions (2) to (4), returning true or false as appropriate.

● EXERCISE 41

How would you design a troll who is afraid of the dark, and needs to be bribed with a light source... so that the troll will be as happy with a goldfish bowl containing a fluorescent jellyfish as he would be with a lamp?

● REFERENCES

For a DarkToDark routine which discourages wandering about caves in the dark, see 'Advent'.   ●It is notoriously tricky to handle the gradual falling of night or a gradual change of visibility. See §51.

§20   Daemons and the passing of time

> Some, such as Sleep and Love, were never human. From this class an individual daemon is allotted to each human being as his 'witness and guardian' through life.
>
> — C. S. Lewis (1898–1963), *The Discarded Image*

> A great Daemon... Through him subsist all divination, and the science of sacred things as it relates to sacrifices, and expiations, and disenchantments, and prophecy, and magic... he who is wise in the science of this intercourse is supremely happy...
>
> — Plato (c.427–347 B.C.), *The Symposium,* in the translation by Percy Bysshe Shelley (1792–1822)

 To medieval philosophers, daemons were the intermediaries of God, hovering invisibly over the world and interfering with it. They may be guardian spirits of places or people. So also with Inform: a daemon is a meddling spirit, associated with a particular game object, which gets a chance to interfere once per turn while it is 'active'. 'Advent' has five: one to deplete the lamp's batteries, three to move the bear, the pirate and the threatening little dwarves and one to close the cave when all the treasures have been collected. Though there isn't much to say about daemons, they are immensely useful, and there are some rule-based design systems for interactive fiction in which the daemon is a more fundamental concept than the object. (The early 1980s system by Scott Adams, for instance.)

The daemon attached to an object is its daemon routine, if one is given. However, a daemon is normally inactive, and must be explicitly activated and deactivated using the library routines

```
StartDaemon(object);
StopDaemon(object);
```

Daemons are often started by a game's Initialise routine and sometimes remain active throughout. When active, the daemon property of the object is called at the end of each turn, regardless of where that object is or what the circumstances, provided only that the player is still alive. This makes daemons useful for 'tidying-up operations', putting rooms back in order after the player has moved on, or for the consequences of actions to catch up with the player.

• △**EXERCISE 42**
Many games contain "wandering monsters", characters who walk around the map. Use a daemon to implement one who wanders as freely as the player, like the gentleman thief in 'Zork'.

• △**EXERCISE 43**
Use a background daemon to implement a system of weights, so that the player can only carry a certain weight before strength gives out and something must be dropped. It should allow for feathers to be lighter than lawn-mowers.

· · · · ·

It's also possible to attach a timer to an object. (In other design languages, timers are called "fuses".) To set up a timer, you need to give an object two properties: time_left and time_out. Like daemons, timers are inactive until explicitly started:

```
StartTimer(object, time);
```

will set object.time_left to time. This value will be reduced by 1 each turn, except that if this would make it negative, the Inform library instead sends the message

```
object.time_out()
```

once and once only, after which the timer is deactivated again. You're free to alter time_left yourself: a value of 0 means "will go off at the end of the present turn", so setting time_left to 0 triggers immediate activation. You can also deactivate the timer, so that it never goes off, by calling

```
StopTimer(object);
```

• **EXERCISE 44**
Construct an egg-timer which runs for three turns.

△   At most 32 timers or daemons can be active at the same time, together with any number of inactive ones. This limit of 32 is easily raised, though: just define the constant MAX_TIMERS to some larger value, putting the definition in your code before "Parser.h" is included.

· · · · ·

There is yet a third form of timed event. If a room provides an each_turn routine, then the library will send the message

```
location.each_turn()
```

at the end of every turn when the player is present. Similarly, for every object O which is near the player and provides each_turn:

```
O.each_turn()
```

will be sent every turn. This would be one way to code the sword of 'Zork', for instance, which begins to glow when monsters are nearby. each_turn is also convenient to run creatures which stay in one place and are only active when the player is nearby. An ogre with limited patience can therefore have an each_turn routine which worries the player ("The ogre stamps his feet angrily!" and so forth) while also having a timer set to go off when patience runs out.

△   "Near the player" actually means "in scope", a term which will be properly defined in §32 but which roughly translates as "in the same place and visible". You can change the scope rules using an InScope routine, say to make the 'Zork I' thief audible throughout the maze he is wandering around in. In case you want to tell whether scope is being worked out for ordinary parsing reasons or instead for each_turn processing, look to see whether the scope_reason variable has the value EACHTURN_REASON. (Again, see §32 for more.)

△   It is safe to move an object when its own each_turn rule is running, but not to move any other objects which are likely to be in scope.

●**EXERCISE 45**
('Ruins'.) Make "the sound of scuttling claws" approach in darkness and, after 4 consecutive turns in darkness, kill the player.

●△**EXERCISE 46**
Now try implementing the scuttling claws in a single object definition, with no associated code anywhere else in the program, not even a line in Initialise, and without running its daemon all the time.

. . . . . .

The library also has a limited ability to keep track of time of day as the game goes on. The current time is held in the variable the_time and runs on a 24-hour clock: this variable holds the number of minutes since midnight, so it takes values between 0 and 1439. The time can be set by

```
SetTime( 60×⟨hours⟩+⟨minutes⟩, ⟨rate⟩ );
```

The rate controls how rapidly time is moving: a rate of 0 means it is standing still, that is, that the library doesn't change it: your routines still can. A positive rate means that that many minutes pass between each turn, while a negative rate means that many turns pass between each minute. It's usual for a timed game to start off the clock by calling SetTime in its Initialise routine. The time will appear on the game's status line, replacing the usual listing of score and turns, if you set

```
Statusline time;
```

as a directive at the start of your source code.

● **EXERCISE 47**
How could you make your game take notice of the time passing midnight, so that the day of the week could be nudged on?

● △**EXERCISE 48**
Make the lighting throughout the game change at sunrise and sunset.

. . . . .

△   Here is exactly what happens at the end of each turn. The sequence is abandoned if at any stage the player dies or wins.

(1) The turns counter is incremented.
(2) The 24-hour clock is moved on.
(3) Daemons and timers are run (in no guaranteed order).
(4) each_turn takes place for the current room, and then for every object in scope.
(5) An entry point called TimePasses is called, if the game provides such a routine.
(6) Light is re-considered (see §19).
(7) Any items the player now holds which have not previously been held are given the moved attribute, and score is awarded if appropriate (see §22).

● △**EXERCISE 49**
Suppose the player is magically suspended in mid-air, but that anything let go of will fall out of sight. The natural way to code this is to use a daemon which gets rid of anything it finds on the floor: this is better than trapping Drop actions because objects might end up on the floor in many different ways. Why is each_turn better still?

● **EXERCISE 50**
How would a game work if it involved a month-long archaeological dig, where anything from days to minutes pass between successive game turns?

● **REFERENCES**

Daemons abound in most games. Apart from 'Advent', see the flying tortoise from 'Balances' and the chiggers from 'Adventureland'. For more ingenious uses of daemon, see the helium balloon and the matchbook from 'Toyshop'.   ●Typical timers include the burning match and the hand grenade from 'Toyshop', the endgame timer from 'Advent' and the 'Balances' cyclops (also employing each_turn).   ●'Adventureland' makes much use of each_turn: see the golden fish, the mud, the dragon and the bees.   ●The chapter of 'Jigsaw' set on the Moon runs the clock at rate −28, to allow for the length of the lunar day.   ●The library extension "timewait.h" by Andrew Clover thoroughly implements time of day, allowing the player to "wait until quarter past three".   ●Whereas Erik Hetzner's "printtime.h" does just the reverse: it prints out Inform's numerical values of time in the form of text like "half past seven". Erik is also author of "timepiece.h", which models watches and clocks, allowing them to run slow or fast compared to the library's absolute notion of time. (As yet nobody has needed a relativistic world model.)

§21   Starting, moving, changing and killing the player

Life's but a walking shadow, a poor player
That struts and frets his hour upon the stage
And then is heard no more; it is a tale
Told by an idiot, full of sound and fury,
Signifying nothing.

— William Shakespeare (1564–1616), *Macbeth* V v

 To recap on §4, an "entry point routine" is one provided by your own source code which the library may call from time to time. There are about twenty of these, listed in §A5, and all of them are optional but one: Initialise. This routine is called before any text of the game is printed, and it *can* do many things: start timers and daemons, set the time of day, equip the player with possessions, make any random settings needed and so on. It *usually* prints out some welcoming text, though not the name and author of the game, because that appears soon after when the "game banner" is printed. The only thing it *must* do is to set the location variable to where the player begins.

This is usually a room, possibly in darkness, but might instead be an enterable object inside a room, such as a chair or a bed. Like medieval romance epics, interactive fiction games often start by waking the player from sleep, sometimes by way of a dream sequence. If your game begins with verbose instructions before the first opportunity for a player to type a command, you may want to offer the chance to restore a saved game at once:

```
print "Would you like to restore a game? >";
if (YesOrNo()) <Restore>;
```

To equip the player with possessions, simply move the relevant objects to player.

The return value from Initialise is ordinarily ignored, whether true or false, and the library goes on to print the game banner. If, however, you return 2, the game banner is suppressed for now. This feature is provided for games like 'Sorcerer' and 'Seastalker' which play out a short prelude first. If you do suppress the banner from Initialise, you should print it no more than a few turns later on by calling the library routine Banner. The banner is familiar to players, reassuringly traditional and useful when testing, because it identifies which version of a game is giving trouble. Like an imprint page with an ISBN, it is invaluable to bibliographers and collectors of story files.

. . . . .

'Ruins' opens in classical fashion:

```
[ Initialise;
  TitlePage();
  location = Forest;
  move map to player;
  move sodium_lamp to player;
  move dictionary to player;
  thedark.description = "The darkness of ages presses in on you, and
      you feel claustrophobic.";
  "^^^Days of searching, days of thirsty hacking through the briars of
  the forest, but at last your patience was rewarded. A discovery!^";
];
```

For the source code of the 'Ruins' TitlePage routine, see the exercises in §42.

. . . . .

The question "where is the player?" can be answered in three different ways. Looking at parent(player) tells you the object immediately containing the player, which can be a location but might instead be a chair or vehicle. So a condition such as:

```
if (player in Bridleway) ...
```

would be false if the player were riding a horse through the Bridleway. The safer alternative is:

```
if (location == Bridleway) ...
```

but even this would be false if the Bridleway were in darkness, because then location would be the special object thedark (see §19). The definitive location value is stored in real_location, so that:

```
if (real_location == Bridleway) ...
```

works in all cases. The condition for "is the player in a dark Bridleway?" is:

```
if (location == thedark && real_location == Bridleway) ...
```

Except for the one time in Initialise, you should not attempt to change either of these variables, nor to move the player-object by hand. One safe way to move the player in your own source code is to cause actions like

```
<Go n_obj>;
```

but for moments of teleportation it's easier to use the library routine `PlayerTo`. Calling `PlayerTo(somewhere)` makes the parent-object of the player somewhere and adjusts the `location` variables accordingly: it also runs through a fair number of standard game rules, for instance checking the light level and performing a Look action to print out the new room description. The value somewhere can be a room, or an enterable object such as a cage or a traction-engine, provided that the cardinal rule is always observed:

> The parent of the player object must at all times be "location-like". An object is "location-like" if either it is a location, or it has `enterable` and its parent is location-like.

In other words, you can't put the player in an enterable cardboard box if that box is itself shut up in a free-standing safe which isn't enterable. And you can't `PlayerTo(nothing)` or `PlayerTo(thedark)` because nothing is not an object and thedark is not location-like.

△   Calling `PlayerTo(somewhere,1)` moves the player without printing any room description. All other standard game rules are applied.

△   Calling `PlayerTo(somewhere,2)` is just like `PlayerTo(somewhere)` except that the room description is in the form the player would expect from typing "go east" rather than from typing "look". The only difference is that in the former case the room is (normally) given an abbreviated description if it has been visited before, whereas in the latter case the description is always given in full.

· · · · ·

△△ It's perhaps worth taking a moment to say what the standard rules upon changing location are. The following rules are applied whenever a Look action or a call to `PlayerTo` take place.

(0) If `PlayerTo` has been called then the parent of the player, `location` and `real_location` are set.

(1) Any object providing `found_in` is checked. If it claims to be `found_in` the location, it is moved to that location. If not, or if it has `absent`, it is removed from the object tree. (See §8.)

(2) The availability of light is checked (see §19), and `location` is set to thedark if necessary.

(3) The "visibility ceiling" of the player is determined. For instance, the *VC* for a player in a closed wooden box is the box, but for a player in a closed glass box it's the location. To be more exact:

    (a) The *VC* of a room is the value of `location`, i.e., either thedark or the room object.

    (b) If the parent of an object is a room or is "see-through" (see §19 for this definition), the *VC* of the object is the *VC* of the parent.

    (c) If not, the *VC* of the object is its parent.

(4) If the *VC* is thedark or (say) a box, skip this rule. Otherwise: if the *VC* has changed since the *previous* time that rule (3) produced a *VC* which wasn't an enterable object, then:

    (a) The message location.initial() is sent, if the location provides an initial rule. If the library finds that the player has been moved in the course of running initial, it goes back to rule (3).

    (b) The game's entry point routine NewRoom is called, if it provides one.

(5) The room description is printed out, unless these rules are being gone through by PlayerTo(somewhere,1). For exactly what happens in printing a room description, see §26.

(6) If the location doesn't have visited, give it this attribute and award the player ROOM_SCORE points if the location has scored. (See §22.) Note that this rule looks at location, not real_location, so no points unless the room is visible.

.   .   .   .   .

In the course of this chapter, rules to interfere with actions have been attached to items, rooms and people, but not yet to the player. In §18 it was set out that an order like "austin, eat tuna" would result in the action Eat tuna being passed to austin.orders, and heavy hints were dropped that orders and actions are more or less the same thing. This is indeed so, and the player's own object has an orders routine. This normally does nothing and always returns false to mean "carry on as usual", but you can install a rule of your own instead:

```
player.orders = MyNewRule;
```

where MyNewRule is a new orders rule. This rule is applied to every action or order issued by the player. The variable actor holds the person asked to do something, usually but not always player, and the variables action, noun and second are set up as usual. For instance:

Example command	actor	action	noun	second
"put tuna in dish"	player	Insert	tuna	dish
"austin, eat tuna"	Austin	Eat	tuna	nothing

For instance, if a cannon goes off right next to the player, a period of partial deafness might ensue:

```
[ MyNewRule;
  if (actor ~= player) rfalse;
  Listen: "Your hearing is still weak from all that cannon-fire.";
  default: rfalse;
];
```

The if statement needs to be there to prevent commands like "helena, listen" from being ruled out – after all, the player can still speak.

- △ **EXERCISE 51**
Why not achieve the same effect by giving the player a react_before rule instead?

- **EXERCISE 52**
(Cf. 'Curses'.) Write an orders routine for the player so that wearing a gas mask will prevent speech.

. . . . .

The player object can not only be altered but switched altogether, allowing the player to play from the perspective of someone or something else at any point in the game. The player who tampers with Dr Frankenstein's brain transference machine may suddenly become the Monster strapped to the table. A player who drinks too much wine could become a drunk player object to whom many different rules apply. The "snavig" spell of 'Spellbreaker', which transforms the player to an animal like the one cast upon, could be implemented thus. Similarly the protagonist of 'Suspended', who telepathically runs a weather-control station by acting through six sensory robots, Iris, Waldo, Sensa, Auda, Poet and Whiz. In a less original setting, a player might have a team of four adventurers exploring a labyrinth, and be able to switch the one being controlled by typing the name. In this case, an AfterLife routine (see below) may be needed to switch the focus back to a still-living member of the team after one has met a sticky end.

   The library routine ChangePlayer(obj) transforms the player to obj. Any object can be used for this. There's no need to give it any name, as the parser always understands pronouns like "me" and "myself" to refer to the current player-object. You may want to set its description, as this is the text printed if the player types "examine myself", or its capacity, the maximum number of items which this form of the player can carry. Finally, this player-object can have its own orders property and thus its own rules about what it can and can't do.

   As ChangePlayer prints nothing, you may want to follow the call with a <<Look>>; action.

△   You can call ChangePlayer as part of a game's Initialise routine, but if so then you should do this before setting location.

△   Calling ChangePlayer(obj,1); does the same except that it makes the game print "(as Whoever)" during subsequent room descriptions.

△   The body dispossessed remains where it was, in play, unless you move it away or otherwise dispose of it. The player-object which the player begins with is a library-defined object called `selfobj`, and is described in room descriptions as "your former self".

● **EXERCISE 53**
In Central American legend, a sorceror can transform himself into a *nagual*, a familiar such as a spider-monkey; indeed, each individual has an animal self or *wayhel*, living in a volcanic land over which the king, as a jaguar, rules. Turn the player into *wayhel* form.

● **EXERCISE 54**
Alter the Wormcast of 'Ruins' (previously defined in §9) so that when in *wayhel* form, the player can pass through into a hidden burial shaft.

● **EXERCISE 55**
To complete the design of this sequence from 'Ruins', place a visible iron cage above the hidden burial shaft. The cage contains skeletons and a warning written in glyphs, but the player who enters it despite these (and they all will) passes into *wayhel* life. (The transformed body is unable to move the sodium lamp, but has nocturnal vision, so doesn't need to.) Unfortunately the player is now outside a cage which has closed around the human self which must be returned to, while the *wayhel* lacks the dexterity to open the cage. The solution is to use the Wormcast to reach the Burial Chamber, then bring its earthen roof down, opening a connection between the chamber below and the cage above. Recovering human form, the player can take the grave goods, climb up into the cage, open it from the inside and escape. Lara Croft would be proud.

·   ·   ·   ·   ·

△△ The situation becomes a little complicated if the same orders routine has to do service in two situations: once while its owner is a character met in the course of play, and then a second time when the player has changed into it. This could be done simply by changing the value of `orders` when the transformation takes place, but an alternative is to arrange code for a single `orders` routine like so:

```
orders [;
    if (player == self) {
        if (actor == self) {
            ! I give myself an action
        }
        else {
            ! I give someone else an order
        }
    }
```

```
        else {
            ! Someone else gives me an order
        }
    ],
```

● △△EXERCISE 56
Write an orders routine for a Giant with a conscience, who will refuse to attack even a
mouse, but so that a player who becomes the Giant can be wantonly cruel.

· · · · ·

"There are only three events in a man's life; birth, life and death; he is not
conscious of being born, he dies in pain and he forgets to live." (Jean de la
Bruyère again.) Death is indeed the usual conclusion of an adventure game,
and occurs when the source code sets the library variable deadflag to true:
in normal play deadflag is always false. The "standard Inform rules" never
lead to the player's death, so this is something the designer must explicitly do.

Unlike life, however, interactive fiction offers another way out: the player
can win. This happens if and when the variable deadflag is set to 2.

Any higher values of deadflag are considered to be more exotic ways the
game can end, requiring text beyond "You have died" or "You have won".
The Inform library doesn't know what this text should be, so it calls the
DeathMessage entry point routine, which is expected to look at deadflag and
can then print something suitable. For instance, 'Ruins' has a chasm subject
to the following before rule:

```
before [;
    Enter: deadflag = 3;
        "You plummet through the silent void of darkness, cracking
        your skull against an outcrop of rock. Amid the pain and
        redness, you dimly make out the God with the
        Owl-Headdress...";
    JumpOver: "It is far too wide.";
],
```

and this means that it needs a DeathMessage routine like so:

```
[ DeathMessage;
    if (deadflag == 3) print "You have been captured";
];
```

Capture was about the worst fate that could befall you in the unspeakably
inhumane world of Maya strife.

'Ruins' doesn't, but many games allow reincarnation or, as David M. Baggett points out, in fact resurrection. You too can allow this, by providing an AfterLife entry point routine. This gets the chance to do as it pleases before any "death message" is printed, and it can even reset deadflag to false, causing the game to resume as though nothing had happened. Such AfterLife routines can be tricky to write, though, because the game often has to be altered to reflect what has happened.

● **REFERENCES**
The magic words "xyzzy" and "plugh" in 'Advent' employ PlayerTo.   ●'Advent' has an amusing AfterLife routine: for instance, try collapsing the bridge by leading the bear across, then returning to the scene after resurrection. 'Balances' has one which only slightly penalises death.

§22 Miscellaneous constants, scoring, quotations

> For when the One Great Scorer comes
> To write against your name,
> He marks – not that you won or lost –
> But how you played the game.
>
> — Grantland Rice (1880–1954), *Alumnus Football*

 There are some constants which, if defined in your code *before* the library files are included, change the standard game rules or tell the Inform library about your game. Two such constants appeared back in §4: the strings of text Story and Headline.

```
Constant Story "ZORK II";
Constant Headline "^An Interactive Plagiarism^
        Copyright (c) 1995 by Ivan O. Ideas.^";
```

. . . . .

The library won't allow the player to carry an indefinite number of objects. As was mentioned in §21, the limit is the value of capacity for the current player-object, which you're free to vary during play. The library sets up the capacity of the usual player-object to be equal to a constant called MAX_CARRIED, which is normally 100. But you can define it differently, and 'Ruins' does:

```
Constant MAX_CARRIED = 7;
```

For these purposes a container counts as only one object, even if it contains hundreds of other objects.

Many games, perhaps too many, involve collecting vast miscellanies of items until a use has been found for each. A small value of MAX_CARRIED will then annoy the player unreasonably, whereas a large one will stretch plausibility. The standard resolution is to give the player a sack for carrying spare objects, and the Inform library provides a feature whereby the designer can nominate a given container to be this "sack":

```
Object satchel "satchel"
    with description "Big and with a smile painted on it.",
        name 'satchel', article 'your',
        when_closed "Your satchel lies on the floor.",
        when_open "Your satchel lies open on the floor.",
    has  container open openable;
Constant SACK_OBJECT = satchel;
```

(This is from 'Toyshop': the 'Ruins' have been sacked too many times as it is.) The convenience this offers is that the game will now automatically put old, least-used objects away into the sack as the game progresses, provided the sack is still being carried:

>get biscuit
(putting the old striped scarf into the canvas rucksack to make room)
Taken.

. . . . .

The "Invisiclues" hints of some of the reissued Infocom games sometimes included a category called "For Your Amusement", listing some of the improbable things the game can do. Only the victorious should read this, as it might spoil surprises for anyone else. You can, optionally, provide such "amusing" information by defining the constant. . .

Constant AMUSING_PROVIDED;

. . . and also providing an entry point routine called Amusing. For a player who has won the game, but not one who has merely died, the usual question

Would you like to RESTART, RESTORE a saved game or QUIT?

will then become

Would you like to RESTART, RESTORE a saved game, see some suggestions for AMUSING things to do or QUIT?

(The best way to provide such suggestions, if there are many, is to use a menu system like that described in §44.) One of the worst-kept secrets of the Inform library is that an option not mentioned by this question is to type "undo", which will undo the last move and restore the player to life. If you feel that this option should be mentioned, define the constant:

Constant DEATH_MENTION_UNDO;

Finally, this end-of-game question will also mention the possibility of typing "full" to see a full score breakdown, if tasks are provided (see below).

. . . . .

The other constants you are allowed to define help keep the score. There are two scoring systems provided by the library, side by side: you can use both or neither. You can always do what you like to the library's score variable in any case, though the "fullscore" verb might not then fully account for what's happened. Whatever scoring system you use, you should define MAX_SCORE, as 'Ruins' for instance does by declaring:

```
Constant MAX_SCORE = 30;
```

This is the value which the library tells to the player as the maximum score attainable in text like:

You have so far scored 0 out of a possible 30, in 1 turn.

Note that the library does *not* check that this is the actual maximum score it's possible to clock up: and nor does it cause the game to be automatically won if the maximum is achieved. The game is won when and only when deadflag is set to 2 (see §21), regardless of score.

The simpler scoring system awards points for the first time certain objects are picked up, and the first time certain places are entered. (As long as there is light to see by: no points unless you can recognise that you've arrived somewhere interesting.) To make an item or a place carry a points bonus, give it the attribute scored. You may also want to vary the amounts of these bonuses by defining two constants:

OBJECT_SCORE   points for picking up a scored object (normally 4);
ROOM_SCORE   points for entering a scored room (normally 5)

The more elaborate scoring system keeps track of which "tasks" the player has accomplished. These are only present if the constant TASKS_PROVIDED is defined, and then the further constant NUMBER_TASKS should indicate how many tasks have to be accomplished. If this value is N, then the tasks are numbered 0, 1, 2, ..., $N - 1$. The number of points gained by solving each task must be defined in a -> array with N entries called task_scores, like so:

```
Constant TASKS_PROVIDED;
Constant NUMBER_TASKS = 5;
Constant MAX_SCORE = 25;
Array task_scores -> 3 7 3 5 7;
```

Thus task 0 scores three points, task 1 scores seven points and so on. Since the entries in a -> array have to be numbers between 0 and 255, no task can have a negative score or a score higher than 255. Besides a points score, each task has a name, and these are printed by an entry point routine called PrintTaskName. For instance ('Toyshop'):

```
[ PrintTaskName task_number;
  switch (task_number) {
      0: "eating a sweet";
      1: "driving the car";
      2: "shutting out the draught";
      3: "building a tower of four";
      4: "seeing which way the mantelpiece leans";
  }
];
```

Finally, the game's source code should call Achieved(task_number) to tell the library that the given task has been completed. If this task has been completed before, the library will do nothing: if not, the library will award the appropriate number of points. The verb "full" will give a full score breakdown including the achieved task in all future listings.

. . . . .

When points are awarded by a call to Achieved, or by the player picking up a scored object, or visiting a scored place, or simply by the source code itself altering the score variable, no text is printed at the time. Instead, the library will normally notice at the end of the turn in question that the score has changed, and will print a message like:

[Your score has gone up by three points.]

Not all players like this feature, so it can be turned on and off with the "notify" verb, but by default it is on. The designer can also turn the feature off and on: it is off if the library's variable notify_mode is false, on if it is true.

. . . . .

Another (optional) entry point routine, called PrintRank, gets the chance to print text additional to the score. It's called PrintRank because the traditional "something additional" is a ranking based on the current score. Here is 'Ruins':

```
[ PrintRank;
  print ", earning you the rank of ";
  if (score == 30) "Director of the Carnegie Institution.";
  if (score >= 20) "Archaeologist.";
  if (score >= 10) "Curiosity-seeker.";
  if (score >= 5) "Explorer.";
  "Tourist.";
];
```

. . . . .

Besides the score breakdown, two more verbs are usually provided to the player: "objects" and "places". The former lists off all the objects handled by the player and where they are now; the latter lists all the places visited by the player. In some game designs, these verbs will cause problems: you can get rid of them both by defining the constant NO_PLACES.

● △EXERCISE 57
Suppose one single room object is used internally for the 64 squares of a gigantic chessboard, each of which is a different location to the player. Then "places" is likely to result in only the last-visited square being listed. Fix this.

. . . . .

The rest of this section runs through some simple "special effects" which are often included in games. See Chapter VII for much more on this, and in particular see §44 for using the "Menus.h" library extension.

The first effect is hardly special at all: to ask the player a yes/no question. To do this, print up the question and then call the library routine YesOrNo, which returns true/false accordingly.

The status line is perhaps the most distinctive feature of Infocom games in play. This is the (usually highlighted) bar across the top of the screen. Usually, the game automatically prints the current game location, and either the time or the score and number of turns taken. It has the score/turns format unless the directive

```
Statusline time;
```

has been written in the program, in which case the game's 24-hour clock is displayed. See §20 for more on time-keeping.

△   If you want to change this, you need to Replace the parser's DrawStatusLine routine. This requires some assembly language programming: there are several examples of altered status lines in the exercises to §42.

. . . . .

Many games contain quotations, produced with box statements like so:

```
box "I might repeat to myself, slowly and soothingly,"
    "a list of quotations beautiful from minds profound;"
    "if I can remember any of the damn things."
    ""
    "-- Dorothy Parker";
```

A snag with printing such boxes is that if you do it in the middle of a turn then it will probably scroll half-off the screen by the time the game finishes printing for the turn. The right time to do so is just after the prompt (usually ">") is printed, when the screen will definitely scroll no more. You could use the Prompt: slot in LibraryMessages to achieve this (see §25), but a more convenient way is to put your box-printing into the entry point routine AfterPrompt, which is called at this time in every turn.

● **EXERCISE 58**
Devise a class Quotation, so that calling QuoteFrom(Q) for any quotation Q will cause it to be displayed at the end of the current turn, provided it hasn't been quoted before.

● **REFERENCES**
'Advent' contains ranks and an Amusing reward (but doesn't use either of the scoring systems provided by the library, instead working by hand).   ●'Balances' uses scored objects (for its cubes).   ●'Toyshop' has tasks, as above.   ●'Adventureland' uses its TimePasses entry point to recalculate the score every turn (and watch for victory).

§23 'Ruins' revisited

> These fragments I have shored against my ruins
> —T. S. Eliot (1888–1965), *The Waste Land*

 Though 'Ruins' is a small world, and distorted in shape by the need to have "one example of everything", it seems worth a few pages to gather together the fragments scattered through the book so far and complete the game.

To begin with, the stage set back in §4 was too generic, too plain. Chosen at random, it may as well become La Milpa, a site rediscovered in dense rainforest by Eric Thompson in 1938, towards the end of the glory days of archaeological exploration. (La Milpa has been sadly looted since.) Though this is something of a cliché of interactive fiction, 'Ruins' contains two objects whose purpose is to anchor the player in time and place. Lining the packing case, we find:

```
Object -> -> newspaper "month-old newspaper"
  with name 'times' 'newspaper' 'paper' 'month-old' 'old',
      description
          "~The Times~ for 26 February, 1938, at once damp and brittle
          after a month's exposure to the climate, which is much the
          way you feel yourself. Perhaps there is fog in London.
          Perhaps there are bombs.";
```

And among the player's initial possessions:

```
Object map "sketch-map of Quintana Roo"
  with name 'map' 'sketch' 'sketch-map' 'quintana' 'roo',
      description
          "This map marks little more than the creek which brought you
          here, off the south-east edge of Mexico and into deepest
          rainforest, broken only by this raised plateau.";
```

To turn from the setting to the prologue, it is a little too easy to enter the structure in the rainforest. And if the steps were always open, surely the rain would sluice in? Recall that the Forest includes inward map connections to the steps, which are a door, instead of to the Square_Chamber directly:

```
          d_to steps, in_to steps,
```

The steps are, however, intentionally blocked by rubble, as happened in the case of the hidden staircase found by Alberto Ruz beneath the Temple of the Inscriptions at another site, Palenque:

```
Object -> steps "stone-cut steps"
  with name 'steps' 'stone' 'stairs' 'stone-cut' 'pyramid' 'burial'
           'structure' 'ten' '10',
       rubble_filled true,
       description [;
           if (self.rubble_filled)
               "Rubble blocks the way after only a few steps.";
           print "The cracked and worn steps descend into a dim
               chamber. Yours might ";
           if (Square_Chamber hasnt visited)
               print "be the first feet to tread";
           else print "have been the first feet to have trodden";
           " them for five hundred years.  On the top step is
           inscribed the glyph Q1.";
       ],
       door_to [;
           if (self.rubble_filled)
               "Rubble blocks the way after only a few steps.";
           return Square_Chamber;
       ],
       door_dir d_to
  has  scenery door open;
```

Next we must face the delicate issue of how to get from the mundane 1930s to a semi-magical Maya world. The stock device of Miguel Angel Asturias's *Leyendas de Guatemala* and other founding works of magic realism (indeed, of *Wuthering Heights* come to think of it) is for the arriving, European rationalist to become fascinated by a long tale told by local peasants. This would take too much code to get right in so small a game, though, and there also remains the unresolved question of what the mushroom is for. So we delete the original before rule for the mushroom, which made eating it potentially fatal, and instead give it an after:

```
Eat: steps.rubble_filled = false;
    "You nibble at one corner, unable to trace the source of an
    acrid taste, distracted by the flight of a macaw overhead
    which seems to burst out of the sun, the sound of the beating
    of its wings almost deafening, stone falling against stone.";
```

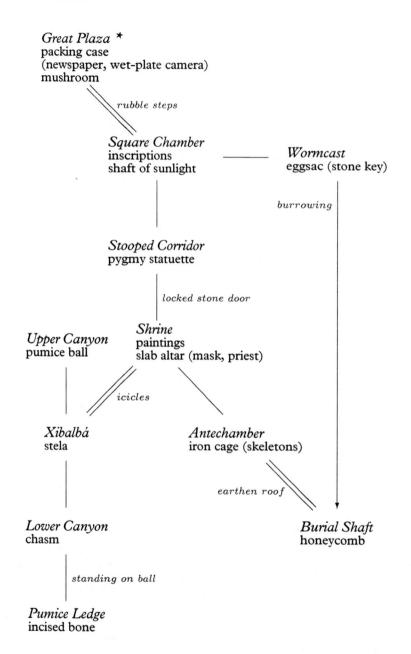

Great Plaza *
packing case
(newspaper, wet-plate camera)
mushroom

rubble steps

Square Chamber
inscriptions
shaft of sunlight

———— Wormcast
eggsac (stone key)

burrowing

Stooped Corridor
pygmy statuette

locked stone door

Upper Canyon
pumice ball

Shrine
paintings
slab altar (mask, priest)

icicles

Xibalbá
stela

Antechamber
iron cage (skeletons)

earthen roof

Lower Canyon
chasm

Burial Shaft
honeycomb

standing on ball

Pumice Ledge
incised bone

---

* The player begins at the Great Plaza, carrying the map, the sodium lamp and Waldeck's Mayan dictionary.

This is fairly authentic, as a cult of hallucinogenic mushrooms seems to have existed. Anyway, the player is getting off pretty lightly considering that Maya lords also went in for narcotic enemas and ritual blood-letting from the tongue and penis, an interactive fiction for which the world is not yet ready.

Descending underground, §8 alluded to an eggsac which burst on contact with natural light. Naturally, this repellent object belongs in the Wormcast, and here is its definition:

```
Object -> eggsac "glistening white eggsac",
  with name 'egg' 'sac' 'eggs' 'eggsac',
       initial "A glistening white eggsac, like a clump of frogspawn
           the size of a beach ball, has adhered itself to something
           in a crevice in one wall.",
       after [;
           Take: "Oh my.";
       ],
       react_before [;
           Go: if (location == Square_Chamber && noun == u_obj) {
                   deadflag = true;
                   "The moment that natural light falls upon the
                   eggsac, it bubbles obscenely and distends. Before
                   you can throw it away, it bursts into a hundred
                   tiny, birth-hungry insects...";
               }
       ];
```

Note the clue that some object is within the egg sac: as it turned out in §8, a stone key, released by putting the egg sac into the shaft of sunlight. The key itself has a very short definition:

```
Object stone_key "stone key"
  with name 'stone' 'key';
```

This is not an easy puzzle, but a further clue is provided by the carvings on the Stone Chamber wall, which can be translated with Waldeck's dictionary to read "becoming the Sun/life".

Given the key, the player must next solve the problem of bringing light to the Stooped Corridor, by pushing the burning sodium lamp south. This means, as promised in §14, adding a before rule to the lamp:

```
PushDir:
    if (location == Shrine && second == sw_obj)
        "The nearest you can do is to push the sodium lamp to
        the very lip of the Shrine, where the cave floor falls
```

```
        away.";
    AllowPushDir(); rtrue;
```

§14 also promised to run down the battery power: although since 100 turns is plenty, this rule doesn't play any real part in the game and is just window-dressing. We need to StartDaemon(sodium_lamp) in the Initialise routine, and define the lamp's daemon along the following lines:

```
daemon [;
    if (self hasnt on) return;
    if (--self.battery_power == 0)
        give self ~light ~on;
    if (self in location) {
        switch (self.battery_power) {
            10: "^The sodium lamp is getting dimmer!";
             5: "^The sodium lamp can't last much longer.";
             0: "^The sodium lamp fades and suddenly dies.";
        }
    }
],
```

With the obligatory light puzzle solved, the Shrine can at last be opened:

```
Object Shrine "Shrine"
  with description
            "This magnificent Shrine shows signs of being hollowed out
            from already-existing limestone caves, especially in the
            western of the two long eaves to the south.",
       n_to StoneDoor, se_to Antechamber,
       sw_to
            "The eaves taper out into a crevice which would wind
            further if it weren't jammed tight with icicles. The glyph
            of the Crescent is not quite obscured by ice.";
```

Looking up the Crescent glyph in the dictionary (§16) reveals that it stands for the word "xibalbá": asking the Priest (§17) brought into existence by wearing the jade mosaic mask (§11) melts the icicles and makes the southwest connection to Xibalbá, of which more later. No Maya game would be complete without their religiously-observed cyclical countings of time:

```
Object -> paintings "paintings"
  with name 'painting' 'paintings' 'lord' 'captive',
        initial "Vividly busy paintings, of the armoured Lord trampling
            on a captive, are almost too bright to look at, the
            graffiti of an organised mob.",
```

```
   description "The flesh on the bodies is blood-red. The markers
       of the Long Count date the event to 10 baktun 4 katun 0 tun
       0 uinal 0 kin, the sort of anniversary when one Lord would
       finally decapitate a captured rival who had been ritually
       tortured over a period of some years, in the Balkanised
       insanity of the Maya city states.",
  has    static;
```

Having called the priest "calendrical", here's another topic to Ask the priest about:

```
'paintings': "The calendrical priest frowns.
    ~10 baktun, 4 katun, that makes 1,468,800 days
    since the beginning of time: in your calendar
    19 January 909.~";
```

And also, to make the point once more, and remind the player once again of distant Europe:

```
Show, Give: ...
   if (noun == newspaper)
       "He looks at the date. ~12 baktun 16 katun 4 tun
       1 uinal 12 kin~, he declares before browsing the
       front page. ~Ah. Progress, I see.~";
```

Perhaps the player will never see either calculation: if so, it doesn't matter, as dates and calendars turn out to be this game's red herring. (Every game should have one.) The Antechamber of the Shrine is an undistinguished room...

```
Object Antechamber "Antechamber"
   with description
           "The southeastern eaves of the Shrine make a curious
           antechamber.",
       nw_to Shrine;
```

... except that this is where the iron cage (§15 and §21) is located, so that the Burial Shaft lies below, with its complex puzzle in which the player is transformed to a warthog and back again, opening the shaft. Lastly, then, in the southwest eaves of the Shrine is a natural cave entrance, which in Mayan mythology leads to the Underworld. There is supposed to be a crossroads here, but in this modest game a three-way junction is all we have space for:

```
Object Junction "Xibalb@'a"
   with description
           "Fifty metres beneath rainforest, and the sound of water
           is everywhere: these deep, eroded limestone caves
```

```
                  extend like tap roots. A slither northeast by a broad
                  collapsed column of ice-covered rock leads back to the
                  Shrine, while a kind of canyon floor extends uphill to
                  the north and downwards to south, pale white like shark's
                  teeth in the diffused light from the sodium lamp above.",
            ne_to Shrine, n_to Canyon_N, u_to Canyon_N,
            s_to Canyon_S, d_to Canyon_S,
      has  light;
Treasure -> stela "stela"
   with name 'stela' 'boundary' 'stone' 'marker',
            initial
                  "A modest-sized stela, or boundary stone, rests on a
                  ledge at head height.",
            description
                  "The carvings appear to warn that the boundary of
                  Xibalb@'a, Place of Fright, is near. The Bird glyph is
                  prominent.";
```

This canyon houses the eight-foot pumice stone ball (see §15) at the north end, and the chasm (§12, §21) at the south:

```
Object Canyon_N "Upper End of Canyon"
   with s_to Junction, d_to Junction,
            description
                  "The higher, broader northern end of the canyon rises only
                  to an uneven wall of volcanic karst.",
      has  light;
Object Canyon_S "Lower End of Canyon"
   with n_to Junction, u_to Junction,
            s_to "Into the chasm?", d_to nothing,
            description
                  "At the lower, and narrower, southern end, the canyon stops
                  dead at a chasm of vertiginous blackness.  Nothing can be
                  seen or heard from below.",
      has  light;
```

As promised in §12, the chasm must react to having the stone ball pushed into it, which means adding this to the chasm's definition:

```
each_turn [;
    if (huge_ball in parent(self)) {
        remove huge_ball; Canyon_S.s_to = On_Ball;
        Canyon_S.description = "The southern end of the canyon
            now continues onto the pumice-stone ball, wedged into
            the chasm.";
```

```
        "^The pumice-stone ball rolls out of control down the
        last few feet of the canyon before shuddering into the
        jaws of the chasm, bouncing back a little and catching
        you a blow on the side of the forehead. You slump
        forward, bleeding, and... the pumice-stone shrinks,
        or else your hand grows, because you seem now to be
        holding it, staring at Alligator, son of seven-Macaw,
        across the ball-court of the Plaza, the heads of his
        last opponents impaled on spikes, a congregation baying
        for your blood, and there is nothing to do but to throw
        anyway, and... but this is all nonsense, and you have
        a splitting headache.";
    }
],
```

(Horribly violent, semi-religious ball-game rituals are common in early central America, though nobody knows why: all substantial Maya cities have prominent ball-courts.) A fat paragraph of text in which fairly interesting things happen, beyond the player's control, is sometimes called a "cut-scene". Most critics dislike the casual use of cut-scenes, and 'Ruins' would be a better game if the confrontation with Alligator were an interactive scene. But this manual hasn't the space. Instead, here is the final location, which represents "standing on the wedged ball":

```
Object On_Ball "Pumice-Stone Ledge"
    with n_to Canyon_S, d_to Canyon_S, u_to Canyon_S,
        description
            "An impromptu ledge formed by the pumice-stone ball,
            wedged into place in the chasm. The canyon nevertheless
            ends here.",
    has  light;
Treasure -> "incised bone"
    with name 'incised' 'carved' 'bone',
        initial
            "Of all the sacrificial goods thrown into the chasm, perhaps
            nothing will be reclaimed: nothing but an incised bone,
            lighter than it looks, which projects from a pocket of wet
            silt in the canyon wall.",
        description
            "A hand holding a brush pen appears from the jaws of
            Itzamn@'a, inventor of writing, in his serpent form.";
```

And this is where Itzamná lays down his brush, for this is the fifth and last of the cultural artifacts to collect. The game ends when they are all deposited in the packing case, a rule which means a slight expansion of the definition of Treasure:

```
after [;
    Insert:
        ...
        if (score == MAX_SCORE) {
            deadflag = 2;
            "As you carefully pack away ", (the) second,
            " a red-tailed macaw flutters down from the tree-tops,
            feathers heavy in the recent rain, the sound of its
            beating wings almost deafening, stone falling against
            stone... As the skies clear, a crescent moon rises above
            a peaceful jungle. It is the end of March, 1938, and it
            is time to go home.";
        }
```

△   The following sequence of 111 moves tests 'Ruins' from beginning to end: "examine case / read newspaper / get newspaper / get camera / down / examine steps / east / up / enter structure 10 / eat mushroom / eat mushroom / down / examine inscriptions / look up arrow in dictionary / east / get eggsac / west / put eggsac in sunlight / get key / drop lamp / light lamp / look / push lamp s / get statuette / drop all except camera / photograph statuette / get key / open door / unlock door with key / open door / drop key / get pygmy / north / up / put pygmy in case / down / south / get dictionary / get newspaper / south / north / push lamp south / examine paintings / drop all but camera / photograph mask / get mask / get dictionary / get newspaper / wear mask / show dictionary to priest / show newspaper to priest / drop newspaper / ask priest about ruins / ask priest about paintings / se / nw / push lamp se / push lamp nw / sw / look up crescent in dictionary / ask priest about xibalba / sw / north / push ball south / push ball south / south / drop all but camera / remove mask / drop mask / photograph bone / get all / north / north / drop all but camera / photograph stela / get all / ne / north / north / up / put bone in case / put stela in case / put mask in case / down / east / nw / west / south / south / push lamp se / examine cage / enter cage / open cage / nw / north / north / east / down / east / up / drop all but camera / photograph honeycomb / get all / up / open cage / out / push lamp nw / north / north / up / put honeycomb in case".

● **REFERENCES**
I am indebted to, which is to say I have roundly travestied, the following: "Mapping La Milpa: a Maya city in northwestern Belize" (Tourtellot, Clarke and Hammond, *Antiquity* 67 (1993), 96–108). All the same 'Ruins' favours old-fashioned ideas of Maya, a good example being the "calendrical priests" fondly imagined by early archaeologists before Maya writing was deciphered.   ●The standard all-in-one-book book is Michael

D. Coe's *The Maya* (fourth edition).   •The same author's history of *Breaking the Maya Code* offers pungently vivid portraits of Sir Eric Thompson and Maximilien Waldeck. The British Museum guide *Maya Glyphs*, by S. D. Houston, is a trifle more reliable than Waldeck's work.   •Numerous colour-postcard photographs by F. Monfort are collected in *Yucatan and the Maya Civilization* (Crescent Books, 1978).

§24   The world model described

This section is a self-contained summary of the concepts and systematic organising principles used by Inform to present the illusion of describing a physically real environment, with which the protagonist of a game interacts. All details of implementation are ignored and Inform jargon is either avoided or explained. While many of the rules are standard to all world models used for interactive fiction, some are not, and the footnotes remark on some of the more interesting cases. The next section, §25, buries itself back into implementation to discuss how to add new rules or to change those rules below which you don't agree with. The description below is arranged as follows: ¶1. Substance; ¶2. Containment; ¶3. Space; ¶4. Sense; ¶5. Time; ¶6. Action.

1. Substance

1.1. Objects make up the substance of the world: its places and their contents, abstract relations between these, transient states the world can be in, actors and trends (such as the flowing of a river).

1.2. At any given time, every object in the world model is one and only one of the following kinds: the player; a room; the darkness object; an item; the compass object; a compass direction; or something which is out of play.[1]

1.2.1. The player object represents the protagonist of the game.

1.2.2. A room represents some region of space, not necessarily with walls or indoors.

1.2.3. The darkness pseudo-room represents the experience of being in a dark place, and has no specific location in space.

---

[1] The compass pseudo-item and the darkness pseudo-room are anomalies. The compass arises from a generic convention which is unrealistic but avoids making the game needlessly tiresome: that the player has a perfect inherent sense of direction. The representation of darkness is less defensible. Although vaguely justifiable from the assumption that the experience of being in one entirely dark place is much like another, it came about instead for reasons of implementation: partly to bundle up various darkness-related texts as though they were room descriptions, and partly because early versions of the Inform run-time format (version 3 of the Z-machine) imposed a restriction that the status line displayed above the screen could only be the short name of an object.

1.2.4. An item represents some body (or group of similar bodies) with a definite spatial position at any given time. It is not necessarily solid but its substance is indivisible.

1.2.5. The compass pseudo-item represents the frame of reference within the protagonist's head, and is not an actual compass with its attendant hazards of being dropped, broken, stolen or becoming invisible in pitch darkness.

1.2.6. A compass direction represents a potential direction of movement, such as "northeast", "down", "in" or "starboard".

1.2.7. Objects out of play represent nothing in the model world and the protagonist does not interact with them. Out of play objects are mostly things which once existed within the model world but which were destroyed, or which have not yet been brought into being.

1.2.8. An object can change its kind as the game progresses: for instance a compass direction can be taken out of play, and certain items can become the player, making the object which was previously the player now merely an item.

1.3. Objects are indivisible even if the player may see internal structure to them, such as the four legs which are part of a chair. Pieces of objects only appear in the model if additional objects are provided for them.[2]

1.4. Objects have internal states and are therefore distinguishable from each other by more than their position in the containment tree. Some are "open", some are "concealed" and so on, and they are given descriptions and other specifications by the designer.

1.4.1. Some objects are "switchable" between two mutually exclusive states, "on" and "off". These represent machines, trapdoors and the like, which behave differently when set to when unset, and which generally have rules about the process of setting and unsetting.

1.4.2. Some objects are "lockable" and someone with the specified "key" object can switch between mutually exclusive states, "locked" and "unlocked". These objects represent containers and doors with locks.

1.4.3. Some objects are "openable" and therefore in one of two mutually exclusive states, "open" and "closed". If such an object is closed and also locked then it cannot be opened. These objects represent containers and doors.

---

[2] The atomic theory of matter. Since there are a finite number of atoms each with a finite range of possible states and positions, Heraclitus' doctrine that one cannot stand in the same river twice is false within the model world, and this can detract from its realism. It is sometimes too easy for the protagonist to exactly undo his actions as if they had never been and to return exactly to the world as it was before. Another problem with ¶1.3 is that liquids need to be divisible ("some water" becoming "some water" and "some water").

2. Containment

2.1. Some objects are contained within other objects in what is sometimes called a tree, meaning that: (i) an object can either be contained in one other object (called its "parent"), or not contained in any; (ii) there is no "loop" of objects such that each is contained in the next and the last is contained in the first. The pattern of containment changes frequently during play but (i) and (ii) always hold.[3]

2.1.1. The objects contained within something are kept in order of how long they have been there. The first possession (sometimes called the "child") is the one most recently arrived, and the last is the one which has been contained for longest.

2.1.2. In some games there are objects called "floating objects" which represent something found in many locations, such as a stream flowing through the map, or a pervasive cloud. These give the appearance of violating rule ¶2.1, but do not: the effect is an illusion brought about by making the floating object belong at all times to the same room as the player.

2.2. The following rules remain true at all times:

2.2.1. A room is not contained.

2.2.2. The darkness object and the compass are not contained.

2.2.3. A compass direction is contained in the compass object but itself contains nothing.

2.2.4. An item is always contained; either in the player, in another item or a room.

2.2.5. The player is always contained in a visitable object. An object is "visitable" if either (a) it is a room, or (b) it is enterable and it has a visitable parent.

2.2.6. An object out of play is either contained in another object out of play, or else not contained at all.[4]

2.3. Containment models a number of subtly different kinds of belonging:

2.3.1. The contents of a room object are near each other (usually within sight and touch) in the space represented by the room. For instance, the player,

---

[3] Infocom world models all included rule (ii) but their implementations made no systematic effort to enforce this, so that Infocom were perpetually fixing bugs arising from putting two containers inside each other.

[4] Without knowing the context, and looking at the object tree alone, it isn't easy to distinguish a room from an object out of play, which can make writing good debugging features tricky.

a wooden door and a table might all be contained in a room representing the inside of a small hut.[5]

2.3.2. The contents of the compass are the compass directions available in principle to an actor. If "north" is removed from the compass, then north becomes meaningless even if an actor is in a room with a north exit; if "aft" is added, then it need not follow that any room actually has an exit leading aft.

2.3.3. The contents of the player fall into two categories: those which are "worn", and the rest.

2.3.3.1. Worn objects represent clothing or accessories held onto the body without the need for hands, such as a belt or a rucksack.

2.3.3.2. The rest represent items being held in the player's hands.

2.3.4. The contents of an item model different kinds of belonging, depending on the nature of the item:[6]

2.3.4.1. Some items are "containers": they represent boxes, bottles, bags, holes in the wall and so on. The contents of a container are considered to be physically inside it. At any given time a container can be "open" or "closed".

2.3.4.2. Some items are "supporters": they represent tables, plinths, beds and so on. The contents of a supporter are considered to be physically on top of it.

2.3.4.3. Some items are "animate": they represent people, sentient creatures generally and higher animals. The contents of an animate object are considered to be carried by it.

2.3.4.4. Some items are "enterable", meaning that it is possible for the player to be contained within them. A large tea-chest might be an enterable container; a bed might be an enterable supporter. In the case of an enterable which is neither container nor supporter, and which contains the player, the player is considered to be confined close to the enterable: for instance, by a pair of manacles.

2.3.4.5. Failing this, the contents of an item represent pieces or components of it, such as a lever attached to machinery, or a slot cut into a slab of masonry.

---

[5] This part of the model was invented by the early mainframe 'Zork'. The Crowther and Woods 'Advent', and later the Scott Adams games, required all objects to belong to a room but had a pseudo-room which represented "being carried by the player". Objects were equated with potential possessions and no object represented the player.

[6] The model in ¶2.3.4 has attracted criticism as being simplistic in three respects: (a) an object is assumed not to be both a container and a supporter, so what about an oven?; (b) while the player has a distinction between items worn and items carried, animate objects do not; (c) being inside and being on top of are modelled, but being underneath or behind are not.

3. Space

3.1. Spatial arrangement on the small scale (at ranges of a few moments' walking distance or less) is modelled by considering some objects to lie close together and others to lie far apart.

3.1.1. Objects ultimately contained in the same room are considered to be close enough together that walking between the two is a largely unconscious act.

3.1.1.1. The model takes no account of directions from one such object to another, except as described in ¶2.3.4 above (e.g., that contents of a supporter are on top of it).

3.1.1.2. All objects with the same parent are considered to be equidistant from, and to have equal access to, each other.[7]

3.1.2. Objects ultimately contained in different rooms are considered to be so far apart that they will not ordinarily interact. Because of this the model takes no account of one being further away than another.[8]

3.2. Spatial arrangement on the large scale (at ranges of an appreciable walking distance or more) is modelled by joining rooms together at their edges, much as a patchwork quilt is made.

3.2.1. Rooms joined together represent areas which are adjacent in that they are separated by so short a walk that the walker does not have opportunity to think twice and turn back, or to stop halfway and do something else.

3.2.2. Rooms are joined either by a map connection or a door.[9]

3.2.2.1. Map connections come in different kinds, representing different directions in the geography of the world. These physical directions are north, south, east, west, northeast, northwest, southeast, southwest, up, down, in and out.

3.2.2.2. Each compass direction corresponds to a single physical direction at any given moment, and this represents the actual direction which a player will walk in if he tries to walk in a given direction within his own frame of reference.[10]

---

[7] In ¶4 it will become apparent that a measure of distance between two objects is given by their distance apart in the containment tree.

[8] Note that ¶3.1.2 says that objects far apart cannot interact, but ¶3.1.1 does *not* say that objects close together can do. A honey bee in a sealed hive cannot interact with or be aware of the delivery man carrying the hive to its new beekeeper. Rules on which close objects can interact are the subject of ¶4.

[9] There is no requirement for such a join to be usable from the other side.

[10] For instance, on board a ship a player may try to walk "starboard", that being a

3.2.2.3. A "door" is an item representing something which comes between two locations, which must be passed through or by in order to go from one to the other, and which it requires some conscious decision to use.[11]

3.2.2.4. As with a compass direction, a door corresponds to a single physical direction at any given moment.

4. Sense

4.1. The senses are used in the world model primarily to determine whether the player can, or cannot, interact with a nearby object. Three different kinds of accessibility are modelled: touch, sight and awareness.[12]

4.2. Awareness = sight + touch, that is, the player is aware of something if it can be seen or touched.[13]

4.2.1. Awareness represents the scope of the player's ability to interact with the world in a single action. Although the player may pursue a grand strategy, he must do so by a series of tactical moves each within the scope of awareness.[14]

4.3. There are only two strengths of light: good enough to read by and pitch blackness, which we shall call "light" and "dark".

4.3.1. Some containers and other items are specified as being transparent to light, meaning that light can pass through from what contains them to what they contain (for instance a glass box or a machine whose contents are the

---

compass direction, but will in fact move in some physical direction such as northeast. Games have also been designed in which the player's frame of reference consists only of "left", "right", "forward", "back", "up" and "down", whose assignment to physical directions changes continuously in play.

[11] Thus a vault door, a plank bridge or a ventilation duct high on one wall would be represented by doors, but an open passageway or a never-locked and familiar door within a house would instead be represented by map connections.

[12] Hearing, taste and smell are not modelled: instead Inform's implementation provides convenient verbs and actions for designers to add their own ad-hoc rules.

[13] Awareness = sense is a strongly restrictive position. Thanks to simplistic parsers, in some early games the player is somehow aware of all objects everywhere, even those not yet encountered. In some more modern games awareness = sense + recent memory. For instance an item dropped in a dark room can be picked up again, since it is assumed that the player can remember where it is.

[14] The Inform parser enforces this by recognising only those typed commands which request interaction with objects the player is aware of at a given time.

buttons on the its front panel), while others are opaque (for instance a wooden box or a spy who keeps all her belongings concealed).

4.3.2. An object is called "see-through" if it is transparent, or if it is a supporter, or if it is an open container, or if it is the player.

4.3.3. Some rooms are specified by the designer as having ambient light (those representing outdoor locations, caves with fluorescent ore formations, strip-lit office buildings and the like); some items are specified as giving off light (those representing torches, lanterns and the like). The room or item is said to be "lit".

4.3.4. There is light for the player to see by only if there is a lit object, close to the player in the sense of ¶3, such that every object between them is see-through. (For instance, if a player is in a sealed glass box in a cupboard which also contains a key, the glass box comes between player and key, but the cupboard does not.)[15]

4.4. What the player can touch depends on whether there is light.

4.4.1. In the light, the player can touch anything close to the player provided that (a) every object between them is see-through and (b) none of the objects between them is a closed container.

4.4.2. In the dark, the player can touch (a) anything contained in the player and (b) the enterable object which the player is contained in (if any).[16]

4.5. What the player can see also depends on whether there is light, but also on whether the designer has specified that any nearby items are "concealed", which models their being hidden from view. Concealed objects remain touchable but you would need to know they were there, since sight alone would not reveal this. On once being picked up, a concealed object ceases to be concealed.

4.5.1. In the light, the player can see any non-concealed object close to the player provided that (a) every object between them is see-through and (b) none of the objects between them is concealed.

4.5.2. In the dark, the player can see nothing.

---

[15] This definition is not as realistic as it looks. Translucency is equated with transparency, presenting problems for glazed glass jars. "Close to the player" implies that light never spills over from one room to another, for instance through an open window on a sunny day.

[16] Equivalently, in the dark you can touch exactly those objects adjacent to you in the containment tree. Thus anything which can be touched in the dark can also be touched in the light but not vice versa.

5. *Time*

5.1. The passage of time is represented by describing and changing the model world at regular intervals, each cycle being called a "turn". The interval from one such moment to the next is considered to be the time occupied by carrying out these changes, so that all basic changes (i.e., actions: see ¶6) consume the same unit of time.

5.2. Changes in the model world are carried out by a number of independent processes called "daemons". Some daemons are built in and others added by the designer of a particular game, conventionally by associating them with certain objects over which they have sway. A turn consists of the daemons being invoked one at a time until each has been given the chance to intervene, or to decline to intervene.

5.2.1. Daemons are invoked in the sequence: action daemon, any designed daemons (in no particular order), each-turn daemon, scoring daemon, clock daemon.

5.2.2. Daemons have the opportunity to carry out arbitrary changes to the state of the objects, but should be designed to violate the rules of the model world as little as possible. The built-in daemons do not violate them at all.

5.2.3. Certain designed daemons are "timers", meaning that they are set to decline to intervene for a set number of turns and will then act once and once only (unless or until reset).

5.3. The action daemon consults the player at the keyboard by asking which action should be performed and then performing it. (See ¶6.) The action daemon is invoked first in each turn.

5.4. The each-turn daemon polls any object of which the player is aware. If it has been specified by the designer as having an each-turn rule, then that rule is applied.

5.5. The scoring daemon keeps track of the length of the game so far by keeping count of the number of turns. It also measures the player's progress by keeping score:

5.5.1. Points are awarded if the player is for the first time carrying an item which the designer has marked as "scored".

5.5.2. Also if the player is for the first time inside a room which the designer has marked as "scored", provided there is light to see by.

5.5.3. The library groups score ranges into ranks, with names such as "Beginner" or "Expert" specified by the designer. If this feature is used at all then every possible score should correspond to one and only one rank.

5.6. The clock daemon records the time of day to the nearest minute. (Day, month and year are not modelled.)

5.6.1. Between one change of state and the next, the clock is normally advanced by one minute, but the designer (not the player) can arrange for this to be varied in play either to several changes per minute, or several minutes per change.

5.6.2. The designer can also change the time at any point.

5.6.3. Time passes at a constant rate for all objects, so that the player's measurement of the passage of time is the same as everybody else's.[17]

5.7. Time stops immediately when any daemon declares the player's death or victory.

5.7.1. Only rules provided by the designer will do this: the model world's normal rules are set up so that, whatever the player asks to do, time will continue indefinitely.[18]

6. Action

6.1. An action is a single impulse by the player to do something, which if feasible would take sufficiently little time to carry out that there would be no opportunity to change one's mind half-way or leave it only partly carried out.

6.1.1. An action "succeeds" if the activity in question does take place within the model world. If not, it "fails".[19]

6.1.2. Not all impulses are sensible or feasible. Some actions fail because circumstances happen to frustrate them, but others could never have succeeded in any circumstances.

6.1.3. Some actions (the so-called "group 3 actions") have a model in which, once the impulse is verified as being feasible, all that happens is that a message along the lines of "nothing much happens" is given.

---

[17] This is a restriction, though not because it ignores relativistic effects (at walking speeds these are of the order of 1 part in 10^{17}). Suppose the player enters a room where time runs slow and all actions take five times longer than they would elsewhere. This means that daemons which handle changes far away from the player also run five times slower than normal, relative to the model world's clock.

[18] Thus victory does not occur automatically when all scored objects are found and all scored rooms visited; death does not occur automatically when the player crosses from a dark room to another dark room, and so on.

[19] It does not necessarily follow that any objects will change their states: an action to look under something will result only in text being printed out, but this is successful because the looking under has become part of the history of the model world.

6.1.4. Some actions imply the need for other actions to take place first. In such cases the first action is tried, and only if this is successful will the second action be tried.

6.1.4.1. An action which requires an object to be held (such as eating) will cause a take action for that object.

6.1.4.2. A particular container, specified by the designer as the "sack object", is such that when the player is carrying the maximum legal number of items, any further take action causes the least recently taken item to be put into the sack first.[20]

6.1.4.3. A drop action for a piece of clothing being worn will cause a remove-clothing action first.

6.1.5. Other actions are recognised as being composites and so are split into a sequence of simpler constituent actions.

6.1.5.1. Actions involving multiple objects specified by the player as a collective batch ("take six buttons", "drop all") are split into one action for each object.

6.1.5.2. Emptying a container is split up into individual remove and drop actions.

6.1.5.3. Entering something which would require intermediate objects to be exited or entered is split into a sequence of exits and entrances.

6.2. An action can involve no objects other than the player, or else one other object of which the player is aware, or else two other objects of which the player is aware.[21]

6.2.1. The following actions fail if the player cannot touch the object(s) acted on: taking, dropping, removing from a container, putting something on or inside something, entering something, passing through a door, locking and unlocking, switching on or off, opening, closing, wearing or removing clothing, eating, touching, waving something, pulling, pushing or turning, squeezing, throwing, attacking or kissing, searching something.

6.2.2. The following actions fail if the player cannot see the object(s) acted on: examining, searching or looking under something.[22]

---

[20] Casual assumptions, in this case that all games have a single rucksack-like container, often make world models needlessly restrictive. Compare the Scott Adams game engine, in which one object is designated as "the lamp".

[21] The Inform parser will not generate actions concerning objects of which the player is unaware.

[22] Thus there is only one action requiring you to both see and touch the object acted on: searching.

6.3. The actions modelled are grouped under five headings below: actions of sense, alteration, arrangement, movement and communication. There is also one inaction: waiting, in which the player chooses to do nothing for the turn.

6.4. Actions of sense are those which seek information about the world without changing it: inventory, examining, consulting, looking, looking under, searching, listening, tasting, touching and smelling.[23]

6.4.1. "Look" describes only those parts of the room which can be seen. (In particular, concealed objects are omitted.) In addition, certain objects are "scenery" and are omitted from specific mention in room descriptions because, although visible, they are either too obvious to mention (such as the sky) or are mentioned already in the room-specific text.

6.5. Actions of alteration are those in which the player changes something without moving it: opening, closing, locking, unlocking, switching on and off, wearing and removing clothing, and eating.

6.5.1. A successful eating action results in the object being taken out of play.[24]

6.6. Actions of arrangement are those in which the player rearranges the spatial arrangement of things: taking, dropping, removing, inserting, putting on top of, transferring, emptying, emptying onto or into, pulling, pushing, turning and throwing.

6.6.1. Pulling, pushing and turning are only minimally provided: they are checked to see if the player can indeed carry out the action, but then nothing happens unless the designer writes code to make it happen, because the model doesn't include directions of pointing.

6.6.2. Actions of arrangement fail if the object is "static", meaning that it is fixed in place.

6.7. Actions of movement are those in which the player moves about: going, entering, exiting, getting off and pushing something from one room to another.

6.7.1. An attempt to enter a container or door fails if it is not open.

6.7.2. Only an enterable object or a door can be entered.

6.7.3. The player can only get off or exit from the enterable object currently holding him.

---

[23] Reading is not distinguished from examining: instead the consult action provides for looking things up in books.

[24] This is the only circumstance in which the rules for the model world destroy an object.

6.7.4. Certain enterable objects are "vehicles". Within a vehicle, movement actions are permitted as if the player were standing on the floor. Otherwise, no movements are permitted if the player is within an enterable object, except to enter or exit.

6.7.4.1. If the player travels in a vehicle, the vehicle object is also moved to the new room, and the player remains within it.

6.7.5. Certain objects are "pushable" and accompany the player on an otherwise normal movement. These, too, move to the new room.

6.7.6. An attempt to move through a concealed door fails as if the door were not there at all.[25]

6.8. Actions of communication are those in which the player relates to other people within the model world: giving, showing, waking somebody up, attacking, kissing, answering, telling, asking about and asking for something.

6.8.1. Actions of communication fail unless the object is animate, except that certain "talkable" objects can be addressed in conversation.

---

[25] I have no idea what this is doing in the Inform world model, but it seems to be there: perhaps the writing-room puzzle in the 'Curses' attic needed it. Andrew Plotkin: "I've always said that the definition of concealed was ad-hoc and not well understood by anybody."

§25   Extending and redefining the world model

A circulating library in a town is as an ever-green tree of diabolical
knowledge! It blossoms through the year!

— R. B. Sheridan (1751–1816), *The Rivals*

 In *The History of Zork*, Tim Anderson summed up the genesis of
the 'Zork I' world model – and perhaps also its exodus, that is, its
adaptation to other games – when he commented that "the general
problem always remained: anything that changes the world you're
modelling changes practically everything in the world you're modelling."
Substantial changes to the world model often have profound implications and
can lead to endless headaches in play-testing if not thought through. Even a
single object can upset the plausibility of the whole: a spray-can, for instance,
unless its use is carefully circumscribed. On the other hand, introducing whole
categories of objects often causes no difficulty at all, if they do not upset
existing ideas such as that of door, location, container and so on. For instance,
the set of collectable Tarot cards in the game 'Curses' have numerous rules
governing their behaviour, but never cause the basic rules of play to alter for
other items or places.

.   .   .   .   .

In making such an extension the natural strategy is simply to define a new
class of objects, and to take advantage of Inform's message system to make
designing such objects as easy and flexible as possible. For example, suppose
we need a class of Egyptian magical amulets, small arrowhead-like totems worn
on the wrist and made of semi-precious minerals, with cartoon-like carvings.
(The Ashmolean Museum, Oxford, has an extensive collection.) Each amulet
is to have the power (but only if worn) to cast a different spell. Almost all of
the code for this will go into a class definition called `Amulet`. This means that

```
if (noun ofclass Amulet) ...
```

provides a convenient test to see if an object noun is an amulet, and so forth.
(This imposes a restriction that an object can't start or stop being an amulet in
the course of play, because class membership is forever. If this restriction were
unacceptable, a new attribute would need to be created instead, in the same
way that the standard world model recognises any object with the attribute
`container` as a container, rather than having a `Container` class.)

Suppose the requirement is that the player should be able to type "cast jasper amulet", which would work so long as the jasper amulet were being worn. It seems sensible to create an action called Cast, and this necessitates creating an action subroutine to deal with it:

```
[ CastSub;
  "Nothing happens.";
];
Verb 'cast' 'invoke' * noun -> Cast;
```

Nothing happens here because the code is kept with the Amulet class instead:

```
Class Amulet
 with amulet_spell "Nothing happens.",
      before [ destination;
          Cast:
              if (self hasnt worn)
                  "The amulet rattles loosely in your hand.";
              destination = self.amulet_spell();
              switch (destination) {
                  false: "Nothing happens.";
                  true: ;
                  default: print "Osiris summons you to...^";
                      PlayerTo(destination);
              }
              rtrue;
      ],
  has clothing;
```

Thus every Amulet provides an amulet_spell message, which answers the question "you have been cast: what happens now?" The reply is either false, meaning nothing has happened; true, meaning that something did happen; or else an object or room to teleport the player to.

From the designer's point of view, once the above extension has been made, amulets are easy to create and have legible code. Here are four example spells:

```
amulet_spell "The spell fizzles out with a dull phut! sound.",
amulet_spell [;
    if (location == thedark) {
        give real_location light;
        "There is a burst of magical light!";
    }
],
amulet_spell HiddenVault,
```

```
amulet_spell [;
    return random(LeadRoom, SilverRoom, GoldRoom);
],
```

An elaborate library extension will end up defining many classes, grammar, actions and verb definitions, and these may neatly be packaged up into an Include file and to be placed among the library files.

△△ Such a file should contain the directive System_file;, as then other designers will be able to Replace routines from it, just as with the rest of the library.

. . . . .

So much for extending the Inform model with new classes: the rest of the section is about modifying what's ordinarily there. The simplest change, but often all that's needed, is to change a few of the standard responses called "library messages", such as the "Nothing is on sale." which tends to be printed when the player asks to buy something, or the "Taken." when something is picked up. (To change every message, and with it the language of the game, see §34.)

To set new library messages, provide a special object called LibraryMessages, which must be defined *between* the inclusion of the "Parser.h" and "Verblib.h" library files. This object should have just one property, a before rule. For example:

```
Object LibraryMessages
  with before [;
          Jump: if (real_location ofclass ISS_Module)
              "You jump and float helplessly for a while in zero
              gravity here on the International Space Station.";
          SwitchOn:
              if (lm_n == 3) {
                  "You power up ", (the) lm_o, ".";
              }
        ];
```

This object is never visible in the game, but its before rule is consulted before any message is printed: if it returns false, the standard message is printed; if true, then nothing is printed, as it's assumed that this has already happened.

The Jump action only ever prints one message (usually "You jump on the spot."), but more elaborate actions such as SwitchOn have several, and Take has thirteen. The library's variable lm_n holds the message number, which counts upwards from 1. In some cases, the object being talked about is held in lm_o. The messages and numbers are given in §A4. New message numbers may possibly be added in future, but old ones will not be renumbered.

An especially useful library message to change is the prompt, normally set to "^>" (new-line followed by >). This is printed under the action Prompt (actually a fake action existing for this very purpose). You can use this to make the game's prompt context-sensitive, or to remove the new-line from before the prompt.

• **EXERCISE 59**
Infocom's game 'The Witness' has the prompt "What should you, the detective, do next?" on turn one and "What next?" subsequently. Implement this.

△ LibraryMessages can also be used as a flexible way to alter the rules governing individual actions. Here are two examples in the guise of exercises.

• △**EXERCISE 60**
Under the standard world model (¶6.7.4 in §24 above), a player standing on top of something is not allowed to type, say, "east" to leave the room: the message "You'll have to get off . . . first" is printed instead. Change this.

• △**EXERCISE 61**
Under standard rules (¶6.6.1 in §24 above), a player trying to "push" something which is not static or scenery or animate will find that "Nothing obvious happens". Add the rule that an attempt to push a switchable item is to be considered as an attempt to switch it on, if it's off, and vice versa. (This might be useful if a game has many buttons and levers.)

· · · · ·

The Library is itself written in Inform, and with experience it's not too hard to alter it if need be. But to edit and change the library files themselves is an inconvenience and an inelegant way to carry on, because it would lead to needing a separate copy of all the files for each project you work on. Because of this, Inform allows you to Replace any routine or routines of your choice from the library, giving a definition of your own which is to be used instead of the one in the standard files. For example, if the directive

```
Replace BurnSub;
```

is placed in your file *before the library files are included*, Inform ignores the definition of BurnSub in the library files. You then have to define a routine called BurnSub yourself: looking in the library file "Verblib.h", the original turns out to be tiny:

```
[ BurnSub; L__M(##Burn,1,noun); ];
```

191

All this does is to print out library message number 1 for Burn, the somewhat preachy "This dangerous act would achieve little." You could instead write a fuller BurnSub providing for a new concept of an object being "on fire".

△△ Inform even allows you to Replace "hardware" functions like random or parent, which would normally be translated directly to machine opcodes. This is even more "at your own risk" than ordinary usages of Replace.

. . . . .

What are the implications of fire likely to be? One way to find out is to read through the world model (§24) and see how fire ought to affect each group of rules. Evidently we have just created a new possible internal state for an object, which means a new rule under ¶1, but it doesn't stop there:

1.4.4. Some objects are "flammable" and therefore in one of two mutually exclusive states, "on fire" and "not on fire".

2.4. If an object on fire is placed in a flammable container or on a flammable supporter, that too catches fire.

2.5. If a container or supporter is on fire, any flammable object within or on top of it catches fire.

4.3.3.1. Any object on fire provides light.

4.4.3. The player cannot touch any object on fire unless (say) wearing the asbestos gloves.

5.4.1. All flammable objects have a "lifespan", a length of time for which they can burn before being consumed. The each-turn daemon subtracts one from the lifespan of any object on fire, and removes it from play if the lifespan reaches zero.

One could go further than this: arguably, certain rooms should also be flammable, so that an object on fire which is dropped there would set the room ablaze; and the player should not survive long in a burning room; and we have not even provided a way to douse the flames, except by waiting for fires to burn themselves out. But the above rules will maintain a reasonable level of plausibility. ¶1.4.4 is provided by defining a new class of Flammable objects, which contains an each_turn routine implementing ¶5.4.1, and an on_fire attribute. The same each_turn can take care of ¶2.4 and ¶2.5, and can give the object light if it's currently on_fire, thus solving ¶4.3.3.1. But, while it would be easy to add simple rules like "you can't *take* an object which is on fire", ¶4.4.3 in its fullest form is more problematic, and means replacing the ObjectIsUntouchable routine. Giving any object on fire a before rule preventing the player from using any of the "touchy" actions on it would go some of the way, but wouldn't handle subtler cases, like a player not being allowed to reach for something through a burning hoop. Nor is this everything: burning objects will need to be talked about differently when alight, and this will call for using the powerful descriptive features in Chapter IV.

● **REFERENCES**

'Balances' implements the 'Enchanter' trilogy's magic system by methods like the above. ●Approximately seventy library extensions have been contributed by members of the Inform community and more are placed at `ftp.gmd.de` with each month that goes by. Often short and legible, they make good examples of Inform coding even if you don't want to use them. Many are cited in "references" paragraphs throughout the book: here are others which seem more appropriate here.   ●`"money.h"`, by Erik Hetzner, is a textbook case of a class-based extension to Inform providing a new aspect to the world model which doesn't much overlap with what's already there: notes and coinage.   ●Conversely, Marnie Parker's `"OutOfRch.h"` exemplifies a change that needs to permeate the existing world model to be effective: it defines which areas of a location are within reach from which other areas, so that for instance a player sitting on a chair might only be able to reach items on the adjacent table and not a window on the far wall.   ●In some graphical adventure games, interactivity sometimes cuts out at a significant event and an unchangeable movie animation is shown instead: this is sometimes called a "cut-scene". Such games sometimes allow the player to replay any movies seen so far, reviewing them for clues missed previously. `"movie.h"`, by L. Ross Raszewski, projects the textual version of movies like this, thus providing a framework for cut-scenes.   ●`"infotake.h"`, by Joe Merical, shifts the Inform model world back to the style of 'Zork': printing Zorkesque messages, providing a "diagnose" verb and so on.   ●Anson Turner's `"animalib"` retains the core algorithms of the Inform library (principally the parser and list-writer) but redesigns the superstructure of properties and attributes with the aim of a cleaner, more consistent world model. Although this alternative library is in its early stages of development, its code makes interesting reading. For instance, some child-objects represent items held inside their parents and others represent items on top of their parents. The standard Inform library distinguishes these cases by looking at the attributes of the parent-object – whether it is a `supporter` or a `container`. Contrariwise, `"animalib"` distinguishes them by looking at attributes of the child, so that the different children of a single parent can all be contained in different ways.

Chapter IV: Describing and Parsing

Language disguises thought... The tacit conventions on which
the understanding of everyday language depends are enormously
complicated.

— Ludwig Wittgenstein (1889–1951), *Tractatus*

§26 Describing objects and rooms

 Talking about the state of the world is much easier than listening
to the player's intentions for it. Despite this, the business of
description takes up a fair part of this chapter since the designer of a
really complex game will eventually need to know almost every rule
involved. (Whereas nobody would want to know everything about the parser.)
The simplest description of an object is its "short name". For instance,

```
print (a) brass_lamp;
```

may result in "an old brass lamp" being printed. There are four such forms of
print:

```
print (the) obj    Print the object with its definite article
print (The) obj    The same, but capitalised
print (a) obj      Print the object with indefinite article
print (name) obj   Print the object's short name alone
```

and these can be freely mixed into lists of things to print or print_ret, as for
example:

```
"The ogre declines to eat ", (the) noun, ".";
```

● **EXERCISE 62**
When referring to animate objects, you sometimes need to use pronouns such as
"him". Define new printing routines so that print "You throw the book at ",
(PronounAcc) obj, "!"; will insert the right accusative pronouns.

194

△△ There is also a special syntax print (object) for printing object names, but *do not use it without good reason*: it doesn't understand some of the features below and is not protected against crashing if you mistakenly try to print the name for an object that doesn't exist.

· · · · ·

Inform tries to work out the right indefinite article for any object automatically. In English-language games, it uses 'an' when the short name starts with a vowel and 'a' when it does not (unless the name is plural, when 'some' is used in either case). You can override this by setting article yourself, either to some text or a routine to print some. Here are some possibilities, arranged as "article / name":

"a / platinum bar", "an / orange balloon", "your / Aunt Jemima",
"some bundles of / reeds", "far too many / marbles",
"The / London Planetarium"

If the object is given the attribute proper then its name is treated as a proper noun taking no article, so the value of article is ignored. Objects representing named people usually have proper, and so might a book like "Whitaker's Almanac".

Definite articles are always "the", except for proper nouns. Thus

"the / platinum bar", "Benjamin Franklin", "Elbereth"

are all printed by print (the) ..., the latter two objects being proper.

A single object whose name is plural, such as "grapes" or "marble pillars", should be given the attribute pluralname. As a result the library might say, e.g., "You can't open those" instead of "You can't open that". As mentioned above, the indefinite article becomes "some", and the player can use the pronoun "them" to refer to the object, so for instance "take them" to pick up the grapes-object.

△ You can give animate objects the attributes male, female or neuter to help the parser understand pronouns properly. animate objects are assumed to be male if you set neither alternative.

△ There's usually no need to worry about definite and indefinite articles for room objects, as the standard Inform rules never print them.

· · · · ·

The short name of an object is normally the text given in double-quotes at the head of its definition. This is very inconvenient to change during play when, for example, "blue liquid" becomes "purple liquid" as a result of a chemical reaction. A more flexible way to specify an object's short name is with the short_name property. To print the name of such an object, Inform does the following:

(1) If the short_name is a string, it's printed and that's all.
(2) If it is a routine, then it is called. If it returns true, that's all.
(3) The text given in the header of the object definition is printed.

For example, the dye might be defined with:

```
short_name [;
    switch(self.colour) {
        1: print "blue ";
        2: print "purple ";
        3: print "horrid sludge"; rtrue;
    }
],
```

with "liquid" as the short name in its header. According to whether its colour property is 1, 2 or 3, the printed result is "blue liquid", "purple liquid" or "horrid sludge".

△   Alternatively, define the dye with short_name "blue liquid" and then simply execute dye.short_name = "purple liquid"; when the time comes.

● **EXERCISE 63**
Design a chessboard of sixty-four locations with a map corresponding to an eight-by-eight grid, so that White advances north towards Black, with pieces placed on the board according to a game position. Hint: using flexible routines for short_name, this can be done with just two objects, one representing all sixty-four squares, the other representing all thirty-two pieces.

· · · · · ·

For many objects the indefinite article and short name will most often be seen in inventory lists, such as:

```
>inventory
You are carrying:
  a leaf of mint
  a peculiar book
  your satchel (which is open)
    a green cube
```

Some objects, though, ought to have fuller entries in an inventory: a wine bottle should say how much wine is left, for instance. The invent property is designed for this. The simplest way to use invent is as a string. For instance, declaring a peculiar book with

```
invent "that harmless old book of Geoffrey's",
```

will make this the inventory line for the book. In the light of events, it could later be changed with a statement like:

```
book.invent = "that lethal old book of Geoffrey's";
```

△   Note that this string becomes the whole inventory entry: if the object were an open container, its contents wouldn't be listed, which might be unfortunate. In such circumstances it's better to write an invent routine, and that's also the way to append text like "(half-empty)".

△   Each line of an inventory is produced in two stages. *First,* the basic line:

(1a) The global variable inventory_stage is set to 1.
(1b) The invent routine is called (if there is one). If it returns true, stop here.
(1c) The object's indefinite article and short-name are printed.

Second, little informative messages like "(which is open)" are printed, and inventories are given for the contents of open containers:

(2a) The global variable inventory_stage is set to 2.
(2b) The invent routine is called (if there is one). If it returns true, stop here.
(2c) A message such as "(closed, empty and providing light)" is printed, as appropriate.
(2d) If it is an open container, or a supporter, or is transparent, then its contents are inventoried.

After each line is printed, linking text such as a new-line or a comma is printed, according to the current "list style".

For example, here is the invent routine used by the matchbook in 'Toyshop':

```
invent [ i;
    if (inventory_stage == 2) {
        i = self.number;
        if (i == 0) print " (empty)";
        if (i == 1) print " (1 match left)";
        if (i > 1)  print " (", i, " matches left)";
    }
],
```

● △△EXERCISE 64

Suppose you want to change the whole inventory line for an ornate box but you can't use an invent string, or return true from stage 1, because you still want stage 2d to happen properly (so that its contents will be listed). How can you achieve this?

. . . . .

The largest and most complicated messages the Inform library ever prints on its own initiative are room descriptions, printed when the Look action is carried out (for instance, when the statement <Look>; triggers a room description). What happens is: the room's short name is printed, usually emphasised in bold-face, then the description, followed by a list of the objects residing there which aren't concealed or scenery.

Chapter III mentioned many different properties – initial, when_on, when_off and so on – giving descriptions of what an object looks like when in the same room as the player: some apply to doors, others to switchable objects and so on. All of them can be routines to print text, instead of being strings to print. The precise rules are given below.

But the whole system can be bypassed using the describe property. If an object gives a describe routine then this takes priority over everything: if it returns true, the library assumes that the object has already been described, and prints nothing further. For example:

```
describe [;
    "^The platinum pyramid catches the light beautifully.";
],
```

Unlike an initial description, this is still seen even if the pyramid has moved, i.e., been held by the player at some stage.

△ Note the initial ^ (new-line) character. The library doesn't print a skipped line itself before calling describe because it doesn't know yet whether the routine will want to say anything. A describe routine which prints nothing and returns true makes an object invisible, as if it were concealed.

△△ Here is exactly how a room description is printed. Recall from §21 that location holds the player's location if there is light, and thedark if not, and see §21 for the definition of "visibility ceiling", which roughly means the outermost thing the player can see: normally the location, but possibly a closed opaque container which the player is inside. First the top line:

(1a) A new-line is printed. The short name of the visibility ceiling is printed, using emphasised type, which on most models of computer appears as bold face.
(1b) If the player is on a supporter, then " (on ⟨something⟩)" is printed; if inside something (other than the visibility ceiling), then " (in ⟨something⟩)".
(1c) " (as ⟨something⟩)" is printed if this was requested by the game's most recent call to ChangePlayer: for instance, " (as a werewolf)". (See §21 for details of ChangePlayer.)
(1d) A new-line is printed.

Now the long description. This step is sometimes skipped, depending on which "look mode" the player has chosen: in the normal mode, it is skipped if the player has just moved by a Go action into a location already visited; in "superbrief" mode it is always skipped, while in "verbose" mode it is never skipped.

(2a) Starting with the visibility ceiling and working down through "levels" of enterable objects containing the player, a long description is printed, as follows:

    (i) If the level is the current value of location, that is, the current room or else thedark, then: if location provides describe then the message location.describe() is sent. If not, then location.description() is sent. Every room is required to provide one or the other. (This is now redundant. In earlier Informs, description could only be a string, so describe was there in case a routine was needed.)

    (ii) If not, the level must be an enterable object E. If E provides it, the message E.inside_description() is sent.

(2b) After the description of each visibility level, the objects contained in that level are "listed" (see below).

The library has now finished, but your game gets a chance to add a postscript by means of an entry point routine:

(3) The entry point LookRoutine is called.

△△ Besides printing room descriptions, the Look action has side-effects: it can award the player some points, or mark a room with the attribute visited. For these rules in full, see §21.

△△ The visited attribute is only given to a room *after* its description has been printed for the first time. This is convenient for making the description different after the first time.

△△ When "listing objects" (as in 3a and 3b above) some objects are given a paragraph to themselves, while others are lumped together in a list at the end. The following objects are not mentioned at all: the player; what the player is in or on (if anything), because this has been taken care of in the short or long description already; and anything which has the attributes scenery or concealed. The remaining objects are looked through, eldest first, as follows:

(1) If the object has a describe routine, run it. If it returns true, stop here and don't mention the object at all.

(2) Work out the "description property" for the object:

    (a) For a container, this is when_open or when_closed;

    (b) Otherwise, for a switchable object this is when_on or when_off;

    (c) Otherwise, for a door this is when_open or when_closed;

    (d) Otherwise, it's initial.

(3) If *either* the object doesn't provide this property *or* the object has moved and the property isn't when_off or when_closed *then* the object will be listed at the end, not given a paragraph of its own.

(4) Otherwise a new-line is printed and the property is printed (if it's a string) or run (if it's a routine). If it is a routine, it had better print something, as otherwise there will be a spurious blank line in the room description.

△   Note that although a supporter which is scenery won't be mentioned, anything on top of it may well be. If this is undesirable, set these objects on top to be concealed.

△   Objects which have just been pushed into a new room are not listed in that room's description on the turn in question. This is not because of any rule about room descriptions, but because the pushed object is moved into the new room only after the room description is made. This means that when a wheelbarrow is pushed for a long distance, the player does not have to keep reading "You can see a wheelbarrow here." every move, as though that were a surprise.

△   You can use a library routine called Locale to perform object listing. See §A3 for details, but suffice to say here that the process above is equivalent to executing

```
if (Locale(location, "You can see", "You can also see"))
    print " here.^";
```

Locale is useful for describing areas of a room which are sub-divided off while remaining part of the same location, such as the stage of a theatre.

● △△EXERCISE 65
As mentioned above, the library implements "superbrief" and "verbose" modes for room description (one always omits long room descriptions, the other never does). How can verbose mode automatically print room descriptions every turn? (Some of the later Infocom games did this.)

● REFERENCES
'Balances' often uses short_name, especially for the white cubes (whose names change) and lottery tickets (whose numbers are chosen by the player). 'Adventureland' uses short_name in simpler ways: see the bear and the bottle, for instance.   ●The scroll class of 'Balances' uses invent.   ●See the ScottRoom class of 'Adventureland' for a radically different way to describe rooms (in pidgin English, like telegraphese, owing to an extreme shortage of memory to store text – Scott Adams was obliged to write for machines with under 16K of free memory).

§27   Listing and grouping objects

As some day it may happen that a victim must be found
I've got a little list – I've got a little list
Of society offenders who might well be underground,
And who never would be missed
Who never would be missed!

— W. S. Gilbert (1836–1911), *The Mikado*

Listing objects tidily in a grammatical sentence is more difficult than it seems, especially when taking plurals and groups of similar objects into account. Here, for instance, is a list of 23 items printed by a room description in the demonstration game 'List Property':

You can see a plastic fork, knife and spoon, three hats (a fez, a Panama and a sombrero), the letters X, Y, Z, P, Q and R from a Scrabble set, Punch magazine, a recent issue of the Spectator, a die and eight coins (four silver, one bronze and three gold) here.

Fortunately, the library's list-maker is available to the public by calling:

```
WriteListFrom(object, style);
```

where the list will start from the given object and go along its siblings. Thus, to list all the objects inside X, list from child(X). What the list looks like depends on a "style" made by adding up some of the following:

ALWAYS_BIT	Always recurse downwards
CONCEAL_BIT	Misses out concealed or scenery objects
DEFART_BIT	Uses the definite article in list
ENGLISH_BIT	English sentence style, with commas and 'and'
FULLINV_BIT	Gives full inventory entry for each object
INDENT_BIT	Indents each entry according to depth
ISARE_BIT	Prints " is " or " are " before list
NEWLINE_BIT	Prints new-line after each entry
NOARTICLE_BIT	Prints no articles, definite or indefinite
PARTINV_BIT	Only brief inventory information after entry
RECURSE_BIT	Recurses downwards with usual rules
TERSE_BIT	More terse English style
WORKFLAG_BIT	At top level (only), only lists objects which have the workflag attribute

Recursing downwards means that if an object is listed, then its children are also listed, and so on for their children. The "usual rules" of RECURSE_BIT are that children are only listed if the parent is transparent, or a supporter, or a container which is open – which is the definition of "see-through" used throughout the Inform library. "Full inventory information" means listing objects exactly as if in an inventory, according to the rigmarole described in §26. "Brief inventory information" means listing as if in a room description: that is, noting whether objects are open, closed, empty or providing light (except that light is only mentioned when in a room which is normally dark).

The best way to decide which bits to set is to experiment. For example, a 'tall' inventory is produced by:

```
WriteListFrom(child(player),
    FULLINV_BIT + INDENT_BIT + NEWLINE_BIT + RECURSE_BIT);
```

and a 'wide' one by:

```
WriteListFrom(child(player),
    FULLINV_BIT + ENGLISH_BIT + RECURSE_BIT);
```

which produce effects like:

```
>inventory tall
You are carrying:
  a bag (which is open)
    three gold coins
    two silver coins
    a bronze coin
  four featureless white cubes
  a magic burin
  a spell book
>inventory wide
```
You are carrying a bag (which is open), inside which are three gold coins, two silver coins and a bronze coin, four featureless white cubes, a magic burin and a spell book.

except that the "You are carrying" part is not done by the list-maker, and nor is the final full stop in the second example.

△ The workflag is an attribute which the library scribbles over from time to time as temporary storage, but you can use it for short periods with care. In this case it makes it possible to specify any reasonable list.

△△ WORKFLAG_BIT and CONCEAL_BIT specify conflicting rules. If they're both given, then what happens is: at the top level, but not below, everything with workflag is included; on lower levels, but not at the top, everything without concealed or scenery is included.

• **EXERCISE 66**

Write a DoubleInvSub action routine to produce an inventory like so:

> You are carrying four featureless white cubes, a magic burin and a spell book.
> In addition, you are wearing a purple cloak and a miner's helmet.

·   ·   ·   ·

Lists are shorter, neater and more elegantly phrased if similar objects are grouped together. For instance, keys, books and torch batteries are all grouped together in lists printed by the game 'Curses'. To achieve this, the objects belonging to such a group (all the keys for instance) provide a common value of the property list_together. If this value is a number between 1 and 1000, the library will unobtrusively group the objects with that value together so that they appear consecutively in any list. For instance 'Curses' includes the following definitions:

```
Constant KEY_GROUP = 1;
...
Object -> -> brass_key "small brass key"
  with ...
        list_together KEY_GROUP;
```

and similarly for the other keys. Alternatively, instead of being a small number the common value can be a string such as "foodstuffs". If so, then it must either be given in a class definition or else as a constant, like so:

```
Constant FOOD_GROUP = "foodstuffs";
```

(In particular, the actual text should only be written out in one place in the source code. Otherwise two or more different strings will be made, which just happen to have the same text as each other, and Inform will consider these to be different values of list_together.) Lists will then cite, for instance,

> three foodstuffs (a scarlet fish, some lembas wafer and an onion)

in running text, or

> three foodstuffs:
>   a scarlet fish
>   some lembas wafer
>   an onion

in indented lists. This only happens when two or more are gathered together. Finally, the common value of list_together can be a routine, such as:

```
list_together [;
    if (inventory_stage == 1) {
        print "heaps of food, notably";
        if (c_style & INDENT_BIT == 0) print " ";
            else print " --^";
    } else if (c_style & INDENT_BIT == 0)
        print " (which only reminds you how hungry you are)";
],
```

Typically this might be part of a class definition from which all the objects in question inherit. Any list_together routine will be called twice: once, with inventory_stage set to 1, as a preamble to the list of items, and once (with 2) to print any postscript required. It is allowed to change c_style, the current list style, without needing to restore the old value and may, by returning true from stage 1, signal the list-maker not to print a list at all. The above example would give a conversational sentence-like list as follows:

> heaps of food, notably a scarlet fish, some lembas wafer and an onion (which only reminds you how hungry you are)

and would also look suitable in sober tall-inventory-like columns:

> heaps of food, notably --
>   a scarlet fish
>   some lembas wafer
>   an onion

△   A list_together routine has the opportunity to look through the objects which are about to be listed together, by looking at some of the list-maker's variables. parser_one holds the first object in the group and parser_two holds the depth of recursion in the list, which might be needed to keep the indentation straight. Applying x = NextEntry(x,parser_two) will move x on from one object to the next in the group being listed.

△   The library variable listing_together is set to the first object of a group being listed, when a group is being listed, or to nothing the rest of the time. This is useful because an object's short_name routine might need to behave differently during a grouped listing to the rest of the time.

● △EXERCISE 67
Implement the Scrabble pieces from the example list above.

• △△EXERCISE 68
Implement the three denominations of coin.

• △△EXERCISE 69
Implement the I Ching in the form of six coins, three gold (goat, deer and chicken), three silver (robin, snake and bison) which can be thrown to reveal gold and silver trigrams.

• △△EXERCISE 70
Design a class called AlphaSorted, members of which are always listed in alphabetical order. Although this *could* be done with list_together, this exercise is here to draw the reader's attention to an ugly but sometimes useful alternative. The only actions likely to produce lists are Look, Search, Open and Inv: so react to these actions by rearranging the object tree into alphabetical order before the list-writer gets going.

• REFERENCES
A good example of WriteListFrom in action is the definition of CarryingClass from the example game 'The Thief', by Gareth Rees. This alters the examine description of a character by appending a list of what that person is carrying and wearing.   •Andreas Hoppler has written an alternative list-writing library extension called "Lister.h", which defines a class Lister so that designers can customise their own listing engines for different purposes in a single game.   •Anson Turner's example program "52.inf" models a deck of cards, and an extensive list_together sorts out hands of cards.

§28 How nouns are parsed

The Naming of Cats is a difficult matter,
It isn't just one of your holiday games;
You may think at first I'm as mad as a hatter
When I tell you, a cat must have THREE DIFFERENT NAMES.

— T. S. Eliot (1888–1965), *The Naming of Cats*

 Suppose we have a tomato defined with

```
    name 'fried' 'green' 'tomato',
```

but which is going to redden later and need to be referred to as "red tomato". The name property holds an array of dictionary words, so that

```
(tomato.#name)/2 == 3
tomato.&name-->0 == 'fried'
tomato.&name-->1 == 'green'
tomato.&name-->2 == 'tomato'
```

(Recall that X.#Y tells you the number of -> entries in such a property array, in this case six, so that X.#Y/2 tells you the number of --> entries, in this case three.) You are quite free to alter this array during play:

```
tomato.&name-->1 = 'red';
```

The down side of this technique is that it's clumsy, when all's said and done, and not so very flexible, because you can't change the length of the tomato.&name array during play. Of course you *could* define the tomato

```
with name 'fried' 'green' 'tomato' 'blank.' 'blank.' 'blank.'
          'blank.' 'blank.' 'blank.' 'blank.' 'blank.' 'blank.'
          'blank.' 'blank.' 'blank.' 'blank.' 'blank.' 'blank.',
```

or something similar, giving yourself another (say) fifteen "slots" to put new names into, but this is inelegant even by Inform standards. Instead, an object like the tomato can be given a parse_name routine, allowing complete flexibility for the designer to specify just what names it does and doesn't match. It is time to begin looking into the parser and how it works.

. . . . .

The Inform parser has two cardinal principles: firstly, it is designed to be as "open-access" as possible, because a parser cannot ever be general enough for every game without being highly modifiable. This means that there are many levels on which you can augment or override what it does. Secondly, it tries to be generous in what it accepts from the player, understanding the broadest possible range of commands and making no effort to be strict in rejecting ungrammatical requests. For instance, given a shallow pool nearby, "examine shallow" has an adjective without a noun: but it's clear what the player means. In general, all sensible commands should be accepted but it is not important whether or not nonsensical ones are rejected.

The first thing the parser does is to read in text from the keyboard and break it up into a stream of words: so the text "wizened man, eat the grey bread" becomes

wizened / man / , / eat / the / grey / bread

and these words are numbered from 1. At all times the parser keeps a "word number" marker to keep its place along this line, and this is held in the variable wn. The routine NextWord() returns the word at the current position of the marker, and moves it forward, i.e., adds 1 to wn. For instance, the parser may find itself at word 6 and trying to match "grey bread" as the name of an object. Calling NextWord() returns the value 'grey' and calling it again gives 'bread'.

Note that if the player had mistyped "grye bread", "grye" being a word which isn't mentioned anywhere in the program or created by the library, then NextWord() returns 0 for 'not in the dictionary'. Inform creates the dictionary of a story file by taking all the name words of objects, all the verbs and prepositions from grammar lines, and all the words used in constants like 'frog' written in the source code, and then sorting these into alphabetical order.

△   However, the story file's dictionary only has 9-character resolution. (And only 6 if Inform has been told to compile an early-model story file: see §45.) Thus the values of 'polyunsaturate' and 'polyunsaturated' are equal. Also, upper case and lower case letters are considered the same. Although dictionary words are permitted to contain numerals or typewriter symbols like -, : or /, these cost as much as two ordinary letters, so 'catch-22' looks the same as 'catch-2' or 'catch-207'.

△△ A dictionary word can even contain spaces, full stops or commas, but if so it is 'untypeable'. For instance, 'in,out' is an untypeable word because if the player were to type something like "go in,out", the text would be broken up into four words, go /

in / , / out. Thus 'in,out' may be in the story file's dictionary but it will never match against any word of what the player typed. Surprisingly, this can be useful, as it was at the end of §18.

. . . . .

Since the story file's dictionary isn't always perfect, there is sometimes no alternative but to actually look at the player's text one character at a time: for instance, to check that a 12-digit phone number has been typed correctly and in full.

The routine WordAddress(wordnum) returns a byte array of the characters in the word, and WordLength(wordnum) tells you how many characters there are in it. Given the above example text of "wizened man, eat the grey bread":

```
WordLength(4) == 3
WordAddress(4)->0 == 'e'
WordAddress(4)->1 == 'a'
WordAddress(4)->2 == 't'
```

because word number 4 is "eat". (Recall that the comma is considered as a word in its own right.)

△ The parser provides a basic routine for comparing a word against the texts '0', '1', '2', ..., '9999', '10000' or, in other words, against small numbers. This is the library routine TryNumber(wordnum), which tries to parse the word at wordnum as a number and returns that number, if it finds a match. Besides numbers written out in digits, it also recognises the texts 'one', 'two', 'three', ..., 'twenty'. If it fails to recognise the text as a number, it returns −1,000; if it finds a number greater than 10,000, it rounds down and returns 10,000.

. . . . .

To return to the naming of objects, the parser normally recognises any arrangement of some or all of the name words of an object as a noun which refers to it: and the more words, the better the match is considered to be. Thus "fried green tomato" is a better match than "fried tomato" or "green tomato" but all three are considered to match. On the other hand, so is "fried green", and "green green tomato green fried green" is considered a very good match indeed. The method is quick and good at understanding a wide variety of sensible texts, though poor at throwing out foolish ones. (An example of the parser's strategy of being generous rather than strict.) To be more precise, here is what happens when the parser wants to match some text against an object:

(1) If the object provides a `parse_name` routine, ask this routine to determine how good a match there is.

(2) If there was no `parse_name` routine, or if there was but it returned −1, ask the entry point routine `ParseNoun`, if the game has one, to make the decision.

(3) If there was no `ParseNoun` entry point, or if there was but it returned −1, look at the name of the object and match the longest possible sequence of words given in the name.

So: a `parse_name` routine, if provided, is expected to try to match as many words as possible starting from the current position of `wn` and reading them in one at a time using the `NextWord()` routine. Thus it must not stop just because the first word makes sense, but must keep reading and find out how many words in a row make sense. It should return:

0   if the text didn't make any sense at all,

k if k words in a row of the text seem to refer to the object, or

−1   to tell the parser it doesn't want to decide after all.

The word marker `wn` can be left anywhere afterwards. For example, here is the fried tomato with which this section started:

```
parse_name [ n colour;
    if (self.ripe) colour = 'red'; else colour = 'green';
    while (NextWord() == 'tomato' or 'fried' or colour) n++;
    return n;
],
```

The effect of this is that if `tomato.ripe` is true then the tomato responds to the names "tomato", "fried" and "red", and otherwise to "tomato", "fried" and "green".

As a second example of how `parse_name` can be useful, suppose you define:

```
Object -> "fly in amber"
  with name 'fly' 'in' 'amber';
```

If the player then types "put fly in amber in hole", the parser will be thrown, because it will think "fly in amber in" is all just naming the object and then it won't know what the word "hole" is doing at the end. However:

```
Object -> "fly in amber"
  with parse_name [;
            if (NextWord() ~= 'fly' or 'amber') return 0;
            if (NextWord() == 'in' && NextWord() == 'amber')
                return 3;
            return 1;
        ];
```

Now the word "in" is only recognised as part of the fly's name if it is followed by the word "amber", and the ambiguity goes away. ("amber in amber" is also recognised, but then it's not worth the bother of excluding.)

△   parse_name is also used to spot plurals: see §29.

● **EXERCISE 71**
Rewrite the tomato's parse_name to insist that the adjectives must come before the noun, which must be present.

● **EXERCISE 72**
Create a musician called Princess who, when kissed, is transformed into "/?%?/ (the artiste formerly known as Princess)".

● **EXERCISE 73**
Construct a drinks machine capable of serving cola, coffee or tea, using only one object for the buttons and one for the possible drinks.

● **EXERCISE 74**
Write a parse_name routine which looks through name in just the way that the parser would have done anyway if there hadn't been a parse_name in the first place.

● △**EXERCISE 75**
Some adventure game parsers split object names into 'adjectives' and 'nouns', so that only the pattern ⟨0 or more adjectives⟩ ⟨1 or more nouns⟩ is recognised. Implement this.

● **EXERCISE 76**
During debugging it sometimes helps to be able to refer to objects by their internal numbers, so that "put object 31 on object 5" would work. Implement this.

● △**EXERCISE 77**
How could the word "#" be made a wild-card, meaning "match any single object"?

● △△**EXERCISE 78**
And how could "*" be a wild-card for "match any collection of objects"? (Note: you need to have read §29 to answer this.)

● **REFERENCES**
Straightforward parse_name examples are the chess pieces object and the kittens class of 'Alice Through the Looking-Glass'. Lengthier ones are found in 'Balances', especially in the white cubes class.   ●Miron Schmidt's library extension "calyx_adjectives.h", based on earlier work by Andrew Clover, provides for objects to have "adnames" as well as "names": "adnames" are usually adjectives, and are regarded as being less good

matches for an object than "names". In this system "get string" would take either a string bag or a ball of string, but if both were present would take the ball of string, because "string" is in that case a noun rather than an adjective.

§29 Plural names for duplicated objects

A notorious challenge for adventure game parsers is to handle a collection of, say, ten gold coins, allowing the player to use them independently of each other, while gathering them together into groups in descriptions and inventories. Two problems must be overcome: firstly, the game has to be able to talk to the player in plurals, and secondly vice versa. First, then, game to player:

```
Class GoldCoin
  with name 'gold' 'coin',
       short_name "gold coin",
       plural "gold coins";
```

(and then similar silver and bronze coin classes)

```
Object bag "bag"
  with name 'bag',
  has  container open openable;
GoldCoin ->;
GoldCoin ->;
GoldCoin ->;
SilverCoin ->;
SilverCoin ->;
BronzeCoin ->;
```

Now we have a bag of six coins. The player looking inside the bag will get

```
>look inside bag
```
In the bag are three gold coins, two silver coins and a bronze coin.

How does the library know that the three gold coins are the same as each other, but the others different? It doesn't look at the classes but the names. It will only group together things which:

(a) have a plural set, and
(b) are "indistinguishable" from each other.

"Indistinguishable" means they have the same name words as each other, possibly in a different order, so that nothing the player can type will separate the two.

△   Actually, it's a little more subtle than this. What it groups together depends slightly on the context of the list being written. When it's writing a list which prints out details of which objects are providing light, for instance (as an inventory does), it won't group together two objects if one is lit but the other isn't. Similarly for objects with visible possessions or which can be worn.

△△ This ramifies further when the objects have a `parse_name` routine supplied. If they have different `parse_name` routines, the library decides that they are distinguishable. But if they have the same `parse_name` routine, for instance by inheriting it from a class definition, then the library has no alternative but to ask them. What happens is that:

(1) A variable called `parser_action` is set to the special value `##TheSame`, a value it never has at any other time;
(2) Two variables, called `parser_one` and `parser_two` are set to the two objects in question;
(3) Their `parse_name` routine is called. If it returns:
-1 the objects are declared "indistinguishable";
-2 they are declared different.
(4) Otherwise, the usual rules apply and the library looks at the ordinary name fields of the objects.

△△ You may even want to provide a `parse_name` routine for objects which otherwise don't need one, just to speed up the process of the library telling if two objects are distinguishable – if there were 30 gold coins in one place the parser would be doing a lot of work comparing names, but you can make the decision much faster.

● △△EXERCISE 79
Perhaps the neatest trick of parsing in any Infocom game occurs in 'Spellbreaker', which has a set of white cubes which are indistinguishable until the player writes words onto them with a magic burin (a medieval kind of pen), after which it's possible to tell them apart. Imitate this in Inform.

·   ·   ·   ·   ·

Secondly, the player talking to the computer. Suppose a game involves collecting a number of similar items, such as a set of nine crowns in different colours. Then you'd want the parser to recognise things like:

```
>drop all of the crowns except green
>drop the three other crowns
```

Putting the word 'crowns' in the name lists of the crown objects is not quite right, because the parser will still think that "crowns" might refer to a single specific item. Instead, put in the word 'crowns//p'. The suffix //p marks out the dictionary word "crowns" as one that can refer to more than one game object at once. (So that you shouldn't set this for the word "grapes" if a bunch of grapes is a single game object; you should give that object the pluralname attribute instead, as in §26 back at the start of this chapter.) For example the GoldCoin class would read:

```
Class GoldCoin
  with name 'gold' 'coin' 'coins//p',
       short_name "gold coin",
       plural "gold coins";
```

Now when the player types "take coins", the parser interprets this as "take all the coins within reach".

△△ The only snag is that now the word 'coins' is marked as //p everywhere in the game, in all circumstances. Here is a more complicated way to achieve the same result, but strictly in context of these objects alone. We need to make the parse_name routine tell the parser that yes, there was a match, but that it was a plural. The way to do this is to set parser_action to ##PluralFound, another special value. So, for example:

```
Class Crown
  with parse_name [ i j;
       for (::) {
           j = NextWord();
           if (j == 'crown' or self.name) i++;
           else {
               if (j == 'crowns') {
                   parser_action = ##PluralFound; i++;
               }
               else return i;
           }
       }
   ];
```

This code assumes that the crown objects have just one name each, their colours.

● **EXERCISE 80**
Write a 'cherub' class so that if the player tries to call them "cherubs", a message like "I'll let this go once, but the plural of cherub is cherubim" appears.

● **REFERENCES**
See the coinage of 'Balances'.

§30 How verbs are parsed

> "...I can see that the grammar gets tucked into the tales and poetry
> as one gives pills in jelly."
>
> — Louisa May Alcott (1832–1888), *Little Women*

 Here is how the parser reads in a whole command. Given a stream of text like

saint / peter / , / take / the / keys / from / paul

it first breaks it into words, as shown, and then calls the entry point routine
BeforeParsing (which you can provide, if you want to, in order to meddle
with the text stream before parsing gets underway). The parser then works
out who is being addressed, if anyone, by looking for a comma, and trying out
the text up to there as a noun matching an animate or talkable object: in
this case St Peter. This person is called the "actor", since he or she is going
to perform the action, and is most often the player (thus, typing "myself, go
north" is equivalent to typing "go north"). The next word, in this case 'take',
is the "verb word". An Inform verb usually has several English verb words
attached, which are called synonyms of each other: for instance, the library is
set up with

$$\text{"take"} = \text{"carry"} = \text{"hold"}$$

all referring to the same Inform verb.

△   The parser sets up variables actor and verb_word while working. (In the example
above, their values would be the St Peter object and 'take', respectively.)

△   This brief discussion is simplified in two ways. Firstly, it leaves out directions,
because Inform considers that the name of a direction-object implies "go": thus
"north" means "go north". Secondly, it misses out the grammar property described in
§18, which can cause different actors to recognise different grammars.

● △EXERCISE 81
Use BeforeParsing to implement a lamp which, when rubbed, produces a genie who
casts a spell to make the player confuse the words "white" and "black".

·   ·   ·   ·   ·

This section is about verbs, which are defined with "grammar", meaning usages of the directives Verb and Extend. The library contains a substantial amount of grammar as it is, and this forms (most of) the library file "Grammar.h". Grammar defined in your own code can either build on this or selectively knock it down, but either way it should be made *after* the inclusion of "Grammar.h".

For instance, making a new synonym for an existing verb is easy:

```
Verb 'steal' 'acquire' 'grab' = 'take';
```

Now "steal", "acquire" and "grab" are synonyms for "take".

△   One can also prise synonyms apart, as will appear later.

.   .   .   .   .

To return to the text above, the parser has now recognised the English word "take" as one of those which can refer to a particular Inform verb. It has reached word 5 and still has "the keys from paul" left to understand.

Every Inform verb has a "grammar" which consists of a list of one or more "grammar lines", each of them a pattern which the rest of the text might match. The parser tries the first, then the second and so on, and accepts the earliest one that matches, without ever considering later ones.

A line is a row of "tokens". Typical tokens might mean 'the name of a nearby object', 'the word 'from'' or 'somebody's name'. To match a line, the parser must match against each token in sequence. Continuing the example, the parser accepts the line of three tokens

⟨one or more nouns⟩ ⟨the word from⟩ ⟨a noun⟩

as matching "the keys from paul".

Every grammar line has the name of an action attached, and in this case it is Remove: so the parser has ground up the original text into just four quantities, ending up with

```
actor = StPeter   action = Remove   noun = gold_keys   second = StPaul
```

The parser's job is now complete, and the rest of the Inform library can get on with processing the action or, as in this case, an order being addressed to somebody other than the player.

△   The action for the line currently being worked through is stored in the variable action_to_be; or, at earlier stages when the verb hasn't been deciphered yet, it holds the value NULL.

. . . . .

The Verb directive creates Inform verbs, giving them some English verb words and a grammar. The library's "Grammar.h" file consists almost exclusively of Verb directives: here is an example simplified from one of them.

```
Verb 'take' 'get' 'carry' 'hold'
    * 'out'                    -> Exit
    * multi                    -> Take
    * multiinside 'from' noun -> Remove
    * 'in' noun                -> Enter
    * multiinside 'off' noun  -> Remove
    * 'off' held               -> Disrobe
    * 'inventory'              -> Inv;
```

(You can look at the grammar being used in a game with the debugging verb "showverb": see §7.) Each line of grammar begins with a *, gives a list of tokens as far as -> and then the action which the line produces. The first line can only be matched by something like "get out", the second might be matched by

"take the banana"
"get all the fruit except the apple"

and so on. A full list of tokens will be given later: briefly, ['out'] means the literal word "out", [multi] means one or more objects nearby, [noun] means just one and [multiinside] means one or more objects inside the second noun. In this book, grammar tokens are written in the style [noun] to prevent confusion (as there is also a variable called noun).

△   Some verbs are marked as meta – these are the verbs leading to Group 1 actions, those which are not really part of the game's world: for example, "save", "score" and "quit". For example:

```
Verb meta 'score' * -> Score;
```

and any debugging verbs you create would probably work better this way, since meta-verbs are protected from interference by the game and take up no game time.

. . . . .

After the -> in each line is the name of an action. Giving a name in this way is what creates an action, and if you give the name of one which doesn't already exist then you must also write a routine to execute the action, even if it's one which doesn't do very much. The name of the routine is always the name of the action with Sub appended. For instance:

```
[ XyzzySub; "Nothing happens."; ];
Verb 'xyzzy' * -> Xyzzy;
```

will make a new magic-word verb "xyzzy", which always says "Nothing happens" – always, that is, unless some before rule gets there first, as it might do in certain magic places. Xyzzy is now an action just as good as all the standard ones: ##Xyzzy gives its action number, and you can write before rules for it in Xyzzy: fields just as you would for, say, Take.

△   Finally, the line can end with the word reverse. This is only useful if there are objects or numbers in the line which occur in the wrong order. An example from the library's grammar:

```
Verb 'show' 'present' 'display'
    * creature held       -> Show reverse
    * held 'to' creature -> Show;
```

The point is that the Show action expects the first parameter to be an item, and the second to be a person. When the text "show him the shield" is typed in, the parser must reverse the two parameters "him" and "the shield" before causing a Show action. On the other hand, in "show the shield to him" the parameters are in the right order already.

·   ·   ·   ·   ·

The library defines grammars for the 100 or so English verbs most often used by adventure games. However, in practice you quite often need to alter these, usually to add extra lines of grammar but sometimes to remove existing ones. For instance, suppose you would like "drop charges" to be a command in a detection game (or a naval warfare game). This means adding a new grammar line to the "drop" verb. The Extend directive is provided for exactly this purpose:

```
Extend 'drop' * 'charges' -> DropCharges;
```

Normally, extra lines of grammar are added at the bottom of those already there, so that this will be the very last grammar line tested by the parser. This may not be what you want. For instance, "take" has a grammar line reading

```
    * multi -> Take
```

quite early on. So if you want to add a grammar line diverting "take ⟨food⟩" to a different action, like so:

```
* edible -> Eat
```

(edible being a token matching anything which has the attribute edible) then it's no good adding this at the bottom of the Take grammar, because the earlier line will always be matched first. What you need is for the new line to go in at the top, not the bottom:

```
Extend 'take' first
    * edible -> Eat;
```

You might even want to throw away the old grammar completely, not just add a line or two. For this, use

```
Extend 'press' replace
    * 'charges' -> PressCharges;
```

and now the verb "press" has no other sense but this, and can't be used in the sense of pressing down on objects any more, because those grammar lines are gone. To sum up, Extend can optionally take one of three keywords:

replace	replace the old grammar with this one;
first	insert the new grammar at the top;
last	insert the new grammar at the bottom;

with last being the default.

△ In library grammar, some verbs have many synonyms: for instance,

```
'attack' 'break' 'smash' 'hit' 'fight' 'wreck' 'crack'
'destroy' 'murder' 'kill' 'torture' 'punch' 'thump'
```

are all treated as identical. But you might want to distinguish between murder and lesser crimes. For this, try

```
Extend only 'murder' 'kill' replace
    * animate -> Murder;
```

The keyword only tells Inform to extract the two verbs "murder" and "kill". These then become a new verb which is initially an identical copy of the old one, but then replace tells Inform to throw that away in favour of an entirely new grammar. Similarly,

```
Extend only 'run' * 'program' -> Compute;
```

makes "run" behave exactly like "go" and "walk", as these three words are ordinarily synonymous to the library, except that it also recognises "program", so that "run program" activates a computer but "walk program" doesn't. Other good pairs to separate might be "cross" and "enter", "drop" and "throw", "give" and "feed", "swim" and "dive", "kiss" and "hug", "cut" and "prune". Bear in mind that once a pair has been split apart like this, any subsequent change to one will not also change the other.

△△ Occasionally verb definition commands are not enough. For example, in the original 'Advent', the player could type the name of an adjacent place which had previously been visited, and be taken there. (This feature isn't included in the Inform example version of the game in order to keep the source code as simple as possible.) There are several laborious ways to code this, but here's a concise way. The library calls the UnknownVerb entry point routine (if you provide one) when the parser can't even get past the first word. This has two options: it can return false, in which case the parser just goes on to complain as it would have done anyway. Otherwise, it can return a verb word which is substituted for what the player actually typed. Here is one way the 'Advent' room-naming might work. Suppose that every room has been given a property called go_verb listing the words which refer to it, so for instance the well house might be defined along these lines:

```
AboveGround Inside_Building "Inside Building"
   with description
            "You are inside a building, a well house for a
            large spring.",
         go_verb 'well' 'house' 'inside' 'building',
   ...
```

The UnknownVerb routine then looks through the possible compass directions for already-visited rooms, checking against words stored in this new property:

```
Global go_verb_direction;
[ UnknownVerb word room direction adjacent;
  room = real_location;
  objectloop (direction in compass) {
      adjacent = room.(direction.door_dir);
      if (adjacent ofclass Object && adjacent has visited
          && adjacent provides go_verb
          && WordInProperty(word, adjacent, go_verb)) {
              go_verb_direction = direction;
              return 'go.verb';
      }
  }
  if (room provides go_verb
      && WordInProperty(word, room, go_verb)) {
      go_verb_direction = "You're already there!";
      return 'go.verb';
  }
  objectloop (room provides go_verb && room has visited
              && WordInProperty(word, room, go_verb)) {
      go_verb_direction = "You can't get there from here!";
      return 'go.verb';
  }
```

```
objectloop (room provides go_verb && room hasnt visited
            && WordInProperty(word, room, go_verb)) {
    go_verb_direction = "But you don't know the way there!";
    return 'go.verb';
}
rfalse;
];
```

When successful, this routine stores either a compass direction (an object belonging to the compass) in the variable go_verb_direction, or else a string to print. (Note that an UnknownVerb routine shouldn't print anything itself, as this might be inappropriate in view of subsequent parsing, or if the actor isn't the player.) The routine then tells the parser to treat the verb as if it were 'go.verb', and as this doesn't exist yet, we must define it:

```
[ Go_VerbSub;
  if (go_verb_direction ofclass String)
      print_ret (string) go_verb_direction;
  <<Go go_verb_direction>>;
];
Verb 'go.verb' * -> Go_Verb;
```

● △△EXERCISE 82

A minor deficiency with the above system is that the parser may print out strange responses like "I only understood you as far as wanting to go.verb." if the player types something odd like "bedquilt the nugget". How can we ensure that the parser will always say something like "I only understood you as far as wanting to go to Bedquilt."?

● REFERENCES

'Advent' makes a string of simple Verb definitions; 'Alice Through the Looking-Glass' uses Extend a little.   ●'Balances' has a large extra grammar and also uses the UnknownVerb and PrintVerb entry points.   ●Irene Callaci's "AskTellOrder.h" library extension file makes an elegant use of BeforeParsing to convert commands in the form "ask mr darcy to dance" or "tell jack to go north" to Inform's preferred form "mr darcy, dance" and "jack, go north".

§31　Tokens of grammar

The complete list of grammar tokens is given in the table below. These tokens are all described in this section except for scope = ⟨Routine⟩ , which is postponed to the next.

`'⟨word⟩'`	that literal word only
`noun`	any object in scope
`held`	object held by the actor
`multi`	one or more objects in scope
`multiheld`	one or more held objects
`multiexcept`	one or more in scope, except the other object
`multiinside`	one or more in scope, inside the other object
`⟨attribute⟩`	any object in scope which has the attribute
`creature`	an object in scope which is `animate`
`noun = ⟨Routine⟩`	any object in scope passing the given test
`scope = ⟨Routine⟩`	an object in this definition of scope
`number`	a number only
`⟨Routine⟩`	any text accepted by the given routine
`topic`	any text at all

To recap, the parser goes through a line of grammar tokens trying to match each against some text from the player's input. Each token that matches must produce one of the following five results:

(a) a single object;
(b) a "multiple object", that is, a set of objects;
(c) a number;
(d) a "consultation topic", that is, a collection of words left unparsed to be looked through later;
(e) no information at all.

Ordinarily, a single line, though it may contain many tokens, can produce at most two substantial results ((a) to (d)), at most one of which can be multiple (b). (See the exercises below if this is a problem.) For instance, suppose the text "green apple on the table" is parsed against the grammar line:

```
* multi 'on' noun -> Insert
```

The |multi| token matches "green apple" (result: a single object, since although |multi| can match a multiple object, it doesn't have to), |'on'| matches "on" (result: nothing) and the second |noun| token matches "the table" (result: a single object again). There are two substantial results, both objects, so the action that comes out is <Insert apple table>. If the text had been "all the fruit on the table", the |multi| token might have resulted in a list: perhaps of an apple, an orange and a pear. The parser would then have generated and run through three actions in turn: <Insert apple table>, then <Insert orange table> and finally <Insert pear table>, printing out the name of each item and a colon before running the action:

>put all the fruit on the table
Cox's pippin: Done.
orange: Done.
Conference pear: Done.

The library's routine InsertSub, which actually handles the action, only deals with single objects at a time, and in each case it printed "Done."

. . . . .

|'⟨word⟩'| This matches only the literal word given, sometimes called a preposition because it usually is one, and produces no resulting information. (There can therefore be as many or as few of them on a grammar line as desired.) It often happens that several prepositions really mean the same thing for a given verb: for instance "in", "into" and "inside" are often synonymous. As a convenient shorthand, then, you can write a series of prepositions (only) with slashes / in between, to mean "one of these words". For example:

```
* noun 'in'/'into'/'inside' noun -> Insert
```

|noun| Matches any single object "in scope", a term defined in the next section and which roughly means "visible to the player at the moment".

|held| Matches any single object which is an immediate possession of the actor. (Thus, if a key is inside a box being carried by the actor, the box might match but the key cannot.) This is convenient for two reasons. Firstly,

many actions, such as Eat or Wear, only sensibly apply to things being held. Secondly, suppose we have grammar

```
Verb 'eat' * held -> Eat;
```

and the player types "eat the banana" while the banana is, say, in plain view on a shelf. It would be petty of the game to refuse on the grounds that the banana is not being held. So the parser will generate a Take action for the banana and then, if the Take action succeeds, an Eat action. Notice that the parser does not just pick up the object, but issues an action in the proper way – so if the banana had rules making it too slippery to pick up, it won't be picked up. This is called "implicit taking", and happens only for the player, not for other actors.

multi   Matches one or more objects in scope. The multi- tokens indicate that a list of one or more objects can go here. The parser works out all the things the player has asked for, sorting out plural nouns and words like "except" in the process. For instance, "all the apples" and "the duck and the drake" could match a multi token but not a noun token.

multiexcept   Matches one or more objects in scope, except that it does not match the other single object parsed in the same grammar line. This is provided to make commands like "put everything in the rucksack" come out right: the "everything" is matched by all of the player's possessions except the rucksack, which stops the parser from generating an action to put the rucksack inside itself.

multiinside   Similarly, this matches anything inside the other single object parsed on the same grammar line, which is good for parsing commands like "remove everything from the cupboard".

⟨attribute⟩   Matches any object in scope which has the given attribute. This is useful for sorting out actions according to context, and perhaps the ultimate example might be an old-fashioned "use" verb:

```
Verb 'use' 'employ' 'utilise'
     * edible    -> Eat
     * clothing  -> Wear
     ...
     * enterable -> Enter;
```

creature   Matches any object in scope which behaves as if living. This normally means having animate: but, as an exceptional rule, if the action on the grammar line is Ask, Answer, Tell or AskFor then having talkable is also acceptable.

noun = ⟨Routine⟩   "Any single object in scope satisfying some condition". When determining whether an object passes this test, the parser sets the variable noun to the object in question and calls the routine. If it returns true, the parser accepts the object, and otherwise it rejects it. For example, the following should only apply to animals kept in a cage:

```
[ CagedCreature;
   if (noun in wicker_cage) rtrue; rfalse;
];
Verb 'free' 'release'
    * noun=CagedCreature -> FreeAnimal;
```

So that only nouns which pass the CagedCreature test are allowed. The CagedCreature routine can appear anywhere in the source code, though it's tidier to keep it nearby.

scope = ⟨Routine⟩   An even more powerful token, which means "an object in scope" where scope is redefined specially. You can also choose whether or not it can accept a multiple object. See §32.

number   Matches any decimal number from 0 upwards (though it rounds off large numbers to 10,000), and also matches the numbers "one" to "twenty" written in English. For example:

```
Verb 'type' * number -> TypeNum;
```

causes actions like <Typenum 504> when the player types "type 504". Note that noun is set to 504, not to an object. (While inp1 is set to 1, indicating that this "first input" is intended as a number: if the noun had been the object which happened to have number 504, then inp1 would have been set to this object, the same as noun.) If you need more exact number parsing, without rounding off, and including negative numbers, see the exercise below.

• **EXERCISE 83**

Some games, such as David M. Baggett's game 'The Legend Lives!' produce footnotes every now and then. Arrange matters so that these are numbered [1], [2] and so on in order of appearance, to be read by the player when "footnote 1" is typed.

△   The entry point ParseNumber allows you to provide your own number-parsing routine, which opens up many sneaky possibilities – Roman numerals, coordinates like "J4", very long telephone numbers and so on. This takes the form

```
[ ParseNumber buffer length;
    ...returning false if no match is made, or the number otherwise...
];
```

and examines the supposed 'number' held at the byte address buffer, a row of characters of the given length. If you provide a ParseNumber routine but return false from it, then the parser falls back on its usual number-parsing mechanism to see if that does any better.

△△ Note that ParseNumber can't return 0 to mean the number zero, because 0 is the same as false. Probably "zero" won't be needed too often, but if it is you can always return some value like 1000 and code the verb in question to understand this as 0. (Sorry: this was a poor design decision made too long ago to change now.)

topic   This token matches as much text as possible, regardless of what it says, producing no result. As much text as possible means "until the end of the typing, or, if the next token is a preposition, until that preposition is reached". The only way this can fail is if it finds no text at all. Otherwise, the variable consult_from is set to the number of the first word of the matched text and consult_words to the number of words. See §16 and §18 for examples of topics being used.

⟨Routine⟩   The most flexible token is simply the name of a "general parsing routine". As the name suggests, it is a routine to do some parsing which can have any outcome you choose, and many of the interesting things you can do with the parser involve writing one. A general parsing routine looks at the word stream using NextWord and wn (see §28) to make its decisions, and should return one of the following. Note that the values beginning GPR_ are constants defined by the library.

GPR_FAIL	if there is no match;
GPR_MULTIPLE	if the result is a multiple object;
GPR_NUMBER	if the result is a number;
GPR_PREPOSITION	if there is a match but no result;

| GPR_REPARSE | to reparse the whole command from scratch; or |
| O | if the result is a single object O. |

On an unsuccessful match, returning GPR_FAIL, it doesn't matter what the final value of wn is. On a successful match it should be left pointing to the next thing *after* what the routine understood. Since NextWord moves wn on by one each time it is called, this happens automatically unless the routine has read too far. For example:

```
[ OnAtorIn;
  if (NextWord() == 'on' or 'at' or 'in') return GPR_PREPOSITION;
  return GPR_FAIL;
];
```

duplicates the effect of ⌐'on'/'at'/'in'⌐, that is, it makes a token which accepts any of the words "on", "at" or "in" as prepositions. Similarly,

```
[ Anything;
  while (NextWordStopped() ~= -1) ; return GPR_PREPOSITION;
];
```

accepts the entire rest of the line (even an empty text, if there are no more words on the line), ignoring it. NextWordStopped is a form of NextWord which returns the special value −1 once the original word stream has run out.

If you return GPR_NUMBER, the number which you want to be the result should be put into the library's variable parsed_number.

If you return GPR_MULTIPLE, place your chosen objects in the table multiple_object: that is, place the number of objects in multiple_object-->0 and the objects themselves in -->1, ...

The value GPR_REPARSE should only be returned if you have actually altered the text you were supposed to be parsing. This is a feature used internally by the parser when it asks "Which do you mean . . .?" questions, and you can use it too, but be wary of loops in which the parser eternally changes and reparses the same text.

. . . . . .

△   To parse a token, the parser uses a routine called ParseToken. This behaves almost exactly like a general parsing routine, and returns the same range of values. For instance,

```
ParseToken(ELEMENTARY_TT, NUMBER_TOKEN)
```

parses exactly as $\boxed{\text{number}}$ does: similarly for NOUN_TOKEN, HELD_TOKEN, MULTI_TOKEN, MULTIHELD_TOKEN, MULTIEXCEPT_TOKEN, MULTIINSIDE_TOKEN and CREATURE_TOKEN. The call

```
ParseToken(SCOPE_TT, MyRoutine)
```

does what $\boxed{\text{scope=MyRoutine}}$ does. In fact ParseToken can parse any kind of token, but these are the only cases which are both useful enough to mention and safe enough to use. It means you can conveniently write a token which matches, say, *either* the word "kit" *or* any named set of items in scope:

```
[ KitOrStuff; if (NextWord() == 'kit') return GPR_PREPOSITION;
  wn--; return ParseToken(ELEMENTARY_TT, MULTI_TOKEN);
];
```

· · · · ·

● **EXERCISE 84**
Write a token to detect small numbers in French, "un" to "cinq".

● **EXERCISE 85**
Write a token called Team, which matches only against the word "team" and results in a multiple object containing each member of a team of adventurers in a game.

● △**EXERCISE 86**
Write a token to detect non-negative floating-point numbers like "21", "5.4623", "two point oh eight" or "0.01", rounding off to two decimal places.

● △**EXERCISE 87**
Write a token to match a phone number, of any length from 1 to 30 digits, possibly broken up with spaces or hyphens (such as "01245 666 737" or "123-4567").

● △△**EXERCISE 88**
(Adapted from code in "timewait.h": see the references below.) Write a token to match any description of a time of day, such as "quarter past five", "12:13 pm", "14:03", "six fifteen" or "seven o'clock".

● △**EXERCISE 89**
Code a spaceship control panel with five sliding controls, each set to a numerical value, so that the game looks like:

>look

Machine Room

There is a control panel here, with five slides, each of which can be set to a numerical value.

>push slide one to 5

You set slide one to the value 5.

>examine the first slide

Slide one currently stands at 5.

>set four to six

You set slide four to the value 6.

● △EXERCISE 90

Write a general parsing routine accepting any amount of text, including spaces, full stops and commas, between double-quotes as a single token.

● △EXERCISE 91

On the face of it, the parser only allows two parameters to an action, noun and second. Write a general parsing routine to accept a third. (This is easier than it looks: see the specification of the NounDomain library routine in §A3.)

● EXERCISE 92

Write a token to match any legal Inform decimal, binary or hexadecimal constant (such as -321, $4a7 or $$1011001), producing the correct numerical value in all cases, while not matching any number which overflows or underflows the legal Inform range of $-32,768$ to 32,767.

● EXERCISE 93

Add the ability to match the names of the built-in Inform constants true, false, nothing and NULL.

● EXERCISE 94

Now add the ability to match character constants like '7', producing the correct character value (in this case 55, the ZSCII value for the character '7').

● △△EXERCISE 95

Next add the ability to match the names of attributes, such as edible, or negated attributes with a tilde in front, such as ~edible. An ordinary attribute should parse to its number, a negated one should parse to its number plus 100. (Hint: the library has a printing rule called DebugAttribute which prints the name of an attribute.)

● △△EXERCISE 96

And now add the names of properties.

● **REFERENCES**

Once upon a time, Andrew Clover wrote a neat library extension called `"timewait.h"` for parsing times of day, and allowing commands such as "wait until quarter to three". L. Ross Raszewski, Nicholas Daley and Kevin Forchione each tinkered with and modernised this, so that there are now also `"waittime.h"` and `"timesys.h"`. Each has its merits.

§32 Scope and what you can see

He cannot see beyond his own nose. Even the fingers he out-stretches from it to the world are (as I shall suggest) often invisible to him.

— Max Beerbohm (1872–1956), of George Bernard Shaw

 Time to say what "in scope" means. This definition is one of the most important rules of play, because it decides what the player is allowed to refer to. You can investigate this experimentally by compiling any game with the debugging suite of verbs included (see §7) and typing "scope" in interesting places. "In scope" roughly means "the compass directions, what you're carrying and what you can see". It exactly means this:

(1) the compass directions;
(2) the player's immediate possessions;
(3) if there is light, then the contents of the player's visibility ceiling (see §21 for definition, but roughly speaking the outermost object containing the player which remains visible, which is usually the player's location);
(4) if there is darkness, then the contents of the library's object thedark (by default there are no such contents, but some designers have been known to move objects into thedark: see 'Ruins');
(5) if the player is inside a container, then that container;
(6) if O is in scope and is see-through (see §21), then the contents of O;
(7) if O is in scope, then any object which it "adds to scope" (see below).

with the proviso that the InScope entry point (see below) can add to or replace these rules, if you write one.

It's significant that rule (3) doesn't just say "whatever is in the current location". For instance, if the player is in a closed cupboard in the Stores Room, then rule (3) means that the contents of the cupboard are in scope, but other items in the Stores Room are not.

Even in darkness the player's possessions are in scope, so the player can still turn on a lamp being carried. On the other hand, a player who puts the lamp on the ground and turns it off then loses the ability to turn it back on again, because it is out of scope. This can be changed; see below.

△ Compass directions make sense as things as well as directions, and they respond to names like "the south wall" and "the floor" as well as "south" and "down".

△   The concealed attribute only hides objects from room descriptions, and doesn't remove them from scope. If you want things to be unreferrable-to, put them somewhere else!

△   The small print: 1. For "player", read "actor". Thus "dwarf, drop sword" will be accepted if the dwarf can see the sword even if the player can't. 2. Scope varies depending on the token being parsed: for the `multi-` tokens, compass directions are not in scope; for `multiexcept` the other object isn't in scope; for `multiinside` only the contents of the other object are in scope.

· · · · ·

Two library routines enable you to see what's in scope and what isn't. The first, TestScope(obj, actor), simply returns true or false according to whether or not obj is in scope. The second is LoopOverScope(routine, actor) and calls the given routine for each object in scope. In each case the actor given is optional, and if it's omitted, scope is worked out for the player as usual.

● **EXERCISE 97**
Implement the debugging suite's "scope" verb, which lists all the objects currently in scope.

● **EXERCISE 98**
Write a "megalook" verb, which looks around and examines everything in scope except the walls, floor and ceiling.

· · · · ·

Formally, scope determines what you can talk about, which usually means what you can see or hear. But what can you touch? Suppose a locked chest is inside a sealed glass cabinet. The Inform parser will allow the command "unlock chest with key" and generate the appropriate action, <Unlock chest key>, because the chest is in scope, so the command at least makes sense.

But it's impossible to carry out, because the player can't reach through the solid glass. So the library's routine for handling the Unlock action needs to enforce this. The library does this using a stricter rule called "touchability". The rule is that you can touch anything in scope unless there's a closed container between you and it. This applies either if you're in the container, or if it is.

Some purely visual actions, such as Examine or LookUnder, don't require touchability. But most actions are tactile, and so are many actions created by designers. If you want to make your own action routines enforce touchability, you can call the library routine ObjectIsUntouchable(obj). This either returns false and prints nothing if there's no problem in touching obj, or returns true and prints a suitable message, such as "The solid glass cabinet is in the way." Thus, the first line of many of the library's action routines is:

```
if (ObjectIsUntouchable(noun)) return;
```

You can also call ObjectIsUntouchable(obj, true) to simply return true or false, printing nothing, if you'd rather provide your own failure message.

· · · · ·

The rest of this section is about how to change the scope rules. As usual with Inform, you can change them globally, but it's more efficient and safer to work locally. To take a typical example: how do we allow the player to ask questions like the traditional "what is a grue"? The "grue" part ought to be parsed as if it were a noun, so that we could distinguish between, say, a "garden grue" and a "wild grue". So it isn't good enough to look only at a single word. Here is one solution:

```
[ QuerySub; noun.description(); return;
];
[ QueryTopic;
  switch (scope_stage) {
      1: rfalse;
      2: ScopeWithin(questions); rtrue;
      3: "At the moment, even the simplest questions confuse you.";
  }
];
Object questions;
```

where the actual questions at any time are the current children of the questions object, like so:

```
Object -> "long count"
  with name 'long' 'count',
       description "The Long Count is the great Mayan cycle of
           time, which began in 3114 BC and will finish with
           the world's end in 2012 AD.";
```

(which might be helpful in 'Ruins') and we also have a grammar line:

```
Verb 'what' * 'is'/'was' scope=QueryTopic -> Query;
```

The individual questions have short names so that the parser might be able to say "Which do you mean, the long count or the short count?" if the player asked "what is the count". (As it stands this won't recognise "what is the count?". Conventionally players are supposed not to type question marks or quotes in their commands. To allow this one could always add 'count?' as one of the names above.)

.   .   .   .   .

Here is the specification. When the parser reaches $\boxed{\texttt{scope=Whatever}}$, it calls the Whatever routine with the variable scope_stage set to 1. The routine should return true if it is prepared to allow multiple objects to be accepted here, and false otherwise. (In the example, as we don't want "what is everything" to list all the questions and answers in the game, we return false.)

A little later the parser calls Whatever again with scope_stage now set to 2. Whatever is then obliged to tell the parser which objects are to be in scope. It can call two parser routines to do this:

```
ScopeWithin(obj)
```

which puts everything inside obj, but not obj itself, into scope, and then works through rules (6) and (7) above, so that it may continue to add the contents of the contents, and so on; and

```
PlaceInScope(obj)
```

which puts just obj into scope. It is perfectly legal to declare something in scope that "would have been in scope anyway": or something which is in a different room altogether from the actor concerned, say at the other end of a telephone line. The scope routine Whatever should then return false if the nominated items are additional to the usual scope, or true if they are the only items in scope. (In the example, QueryTopic returns true because it wants the only items in scope to be its question topics, not the usual miscellany near the player.)

This is fine if the token is correctly parsed. If not, the parser may choose to ask the token routine to print a suitable error message, by calling Whatever with scope_stage set to 3. (In the example, this will happen if the player types "what is the lgon count", and QueryTopic replies "At the moment, even the simplest questions confuse you.", because it comes from a faintly dream-like game called 'Balances'.)

● **EXERCISE 99**
Write a token which puts everything in scope, so that you could have a debugging "purloin" which could take anything, regardless of where it was and the rules applying to it.

.   .   .   .   .

△   The global scope rules can be tampered with by providing an entry point routine
called InScope(actor), where actor is the actor whose scope is worked out. In effect,
this defines the "ordinary" scope by making calls to ScopeWithin and PlaceInScope,
then returning true or false, exactly as if it were a scope token at stage 2. For instance,
here as promised is how to change the rule that "things you've just dropped disappear
in the dark":

```
[ InScope person i;
  if (person == player && location == thedark)
      objectloop (i in parent(player))
          if (i has moved) PlaceInScope(i);
  rfalse;
];
```

With this routine added, objects near the player in a dark room are in scope only if
they have moved (that is, have been held by the player in the past), and even then are
in scope only to the player, not to anyone else.

△   The token scope=⟨Routine⟩ takes precedence over InScope, which will only be
reached if the routine returns false to signify "carry on".

△△ There are seven reasons why InScope might be being called; the scope_reason
variable is set to the current one:

PARSING_REASON   The usual reason. Note that action_to_be holds NULL in
                         the early stages (before the verb has been decided) and later
                         on the action which would result from a successful match.
TALKING_REASON   Working out which objects are in scope for being spoken to
                         (see the end of §18 for exercises using this).
EACHTURN_REASON   When running each_turn routines for anything nearby, at
                         the end of each turn.
REACT_BEFORE_REASON   When running react_before.
REACT_AFTER_REASON   When running react_after.
TESTSCOPE_REASON   When performing a TestScope.
LOOPOVERSCOPE_REASON   When performing a LoopOverScope.

• △△EXERCISE 100
Construct a long room divided by a glass window. Room descriptions on either side
should describe what's in view on the other; the window should be possible to look
through; objects on the far side should be in scope, but not manipulable.

• △△EXERCISE 101
Code the following puzzle. In an initially dark room there is a light switch. Provided
you've seen the switch at some time in the past, you can turn it on and off – but before
you've ever seen it, you can't. Inside the room is nothing you can see, but you can hear
the distinctive sound of a dwarf breathing. If you tell this dwarf to turn the light on, he
will.

·   ·   ·   ·   ·

Each object has the ability to drag other objects into scope whenever it is in scope. This is especially useful for giving objects component parts: e.g., giving a washing-machine a temperature dial. (The dial can't be a child object because that would throw it in with the clothes: and it ought to be attached to the machine in case the machine is moved from place to place.) For this purpose, the property add_to_scope may contain a list of objects to add.

△   Alternatively, it may contain a routine. This routine can then call AddToScope(x) to add any object x to scope. It may not, however, call ScopeWithin or any other scoping routines.

△△ Scope addition does *not* occur for an object moved into scope by an explicit call to PlaceInScope, since this must allow complete freedom in scope selections. But it does happen when objects are moved in scope by calls to ScopeWithin(domain).

● **EXERCISE 102**
(From the tiny example game 'A Nasal Twinge'.) Give the player a nose, which is always in scope and can be held, reducing the player's carrying capacity.

● **EXERCISE 103**
(Likewise.) Create a portable sterilising machine, with a "go" button, a top which things can be put on and an inside to hold objects for sterilisation. Thus it is a container, a supporter and a possessor of sub-objects all at once.

● △△**EXERCISE 104**
Create a red sticky label which the player can affix to any object in the game. (Hint: use InScope, not add_to_scope.)

● **REFERENCES**
'Balances' uses scope = ⟨routine⟩ tokens for legible spells and memorised spells. ●Jesse Burneko's library extension "Info.h" is a helpful model to follow: using a simple scope token, it allows for "consult" and "ask" commands to access topics which are provided as objects.   ●See also the exercises at the end of §18 for further scope trickery.   ●Similarly, L. Ross Raszewski's "whatis.h" (adapted to Inform 6 by Andrew C. Murie) and David Cornelson's "whowhat.h" field questions such as "what is..." and "who is...".

§33 Helping the parser out of trouble

Once you begin programming the parser on a large scale, you soon reach the point where the parser's ordinary error messages no longer appear sensible. The ParserError entry point can change the rules even at this last hurdle: it takes one argument, the error type, and should return true to tell the parser to shut up, because a better error message has already been printed, or false, to tell the parser to print its usual message. The error types are defined as constants:

STUCK_PE	I didn't understand that sentence.
UPTO_PE	I only understood you as far as...
NUMBER_PE	I didn't understand that number.
CANTSEE_PE	You can't see any such thing.
TOOLIT_PE	You seem to have said too little!
NOTHELD_PE	You aren't holding that!
MULTI_PE	You can't use multiple objects with that verb.
MMULTI_PE	You can only use multiple objects once on a line.
VAGUE_PE	I'm not sure what 'it' refers to.
EXCEPT_PE	You excepted something not included anyway!
ANIMA_PE	You can only do that to something animate.
VERB_PE	That's not a verb I recognise.
SCENERY_PE	That's not something you need to refer to...
ITGONE_PE	You can't see 'it' (the *whatever*) at the moment.
JUNKAFTER_PE	I didn't understand the way that finished.
TOOFEW_PE	Only five of those are available.
NOTHING_PE	Nothing to do!
ASKSCOPE_PE	*whatever the scope routine prints*

Each unsuccessful grammar line ends in one of these conditions. By the time the parser wants to print an error, every one of the grammar lines in a verb will have failed. The error message chosen it prints is the most "interesting" one: meaning, lowest down this list.

If a general parsing routine you have written returns GPR_FAIL, then the grammar line containing it normally ends in plain STUCK_PE, the least interesting of all errors (unless you did something like calling the library's ParseToken routine before giving up, which might have set a more interesting error like CANTSEE_PE). But you can choose to create a new error and put it in the parser's variable etype, as in the following example:

```
[ Degrees d;
  d = TryNumber(wn++);
```

```
        if (d == -1000) return GPR_FAIL;
        if (d <= 360) { parsed_number = d; return GPR_NUMBER; }
        etype = "There are only 360 degrees in a circle.";
        return GPR_FAIL;
    ];
```

This parses a number of degrees between 0 and 360. Although etype normally
only holds values like VERB_PE, which are numbers lower than 100, here we've
set it equal to a string. As this will be a value that the parser doesn't recognise,
we need to write a ParserError routine that will take care of it, by reacting to
a string in the obvious way – printing it out.

```
[ ParserError error_type;
    if (error_type ofclass String) print_ret (string) error_type;
    rfalse;
];
```

This will result in conversation like so:

```
>steer down
```
I didn't understand that sentence.
```
>steer 385
```
There are only 360 degrees in a circle.

In the first case, Degrees failed without setting any special error message on
finding that the second word wasn't a number; in the second case it gave the
new, specific error message.

. . . . .

The VAGUE_PE and ITGONE_PE errors apply to all pronouns (in English, "it",
"him", "her" and "them"). The variable vague_word contains the dictionary
address of whichever pronoun is involved ('it', 'him' and so on).

You can find out the current setting of a pronoun using the library's
PronounValue routine: for instance, PronounValue('it') gives the object
which "it" currently refers to, possibly nothing. Similarly SetPronoun('it',
magic_ruby) would set "it" to mean the magic ruby object. You might want
this because, when something like a magic ruby suddenly appears in the
middle of a turn, players will habitually call it "it". A better way to adjust
the pronouns is to call PronounNotice(magic_ruby), which sets whatever
pronouns are appropriate. That is, it works out if the object is a thing or
a person, of what number and gender, which pronouns apply to it in the
parser's current language, and so on. In code predating Inform 6.1 you may
see variables called itobj, himobj and herobj holding the English pronoun
values: these still work properly, but please use the modern system in new
games.

.   .   .   .   .

△   The Inform parser resolves ambiguous object names with a pragmatic algorithm which has evolved over the years (see below). Experience also shows that no two people ever quite agree on what the parser should "naturally" do. Designers have an opportunity to influence this by providing an entry point routine called ChooseObjects:

```
ChooseObjects(obj, code)
```

is called in two circumstances. If code is false or true, the parser is considering including the given obj in an "all": false means the parser has decided against, true means it has decided in favour. The routine should reply

0   to accept the parser's decision;
1   to force the object to be included; or
2   to force the object to be excluded.

It may want to decide using verb_word (the variable storing the current verb word, e.g., 'take') and action_to_be, which is the action which would happen if the current line of grammar were successfully matched.

The other circumstance is when code is 2. This means the parser is choosing between a list of items which made equally good matches against some text, and would like a hint. ChooseObjects should then return a number from 0 to 9 to give obj a score for how appropriate it is.

For instance, some designers would prefer "take all" not to attempt to take scenery objects (which Inform, and the parsers in most of the Infocom games, will do). Let us code this, and also teach the parser that edible things are more likely to be eaten than inedible ones:

```
[ ChooseObjects obj code;
  if (code < 2) { if (obj has scenery) return 2; rfalse; }
  if (action_to_be == ##Eat && obj has edible) return 3;
  if (obj hasnt scenery) return 2;
  return 1;
];
```

Scenery is now excluded from "all" lists; and is further penalised in that non-scenery objects are always preferred over scenery, all else being equal. Most objects score 2 but edible things in the context of eating score 3, so "eat black" will now always choose a Black Forest gateau in preference to a black rod with a rusty iron star on the end.

• △EXERCISE 105
Allow "lock" and "unlock" to infer their second objects without being told, if there's an obvious choice (because the player's only carrying one key), but to issue a disambiguation question otherwise. (Use Extend, not ChooseObjects.)

• △EXERCISE 106

Joyce Haslam's Inform edition of the classic Acornsoft game 'Gateway to Karos' requires a class called `FaintlyLitRoom` for rooms so dimly illuminated that "take all" is impossible. How might this work?

. . . . .

△△ Suppose we have a set of objects which have all matched equally well against the textual input, so that some knowledge of the game world is needed to resolve which of the objects – possibly only one, possibly more – is or are intended. Deciding this is called "disambiguation", and here in full are the rules used by library 6/10 to do it. The reader is cautioned that after six years, these rules are still evolving.

(1) Call an object "good" according to a rule depending on what kind of token is being matched:

`held`	Good if its parent is the actor.
`multiheld`	Good if its parent is the actor.
`multiexcept`	Good if not also the second object, if that's known yet.
`multiinside`	Good if not inside the second object, if that's known yet.
`creature`	Good if animate, or if the proposed action is Ask, Answer, Tell or AskFor and the object is `talkable`.
other tokens	All objects are good.

If only a single object is good, this is immediately chosen.

(2) If the token is `creature` and no objects are good, fail the token altogether, as no choice can make sense.

(3) Objects which don't fit "descriptors" used by the player are removed:

if "my", an object whose parent isn't the actor is discarded;

if "that", an object whose parent isn't the actor's location is discarded;

if "lit", an object which hasn't `light` is discarded;

if "unlit", an object which has `light` is discarded;

if "his" or some similar possessive pronoun, an object not owned by the person implied is discarded.

Thus "his lit torches" will invoke two of these rules at once.

(4) If there are no objects left, fail the token, as no choice can make sense.

(5) It is now certain that the token will not fail. The remaining objects are assigned a score as follows:

(i) $1000 \times C$ points, where C is the return value of `ChooseObjects(object,2)`. ($0 \le C \le 9$. If the designer doesn't provide this entry point at all then $C = 0$.)

(ii) 500 points for being "good" (see (1) above).

(iii) 100 points for not having `concealed`.

(iv) P points depending on the object's position:

$$P = \begin{cases} A & \text{if object belongs to the actor,} \\ L & \text{if object belongs to the actor's visibility ceiling,} \\ 20 & \text{if object belongs anywhere else except the compass,} \\ 0 & \text{if object belongs to the compass.} \end{cases}$$

(Recall that "visibility ceiling" usually means "location" and that the objects belonging to the compass are exactly the compass directions.) The values A and L depend on the token being parsed:

$$\begin{cases} A = 60 & L = 40 & \text{for } \boxed{\text{held}} \text{ or } \boxed{\text{multiheld}} \text{ tokens,} \\ A = 40 & L = 60 & \text{otherwise.} \end{cases}$$

(v) 10 points for not having scenery.

(vi) 5 points for not being the actor object.

(vii) 1 point if the object's gender, number and animation (GNA) matches one possibility implied by some pronoun typed by the player: for instance "them" in English implying plural, or "le" in French implying masculine singular.

(6d) In "definite mode", such as if the player has typed a definite article like "the", if any single object has highest score, choose that object.

(7ip) The following rule applies only in indefinite mode and provided the player has typed something definitely implying a plural, such as the words "all" or "three" or "coins". Here the parser already has a target number of objects to choose: for instance 3 for "three", or the special value of 100, meaning "an unlimited number", for "all" or "coins".

Go through the list of objects in "best guess" order (see below). Mark each as "accept" unless:

(i) it has worn or concealed;

(ii) or the action is Take or Remove and the object is held by the actor;

(iii) or the token is $\boxed{\text{multiheld}}$ or $\boxed{\text{multiexcept}}$ and the object isn't held by the actor;

(iv) or the target number is "unlimited" and $S/20$ (rounded down to the nearest integer) has fallen below its maximum value, where S is the score of the object.

The entry point ChooseObjects(object,accept_flag) is now called and can overrule the "accept"/"reject" decision either way. We keep accepting objects like this until the target is reached, or proves impossible to reach.

(8) The objects are now grouped so that any set of indistinguishable objects forms a single group. "Indistinguishable" means that no further text typed by the player could clarify which is meant (see §29). Note that there is no reason to suppose that two indistinguishable objects have the same score, because they might be in different places.

(9d) In definite mode, we know that there's a tie for highest score, as otherwise a choice would have been made at step (6d). If these highest-scoring objects belong to more than one group, then ask the player to choose which group:

You can see a bronze coin and four gold coins here.
>get coin
Which do you mean, the bronze coin or a gold coin?
>gold

The player's response is inserted textually into the original input and the parsing begins again from scratch with "get gold coin" instead of "get coin".

(10) Only two possibilities remain: either (i) we are in indefinite but singular mode, or (ii) we are in definite mode and there is a tie for highest-scoring object and all of these equal-highest objects belong to the same group. Either way, choose the "best guess" object (see below). Should this parsing attempt eventually prove successful, print up an "inference" on screen, such as

>get key
(the copper key)

only if the number of groups found in (8) is more than 1.

(BG) It remains to define "best guess". From a set of objects, the best guess is the highest-scoring one not yet guessed; and if several objects have equal highest scores, it is the earliest one to have been matched by the parser. In practice this means the one most recently taken or dropped, because the parser tries to match against objects by traversing the object-tree, and the most recently moved object tends to be the first in the list of children of its parent.

• REFERENCES

See 'Balances' for a usage of ParserError. •Infocom's parser typically produces error messages like "I don't know the word 'tarantula'." when the player types a word not in the game's dictionary, and some designers prefer this style to Inform's give-nothing-away approach (Inform tries not to let the player carry out experiments to see what is, and what is not, in the dictionary). Neil Cerutti's "dunno.h" library extension restores the Infocom format. •The library extension "calyx_adjectives.h", which resolves ambiguities in parsing by placing more weight on matches with nouns than with adjectives, works by using ChooseObjects.

Chapter V: Natural Language

Westlich von Haus
Du stehst auf freiem Feld westlich von einem weißen Haus, dessen Haustür
mit Brettern vernagelt ist. Hier ist ein kleiner Briefkasten.
— 'Zork I: Das Große Unterweltreich'

§34   Linguistics and the Inform parser

¡Bienvenido a Aventura! Despite the English-language bias of early
computers and their manuals, interactive fiction has a culture and
a history beyond English, not least in Germany. Like the Monty
Python team and the Beatles, Infocom made a German translation
of their defining work, when in early 1988 Jeff O'Neill coded up 'Zork I:
Das Große Unterweltreich'. It came at a sorry time in Infocom's fortunes
and remains officially unreleased, in part because the translator recruited had
rendered the text in a stilted, business-German manner, though a beta-test
of the story file circulates to this day. But O'Neill's work was not in vain,
as it left another important legacy: an upgrading of the Z-machine format
to allow for accented characters, which opened the door to non-English IF
on the Z-machine. Jose Luiz Diaz's translation of 'Advent' into Spanish,
as 'Aventura', stimulated much of the 1996 development of Inform as a
multilingual system, and Toni Arnold's game 'Rummelplatzgeschichte' (1998)
also deserves mention, as does advice from Inform users across four continents,
among them Torbjörn Andersson, Joachim Baumann, Paul David Doherty,
Bjorn Gustavsson, Aapo Haapanen, Ralf Herrmann, J. P. Ikaheimonen, Ilario
Nardinocchi, Bob Newell, Giovanni Riccardi and Linards Ticmanis. If nothing
else, I am glad to have learned the palindromic Finnish word for soap dealer,
"saippuakauppias".

The standard English-language release of the Inform library now consists
of eight files of code. Of these eight, only two need to be replaced to make
a translation to another language: "Grammar.h", which contains grammars
for English verbs like "take" and "drop"; and a "language definition file"
called "English.h". For instance, in Ilario Nardinocchi's translation these

two files are replaced by `"ItalianG.h"` and `"Italian.h"`, in Jose Luis Diaz's translation they become `"SpanishG.h"` and `"Spanish.h"` and so on. Language definition files can be useful for more, or rather less, than just translation. 'The Tempest' (1997), for instance, uses a language definition file to enable it to speak in Early Modern English verse and to recognise pronouns like "thee" and "thy". A suitable language definition file could also change the persona of an Inform game from second-person ("You fall into a pit!") to first-person ("I have fallen into a pit!") or third ("Bilbo falls into a pit!"), or from present to past tenses, as Jamie Murphy's game 'Leopold the Minstrel' (1996) did.

This section goes into the linguistics of the Inform parser, and how to add new grammatical concepts to it using grammar tokens. The next goes into full-scale translation and how to write new language definition files.

· · · · ·

Language is complex, computers are simple. Modern English is a mostly non-inflected language, meaning that words tend not to alter their spelling according to their usage, but even here the parser has to go to some trouble to cope with one of its remaining inflections ("take coin" but "take six coins": see §29). The range of variation in human languages is large and as many are heavily inflected the task at first seems hopeless.†

On the other hand, Inform is mainly used with Romance-family languages, where commands are formed roughly as they are in English. The language understood by the parser is a simple one, called Informese. It has three genders, two numbers, a concept of animate versus inanimate nouns and a clear understanding of articles and pronouns, but all verbs are imperative, the only tense is the present, there are no cases of nouns (but see §35) and adjectives are not distinguished from nouns (but see §26). Informese is based on a small part of English, but the proposition of this chapter is that (with some effort) you can find Informese at the core of many other languages as well.

Changes of vocabulary are obviously needed: for instance, where an English game recognises "other", a French one must recognise "autre". But, as the following example shows, vocabulary changes are not enough:

jetez la boule dedans   *throw the ball into it* (French)

has no word-for-word translation into Informese, because "dedans" (into it) is a pronominal adverb, and Informese doesn't have pronominal adverbs.

---

† In fact the difficult languages to parse are not those with subtleties of spelling but those where even word-recognition can be a matter of context and guesswork, such as Hebrew, where all vowels are conventionally omitted.

Instead, a transformational rule like this one must be applied:

dedans *inside it* $\mapsto$ dans lui

Transformational rules like this one bring new grammatical structures into the Inform parser. The rest of this section is occupied with describing what is present already.

·   ·   ·   ·   ·

The following is a short grammar of Informese. Both here and in the General Index, grammatical concepts understood by the parser are written in angle brackets ⟨like so⟩.

(1) *Commands*

A command to an Inform game should be one of:

⟨oops-word⟩ ⟨word⟩
⟨action phrase⟩
⟨noun phrase⟩, ⟨action phrase⟩

An ⟨oops-word⟩ corrects the last command by putting the ⟨word⟩ in to replace whatever seemed to be incorrect. In "English.h", the only words in the ⟨oops-word⟩ category are "oops" and its abbreviation "o". An ⟨action phrase⟩ instructs the player to perform an action, unless it is preceded by a ⟨noun phrase⟩ and a comma, in which case someone else is instructed to perform an action.

An ⟨action phrase⟩ consists of a sequence of verb phrases, divided up by full stops or then-words: a ⟨then-word⟩ is a word like the English "then" or a full stop. For instance "take sword. east. put sword in stone" is broken into a sequence of three verb phrases, each parsed and acted on in turn. (It's important not to parse them all at once: the meaning of the noun phrase "stone" depends on where the player is by then.)

(2) *Verb phrases*

A ⟨verb phrase⟩ is one of:

⟨again-word⟩
⟨imperative verb⟩ ⟨grammar line⟩

Again-words are another category: in "English.h" these are "again" and its abbreviation "g". An ⟨again-word⟩ is understood as "the ⟨verb phrase⟩ most recently typed in which wasn't an ⟨again-word⟩".

The imperative is the form of the verb used for orders or instructions. In English the imperative ("open the window") looks the same as the infinitive ("to open"), but in most languages they differ (French "ouvrez" is imperative, "ouvrir" infinitive). Even in many languages where verbs usually follow objects, such as Latin, the imperative comes at the start of a verb phrase, and Informese insists on this. Informese also wants the ⟨imperative verb⟩ to be a single word, but programming can get around both requirements.

Grammar lines are sequences of tokens. Each token results in one of four grammatically different outcomes:

> ⟨noun phrase⟩
> ⟨preposition⟩
> ⟨number⟩
> ⟨unparsed text⟩

For instance, a successful match for the tokens `noun` or `multiheld` would produce a ⟨noun phrase⟩, whereas a match for `'into'` would produce a ⟨preposition⟩. Note that a general parsing routine can produce any of these four outcomes.

(3) *Prepositions*

Any word written in quotes as a grammar token. This is normally also a preposition in the ordinary grammatical sense, but not always, as the "press charges" example in §30 shows. In "English.h", "look under table" and "switch on radio" contain two words considered to be prepositions in Informese: "under" and "on".

(4) *Numbers*

Include at least the numbers 1 to 20 written out in words. "At least" because a language definition file is free to include more, but should not include less.

(5) *Noun phrases*

A string of words which refer to a single object or collection of objects, with more or less exactness. Here are some typical examples of "English.h" noun phrases:

> it
> rucksack
> brown bag, pepper
> a box and the other compass
> nine silver coins
> everything except the rucksack
> smooth stones

A noun phrase is a list of basic noun phrases:

> ⟨basic np⟩ ⟨connective⟩ ⟨basic np⟩ ⟨connective⟩ ... ⟨connective⟩ ⟨basic np⟩

and there are two kinds of connective: an ⟨and-word⟩ (conjunction), and a ⟨but-word⟩ (disjunction). The Inform parser always regards a comma in a ⟨noun phrase⟩ (other than one used at the start of a command: see (1) above) as an ⟨and-word⟩, and the definition of "English.h" gives "and" as another. "English.h" has two ⟨but-words⟩: "but" and "except".

⟨Noun phrases⟩ being parsed are assigned several properties. They are declared *definite* if they carry no article, or a definite article which is not qualified by an all-word or a demanding number, and are otherwise *indefinite*. (Except that a noun-phrase containing a dictionary word flagged as likely to be referring to plural objects, such as 'crowns//p', is always indefinite.) Definiteness affects disambiguation and the parser's willingness to make guesses, as the description of the parser's disambiguation algorithm at the end of §33 shows.

Indefinite noun phrases also have a target quantity of objects being referred to: this is normally 1, but 7 for "seven stones" and 100, used internally to mean "as many as possible", for "crowns" or "all the swords". Noun phrases also have a *gender-number-animation* combination, or "GNA":

Gender: in most European languages, nouns divide up into masculine, feminine or neuter, the three genders in Informese. Gender is important when parsing noun phrases because it can distinguish otherwise identical nouns, as in French: "le faux", the forgery, "la faux", the scythe. As in German, there may be no satisfactory way to determine the gender of a noun by any automatic rules: see the next section for how Inform assigns genders to nouns.

Number: singular ("the hat") or plural ("the grapes"). Individual objects in Inform games can have names of either number. Languages with more than two numbers are rare, but Hebrew has a "pair of" number. This would have to be translated into a demanding number (see (7d) below) for Informese.

Animation: Informese distinguishes between the animate (people and higher animals) and the inanimate (objects, plants and lower animals).

With three genders, two numbers and two animations, Informese has twelve possible GNA combinations, and these are internally represented by the numbers 0 to 11:

0	animate	singular	masculine
1			feminine
2			neuter
3		plural	masculine
4			feminine
5			neuter
6	inanimate	singular	masculine
7			feminine
8			neuter
9		plural	masculine
10			feminine
11			neuter

Not all possible GNAs occur in all natural languages. In English, cases 6, 7, 9 and 10 never occur, except perhaps that ships are sometimes called "she" and "her" without being animate (GNA 7). In French, 2, 5, 8 and 11 never occur. The parser actually works by assigning sets of possible GNA values to each noun phrase: so, in French, "le faux" carries the set $\{6\}$, while the more ambiguous noun phrase "les" carries $\{3, 4, 9, 10\}$.

(6) Basic noun phrases

These take the following form, in which both lists can have any number of words in, including none, and in any order:

⟨list of descriptors⟩ ⟨list of nouns⟩

For instance "the balloon" has one descriptor and one noun; "red balloon" has just two nouns; "all" has just one descriptor.

(7) Descriptors

There are five kinds of ⟨descriptor⟩, as follows:

(a) An ⟨article⟩ is a word indicating whether a particular object is being referred to, or merely one of a range. Thus there are two kinds of article, *definite* and *indefinite*. "English.h" has four articles: "the" is definite, while "a", "an" and "some" are indefinite.

(b) An ⟨all-word⟩ is a word which behaves like the English word "all", that is, which refers to a whole range of objects. Informese, like some natural languages (such as Tagalog), handles this as a kind of article but which pluralises what follows it.

(c) An ⟨other-word⟩ is a word behaving like "other", which Informese understands as "other than the one I am holding". Thus, if the player is holding a sword in a room where there's also a sword on the floor, then "examine other sword" would refer to the one on the floor.

(d) A ⟨demanding number⟩ is a word like "nine" in "nine bronze coins", which demands that a certain number of items are needed.

(e) A ⟨possessive adjective⟩ is a word indicating ownership by someone or something whose meaning is held in a pronoun. Among others "English.h" has "my" (belonging to "me"); French has "son" (belonging to "lui"). Informese also counts ⟨demonstrative adjectives⟩ like "this", "these", "that" and "those" as possessives, though demonstratives are hardly ever used by players and may not be worth providing in other languages. In Spanish, for instance, there would have to be twelve, for "this", "that" (nearby) and "that" (far away), each in masculine, feminine, singular and plural forms; and the structure of "celui-ci" and "celui-la" in French is too complex to be worth the effort of parsing.

(8) Nouns

There are three kinds of ⟨noun⟩, as follows:

(a) A ⟨name⟩ is a word matched against particular objects. Unless an object has a parse_name routine attached, which complicates matters, these will be the words in its name array. For instance:

```
Object -> "blue box" with name 'blue' 'box';
```

has two possible names in Informese, "blue" and "box".

(b) A ⟨me-word⟩ is a word which behaves like the English word "me", that is, which refers to the player-object. Most languages would think these are just examples of relative pronouns, but Informese considers them to be in a category of their own. Note that they refer to the player, whoever is addressed: in "mark, give me the bomb", "me" refers to the speaker, not to Mark.

(c) A ⟨pronoun⟩ is a word which stands in the place of nouns and can only be understood with reference back to what has previously been said. "it", "him", "her" and "them" are all pronouns in "English.h". (Though "her" can also be a possessive adjective, as in (7e) above.)

.   .   .   .   .

It is worth mentioning a number of grammatical features which are *not* contained in Informese, along with some ways to simulate them.

adverbs such as "quickly" in "run quickly east". These are not difficult to implement:

```
Verb 'run'
    * noun=ADirection -> Go
    * 'quickly' noun=ADirection -> GoQuickly
    * noun=ADirection 'quickly' -> GoQuickly;
```

However, "The authors of Zork have thought about several possible extensions to the Zork parser. One that has come up many times is to add adverbs. A player should be able to do the following:

>go north quietly
You sneak past a sleeping lion who sniffs but doesn't wake up.

The problem is to think of reasons why you would not do everything 'quietly', 'carefully' or whatever." (P. David Lebling, "Zork and the Future of Computerized Fantasy Simulations", *Byte*, December 1980.) A further problem is the impracticality of modelling the game world closely enough to differentiate between ways to achieve the same action. In Melbourne House's 'The Hobbit' adverbs influence the probability of success in randomised events, so for instance "throw rope vigorously across river" is more likely to succeed than "throw rope across river", but those few players who discovered this were not pleased. Twenty years on from 'Zork', adverbs remain largely unused in the medium.

adjectives are not distinguished from nouns, although it can be useful to do so when resolving ambiguities. See §28 for remedies.

genitives: objects are not normally named by description of their circumstances, so "the box on the floor" and "the priest's hat" would not normally be understood. Designers can still define objects like

```
Object -> "priest's hat"
    with name 'hat' 'priest^s';
```

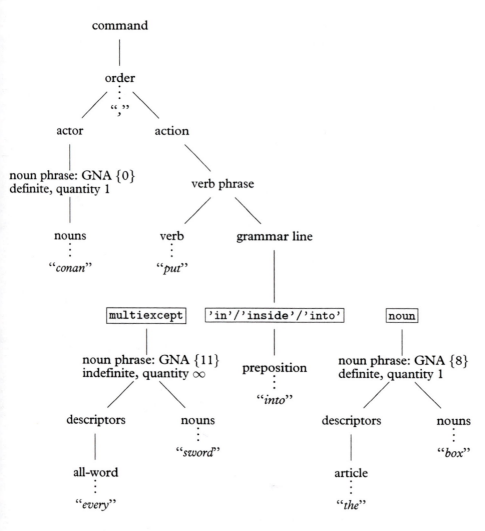

An example of parsing Informese. This diagram shows the result of parsing the text "conan, put every sword into the box", assuming that the verb "put" has a grammar line reading

```
* multiexcept 'in'/'inside'/'into' noun -> Insert
```

as indeed it does have in the "English.h" grammar.

in which the genitive "priest's" is a noun like any other.

pronouns of other kinds, notably: nominative pronouns ("I" in "I am happy"); interrogative pronouns ("What" in "What are you doing?"), although these are often simulated by making "what" an Informese verb; demonstrative pronouns ("that" in "eat that"), although in "English.h" the parser gets this right because they look the same as demonstrative adjectives with no noun attached; possessive pronouns ("mine" in "take the troll's sword. give him mine", which should expand "mine" to "my X", where X is the current value of "it").

pronominal adverbs are not found in English, but are common in other languages: for instance "dessous" (French: "under it"). The next section suggests how these can be achieved.

§35   Case and parsing noun phrases

 As this section and the next use a variety of linguistic terms, here are some definitions. "Flexion" is the changing of a word according to its situation, and there are several kinds:

inflection: a variable ending for a word, such as "a" becoming "an".

agreement: when the inflection of one word is changed to match another word which it goes with. Thus "grand maison" but "grande dame" (French), where the inflection on "grand" agrees with the gender of the noun it is being applied to.

affix: part of a word which is attached either at the beginning (*prefix*), the end (*suffix*) or somewhere in the middle (*infix*) of the ordinary word (the *stem*) to indicate, for instance, person or gender of the objects attached to a verb. The affix often plays a part that an entirely separate word would play in English. For instance, "donnez-lui" (French: "give to him"), where the suffix is "-lui", or "cogela" (Spanish: "take it"), where the suffix is "la".

enclitic: an affix, usually a suffix, meaning "too" or "and" in English. For instance, "que" (Latin).

agglutinization: the practice of composing many affixes to a single word, so that it may even become an entire phrase. For instance:

   kirjoitettuasi   *after you had written* (Finnish)

. . . . .

In most languages, noun phrases have different *cases* according to their situation in a sentence. In the English sentence "Emily ate one bath bun and gave Beatrice the other", the noun phrase "Emily" is *nominative*, "one bath bun" and "the other" are *accusative* and "Beatrice" is *dative*. These last two are the cases most often occurring in Inform commands, as in the example

   leg den frosch auf ihn   *put the frog on him* (German)
   nimm den frosch von ihm   *take the frog from him*

where the noun phrase "den frosch" is accusative both times, but "ihn" and "ihm" are the same word ("him") in its accusative and dative forms. In some languages a *vocative* case would also be needed for the name of someone being addressed:

   domine, fiat lux   *Lord, let there be light* (Latin)

since "domine" is the vocative form of "dominus". Latin also has genitive and ablative cases, making six in all, but this pales by comparison with Finnish, which has about thirty. In effect, a wide range of English prepositional phrases like "into the water" are written as just the noun phrase "water" with a suffix meaning "into".

. . . . .

To parse any of these languages, and even in some circumstances to parse special effects in English-language games, it's useful to have further control over the way that the parser recognises noun phrases.

The words entered into an object's name property normally take the accusative case, the one most often needed in commands, as for example in the grammar line:

```
Verb 'take' * noun -> Take;
```

On the other hand, the nouns in the following grammar lines aren't all accusative:

```
Verb 'give'
    * noun 'to' noun -> Give
    * noun noun      -> Give reverse;
```

This matches "give biscuit to jemima" and "give jemima biscuit", "biscuit" being accusative in both cases and "to jemima" and "jemima" both dative. In a language where the spelling of a word can tell a dative from an accusative, such as German, we could instead use grammar like this:

```
Verb 'give'
    * noun dativenoun -> Give
    * dativenoun noun -> Give reverse;
```

where dativenoun is some token meaning "like noun , but in the dative case instead of the accusative". This could be used as the definition of a German verb "gib", in which case both of the following would be parsed correctly:

gib die blumen dem maedchen   *give the flowers to the girl*
gib dem maedchen die blumen   *give the girl the flowers*

Unfortunately Inform doesn't come with a token called dativenoun built in, so you have to write one, using a general parsing routine (see §31). For the sake of an example closer to English, suppose a puzzle in which the Anglo-Saxon hero Beowulf will do as he is asked to, but only if addressed in Old English:

beowulf, gief gold to cyning   *beowulf, give gold to king* (Old English)

The grammar would be much like that for German, and indeed English:

```
Verb 'gief' * noun dativenoun -> OEGive;
```

and here is a simple version of dativenoun :

```
[ dativenoun;
  if (NextWord() == 'to')
      return ParseToken(ELEMENTARY_TT, NOUN_TOKEN);
  return GPR_FAIL;
];
```

Read this as: "if the next word is "to", try and match a noun following it; otherwise it isn't a dative". A more likely form of the command is however

beowulf, gief gold cyninge   *beowulf, give gold to king* (Old English)

where "cyninge" is the dative form of "cyning". The ending "-e" often indicates a dative in Old English, but there are irregularities, such as "searo" (device), whose dative is "searwe", not "searoe". In the unlikely event of Beowulf confronting a vending machine:

beowulf, gief gold to searo   *beowulf, give gold to device* (Old English)
beowulf, gief gold searwe   *beowulf, give gold to device*

How to manage all this? Here is a laborious way:

```
Object -> "searo"
  with name 'searo', dativename 'searwe';
Object -> "Cyning"
  with name 'cyning', dativename 'cyninge';
[ dativenoun;
  if (NextWord() ~= 'to') {
      wn--; parser_inflection = dativename;
  }
  return ParseToken(ELEMENTARY_TT, NOUN_TOKEN);
];
```

The variable `parser_inflection` tells the parser where to find the name(s) of an object. It must always be equal to *either* a property *or* a routine. Most of the time it's equal to the property `name`, the accusative case as normal. If it equals another property, such as `dativename`, then the parser looks in that property for name-words instead of in `name`.

The above solution is laborious because it makes the game designer write out dative forms of every name, even though they are very often the same but with "-e" suffixed. It's for this kind of contingency that `parser_inflection` can be set to a routine name. Such an "inflection routine" is called with two arguments: an object and a dictionary word. It returns `true` if the dictionary word can mean the object and `false` if not. The word number `wn` is always set to the number of the next word along, and it should not be moved. Two library routines may be particularly helpful:

```
DictionaryLookup(text, length)
```

returns 0 if the word held as a `->` array of characters

```
text->0, text->1, ..., text->(length-1)
```

is not in the game's dictionary, or its dictionary entry if it is.

```
WordInProperty(word, object, property)
```

to see if this is one of the words listed in `object.property`. It may also be useful to know that the variable `indef_mode` is always set to `true` when parsing something known to be indefinite (e.g., because an indefinite article or a word like "all" has just been typed), and `false` otherwise.

- △**EXERCISE 107**
Rewrite the `dativenoun` token so that "-e" is recognised as a regular suffix indicating the dative, while still making provision for some nouns to have irregular dative forms.

- △**EXERCISE 108**
Now add an (imaginary, not Old English) dative pronominal adverb "toit", which is to be understood as "to it".

- △△**EXERCISE 109**
Define a token ⟨swedishnoun⟩ to make nouns and adjectives agree with the article (definite or indefinite) applied to them, so for instance:

en brun hund   *a brown dog* (Swedish)
den bruna hunden   *the brown dog*
ett brunt hus   *a brown house*
det bruna huset   *the brown house*

△△ The use of grammar tokens is only one way of dealing with flexion and pronominal adverbs. The alternative is to alter the text typed until it resembles normal Informese:

gief gold cyninge	⟼	gief gold to cyning
gief gold toit	⟼	gief gold to it
den bruna hunden	⟼	den brun hund
det bruna huset	⟼	det brun hus

See §36 below. In a heavily inflected language with many irregularities, a combination of the two techniques may be needed.

§36   Parsing non-English languages

It, hell. She had *Those*.

— Dorothy Parker (1893–1967), reviewing the romantic novel '*It*'

Before embarking on a new language definition file, the translator may want to consider what compromises are worth making, omitting tricky but not really necessary features of the language. For instance, in German, adjectives take forms agreeing with whether their noun takes a definite or indefinite article:

ein großer Mann   *a tall man* (German)
der große Mann   *the tall man*

This is an essential. But German also has a "neutral" form for adjectives, used in sentences like

Der Mann ist groß   *The man is tall*

Now it could be argued that if the parser asks the German equivalent of

Whom do you mean, the tall man or the short man?

then the player ought to be able to reply "groß". But this is probably not worth the effort.

As another example from German, is it essential for the parser to recognise commands put in the polite form when addressed to somebody other than the player? For instance,

freddy, öffne den ofen   *Freddy, open the oven*
herr krüger, öffnen sie den ofen   *Mr Krueger, open the oven*

indicate that Freddy is a friend but Mr Krueger a mere acquaintance. A translator might go to the trouble of implementing this, but equally might not bother, and simply tell players always to use the familiar form. It's harder to avoid the issue of whether the computer is familiar to the player. Does the player address the computer or the main character of the game? In English it makes no difference, but there are languages where an imperative verb agrees with the gender of the person being addressed. Is the computer male? Is it still male if the game's main character is female?

Another choice is whether to require the player to use letters other than 'a' to 'z' from the keyboard. French readers are used to seeing words written in capital letters without accents, so that there is no need to make the player type accents. In Finnish, though, 'ä' and 'ö' are significantly different from 'a' and 'o': "vaara" means "danger", but "väärä" means "wrong".

Finally, there are also dialect forms. The number 80 is "quatre-vingt" in metropolitan French, "octante" in Belgian and "huitante" in Swiss French. In such cases, the translator may want to write the language definition file to cope with all possible dialects. For example, something like

```
#ifdef DIALECT_FRANCOPHONE; print "septante";
#ifnot; print "soixante-dix";
#endif;
```

would enable the same definition file to be used by Belgian authors and members of the Académie française alike. The standard "English.h" definition already has such a constant: DIALECT_US, which uses American spellings, so that if an Inform game defines

```
Constant DIALECT_US;
```

before including Parser, then (for example) the number 106 would be printed in words as "one hundred six" instead of "one hundred and six".

△   An alternative is to allow the player to change dialect during play, and to encode all spelling variations inside variable strings. Ralf Herrmann's "German.h" does this to allow the player to choose traditional, reformed or Swiss German conventions on the use of "ß". The low string variables @30 and @31 each hold either "ss" or "ß" for use in words like "schlie@30t" and "mu@31t".

· · · · ·

Organisation of language definition files

A language definition file is itself written in Inform, and fairly readable Inform at that: you may want to have a copy of "English.h" to refer to while reading the rest of this section. This is divided into four parts:
  I. Preliminaries
  II. Vocabulary
  III. Translating to Informese
  IV. Printing

It is helpful for all language definitions to follow the order and layout style of "English.h". The example used throughout the rest of the section is of developing a definition of "French.h".

(I.1) Version number and alphabet

The file should begin as follows:

```
!  ============================================================
!   Inform Library Definition File: French
!
!   (c) Angela M. Horns 1996
!  ------------------------------------------------------------
System_file;
!  ------------------------------------------------------------
!   Part I.   Preliminaries
!  ------------------------------------------------------------
Constant LanguageVersion
    = "Traduction fran@ccais 961205 par Angela M. Horns";
```

("English.h" defines a constant called EnglishNaturalLanguage here, but this is just to help the library keep old code working with the new parser: don't define a similar constant yourself.) Note the c-cedilla written using escape characters, @cc not c, which is a precaution to make absolutely certain that the file will be legible on anyone's system, even one whose character set doesn't have accented characters in the normal way.

The next ingredient of Part I is declaring the accented letters which need to be "cheap" in the following sense. Inside story files, dictionary words are stored to a "resolution" of nine Z-characters: that is, only the first nine Z-characters are looked at, so that

"chrysanthemum" is stored as 'chrysanth'
"chrysanthemums" is stored as 'chrysanth'

(This is one of the reasons why Informese doesn't make linguistic use of word-endings.) Normally no problem, but unfortunately Z-characters are not the same as letters. The letters 'A' to 'Z' are "cheap" and take only one Z-character each, but accented letters like 'é' normally take out four Z-characters. If your translation is going to ask the player to type accented letters at the keyboard (which even a French translation need not do: see above), the resolution may be unacceptably low:

"télécarte" is stored as 't@'el'
"téléphone" is stored as 't@'el'

as there are not even enough of the nine Z-characters left to encode the second 'é', let alone the 'c' or the 'p' which would distinguish the two words. Inform therefore provides a mechanism to make up to about 10 common accents cheaper to use, in that they then take only two Z-characters each, not four. In the case of French, we might write:

```
Zcharacter '@'e';     ! E-acute
Zcharacter '@`e';     ! E-grave
Zcharacter '@`a';     ! A-grave
Zcharacter '@`u';     ! U-grave
Zcharacter '@^a';     ! A-circumflex
Zcharacter '@^e';     ! E-circumflex
```

(Note that since the Z-machine automatically reduces anything the player types into lower case, we need only include lower-case accented letters here. Note also that there are plenty of other French accented letters (î, û and so forth) but these are uncommon enough not to matter here.) With this change made,

"télécarte" is stored as 't@'el@'ecar'
"téléphone" is stored as 't@'el@'epho'

enabling a phone card and a phone to be correctly distinguished by the parser.

△△ In any story file, 78 of the characters in the ZSCII set are designated as "cheap" by being placed into what's called the "alphabet table". One of these is mandatorily new-line, another is mandatorily double-quote and a third cannot be used, leaving 75. Zcharacter moves a ZSCII character into the alphabet table, throwing out a character which hasn't yet been used to make way. Alternatively, and provided no characters have so far been used at all, you can write a Zcharacter directive which sets the entire alphabet table. The form required is to give three strings containing 26, 26 and 23 ZSCII characters respectively. For instance:

```
Zcharacter "abcdefghijklmnopqrstuvwxyz"
           "ABCDEFGHIJKLMNOPQRSTUVWXYZ"
           "0123456789!$&*():;.,<>@{386}";
```

Characters in alphabet 1, the top row, take only one Z-character to print; characters in alphabets 2 and 3 take two Z-characters to print; characters not in the table take four. Note that this assumes that Unicode $0386 (Greek capital Alpha with tonos accent, as it happens) is present in ZSCII. Ordinarily it would not be, but the block of ZSCII character codes between 155 and 251 is configurable and can in principle contain any Unicode characters of your choice. By default, if Inform reads ISO 8859-n (switch setting -Cn) then this block is set up to contain all the non-ASCII letter characters in ISO 8859-n. In the most common case, -C1 for ISO Latin-1, the ligatures 'œ' and 'Œ' are then added, but this still leaves 28 character codes vacant.

```
Zcharacter table + '@{9a}';
```

adds Unicode character $009a, a copyright symbol, to ZSCII. Alternatively, you can instruct Inform to throw away all non-standard ZSCII characters and replace them with a fresh stock. The effect of:

```
Zcharacter table '@{9a}' '@{386}' '@^a';
```

is that ZSCII 155 will be a copyright symbol, 156 will be a Greek capital alpha with tonos, 157 will be an a-circumflex and 158 to 251 will be undefined; and all other accented letters will be unavailable. Such Zcharacter directives must be made before the characters in question are first used in game text. You don't need to know the ZSCII values, anyway: you can always write @{9a} when you want a copyright symbol.

(I.2) Compass objects

All that is left in Part I is to declare standard compass directions. The corresponding part of "English.h", given below, should be imitated as closely as possible:

```
Class CompassDirection
 with article "the", number
  has scenery;
Object Compass "compass" has concealed;
Ifndef WITHOUT_DIRECTIONS;
CompassDirection -> n_obj "north wall"
                   with name 'n//' 'north' 'wall',      door_dir n_to;
CompassDirection -> s_obj "south wall"
                   with name 's//' 'south' 'wall',      door_dir s_to;
CompassDirection -> e_obj "east wall"
                   with name 'e//' 'east' 'wall',      door_dir e_to;
CompassDirection -> w_obj "west wall"
                   with name 'w//' 'west' 'wall',      door_dir w_to;
CompassDirection -> ne_obj "northeast wall"
                   with name 'ne' 'northeast' 'wall', door_dir ne_to;
CompassDirection -> nw_obj "northwest wall"
                   with name 'nw' 'northwest' 'wall', door_dir nw_to;
CompassDirection -> se_obj "southeast wall"
                   with name 'se' 'southeast' 'wall', door_dir se_to;
CompassDirection -> sw_obj "southwest wall"
                   with name 'sw' 'southwest' 'wall', door_dir sw_to;
CompassDirection -> u_obj "ceiling"
                   with name 'u//' 'up' 'ceiling',      door_dir u_to;
CompassDirection -> d_obj "floor"
                   with name 'd//' 'down' 'floor',      door_dir d_to;
Endif;
CompassDirection -> out_obj "outside"
                   with                                door_dir out_to;
```

```
CompassDirection -> in_obj "inside"
                         with                          door_dir in_to;
```

For example, "French.h" would contain:

```
Class  CompassDirection
  with article "le", number
  has  scenery;
Object Compass "compas" has concealed;
...
CompassDirection -> n_obj "mur nord"
                         with name 'n//' 'nord' 'mur',      door_dir n_to;
```

(II.1) Informese vocabulary: the small categories

This is where small grammatical categories like ⟨again-word⟩ are defined. The following constants must be defined:

AGAIN*__WD	words of type ⟨again-word⟩
UNDO*__WD	words of type ⟨undo-word⟩
OOPS*__WD	words of type ⟨oops-word⟩
THEN*__WD	words of type ⟨then-word⟩
AND*__WD	words of type ⟨and-word⟩
BUT*__WD	words of type ⟨but-word⟩
ALL*__WD	words of type ⟨all-word⟩
OTHER*__WD	words of type ⟨other-word⟩
ME*__WD	words of type ⟨me-word⟩
OF*__WD	words of type ⟨of-word⟩
YES*__WD	words of type ⟨yes-word⟩
NO*__WD	words of type ⟨no-word⟩

In each case * runs from 1 to 3, except for ALL*__WD where it runs 1 to 5 and OF*__WD where it runs 1 to 4. ⟨of-words⟩ have not been mentioned before: these are used in the sense of "three of the boxes", when parsing a reference to a given number of things. They are redundant in English because the player could have typed simply "three boxes", but Inform provides them anyway.

In French, we might begin with:

```
Constant AGAIN1__WD    = 'encore';
Constant AGAIN2__WD    = 'c//';
Constant AGAIN3__WD    = 'encore';
```

Here we can't actually think of a third synonymous word for "again", but we must define AGAIN3__WD all the same, and must not allow it to be zero. And so on, through to:

```
Constant YES1__WD    = 'o//';
Constant YES2__WD    = 'oui';
Constant YES3__WD    = 'oui';
```

⟨yes-words⟩ and ⟨no-words⟩ are used to parse the answers to yes-or-no questions (oui-ou-non questions in French, of course). It causes no difficulty that the word "o" is also an abbreviation for "ouest" because they are used in different contexts. On the other hand, ⟨oops-words⟩, ⟨again-words⟩ and ⟨undo-words⟩ should be different from any verb or compass direction name.

After the above, a few further words have to be defined as possible replies to the question asked when a game ends. Here the French example might be:

```
Constant AMUSING__WD    = 'amusant';
Constant FULLSCORE1__WD = 'grandscore';
Constant FULLSCORE2__WD = 'grand';
Constant QUIT1__WD      = 'a//';
Constant QUIT2__WD      = 'arret';
Constant RESTART__WD    = 'reprand';
Constant RESTORE__WD    = 'restitue';
```

(II.2) Informese vocabulary: pronouns

Part II continues with a table of pronouns, best explained by example. The following table defines the standard English accusative pronouns:

```
Array LanguagePronouns table
  !  word         possible GNAs:                connected to:
  !                a   i
  !                s  p  s  p
  !                mfnmfnmfnmfn
     'it'          $$001000111000               NULL
     'him'         $$100000100000               NULL
     'her'         $$010000010000               NULL
     'them'        $$000111000111               NULL;
```

The "connected to" column should always be created with NULL entries. The pattern of 1 and 0 in the middle column indicates which types of ⟨noun phrase⟩ might be referred to with the given ⟨pronoun⟩. This is really a concise way of expressing a set of possible GNA values, saying for instance that "them" can match against noun phrases with any GNA in the set $\{3, 4, 5, 9, 10, 11\}$.

The accusative and dative pronouns in English are identical: for instance "her" in "give her the flowers" is dative and in "kiss her" is accusative. French is richer in pronoun forms:

> donne-le-lui *give it to him/her*
> mange avec lui *eat with him*

Here "-lui" and "lui" are grammatically quite different, with one implying masculinity where the other doesn't. The table needed is:

```
Array LanguagePronouns table
```

```
! word         possible GNAs:                connected to:
!              a    i
!              s  p  s  p
!              mfnmfnmfnmfn
  '-le'        $$100000100000                NULL
  '-la'        $$010000010000                NULL
  '-les'       $$000110000110                NULL
  '-lui'       $$110000110000                NULL
  '-leur'      $$000110000110                NULL
  'lui'        $$100000100000                NULL
  'elle'       $$010000010000                NULL
  'eux'        $$000100000100                NULL
  'elles'      $$000010000010                NULL;
```

This table assumes that "-le" can be treated as a free-standing word in its own right, not as part of the word "donne-le-lui", and section (III.1) below will describe how to bring this about. Note that "-les" and "-leur" are treated as synonymous: Informese doesn't (ordinarily) care that dative and accusative are different.

Using the "pronouns" verb in any game will print out current values, which may be useful when debugging the above table. Here is the same game position, inside the building at the end of the road, in parallel English, German and Spanish text:

English: 'Advent'
At the moment, "it" means the small bottle, "him" is unset, "her" is unset and "them" is unset.

German: 'Abenteuer'
Im Augenblick, "er" heisst der Schlüsselbund, "sie" heisst die Flasche, "es" heisst das Essen, "ihn" heisst der Schlüsselbund, "ihm" heisst das Essen und "ihnen" ist nicht gesetzt.

Spanish: 'Aventura'
En este momento, "-lo" significa el grupo de llaves, "-los" no está definido, "-la" significa la pequeña botella, "-las" significa las par de tuberí as de unos 15 cm de diámetro, "-le" significa la pequeña botella, "-les" significa las par de tuberí as de unos 15 cm de diámetro, "él" significa el grupo de llaves, "ella" significa la pequeña botella, "ellos" no está definido y "ellas" significa las par de tuberí as de unos 15 cm de diámetro.

(II.3) Informese vocabulary: descriptors

Part II continues with a table of descriptors, in a similar format.

```
Array LanguageDescriptors table
  ! word         possible GNAs    descriptor      connected
  !              to follow:       type:           to:
  !              a    i
  !              s  p  s  p
```

```
   !                  mfnmfnmfnmfn
     'my'       $$111111111111    POSSESS_PK      0
     'this'     $$111000111000    POSSESS_PK      0
     'these'    $$000111000111    POSSESS_PK      0
     'that'     $$111111111111    POSSESS_PK      1
     'those'    $$000111000111    POSSESS_PK      1
     'his'      $$111111111111    POSSESS_PK      'him'
     'her'      $$111111111111    POSSESS_PK      'her'
     'their'    $$111111111111    POSSESS_PK      'them'
     'its'      $$111111111111    POSSESS_PK      'it'
     'the'      $$111111111111    DEFART_PK       NULL
     'a//'      $$111000111000    INDEFART_PK     NULL
     'an'       $$111000111000    INDEFART_PK     NULL
     'some'     $$000111000111    INDEFART_PK     NULL;
```

This gives three of the four types of ⟨descriptor⟩. The constant POSSESS_PK signifies a ⟨possessive adjective⟩, connected either to 0, meaning the player-object, or to 1, meaning anything other than the player-object (used for "that" and similar words) or to the object referred to by the given ⟨pronoun⟩, which must be one of those in the pronoun table. DEFART_PK signifies a definite ⟨article⟩ and INDEFART_PK an indefinite ⟨article⟩: these should both give the connected-to value of NULL in all cases.

The fourth kind allows extra descriptors to be added which force the objects that follow to have, or not have, a given attribute. For example, the following three lines would implement "lit", "lighted" and "unlit" as adjectives automatically understood by the English parser:

```
     'lit'       $$111111111111    light       NULL
     'lighted'   $$111111111111    light       NULL
     'unlit'     $$111111111111    (-light)    NULL
```

An attribute name means "must have this attribute", while the negation of it means "must not have this attribute".

To continue the example, "French.h" needs the following descriptors table:

```
Array LanguageDescriptors table
   !   word          possible GNAs    descriptor       connected
   !                 to follow:       type:            to:
   !                 a     i
   !                 s  p  s  p
   !                 mfnmfnmfnmfn
     'le'       $$100000100000    DEFART_PK       NULL
     'la'       $$010000010000    DEFART_PK       NULL
     'l^'       $$110000110000    DEFART_PK       NULL
     'les'      $$000110000110    DEFART_PK       NULL
     'un'       $$100000100000    INDEFART_PK     NULL
```

'une'	$$010000010000	INDEFART_PK	NULL
'des'	$$000110000110	INDEFART_PK	NULL
'mon'	$$100000100000	POSSESS_PK	0
'ma'	$$010000010000	POSSESS_PK	0
'mes'	$$000110000110	POSSESS_PK	0
'son'	$$100000100000	POSSESS_PK	'-lui'
'sa'	$$010000010000	POSSESS_PK	'-lui'
'ses'	$$000110000110	POSSESS_PK	'-lui'
'leur'	$$110000110000	POSSESS_PK	'-les'
'leurs'	$$000110000110	POSSESS_PK	'-les' ;

(recall that in dictionary words, the apostrophe is written ^). Thus, "son oiseau" means "his bird" or "her bird", according to the current meaning of "-lui", i.e., according to the gender of the most recent singular noun referred to.

The parser automatically tries both meanings if the same word occurs in both pronoun and descriptor tables. This happens in English, where "her" can mean either a feminine singular possessive adjective ("take her purse") or a feminine singular object pronoun ("wake her up").

(II.4) Informese vocabulary: numbers

An array should be given of words having type ⟨number⟩. These should include enough to express the numbers 1 to 20, as in the example:

```
Array LanguageNumbers table
    'un' 1 'une' 1 'deux' 2 'trois' 3 'quatre' 4 'cinq' 5
    'six' 6 'sept' 7 'huit' 8 'neuf' 9 'dix' 10
    'onze' 11 'douze' 12 'treize' 13 'quatorze' 14 'quinze' 15
    'seize' 16 'dix-sept' 17 'dix-huit' 18 'dix-neuf' 19 'vingt' 20;
```

In some languages, such as Russian, there are numbers larger than 1 which inflect with gender: please recognise all possibilities here. If the same word appears in both numbers and descriptors tables, its meaning as a descriptor takes priority, which is useful in French as it means that the genders of "un" and "une" are recognised after all.

(III.1) Translating natural language to Informese

Part III holds the routine to convert what the player has typed into Informese. In "English.h" this does nothing at all:

```
[ LanguageToInformese; ];
```

This might just do for Dogg, the imaginary language in which Tom Stoppard's play *Dogg's Hamlet* is written, where the words are more or less English words rearranged. (It begins with someone tapping a microphone and saying "Breakfast, breakfast... sun, dock, trog...", and "Bicycles!" is an expletive.) Other languages are structurally unlike

266

English and the task of LanguageToInformese is to rearrange or rewrite commands to make them look more like English ones. Here are some typical procedures for LanguageToInformese to follow:

(1) Strip out optional accents. For instance, "German.h" looks through the command replacing ü with ue and so forth, and replacing ß with ss. This saves having to recognise both spelling forms.

(2) Break up words at hyphens and apostrophes, so that:

> donne-lui l'oiseau   *give the bird to him*   ↦   donne -lui l' oiseau

(3) Remove inflections which don't carry useful information. For instance, most German imperatives can take two forms, one with an 'e' on the end: "lege" means "leg" (German: "put") and "schaue" means "schau" (German: "look"). It would be helpful to remove this "e", if only to avoid stuffing game dictionaries full of essentially duplicate entries. (Toni Arnold's "German.h" goes further and strips all inflections from nouns, while Ralf Herrmann's preserves inflections for parsing later on.)

(4) Break affixes away from the words they're glued to. For instance:

> della   *of the* (Italian)   ↦   di la
> cogela   *take it* (Spanish)   ↦   coge la

so that the affix part "la" becomes a separate word and can be treated as a pronoun.

(5) Replace parts of speech not existing in Informese, such as pronominal adverbs, with a suitable alternative. For instance:

> dessus   *on top of it* (French)   ↦   sur lui
> dedans   *inside it*   ↦   dans lui

(6) Alter word order. For instance, break off an enclitic and move it between two nouns; or if the definite article is written as a suffix, cut it free and move it before the noun:

> arma virumque   *arms and the man* (Latin)   ↦   arma et virum
> kakane   *the cakes* (Norwegian)   ↦   ne kake

When the call to LanguageToInformese is made, the text that the player typed is held in a -> array called buffer, and some useful information about it is held in another array called parse. The contents of these arrays are described in detail in §2.5.

The translation process has to be done by shifting characters about and altering them in buffer. Of course the moment anything in buffer is changed, the information in parse becomes out of date. You can update parse with the assembly-language statement

```
@tokenise buffer parse;
```

(And the parser does just this when the LanguageToInformese routine has finished.) The most commonly made alterations come down to inserting characters, often spaces, in between words, and deleting other characters by overwriting them with spaces. Inserting characters means moving the rest of buffer along by one character, altering the length buffer->1, and making sure that no overflow occurs. The library therefore provides a utility routine

```
LTI_Insert(position, character)
```

to insert the given character at the given position in buffer.

● **EXERCISE 110**
Write a LanguageToInformese routine to insert spaces before each hyphen and after each apostrophe, so that:

donne-lui l'oiseau   *give the bird to him*   ↦   donne -lui l' oiseau

● **EXERCISE 111**
Make further translations for French pronominal adverbs:

dessus   *on top of it*   ↦   sur lui
dedans   *inside it*   ↦   dans lui

● △**EXERCISE 112**
Write a routine called LTI_Shift(from,chars), which shifts the tail of the buffer array by chars positions to the right (so that it moves leftwards if chars is negative), where the "tail" is the part of the buffer starting at from and continuing to the end.

● △**EXERCISE 113**
Write a LanguageToInformese routine which sorts out German pronominal adverbs, which are made by adding "da" or "dar" to any preposition. Beware of breaking a name like "Darren" which might have a meaning within the game, though, so that:

davon   ↦   von es
darauf   ↦   auf es
darren   ↦̸   ren es

§37 Names and messages in non-English languages

The fourth and final part of the language definition file is taken up with rules on printing out messages and object names in the new language. The *gender-number-animation (GNA)* combination is considerably more important when printing nouns than when parsing them, because the player is less forgiving of errors. Few errors are as conspicuous or as painful as "You can see a gloves here.", in which the library's list-writer has evidently used the wrong GNA for the gloves. Here is a more substantial example:

> *Volière*
> Une jungle superbe, avec des animaux et des arbres.
> On peut voir ici trois oiseaux (une oie, un moineau et un cygne blanc), cinq boîtes, une huître, Edith Piaf et des raisins.

To print this, the list-writer needs to know that "oie" is feminine singular, "cygne blanc" is masculine singular and so on. In short, it must be told the GNA of every object name it ever prints, or it will append all the wrong articles.

The translator will need first to decide how the genders are to be used. Inform allows for three genders, called `male`, `female` and `neuter` because they are usually used for masculine, feminine and neuter genders. Different natural languages will use these differently. In English, all nouns are neuter except for those of people (and sometimes higher animals), when they follow the gender of the person. Latin, German and Dutch use all three genders without any very logical pattern, while French, Spanish and Italian have no neuter. In Norwegian even the number of genders is a matter of dialect: traditional Norwegian has two genders, "common" and "neuter", but more recently Norwegian has absorbed a new feminine gender from its rural dialects. One way to achieve this in Inform would be to use `male` for common, `female` for the rural feminine and `neuter` for neuter. To avoid confusion it might be worth making the definition

```
Attribute common alias male;
```

which makes `common` equivalent to writing `male`. (The keyword `alias` is used, though very seldom, for making alternative names for attributes and properties.)

Here's how the library determines the GNA of an object's short name. The A part is easy: all objects having the `animate` attribute are animate and all others are inanimate. Similarly for the N part: objects having `pluralname` are plural, all others singular. (An object having `pluralname` is nevertheless only one object: for example an object called "doors" which represents a pair of doubled doors, or "grapes" representing a bunch of grapes.) If the object has `male`, `female` or `neuter` then the short name has masculine, feminine or neuter gender accordingly. If it has none of these, then it defaults to the gender `LanguageAnimateGender` if animate and `LanguageInanimateGender` otherwise. (These are constants set by the language definition file: see (IV.1) below.) You can find the GNA associated with an object's short name by calling the library routine

```
GetGNAOfObject(obj);
```

which returns the GNA number, 0 to 11.

- **EXERCISE 114**
Devise a verb so that typing "gna frog" results in "frog: animate singular neuter (GNA 2) / The frog / the frog / a frog", thus testing all possible articled and unarticled forms of the short name.

. . . . .

In some languages, though not English, short names are inflected to make them agree with the kind of article applied to them:

das rote Buch   *the red book* (German)
ein rotes Buch   *a red book*

In printing as in parsing, the library variable indef_mode holds true if an indefinite article attaches to the noun phrase and false otherwise. So one rather clumsy solution would be:

```
Object Buch
  with ...
        short_name [;
          if (indef_mode) print "rotes Buch"; else print "rote Buch";
          rtrue;
        ];
```

In fact, though, the library automatically looks for a short_name_indef property when printing short names in indefinite cases, and uses this instead of short_name. So:

```
Object Buch
  with short_name "rote Buch", short_name_indef "rotes Buch";
```

An automatic system for regular inflections of short names is possible but not easy to get right.

In languages other than English, short names also inflect with case, and the best way to handle this may be to provide new printing rules like dative_the, enabling the designer to write code like so:

```
"You give ", (the) noun, " to ", (dative_the) second, ".";
```

(IV.1) Default genders and contraction forms

Part IV of a language definition file opens with declarations of the default gender constants mentioned above. "English.h" has

```
Constant LanguageAnimateGender   = male;
Constant LanguageInanimateGender = neuter;
```

whereas French would define both to be male.

Inform uses the term *contraction form* to mean a textual feature of a noun which causes any article in front of it to inflect. English has two contraction forms, "starting with a vowel" and "starting with a consonant", affecting the indefinite article:

a + orange = an orange
a + banana = a banana

The first constant to define is the number of contraction forms in the language. In the case of "French.h" there will be two:

```
Constant LanguageContractionForms = 2;
```

Of these, form 0 means "starting with a consonant" and 1 means "starting with a vowel or mute h". (It's up to you how you number these.) You also have to provide the routine that decides which contraction form a piece of text has. Here is an abbreviated version for French, abbreviated in that it omits to check accented vowels like 'é':

```
[ LanguageContraction text;
   if (text->0 == 'a' or 'e' or 'i' or 'o' or 'u' or 'h' or
                  'A' or 'E' or 'I' or 'O' or 'U' or 'H') return 1;
   return 0;
];
```

The text array holds the full text of the noun, though this routine would normally only look at the first few letters at most. The routine is only ever called when it is necessary to do so: for instance, when the library prints "the eagles", LanguageContraction is not called because the article would be the same regardless of whether "eagles" has contraction form 0 or 1.

● **EXERCISE 115**

Italian has three contraction forms: starting with a vowel, starting with a 'z' or else 's'-followed-by-a-consonant, and starting with a consonant. Write a suitable LanguageContraction routine.

(IV.2) How to print: articles

English needs two sets of articles: one set for singular nouns, which we shall call article set 0, another for plurals, article set 1. We need to define an array to show which GNAs result in which article set:

```
            !                a            i
            !                s     p      s      p
            !                m f n m f n m f n m f n
   Array LanguageGNAsToArticles --> 0 0 0 1 1 1 0 0 0 1 1 1;
```

(The number of article sets is not defined as a constant, but instead by the contents of this array: here the only values are 0 and 1, so there need to be two article sets.) We also need to define the article sets themselves. There are three articles for each combination of contraction form and article set. For example, "English.h" has two contraction forms and two article sets, so we supply twelve articles:

```
   Array LanguageArticles -->
    !  Contraction form 0:      Contraction form 1:
    !  Cdef    Def    Indef     Cdef    Def    Indef
       "The " "the " "a "       "The " "the " "an "      ! Set 0
       "The " "the " "some "    "The " "the " "some ";   ! Set 1
```

That defines the automatic rules used to apply articles to nouns, but there are two ways to override this: the property `article`, if present, specifies an explicit indefinite article for an object; and the property `articles`, if present, specifies an explicit set of three articles. This is useful for nouns whose articles are irregular, such as the French "haricot": the regular definite article would be "l'haricot", but by an accident of history "le haricot" is correct, so:

```
   Object "haricot"
     with articles "Le " "le " "un ", ...
```

● EXERCISE 116
Construct suitable arrays for the regular French articles.

● EXERCISE 117
Likewise for Italian, where Inform needs to be able to print a wider selection: un, un', una, uno, i, il, gli, l', la, le, lo.

● EXERCISE 118
At the other extreme, what if (like Latin: "vir" *man* or *a man* or *the man*) a language has no articles?

(IV.3) How to print: direction names

Next is a routine called LanguageDirection to print names for direction properties (*not* direction objects). Imitate the following, from "French.h":

```
[ LanguageDirection d;
  switch (d) {
        n_to:    print "nord";        s_to:    print "sud";
        e_to:    print "est";         w_to:    print "ouest";
        ne_to:   print "nordest";     nw_to:   print "nordouest";
        se_to:   print "sudest";      sw_to:   print "sudouest";
        u_to:    print "haut";        d_to:    print "bas";
        in_to:   print "dans";        out_to:  print "dehors";
        default: RunTimeError(9,d);
  }
];
```

(IV.4) How to print: numbers

Next is a routine called LanguageNumber which takes a number N and prints it out in textual form. N can be anything from −32767 to 32767 and the correct text should be printed in every case. In most languages a recursive approach makes this routine less enormous than it might sound.

● **EXERCISE 119**
Write LanguageNumber for French.

(IV.5) How to print: the time of day

Even mostly numeric representations of the time of day vary from language to language: when it's 1:23 pm in England, it's 13h23 in France. A routine called LanguageTime-OfDay should print out the language's preferred form of the time of day, like so:

```
[ LanguageTimeOfDay hours mins;
  print hours/10, hours%10, "h", mins/10, mins%10;
];
```

● **EXERCISE 120**
Write the corresponding English version.

(IV.6) How to print: verbs

The parser sometimes needs to print verbs out, in messages like:

> I only understood you as far as wanting to *take* the red box.

It normally does this by simply printing out the verb's dictionary entry. However, dictionary entries tend to be cut short (to the first 9 letters or so) or else to be

273

abbreviations (rather as "i" means "inventory"). In your language, verbs might also need to inflect in a sentence like the one above, which assumes that the infinitive and imperative are the same. You might get around that by rewording the statement as:

I only understood you as far as "*take* the red box".

Even so, how to print out verbs depends on the language, so you need to give a routine called LanguageVerb which looks at its argument and either prints a textual form and returns true, or returns false to let the library carry on as normal. In English, only a few of the more commonly-used abbreviations are glossed, and "x" for "examine" is the only one that really matters:

```
[ LanguageVerb verb_word;
  switch (verb_word) {
      'l//': print "look";
      'z//': print "wait";
      'x//': print "examine";
      'i//', 'inv', 'inventory': print "inventory";
      default: rfalse;
  }
  rtrue;
];
```

(IV.7) How to print: menus

Next, a batch of definitions should be made to specify the look of menus and which keys on the keyboard navigate through them. Imitate the following "English.h" definitions, if possible keeping the strings the same length (padding out with spaces if your translations are shorter than the English original):

```
Constant NKEY__TX    = "N = next subject";
Constant PKEY__TX    = "P = previous";
Constant QKEY1__TX   = "  Q = resume game";
Constant QKEY2__TX   = "Q = previous menu";
Constant RKEY__TX    = "RETURN = read subject";
Constant NKEY1__KY   = 'N';
Constant NKEY2__KY   = 'n';
Constant PKEY1__KY   = 'P';
Constant PKEY2__KY   = 'p';
Constant QKEY1__KY   = 'Q';
Constant QKEY2__KY   = 'q';
```

(IV.8) How to print: miscellaneous short messages

These are phrases or words so short that the author decided they probably weren't worth putting in the LibraryMessages system (he now thinks otherwise: code in haste, repent at leisure). Here are some French versions with notes.

```
Constant SCORE__TX    = "Score: ";
Constant MOVES__TX    = "Tours: ";
Constant TIME__TX     = "Heure: ";
```

which define the text printed on the status line: in English, "Score" and "Turns" or "Time";

```
Constant CANTGO__TX   = "On ne peut pas aller en ce direction.";
```

the default "You can't go that way" message;

```
Constant FORMER__TX   = "votre m@^eme ancien";
```

the short name of the player's former self, after the player has become somebody else by use of the ChangePlayer routine;

```
Constant YOURSELF__TX = "votre m@^eme";
```

the short name of the player object;

```
Constant DARKNESS__TX = "Obscurit@'e";
```

the short name of a location in darkness;

```
Constant NOTHING__TX  = "rien";
```

the short name of the nothing object, caused by print (name) 0;, which is not strictly speaking legal anyway;

```
Constant THAT__TX     = "@cca";
Constant THOSET__TX   = "ces choses";
```

(THOSET stands for "those things") used in command printing. There are three circumstances in which all or part of a command can be printed by the parser: for an incomplete command, a vague command or an overlong one. Thus

>take out
What do you want to take out?
>give frog
(to Professor Moriarty)

```
>take frog within cage
```
I only understood you as far as wanting to take the frog.

In such messages, the THOSET__TX text is printed in place of a multiple object like "all" while THAT__TX is printed in place of a number or of something not well understood by the parser, like the result of a topic token.

```
Constant OR__TX        = " ou ";
```

appears in the list of objects being printed in a question asking you which thing you mean: if you can't find anything grammatical to go here, try using just ", ";

```
Constant AND__TX       = " et ";
```

used to divide up many kinds of list;

```
Constant WHOM__TX      = "qui ";
Constant WHICH__TX     = "lequel ";
Constant IS2__TX       = "est ";
Constant ARE2__TX      = "sont ";
```

used only to print text like "inside which is a duck", "on top of whom are two drakes";

```
Constant IS__TX        = " est";
Constant ARE__TX       = " sont";
```

used only by the list-maker and only when the ISARE_BIT is set; the library only does this from within LibraryMessages, so you can avoid the need altogether.

(IV.9) How to print: the Library Messages

Finally, Part IV contains an extensive block of translated library messages, making up at least half the bulk of the language definition file. Here is the entry for a typical verb in "English.h":

```
SwitchOn:
    switch (n) {
        1: print_ret (ctheyreorthats) x1,
                " not something you can switch.";
        2: print_ret (ctheyreorthats) x1,
                " already on.";
        3: "You switch ", (the) x1, " on.";
    }
```

You have to translate every one of these messages to at least a near equivalent. It may be useful to define new printing rules, just as "English.h" does:

```
[ CTheyreorThats obj;
   if (obj == player) { print "You're"; return; }
   if (obj has pluralname) { print "They're"; return; }
   if (obj has animate)
   {   if (obj has female) { print "She's"; return; }
       else if (obj hasnt neuter) { print "He's"; return; }
   }
   print "That's";
];
```

• **EXERCISE 121**

Write a printing rule called FrenchNominativePronoun which prints the right one out of il, elle, ils, elles.

• **REFERENCES**

Andreas Hoppler's alternative list-writing library extension "Lister.h" is partly designed to make it easier for inflected languages to print out lists.

Chapter VI: Using the Compiler

I was promised a horse, but what I got instead
was a tail, with a horse hung from it almost dead.

— Palladas of Alexandria (319?–400?),
translated by Tony Harrison (1937–)

§38   Controlling compilation from within

Inform has a number of directives for controlling which pieces of source code are compiled: for instance, you can divide your source code into several files, compiled together or separately, or you can write source code in which different passages will be compiled on different occasions. Most of these directives are seldom seen, but almost every game uses:

```
Include "filename";
```

which instructs Inform to glue the whole of that source code file into the program right here. It is exactly equivalent to removing the Include directive and replacing it with the whole file "filename". (The rules for how Inform interprets "filename" vary from machine to machine: for instance, it may automatically add an extension such as ".inf" if your operating system normally uses filename extensions and it may look in some special directory. Run Inform with the -h1 switch for further information.) Note that you can write

```
Include ">shortname";
```

to mean "the file called "shortname" which is in the same directory that the present file came from". This is convenient if all the files making up the source code of your game are housed together.

Next, there are a number of "conditional compilation" directives. They take the general form of a condition:

```
Ifdef ⟨name⟩;        Is ⟨name⟩ defined as having some meaning?
Ifndef ⟨name⟩;       Is ⟨name⟩ undefined?
Iftrue ⟨condition⟩;  Is this ⟨condition⟩ true?
Iffalse ⟨condition⟩; Is this ⟨condition⟩ false?
```

followed by a chunk of Inform and then, optionally,

```
Ifnot;
```

and another chunk of Inform; and finally

```
Endif;
```

At this point it is perhaps worth mentioning that (most) directives can also be interspersed with statements in routine declarations, provided they are preceded by a # sign. For example:

```
[ MyRoutine;
#Iftrue MAX_SCORE > 1000;
   print "My, what a long game we're in for!^";
#Ifnot;
   print "Let's have a quick game, then.^";
#Endif;
   PlayTheGame();
];
```

which actually only compiles one of the two print statements, according to what the value of the constant MAX_SCORE is.

△   One kind of "if-defined" manoeuvre is so useful that it has an abbreviation:

```
Default ⟨name⟩ ⟨value⟩;
```

defines ⟨name⟩ as a constant if it wasn't already the name of something: so it's equivalent to

```
Ifndef ⟨name⟩; Constant ⟨name⟩ = ⟨value⟩; Endif;
```

Similarly, though far less often used, Stub <name> <number>; defines a do-nothing routine with this name and number (0 to 3) of local variables, if it isn't already the name of something: it is equivalent to

```
Ifndef ⟨name⟩; [ ⟨name⟩ x1 x2 ... x⟨number⟩; ]; Endif;
```

279

. . . . .

Large standard chunks of Inform source code are often bundled up into "libraries" which can be added to any Inform story file using the Include directive. Almost all Inform adventure games include three library files called "Parser", "VerbLib" and "Grammar", and several dozen smaller libraries have also been written. Sometimes, though, what you want to do is "include all of this library file except for the definition of SomeRoutine". You can do this by declaring:

```
Replace SomeRoutine;
```

before the relevant library file is included. You still have to define your own SomeRoutine, hence the term "replace".

△△ How does Inform know to ignore the SomeRoutine definition in the library file, but to accept yours as valid? The answer is that a library file is marked out as having routines which can be replaced, by containing the directive

```
System_file;
```

All eight of the standard Inform library files (the three you normally Include in games, plus the five others which they Include for you) begin with this directive. It also has the effect of suppressing all compilation warnings (but not errors) arising from the file.

. . . . .

One way to follow what is being compiled is to use the Message directive. This makes the compiler print messages as it compiles:

```
Message "An informational message";
Message error "An error message";
Message fatalerror "A fatal error message";
Message warning "A warning message";
```

Errors, fatal errors and warnings are treated as if they had arisen from faults in the source code in the normal way. See §40 for more about the kinds of error Inform can produce, but for now, note that an error or fatal error will prevent any story file from being produced, and that messages issued by Message warning will be suppressed if they occur in a "system file" (one that you have marked with a System_file directive). Informational messages are simply printed:

```
Message "Geometry library by Boris J. Parallelopiped";
```

prints this text, followed by a new-line.

△   One reason to use this might be to ensure that a library file fails gracefully if it needs to use a feature which was only introduced on a later version of the Inform compiler than the one it finds itself running through. For example:

```
Ifndef VN_1610;
Message fatalerror
    "The geometry extension needs Inform 6.1 or later";
Endif;
```

By special rule, the condition "VN_1610 is defined" is true if and only if the compiler's release number is 6.10 or more; similarly for the previous releases 6.01, first to include message-sending, 6.02, 6.03, 6.04, 6.05, 6.10, which expanded numerous previous limits on grammar, 6.11, 6.12, which allowed Inform to read from non-English character sets, 6.13, 6.15, which allowed parametrised object creation, 6.20, which introduced strict error checking, and finally (so far) 6.21, the first to feature Infix. A full history can be found in the *Technical Manual*.

·   ·   ·   ·   ·

Inform also has the ability to link together separately-compiled pieces of story file into the current compilation. This feature is provided primarily for users with slowish machines who would sooner not waste time compiling the standard Inform library routines over and over again. Linking isn't something you can do entirely freely, though, and if you have a fast machine you may prefer not to bother with it: the time taken to compile a story file is now often dominated by disc access times, so little or no time will be saved.

The pieces of pre-compiled story file are called "modules" and they cannot be interpreted or used for anything other than linking.

The process is as follows. A game being compiled (called the "external" program) may Link one or more pre-compiled sections of code called "modules". Suppose the game Jekyll has a subsection called Hyde. Then these two methods of making Jekyll are, very nearly, equivalent:

(1) Putting Include "Hyde"; in the source for "Jekyll", and compiling "Jekyll".
(2) Compiling "Hyde" with the -M ("module") switch set, then putting Link "Hyde"; into the same point in the source for "Jekyll", and compiling "Jekyll".

Option (2) is faster as long as "Hyde" does not change very often, since its ready-compiled module can be left lying around while "Jekyll" is being developed.

Because "linking the library" is by far the most common use of the linker, this is made simple. All you have to do is compile your game with the -U switch set, or, equivalently, to begin your source code with

```
Constant USE_MODULES;
```

This assumes that you already have pre-compiled copies of the two library modules: if not, you'll need to make them with

```
inform -M library/parserm.h
inform -M library/verblibm.h
```

where `library/parserm.h` should be replaced with whatever filename you keep the library file "parserm" in, and likewise for "verblibm". This sounds good, but here are four caveats:

(1) You can only do this for a game compiled as a Version 5 story file. This is the version Inform normally compiles to, but some authors of very large games need to use Version 8. Such authors usually have relatively fast machines and don't need the marginal speed gain from linking rather than including.

(2) It's essential not to make any `Attribute` or `Property` declarations *before* the `Include "Parser"` line in the source code, though *after* that point is fine. Inform will warn you if you get this wrong.

(3) Infix debugging, -X, is not compatible with linking, and strict error checking -S does not apply within modules.

(4) The precompiled library modules always include the -D debugging verbs, so when you come to compile the final release version of a game, you'll have to compile it the slow way, i.e., without linking the library.

△△ If you intend to write your own pre-compilable library modules, or intend to subdivide a large game into many modular parts, you will need to know what the limitations are on linking. (In the last recourse you may want to look at the *Technical Manual*.) Here's a brief list:

(1) The module must make the same `Property` and `Attribute` directives as the main program and in the same order. Including the library file `"linklpa.h"` ("link library properties and attributes") declares the library's own stock, so it might be sensible to do this first, and then include a similar file defining any extra common properties and attributes you need.

(2) The module cannot contain grammar (i.e., use `Verb` or `Extend` directives) or create "fake actions".

(3) The module can only use global variables defined outside the module if they are explicitly declared before use using the `Import` directive. For example, writing `Import global frog;` allows the rest of the module's source code to refer to the

variable frog (which must be defined in the outside program). Note that the
Include file "linklv.h" ("link library variables") imports all the library variables,
so it would be sensible to include this.
(4) An object in the module can't inherit from a class defined outside the module.
(But an object outside can inherit from a class inside.)
(5) Certain constant values in the module must be known at module-compile-time
(and must not, for instance, be a symbol only defined outside the module). For
instance: the size of an array must be known now, not later; so must the number
of duplicate members of a Class; and the quantities being compared in an Iftrue
or Iffalse.
(6) The module can't: define the Main routine; use the Stub or Default directives; or
define an object whose parent object is not also in the same module.

These restrictions are mild in practice. As an example, here is a short module to play
with:

```
Include "linklpa";        ! Make use of the properties, attributes
Include "linklv";         ! and variables from the Library
[ LitThings x;
   objectloop (x has light)
       print (The) x, " is currently giving off light.^";
];
```

It should be possible to compile this -M and then to Link it into another game, making
the routine LitThings exist in that game.

· · · · ·

Every story file has a release number and a serial code. Games compiled
with the Inform library print these numbers in one line of the "banner". For
instance, a game compiled in December 1998 might have the banner line:

Release 1 / Serial number 981218 / Inform v6.20 Library 6/8

The release number is 1 unless otherwise specified with the directive

```
Release <number>;
```

This can be any Inform number, but convention is for the first published copy
of a game to be numbered 1, and releases 2, 3, 4, . . . to be amended re-releases.

The serial number is set automatically to the date of compilation in the
form "yymmdd", so that 981218 means "18th December 1998" and 000101
means "1st January 2000". You can fix the date differently by setting

```
Serial "dddddd";
```

where the text must be a string of 6 (decimal) digits. Inform's standard example
games do this, so that the serial number will be the date of last modification of
the source code, regardless of when the story file is eventually compiled.

△   The Inform release number is written into the story file by Inform itself, and you can't change it. But you can make the story file print out this number with the special statement inversion;.

§39   Controlling compilation from without

The Inform compiler has the equivalent of a dashboard of "command line switches", controlling its behaviour. Most of these have only two settings, off or on, and most of them are off most of the time. Others can be set to a number between 0 and 9. In this book switches are written preceded by a minus sign, just as they would be typed if you were using Inform from the command line of (say) Unix or RISC OS. Setting -x, for instance, causes Inform to print a row of hash signs as it compiles:

```
inform -x shell
RISC OS Inform 6.20 (10th December 1998)
::###############################################################
################
```

One hash sign is printed for every 100 textual lines of source code compiled, so this row represents about eight thousand lines. (During the above compilation, carried out by an Acorn Risc PC 700, hashes were printed at a rate of about thirty per second.) -x is provided not so much for information as to indicate that a slow compilation is continuing normally. Contrariwise, the -s switch offers more statistics than you could possibly have wanted, as in the following monster compilation (of 'Curses'):

```
RISC OS Inform 6.20 (10th December 1998)
In: 25 source code files        17052 syntactic lines
 22098 textual lines           860147 characters (ISO 8859-1 Latin1)
Allocated:
  1925 symbols (maximum 10000)  1022182 bytes of memory
Out:   Version 8 "Extended" story file 17.981218 (343.5K long):
    37 classes (maximum 64)        579 objects (maximum 639)
   169 global vars (maximum 233)  4856 variable/array space (m. 8000)
   153 verbs (maximum 200)        1363 dictionary entries (m. 2000)
   318 grammar lines (version 2)   490 grammar tokens (unlimited)
   167 actions (maximum 200)        34 attributes (maximum 48)
    51 common props (maximum 62)   153 individual props (unlimited)
267892 characters used in text  195144 bytes compressed (rate 0.728)
     0 abbreviations (maximum 64)  891 routines (unlimited)
 25074 instructions of Z-code   10371 sequence points
 52752 bytes readable memory used (maximum 65536)
351408 bytes used in Z-machine  172880 bytes free in Z-machine
Completed in 8 seconds
```

The complete list of switches is listed when you run Inform with -h2, and also in Table 3 at the back of this book, where there are notes on some of the odder-looking ones.

When the statistics listing claims that, for instance, the maximum space for arrays is 10,000, this is so because Inform has only allocated enough memory to keep track of 10,000 entries while compiling. This in turn is because Inform's "memory setting" $MAX_STATIC_DATA was set to 10,000 when the compilation took place.

Between them, the "memory settings" control how much of your computer's memory Inform uses while running. Too little and it may not be able to compile games of the size you need, but too much and it may choke any other programs in the computer for space. It's left up to you to adjust the memory settings to suit your own environment, but most people leave them alone until an error message advises a specific increase.

Finally, Inform has "path variables", which contain filenames for the files Inform uses or creates. Usage of these varies widely from one operating system to another. Run Inform with the -h1 switch for further information.

.   .   .   .   .

Inform's switches, path variables and memory settings are set using "Inform Command Language" or ICL. The usual way to issue ICL commands, at least on installations of Inform which don't have windowed front-ends, is to squeeze them onto the command line. The standard command line syntax is

```
inform ⟨ICL commands⟩ ⟨source file⟩ ⟨output file⟩
```

where only the ⟨source file⟩ is mandatory. By default, the full names to give the source and output files are derived in a way suitable for the machine Inform is running on: on a PC, for instance, advent may be understood as asking to compile advent.inf to advent.z5. This is called "filename translation". No detailed information on filenaming rules is given here, because it varies so much from machine to machine: see the -h1 on-line documentation. Note that a filename can contain spaces if it is written in double-quotes and if the operating system being used can cope with spaces (as Mac OS can, for instance).

To specify sprawling or peculiar projects may need more ICL commands than can fit comfortably onto the command line. One possible ICL command, however, is to give a filename in (round) brackets: e.g.,

```
inform -x (skyfall_setup) ...
```

which sets the -x switch, then runs through the text file skyfall_setup executing each line as an ICL command. This file then look like this:

```
! Setup file for "Skyfall"
-d                    ! Contract double spaces
$max_objects=1000     ! 500 of them snowflakes
(usual_setup)         ! include my favourite settings, too
+module_path=mods     ! keep modules in the "mods" directory
```

ICL can include comments if placed after !, just as in Inform. Otherwise, an ICL file has only one command per line, with no dividing semicolons. Using ICL allows you to compile whole batches of files as required, altering switches, path variables and memory settings as you go. Notice that ICL files can call up other ICL files, as in the example above: don't allow a file to call up another copy of itself, or the compilation will all end in tears.

△ When typing such a command into a shell under a Unix-like operating systems, you may need to quote the parentheses:

```
inform -x '(skyfall_setup)' ...
```

This instructs the shell to pass on the command literally to Inform, and not to react to unusual characters like $, ?, (or) in it. The same may be needed for other ICL commands such as:

```
inform -x '$MAX_OBJECTS=2000' ...
```

△ Windowed front-ends for Inform sometimes work by letting the user select various options and then, when the "Go" button is pressed, convert the state of the dialogue box into an ICL file which is passed to Inform.

△△ If you need to use Inform without benefit of either a command line or a fancy front-end, or if you want your source code to specify its own switch settings, you can still set (most) switches by placing the directive

```
Switches ⟨some settings⟩;
```

at the very beginning of your source code. (So that you can still override such settings, the switch -i tells Inform to ignore all Switches directives.)

. . . . .

The ICL commands are as follows:

-⟨switches⟩
Set these switches; or unset any switch preceded by a tilde ~. (For example, -a~bc sets a, unsets b and sets c.)

$list
List current memory settings.

$?⟨name⟩
Ask for information on what this memory setting is for.

$small
Set the whole collection of memory settings to suitable levels for a small game.

$large
Ditto, for a slightly larger game.

$huge
Ditto, for a reasonably big one.

$⟨name⟩=⟨quantity⟩
Alter the named memory setting to the given level.

+⟨name⟩=⟨filename⟩
Set the named pathname variable to the given filename, which should be one or more filenames of directories, separated by commas.

compile ⟨filename⟩ ⟨filename⟩
Compile the first-named file, containing source code, writing the output program to the (optional) second-named file.

(⟨filename⟩)
Execute this ICL file (files may call each other in this way).

·   ·   ·   ·   ·

It's a nuisance to have to move all the memory settings up or down to cope with a big game or a small computer, so $small, $large and $huge are provided as short cuts. Typically these might allocate 350K, 500K or 610K respectively. Running

```
inform $list
```

will list the various settings which can be changed, and their current values. Thus one can compare small and large with:

```
inform $small $list
inform $large $list
```

If Inform runs out of allocation for something, it will generally print an error message like:

```
"Game", line 1320: Fatal error: The memory setting MAX_OBJECTS
(which is 200 at present) has been exceeded.  Try running Inform
again with $MAX_OBJECTS=<some-larger-number> on the command line.
```

and it would then be sensible to try

```
inform $MAX_OBJECTS=250 game
```

which tells Inform to try again, reserving more memory for objects this time. ICL commands are followed from left to right, so

```
inform $small $MAX_ACTIONS=200 ...
```

will work, but

```
inform $MAX_ACTIONS=200 $small ...
```

will not because the $small changes MAX_ACTIONS back again. Changing some settings has hardly any effect on memory usage, whereas others are expensive to increase. To find out about, say, MAX_VERBS, run

```
inform $?MAX_VERBS
```

(note the question mark) which will print some very brief comments.

§40   Error messages

Five kinds of error are reported by Inform: a fatal error is a breakdown severe enough to make Inform stop working at once; an error allows Inform to continue for the time being, but will normally cause Inform not to output the story file (because it is suspected of being damaged); and a warning means that Inform suspects you may have made a mistake, but will not take any action itself. The fourth kind is an ICL error, where a mistake has been made in a file of ICL commands for Inform to follow: an error on the command line is called a "command line error" but is just another way to get an ICL error. And the fifth is a compiler error, which appears if Inform's internal cross-checking shows that it is malfunctioning. The text reporting a compiler error asks the user to report it the author of Inform.

Fatal errors

1. *Too many errors*

```
Too many errors: giving up
```

After 100 errors, Inform stops, in case it has been given the wrong source file altogether, such as a program written in a different language.

. . . . .

2. *Input/output problems*

Most commonly, Inform has the wrong filename:

```
Couldn't open source file ⟨filename⟩
Couldn't open output file ⟨filename⟩
```

(and so on). More seriously the whole process of file input/output (or "I/O") may go wrong for some reason to do with the host computer: for instance, if it runs out of disc space. Such errors are rare and look like this:

```
I/O failure: couldn't read from source file
I/O failure: couldn't backtrack on story file for checksum
```

and so forth. The explanation might be that two tasks are vying for control of the same file (e.g., two independent Inform compilations trying to write a debugging information file with the same name), or that the file has somehow been left "open" by earlier, aborted compilation. Normally you can only have at most 256 files of source code in a single compilation. If this limit is passed, Inform generates the error

```
Program contains too many source files: increase #define
    MAX_SOURCE_FILES
```

This might happen if file A includes file B which includes file C which includes file A which... and so on. Finally, if a non-existent pathname variable is set in ICL, the error

```
No such path setting as ⟨name⟩
```

is generated.

· · · · ·

3. *Running out of things*

If there is not enough memory even to get started, the following appear:

```
Run out of memory allocating ⟨n⟩ bytes for ⟨something⟩
Run out of memory allocating array of ⟨n⟩x⟨m⟩ bytes for ⟨something⟩
```

More often memory will run out in the course of compilation, like so:

```
The memory setting ⟨setting⟩ (which is ⟨value⟩ at present) has
    been exceeded. Try running Inform again with $⟨setting⟩=⟨larger-value⟩
    on the command line.
```

(For details of memory settings, see §39 above.) In a really colossal game, it is just conceivable that you might hit

```
One of the memory blocks has exceeded 640K
```

which would need Inform to be recompiled to get around (but I do not expect anyone ever to have this trouble, because other limits would be reached first). Much more likely is the error

```
The story file/module exceeds version ⟨n⟩ limit (⟨m⟩K) by ⟨b⟩ bytes
```

If you're already using version 8, then the story file is full: you might be able to squeeze more game in using the Abbreviate directive, but basically you're near to the maximum game size possible. Otherwise, the error suggests that you might want to change the version from 5 to 8, and the game will be able to grow at least twice as large again. It's also possible to run out not of story file space but of byte-accessible memory:

```
This program has overflowed the maximum readable-memory size of the
    Z-machine format. See the memory map below: the start of the
    area marked "above readable memory" must be brought down to
    $10000 or less.
```

Inform then prints out a memory map so that you can see what contributed to the exhaustion: there is detailed advice on this vexatious error in §45. Finally, you can also exhaust the number of classes:

```
Inform's maximum possible number of classes (whatever amount of memory
    is allocated) has been reached. If this causes serious
    inconvenience, please contact the author.
```

At time of writing, this maximum is 256 and nobody has yet contacted the author.

Errors

In the following, anything in double-quotes is a quotation from your source code; other strings are in single-quotes. The most common error by far takes the form:

```
Expected ⟨...⟩ but found ⟨...⟩
```

There are 112 such errors, most of them straightforward to sort out, but a few take some practice. One of the trickiest things to diagnose is a loop statement having been misspelt. For example, the lines

```
    pritn "Hello";
    While (x == y) print "x is still y^";
```

produce one error each:

```
    line 1: Error: Expected assignment or statement but found pritn
    line 2: Error: Expected ';' but found print
```

The first is fine. The second is odd: a human immediately sees that While is meant to be a while loop, but Inform is not able to make textual guesses like this. Instead Inform decides that the code intended was

```
    While (x == y); print "x is still y^";
```

with While assumed to be the name of a function which hasn't been declared yet. Thus, Inform thinks the mistake is that the ; has been missed out.

In that example, Inform repaired the situation and was able to carry on as normal in subsequent lines. But it sometimes happens that a whole cascade of errors is thrown up, in code which the user is fairly sure must be nearly right. What has happened is that one syntax mistake threw Inform off the right track, so that it continued not to know where it was for many lines in a row. Look at the first error message, fix that and then try again.

.   .   .   .   .

1. *Reading in the source-code*

```
Unrecognised combination in source: ⟨text⟩
Alphabetic character expected after ⟨text⟩
Name exceeds the maximum length of ⟨number⟩ characters: ⟨name⟩
Binary number expected after '$$'
Hexadecimal number expected after '$'
Too much text for one pair of quotations '...' to hold
Too much text for one pair of quotations "..." to hold
No text between quotation marks ''
Expected 'p' after '//' to give number of dictionary word ⟨word⟩
```

In that last error message, "number" is used in the linguistic sense, of singular versus plural.

.   .   .   .   .

2. *Characters*

```
Illegal character found in source: ⟨char⟩
No such accented character as ⟨text⟩
'@{' without matching '}'
At most four hexadecimal digits allowed in '@{...}'
'@{...}' may only contain hexadecimal digits
'@..' must have two decimal digits
Character can be printed but not input: ⟨char⟩
Character can be printed but not used as a value: ⟨char⟩
Alphabet string must give exactly 23 [or 26] characters
Character can't be used in alphabets unless entered into Zcharacter
    table: ⟨char⟩
Character must first be entered into Zcharacter table: ⟨char⟩
Character can only be used if declared in advance as part of
    'Zcharacter table': ⟨char⟩
Character duplicated in alphabet: ⟨char⟩
No more room in the Zcharacter table
```

Characters are given by ISO Latin-1 code number if in this set, and otherwise by Unicode number, and are also printed if this is possible. For instance, if you try to use an accented character as part of an identifier name, you cause an error like so:

```
Error:  Illegal character found in source: (ISO Latin1) $e9, i.e., 'e'
> Object cafe
```

because identifiers may only use the letters A to Z, in upper and lower case, the digits 0 to 9 and the underscore character _. The same kind of error is produced if you try to use (say) the ^ character outside of quotation marks. The characters legal in unquoted Inform source code are:

⟨new-line⟩ ⟨form-feed⟩ ⟨space⟩ ⟨tab⟩
0123456789
abcdefghijklmnopqrstuvwxyz
ABCDEFGHIJKLMNOPQRSTUVWXYZ
()[]{}<>"',.:;?!+-*/%=&|~#@_

. . . . .

3. *Variables and arrays*

```
Variable must be defined before use: ⟨name⟩
'=' applied to undeclared variable
Local variable defined twice: ⟨name⟩
All 233 global variables already declared
No array size or initial values given
Array sizes must be known now, not externally defined
An array must have a positive number of entries
A 'string' array can have at most 256 entries
An array must have between 1 and 32767 entries
Entries in byte arrays and strings must be known constants
Missing ';' to end the initial array values before "[" or "]"
```

The limit of 233 global variables is absolute: a program even approaching this limit should probably be making more use of object properties to store its information. "Entries... must be known constants" is a restriction on what byte or string arrays may contain: basically, numbers or characters; defined constants (such as object names) may only be used if they have already been defined. This restriction does not apply to the more normally used word and table arrays.

. . . . .

4. *Routines and function calls*

```
No 'Main' routine has been defined
It is illegal to nest routines using '#['
A routine can have at most 15 local variables
Argument to system function missing
System function given with too many arguments
Only constants can be used as possible 'random' results
```

```
A function may be called with at most 7 arguments
Duplicate definition of label: ⟨name⟩
The following name is reserved by Inform for its own use as a
    routine name; you can use it as a routine name yourself
    (to override the standard definition) but cannot use it for
    anything else: ⟨name⟩
```

Note that the system function random, when it takes more than one argument, can only take constant arguments, as this enables the possibilities to be stored efficiently within the program. Thus random(random(10), location) will produce an error. To make a random choice between non-constant values, write a switch statement instead.

. . . . .

5. *Expressions and arithmetic*

```
Missing operator: inserting '+'
Evaluating this has no effect: ⟨operator⟩
'=' applied to ⟨operator⟩
Brackets mandatory to clarify order of: ⟨operator⟩
Missing operand for ⟨operator⟩
Missing operand after ⟨something⟩
Found '(' without matching ')'
No expression between brackets '(' and ')'
'or' not between values to the right of a condition
'has'/'hasnt' applied to illegal attribute number
Division of constant by zero
Signed arithmetic on compile-time constants overflowed the range
    -32768 to +32767: ⟨calculation⟩
Label name used as value: ⟨name⟩
System function name used as value: ⟨name⟩
No such constant as ⟨name⟩
The obsolete '#w$word' construct has been removed
```

"Operators" include not only addition +, multiplication * and so on, but also higher-level things like --> ("array entry") and . ("property value") and :: ("superclass"). An example of an operator where "Evaluating this has no effect" is in the statement

```
    34 * score;
```

where the multiplication is a waste of time, since nothing is done with the result. "= applied to ⟨operator⟩" means something like

```
    (4 / fish) = 7;
```

which literally means "set 4/fish to 7" and gives the error "= applied to /".

"Brackets mandatory to clarify order" means that an expression is unclear as written, and this is often a caution that it would be wrong either way and needs to be reconsidered. For instance:

```
if (parent(axe) == location == Hall_of_Mists) ...
```

This looks as if it might mean "if these three values are all equal", but does not: the result of == is either true or false, so whichever comparison happens first, the other one compares against one of these values.

· · · · ·

6. *Miscellaneous errors in statements*

```
'do' without matching 'until'
'default' without matching 'switch'
'else' without matching 'if'
'until' without matching 'do'
'break' can only be used in a loop or 'switch' block
At most 32 values can be given in a single 'switch' case
Multiple 'default' clauses defined in same 'switch'
'default' must be the last 'switch' case
'continue' can only be used in a loop block
A reserved word was used as a print specification: ⟨name⟩
No lines of text given for 'box' display
In Version 3 no status-line drawing routine can be given
The 'style' statement cannot be used for Version 3 games
```

For instance, print (bold) X gives the "reserved word in print specification" error because bold is a keyword that has some meaning already (the statement style bold; changes the type face to bold). Anyway, call such a printing routine something else.

· · · · ·

7. *Object and class declarations*

```
Two textual short names given for only one object
The syntax '->' is only used as an alternative to 'Nearby'
Use of '->' (or 'Nearby') clashes with giving a parent
'->' (or 'Nearby') fails because there is no previous object
'-> -> ...' fails because no previous object is deep enough
Two commas ',' in a row in object/class definition
Object/class definition finishes with ','
```

⟨name⟩ is a name already in use (with type ⟨type⟩) and may not be
    used as a property name too
Property given twice in the same declaration, because the names
    '⟨name⟩' and '⟨name⟩' actually refer to the same property
Property given twice in the same declaration: ⟨name⟩
Property should be declared in 'with', not 'private': ⟨name⟩
Limit (of 32 values) exceeded for property ⟨name⟩
An additive property has inherited so many values that the list has
    overflowed the maximum 32 entries
Duplicate-number not known at compile time
The number of duplicates must be 1 to 10000

Note that "common properties" (those provided by the library, or those declared with Property) cannot be made private. All other properties are called "individual". The "number of duplicates" referred to is the number of duplicate instances to make for a new class, and it needs to be a number Inform can determine now, not later on in the source code (or in another module altogether). The limit 10,000 is arbitrary and imposed to help prevent accidents: in practice available memory is very unlikely to permit anything like this many instances.

                    .   .   .   .   .

8. *Grammar*

Two different verb definitions refer to ⟨name⟩
There is no previous grammar for the verb ⟨name⟩
There is no action routine called ⟨name⟩
No such grammar token as ⟨text⟩
'=' is only legal here as 'noun=Routine'
Not an action routine: ⟨name⟩
This is a fake action, not a real one: ⟨name⟩
Too many lines of grammar for verb: increase #define MAX_LINES_PER_VERB
'/' can only be used with Library 6/3 or later
'/' can only be applied to prepositions
The 'topic' token is only available if you are using Library
    6/3 or later
'reverse' actions can only be used with Library 6/3 or later

At present verbs are limited to 20 grammar lines each, though this would be easy to increase. (A grammar of this kind of length can probably be written more efficiently using general parsing routines, however.)

                    .   .   .   .   .

9. *Conditional compilation*

```
'Ifnot' without matching 'If...'
'Endif' without matching 'If...'
Second 'Ifnot' for the same 'If...' condition
End of file reached in code 'If...'d out
This condition can't be determined
```

"Condition can't be determined" only arises for Iftrue and Iffalse, which make numerical or logical tests: for instance,

```
Iftrue #strings_offset == $4a50;
```

can't be determined because, although both quantities are constants, the value of #strings_offset will not be known until compilation is finished. On the other hand, for example,

```
Iftrue #version_number > 5;
```

can be determined at any time, as the version number was set before compilation.

·   ·   ·   ·   ·

10. *Miscellaneous errors in directives*

```
You can't 'Replace' a system function already used
Must specify 0 to 3 local variables for 'Stub' routine
A 'Switches' directive must come before the first constant definition
All 62 properties already declared
'alias' incompatible with 'additive'
The serial number must be a 6-digit date in double-quotes
A definite value must be given as release number
A definite value must be given as version number
Grammar__Version must be given an explicit constant value
Once a fake action has been defined it is too late to change the
     grammar version. (If you are using the library, move any
     Fake_Action directives to a point after the inclusion of "Parser".)
The version number must be in the range 3 to 8
All 64 abbreviations already declared
All abbreviations must be declared together
It's not worth abbreviating ⟨text⟩
'Default' cannot be used in -M (Module) mode
'LowString' cannot be used in -M (Module) mode
```

·   ·   ·   ·   ·

11. *Linking and importing*

```
File isn't a module: ⟨name⟩
Link: action name clash with ⟨name⟩
Link: program and module give differing values of ⟨name⟩
Link: module (wrongly) declared this a variable: ⟨name⟩
Link: this attribute is undeclared within module: ⟨name⟩
Link: this property is undeclared within module: ⟨name⟩
Link: this was referred to as a constant, but isn't: ⟨name⟩
Link: ⟨type⟩ ⟨name⟩ in both program and module
Link: ⟨name⟩ has type ⟨type⟩ in program but type ⟨type⟩ in module
Link: failed because too many extra global variables needed
Link: module (wrongly) declared this a variable: ⟨name⟩
Link: this attribute is undeclared within module: ⟨name⟩
Link: this property is undeclared within module: ⟨name⟩
Link: this was referred to as a constant, but isn't: ⟨name⟩
Link: module and game use different character sets
Link: module and game both define non-standard character sets, but they
    disagree
Link: module compiled as Version ⟨number⟩ (so it can't link into this
    V⟨number⟩ game
'Import' cannot import things of this type: ⟨name⟩
'Import' can only be used in -M (Module) mode
```

Note that the errors beginning "Link:" are exactly those occurring during the process of linking a module into the current compilation. They mostly arise when the same name is used for one purpose in the current program, and a different one in the module.

·   ·   ·   ·   ·

12. *Assembly language*

```
Opcode specification should have form "VAR:102"
Unknown flag: options are B (branch), S (store),
    T (text), I (indirect addressing), F** (set this Flags 2 bit)
Only one '->' store destination can be given
Only one '?' branch destination can be given
No assembly instruction may have more than 8 operands
This opcode does not use indirect addressing
Indirect addressing can only be used on the first operand
Store destination (the last operand) is not a variable
Opcode unavailable in this Z-machine version: ⟨name⟩
Assembly mistake: syntax is ⟨syntax⟩
```

```
Routine contains no such label as ⟨name⟩
For this operand type, opcode number must be in range ⟨range⟩
```

.   .   .   .   .

13. *Deliberate "errors"*

Finally, error messages can also be produced from within the program (deliberately) using Message. It may be that a mysterious message is being caused by an included file written by someone other than yourself.

Warnings

1. *Questionable practices*

⟨type⟩ ⟨name⟩ declared but not used

For example, a Global directive was used to create a variable, which was then never used in the program.

'=' used as condition: '==' intended?

Although a line like

```
    if (x = 5) print "My name is Alan Partridge.";
```

is legal, it's probably a mistake: x = 5 sets x to 5 and results in 5, so the condition is always true. Presumably it was a mistype for x == 5 meaning "test x to see if it's equal to 5".

Unlike C, Inform uses ':' to divide parts of a 'for' loop
    specification: replacing ';' with ':'

Programmers used to the C language will now and then habitually type a for loop in the form

```
    for (i=0; i<10; i++) ...
```

but Inform needs colons, not semicolons: however, as it can see what was intended, it makes the correction automatically and issues only a warning.

`Missing ','? Property data seems to contain the property name <name>`

The following, part of an object declaration, is legal but unlikely:

```
with found_in MarbleHall
        short_name "conch shell", name "conch" "shell",
```

As written, the `found_in` property has a list of three values: `MarbleHall`, `short_name` and `"conch shell"`. `short_name` throws up the warning because Inform suspects that a comma was missed out and the programmer intended

```
with found_in MarbleHall,
        short_name "conch shell", name "conch" "shell",
```

`This is not a declared Attribute: ⟨name⟩`

Similarly, suppose that a game contains a pen. Then the following `give` statement is dubious but legal:

```
give MarbleDoorway pen;
```

The warning is caused because it's far more likely to be a misprint for

```
give MarbleDoorway open;
```

`Without bracketing, the minus sign '-' is ambiguous`

For example,

```
Array Doubtful --> 50 10 -20 56;
```

because Inform is not sure whether this contains three entries (the middle one being $10 - 20 = -10$), or four. It guesses four, but suggests brackets to clarify the situation.

`Entry in '->' or 'string' array not in range 0 to 255`

Byte `->` and `string` arrays can only hold numbers in the range 0 to 255. If a larger entry is supplied, only the remainder mod 256 is stored, and this warning is issued.

This statement can never be reached

There is no way that the statement being compiled can ever be executed when the game is played. Here is an obvious example:

    return; print "Goodbye!";

where the print statement can never be reached, because a return must just have happened. Beginners often run into this example:

    "You pick up the gauntlet."; score = score + 5; return;

Here the score = score + 5 statement is never reached because the text, given on its own, means "print this, then print a new-line, then return from the current routine". The intended behaviour needs something like

    score = score + 5; "You pick up the gauntlet.";

Verb disagrees with previous verbs: ⟨verb⟩

The Extend only directive is used to cleave off a set of synonymous English verbs and make them into a new Inform verb. For instance, ordinarily "take", "get", "carry" and "hold" are one single Inform verb, but this directive could split off "carry" and "get" from the other two. The warning would arise if one tried to split off "take" and "drop" together, which come from different original Inform verbs. (It's still conceivably usable, which is why it's a warning, not an error.)

This does not set the final game's statusline

An attempt to choose, e.g., Statusline time within a module, having no effect on the program into which the module will one day be linked. Futile. Finally a ragbag of unlikely and fairly self-explanatory contingencies:

This version of Inform is unable to produce the grammar table format
    requested (producing number 2 format instead)
Grammar line cut short: you can only have up to 6 tokens in any line
    (unless you're compiling with library 6/3 or later)
Version 3 limit of 4 values per property exceeded (use -v5 to get 32),
    so truncating property ⟨name⟩
The 'box' statement has no effect in a version 3 game
Module has a more advanced format than this release of the
    Inform 6 compiler knows about: it may not link in correctly

The last of these messages is to allow for different module formats to be introduced in future releases of Inform, but so far there has only ever been module format 1, so nobody has ever produced this error.

. . . . .

2. Obsolete usages

```
more modern to use 'Array', not 'Global'
use '->' instead of 'data'
use '->' instead of 'initial'
use '->' instead of 'initstr'
ignoring 'print_paddr': use 'print (string)' instead
ignoring 'print_addr': use 'print (address)' instead
ignoring 'print_char': use 'print (char)' instead
use 'word' as a constant dictionary address
'#a$Act' is now superseded by '##Act'
'#n$word' is now superseded by ''word''
'#r$Routine' can now be written just 'Routine'
all properties are now automatically 'long'
use the ^ character for the apostrophe in ⟨dictionary word⟩
```

These all occur if Inform compiles a syntax which was correct under Inform 5 (or earlier) but has now been withdrawn in favour of something better.

△△ No Inform library file (or any other file marked System_file) produces warning messages. It may contain many declared but unused routines, or may contain obsolete usages for the sake of backward compatibility.

Chapter VII: The Z-Machine

§41 Architecture and assembly

Infocom's games of 1979–89 were written in a language called ZIL, the Zork Implementation Language. At first sight this is outlandishly unlike Inform, but appearances are deceptive. The following source code describes toy boats in Kensington Park, from a game widely considered a masterpiece: 'Trinity' (1986), by Brian Moriarty.

```
<OBJECT BOAT
        (LOC ROUND-POND)
        (DESC "toy boats")
        (FLAGS TRYTAKE NODESC PLURAL)
        (SYNONYM BOAT BOATS TOYS)
        (ADJECTIVE TOY)
        (ACTION BOAT-F)>
<ROUTINE BOAT-F ()
        <COND (<VERB? EXAMINE WATCH>
              <TELL CTHEO
" are crafted of paper and sticks. They bob freely among the "
D ,POND-BIRDS ", who can barely conceal their outrage." CR>
              <RTRUE>)
              (<VERB? SWIM DIVE WALK-TO FOLLOW SIT LIE-DOWN ENTER>
              <DO-WALK ,P?IN>
              <RTRUE>)
              (<INTBL? ,PRSA ,TOUCHVERBS ,NTOUCHES>
              <TELL CTHE ,BOAT " are far out of reach." CR>
              <RTRUE>)
              (T
              <RFALSE>)>>
```

Inform and ZIL each have objects, with properties and attributes. They're called different things, true: ZIL has its dictionary words in SYNONYM and ADJECTIVE where Inform uses name, ZIL calls attributes "flags" and has NODESC where Inform would have scenery, but the similarity is striking. Both languages have routines with a tendency to return true and false, too.

The underlying similarity is the Z-machine, which both languages make use of. The Z-machine is an imaginary computer: created on Joel Berez's mother's coffee table in Pittsburgh in 1979, it has never existed as circuitry.

Instead, almost every real computer built in the 1980s and 1990s has been taught to emulate the Z-machine, and so to run story files.

This chapter contains what the advanced Inform programmer needs, from time to time, to know about the Z-machine. The reader who only wants to get at fairly easy screen effects like coloured text may want to turn straight to the references to §42, where a number of convenient library extensions are listed.

In any case this chapter is by no means the full story, which is contained in *The Z-Machine Standards Document*. It seems nonetheless appropriate to acknowledge here the work of the Z-machine's architects: Joel Berez, Marc Blank, P. David Lebling, Tim Anderson and others.

· · · · ·

The Z-machine as conceived in 1979 is now known as "version 1", and there have been seven subsequent versions to date. Inform normally produces version 5 story files, but this can be controlled with the -v switch: so -v6 compiles a version 6 story file, for instance. Briefly, the versions are:

Versions 1 and 2. Early draft designs by Infocom, used only in the first release of the 'Zork' trilogy. Inform cannot produce them.

Version 3. The standard Infocom design, limited in various ways: to 255 objects, 32 attributes, at most 4 entries in a property array, at most 3 arguments in a routine call and a story file at most 128K in size. Inform can produce version 3 files but this is not recommended and some advanced features of the language, such as message-sending, will not work.

Version 4. A partial upgrade, now seldom used.

Version 5. The advanced Infocom design and the one normally used by Inform. Limits are raised to 65,535 objects, 48 attributes, 32 entries in a property array, 7 arguments in a routine call and a story file at most 256K in size.

Version 6. Similar, though not identical, in architecture to Version 5, but offering support for pictures. Inform will compile to this, but there are two further obstructions: you need a way to package up the sounds and images to go with the story file (see §43), and then players need an interpreter able to make use of them.

Version 7. An intermediate version which has never proved useful, and whose use is now deprecated.

Version 8. Identical to version 5 except that it allows story files up to 512K long. Most of the largest Inform games use version 8.

· · · · ·

The native language of the Z-machine is neither Inform nor ZIL, but an intermediate-level code which we'll call "assembly language". It's tiresome to write a program of any complexity in assembly language. For instance, here are two equivalent pieces of Inform: first, a statement in ordinary code:

```
"The answer is ", 3*subtotal + 1;
```

Secondly, assembly language which achieves the same end:

```
@print "The answer is ";
@mul 3 subtotal -> x;
@add x 1 -> x;
@print_num x;
@new_line;
@rtrue;
```

(Here we've used a variable called x.) Inform allows you to mix assembly language and ordinary Inform source code freely, but all commands in assembly language, called "opcodes", are written with an @ sign in front, to distinguish them. The values supplied to opcodes, such as 3 and subtotal, are called "operands". The -> arrow sign is read "store to" and indicates that an answer is being stored somewhere. So, for instance, the line

```
@add x 1 -> x;
```

adds x and 1, storing the result of this addition back in x. Operands can only be constants or variables: so you can't write a compound expression like my_array-->(d*4).

As can be seen above, some opcodes store values and some don't. Another important category are the "branch" opcodes, which result in execution jumping to a different place in the source code if some condition turns out to be true, and not otherwise. For instance:

```
@je x 1 ?Xisone;
@print "x isn't equal to 1.";
.Xisone;
```

Here, Xisone is the name of a label, marking a point in the source code which a branch opcode (or an Inform jump statement) might want to jump to. (A label can't be the last thing in a function, but if you needed this, you could always finish with a label plus a return statement instead.) @je means "jump if equal", so the code tests x to see if it's equal to 1 and jumps to Xisone if so. Inform will only allow branches to labels in the same routine. Note that inserting a tilde,

```
@je x 1 ?~Xisntone;
```

reverses the condition, so this opcode branches if x is not equal to 1.

The full specification of Inform's assembly-language syntax is given in §14 of *The Z-Machine Standards Document*, but this will seldom if ever be needed, because the present chapter contains everything that can't be done more easily without assembly language anyway.

. . . . .

△   The rest of this section sketches the architecture of the Z-machine, which many designers won't need to know about. Briefly, it contains memory in three sections: readable and writeable memory at byte addresses 0 up to $S - 1$, read-only memory from S up to $P - 1$ and inaccessible memory from P upwards. (In any story file, the Inform expression 0-->2 gives the value of P and 0-->7 gives S.) The read-write area contains everything that needs to change in play: variables, object properties and attributes, arrays and certain other tables; except for the stack and the "program counter", its marker as to which part of some routine it is currently running. The beginning of the read-write area is a 64-byte "header". Byte 0 of this header, and so of an entire story file, contains the version number of the Z-machine for which it is written. (The expression 0->0 evaluates to this.)

The read-only area contains tables which the Inform parser needs to make detailed use of but never alters: the grammar lines and the dictionary, for instance. The "inaccessible" area contains routines and static (that is, unalterable) strings of text. These can be called or printed out, which is access of a sort, but you can't write code which will examine them one byte at a time.

In addition to local and global variables, the Z-machine contains a "stack", which is accessed with the name sp for "stack pointer". The stack is a pile of values. Each time sp is written to, a new value is placed on top of the pile. Each time it is read, the value being read is taken off the pile. At the start of a routine, the stack is always empty.

There is no access to the outside world except by using certain opcodes. For instance, @read and @read_char allow use of the keyboard, whereas @print and @draw_picture allow use of the screen. (The screen's image is not stored anywhere in memory, and nor is the state of the keyboard.) Conversely, hardware can cause the Z-machine to "interrupt", that is, to make a spontaneous call to a particular routine, interrupting what it was previously working on. This happens only if the story file has previously requested it: for example, by setting a sound effect playing and asking for a routine to be called when it finishes; or by asking for an interrupt if thirty seconds pass while the player is thinking what to type.

§42   Devices and opcodes

This section covers the only opcodes which designers are likely to have occasional need of: those which drive powerful and otherwise inaccessible features of the Z-machine's "hardware", such as sound, graphics, menus and the mouse. There's no need to be fluent in assembly language to use these opcodes, which work just as well if used as incantations from a unfamiliar tongue.

- **WARNING**

Some of these incantations may not work well if a story file is played on old interpreters which do not adhere to the Z-Machine Standard. Standard interpreters are very widely available, but if seriously worried you can test in an Initialise routine whether your game is running on a good interpreter, as in the following code.

```
if (standard_interpreter == 0) {
    print "This game must be played on an interpreter obeying the
            Z-Machine Standard.^";
    @quit;
}
```

The library variable `standard_interpreter` holds the version number of the standard obeyed, with the upper byte holding the major and the lower byte the minor version number, or else zero if the interpreter isn't standard-compliant. Thus $002 means 0.2 and $100 means 1.0. Any standard interpreter will carry out the opcodes in this chapter correctly, or else provide fair warning that they cannot. (For instance, an interpreter running on a palm-top personal organiser without a loudspeaker cannot provide sound effects.) Here is how to tell whether a standard interpreter can or can't provide the feature you need.

Feature	Versions	Available if
auxiliary files	5,6,8	(true)
coloured text	5,6,8	((0->1) & 1 ~= 0)
input streams	5,6,8	(true)
menus	6	(($10-->0) & 256 ~= 0)
mouse	5,6	(($10-->0) & 32 ~= 0)
output streams	5,6,8	(true)
pictures	6	(($10-->0) & 8 ~= 0)
sounds	5,6,8	(($10-->0) & 128 ~= 0)
throw/catch stack frames	5,6,8	(true)
timed keyboard interrupts	5,6,8	((0->1) & 128 ~= 0)

For instance, if coloured text is essential (for instance if red and black letters have to look different because it's a vital clue to some puzzle), you may want to add a test like the following to your Initialise routine:

```
if ((0->1) & 1 == 0)
        print "*** This game is best appreciated on an interpreter
            capable of displaying colours, unlike the present
            one. Proceed at your own risk! ***^";
```

· · · · ·

△   Text flows in and out of the Z-machine continuously: the player's commands flow in, responses flow out. Commands can come in from two different "input streams", only one of which is selected at any given time: stream 0 is the keyboard and stream 1 is a file on the host computer. The stream is selected with:

`@input_stream number`

The Inform debugging verb "replay" basically does no more than switch input to stream 1.

△   There are four output streams for text, numbered 1 to 4. These are: (1) the screen, (2) the transcript file, (3) an array in memory and (4) a file of commands on the host computer. These can be active in any combination, except that at all times either stream 1 or stream 3 is active and not both. Inform uses stream 3 when the message print_to_array is sent to a string, and streams 2 and 4 in response to commands typed by the player: "script on" switches stream 2 on, "script on" switches it off; "recording on" and "off" switch stream 4 on and off. The relevant opcode is:

`@output_stream number arr`

If number is 0 this does nothing. +n switches stream n on, −n switches it off. The arr operand is omitted except for stream 3, when it's a table array holding the text printed: that is, arr-->0 contains the number of characters printed and the text printed is stored as ZSCII characters in arr->2, arr->3, ...

△   As the designer, you cannot choose the filename of the file of commands used by input stream 1 or output stream 4. Whoever is playing the story file will choose this: perhaps after being prompted by the interpreter, perhaps through a configuration setting on that interpreter.

● △△EXERCISE 122
Implement an Inform version of the standard 'C' routine printf, taking the form

```
printf(format, arg1, ...)
```

to print out the format string but with escape sequences like %d replaced by the arguments (printed in various ways). For example,

```
printf("The score is %e out of %e.", score, MAX_SCORE);
```

should print something like "The score is five out of ten."

△   In Version 6 story files, only, @output_stream can take an optional third operand when output stream 3 is being enabled. That is:

`@output_stream 3 arr width`

If width is positive, the text streamed into the array will be word-wrapped as if it were on a screen width characters wide; if width is negative, then as if on a screen -width pixels wide. The text going into arr is in the form of a sequence of lines, each consisting of a word containing the number of characters and then the ZSCII characters themselves in bytes. The sequence of lines finishes with a zero word. Such an array is exactly what is printed out by the opcode @print_form arr.

.   .   .   .   .

△   The Z-machine has two kinds of "screen model", or specification for what can and can't be done to the contents of the screen. Version 6 has an advanced graphical model, whereas other versions have much simpler textual arrangements. Early versions of the Z-machine are generally less capable here, so this section will document only the Version 5 and Version 6 models. (Versions 7 and 8 have the same model as Version 5.)

The version 5 screen model. The screen is divided into an upper window, normally used for a status line and sometimes also for quotations or menus, and a lower window, used for ordinary text. At any given time the upper window has a height H, which is a whole number of lines: and H can be zero, making the upper window invisible. (The story file can vary H from time to time and many do.) When text in the upper and lower windows occupy the same screen area, it's the upper window text that's visible. This often happens when quotation boxes are displayed.

`@split_window H`

Splits off an upper-level window of the given number of lines H in height from the main screen. Be warned that the upper window doesn't scroll, so you need to make H large enough for all the text you need to fit at once.

`@set_window window`

Selects which window text is to be printed into: (0) the lower one or (1) the upper one. Printing on the upper window overlies printing on the lower, is always done in a fixed-pitch font and does not appear in a printed transcript of the game.

`@set_cursor line column`

Places the cursor inside the upper window, where (1, 1) is the top left character.

`@buffer_mode flag`

This turns on (flag==true) or off (flag==false) word-breaking for the current window: that is, the practice of printing new-lines only at the ends of words, so that text is neatly formatted.

`@erase_window window`

Blanks out window 0 (lower), window 1 (upper) or the whole screen (if window=-1).

Using fixed-pitch measurements, the screen has dimensions X characters across by Y characters down, where X and Y are stored in bytes \$21 and \$20 of the header respectively. It's sometimes useful to know this when formatting tables:

```
print "My screen has ", 0->$20, " rows and ", 0->$21, " columns.^";
```

Be warned: it might be 80 × 210 or then again it might be 7 × 40. Text printing has a given foreground and background colour at all times. The standard stock of colours is:

0	*current colour*	5	yellow
1	*default colour*	6	blue
2	black	7	magenta
3	red	8	cyan
4	green	9	white

`@set_colour foreground background`

If coloured text is available, this opcode sets text to be foreground against background. (But bear in mind that not all interpreters can display coloured text, and not all players enjoy reading it.) Even in a monochrome game, text can be set to print in "reverse colours": background on foreground rather than vice versa. Status lines are almost always printed in reverse-colour, but this is only a convention and is not required by the Z-machine. Reverse is one of five possible text styles: roman, bold, underline (which many interpreters will render with italic), reverse and fixed-pitch. (Inform's style statement chooses between these.)

- △EXERCISE 123
Design a title page for 'Ruins', displaying a more or less apposite quotation and waiting for a key to be pressed. (For this last part, see below.)

- △EXERCISE 124
Change the status line so that it has the usual score/moves appearance except when a variable `invisible_status` is set to true, when it's invisible.

• △EXERCISE 125
Alter the 'Advent' example game to display the number of treasures found instead of the score and turns on the status line.

• △EXERCISE 126
(From code by Joachim Baumann.) Put a compass rose on the status line, displaying the directions in which the room can be left.

• △△EXERCISE 127
(Cf. 'Trinity'.) Make the status line consist only of the name of the current location, centred in the top line of the screen.

The version 6 screen model. We are now in the realm of graphics, and the screen is considered to be a grid of pixels: coordinates are usually given in the form (y, x), with $(1, 1)$ at the top left. y and x are measured in units known, helpfully enough, as "units". The interpreter decides how large "1 unit" is, and it's not safe to assume that 1 unit equals 1 pixel. All you can tell is what the screen dimensions are, in units:

```
print "The screen measures ", $22-->0, " units across and ",
    $22-->1, " units down.^";
```

There are eight windows, numbered 0 to 7, which text and pictures can currently be printing to: what actually appears on the screen is whatever shows through the boundaries of the window at the time the printing or plotting happens. Window number −3 means "the current one". Windows have no visible borders and usually lie on top of each other. Subsequent movements of the window do not move what was printed and there is no sense in which characters or graphics "belong" to any particular window once printed. Each window has a position (in units), a size (in units), a cursor position within it (in units, relative to its own origin), a number of flags called "attributes" and a number of variables called "properties". If you move a window so that the cursor is left outside, the interpreter automatically moves the cursor back to the window's new top left. If you only move the cursor, it's your responsibility to make sure it doesn't leave the window.

The attributes are (0) "wrapping", (1) "scrolling", (2) "copy text to output stream 2 if active" and (3) "buffer printing". Wrapping means that when text reaches the right-hand edge it continues from the left of the next line down. Scrolling means scrolling the window upwards when text printing reaches the bottom right corner, to make room for more. Output stream 2 is the transcript file, so the question here is whether you want text in the given window to appear in a transcript: for instance, for a status line the answer is probably "no", but for normal conversation it would be "yes". Finally, buffering is a more sophisticated form of wrapping, which breaks lines of text in between words, but which (roughly speaking) means that no line is printed until complete. Note that ordinary printing in the lower window has all four of these attributes.

```
@window_style window attrs operation
```

Changes window attributes. `attrs` is a bitmap in which bit 0 means "wrapping", bit 1 means "scrolling", etc. `operation` is 0 to set to these settings, 1 to set only those attributes which you specify in the bitmap, 2 to clear only those and 3 to reverse them. For instance,

`@window_style 2 $$1011 0`

sets window 2 to have wrapping, scrolling and buffering but not to be copied to output stream 2, and

`@window_style 1 $$1000 2`

clears the buffer printing attribute of window 1.

Windows have 16 properties, numbered as follows:

0	*y coordinate*	8	newline interrupt routine
1	*x coordinate*	9	interrupt countdown
2	*y size*	10	*text style*
3	*x size*	11	*colour data*
4	*y cursor*	12	*font number*
5	*x cursor*	13	*font size*
6	*left margin size*	14	*attributes*
7	*right margin size*	15	line count

The x and y values are all in units, but the margin sizes are in pixels. The font size data is $256*h+w$, where h is the height and w the width in pixels. The colour data is $256*b+f$, where f and b are foreground and background colour numbers. The text style is a bitmap set by the Inform `style` statement: bit 0 means Roman, 1 is reverse video, 2 is bold, 3 is italic, 4 is fixed-pitch. The current value of any property can be read with:

`@get_wind_prop window prop -> r`

Those few window properties which are not italicised in the table (and only those few) can be set using:

`@put_wind_prop window prop value`

Most window properties, the ones with italicised text in the table above, are set using specially-provided opcodes:

`@move_window window y x`

Moves to the given position on screen. Nothing visible happens, but all future plotting to the given window will happen in the new place.

`@window_size window y x`

Changes window size in pixels. Again, nothing visible happens.

`@set_colour foreground background window`

Sets the foreground and background colours for the given window.

`@set_cursor line column window`

Moves the window's cursor to this position, in units, relative to $(1, 1)$ in the top left of the window. If this would lie outside the margin positions, the cursor moves to the left margin of its current line. In addition, `@set_cursor -1` turns the cursor off, and `@set_cursor -2` turns it back on again.

`@get_cursor arr`

Writes the cursor row of the current window into `arr-->0` and the column into `arr-->1`, in units.

`@set_font font -> r`

(This opcode is available in Versions 5 and 8 as well as 6.) Selects the numbered font for the current window, and stores a positive number into r (actually, the previous font number) if available, or zero if not available. Font support is only minimal, for the sake of portability. The possible font numbers are: 1 (the normal font), 3 (a character graphics font: see §16 of *The Z-Machine Standards Document*), 4 (a fixed-pitch Courier-like font). Owing to a historical accident there is no font 2.

`@set_margins left right window`

Sets margin widths, in pixels, for the given window. If the cursor is overtaken in the process and now lies outside these margins, it is moved back to the left margin of the current line.

△   "Interrupt countdowns" are a fancy system to allow text to flow gracefully around obstructions such as pictures. If property 9 is set to a non-zero value, then it'll be decremented on each new-line, and when it hits zero the routine in property 8 will be called. This routine should not attempt to print any text, and is usually used to change margin settings.

• **EXERCISE 128**
(Version 6 games only.) Set up wavy margins, which advance inwards for a while and then back outwards, over and over, so that the game's text ends up looking like a concertina.

Here are two useful tricks with windows:

`@erase_window window`

Erases the window's whole area to its background colour.

`@scroll_window window pixels`

Scrolls the given window by the given number of pixels. A negative value scrolls backwards, i.e., moving the body of the window down rather than up. Blank (background colour) pixels are plotted onto the new lines. This can be done to any window and is not related to the "scrolling" attribute of a window.

△   Finally, Version 6 story files (but no others) are normally able to display images, or "pictures". To the Z-machine these are referred to only by number, and a story file does not "know" how pictures are provided to it, or in what format they are stored. For the mechanics of how to attach resources like pictures to a story file, see §43. Four opcodes are concerned with pictures:

`@draw_picture pn y x`

Draws picture number pn so that its top left corner appears at coordinates (y, x) in units on the screen. If y or x are omitted, the coordinate of the cursor in the current window is used.

`@erase_picture pn y x`

Exactly as `@draw_picture`, but erases the corresponding screen area to the current background colour.

`@picture_data pn arr ?Label`

Asks for information about picture number pn. If the given picture exists, a branch occurs to the given `Label`, and the height and width in pixels of the image are written to the given array arr, with arr-->0 being the height and arr-->1 the width. If the given picture doesn't exist, no branch occurs and nothing is written, *except* that if pn is zero, then arr-->0 is the number of pictures available to the story file and arr-->1 the "release number" of the collection of pictures. (Or of the Blorb file attached to the story file, if that's how pictures have been provided to it.)

`@picture_table tarr`

Given a `table` array tarr of picture numbers, this warns the Z-machine that the story file will want to plot these pictures often, soon and in quick succession. Providing such a warning is optional and enables some interpreters to plot more quickly, because they can cache images in memory somewhere.

·   ·   ·   ·   ·

△   Sound effects are available to story files of any Version from 5 upwards. Once again, to the Z-machine these are referred to only by number, and a story file does not "know" how sounds are provided to it, or in what format they are stored. For the mechanics of how to attach resources like sound effects to a story file, see §43. There is only one sound opcode, but it does a good deal. The simplest form is:

`@sound_effect number`

which emits a high-pitched bleep if number is 1 and a low-pitched bleep if 2. No other values are allowed.

@sound_effect number effect volrep routine

The given **effect** happens to the given sound **number**, which must be 3 or higher and correspond to a sound effect provided to the story file by the designer. Volume is measured from 1 (quiet) to 8 (loud), with the special value 255 meaning "loudest possible", and you can also specify between 0 and 254 repeats, or 255 to mean "repeat forever". These two parameters are combined in **volrep**:

```
volrep = 256*repeats + volume;
```

The **effect** can be: 1 (prepare), 2 (start), 3 (stop), 4 (finish with). You may want to "warn" the Z-machine that a sound effect will soon be needed by using the "prepare" effect, but this is optional: similarly you may want to warn it that you've finished with the sound effect for the time being, but this too is optional. "Start" and "stop" are self-explanatory except to say that sound effects can be playing in the background while the player gets on with play: i.e., the Z-machine doesn't simply halt until the sound is complete. The "stop" effect makes the sound cease at once, even if there is more still to be played. Otherwise, unless set to repeat indefinitely, it will end by itself in due course. If a **routine** has been provided (this operand is optional, and takes effect only on **effect** 2), this routine will then be called as an interrupt. Such routines generally do something like play the sound again but at a different volume level, giving a fading-away effect.

. . . . .

△   In addition to reading entire lines of text from the keyboard, which games normally do once per turn, you can read a single press of a key. Moreover, on most interpreters you can set either kind of keyboard-reading to wait for at most a certain time before giving up.

@aread text parse time function -> result

This opcode reads a line of text from the keyboard, writing it into the **text** string array and 'tokenising' it into a word stream, with details stored in the **parse** string array (unless this is zero, in which case no tokenisation happens). (See §2.5 for the format of **text** and **parse**.) While it is doing this it calls **function()** every **time** tenths of a second: the process ends if ever this function returns true. The value written into **result** is the "terminating character" which finished the input, or else 0 if a time-out ended the input.

@read_char 1 time function -> result

Results in the ZSCII value of a single keypress. Once again, **function(time)** is called every **time** tenths of a second and may stop this process early. (The first operand is always 1, meaning "from the keyboard".)

`@tokenise text parse dictionary`

This takes the text in the text buffer (in the format produced by @aread) and tokenises it, i.e., breaks it up into words and finds their addresses in the given dictionary. The result is written into the parse buffer in the usual way.

`@encode_text    zscii-text length from coded-text`

Translates a ZSCII word to the internal, Z-encoded, text format suitable for use in a @tokenise dictionary. The text begins at from in the zscii-text and is length characters long, which should contain the right length value (though in fact the interpreter translates the word as far as a zero terminator). The result is 6 bytes long and usually represents between 1 and 9 letters.

It's also possible to specify which ZSCII character codes are "terminating characters", meaning that they terminate a line of input. Normally, the return key is the only terminating character, but others can be added, and this is how games like 'Beyond Zork' make function keys act as shorthand commands. For instance, the following directive makes ZSCII 132 (cursor right) and 136 (function key f4) terminating:

```
Zcharacter terminating 132 136;
```

The legal values to include are those for the cursor, function and keypad keys, plus mouse and menu clicks (see Table 2 for values). The special value 255 makes all of these characters terminating. (For other uses of Zcharacter, see §36.)

- **EXERCISE 129**
Write a "press any key to continue" routine.

- **EXERCISE 130**
And another routine which determines if any key is being held down, returning either its ZSCII code or zero to indicate that no key is being held down.

- **EXERCISE 131**
Write a game in which a player taking more than ten seconds to consider a command is hurried along.

- **EXERCISE 132**
And if thirty seconds are taken, make the player's mind up for her.

- **EXERCISE 133**
Design an hourglass fixed to a pivot on one room's wall, which (when turned upright) runs sand through in real time, turning itself over automatically every forty seconds.

. . . . .

△   Besides the keyboard, Version 6 normally supports the use of a mouse. In theory this can have any number of buttons, but since some widely-used computers have single-button mice (e.g., the Apple Macintosh) it's safest not to rely on more than one.

The mouse must be attached to one of the eight windows for it to register properly. (Initially, it isn't attached to any window and so is entirely inert.) To attach it to the window numbered wnum, use the opcode:

```
@mouse_window wnum
```

Once attached, a click within the window will register as if it were a key-press to @read_char with ZSCII value 254, unless it is a second click in quick succession to a previous click in the same position, in which case it has ZSCII value 253. Thus, a double-clicking registers twice, once as click (254) and then as double-click (253).

At any time, the mouse position, measured in units, and the state of its buttons, i.e., pressed or not pressed, can be read off with the opcode:

```
@read_mouse mouse_array
```

places (x, y) coordinates of the click in mouse_array-->0 and mouse_array-->1 and the state of the buttons as a bitmap in mouse_array-->2, with bit 0 representing the rightmost button, bit 1 the next and so on. In practice, it's safest simply to test whether this value is zero (no click) or not (click). The array mouse_array should have room for 4 entries, however: the fourth relates to menus (see below).

● EXERCISE 134
Write a test program to wait for mouse clicks and then print out the state of the mouse.

△   The mouse also allows access to menus, on some interpreters, though in Version 6 only. The model here is of a Mac OS-style desktop, with one or more menus added to the menu bar at the top of the screen: games are free to add or remove menus at any time. They are added with:

```
@make_menu number mtable ?IfAbleTo;
```

Such menus are numbered from 3 upwards. mtable is a table array of menu entries, each of which must be itself a string array giving the text of that option. IfAbleTo is a label, to which the interpreter will jump if the menu is successfully created. If mtable is zero, the opcode instead removes an already-existing menu. During play, the selection of a menu item by the player is signalled to the Z-machine as a key-press with ZSCII value 252, and the game receiving this can then look up which item on which menu was selected by looking at entry -->3 in an array given to read_mouse. The value in this entry will be the menu number times 256, plus the item number, where items are numbered from 0. If the game has 252 listed as a "terminating character" (see above), then menu selection can take the place of typing a command.

● EXERCISE 135
Provide a game with a menu of common commands like "inventory" and "look" to save on typing.

. . . . .

△ The Z-machine can also load and save "auxiliary files" to or from the host machine. These should have names adhering to the "8 + 3" convention, that is, one to eight alphanumeric characters optionally followed by a full stop and one to three further alphanumeric characters. Where no such extension is given, it is assumed to be .AUX. Designers are asked to avoid using the extensions .INF, .H, .SAV or .Z5 or similar, to prevent confusion. Note that auxiliary files from different games may be sharing a common directory on the host machine, so that a filename should be as distinctive as possible. The two opcodes are:

```
@save buffer length filename -> R
```

Saves the byte array buffer (of size length) to a file, whose (default) name is given in the filename (a string array). Afterwards, R holds true on success, false on failure.

```
@restore buffer length filename -> R
```

Loads in the byte array buffer (of size length) from a file, whose (default) name is given in the filename (a string array). Afterwards, R holds the number of bytes successfully read.

● EXERCISE 136
How might this assist a "role-playing game campaign" with several scenarios, each implemented as a separate Inform game but sharing a player-character who takes objects and experience from one scenario to the next?

● EXERCISE 137
Design catacombs in which the ghosts of former, dead players from previous games linger.

. . . . .

△ Finally, the Z-machine supports a very simple form of exception-handling like that of the C language's long jump feature. This is very occasionally useful to get the program out of large recursive tangles in a hurry.

```
@catch -> result
```

The opposite of @throw, @catch preserves the "stack frame" of the current routine in the variable result: roughly speaking, the stack frame is the current position of which routine is being run and which ones have called it so far.

```
@throw value stack-frame
```

This causes the program to execute a return with value, but as if it were returning from the routine which was running when the stack-frame was "caught", that is, set up by a corresponding @catch opcode. Note that you can only @throw back to a routine which is still running, i.e., to which control will eventually return anyway.

• △△EXERCISE 138

Use @throw and @catch to make an exception handler for actions, so that any action subroutine getting into recursive trouble can throw an exception and escape.

• REFERENCES

The assembly-language connoisseur will appreciate 'Freefall' by Andrew Plotkin and 'Robots' by Torbjörn Andersson, although the present lack of on-line hints make these difficult games to win.   •Gevan Dutton has made an amazing port of the classic character-graphic maze adventure 'Rogue' to Inform, taking place entirely in the upper window.   •Similarly, 'Zugzwang' by Magnus Olsson plots up a chess position.   •The function library "text_functions.h", by Patrick Kellum, offers text styling and colouring. These routines are entirely written in assembler. Similar facilities are available from Chris Klimas's "style.h" and L. Ross Raszewski's "utility.h". •Jason Penney's "V6Lib.h" is a coherent extension to the Inform library for Version 6 games (only), offering support for multiple text windows, images and sounds by means of class definitions and high-level Inform code.   •More modestly, but applicably to Version 5 and 8 games, L. Ross Raszewski's "sound.h" function library handles sound effects.

§43 Pictures, sounds, blurbs and Blorb

> The blorb spell (safely protect a small object as though in a strong box).
>
> — Marc Blank and P. David Lebling, 'Enchanter'

Pictures may, but need not, accompany a Version 6 game. They are not stored in the story file itself, and different interpreters make different arrangements for getting access to them. Some interpreters can only read low-resolution, low-colour-range images in the awkward format used by Infocom's graphical games. Others take pictures from a "Blorb file" which can hold high-resolution and riotously colourful images in a format called PNG. The story file neither knows nor cares which, and refers to pictures only by their numbers.

A Blorb file can also safely protect sound effects and even the story file itself, so that a game and its multi-media resources can be a single file. Blorb is a simple format largely devised by Andrew Plotkin (partly based on the same author's earlier "Pickle"); it has been fully implemented in Kevin Bracey's 'Zip2000' interpreter for Acorn RISC OS machines, and is also used by the new "glulx" format of story files.

A Perl script called perlBlorb, runnable on many models of computer, gathers together sounds and images and constructs Blorb files as needed, from a list of instructions called a "blurb file". For instance:

```
! Example of a blurb file
copyright "Angela M. Horns 1998"
release 17
palette 16 bit
resolution 600x400
storyfile "games/sherbet.z5"
sound    creak   "sounds/creaking.snd"
sound    wind    "sounds/wind.snd"
picture  flag     "flag.png"       scale 3/1
picture  pattern  "backdrop.png"
```

When run through perlBlorb, the above produces the text below:

```
! perlBlorb 1.0 [executing on 980124 at 15:31.33]
Constant SOUND_creak = 3;
```

```
Constant SOUND_wind = 4;
Constant PICTURE_flag = 1;
Constant PICTURE_pattern = 2;
! Completed: size 45684 bytes (2 pictures, 2 sounds)
```

This output text looks like Inform source code, and this is not an accident: the idea is that it can be used as an Include file to give sensible names to the sound and picture numbers, so that the rest of the code can include statements like this one:

```
@sound_effect SOUND_creak 2 128 255;
```

("start playing this effect at about half maximum volume, repeating it indefinitely"). An attractive alternative is to use a convenient class library, such as "V6Lib.h" by Jason Penney, to avoid messing about with assembly language.

You're free to specify the numbering yourself, and you need not give names for the pictures and sounds. A blurb command like:

```
picture "backdrop.png"
```

gives this image the next picture number: i.e., the previous picture number plus 1, or just 1 if it's the first specified picture. On the other hand, a blurb command like:

```
picture 100 "backdrop.png"
```

gives it picture number 100. The only restriction is that pictures must be given in increasing numerical order. The numbering of sounds is similar.

· · · · ·

△   The full specification for the "blurb" language is as follows. With one exception (see palette below) each command occupies one and only one line of text. Lines are permitted to be empty or to contain only white space. Lines whose first non-white-space character is an exclamation mark are treated as comments, that is, ignored. ("White space" means spaces and tab characters.)

⟨string⟩ means any text within double-quotes, not containing either double-quote or new-line characters

⟨number⟩ means a decimal number in the range 0 to 32767

⟨id⟩ means either nothing at all, or a ⟨number⟩, or a sequence of up to 20 letters, digits or underscore characters _

⟨dim⟩ indicates screen dimensions, and must take the form ⟨number⟩x⟨number⟩

⟨ratio⟩ is a fraction in the form ⟨number⟩/⟨number⟩. 0/0 is legal but otherwise both numbers must be positive

⟨colour⟩ is a colour expressed as six hexadecimal digits, as in some HTML tags: for instance F5DEB3 is the colour of wheat, with red value F5 (on a scale 00, none, to FF, full), green value DE and blue value B3. Hexadecimal digits may be given in either upper or lower case.

With the exception of picture and sound, each type of command can only occur at most once in any blurb file. Commands can be used in any order or not at all: an empty "blurb" file results in a perfectly legal, if useless, Blorb file. The full set of commands is as follows:

```
copyright ⟨string⟩
```

Adds this copyright declaration to the file. It would normally consist of the author's name and the date.

```
release ⟨number⟩
```

Gives this release number to the file. This is the number returned by the opcode @picture_data 0 within any game using the Blorb file, and might be used when printing out version information.

```
palette 16 bit
palette 32 bit
palette { ⟨colour-1⟩ ... ⟨colour-N⟩ }
```

Blorb allows designers to signal to the interpreter that a particular colour-scheme is in use. The first two options simply suggest that the pictures are best displayed using at least 16-bit, or 32-bit, colours. The third option specifies colours used in the pictures in terms of red/green/blue levels, and the braces allow the sequence of colours to continue over many lines. At least one and at most 256 colours may be defined in this way. This is only a "clue" to the interpreter; see the Blorb specification for details.

```
resolution ⟨dim⟩
resolution ⟨dim⟩ min ⟨dim⟩
resolution ⟨dim⟩ max ⟨dim⟩
resolution ⟨dim⟩ min ⟨dim⟩ max ⟨dim⟩
```

Allows the designer to signal a preferred screen size, in real pixels, in case the interpreter should have any choice over this. The minimum and maximum values are the extreme values at which the designer thinks the game will be playable: they're optional, the default values being 0x0 and infinity by infinity.

```
storyfile ⟨string⟩
```

323

```
storyfile ⟨string⟩ include
```

Tells perlBlorb the filename of the Z-code story file which these resources are being provided for. (There is no need to do this if you prefer not to.) Usually the Blorb file simply contains a note of the release number, serial code and checksum of the story file, which an interpreter can try to match at run-time to see if the Blorb file and story file go together. If the include option is used, however, the entire story file is embedded within the Blorb file, so that game and resources are all bound up in one single file.

```
sound ⟨id⟩ ⟨string⟩
sound ⟨id⟩ ⟨string⟩ repeat ⟨number⟩
sound ⟨id⟩ ⟨string⟩ repeat forever
sound ⟨id⟩ ⟨string⟩ music
sound ⟨id⟩ ⟨string⟩ song
```

Tells perlBlorb to take a sound sample from the named file and make it the sound effect with the given number. The file should be an AIFF file unless music is specified, in which case it should be a MOD file (roughly speaking a SoundTracker file); or unless song is specified, in which case it should be a song file (roughly, a SoundTracker file using other Blorb sound effects as note samples). Note that repeat information (the number of repeats to be played) is meaningful only with version 3 story files using sound effects, as only Infocom's 'The Lurking Horror' ever has.

```
picture ⟨id⟩ ⟨string⟩
picture ⟨id⟩ ⟨string⟩ scale ⟨ratio⟩
picture ⟨id⟩ ⟨string⟩ scale min ⟨ratio⟩
picture ⟨id⟩ ⟨string⟩ scale ⟨ratio⟩ min ⟨ratio⟩
```
and so on

Similarly for pictures: the named file must be a PNG-format image. Optionally, the designer can specify a scale factor at which the interpreter will display the image – or, alternatively, a range of acceptable scale factors, from which the interpreter may choose its own scale factor. (By default an image is not scaleable and an interpreter must display it pixel-for-pixel.) There are three optional scale factors given: the preferred scale factor, the minimum and the maximum allowed. The minimum and maximum each default to the preferred value if not given, and the default preferred scale factor is 1. Scale factors are expressed as fractions: so for instance,

```
picture "flag/png" scale 3/1
```

means "always display three times its normal size", whereas

```
picture "backdrop/png" scale min 1/10 max 8/1
```

means "you can display this anywhere between one tenth normal size and eight times normal size, but if possible it ought to be just its normal size".

● **REFERENCES**

The Perl script 'perlBlorb' is available from the Inform web-page.   ●The source code to Kevin Bracey's fully Blorb-compliant standard interpreter 'Zip2000' is public.   ●Andrew Plotkin has published generic C routines for handling Blorb files. ●Numerous utility programs exist which will convert GIF or JPEG images to PNG format, or WAV and MPEG sounds to AIFF.

§44   Case study: a library file for menus

> Yes, all right, I won't do the menu. . . I don't think you realise how
> long it takes to do the menu, but no, it doesn't matter, I'll hang
> the picture now. If the menus are late for lunch it doesn't matter,
> the guests can all come and look at the picture till they are ready,
> right?
>
> — John Cleese and Connie Booth, *Fawlty Towers*

 Sometimes one would like to provide a menu of text options, offered
to the player as a list on screen which can be rummaged through
with the cursor keys. For instance, the hints display in the "solid
gold" edition of Infocom's 'Zork I' shows a list of "Invisiclues":
"Above Ground", "The Cellar Area", and so on. Moving a cursor to one of
these options and pressing RETURN brings up a sub-menu of questions on the
general topic chosen: for instance, "How do I cross the mountains?" Besides
hints, many modern games use menu displays for instructions, background
information, credits and release notes.

An optional library file called "Menus.h" is provided to manage such
menus. If you want its facilities then, where you previously included Verblib,
now write:

```
Include "Verblib";
Include "Menus";
```

And this will make the features of Menus.h available. This section describes
what these simple features are, and how they work, as an extended example of
Z-machine programming.

The designer of this system began by noticing that menus and submenus
and options fit together in a tree structure rather like the object tree:

Hints for 'Zork I' (menu)
  ⟶ Above Ground (submenu)
    ⟶ How do I cross the mountains? (option)
      ⟶ *some text is revealed*
  ⟶ The Cellar Area (submenu)
    ⟶ . . .

The library file therefore defines two classes of object, Menu and Option. The short name of a menu is its title, while its children are the possible choices, which can be of either class. (So you can have as many levels of submenu as needed.) Since choosing an Option is supposed to produce some text, which is vaguely like examining objects, the description property of an Option holds the information revealed. So, for instance:

```
Menu hints_menu "Hints for Zork I";
Menu -> "Above Ground";
Option -> -> "How do I cross the mountains?"
  with description "By ...";
Menu -> "The Cellar Area";
```

Note that such a structure can be rearranged in play just as the rest of the object tree can, which is convenient for "adaptive hints", where the hints offered vary with the player's present travail.

How does this work? A menu or an option is chosen by being sent the message select. So the designer will launch the menu, perhaps in response to the player having typed "hints", like so:

```
[ HintsSub;
  hints_menu.select();
];
```

As the player browses through the menu, each menu sends the select message to the next one chosen, and so on. This already suggests that menus and options are basically similar, and in fact that's right: Menu is actually a subclass of Option, which is the more basic idea of the two.

. . . . .

The actual code of Menus.h is slightly different from that given below, but only to fuss with dealing with early copies of the rest of the library, and to handle multiple languages. It begins with the class definition of Option, as follows:

```
Class Option
 with select [;
        self.emblazon(1, 1, 1);
        @set_window 0; font on; style roman; new_line; new_line;
        if (self provides description) return self.description();
        "[No text written for this option.]^";
     ],
```

The option sends itself the message emblazon(1,1,1) to clear the screen and put a bar of height 1 line at the top, containing the title of the option centred. The other two 1s declare that this is "page 1 of 1": see below. Window 0 (the ordinary, lower window) is then selected; text reverts to its usual state of being roman-style and using a variable-pitched font. The screen is now empty and ready for use, and the option expects to have a description property which actually does any printing that's required. To get back to the emblazoning:

```
emblazon [ bar_height page pages temp;
    screen_width = 0->33;
    !   Clear screen:
    @erase_window -1;
    @split_window bar_height;
    !   Black out top line in reverse video:
    @set_window 1;
    @set_cursor 1 1;
    style reverse; spaces(screen_width);
    if (standard_interpreter == 0)
        @set_cursor 1 1;
    else {
        ForUseByOptions-->0 = 128;
        @output_stream 3 ForUseByOptions;
        print (name) self;
        if (pages ~= 1) print " [", page, "/", pages, "]";
        @output_stream -3;
        temp = (screen_width - ForUseByOptions-->0)/2;
        @set_cursor 1 temp;
    }
    print (name) self;
    if (pages ~= 1) print " [", page, "/", pages, "]";
    return ForUseByOptions-->0;
];
```

That completes Option. However, since this code refers to a variable and an array, we had better write definitions of them:

```
Global screen_width;
Global screen_height;
Array ForUseByOptions -> 129;
```

(The other global variable, screen_height, will be used later. The variables are global because they will be needed by all of the menu objects.) The emblazon code checks to see if it's running on a standard interpreter. If so, it uses output stream 3 into an array to measure the length of text like "The

Cellars [2/3]" in order to centre it on the top line. If not, the text appears at the top left instead.

So much for Option. The definition of Menu is, inevitably, longer. It inherits emblazon from its superclass Option, but overrides the definition of select with something more elaborate:

```
Class Menu class Option
 with select [ count j obj pkey line oldline top_line bottom_line
       page pages options top_option;
         screen_width = 0->33;
         screen_height = 0->32;
         if (screen_height == 0 or 255) screen_height = 18;
         screen_height = screen_height - 7;
```

The first task is to work out how much room the screen has to display options. The width and height, in characters, are read out of the story file's header area, where the interpreter has written them. In case the interpreter is *really* poor, we guess at 18 if the height is claimed to be zero or 255; since this is a library file and will be widely used, it errs on the side of extreme caution. Finally, 7 is subtracted because seven of the screen lines are occupied by the panel at the top and white space above and below the choices. The upshot is that screen_height is the actual maximum number of options to be offered per page of the menu. Next: how many options are available?

```
         options = 0;
         objectloop (obj in self && obj ofclass Option) options++;
         if (options == 0) return 2;
```

(Note that a Menu is also an Option.) We can now work out how many pages will be needed.

```
         pages = options/screen_height;
         if (options%screen_height ~= 0) pages++;
         top_line = 6;
         page = 1;
         line = top_line;
```

top_line is the highest screen line used to display an option: line 6. The local variables page and line show which line on which page the current selection arrow points to, so we're starting at the top line of page 1.

```
         .ReDisplay;
         top_option = (page - 1) * screen_height;
```

This is the option number currently selected, counting from zero. We display the three-line black strip at the top of the screen, using emblazon to create the upper window:

```
self.emblazon(7 + count, page, pages);
@set_cursor 2 1; spaces(screen_width);
@set_cursor 2 2; print "N = next subject";
j = screen_width-12; @set_cursor 2 j; print "P = previous";
@set_cursor 3 1; spaces(screen_width);
@set_cursor 3 2; print "RETURN = read subject";
j = screen_width-17; @set_cursor 3 j;
```

The last part of the black strip to print is the one offering Q to quit:

```
if (sender ofclass Option) print "Q = previous menu";
else print "  Q = resume game";
style roman;
```

The point of this is that pressing Q only takes us back to the previous menu if we're inside the hierarchy, i.e., if the message select was sent to this Menu by another Option; whereas if not, Q takes us out of the menu altogether. Next, we count through those options appearing on the current page and print their names.

```
count = top_line; j = 0;
objectloop (obj in self && obj ofclass Option) {
    if (j >= top_option && j < (top_option+screen_height)) {
        @set_cursor count 6;
        print (name) obj;
        count++;
    }
    j++;
}
bottom_line = count - 1;
```

Note that the name of the option begins on column 6 of each line. The player's current selection is shown with a cursor > appearing in column 4:

```
oldline = 0;
for (::) {
    ! Move or create the > cursor:
    if (line ~= oldline) {
        if (oldline ~= 0) {
            @set_cursor oldline 4; print " ";
        }
        @set_cursor line 4; print ">";
```

```
    }
    oldline = line;
```

Now we wait for a single key-press from the player:

```
@read_char 1 -> pkey;
if (pkey == 'N' or 'n' or 130) {
    ! Cursor down:
    line++;
    if (line > bottom_line) {
        line = top_line;
        if (pages > 1) {
            if (page == pages) page = 1; else page++;
            jump ReDisplay;
        }
    }
    continue;
}
```

130 is the ZSCII code for "cursor down key". Note that if the player tries to move the cursor off the bottom of the list, and there's at least one more page, we jump right out of the loop and back to ReDisplay to start again from the top of the next page. Handling the "previous" option is very similar, and then:

```
if (pkey == 'Q' or 'q' or 27 or 131) break;
```

Thus pressing lower or upper case Q, escape (ZSCII 27) or cursor left (ZSCII 131) all have the same effect: to break out of the for loop. Otherwise, one can press RETURN or cursor right to select an option:

```
if (pkey == 10 or 13 or 132) {
    count = 0;
    objectloop (obj in self && obj ofclass Option) {
        if (count == top_option + line - top_line) break;
        count++;
    }
    switch (obj.select()) {
        2: jump ReDisplay;
        3: jump ExitMenu;
    }
    print "[Please press SPACE to continue.]^";
    @read_char 1 -> pkey;
    jump ReDisplay;
}
```

(No modern interpreter should ever give 10 for the key-code of RETURN, which is ZSCII 13. Once again, the library file is erring on the side of extreme caution.) An option's `select` routine can return three different values for different effects:

2	Redisplay the menu page that selected me
3	Exit from that menu page
anything else	Wait for SPACE, then redisplay that menu page

Finally, the exit from the menu, either because the player typed Q, escape, etc., or because the selected option returned 3:

```
    .ExitMenu;
    if (sender ofclass Option) return 2;
    font on; @set_cursor 1 1;
    @erase_window -1; @set_window 0;
    new_line; new_line; new_line;
    if (deadflag == 0) <<Look>>;
    return 2;
];
```

And that's it. If this menu was the highest-level one, it needs to resume the game politely, by clearing the screen and performing a Look action. If not, then it needs only to return 2, indicating "redisplay the menu page that selected me": that is, the menu one level above.

The only remaining code in "Menus.h" shows some of the flexibility of the above design, by defining a special type of option:

```
Class SwitchOption class Option
   with short_name [;
           print (object) self, " ";
           if (self has on) print "(on)"; else print "(off)";
           rtrue;
       ],
       select [;
           if (self has on) give self ~on; else give self on;
           return 2;
       ];
```

Here is an example of SwitchOptions in use:

```
Menu settings "Game settings";
SwitchOption -> FullRoomD   "full room descriptions" has on;
SwitchOption -> WordyP       "wordier prompts";
SwitchOption -> AllowSavedG "allow saved games" has on;
```

So each option has the attribute on only if currently set. In the menu, the option FullRoomD is displayed either as "full room descriptions (on)" or "full room descriptions (off)", and selecting it switches the state, like a light switch. The rest of the code can then perform tests like so:

```
if (AllowSavedG hasnt on) "That spell is forbidden.";
```

. . . . .

Appearance of the final menu on a screen 64 characters wide:

```
line 1                      Hints for Zork I [1/2]
line 2   N = next subject                        P = previous
line 3   RETURN = read subject                   Q = resume game
line 4
line 5
line 6        Above Ground
line 7      > The Cellar Area
line 8        The Maze
line 9        The Round Room Area
```

• REFERENCES

Because there was a crying need for good menus in the early days of Inform, there are now numerous library extensions to support menus and interfaces built from them. The original such was L. Ross Raszewski's "domenu.h", which provides a core of basic routines. "AltMenu.h" then uses these routines to emulate the same menu structures coded up in this section. "Hints.h" employs them for Invisiclues-style hints; "manual.h" for browsing books and manuals; "converse.h" for menu-based conversations with people, similar to those in graphical adventure games. Or indeed to those in Adam Cadre's game 'Photopia', and Adam has kindly extracted his menu-based conversational routines into an example program called "phototalk.inf". For branching menus, such as a tree of questions and answers, try Chris Klimas's "branch.h". To put a menu of commands at the status line of a typical game, try Adam Stark's "action.h".

§45 Limitations and getting around them

How wide the limits stand
Between a splendid and an happy land.
— Oliver Goldsmith (1728–1774), *The Deserted Village*

 The Z-machine is well-designed, and has three major advantages: it is compact, widely portable and can be quickly executed. Nevertheless, like any rigidly defined format it imposes limitations. This section is intended to help those few designers who encounter the current limits. Some of the economy-measures below may sound like increasingly desperate manoeuvres in a lost battle, but if so then the cavalry is on its way: Andrew Plotkin has written a hybrid version of Inform which removes almost every restriction. Although it doesn't quite have all the nooks and crannies of Inform yet working, it does allow most games to compile without difficulty to a very much larger virtual machine than the Z-machine called "glulx".

1. Story file size. The maximum size of a story file (in K) is given by:

V3	V4	V5	V6	V7	V8
128	256	256	512	320	512

Because the centralised library of Inform is efficient in terms of not duplicating code, even 128K allows for a game at least half as large again as a typical old-style Infocom game. Inform is normally used only to produce story files of Versions 5, 6 and 8. Version 5 is the default; Version 6 should be used where pictures or other graphical features are essential to the game; Version 8 is a size extension for Version 5, allowing games of fairly gargantuan proportions.

△ If story file memory does become short, a standard mechanism can save about 8–10% of the total memory, though it will not greatly affect readable memory extent. Inform does not usually trouble with this economy measure, since there's very seldom any need, and it makes the compiler run about 10% slower. What you need to do is define abbreviations and then run the compiler in its "economy" mode (using the switch -e). For instance, the directive

```
Abbreviate " the ";
```

(placed before any text appears) will cause the string " the " to be internally stored as a single 'letter', saving memory every time it occurs (about 2,500 times in 'Curses', for

334

instance). You can have up to 64 abbreviations. When choosing abbreviations, avoid proper nouns and instead pick on short combinations of a space and common two- or three-letter blocks. Good choices include " the ", "The ", ", ", " and ", "you", " a ", "ing ", " to". You can even get Inform to work out by itself what a good stock of abbreviations would be, by setting the -u switch: but be warned, this makes the compiler run about 29,000% slower.

2. *Readable memory size.* In a very large game, or even a small one if it uses unusually large or very many arrays, the designer may run up against the following Inform fatal error message:

> This program has overflowed the maximum readable-memory size of the Z-machine format. See the memory map below: the start of the area marked "above readable memory" must be brought down to $10000 or less.

In other words, the readable-memory area is absolutely limited to 65,536 bytes in all Versions. Using the -D debugging option increases the amount of readable-memory consumed, and the Infix -X switch increases this further yet. (For instance 'Advent' normally uses 24,820 bytes, but 25,276 with -D and 28,908 with -X.) The following table suggests what is, and what is not, worth economising on.

Each. . .	Costs. . .
Routine	0
Text in double-quotes	0
Object or class	26
Common property value	3
Non-common property value	5
If a property holds an array	add 2 for each entry after the first
Dictionary word	9
Verb	3
Different action	4
Grammar token	3
--> or table array entry	2
-> or string array entry	1

To draw some morals: verbs, actions, grammar and the dictionary consume little readable memory and are too useful to economise on. Objects and arrays are where savings can be made. Here is one strategy for doing so.

2a. *Economise on arrays.* Many programmers create arrays with more entries than needed, saying in effect "I'm not sure how many this will take, but it's bound to be less than 1,000, so I'll say 1,000 entries to be on the safe side." More thought will often reduce the number. If not, look at the typical contents. Are the possible values always between 0 and 255? If so, make it a -> or string array and the consumption of readable memory is halved. Are the possible values always true or false? If so, Adam Cadre's "flags.h" library extension offers a slower-access form of array but which consumes only about 1/8th of a byte of readable memory per array entry.

2b. Turn arrays of constants into routines.   Routines cost nothing in readable memory terms, but they can still store information as long as it doesn't need to vary during play. For instance, 'Curses' contains an array beginning:

```
Array RadioSongs table
    "Queen's ~I Want To Break Free~."
    "Bach's ~Air on a G-string~."
    "Mozart's ~Musical Joke~."
```

and so on for dozens more easy-listening songs which sometimes play on Aunt Jemima's radio. It might equally be a routine:

```
[ RadioSongs n;
    switch (n) {
        0: return 100; ! Number of songs
        1: return "Queen's ~I Want To Break Free~.";
        2: return "Bach's ~Air on a G-string~.";
        3: return "Mozart's ~Musical Joke~.";
```

and so on. Instead of reading RadioSongs-->x, one now reads RadioSongs(x). Not an elegant trick, but it saves 200 bytes of readable memory.

2c. Economise on object properties.   Each time an object provides a property, readable memory is used. This is sometimes worth bearing in mind when writing definitions of classes which will have many members. For instance:

```
Class Doubloon(100)
  with name 'gold' 'golden' 'spanish' 'doubloon' 'coin' 'money'
           'coins//p' 'doubloons//p',
       . . .
```

Each of the hundred doubloons has a name array with eight entries, so 1700 bytes of readable memory are consumed. This could be reduced to 300 like so:

```
Class Doubloon(100)
  with parse_name [;
       ! A routine detecting the same name-words
       . . .
       ],
```

336

2d. Make commonly occurring properties common.   Recall that properties declared with the Property directive are called "common properties": these are faster to access and consume less memory. If, for instance, each of 100 rooms in your game provides a property called time_zone, then the declaration

```
Property time_zone;
```

at the start of your code will save 2 bytes each time time_zone is provided, saving 200 bytes in all. (The library's properties are all common already.)

2e. Economise on objects.   In a room with four scenery objects irrelevant to the action, say a window, a chest of drawers, a bed and a carpet, is it strictly necessary for each to have its own object? Kathleen Fischer: "parse_name is your friend... a single object with an elaborate parse_name can be used to cover a whole lot of scenery." In Kathleen's technique, it would use parse_name to record which of the words "window", "chest", "bed" or "carpet" was used, storing that information in a property: other properties, like description, would be routines which produced text depending on what the object is representing this turn.

2f. Reuse objects.   This is a last resort but L. Ross Raszewski's "imem.h" has helped several designers through it. Briefly, just as an array was converted to a routine in (1) above, "imem.h" converts object definitions to routines, with a minimal number of them "swapped in" as real objects at any given time and the rest – items of scenery in distant locations, for instance – "swapped out".

3. Grammar.   There can be up to 256 essentially different verbs, each with up to 32 grammar lines. Using the UnknownVerb entry point will get around the former limit, and general parsing routines can make even a single grammar line match almost any range of syntax.

4. Vocabulary.   There is no theoretical limit except that the dictionary words each take up 9 bytes of readable memory, which means that 4,000 words is probably the practical limit. In practice games generally have vocabularies of between 500 and 2,000 words.

5. Dictionary resolution.   Dictionary words are truncated to their first 9 letters (except that non-alphabetic characters, such as hyphens, count as 2 "letters" for this purpose: look up Zcharacter in the index for references to more on this). Upper and lower case letters are considered equal. Since general parsing routines, or parse_name routines, can look at the exact text typed by the player, finer resolution is easy enough if needed.

6. Attributes, properties, names.   There can be up to 48 attributes and an unlimited number of properties, at most 63 of these can be made common by

337

being declared with Property. A property entry can hold up to 64 bytes of data. Hence, for example, an object can have up to 32 names. If an object must respond to more, give it a suitable parse_name routine.

7. Objects and classes. The number of objects is unlimited so long as there is readable memory to hold their definitions. The number of classes is presently limited to 256, of which the library uses only 1.

8. Global variables. There can only be 240 of these, and the Inform compiler uses 5 as scratch space, while the library uses slightly over 100; but since a typical game uses only a dozen of its own, code being almost always object-oriented, the restriction is never felt.

9. Arrays. An unlimited number of Array statements is permitted, although the entries in arrays consume readable memory (see above).

10. Function calls and messages. A function can be called with at most seven arguments. A message can be called with at most five.

11. Recursion and stack usage. The limit on this is rather technical (see *The Z-Machine Standards Document*). Roughly speaking, recursion is permitted to a depth of 90 routines in almost all circumstances, and often much deeper. Direct usage of the stack via assembly language must be modest.

Chapter VIII: The Craft of Adventure

Designing is a craft as much as an art. Standards of workmanship, of "finish", are valued and appreciated by players, and the craft of the adventure game has developed as it has been handed down. The embryonic 'Zork' (Tim Anderson, Marc Blank, Bruce Daniels, Dave Lebling, 1977) – shambolic, improvised, frequently unfair – was thrown together in a fortnight of spare time. 'Trinity' (Brian Moriarty, 1986), plotted in synopsis in 1984, required thirteen months to design and test.

'Spellbreaker' (Dave Lebling, 1985) is a case in point. A first-rate game, it advanced the state of the art by allowing the player to name items. It brought a trilogy to a satisfying conclusion, while standing on its own merits. A dense game, with more content per location than ever before, it had a structure which succeeded both in being inexplicable at first yet inevitable later. With sly references to string theory and to Aristophanes' *The Frogs*, it was cleverer than it looked. But it was also difficult and, at first, bewildering, with the rewards some way off. What kept players at it were the "cyclopean blocks of stone", the "voice of honey and ashes", the characters who would unexpectedly say things like "You insult me, you insult even my dog!". Polished, spare text is almost always more effective than a discursive ramble, and many of the room descriptions in 'Spellbreaker' are nicely judged:

Packed Earth
This is a small room crudely constructed of packed earth, mud, and sod.
Crudely framed openings of wood tied with leather thongs lead off in each of
the four cardinal directions, and a muddy hole leads down.

In short, it was masterly craftsmanship (in what was Lebling's seventh title) which made this exercise in pushing the boundaries of difficulty and connectedness possible.

Classics like 'Spellbreaker' cast long shadows and have endured beyond all expectation: 'Zork II', for instance, has been continuously on sale in the high street since 1981, a record matched by only about two dozen of that year's novels. But the story of interactive fiction is *not* the story of the production company Infocom, Inc., alone. Many hundreds of plays were performed in late sixteenth-century London, but today only Shakespeare's three dozen are familiar, even the weakest protected from neglect by the gilding of being canonical. The resulting attention may be justified on literary grounds, but perhaps not historical, since it gives a picture wholly unlike the regular diet of the contemporary audience. So with Infocom. Many 1980s adventure players seldom if ever played their works, or not until years later. Their real importance, besides quality and familiarity, is that they were foundational, in the same way that Hergé's pre-war *Tintin* albums evolved the visual grammar of the European graphic novel, from layout rules for speech bubbles and panels to how sudden motion should be depicted. Tintin and his dog Snowy began to walk from left to right (the direction of reading) when making progress, but from right to left after a setback. Snowy lost first the ability to speak, then the ability to understand Tintin's speech. Infocom had a similar effect in laying down the mechanics of interactive fiction, the conventions of which are subliminally accepted by players (and silently perpetuated by Inform). For instance, it was the Infocom games of 1986 which began the now familiar use of pop-up literary quotations as a stylish form of commentary or signposting, a development which might be compared to exclamation marks appearing over the heads of surprised characters in *Tintin*.

The mechanics of reading a novel are almost unconscious, but the mechanics of interactive fiction are far less familiar, and it is a uniquely unforgiving medium. A technical mistake by a novelist, say an alternating dialogue so long that it becomes unclear who is speaking, does not make it impossible for the reader to continue, as if the last hundred pages of the book had been glued together. The designer of an interactive fiction has continually to worry over the order in which things happen, the level of difficulty, the rate at which new material is fed out and so on. Meanwhile, even the designer's footing seems uncertain, for the form itself is a wavering compromise. An interactive fiction is not a child's puzzle-book, with a maze on one page and a rebus on the next, but nor is it a novel. Neither pure interaction nor pure fiction, it lies in a strange and still largely unexplored land in between.

● **REFERENCES**

In this chapter, a game is cited by designer and date when first mentioned but subsequently by title alone. Details of availability may be found in the bibliography of cited works.　●Unattributed quotations from Infocom designers are all to be found in the ftp.gmd.de archive of 1980s computing press articles. My choice has been skewed by availability: Lebling is quoted frequently not because he was a great designer (though he was) but because he often went on the record. Marc Blank, among other notable figures, spent less time entertaining the press.　●Some thousands of internal Infocom email messages (1982–) have been quietly preserved. Except at the end the overall impression is of a sensible workplace with engagingly warm moments, and a number of unsung figures emerge from the shadows. Much of this material is unlikely to become public because of its personal nature. To respect this, I have quoted nothing directly from *unpublished* email and have avoided attributing specific opinions to named people. I do quote from the handful of relatively innocuous emails published on Activision's *Masterpieces of Infocom* compact disc, though note that these were stripped of all context. For instance the most interesting, a 1987 memo about which way to take text games now (discussed briefly in §49 below), is not as it seems a minute of a committee but was typed up as an apology to two people offended at being excluded from a low-key crisis meeting, held covertly off the premises.   •A happier example is a sketch written by Stu Galley in response to an email circular asking for a job description: the so-called 'Implementors' Creed'. Despite the style – fifty percent mission statement, fifty percent Martin Luther King – this manifesto is worth reading, because it is conscious of working in an experimental and artistic medium: "I am exploring a new medium for telling stories. My readers should become immersed in the story and forget where they are. They should forget about the keyboard and the screen, forget everything but the experience. My goal is to make the computer invisible. ... None of my goals is easy. But all are worth hard work. Let no one doubt my dedication to my art."   •Another true believer was Cleveland M. Blakemore, in his treatise in issue 54 of *Ahoy!* magazine: "Every human being on earth is a natural dynamo of creative energy. Learning how to tap this energy and translate it to a book, a canvas, or a computer's memory, is a skill that can be learned."

§46 A short history of interactive fiction

The history of interactive fiction in the twentieth century has yet to be written. One outline might be as follows: an age of precursors and university games, 1972–81; the commercial boom, 1982–6; a period of nostalgia among Internet users for text while the industry completed the move to graphical games, 1987–91; and the age of the Usenet newsgroup `rec.arts.int-fiction` and its annual competition, of shorter stories moving away from genres and puzzles, 1992–9.

§46.1 Precursors and university games 1972–81

Perhaps the first adventurer was a mulatto slave named Stephen Bishop, born about 1820: "slight, graceful, and very handsome"; a "quick, daring, enthusiastic" guide to the Mammoth Cave in the Kentucky karst. The story of the Cave is a curious microcosm of American history. Its discovery is a matter of legend dating back to the 1790s; it is said that a hunter, John Houchin, pursued a wounded bear to a large pit near the Green River and stumbled upon the entrance. The entrance was thick with bats and by the War of 1812 was intensively mined for guano, dissolved into nitrate vats to make saltpetre for gunpowder. After the war prices fell, but the Cave became a minor side-show when a desiccated Indian mummy was found nearby, sitting upright in a stone coffin, surrounded by talismans. In 1815, Fawn Hoof, as she was nicknamed after one of the charms, was taken away by a circus, drawing crowds across America (a tour rather reminiscent of Don McLean's song "The Legend of Andrew McCrew"). She ended up in the Smithsonian but by the 1820s the Cave was being called one of the wonders of the world, largely due to her posthumous efforts.

By the early nineteenth century European caves were big tourist attractions, but hardly anyone visited the Mammoth, "wonder of the world" or not. Nor was it then especially large, as the name was a leftover from the miners, who boasted of mammoth yields of guano. In 1838, Stephen Bishop's owner bought up the Cave. Stephen, as (being a slave) he was invariably called, was by any standards a remarkable man: self-educated in Latin and Greek, he became famous as the "chief ruler" of his underground realm. He explored and named much of the layout in his spare time, doubling the known map in a year. The distinctive flavour of the Cave's names – half homespun American, half classical – started with Stephen: the River Styx, the Snowball Room, Little Bat Avenue, the Giant Dome. Stephen found strange blind fish, snakes, silent crickets, the remains of cave bears (savage, playful creatures, five feet long and four high, which became extinct at the end of the last Ice Age), centuries-old Indian gypsum workings and ever more cave. His 1842 map, drafted entirely from memory, was still in use forty years later.

After a brief period of misguided philanthropy in which the caves were used as a sanatorium for tuberculosis patients, tourism took over. By the twentieth century nearby caves were being hotly seized and legal title endlessly challenged. The neighbouring chain, across Houchins Valley in the Flint Ridge, opened the Great Onyx Cave in 1912. By the 1920s, the Kentucky Cave Wars were in full swing. Rival owners diverted tourists with fake policemen, employed stooges to heckle each other's guided tours, burned down ticket huts, put out libellous and forged advertisements. Cave exploration became so dangerous and secretive that finally in 1941 the U.S. Government stepped in, made much of the area a National Park and effectively banned caving. The gold rush of tourists was, in any case, waning.

Convinced that the Mammoth and Flint Ridge caves were all linked in a huge chain, of perhaps four hundred miles in extent, explorers tried secret entrances for years, eventually winning official backing. Throughout the 1960s all connections from Flint Ridge – difficult and water-filled tunnels – ended frustratingly in chokes of boulders. A "reed-thin" physicist, Patricia Crowther, made the breakthrough in 1972 when she got through the Tight Spot and found a muddy passage: it was a hidden way into the Mammoth Cave.

Under the terms of his owner's will, Stephen Bishop was freed in 1856, at which time the cave boasted 226 avenues, 47 domes, 23 pits and 8 waterfalls. He died a year later, before he could buy his wife and son, and achieve his ambition of farming in Argentina. In the 1970s, Crowther's muddy passage was found on his map.

. . . . .

One of Pat Crowther's caving companions was her husband, Will, who had already used computer plotters to draw the group's maps. He takes up the story:

> I had been involved in a non-computer role-playing game called *Dungeons and Dragons* at the time [c. 1975], and also I had been actively exploring in caves ... Suddenly, I got involved in a divorce, and that left me a bit pulled apart in various ways. In particular I was missing my kids. Also the caving had stopped, because that had become awkward, so I decided I would fool around and write a program that was a re-creation in fantasy of my caving,

and also would be a game for the kids ... My idea was that it would be a computer game that would not be intimidating to non-computer people, and that was one of the reasons why I made it so that the player directs the game with natural language input, instead of more standardized commands.

(Quoted in Dale Peterson, *Genesis II: Creation and Recreation with Computers*, 1983.) It's hard not to feel a certain sadness that the first adventure game is shaped by these two lost souls, Bishop and Crowther, each like Orpheus unable to draw his wife out of the underworld.

Crowther's program (c. 1975), then, was a simulation of the Bedquilt Cave area, owing its turn-based conversational style to a medieval-fantasy adaptation of tabletop wargaming: E. Gary Gygax and Dave Arneson's *Dungeons and Dragons* (1973-4). Nor was the program without precedent, either in computing – 'Hunt the Wumpus' (Gregory Yob, 1972) was a textual maze game, while 'SHRDLU' (Terry Winograd, 1972) had a recognisably adventure-like parser – or in literature, where OuLiPo and other ludic literary genres, especially in France, had tried almost every permutation to make physical books more open-ended: Raymond Queneau's *Cent mille milliards de poèmes* (1962) cut its pages into strips so that the lines of ten sonnets could be mingled to form 10^{14} different outcomes.† But the OuLiPo writers, and earlier futurists, had thought more in terms of clockwork than the computer: the literature machine's unashamed mindlessness a provocation to the reader, in whom associations will be triggered. Italo Calvino (in his 1969 lecture *Cybernetics and Ghosts*):

> It will be the shock that occurs only if the writing machine is surrounded by the hidden ghosts of the individual and of his society.

To all intents and purposes, then, 'Advent' had invented a new category of computer program and of literature. The aim was to explore, with five treasures hidden below and only a few of the more "natural" puzzles as obstacles, such as the snake, the dwarves and pirate, the first of the mazes and the limited battery span of the caver's essential companion, the carbide lamp. Like the real Bedquilt, the simulation has a map on about four levels of depth and is rich in geological detail:

> YOU ARE IN A SPLENDID CHAMBER THIRTY FEET HIGH. THE WALLS ARE FROZEN RIVERS OF ORANGE STONE. AN AWKWARD CANYON AND A GOOD PASSAGE EXIT FROM EAST AND WEST SIDES OF THE CHAMBER.

---

† Queneau's novel *Zazie dans le métro* is freely adapted, and translated into Italian, by Luca Melchionna's Inform game 'Zazie – Una lettura interattiva' (1999).

There are photographs of this chamber and of the column that descends to it, which is of travertine, an orange mineral found in wet limestone. The game's language is loaded with references to caving, to "domes" and "crawls". A "slab room", for instance, is a very old cave whose roof has begun to break away into sharp flakes which litter the floor in a crazy heap.

Working at SAIL, the Stanford Artificial Intelligence Laboratory, in the spring of 1976, Don Woods discovered Crowther's game among a number available to be played across the burgeoning (110-computer) network ARPANET, the child of a shotgun wedding in 1969 between university and Department of Defense PDP-10 (and some other) computers. The PDP-10, whose character set did not include lower case letters – hence the capitals above, although elsewhere in the book quotations from 'Advent' have been normalised – was widely found to be a "friendly" computer for recreational use, but more to the point it was a time-sharing computer on which individual users could run programs much larger and more complex than traditional games like the PDP-1's *Spacewar!*. With Crowther's eventual blessing, but working entirely independently, Woods reworked the caves and stocked them with magical items and puzzles, liberally ignoring the original style from time to time. Much of the game's classic quality comes from the tension between the original simulation, the earnestly discovered caves with their mysterious etched markings and spectacular chambers, and the cartoonish additions – the troll bridge, the giant's house, the Oriental Room, the active volcano. Crowther contributed an austere, Tolkienesque feel, in which magic is scarce, and a well-judged geography, especially around the edges of the map: the outside forests and gullies, the early rubble-strewn caves, the Orange River Rock. Some of Woods's additions, such as the bear, were sympathetic but others, such as the vending machine for fresh lamp batteries, clashed against the original. But their strange collaboration is somehow consistent. Stretching a point, you could say that there is a Crowther and a Woods in every designer, the one intent on recreating an experienced world, the other with a really neat puzzle which ought to fit *somewhere*.

By 1977 tapes of 'Advent' were being circulated widely, by the Digital user group DECUS, amongst others, taking over lunchtimes and weekends wherever they went. The idea spread, and diffused, as it surprised members of the general public who were shown it by friends. In Tracy Kidder's Pulitzer prize-winning book *The Soul of a New Machine* (1981), a journalist's-eye-view of the building of a new model of company-sized computer, 'Advent' appears as an addiction, but more: while the engineers use the program as a convenient endurance-test, for Kidder it is a cypher for an absorbing inner world and, perhaps, an emerging personality. Another fascinated visitor, the television producer Patrick Dowling, created *The Adventure Game* (BBC1 and BBC2, May 1980 to February 1986): by a curious coincidence, his first choice as puzzle-deviser and scriptwriter was Douglas Adams, then at the BBC but as it turned out unavailable. Adams will reappear later. In the *Game*, Earth-people were tested by the alien Argonds by being made to explore rooms stocked with items and quite difficult puzzles in hope of finding drognas (the currency of Arg), payment of which might placate His Highness the Rangdo, who had adopted the body of an aspidistra plant with a tendency to shake and roar when irritable. (And there may have been other anagrams of "dragon".) A recurring puzzle was a simple adventure game running on, naturally, a BBC Micro, so that each week viewers would see fresh contestants sit at the keyboard and twig, eventually, that the "scarlet fish" was a red herring.

Most of the university departments then connected to the ARPANET specialised in computer science, where any program is an invitation to develop a further one. At Essex University, England, Roy Trubshaw and Richard Bartle developed the concept of 'Advent' into 'Essex MUD' (which ran from late 1979 to September 1987 and continues in different forms even today). MUD was a Multi-User Dungeon to which remote users logged on during the night, competing sometimes unkindly with each other – killing another player netted 1/24th of their points, which must otherwise be earned by the troublesome business of finding treasures and dropping them into a swamp – to become "wizards" in a fantasy landscape anglicised slightly by the presence of a thatched cottage. To early phone-line networks such as British Telecom's Prestel Gold and CompuServe, running MUDs was (briefly) lucrative, and in a sense the Internet-connected "deathmatch" tournaments of today's games like 'Quake' are the legacy of MUDs.

In 1979–81, "game assemblers" were written in at least three departments to make new "Adventure-like programs" – the plural "adventures" seems not yet to have been used. Chris Gray and Alan Covington's "Six/Fant" at the University of Alberta, Canada, and the UCLA Computer Club's "Dungeon Definition Language" (which later evolved into Tim Brengle and Ross Cunniff's ADL (1987)) deserve mention. At Cambridge University, England, however, the assembler by David Seal and Jonathan Thackray may have been the first "adventure design system" to be used more widely than by its creators. Here is some typical code, allowing the player to jump up to a hole only if carrying the chair and in the room which actually has the hole:

```
JUMPHOLE:
SKIP UNLESS R (CHAIR)R EQ HOLEROOM
SKIP UNLESS H CHAIR PLAYER
PRINTRET HOLEHIGH
```

```
MOVE PLAYER WITH TO UPROOM
PRINTRET CHAIRJUMP
```

The assembler was used to build sixteen games which were the chief recreation on "Phoenix", the IBM 370 mainframe used by undergraduates and academic staff throughout the 1980s. These were large, computationally expensive games, traditional in form and very difficult, played outside of prime time when research palled. "Well go and do some work then" is the parting shot of 'Fyleet' (Jonathan Partington, 1985). Titles tended to be distinctive one-word commands, supposedly the names of ancient lands. Some games were later released by Acornsoft and some later again by Topologika, so that these are sometimes vaguely called "the Topologika games". But to anyone who was there, they are as redolent of late nights in the User Area as the soapy taste of Nestlé's vending machine chocolate or floppy, rapidly-yellowing line printer paper. Adam Atkinson (author of 'Nidus', 1987), who still has faint sketch-maps drawn on that paper more than ten years ago, has recently worked with Paul David Doherty and Gunther Schmidl to recover much of the Phoenix source code; many of the games have now returned to play through mechanical translation to Inform.

'Advent' had no direct sequel as such, but for the five years to 1982 almost every game created was another 'Advent'. The standard prologue – middle game – end game form would have, for prologue, a tranquil outside world (almost always with a little building offering two out of three of a bunch of keys, a bottle and a lamp); the middle game would be a matter of collecting treasures from a cave and depositing them somewhere, while the end would be called a "Master Game". The secret canyons, cold spring streams, wizards' houses, passive dragons, bears, trolls on bridges, volcanos, mazes, silver bars, magic rings, lamps with limited battery power, octagonal caverns with exits in all directions and so forth recur endlessly in a potent, immediately recognisable blend. Publicity surrounding the notorious Ace Paperbacks pirate edition (1965) of *The Lord of the Rings* had helped make Tolkien's epic an American campus classic of the late 1960s: ten years later, most of the cave games can be seen to have superficial Tolkienisms, with elves, dwarves (note the spelling) and dungeons called Moria. Unsurprisingly, then, the first book adaptation in interactive fiction seems to have been 'Lord' (Olli J. Paavola, c. 1980), initially a mainframe game at Helsinki.† (The earliest ARPANET connections outside America were to Britain and Scandinavia.) 'Lord' took pains to be faithful to

---

† 'Journey to the Center of the Earth' (1978), by the remarkable Greg Hassett – then aged twelve – had better be disqualified, unless Jules Verne's original really has a coke machine, a troll's palace and a car repair shop.

the text, even to including the ballads.

> You are standing now in Longbottom where Tobold Hornblower once lived,
> the one who first grew the true pipe-weed in his gardens, about the year 1070
> according to Shire reckoning. To the south-east is a narrow path.

It was characteristic of Tolkien, who died in 1973, to think the Hobbit tobacco industry as "real" as the story of the Ring, but it has been characteristic of Tolkien's imitators and adaptors to prefer orcs and magic: 'Lord', though never completed, has a true authenticity. Even here, though, the myth of the cave game – the underground labyrinth linking the computers – is as strong as the myth of Middle Earth. 'Lord' also has a Flathead coin and a postage stamp, in clear reference to 'Dungeon', the 1978 mainframe distribution of the game before and afterwards called 'Zork'.

At one extreme of the cave game is 'Adventureland' (Scott Adams, 1978), the first commercial game to reach the home: a tiny set-piece for cassette tape-based microcomputers, written under vicious memory constraints. "I'm in a temple" is as detailed as it gets, but Adams's games are distinguished by weirdly errant grammar, a wide vocabulary and a talent for arranging diverse objects in a room to portray it:

> I'm in a dismal swamp.
> Obvious exits: North, South, East, West, Up.
> I can also see: cypress tree – evil smelling mud – swamp gas – floating patch
> of oily slime – chiggers

At the other extreme is 'Acheton' (David Seal, Jonathan Thackray, Jonathan Partington, 1978–80), probably the largest game in the world in 1980, with 162 objects in 403 locations. (The title is a confection of Acheron, the underworld, and Achates, a character from the Aeneid.) Here is the lodestone room:

> You are in a large featureless room whose walls are composed entirely of
> a black magnetic material. Your compass seems incapable of fixing on any
> direction as being north. Several passages lead off to other parts of the cave.

This might easily be a room from 'Advent': and for all that they vastly differ in scale, 'Acheton' and 'Adventureland' are recognisably the same game.

△   As 'Advent' spread through universities, so it was often reworked and altered. As with Chaucer's *Canterbury Tales*, the vast number of mutated versions is evidence of popularity not just with the audience (players) but with those who told the tale (programmers). Chaucer's original manuscript is lost but all 83 surviving variants are thought to derive from a single version copied from it. Here, it is Crowther's 5-treasure original (c. 1975) which is gone, and all known forms of 'Advent' build on Woods's 15-treasure extension of June 1977, further diluting Crowther's contribution, that is, the simulation aspect of play. (For a "filiation" almost as complicated as Chaucer's, that is, a family tree showing how the many versions relate to each other, see ftp.gmd.de.)

Most of these extensions are inferior works, making nervous and minor additions, but three deserve passing mention. Don Woods made a further extension in Autumn 1978 to a "20-treasure version (Revision 2)", which he still considers definitive: it made the modest addition of a reservoir and cliff, scoring from 430 rather than 350 points. David Platt's 550-point version (1979) has a "Valley of the Stone Faces" and a puzzle bringing the volcano into play. Like Platt, David Long (1978) also felt the need to add a sword-in-the-stone puzzle: Long's 501-point version has some painful incongruities, such as a Wumpus and a telephone box, but is actually not too bad.

△   A port by Jay Jaeger for a (substantially souped-up) kit-built Altair 8800 is claimed to be the first microcomputer version: if so, it was not alone for long. Microsoft and Apple, unequal titans of the future but contenders even then, followed with 'Microsoft Adventure' (Gordon Letwin, 1979) and 'Apple Adventure' (Peter Schmuckal and Leonard Barshack, 1980) for Apple II and TRS-80. Early commercial versions were faithful or trimmed, although Microsoft added a "Software Den", north of the Soft Room, containing computers and a bearded programmer whose "spells help keep this cave together". (Cf. the RAM location in 'Adventureland', or the appearance in person of the programmers of 'Enchanter'.) Level 9's multi-platform 'Colossal Adventure' (1983) also has a classic feel but makes a confident extension, with a fleshed-out landscape above ground including a spire and a hawthorn wood, and a more satisfying end-game. The authors of the little-known but rather good Spectrum 128K version 'The Serf's Tale' (Nigel Brooks and Said Hassan, Players, 1986) seem familiar with Level 9's, and add a mild intrigue (in cut-scenes, the player searches a dead body for keys, and is helped by an innkeeper) on the way to the caves. 'The Serf's Tale' takes embellishment to baroque extremes: "You are in a splendid chamber shaped like the inside of an Arabian tower. The walls are frozen rivers of orange stone that curve gently up to a shadowy apex some thirty feet above your head. From this a huge stalactite hangs like an inverted spire above the centre of the room." One wonders if Crowther would still have known his place.

§46.2   *The commercial boom 1982–6*

"Then Adventure hit MIT and everything changed." The response of a disparate group of students, an improvised imitation called 'Zork', led to the founding of Infocom, in June 1979, which at its height six years later employed a hundred people: its mainframe, "a fleet of red refridgerators" (Brian Moriarty), had the electricity bill you would expect "if you were running an aluminum smelter" (Marc Blank). An engaging image, but extensive testing and packaging were also critical in establishing Infocom as a quality brand in a self-created niche market. Infocom's glory years have been romanticised by talk of its free soda, aloha shirts and the Tuesday lunchtime meetings of the

Implementors of games – of whom there were never more than ten, and who were by no means as free to do whatever they liked as their image suggested. Too little credit has been given to department heads who were at least as responsible for Infocom's artistic texture, notably John Prince (book editor, lunch host and low-key manager of the Implementors) and Liz Cyr-Jones (chief of testing, and the only woman to substantially influence the creative process). "The staff dresses casually, and it appears as if some of them have slept in their clothes, if they have slept at all...", wrote Richard Dyer in the *Boston Globe* (6 May 1984), the most perceptive and least wide-eyed of their many journalist visitors. There was pain on the way, particularly in the discovery that games were to be the only viable product of the former MIT Dynamic Modelling Group, and not merely an interim line. Unsavoury corporate dealings after a buyout by another ailing company, together with the Implementors' own faltering belief in text as the medium and the exhaustion of key members of staff, made the winding-down of 1988–9 unnecessarily dispiriting. But former hands mostly look back on the heyday as a happy, one-time thing, like a summer romance.

Infocom was dominant for a period in the higher-end, chiefly American market: in 1985 it always occupied several of the top twenty positions in the SoftSel Hot List – industry-wide sales charts run by a major US distributor – and one game held the number one slot for nine months. But the company was not nearly so visible outside the USA, where disc drives were less affordable, and in any case had no monopoly on the basic idea. "The 'adventure boom' is on – witness the rash of new programs, books and even a specialist magazine."‡ Although many were short-lived in what was something of a cottage industry, Hans Persson's catalogue cites 329 production companies. For instance, in the UK, Acornsoft made an early start: based in Cambridge and with close links to the university, it had a ready-made supply of adventure designs and quickly released reworkings of the Phoenix mainframe games for the BBC Micro – Acorn's computer, but built to spearhead a national computer literacy campaign supported by television programmes. Some of Acornsoft's titles

---

‡ Thus A. J. Bradbury, in *Adventure Games for the Commodore 64* (1984, with variant editions for other microcomputers), a wide-ranging and thoughtful book: for instance Bradbury discusses defects in 'Philosopher's Quest' (arbitrary) and 'The Hobbit' (too little thought to different possible orders of play – perhaps this is why many winning lines score more than 100%), advocates mapping on a linked-octagon grid and so on. The magazine alluded to is *Micro Adventurer*, edited by Graham Cunningham and published by the small press Sunshine Books. It ran for thirteen issues from November 1983, moving gradually away from snippets of program listings as reviews and general articles took over.

made tidy business (one of its authors earned royalties of around £35,000 on games originally written with no thought of profit), but in the end a market limited to a single model of microcomputer was insufficient to support a large games company.

Looking back at the early microcomputers is like looking at the fossils in ancient shale, before evolution took out three quarters of the species, some of them weirder than anything living today. The market had been entered by Apple, Commodore, Tandy (1977), Atari, Exidy (1978), Acorn (1979), Sinclair (1980), Osborne, IBM (1981) and a dozen others, whose machines were mutually incompatible in that software could not easily be transferred from one model to another. Text adventures were an exception, using little of the more complex hardware (for graphics and sound) which really differentiated designs: also because a typical adventure program is 90% map, text and other data tables, so that only 10% would need rewriting to move to a new machine. The more specialised design companies got this division down to a fine art, and 'Zork I' was offered for 23 different microcomputers.

Infocom was incomparably the largest of these specialist houses, the others directly employing five or six people at most. On paper the main rivals were, in America, Scott Adams's Adventure International (seventeen games, 1979–85); in Australia, Melbourne House (seventeen highly variable games from different sources); in Britain, Level 9 (twenty games 1981–91, founded by the brothers Pete, Mike and Nick Austin) and later Magnetic Scrolls (seven games 1984–90, founded by Anita Sinclair and Ken Gordon, 1984). In practice their markets – geographical and by computer ownership – overlapped little so that competition came not from each other, but from different genres of game.

Right through the "golden age of text adventures", around two-thirds of the perhaps 1,000 adventure games published mixed graphics with text, usually in the form of a picture accompanying each room description. Sierra, still a major player in the games industry today for its long-running *King's Quest* series, began this trend as early as 1980 with 'Mystery House' (Roberta Williams). Sales were so good that board game companies (Avalon Hill, Games Workshop) dabbled in the market, and spin-offs from books, film and television began to appear, though play seldom really engaged with the subject matter. When 'Dallas Quest' (James Garon, 1984) confronts the player with Miss Ellen, a bugle and a rifle, it is easy to guess which of the three will prove to be decoration. Spinnaker/Telarium Software's adaptations of two classics of science fiction, Arthur C. Clarke's 'Rendezvous with Rama' (Ronald Martinez, 1984) and Ray Bradbury's 'Fahrenheit 451' (Len Neufeld and Byron Preiss, 1984) deserve mention, though, as does the same company's

'Amazon' (1984), by the novelist and screen-writer Michael Crichton, later to become famous for *Jurassic Park* but already hot property in Hollywood. Thomas M. Disch, another novelist of real powers, went through a wild surge of enthusiasm writing 'Amnesia' (1986), to be followed by total disillusion when it was not marketed and received as a novel might be. "The notion of trying to superimpose over this structure [i.e., the adventure game] a *dramatic conception* other than a puzzle was apparently too much for the audience." (*Interviews with Contemporary American Science Fiction Writers*, 1990). The poet Robert Pinsky was more obliging with puzzle-based play, as we shall see.

△   "Once I was deluxe; now I am debris" (Adrian Belew). 1980s graphics are often crude and few players can tolerate them, so that these 600 or so games lie in almost total neglect today and even Infocom's four late graphical titles are made playable on modern machines more out of piety than appreciation.† Nevertheless, graphical adventures were once formidable rivals and the idea that graphics should voluntarily be given up required selling. "You'll never see Infocom's graphics on any computer screen," boasted early advertisements, making a virtue of necessity: the games were supposedly too evocative and too cerebral, as was implied by the photograph of a brain. It would be truer to say that Infocom's graphics were instead in the highly crafted and colourful booklet built into each game's box lid, which often contained clues (partly as an anti-piracy measure). Inspired perhaps by the success of Kit Wright's book of paintings *Masquerade*, which encoded the location of a buried golden hare, Acornsoft offered a prize for the first correct solution of 'Castle of Riddles' (Peter Killworth, 1984) which – it was laid on pretty thick – was so fiendish that the prize would take quite some winning. A similar prize for 'Eureka' (Ian Livingstone, Domark, 1984) offered a whopping £25,000. Another strategy was to extol the sophistication of a parser, and how very far it soared above the mulish ignorance of a shoddy two-word job. Thus Magnetic Scrolls's 'The Pawn' was sold partly on its celebrated claim to understand "use the trowel to plant the pot plant in the plant pot". Publicity for Melbourne House's 'The Hobbit', a huge success in Britain, stressed that only the presence on the programming team of an expert in linguistics (Stuart Richie) had enabled the invention of "Inglish", as the parser's subset of English was called. In a similar bid for dignity, Infocom soon distanced itself from the boy-scout "adventure game" and the nerdile "computerized fantasy simulation", instead billing its product first as "Interlogic" (1982) and then "interactive fiction" (1984), which remains the preferred euphemism today.

·   ·   ·   ·   ·

---

† While Spectrum and early PC graphics are often unbearable, the Atari ST and Amiga offered a better colour palette and resolution: in these versions, the Magnetic Scrolls games were well illustrated. Of lower-resolution games, 'Asylum' (William Denman), 'Sherwood Forest' and 'Masquerade' (Dale Johnson) are recommendable.

Though cave games became old hat, more cohesive fantasies and overt miscellanies and treasure hunts had continued unabated as the mechanics of 'Advent' lived on in the guise of different genres. John Laird's 'Haunt' (begun 1978, and known to the authors of 'Zork') may in fact be the first non-cave game, but its vampire-haunted house has 'Advent'-like puzzles based on combining objects (throw turpentine on a poor painting to reveal a Rembrandt). 'Haunt' is not inspired, but the knockabout style and the unexpected arrival of James Watt from the Department of the Interior wanting to buy the house for $10,000,000 liven things up. Camp horror-movie settings, usually featuring Dracula or Frankenstein and set in large houses even more haphazardly stocked than caves (Chris Gray's 'Mansion' (1980) somehow works in a submarine), vied with science fiction and spy thrillers as the most popular variations. Alien worlds and derelict spacecraft, caves of steel so to speak, initially lent themselves to works of fairly high seriousness such as 'Starcross' (Dave Lebling, 1982), which is heavily indebted to Arthur C. Clarke's *Rendezvous with Rama* (again) and to Larry Niven's *Known Space* stories, from which it borrowed red and blue stepping discs. Level 9's 'Snowball' (Mike, Nick and Pete Austin, 1983), set on an interstellar colony ship, and Peter Killworth's 'Countdown to Doom' (1984) for Acornsoft and Topologika, set on Doomawangara (a hostile planet, not a region of the Australian outback), are equally steeped in golden-age science fiction.

More often, the future became a vehicle for comedy, usually in the form of sending up or camping up traditional science fiction, with one notable exception. Douglas Adams's radio series and novel *The Hitchhiker's Guide To The Galaxy*, the *Three Men in a Boat* of the 1970s, achieved enormous success. To computer hackers it became a devotional text, like the Monty Python sketches it owed considerable debts to,† especially in Adams's invariable practice of having the "straight man" in any conversation argue back. For all its playful anything-goes imagination, it is not a send-up but a genuine work of science fiction in the sense of social analysis: Adams mocks something large enough to be worth mocking, i.e., real life, rather than pulp sci-fi and flying-saucer movies. With an electronic, interactive encyclopaedia as narrator and an author fascinated by textual gadgetry, Adams's comedy was a natural for adaptation to adventure-game form and his collaboration with Steve Meretzky at Infocom produced their bestselling title (1984). Imitations became commonplace.

It is often forgotten, because this is not how we think of "classic text

---

† 'Advent' quotes from Python's *Parrot Sketch*: try feeding the bird. As for Adams, 'Lord' has a babel fish and 'Acheton' a ningy.

adventures", that many early games were earnestly or drably serious in tone. 'Advent' itself contains relatively little humour, despite one comedy room (Witt's End) and infrequent moments of drollery from the narrator:

> A glistening pearl falls out of the clam and rolls away. Goodness, this must really be an oyster. (I never was very good at identifying bivalves.)

The distinctive comedy running, sometimes only as an underground stream, through all of Infocom's games has its source instead in 'Zork' which, partly because it contains many more inessential responses than 'Advent' (responses, that is, which a player winning the game need never see), gives a much stronger impression of personality: shaped by 'Zork', by inheritance of parsing code from one game to another and by a shared in-house testing team, the strongest unity of style between the Infocom games is that they seem told by essentially the same narrator. This is a theme that will recur in §48.

With a growing catalogue in the mid-1980s, Infocom's mature style was to make conscious use of genre to differentiate its products, essential since a core audience, subscribing to a newsletter, had formed and would buy many of its titles: also, of course, for the fun of it. Any player dropped into the middle of one of 'The Lurking Horror' (H. P. Lovecraft horror), 'Leather Goddesses of Phobos' (racy send-up of 1930s space opera) or 'Ballyhoo' (mournfully cynical circus mystery) would immediately be able to say which it was. ('TLH', Dave Lebling, 1987; 'LGOP', Steve Meretzky, 1986; 'BH', Jeff O'Neill, 1985.) Infocom also evolved a police procedural "detective novel" format rarely used since, which differed from any number of spy intrigues in that it involved character interaction and a developing case, rather than simply an 'Advent'-style exploration in which an enemy base replaced the caves. Today's designers are not always so definite in keying a game to an established genre of fiction, but the first decisions remain to choose the style, the mood, the character of the protagonist and above all the fictional world of which the story itself will remain only a part.

Infocom achieved popular success in the mid-1980s and continues to be highly rated now, but to some extent for different games. The 1984 and 1985 bestsellers, 'The Hitchhiker's Guide To The Galaxy' and 'Wishbringer' (Brian Moriarty) are now found solidly mediocre, charming but insubstantial. Critical acclaim flickers instead to 'Trinity' (1986), as lightning flickers to an aerial, because the game opens with something of the mood of an art-house movie, because it is bookish and purposeful – a research bibliography is supplied – and because it is obtrusively trying to be what today's critics most wish to find: literature. Here is Brian Moriarty, a self-analysing and intensely driven designer, ambitious for worldly success but describing himself in the credits as a member of the Nathaniel Hawthorne Society, and a man who remains a name in the games industry today:

> I amassed a pretty substantial library on the history of the atomic bomb ... I
> went to the Trinity site [of Oppenheimer's first test] itself, visited Los Alamos
> and a lot of museums and I talked to a couple of people who were actually
> there ... I wanted people, when playing the game, to feel their helplessness.
> Because that's what I felt when I was reading and talking to these people and
> seeing these places. You could just feel the weight of history on you.

'Trinity' is not altogether dark, nor innovative in its basic mechanics, with
an extensive slice of 'Zork'-like terrain and some mischievous animals. A
black cover with mushroom cloud wrapped a typically deluxe and supportive
book-shaped package which included a map of the Trinity test site, a sundial,
instructions for folding an origami crane and a spoof 1950s *The Illustrated
History of the Atom Bomb* comic for boys (by Carl Genatossio). Sales were tepid
at best, albeit in part because the game played only on larger and therefore
less widely owned computers. Had it sold no further even than to his mother,
though, Moriarty's reputation would still rest secure upon 'Trinity' today.

All the same, for the origins of the deliberate artistic statement in interactive fiction one should look further back. Mike Berlyn had been instrumental
in subverting the genre's initial "puzzles for treasures" definition, and the
closing scenes of his 'Infidel' (1983, with Patricia Fogleman), re-enacting
the Egyptian *Book of the Dead*, are arguably the earliest to be guided for
consciously literary ends. Where 'Infidel' is clearly a plotted novel, 'Mindwheel' (Robert Pinsky, coding by Steve Hales and William Mataga, Synapse,
1984) is a puckish dream-poem, Dante meets *Alice Through the Looking-Glass*.
The protagonist wakes to find that one Doctor Virgil is guiding him to meet
some popular entertainers (rock singers and baseball players), some chatty,
debauched insects and "your broccoli-coloured companion", a frog who keeps
up self-deprecating chatter throughout the game:

> "Again!" says the frog. "Again we're in a situation of this kind. And I turned
> down a nice job, summer replacement for the little dog in Monopoly!"

But there are also transfigured victims out of Bruegel or Bosch, such as the
children with the heads of birds who police the snowy, complacent mind
of a Generalissimo. Opposition is provided by the more playful Spaw, a
demon wearing "lawyerskin boots". Puzzles include sonnet-writing and an
end-game based on human chess with different puzzles on each square, the
player advancing pawn-like (there are several possible paths, since captures
can be made) to the eighth rank. Pinsky – noted for semi-formal verse with a
social aspect – was named the US Poet Laureate in 1997, and what he now
calls his "computerized novel" is not easy to dismiss. 'Mindwheel' was the first
of four nightmarish games by Synapse Software: 'Breakers' (Rod Smith, Joe

Vierra and William Mataga, 1986) is a tale of indentured labour with "coercive interrogation techniques" and the starship 'Essex' (Bill Darrah, 1985) lends a similar mood of persecution. Only 'Brimstone: The Dream of Gawain' (James Paul, David Bunch and Bill Darrah, 1985) – doubly unreal as a dream by an Arthurian knight – resembled ordinary adventure fodder. The line was terminated by Broderbund in 1986, which had bought the company but was now alarmed by a rape scene and some Chinese black magic. The computer games audience was sliding downward in age.

△   Infocom's intention to explore byways of the new medium was genuine, but not of course altruistic, and its business history throws a good deal of light on its decisions. The extent of Infocom's commercial success is often exaggerated, not in its scale (at one time a quarter of U.S. homes owning computers had bought the product) but in its duration. Typical sales per new title rose from 10,000 in 1981 to 50,000 in 1983–6, falling below 20,000 again in 1987–9. The exceptions were the 'Zork' trilogy, which sold 1,000,000 units over the decade – which explains if not excuses the later sequels – and 'The Hitchhiker's Guide To The Galaxy' at 250,000, which explains Infocom's eagerness to write 'The Restaurant at the End of the Universe'. Sales were further buttressed by customer loyalty, carefully nurtured by large direct mail shots (at end of 1986, circulation of the newsletter was 240,000); by repackaging of 1980–2 titles; and by a no-returns policy in distribution (ended in 1987) obliging shopkeepers to treat Infocom's wares as luxury goods, kept on shelves until they sold. Remarkably, 'Suspended' (1983), not an obvious money-spinner, was to receive a Gold certificate for 100,000 sales in 1986: typical shelf times today are measured in months or even weeks. Infocom's customers were, according to market research, adult (75% over 25) – which is not so surprising given prices of $40 to $50 – and heavy readers, 80% of them men, though specific products were designed to appeal to women (such as 'Plundered Hearts' and the mysteries) and to children (Stu Galley adapted the 'Seastalker' parser to children's sentence structures, observed during testing). The work force had grown fast (1981, two; 1982, four; 1983, twenty; 1984, fifty; 1985, one hundred) but was increasingly preoccupied with managing itself and with Infocom's one business product, the database 'Cornerstone' (1986). It was intended to capitalise on Infocom's expertise in virtual machines, which allowed large programs – adventure games – to run on a variety of different designs of small computer: but this was not the strength in 1986 that it would have been in 1982, since the IBM PC had grown in capacity and cornered the business market, most of the rival manufacturers having gone bust in 1983–4. 'Cornerstone' sold 10,000 but only after a price reduction from $495 to $100, and by then Infocom had turned the corner into loss. In June 1986 Activision had bought Infocom, in what amounted to an agreed merger, for stock valued at around $8 million: at about five years' gross income, this was a high price, or would have been if the stock had in fact been worth that. Infocom still had fifteen titles ahead, including a few of its best, but disputes over branding, marketing and the division of profits and losses produced disquiet, as did a time-consuming lawsuit about the state of the books when the company changed hands; while Activision had its own travails. Expected sales from the Hitchhiker's sequel 'Restaurant' were an essential part of the business plan every year from 1985 to 1989, while Meretzky, Lebling, Jeff O'Neill and Amy Briggs were each briefly in the frame as the unlucky programmer. The project was stymied in 1985–6 by Douglas Adams's inability to get out of the bath when copy deadlines loom – "you can't fault him for personal hygiene in a crisis" (Geoffrey Perkins) – and by 1987–9 meant impossible collaborations with the British firm Magnetic Scrolls and other intermediaries, whom the Implementors were unable to establish working relationships with. Games by out-house employees got a little further: though Berlyn's came to nothing, Blank wrote 'Journey' from California and newcomer Bob Bates designed 'Sherlock' and 'Arthur'. (Bates worked from his notionally independent company Challenge, but its finances were at that time heavily dependent on advances from Infocom.) Without conscious decision, Infocom was becoming a commissioning house rather than a workshop. The testing department was involved so late on that the new management saw it as largely an obstruction. Artistic collapse came in 1988, when four of the six remaining creative figures were fired or felt unable to go on (editor John Prince, tester Liz Cyr-Jones, Implementors Jeff O'Neill and Amy Briggs). Meretzky and Lebling remained, sometimes despondent, sometimes cheerful, doing largely terrible work. The weekly game-design lunches became at the last a charade, attended by random managers whom they barely knew. Infocom never went bust as such, but by 1989 market conditions would have obliged any management to salvage the Infocom brand-names while abandoning text for largely graphical games. The company now called Activision (following a second, happier merger) did just this with a fresh generation of game designers in the 1990s. For all that they were doing something quite different and thousands of miles away, many had a keen sense of standing in an Infocom tradition. Activision's omnibus 1990s reissues of the Infocom text games achieved unexpectedly high sales, to everybody's pleasure.

§46.3   The growth of a community c. 1985–91

One by one, the companies ceased to publish text-based games: Adventure International (1985), Synapse (1986), Infocom (1989), Level 9 (1991), Topologika (1992), Magnetic Scrolls (1992). The last stalwart, Legend Entertainment – which had inherited two of the designers of Infocom's last days, Bob Bates and Steve Meretzky – made the last mainstream release of a game with a parser in 1993 ('Gateway II: Homeworld', by Mike Verdu and Glen Dahlgren) and so, according to some, the dark ages began: the adventure games which flourished in the marketplace were fiction of a kind, and steerable, but no longer interactive in any conversational sense. Yet the same advance of technology which drove the irresistable rise of graphics and animation also brought interactive fiction writing into the home. Between 1980 and 1990 the personal computer went from being barely able to play a text game to being easily able to compile one.

To be able to program a PDP-10, as Crowther and Woods had, was a professional qualification, but early microcomputers came with the easily learned programming language BASIC built in, and also with manuals which emphasised that computers were more for writing your own programs than for using other people's. Minimal adventure programming is not complicated – indeed adventure game-writing has been used to teach children about computing (*Creating a Database*, 1985, Steve Rodgers and Marcus Milton) – and the slowness of a program written in BASIC does not much matter for a text adventure. So, parallel to the commercial market and at the cheaper end merging into it, hobbyists had had been devising their own adventures since at least May 1979, when Lance Micklus published 'Dog Star Adventure' in a computing magazine. This was the first of many type-it-in-yourself games which some readers, at least, adapted and reworked as they typed. Scott Adams's 'Adventureland' source was itself published in *Byte* (1980) and, within a year, reworked into the core of Brian Howarth's rival 'Mysterious Adventures'. (No less than three Scott Adams-format adventure-making programs existed for the TI-99/4a microcomputer alone, and Adams-format games in circulation outnumber his official titles by at least three to one.) Dozens of books with titles like *Adventure Games For Your Commodore 64* (Duncan Quirie, 1984) consisted of little more than unannotated and – partly because of the need to save every possible byte of memory – almost incomprehensible BASIC listings, often rushed into print by coders with more enthusiasm than skill, and seldom properly tested.

The major companies each had in-house systems for designing adventure games (see §41 for a sample of Infocom's ZIL): these never emerged into the public eye. But a popular design tool called *The Quill* (Graeme Yeandle, 1983), running on the Sinclair Spectrum and Commodore 64 microcomputers, allowed many hobbyists working from home to sell their wares. Yeandle's generous acknowledgement in the manual that the system "has its origins in an article written by Ken Reed and published in the August 1980 issue of Practical Computing" is further testament to the influence of 1979–80 magazines in spreading the word. At least 60 commercial releases in the period 1983–6 were Quilled. (*Graphic Adventure Creator* (Sean Ellis, 1986), was also popular later on. Two corresponding American commercial systems, *Adventure Writer* and *Adventure Master* were less fruitful.) Yet tiny BASIC games were inevitably toy models of the real thing, and even *The Quill* could not then build a port of 'Advent' (though extensions of it, such as the *Professional Adventure Writer* (1987), later did), let alone an Infocom-scale game.

Some 33 non-commercial design systems are now present at ftp.gmd.de, though some have fallen into disuse, some are flimsy at best and others are exercises in writing a Pascal-like compiler, or a LISP-like compiler, which pay too much attention to syntax and do not engage with the real issue: the world model and how designers can work with and alter it. During 1995–9, only two systems have been widely used: the Text Adventure Development System (or TADS, Mike Roberts, 1987) and Inform (Graham Nelson, 1993). A further two retain interested minorities and remain in the running: Hugo (Kent Tessman, 1994) and revamped forms of the Adventure Game Toolkit (AGT, David R. Malmberg and Mark Welch, 1985–7). Note the dates, implying both the durability of a capable system and the difficulty in getting a new one off the ground. All four have been continuously developed since their inception, to some extent bidding each other up in richness or complexity.

Design systems of the 1980s had the consistent ambition of easing the way of the neophyte programmer, who would if possible never be asked really to program at all: only to supply textual descriptions, in effect filling in a database. "Alan is not a *programming* language. Instead Alan takes a descriptive view," says its manual (by Thomas Nilsson), and the Generic Adventure Games System manual (Mark Welch) concurs:

> It [GAGS] *cannot* be used to write an adventure game with as many complex features as Infocom's. To do so . . . would require adventure-game writers to learn a very complex set of rules.

This is the bargain that was, with some reluctance, accepted around 1992 – a crucial year, as we shall see.

.   .   .   .   .

Changing conditions of computer networking have, throughout this story, had greater effect than the changing technology of the computers themselves. In the late 1960s and early 1970s, tools such as Unix and games like 'Space-war!'spread through outposts of the early Internet much as, in the dark ages, classical texts flowed down monastic libraries along the Rhine and the Loire, always subtly rewritten until it seemed no definitive version remained. (We have already seen what this did to 'Advent'.) By the mid-1980s, universities and institutions across at least the Western world were securely networked, but the same could not yet be said of home computers and small businesses.

Enthusiasts for writing interactive fiction could achieve little until there was enough mutual contact for non-commercially distributed design systems and games to spread around. Usenet, a wide-ranging system of discussion forums or "newsgroups", was created in 1979 and roughly doubled in usage each year: but in 1985 it still only accounted for 375 postings per day, across all topics combined, and as late as 1989 it was still possible for a single person to skim through the entire traffic. In America, the hundreds of local dial-up bulletin board systems (BBSs) and their big brother, the American CompuServe service, had greater effect. Much as the creators of Usenet called it "the poor man's ARPANET", bulletin boards were a poor man's FTP: allowing downloading of files from archives with only a modem and without the need for a university or corporate Internet connection. Even as late as 1993, downloads of 'Curses' (say) from CompuServe rivalled those from ftp.gmd.de. From 1982, when the concept of "shareware" was invented, quality home-made software was routinely "shared" on these boards and via discs ordered from the Public Software Library, subject to a moral obligation for users to "register" by paying the original author a small fee. TADS and some of the better early TADS games were administered as shareware by High Energy Software, a company with its own BBS. AGT was also available from the BBS community, and the Byte Information Exchange, and as discs which could be ordered from Softworks, a member company of the Association of Shareware Professionals.

Judith Pintar's story (from an interview in *XYZZYnews* 11) shows how fruitful this contact could be:

> I started writing IF in the mid-80s, when the XT I bought happened to have GAGS [1985] on it ... When I joined CompuServe in 1990, I tried to find Mark Welch, to register GAGS, and discovered that it had become AGT and was administered by the co-author, David R. Malmberg. He had run several annual game-writing contests, and I was determined to enter ... 'CosmoServe' [1991] tied for first place. [In 1992] I had the idea of writing a game as part of a group venture. I posted this idea in CompuServe's Gamer's forum, and a small group of people responded. ... We were given a private area on the forum to post our messages to one another and to share game files.

'Shades of Gray' (1992), by Mark Baker, Steve Bauman, Elizabeth Ellison, Mike Laskey, Hercules, Cynthia Yans and Pintar herself, duly won. The AGT contest began as a GAGS contest in 1986, to promote interest, then ran annually 1987-93 and, though no longer tied to any game design system, essentially resumed in 1995 as the rec.arts.int-fiction competition.

§46.4 Newsgroups and revival 1992–

The rest of the infrastructure of the present interactive fiction community was created by four almost simultaneous events: first, the creation of specific Usenet newsgroups (on or before 21 March 1992, 21 September 1992), moving away from sporadic and easily drowned-out talk in the early net.games and the later rec.games.programming, while asserting an artistic medium by moving to the rec.arts.* sub-hierarchy, where theatre and the novel are also discussed. Next, the founding of the interactive fiction archive at ftp.gmd.de by Volker Blasius and David M. Baggett (24 November 1992), the release of TADS 2.0 (6 December 1992), significant because it established the dominance of TADS, and the release of Inform 1 (10 May 1993), though not until 1995 was Inform seriously used.

The proximity of these dates is no coincidence: they followed the sudden, widespread and cheap release of the entire Infocom back catalogue, in two volumes, *Lost Treasures of Infocom I* (January 1992) and *II* (July 1992), which stimulated a revival both of the cult of Infocom and of interactive fiction in general. If Infocom is to be compared with Shakespeare then this was the First Folio. Anybody who had occasionally liked Infocom's games in the past suddenly had all of them, while players' expectations of quality rose. Infocom antiquarianism occupies much of the early newsgroup traffic; much of the initial stock at ftp.gmd.de consisted of fact-sheets on Infocom story files; and the collectors of these diamonds were provided with a rhinestone machine when Inform, which compiled Infocom-format story files, appeared. Design systems successful in the mid-1980s, which were not well-adapted to build Infocom-scale games, quickly died out. Instead TADS and Inform were used for a clump of large games plausibly imitating Infocom's production values, among them 'Save Princeton' (Jacob Solomon Weinstein, 1992), 'Horror of Rylvania' (Dave Leary, 1993), 'Curses' (Graham Nelson, 1993), 'The Legend Lives!' (David M. Baggett, 1993), 'Theatre' (Brendon Wyber, 1994), 'Christminster' (Gareth Rees, 1995), 'Jigsaw' (Graham Nelson, 1995), 'Perdition's Flames' (Mike Roberts, 1995) and so on.

The revival by Gerry Kevin Wilson of an annual game-designing competition, fondly remembered by AGT and CompuServe users, took place in September 1995, though the 1996 event (with 26 entries) marked the beginning of its real importance. There was no restriction to any specific design system, as was typical of a newsgroup which has consistently voted against dividing itself off into subsections such as comp.lang.tads or comp.lang.inform. However, the rule that a contest game should be solvable in two hours, albeit often more honoured in the breach, has had a decisive effect in diverting designers from Infocom-sized "novels" into short stories. This freed up the form for greater experimentation, but meant that few large games were created in the late 1990s. The annual September event – shrewdly timed, after long university vacations – has also had the unfortunate effect that games are held back and then all released at once, in the breaking of a monsoon after a parched summer. But for the quantity of fine work stimulated, and the number of newcomers attracted, the competition can only be considered a triumph. Its success has also spun off a number of alternative contests and forms of recognition, such as the annual and Oscar-like XYZZY Awards. The most ludic, madcap events are the SpeedIF contests, begun by David Cornelson in October 1998, in which just two hours are allowed to write a complete game. The rubric for SpeedIF 13: "The game will take place in a Chinese restaurant. It will feature one or more of the following animals: pigeon, elephant or badger. There will be some kind of sculpture made of mud, and some character will be obsessed with either HAL or Doraemon, the robot-cat from the future (or both)..."

A growing appreciation of the medium's potential for art has characterised turn of the century interactive fiction. One provocative example was Nick Montfort's showing of a *hardback* edition of 'Winchester's Nightmare' at Digital Arts and Culture in Atlanta, in October 1999: ten decommissioned laptops converted to run an Inform game. Formerly property of the Internal Revenue Service, several still bore the U.S. Treasury seal of an eagle holding a key. Even shown in images on a web page, it was startling as a work of conceptual art, and challenged the unconscious assumption that an interactive fiction need be intrinsically unlike a material book. Chris Klimas's affecting short story 'Mercy', and Andrew Plotkin's shifting vignette 'The Space Under The Window', were influential in the late 1990s style for non-game games. Marnie Parker organises art shows which challenge traditional aspirations for IF by encouraging artistic expression. Making an exception to this chapter's general rule of stopping history at the close of 1999, it seems appropriate to finish with two fine debut pieces which took awards in the 2000 Art Show: 'Galatea' (Emily Short, 2000), a conversation with an animated sculpture which breaks new ground in interactive dialogue; and 'The Cove' (Kathleen Fischer, 2000), an evocative seascape which is also a gathering of memories. Interactive fiction will always appreciate what in theatre used to be called "the well-made play", the polished entertainment on traditional lines, but without its radicals it will die. Though the grail of puzzle-free yet interactive literature seems as elusive as ever, it is too soon to stop looking.

△   And what of the history of the *theory* of interactive fiction? For most of the last twenty years, the best published sources are chapters which, like this one, hide at the back of books on game programming: thus, Chapter 8 of Peter Killworth's *How to Write Adventure Games for the BBC Microcomputer Model B and Acorn Electron* (1984), Chapter 7 of the Alan manual, Appendix B to the TADS manual. (Even people who don't intend ever to use TADS should read the delightfully written TADS manual.) Most are couched in the form of avuncular advice ("No matter how small an Adventure you write, it will take far, far more time and effort than you thought it would" – Killworth) but there are often clear signs of groping towards a systematic critical model of what the essential ingredients of a game might be. *Basic Adventure and Strategy Game Design for the TRS-80* (Jim Menick, 1984), a turgid work, talks about "layering" complications into "phases". Others, such as A. J. Bradbury's book, quoted above, or the somewhat gauche *Player's Bill of Rights* (Usenet posting, 1993), boil opinions down to (usually ten) golden rules. Bradbury's are well-supported by argument and engage with the underlying fiction and not simply the surface puzzles: for instance, "resist the urge to create a superhero" of the game's protagonist.

● **REFERENCES**

For interactive fiction history, see the *Infocom Fact Sheet* by Paul David Doherty, the *Level 9 Fact Sheet* by Miron Schmidt and Manuel Schulz and the *Magnetic Scrolls Fact Sheet* by Stefan Meier and Gunther Schmidl. Hans Persson's *Adventureland* catalogue and the master index of ftp.gmd.de are also indispensable. On connections with literary precursors, see Gareth Rees's 1994 article *Tree fiction*. The number of games said to have origins before 1979 is somewhat akin to the number of American families claiming descent from the *Mayflower* pilgrims and one must approach claims to priority with caution. But it is clear that too little is known about the games libraries in circulation in the mid-1970s. Peter Langston's 'Wander' (1974), a text-based world modelling program included in his PSL games distribution for Unix and incorporating rooms, states and portable objects, was at least a proto-adventure: perhaps many others existed, but failed to find a Don Woods to complete the task? So much appears lost that even Crowther's original source code, the most important document we might want to see, appears not to have existed anywhere since 1977. (Crowther confirms that he now has no printouts or notes of it.) In the discussion of authorship above I have therefore relied on anecdotal accounts in print quoting Crowther and Woods, and on recent and valuable research by Dennis G. Jerz.   ●*The Longest Cave*, by Roger Brucker and Richard Watson, includes a history of the Bedquilt Cave.   ●It is difficult to estimate the extent of the literature with any reliability. The ftp.gmd.de archive contains over 1,700 games which have been finished and offered to some kind of audience, and this necessarily excludes some material still under copyright or simply lost. Hans Persson's catalogue (surely incomplete) lists around 800 commercial publications in the 1980s, of which 330 are purely textual. The well-established canon of "important" or "classic" games still talked about today consists of about 100 titles. At most fifty titles of the 1990s remain in regular play through being rediscovered.   ●*The Quill* and its variants continued even into the 1990s, at least for the prolific Dorothy Millard, whose games are off-beat variations of "you are stranded": the most off-beat of all being 'Yellow Peril' (1994), in which the entire world has become yellow.   ●1993 was the year of the explosion of the World Wide Web, during which it grew by a factor of 3,000. But in 1992, personal web pages barely existed, and it seemed not only natural but unavoidable to house games at a centralised library, ftp.gmd.de. The continued importance of this IF-archive is a major part of the solidarity of today's community.

§47 Realities

> As we ranged by Gratiosa, on the tenth of September, about
> twelve a clocke at night, we saw a large and perfect Rainbow by
> the Moone light, in the bignesse and forme of all other Rainbows,
> but in colour much differing, for it was more whitish, but chiefly
> inclining to the colour of the flame of fire.
>
> — Arthur Gorges, ordinary seaman aboard Sir Walter Raleigh's
> expedition (1597)

"Explain why the game-world exists and thus give a consistency
to the text that you will present to the player" (Thomas Nilsson,
in the Alan manual). It is worth a look back to compare 'Advent'
and 'Zork', the alpha and omega of the cave game. 'Zork' is
better laid out and its middle segments (now called 'Zork II') are among the
smoothest and best structured of any game in the literature. And yet for all its
dead ends and hidden canyons, 'Advent' is essentially the better work, more
memorable and more atmospheric, because its roots lie in a true experience.
The mythology of 'Zork' is far less well-grounded: the long-gone Flathead
dynasty, beginning in a few throwaway jokes, ended up downright tiresome
by the time of the later sequels, when the "legend of the Flatheads" had
become, by default, the distinguishing feature of Zorkness. Though perfectly
engineered, 'Zork' lacks authenticity.

The most telling argument in favour of a clear fictional backdrop is
provided by the games which did not have one, and which were merely surreal
miscellanies of the medieval and the modern. A very few, such as 'Brand X' by
Peter Killworth and the chess grandmaster Jonathan Mestel (1982: later called
'Philosopher's Quest'), came stubbornly alive through their ruthless difficulty.
'Brand X' lacks even a descriptive title – there is no setting or plot to describe –
and the overture reads: "You don't need instructions, so you won't get any."
But in the main such games are indistinguishable from each other and are
justly forgotten.

· · · · ·

Here is a revealing moment from 'The Hitchhiker's Guide To The Galaxy'
(Steve Meretzky and Douglas Adams, 1984):

Ford yawns. "Matter transference always tires me out. I'm going to take a
nap." He places something on top of his satchel. "If you have any questions,

here's The Hitchhiker's Guide to the Galaxy" (Footnote 14). Ford lowers his voice to a whisper. "I'm not supposed to tell you this, but you'll never be able to finish the game without consulting the Guide about lots of stuff." As he curls up in a corner and begins snoring, you pick up The Hitchhiker's Guide.

Why does Ford feel the need to whisper? Who supposes that Ford should not say such things? Roger Giner-Sorolla does, for one. His 1996 essays *Crimes Against Mimesis* put the case for the prosecution of such passages:

> I see successful fiction as an imitation or "mimesis" of reality, be it this world's or an alternate world's. Well-written fiction leads the reader to temporarily enter and believe in the reality of that world. A crime against mimesis is any aspect ... that breaks the coherence of its fictional world as a representation of reality.

This elegant polemic, posted to `rec.arts.int-fiction`, provided the *mise au point* for a debate which rumbled on for some months.† The target was not so much the tripping over of mimesis in a pratfall, as in the passage above, but the accidental undermining of mimesis by careless authors. The placing of objects out of context or of characters without motivation, the bending of genres to include whimsical anachronisms or the use of puzzles which are out of context (a sliding block puzzle to solve in a ruined crypt) are problematic because they emphasise exactly what ought to be concealed, that the game is a collection of puzzles to solve. From this view it follows that a game should have a coherent fictional world and its puzzles should be seamlessly joined to the textual fabric, appearing to occur naturally.

.   .   .   .   .

The secret of success in designing the backdrop is originality: once you can imitate that, all else will follow. Probably the most popular source is real life, and for many games design begins with, and is periodically interrupted by, research. If constructing geography, maps of real mountain ranges, river valleys and cave systems can be a helpful reminder that real geography is convoluted and continuous – if a river passes through a given location, it must continue elsewhere, and so on. (More on this in §51.)

For 'Jigsaw' (Graham Nelson, 1995), a game containing historical re-enactments, the present author began by wandering along the open shelves of Oxford County Library with pockets full of coins to photocopy pages at random. Later there came the 1956 run of the *Eagle* comic in facsimile (for views of the British Empire at the time of Suez as expressed in fiction for boys),

---

† To be parodied in Adam Thornton's game 'Sins Against Mimesis' (1997).

the Apollo 17 Lunar Surface Journal (Eric Jones's superb Internet resource, now officially adopted by NASA) and, for the 1900 sequence of the game, Stephen Poliakoff's excellent film *Century*. As this may suggest, research can be overdone. Here is Stu Galley, on writing the Chandleresque murder mystery 'The Witness' (1983):

> Soon my office bookshelf had an old Sears catalogue and a pictorial history of advertising (to help me furnish the house and clothe the characters), the *Dictionary of American Slang* (to add colour to the text) and a 1937 desk encyclopaedia (to weed out anachronisms).

And so we walk up the peastone drive of the Linder house to meet Monica, who has dark waved hair and wears a navy Rayon blouse, tan slacks and tan pumps with Cuban heels, and she treats us like a masher who just gave her a whistle. In a game which is intended to be a little kitsch, this is all in good fun. In a more serious work it would be way off balance.

. . . . .

Book adaptations present two main problems for interactive fiction. Plenty have been made: Frederik Pohl's *Gateway*, a masterpiece of "hard" science fiction, and the books of J. R. R. Tolkien, Terry Pratchett and Enid Blyton have all lent their extensive imaginary worlds. But in each case by permission. Even if no money changes hands, copyright law is enforceable until fifty or seventy years (depending on jurisdiction) after the death of the author or the author's spouse. There are nineteenth-century novels still subject to copyright and numerous characters have been trademarked. Some literary estates, that of Tintin for instance, are highly protective, and the rights managers of Anne McCaffrey's "Dragon" books or Paramount's *Star Trek* franchise are assiduous in watching for abuse of their property by authors on the Internet: understandably, since a venture by Marion Zimmer Bradley in authorising fan fiction ended in miserable litigation. The Commodore 64 game 'HitchHiker-64' (Bob Chappell, 1984), an unauthorised work loosely based on Douglas Adams's comedy had to be hastily rewritten as 'Cosmic Capers', with the Ravenous Bugblatter Beast of Traal becoming the somehow less satisfying Barbaric Binge Beast of Bongo.

The second problem is that, in any case, a direct linear plot simply does not work as an adventure game and a novel is too long for a game, just as it is for a film: both are nearer to a longish short story. Dave Lebling reckoned 'Shogun' (1989), an authorised version of James Clavell's epic novel, the worst not only of his own games but of all Infocom's too. (Graeme Cree: "Too often the story just seems to go on around you while you get meaningless points for smiling, nodding, or bowing at the right times." Torbjörn Andersson:

"it never lets you stray more than a few baby-steps from the pre-determined story".) 'Sherlock' (Bob Bates, 1987) was on the whole more successful, not because Conan Doyle is more interesting – he is so familiar that the reverse is true, and besides, Bates overplayed the camp humour – but because the game was a pastiche, not a slavish adaptation.   The same can be said of 'Wonderland' (David Bishop, 1990), one of the few Alice-based games not to follow the text.   Shakespeare's 'The Tempest' has been adapted at least twice for interactive fiction (David R. Grigg, 1992; Graham Nelson, 1997) but Jonathan Partington's confection of Shakespearian settings, 'Avon' (1982), is more fun than either.   Puzzles range across most of the plays in a mad rush, from hiding in a laundry basket (*The Merry Wives of Windsor*) to borrowing three thousand ducats (*The Merchant of Venice*) and one is really best advised not to eat the pie from *Titus Andronicus*.

● **REFERENCES**

The tension between open-ended simulation and narrative has attracted much comment. David Graves's three papers *Second Generation Adventure Games* (J. of Computer Game Design, 1987) have little to say. Gerry Kevin Wilson observes that "The Minimalists argue that games should be an experience in exploration and simulation. They want to be able to start their own plots and toss them aside at will. In my opinion, they are very dangerous people." Mike Roberts, in the appendix to *The TADS Author's Manual*, writes: "Adventure games all have a major problem: they pretend to be what they're not ... Adventures are simulations. Unfortunately, most adventures claim to be simulations of the real world... The key is to choose a small universe that you can model completely." He develops this idea of self-containment by suggesting that design should concentrate on a single important usage for each object, with irrelevant connections added only later.

§48 A triangle of identities

> "Queer grammar!" said Holmes with a smile as he handed the
> paper back to the inspector. "Did you notice how the 'he' suddenly
> changed to 'my'? The writer was so carried away by his own story
> that he imagined himself at the supreme moment to be the hero."
>
> — Sir Arthur Conan Doyle (1859–1930), *Three Gables*

 In books like this one the word "player" is overused. There are at
least three identities involved in play: the person typing and reading
("player"), the main character within the story ("protagonist"),
and the voice speaking about what this character sees and feels
("narrator"). There is a triangle of relationships between them, and it's a
triangle with very different proportions in different games.

1. Protagonist and player.   "What should you, the detective, do now?" asks
'The Witness' pointedly on its first turn. Numerous games ('Zork', for instance)
take the attitude that anyone who turns up can play, as themselves, regardless
of gender or attitudes. This is to equate player with protagonist, making them
almost the same. Sometimes the equation is actually engineered: 'Leather
Goddesses of Phobos' notices into which bathroom the player chooses to move
the protagonist and decides the protagonist's gender accordingly. 'Seastalker'
(Stu Galley and Jim Lawrence, 1984), aimed at a younger audience, asks for
the player's name and gives it to the protagonist, too. At the other extreme is
Amy Briggs's much underplayed 'Plundered Hearts' (1987), which has as its
heroine a specific girl whisked away by pirates in the West Indies. Reviewing
in *SPAG* 4, Graeme Cree wrote that:

> In 'Zork', you're just some anonymous guy who was walking by the white
> house. You have no particular personality, or history before this point.
> 'Planetfall' makes an effort to paint your character with the enclosed diary,
> but it is all chrome ... 'Plundered Hearts', more than any other game gave
> me the feeling of really being inside someone *else's* head. Throughout the
> game, who you are plays an important part. Disguising your identity and
> altering your appearance is important in several places to elicit a desired
> reaction from other characters ...

Either approach presents difficulties. If the protagonist is uncharacterised,
the story may lack literary interest. If heavily determined, the protagonist is
likely to be highly unlike the player and this risks losing the player's sense of
engagement.

△ Few players have minded becoming the Reverend Stephen Dawson, the middle-aged clergyman of 'Muse, an Autumn Romance' (Christopher Huang, 1998), whose behaviour is constrained by his emotional blockage. But there are players who resent being obliged to identify with gay protagonists. On the whole this is their problem, not the game's, and it was for them that Neil James Brown wrote his pointed spoof 'The Lost Spellmaker' (1997), the exploit of Mattie, a lesbian dwarf Secret Service agent addicted to sweets.

· · · · ·

In an interactive medium, the beliefs and abilities of the protagonist are more than simply a painted backcloth, because the player participates in them. These special abilities might be called the "magic" in the game's model world, in the broadest sense:

> For magic and applied science alike the problem is how to subdue reality to the wishes of man.

(C. S. Lewis, *The Abolition of Man*.) In 'The Witness', for instance, the magic might be said to be the detective's ability to arrest or call for forensic analysis, and in 'Ruins' we have the camera and the packing case. The magic is the imaginary fabric of the world, and it is as essential for the magic to have a coherent rationale as it is for the map to suggest a coherent geography.

Because the magic is part of the background, it should not be allowed to become too crudely a way to solve puzzles. An "open door" spell should be a general technique, with several different applications across its game. Better yet, these techniques should be used indirectly and with ingenuity, for instance opening a locked door by casting a "cause to rust" spell on its hinges. And plenty of puzzles should have solutions which don't involve the magic at all, or else the player will start to feel that it would save a good deal of time and effort just to find the "win game" spell and be done with it.

△ In a few games a linguistic surrealism is the reality: for instance 'Nord and Bert Couldn't Make Head or Tail of It' (Jeff O'Neill, 1987) is entirely based on puns and the T-Removing Machine of 'Leather Goddesses of Phobos' can transform a rabbit into a rabbi. A literary critic might call this a "postmodern" magic, which dislocates language from what is "really" happening in the game. This is exceptionally hard to do well.

△ Games with magic in the authentic fantasy sense seldom follow the austere example of Tolkien, where – although there are spells, as where Gandalf sets light to fir cones in (the book) *The Hobbit* – the sign of a wizard is more often a priest-like ability to question out motives in what people say and a sage-like wisdom about nature and history. Instead, perhaps for easy parsing and convenient subdivision and perhaps simply to imitate Gary Gygax's role-playing game *Dungeons and Dragons*, interactive fiction has tended to follow the *Dying Earth* stories (c. 1950) of Jack Vance† where spells are at once dramatic flourishes, complex mental exercises which must be memorised, and highly specific tools with outré names like "Xarfaggio's Physical Malepsy" and "The Excellent Prismatic Spray". Many schemes of magic have been tried, and naturally each designer wants to find a new one. Sometimes spells take place in the mind ('Enchanter'), sometimes with the aid of certain objects ('Curses'); sometimes half-way between (Level 9's 'Magik' games, David Williamson and Pete Austin, 1985–6). Keying magic to objects is advantageous because objects are tactile and part of the game's other play. In other respects, too, magic needs to be subject to the discipline of being easily subdivided and described. "Change a belt or staff into a small poisonous serpent" is far more amenable to designing (and parsing) than "convert up to 1000 cubic feet of rock to mud or quicksand".

△   If the map is very large, or a good deal of moving to-and-fro is called for, designers have frequently used magic to provide rapid transport: such as the magic words in 'Advent', or the eight colour-coded collars in 'Dungeon Adventure', or the teleport booths in 'Planetfall' (Steve Meretzky, 1983), or the black and white dots in 'Adventure Quest' (Mike, Nick and Pete Austin, 1984, 1983). Finding and deducing how to use this transport system can be a puzzle in itself, one whose solution is optional but rewarding.

. . . . .

2. Narrator and protagonist.   Some narrators behave like a French "new novelist", reporting only what the protagonist is currently seeing and doing. Others enjoy access to what the protagonist thinks and believes:

> Aunt Jemima has two cats, Jane and Austin, but she finds Austin especially annoying – this ought to make Austin your natural ally, but as it is you tend to glower at each other.

Here the narrator of 'Curses' (Graham Nelson, 1993) tells the player that the protagonist doesn't like somebody. In a different game this could have been established by events, showing rather than telling. Indeed, the protagonist's relationship with Austin might have been neutral until established by the player's choices.

It is the narrator who speaks the game's opening words, sometimes called the "overture" and conventionally used to say what sort of person the protagonist is, and what he or she is trying to do. Overtures vary widely in how direct and indeed how honest they are. Many, like 'Curses', leave the player guessing or misdirect as a form of tease. This is a reaction against the overture style of the 1980s, exemplified by 'Snowball' (original version):

---

† Though Dave Lebling cites the *Earthsea* novels of Ursula K. LeGuin as the main influence behind 'Enchanter'.

The interstar freezer, Snowball 9, has entered its target starsystem. And it will soon enter the star unless you can do something!

Such directness was itself a necessity considering that players of the day expected any game to be a treasure hunt unless they were told otherwise. The overtures to quest games became highly predictable: here is 'Enchanter' (Marc Blank and Dave Lebling, 1983):

You, a novice Enchanter with but a few simple spells in your Book, must seek out Krill, explore the Castle he has overthrown, and learn his secrets. Only then may his vast evil. . .

And so on and so forth. What makes such briefings disappointing is partly that they often run on far too long and are full of words like "dread" and "imbue", and either take themselves very seriously or, which is worse, don't. Here is about a quarter of the "overture", or opening text, of 'Beyond Zork' (Brian Moriarty, 1987), a game not meant as a comedy:

Y'Gael's dry chuckle stilled the murmur of the crowd. "You forget your own history, Gustar. Are you not author of the definitive scroll on the Coconut of Quendor?"
A tumult of amphibious croaks and squeals drowned out Gustar's retort. Y'Gael hobbled over to a table laden with mystical artifacts, selected a small stone and raised it high.
"The Coconut is our only hope," she cried, her eyes shining in the stone's violet aura. "Its seed embodies the essence of our wisdom. Its shell is impervious to the ravages of Time. We must reclaim it from the Implementors, and hide it away before its secrets are forgotten!"

Self-indulgent, self-parodying, slack, told in the past tense, uninteractive and basically dumb. If Moriarty felt that the quest of the game was hackneyed, a better response would have been to restructure the game, not to allow the narrator to show disdain for it. The same author's overture to 'Trinity' was by contrast honed to perfection:

Sharp words between the superpowers. Tanks in East Berlin. And now, reports the BBC, rumors of a satellite blackout. It's enough to spoil your continental breakfast.
But the world will have to wait. This is the last day of your $599 London Getaway Package, and you're determined to soak up as much of that authentic English ambience as you can. So you've left the tour bus behind, ditched the camera and escaped to Hyde Park for a contemplative stroll through the Kensington Gardens.

A good deal has been achieved in these two paragraphs. Apart from details – mention of the BBC, of continental breakfasts, of the camera and the tour bus – you know who you are (an unadventurous American tourist, of no consequence to the world), where you are (Kensington Gardens, Hyde Park, London, England), and what is going on in the world beyond (bad news: World War III is about to break out). Also, nobody knows where you've gone. In style, the opening of 'Trinity' is escapism from a disastrous world out of control, and notice the way the first paragraph is in tense, blunt, headline-like sentences, whereas the second is much more relaxed. For a second example, 'Ballyhoo':

> As you trudge along in the wake of the outflowing crowd, you thumb through your memories of this evening. Your experience of the circus, with its ballyhooed promises of wonderment and its ultimate disappointment, has been to sink your teeth into a candy apple whose fruit is rotten.
> Never mind the outrageous prices, the Mt. Everest vantage point, the communistically long lines, the audience more savage than the lion act. And it wasn't the shabbiness of the performances themselves that's got you soured on Spangleland. No, instead it's that the circus is a reminder of your own secret irrational desire to steal the spotlight, to defy death, and to bask in the thunder of applause.

Many players will have no desire for any of that: but then the narrator is not talking about the player, only the protagonist.

△   More detailed briefing information, if it is needed at all, can be placed interactively into the game – and not necessarily made available all at once: see the books in the library of 'Christminster' (Gareth Rees, 1995).

·   ·   ·   ·   ·

3. Player and narrator.   The narrator chooses how much to tell the player and which scenes to show instead. When the game lapses into a cut-scene, a passage of text in which something happens which the player cannot interact with, it is because the narrator has chosen to override the player. Gareth Rees (Usenet posting 8/8/95):

> I decided not to use this technique, partly because I think it's an admission of defeat, a statement that the medium of adventure games is too inflexible to write the kind of character interaction we want to.

Cut-scenes risk dislocating the player's engagement with the game, and the level of trust between player and narrator. By the end of a successful game, the narrator can take greater risks, taking advantage of friendship so to speak. At the start, and especially in the overture text, the narrator does well to avoid cut-scenes and presumptions. Thomas Nilsson advises designers to

> Create an image of him or it [the narrator] and stick to it. Receiving comments about your (limited) progress in the game might be funny, as long as they are not out of character.

Indeed many narrators are self-effacing and unintrusive so long as the player pursues the "correct" line of choices, but immediately emerge as wry, sardonic or knowing once this line is deviated from. The tiniest phrases betray this:

>wave
You wave, but nobody waves back. Life's like that.

>look behind hanging
Nope, no more keys.

You are falling towards the ground, wind whipping around you.
>east
Down seems more likely.

Austin, your incorrigible ginger cat, lounges around here.
>austin, go south
I can see you've never had a cat.

'Kingdom of Hamil'; 'Sorcerer'; 'Spellbreaker'; 'Curses'. It is no coincidence that these responses are often jibes at the player's progress. Like the player, but unlike every character in the game (including the protagonist), the narrator knows that it *is* a game: it's the narrator who announces the rules, awards points and offers clues. The un-mimetic passage from 'The Hitchhiker's Guide To The Galaxy' quoted in the previous section...

Ford lowers his voice to a whisper. "I'm not supposed to tell you this, but you'll never be able to finish the game without consulting the Guide about lots of stuff."

... is funny (if it is) because Ford is usurping the narrator. Nobody would turn a hair at the more conventional alternative:

Ford hands over the book and turns away.
[Please type "consult guide about stuff" to look up its entry on "stuff", and so on.]

Indeed in some games it might be said that the parser, who asks questions like "Which do you mean...?" and in some games speaks only in square brackets, is a fourth character, quite different from the narrator.

Playing games with the narrator is one of Steve Meretzky's favourite comic techniques. Here is a more moderate, more typical example:

(It's no wonder this section of Mars is considered the Ruined Castle Capital of the Solar System.)

More moderate, yet even in 'Leather Goddesses of Phobos' such a remark feels the need for parentheses. It is only in parody that the narrator goes in for commentary full-time.

△   This is a common tactic for designers of juvenile or silly games, who hope thereby to suggest that because the game is knowing about its shortcomings it is therefore more sophisticated, more mature. But it seldom is. Cf. the numerous 'Zork' pastiches which were intended to be parodies, or Big Al's 'BJ Drifter' (1998).

● REFERENCES
For surveys of the quite extensive range of approaches to player identity in the canonical games, see 'Character Gender in Interactive Fiction', parts I and II, by Doug Anderson (*XYZZYnews* 3 and 6) and 'Player Character Identity in IF', John Wood (*XYZZYnews* 9). Notable gender ambiguities include the 'Snowball' trilogy, whose protagonist is one Kim Kimberley, and 'Jigsaw', which attempts a romantic sub-plot without specified genders on either part.   ●In later life, W. H. Auden (1907–73) considered the ghostly identity narrating a poem to be one of its two gifts to the reader: "The first question [the reader asks] is technical: 'Here is a verbal contraption. How does it work?' The second is, in the broadest sense, moral: 'What kind of guy inhabits this poem?' "

§49   Structure

Games from all of the major design houses of the 1980s share a common structure, partly because they were planned as if they were Hollywood films, which even today retain the shape of a three-act play from nineteenth-century theatre. Designers would begin by making a formal pitch, writing two or three-page synopses of the action, and serious coding did not begin until such a synopsis had been talked through. Structural breakdowns of what they produced are often revealing.

· · · · · ·

Size and density.   There was a time when the sole measure of quality in advertisements for cheaper adventure games was the number of rooms. Level 9's most original work, 'Snowball', claimed to have over 7,000 locations, of which 6,800 made up an unusually wearisome maze. Even a 200-room game meant only minimal room descriptions and simple puzzles, scattered thinly over the map. Whereas ten of the Infocom games have fewer than sixty rooms, with 'Seastalker' (30 rooms), 'The Witness' (30) and 'The Hitchhiker's Guide To The Galaxy' (31) the most geographically concise. Today's custom is that, barring a few junctions and corridors, there should be something interactive in every room.

Today's design systems impose few restrictions on game size or construction, but designers still have an unconscious idea of a "budget" for a game design, if only to keep its proportions in balance. A typical medium-to-large game contains 250 objects, counting items, rooms and other sundries (the player, the compass directions) as objects. Many items are not portable but are instead walls, tapestries, thrones, control panels, coal-grinding machines and, as a rule of thumb, three items to one room is about right. We might therefore expect 60 rooms, and the next step in budgeting would be to share these out among game regions. The 180 or so items might divide as 50 portable items and 130 furnishings. ('Wishbringer': 250 objects, 52 rooms, 34 takeable items.) As for the text, 'Enchanter' contains 20,100 words, 'Trinity' 32,200 and 'Curses' 44,000, but the latter are large games and 25,000 words is more typical: around a quarter of the length of a typical novel, for an average of only 400 words per location. The size of the source code varies dramatically with the design system, but for instance: 'Spellbreaker' 17,800 lines, 'Christminster' 13,000, 'Once and Future' (Gerry Kevin Wilson, 1998) 35,000.

Limitations can be a blessing in disguise, because they force a designer to keep asking if this part or that part is altogether necessary. Here is Brian Moriarty, whose research went as far as looking up geological surveys:

> The first thing I did was sit down and make a map of the Trinity site. It was changed about 50 times trying to simplify it and get it down from over 100 rooms to the 40 or so rooms that now comprise it. It was a lot more accurate and very detailed, but a lot of that detail was totally useless.

This reduction to 40 rooms would have been worthwhile even if memory and disc space had been unlimited. Redundant locations can be an indication of too much prose and too little interaction. 'The Light: Shelby's Addendum' (C. A. McCarthy, 1995) contains much that is praiseworthy but its reviewers took a dim view of its having over twenty locations in which nothing happens.

△   It is not always realised how technical constraints have influenced the literary style of the classic games, and so of what we consider to be good today. Infocom's writers were mostly working under an absolute ceiling of 255 objects (including rooms) and memory was more pressing still. Lebling summarised the implementor's frustration *en passant* in a 1987 memo: "I made a pitch for a more-unlimited game system... Brian [Moriarty] is already running out of table space in his game, Amy [Briggs]'s game is too big and not even in Beta yet, all our EZIP games have had to be cut, and 'Bureaucracy' [Douglas Adams, 1987] had to become EZIP instead of LZIP." (We would now call both EZIP and LZIP version 4 of the Z-machine, but LZIP games were small enough to run on a Commodore 64 – the biggest source of sales – and EZIPs weren't.) Lebling lamented in 1998 that "a lot of lovely shivers" had to be cut out of his almost-finished 'The Lurking Horror' as a result: whereas in spite of the amount of her game ('Plundered Hearts') that ended on the cutting-room floor, Amy Briggs felt that "The constraints of running on the Commodore 64 helped the games be richer, I believe, than if we had been writing then for the Pentium Pro" (*XYZZYnews* 12). Similarly, Scott Adams's games, running on smaller computers with tape decks instead of disc drives, were obliged to show extreme economy with objects and textual messages, but coded rules and what we would now call daemons so efficiently that these few objects ended up tightly interlinked, with side effects and multiple uses.

· · · · ·

The prologue.   Most games divide into three phases: prologue, middle game and end game. These phases are often closed off from each other, so that once a phase has ended it cannot be returned to, though the prologue sometimes offers premonitions of the end, or conversely the end game echoes back to the prologue. Like the children in C. S. Lewis's tales of Narnia, the player is always going "further up, and further in". Stu Galley, in debugging the mystery 'The Witness', found himself obliged to enforce the plotting of the passage between prologue and middle game:

[The play-testers] discovered significant "branches" in the story that I had overlooked. For example, what if the player sneaks into the house or doesn't go in at all until too late? The first possibility raised too many complications, so we decided to lock all the outside doors.

The duties of the prologue are to establish an atmosphere, to foreshadow what is to come and give out a little background information, while giving the player enough entertainment to want to continue. The interactive aspect of this is that the player has to pick up the game's special skills, using commands, tools or actions special to the setting. (The prologue to 'The Meteor, The Stone and a Long Glass of Sherbet' (Angela M. Horns, 1997) uses an easy puzzle involving a telescope and a guide book to provide practice with them.)

The task of passing into the middle game should be reasonably straightforward, but at the same time involved enough that the player has a feeling that time spent on the game is time rewarded. The designer would be wise to imagine that the player of the prologue is really only toying with the game at this stage, and isn't drawing a map or being at all careful. If the prologue is too big, the player will quickly get lost and give up. If it is too hard, then many players simply won't reach the middle game.

△   The passage from the prologue to the middle game is often also the passage from the mundane to the fantastical, so that the prologue answers the question "How did I get into all this?" The prologue of 'Advent' is an above-ground landscape, whose presence lends a much greater sense of claustrophobia and depth to the underground bulk of the game. On the other hand, a few games drop the player right in at the deep end, as in 'Plundered Hearts', which opens to a sea battle in full swing.

△   Notable prologues include the streets and meadows outside the apparently impenetrable 'Christminster' college (4 locations), the undemolished planet Earth of 'The Hitchhiker's Guide To The Galaxy' (6) or 221B Baker Street in 'Sherlock' (again, 6), but some have been as large as the guild house of 'Sorcerer' (Steve Meretzky, 1984), at 13 locations, or the seaport of 'Crobe' (Jonathan Partington, 1986), at 18. 'Advent' in its classical form had an 8-location prologue, but some extensions (such as Level 9's) fleshed out the above-ground substantially, making the volcano visible as a precursor to its underground discovery late in the middle game.

·   ·   ·   ·   ·

The middle game.   The middle game is the one which least needs detailed planning in advance, because it is the one which comes nearest to being a miscellaneous collection of puzzles. On the other hand, since it is also the largest part it is the most in need of some rough subdivision into segments. Working through these segments, one by one, provides a sequence of problems and rewards for the player. A first-draft design of the middle game may just consist of a rough sketch of these segments, with some general ideas for objects, places and characters. Slotting actual puzzles in can come later in a more improvisatory, freewheeling sort of way.

The obvious way to subdivide is to carve up the map, perhaps with a pattern to the regions, perhaps even sharing regions out to different authors (as in the AGT game, 'Shades of Gray', 1993). Regions correspond perhaps to time zones, to the four winds or the twelve signs of the Zodiac, or else are delineated from each other through simple geography: cave games are especially prone to this, often having a node-like room with exits in all eight cardinal directions. Thus 'Zork II' (Marc Blank and Dave Lebling, 1981) has seven areas arranged at compass points around the Carousel Room, with the area northeast serving as prologue. Sometimes the same locale occurs more than once, revisited with a different perspective. The innovative 'Spider and Web' (Andrew Plotkin, 1998), in which a player is being interrogated about what really happened when a secret installation was broken into, features repeated but varying hypothetical versions set in the same locations.

Other designers structure the game around performances: in 'Ballyhoo' the player enacts the full repertoire of circus skills, and in a region of 'The Quest for the Sangraal' all seven deadly sins must be committed. More often, though, dramatic actions are intended to become the turning points in a story. Gareth Rees (in *XYZZYnews* 6):

> In 'Christminster', I identified a set of key scenes each of which was an event or experience that affected the player character, and moved the story forwards towards the conclusion, and yet could plausibly be implemented as a section of an adventure game.

In chronological terms, the plot literally moved forwards: the clock, in 'Christminster', chimes the half-hour when a key event takes place, advancing towards dinner in hall, but time hangs heavy in an endless Cambridge afternoon while the player is stuck. Puzzles were slotted in later, often around the needs of the plot. One of the game's most enjoyable sequences, with the player exploring a pitch-dark secret tunnel in the company of Professor Wilderspin, in fact exists only to oblige the player to spend time in the Professor's company so that he can do a good deal of talking. Like most traditional interactive fiction, 'Christminster' has a plot with little overall variation except for the order in which the player does things. But some radical designers see events not as milestones but forks in the plot. Thomas M. Disch:

> ... any computer-interactive text deconstructs itself as you write because it's always stopping and starting and branching off this way and that ... With 'Amnesia', I found myself working with a form that allowed me to display these erasures, these unfollowed paths.

There are games, though, in which an entirely improvised middle game is compensated for by a tautly controlled prologue and end game. Andrew Plotkin (in *XYZZYnews* 14):

> Since 'So Far' [1996] is pretty much pure surrealism, I didn't *have* a plot in mind originally. I had a theme, and was co-inventing puzzles and scenes and events all at the same time.

This sounds potentially shambolic, but in an interview (*XYZZYnews* 13) in the immediate aftermath of testing 'So Far', Michael Kinyon found it enormously affecting. Steve Meretzky:

> Sometimes you have only a sketchy outline and are just beginning to coalesce the geography. Sometimes the geography coalesces around the puzzles. Sometimes it's both together.

Geography coalescing around puzzles is evident in Meretzky's work, in which events often spread across multiple locations, as in the case of the 'Sorcerer' flume ride.

△   The middle game is likely to have the largest area of playable map that the player will face. In laying this out, it adds to the interest to make connections in the half-cardinal compass directions – northeast, northwest, southeast, southwest – and to steer away from a feeling that the game has a square grid. (One of the few defects of the 'Trinity' middle game, though possibly that was the price to be paid for one of its better puzzles.) Equally, a few, possibly long, loops which can be walked around reduce retracing of steps and avoid the appearance of a bus service map in which half a dozen lines have only one exchange.

△   The passage from middle game to end game often takes the form of a scavenger hunt: throughout the middle game a number of well-hidden objects are collected and only when they are combined can the end game be entered. See 'Lords of Time' (Sue Gazzard, 1983) or indeed almost any game produced in the wake of 'Advent', as it was almost taken for granted that any game must have "treasures". Soon enough it became a cliché, and one which games like 'Leather Goddesses of Phobos' or 'Hollywood Hijinx' ("Hollywood" Dave Anderson and Liz Cyr-Jones, 1986) send up, but it's still not a bad idea, because it enables many different problems to be open at once. You can be stuck finding sprocket 2 and go and work on finding sprocket 5 for a while instead.

·   ·   ·   ·   ·

End game.   End games serve two purposes. First, they give the player a sense of being near to success (they used to be called the "Master Game"), and can be used to culminate the plot, to reveal the game's secrets. They also serve to stop the final stage of the game from being too hard to play, narrowing it to only a few accessible rooms or objects. In cave games like 'Zork', the final puzzle would be made exceptionally difficult but today's designers usually prefer to give the player the satisfaction of finishing, and themselves the satisfaction of knowing that their story has been completed.

A mark of the last pieces of the puzzle falling into place is that loose ends are tied neatly up and the characters sent away with their fates worked out and futures settled. Looking back, from the point of view of a winning player, can you understand what has happened and why? Can you also see what is to happen to the protagonist next?

The final message is another important one and, as with the overture, the coda is all the better for being brief. To quote examples would only spoil their games. A popular device is to make the two scenes which open and close the story "book-ends" for each other, symmetrical and matching.

△   To speak of "the" final message or "the" last step is a little presumptive. Multiple outcomes are not to every designer's taste, but Daniel Ravipinto's 'Tapestry' (1996), with its sense of tragedy, and its misleading portents and advice, drew much of its strength from an open end. (Its plot owes much to the 1993 *Star Trek: The Next Generation* episode of the same name.)

△   Gerry Kevin Wilson suggests that the end game should feature "your Big Nasty^{TM}. The Big Nasty^{TM} is the final challenge, be it monster, man, maze, or whatever. This is where you want to ham up your writing and get a sense of urgency going. There needs to be a time limit . . ." In this view, which is not universally shared, the end game is like a video game's "Boss Level".

△   Like prologues, end games vary in size: from a one or two location single closing scene ('The Lurking Horror', 'Sorcerer') to a new game region (the Dungeon Master's lair in 'Zork III' (Marc Blank and Dave Lebling, 1982), 7 locations, or Roman Britain in 'Curses', 16).

. . . . . .

Games in the style of 'Advent' are very wide, with around thirty or so puzzles, all easily available and soluble in any order. Others, such as the Melbourne House adaptation of Tolkien ('Lord of the Rings Game One' (later a.k.a. 'The Fellowship of the Ring'), 'Shadows of Mordor', 'The Crack of Doom', Philip Mitchell, 1985, 1987, 1989), are very narrow: a long sequence of puzzles, each of which leads only to a chance to solve the next. Wide games are dull, since no problem solved will lead to any radical change. Narrow games are difficult to pitch: if the one puzzle open at a time is easy then play is too rapid, but if it is hard then the player will be abruptly slammed into a wall of frustration.

Towards the end of design it can be helpful to draw out a lattice diagram of the puzzles. At the top is a node representing the start of the game, and then lower nodes represent solved puzzles. An arrow is drawn between two puzzles if one has to be solved before the other can be. Here is the lattice diagram for

'Ruins', with subscripted numbers showing the points scored on reaching each given position: each of the artifacts is worth 5 except the jade mask, worth 10.

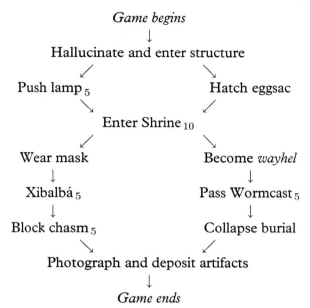

Game begins
↓
Hallucinate and enter structure
↙   ↘
Push lamp $_5$ Hatch eggsac
↘   ↙
Enter Shrine $_{10}$
↙   ↘
Wear mask   Become *wayhel*
↓   ↓
Xibalbá $_5$ Pass Wormcast $_5$
↓   ↓
Block chasm $_5$ Collapse burial
↘   ↙
Photograph and deposit artifacts
↓
Game ends

This diagram is useful for three reasons. Firstly, it checks that the game is soluble at all: for example, if the jade mask had been kept in Xibalbá, there would be no solution. Secondly, it shows how much of the game happens in different areas. Most usefully of all, the diagram shows whether the game is wide or narrow and which puzzles are likely to be bottlenecks, with large parts of the game depending on their solution. This tall, spindly diagram is indicative of a fairly linear plot, not surprisingly as the game is so small. The problem of entering the Shrine is evidently a bottleneck.

△   A long arrow on a lattice diagram is a caution that some action very early in play is essential even though it has no effect until some other action much later on. If the early action becomes impossible later, for instance because it is in a prologue which cannot be returned to, the player will legitimately feel aggrieved. In 'Christminster', "getting invited to dinner" is theoretically an early puzzle because access to the Master's lodgings occurs at the outset of the middle game, but the puzzle never goes away and remains accessible right up to dinner time.

● **REFERENCES**
C. E. Forman exhibits the lattice diagram for 'Enchanter', which clearly shows its prologue, middle game, end game structure, in *XYZZYnews* 4. Replying in issue 6, Gareth Rees argues that game analysis is an aid to, rather than an integral part of, game design.

§50   The design of puzzles

The odyssey of 'Zork: Mimesis' begins in a field behind a white house. You climb in through an open window, take the water and sack lunch from the table, go in the living room and move the rug aside to reveal – a blank floor! … Soon the owner of the house – an underemployed, alcoholic bricklayer – is covering you with a shotgun as his unfaithful, neurotic wife dials 911. The puzzle-free, super-literary action continues as you are funneled through the criminal justice system…

— Roger Giner-Sorolla, conceding that mimesis is not everything

 Without puzzles, or problems, or mechanisms to allow the player to receive the text a little at a time – whichever phrase you prefer – there is no interaction. Inevitably, puzzles are obstacles. Here, Arthur Dent will not be able to meet aliens and have a generally wild time until he has got hold of a babel fish:

>examine machine
The dispenser is tall, has a button at around eye-level, and says "Babel Fish" in large letters. Anything dispensed would probably come out the slot at around knee-level. It bears a small label which reads "Another fine product of the Sirius Cybernetics Corporation."
>press dispenser button
A single babel fish shoots out of the slot. It sails across the room and through a small hole in the wall, just under a metal hook.
>remove dressing gown
Okay, you're no longer wearing your gown.
>hang gown on hook
The gown is now hanging from the hook, covering a tiny hole.
>push dispenser button
A single babel fish shoots out of the slot. It sails across the room and hits the dressing gown. The fish slides down the sleeve of the gown and falls to the floor, vanishing through the grating of a hitherto unnoticed drain.
>put towel over drain
The towel completely covers the drain.

(For the final solution, still some way off, see 'The Hitchhiker's Guide To The Galaxy'.) A good game mixes easy puzzles with hard, but no puzzle should be so simple that one obvious command solves it. On the other hand nor should its solution, once guessed, take ridiculously long to achieve, or require endless repetition: such as to fetch something pointlessly distant, or to solve an eight-discs Tower of Hanoi, or to keep juggling objects so that only three are carried at any one time. Here are two basic pitfalls:

The "Get–X–Use–X" syndrome.   By convention, every word or phrase in a cryptic crossword clue is used exactly once to account for some part of the answer. The equivalent in adventure games is the equation "one object = one puzzle solved", where the player picks up a bicycle pump and looks for a bicycle, picks up a pin and looks for a balloon, and so on. Once used, an object can be dropped, for it surely will not be needed again. But this convention rapidly drains away realism, and most designers try to break the equation in every way possible: with red herrings (one object = no solutions), collection puzzles (many objects = one solution), multiple solutions (any of several objects = one solution) and multiple usages (one object = many solutions).

The "What's-the-Verb" syndrome.   In 'Ballyhoo', "whip lion" and "hit lion with whip" are inequivalent and only one of them does any taming. The following, from 'Sorcerer', can only be called a bug:

>unlock journal
(with the small key)
No spell would help with that!
>open journal
(with the small key)
The journal springs open.

(For a third example, the wording needed to use the brick in 'Zork II' is most unfair.) In many games the "examine", "search" and "look inside" verbs all perform different actions, and it is easy to accidentally design a hidden treasure in such a way that only one of these will find it. (Though at the other extreme, excessive tolerance for verbs leads to everything being "moved", not "pushed", "pulled" or "rotated".) Similarly, in the *"What's-the-Noun" syndrome*, an object stubbornly fails to respond to reasonable synonyms, such as "sword" for "gladius" or "football" for a soccer ball. But perhaps a remark on a sad subject might be intruded here. The Japanese woman near the start of 'Trinity' can be called "yellow" and "Jap", terms with a grisly resonance. The game shows nothing but respect for her: should it allow the player to do otherwise?

Variety is valuable, but logic and fairness are paramount. "Is the writer pulling a rabbit out of a hat or do you see the fuzzy ears first?" (Dave Lebling). Gareth Rees suggests that one way to ensure that puzzles are consistent with the game containing them is to write a sample transcript of play first:

It stops me coding anything until I have a puzzle fairly well fleshed out in my mind. Too often it's tempting to start coding something one way and then discover that later developments need a different approach.

It makes me think like a player (I try to ... include a selection of the silly things that I would be liable to type if I were playing the game ...). Often when coding it becomes habit just to fail to deal with situations and responses that are tricky to write. Having them appear on the script forces me to say to myself, 'It may be tough to code but it'll appear natural in the game and that's worth it'. I also find it hard to get into the habit of providing interesting responses to failed actions, and the script helps with this.

Another approach is to chain backwards from a goal, repeatedly asking "how can I obstruct this further?", so that the plot line becomes, like a computer drawing of a fractal curve, more crinkly with each iteration. Peter Killworth, in his book *How to Write Adventure Games for the BBC Microcomputer Model B and Acorn Electron* (whose opening words are "Adventure games are like avocado pears") describes an entire game this way ('Roman', 1984). Thus you need to pay a debt to a Senator, so you need to steal a bust from a temple, but that means impersonating a priest, by sacrificing a chicken with a gladius, which means catching a chicken (you scare it with a cat, but the cat must be attracted by a mouse, which you need to catch with a mousetrap): and the gladius isn't just lying around, either. You also need a torch, which

... needs soaking in oil first, just as candles need wax to burn. So we'd better organise a pool of oil through which the player can walk ... When the player gets to a source of flame – how about a brazier of coals, which will have to be untakeable? – he can attempt to light his torch. It isn't oily, it burns to a stump well-nigh instantly ... If it is oily, it'll catch fire ... No, that's too simple. If a player is soaked in oil too, he'll probably catch fire too! ... We'll create a damp, misty area, where the player is assassinated by a runaway slave, unless he enters while on fire. Then he will be safe, because the mist will condense on his body ... So the poor player, staggering around and on fire, will try the mist, but to his disappointment the torch will go out permanently too! The solution is trivial – he must drop the torch before entering the mist.

(Killworth's games are not known for their qualms and the player, it will be noted, forfeits the game without any warning by lighting the unoily torch or exploring the misty area.) This kind of plotting, with puzzles strung together like beads onto a necklace, offers the considerable advantage of lending coherency. But it is also liable to make long, linear sequences of puzzles which must be completed in an exact order. "I've found it incredibly hard to keep the puzzles from leading the whole story" (David M. Baggett, 1994).

. . . . .

Mazes.   In the *Traité des systèmes* of 1749, Condillac wrote: "What could be more ridiculous than that men awakening from a profound sleep, and finding themselves in the middle of a labyrinth, should lay down general principles for discovering the way out?" Ridiculous, but very human, because the dogged exploration of a maze is dull indeed, repetitive and irritatingly drawn-out: far more enjoyment is to be found in the working-out of its general principles.

Be it clearly said: it is designers who like mazes ("Concocting such mazes is one of my delights" – Peter Killworth); players do *not* like mazes. In the original puzzle, a tangled set of rooms have indistinguishable descriptions so that mapping becomes impossible: the original solution is to make the rooms distinguishable again by littering them with objects as markers. This solution is easily obstructed (the 'Advent' pirate and the 'Zork I' thief wander around picking the objects up again), but this only makes the experience more tiresome. When David Baggett was asked "How do I make my maze so that it doesn't have the standard solution?", his entire reply was: "Omit it."

Nevertheless, like the writing of locked-room mysteries, the devising of new solutions for mazes – usually involving guides, or hidden signs, or ways to see – is a modest art form in its own right: novelty being the essential point, though it is equally important to signal to the player that a novel solution exists. The unique *The Adventure Gamer's Manual* (1992), by the Cornish vicar and eccentric writer Bob Redrup, devotes all of Chapters 7 and 8 to solving maze variants: a faintly weary tone is maintained throughout. Redrup was an aficionado of the Topologika, and thus of the formerly Cambridge University games, which are simply riddled with mazes. Here, in 'Crobe' (1986) by the indefatigable maze-maker Jonathan Partington, the player is evidently not expected to explore haphazardly:

> You are in an underground marsh, a treacherous place where everything looks alike and water and slime lap around your feet. One false move would mean death, but you do at least have the choice of 8 horizontal directions to wander in.

Because lethal unless solved utterly, this is a benign sort of maze. Likewise, in 'Kingdom of Hamil' (1982):

> You are in the Maze of Hamil. Light streams in through many gaps in the rocks. There is the constant sound of rockfalls, distant and not-so-distant.
> There is a small nickel hexagon here, with the inscription "1 PFENTIME".

Whatever is going on here, it doesn't look like a simple matter of dropping marker-objects. Partington also has a (thoroughly unfashionable) penchant for elements of randomness which a player can overcome with great difficulty by careful planning. The caryatid maze from 'Fyleet' (1985) makes the novel twist of imposing random obstacles on a determined layout, and in 'The Quest

385

for the Sangraal' (1987): "There are exits in various directions, but, since the island is rotating, these directions change continually." Infocom's output has its share of mazes, too, one per game: those in 'Starcross' and the 'Enchanter', 'Sorcerer', 'Spellbreaker' trilogy are the most satisfying.

Light source puzzles.   Almost as disliked, but offering a little more scope to the designer, is the "bringing light to darkness" puzzle. The two standards reduce to refilling a lamp with limited oil and bringing light to a dark room which can apparently only be reached by a player who *hasn't* got a light source. ('Advent' includes both. The lake and aqueduct areas of 'Zork III' have an elegant light puzzle, probably the best thing in an otherwise so-so game.) Darkness need not be a problem to be solved, though: it might be a fact of life. Though few games have tried this (but visit the secret passage in 'Christminster'), a large permanently dark area might still be explored with the other senses.

Capacity and exhaustion puzzles.   Again, unpopular because their solution is normally tiresomely repetitive, forcing the player to keep putting things down and picking them up again. It can seem ridiculous that the protagonist can carry hundreds of bulky and fiddly things around all the time, so many designers impose a limit for realism's sake, typically of seven objects. It is bad form to set puzzles making life difficult because the limit is four and not five (after all, in emergency anyone can always carry one more item). In some games the limit is instead on total weight. Taking realism further, some games measure a state of health or even numerical levels of "strength" and "constitution" during play. The protagonist grows hungry and needs food, tired and needs sleep (in 'Enchanter' he is positively narcoleptic), wounded and needs recuperation. 'Planetfall' simulated a progressive illness whose symptoms are increasing need for food and sleep, and put many players off this kind of puzzle for life. Exhaustion rules are difficult to make fair. A rule requiring a return to an orchard for fruit should be watched carefully, as it will irritate a player to have to do this for a second, a third or a tenth time.

Timed puzzles.   Completing this round-up of unpopular but still sometimes justified puzzles are those which involve timed events, running along a script which requires the player to do something specific at one particular moment. In the prologue to 'The Hitchhiker's Guide To The Galaxy', why would any player buy the cheese sandwich in the pub and then feed it to the dog in the lane, on the one and only turn in which this is possible? Admittedly, an alternative exists later on, but this is not evident at the time. Mike Roberts (Usenet posting, 1999):

Aside from the annoyance, the reason I try to avoid timed puzzles is that they make you acutely aware that you're playing a game. As soon as I get into a save-try-restore loop, any sense of immersion is destroyed for me; I instead feel like I'm debugging a program, since I'm running through a series of inputs to figure out how the game responds.

This "sense of immersion" can partly be restored by keying events not to game turns but to the time of day, provided this fits the scenario, and making each stage last for a great many more turns than are strictly needed to solve the puzzles. Events which come only to he who waits are also problematic. In the Land of Shadow of 'Zork III', only the player who decides for some reason to wait on a fairly uninteresting Ledge will be rewarded with a visitor. (This case is defensible on grounds of context, but only just.)

Utility objects.   A designer who wants players to think of some items as useful needs to provide many situations – more than one, anyway – in which they can be used. A hallmark of better-designed games is that the player accumulates a few useful tools during play and wants to keep them to hand thereafter. (Cf. the crowbar and gloves in 'The Lurking Horror'.)

Keys and doors.   Almost all games close off segments of the map on a temporary basis by putting them behind locked doors. Many variations on this theme are extant in the literature: coded messages on the door, illusory defences, gate-keepers, the key being in the lock on the wrong side and so on. More usually a locked door signals to the player that a different puzzle (i.e., finding the key) has to be solved before this one can be, so that a designer uses it to impose a chronology on events. Questions to ask here include: if there are people just inside, do they react when the protagonist knocks on the door, or tries to break it down or ram it? Can the door be opened, closed, locked or unlocked from both sides? Are there skeleton or master-keys capable of opening many different doors? Are the keys which do open different doors sufficiently distinctive in appearance? Roger Giner-Sorolla commented that keys are the most naked kind of Get–X–Use–X puzzle:

> One can only find so many keys inside fishes' bellies, lost in the wainscotting, dropped at random in corridors, or hanging around guard dogs' necks before the artifice of the puzzle structure becomes painfully clear. By contrast, all six of the keys in 'Christminster' are hidden in places where one might actually keep a key, and all their locks are guarding places that one would expect to be locked; moreover, we end the game with a pretty clear idea of who normally uses each key and why.

Machinery and vehicles.   Machines are among the easiest puzzles to design: they have levers or ropes to pull, switches to press, cogs to turn. They need not make conversation or respond to anything beyond their function. They often require specialised tools, which brings in objects. They can transform the game in a semi-magical way; time travel or transforming coal to diamond being the clichés. They can also connect together different locations: chains, swinging arms and chutes may run across the map, and help to glue it together. Writing in the TADS manual, Mike Roberts makes the useful point that machines assist interactivity:

> For example, you might design a machine, described as "a small metal box with a button, a short plastic hose on one side, and a large metal pipe on the other side." When the button is pushed, "a loud hissing comes from the plastic hose for a moment, then a large drop of clear liquid drops out of the pipe, which hits the floor and quickly evaporates into a white cloud of vapor." If the player puts the plastic hose in a glass of water and the button is pushed, "the water is sucked into the plastic tube, and few moments later a block of ice is dropped out of the pipe." This allows the player to learn by experimentation what the machine does, which is more fun for the player than if you had labelled the machine "a freezer" or some such.

In machine puzzles, then, the player experiments with the controls and forms a theory of what is happening. With larger machines this involves visualising the physical construction of the components and how they affect each other: 'Hollywood Hijinx' is a tour de force of such puzzles, with a see-saw and a suspended safe. But the literature also includes highly complex self-contained machines presenting something of a black box whose internals must be deduced, such as a B-52 bomber and an Enigma cipher machine ('Jigsaw') and a computer which is programmable in the language Scheme ('Lists and Lists', Andrew Plotkin, 1996). Vehicles in games to date have included cars, tractors, fork-lift trucks, boats, hot-air balloons, log flumes, punts and elephant rides. Vehicles increase the realism of a landscape, by making it more than a set of rules about walking. They nevertheless need a little care to code: for instance, to disallow driving up ladders or through a narrow crevice.

Fire. The elements all tangle up code but add to the illusion. Fire has many useful properties – it makes light, it destroys things, it can cause explosions and chemical reactions, it cooks food, it softens materials, it can be passed from one object to another – but in the end it spreads, whereas the game's understanding doesn't. If the player is allowed to carry a naked flame, then the game is likely to need a rule to tell it whether or not every other item is flammable, and so on.

Water. In any location where water is available, players will try drinking, swimming, washing, diving. They will try to walk away with, indeed on, the water. Liquids make poor objects, because they need to be carried in some container yet can be poured from one to another, and because they are endlessly divisible. "Some water" can easily be made into "some water" and "some water". If there's more than one liquid in the game, can they be mixed? Pouring liquid over something is likely to make a mess of it: yet why should it be impossible? And so on. The compromise solution is usually to have a bottle with a capacity of, say, 5 units of water, which can be refilled in any room where there is water and so that 1 unit is drunk at a time. The player who tries to pour water over most things is simply admonished and told not to. Implementing swimming, or being underwater, is a different order of difficulty again, and many games agree with 'Parc' (John Rennie, 1983) that "since you cannot free yourself, and since you are by nature an air-breathing mammal I'm afraid you drown!". (Level 9's game 'Adventure Quest' is rare in containing a coherently worked out underwater section, though many games have the odd turn's-worth of diving. 'Jinxter' (Georgina Sinclair and Michael Bywater, 1987), also has an elaborate underwater section, with a seldom-discovered shipwreck to boot.) What happens to objects being held? Can the protagonist swim while wearing heavy clothes, or carrying many things? Is it possible to dive?

Air.   Smoke and fog can obscure the scene, but puzzles involving air are mainly about its absence. The lack of oxygen to breathe has featured in many games, not always through being underwater: 'Zork I' and 'Sorcerer' share a mine with poor air, 'Starcross' and 'Trinity' include locations in the vacuum of space. A scuba mask, space helmet or some other kind of breathing apparatus is called for. (Other gases simulated include helium, explosive hydrogen and laughing gas.) Can the protagonist speak, or eat, or listen, or taste while wearing this apparatus?

Earth.   Digging for buried treasure... the shovel can be found in just about every traditional-style game and a good many others which ought to know better besides. The problem is that the player may want to dig anywhere and everywhere, which the game will probably not want to implement: to dig may artificially create a new location, or a new map connection, or a new container – the hole left in the ground, that is. (The prologue to 'Infidel', though the least interesting part of the game from the point of view of playing, has a good implementation of digging through sand.)

Plants.   Vegetation fits into almost any landscape, and on the grounds of interactivity generally plays some part in the game, which is good for variety, because people deal differently with plants from machines and people. Undergrowth can be pulled away from something obscured, or useful plants picked. Trees and creeping plants ought to be climbable: players nearly always try.

Animals.   In many ways preferable to people, animals add a splash of colour, and what would the Garden of Eden have been without elephants, rabbits, leopards and guinea pigs? They move and behave in curious and obsessive ways, displaying what human characteristics they like but not needing to react to conversation or to show human curiosity or surprise at what happens. This makes them much easier to design, but it doesn't exempt them from characterisation. It's a little predictable to make the player feed an animal into obedience and then get it do something. (The bird in 'Advent' is nicely characterised, in that it is frightened by the rusty iron rod with a star on one end. 'Trinity' is positively overrun with animal life, with some critics having called its roadrunner the most important character.)

Monsters.   Many of the early adventure games included trolls, orcs and dragons, or else Frankenstein's Monster, Dracula and vampire bats: some, like 'Zork I', allow hack-and-slay combat in the style of a role-playing game like *Dungeons and Dragons*. Others, like the heavily infested and therefore somewhat repetitive 'Murdac' (Jonathan Partington, 1982), base all their puzzles on getting past or getting rid of things. "Getting past" occurs often because most monster puzzles are no more than doors with the decoration of slavering fangs. Even when monsters wander, they are generally dull because – being monsters – they have no unpredictable behaviour. Whereas the capacious underworld of the same author's 'Kingdom of Hamil' houses a baby hexapod (a what?) and a Conan Doyle-like Lost World of dinosaurs, which is much more the thing.

People.   So dawns the sixth day of creation: we have the mountains, rivers, plants and animals, but as yet no people. The nightmare of coding real characters is illustrated well by one of Dave Lebling's example bugs from 'Suspect' (1984):

```
>show corpse to michael
Michael doesn't appear interested.
```

The body is that of Veronica, Michael's wife. Objects representing people often take extensive code, perhaps five times that needed for even a complicated room, because they may need to react to events, follow instructions ("robot, go

390

south"), wander around the map and make conversation of sorts (the woman selling bread-crumbs in 'Trinity', who plays only a minor role, can say over 50 different things). Games with strongly-defined protagonists tend to have a stronger supporting cast, too:

> 'Christminster' does an exceptionally good job of outlining Christabel's role as a woman by limiting her actions (she can't enter chapel bareheaded) and through ... dialogue (the villains and the Master are condescending, while young Edward sees her as a confidante).

(Roger Giner-Sorolla.) What distinguishes a character from, say, a spanner is that it has an attitude to the protagonist. One model of this has the current attitude as a position in a "mood maze", with different moods being like locations and stimuli applied by the protagonist being like directions:

$$\text{Suspicious}$$
$$\downarrow \textit{reassure}$$
$$\text{Hungry} \quad \xrightarrow{feed} \quad \text{Grateful}$$

(Setting out in the "feed" direction from Suspicious leads nowhere, as the food is not accepted.) Such a person is no more than a plaything, entirely reactive and without memory, so most designers would want to conceal this fact by adding spontaneous or even random behaviour, startling the player from time to time. Or, of course, by simulating some memory of events. Adam Cadre's 'Varicella' (1999) handles conversation using around 450 flag variables to remember which questions have been asked and answered before. It also reformulates conversation. Here, the protagonist Varicella – as bad as the rest of them, Cadre having a rare gift for the amoral – encounters Miss Sierra, the King's mistress:

```
>ask sierra about king
```
"What can you tell me about the King?" you ask. "You seem to have known him better than anyone else..."
Miss Sierra scowls at you. "That had better not be an attempt at a personal question," she says. "If you're expecting a rhapsody about how he won my girlish heart, think again. ..."
```
>ask sierra about king
```
"Is there anything else you care to say about the King?" you ask.

Elsewhere, "ask guard about rico" can come out as "Is Rico in?", "ask queen about prince" as "How is Prince Charles?" and so on according to what would make sense in context. Such programming is exhausting but fruitful in a game placing great reliance on conversation.

391

Ropes and chains.   Are notoriously troublesome to implement consistently:

> [Someone will] say "Well, I've got this rope... how do I do a rope? It can be in two rooms at once if you tie it to something and take the end with you, and can you tie things up with it and drag them around with you?"
>
> Then we'll stop and think and say, "You don't want to have a rope in your game," and that makes it much easier for the new writers, you see.
>
> My new game ['The Lurking Horror'] has a chain in it, and it's even worse than a rope in almost every respect you can imagine and it's caused me no end of horror... the number of bugs that have come in on this chain alone would stack from here to there and back again.

(Dave Lebling again. But the chain puzzle in 'Lurking' is a masterstroke.) 'The Meteor, The Stone and a Long Glass of Sherbet' has a rope solving several puzzles whose source code runs to 300 lines of Inform, which is more than the whole "lily pond" region took: put another way, 5% of the entire code is occupied describing the rope. There is also a long ladder which is nearly as bad, and which the player is *not* allowed to tie the rope to.

Riddles.   Numerous games ('Beyond Zork', 'The Path to Fortune' (Jeff Cassidy and C. E. Forman, 1995)) include sphinxes or talking doors which pose riddles to passing strangers, and the writing of good riddles is an art form in itself. But who put these puzzle-obsessed doorkeepers there, and why? The knock-knock joke door in Irene Callaci's 'Mother Loose' (1998) sits much more happily, as the game is a wry mingling of nursery-rhyme stories for her six-year-old granddaughter (and indeed for the rest of us).

Decipherment.   Perhaps the most abstract and, if done well, the most satisfying of puzzles are those which present a system of coded messages, clues to the meaning of which are scattered across the game. 'Infidel' has hieroglyphics. 'Edifice' (Lucian Smith, 1997) requires the player to learn the language of Nalian, a puzzle which won considerable plaudits from players. But there are non-linguistic decipherments, too: in a sense the map of 'Spellbreaker' is itself a cipher. On a smaller scale, several Cambridge University games contain tricky cipher puzzles not unrelated to recreational mathematics. 'Avon', for instance, has a substitution code which is insoluble, but which it is possible to make partial deductions about: just enough to solve the problem at hand.

· · · · ·

Clues.   At least in one view of interactive fiction, clues are essential and the principle should be that an ideally perceptive player could win on his or her first attempt, without recourse to saved games: in particular, without knowledge of past lives or of future events. (The exact opposite, in fact, of what 'Brand

X' does. The player begins in a shop containing an aqualung, a cushion, a bunch of keys, a piece of sausage, a teabag and a sign declaring that "only two implements may be removed from this shop under penalty of death, so choose carefully".) Here are three clues which did not carry:

(1) In 'Dungeon Adventure', a pride of lions is carved over a doorway. Any player walking through falls into a lethal pit. Did you miss the clue?†

(2) The diamond maze in 'Zork II' is almost impossible to fathom unless (or even if) you are familiar with a certain multiple-innings team sport played only in America. In the words of even its designer: "always annoyed me... pretty lame."

(3) Almost every player of 'Advent' has considered the rock marked Y2 to be a decoy, emblematic of the mysterious cave. But it was meant as a clue: on the cave maps used by Will Crowther's group, "Y2" denoted a secondary cave entrance, which in a certain sense is what this location is.‡

(1) is a bad pun, (2) an unconscious assumption and (3) an in-joke. Games that are entirely in-jokes, like the subgenre of college campus simulations ('The Lurking Horror' features MIT, Infocom's alma mater) are at least deliberately so, but it is all too easy for designers to include familiar objects from their own lives into any game, and unconsciously assume that the player shares this familiarity. When that familiarity is needed to solve a puzzle, the game may become unplayable.

Luck and accidental solutions.   Small chance variations add to the fun, but only small ones. The thief in 'Zork I' seems to me to be just about right in this respect, and similarly the spinning room in 'Zork II', but a ten-ton weight which falls down and kills the player at a certain point in half of all games would simply irritate. A particular danger occurs with low-probability events, one or a combination of which might destroy the player's chances. For instance, in the earliest edition of 'Adventureland', the bees have an 8% chance of suffocation each turn carried in the bottle: one needs to carry them for 10 or 11 turns, giving the bees only a 40% chance of surviving to their destination.

Even in a puzzle with no element of luck, many problems are solved by accident or trial and error. (The notorious Bank of Zork puzzle in 'Zork II' has been understood by almost nobody who solved it.) This is unsatisfying for

---

† Pride comes before a fall.

‡ Several Cambridge University games, written by mathematicians, refer to "J4": 'Acheton', for instance, has a "J4 room" rather like the "Y2 rock room". The then-recent construction of the previously only hypothetical group J_4 had completed the classification theorem for finite simple groups, and was a departmental triumph. The sign "$\exists J_4$" remained above a doorframe for some years.

both player and designer, and some games take steps to try to avoid it. The gold-assaying puzzle in 'Spellbreaker' is such that a shrewd strategy will always succeed, but in principle even a random strategy *might* succeed. The game rigs the odds to ensure that it never does.

Optional, partial and multiple solutions.   Most designers like to give two or more different solutions to a few puzzles in a game: it seems more real, it means that even a winning player hasn't found all of the game's secrets and it makes a difficult puzzle easier. (There are seven ways to open the child-proof medicine bottle in 'Curses'.) Multiple solutions to the same puzzle need to be equally valid. The designer should not think of one solution as the "real" one, or allow another "short cut" one to skip critical plot events – this would short-change the player. On the other hand the designer must be relaxed about the inevitability that some part of his golden prose will never be seen whichever path the player takes. Most additional solutions are added in play-testing, but here is Brian Moriarty on 'Wishbringer' (1985):

> Most of the problems in the story have two or more solutions. The easy way out is to use Wishbringer. If a beginner gets frustrated, he can whip out the magic stone, mumble a wish and keep on playing. Experienced players can search for one of the logical solutions – a bit harder, perhaps, but more satisfying. It's possible to complete the story without using any of the stone's seven wishes. In fact, that's the only way to earn the full 100 points.
>
> The puzzles are highly interconnected. Once you start wishing your problems away, it's very hard to continue playing without relying more and more on the magic stone.   The impotence of idle wishing – that's the moral of 'Wishbringer'. All really good stories have a moral.

Analogous perhaps to the Wishbringer stone, 'Enchanter' has a one-use-only anti-magic spell. Although this solves one in particular of the more difficult puzzles, to use it up so early forfeits the game, since it is needed later. If you do fall into this trap, one of the ingenious dream sequences offers an oblique warning:

> You dream of climbing in an unfamiliar place. You seem to climb forever, beyond reason. A fleeting hope arises in you, and you search furiously in your spell book and possessions for something. After a moment, you become frantic as you realize that you don't have it! You bolt awake in a cold sweat.

Rewards.   What reward for solving a puzzle? One is obvious: the game state advances a little towards its completion. But the player at the keyboard needs a reward as well: that the game should offer something new to look at. The white cubes in 'Spellbreaker', with the power to teleport the protagonist to new areas, are far more alluring than, say, the "platinum pyramid" of 'Advent', which is only a noun with a few points attached and opens up no further map.

● **REFERENCES**

"[A puzzle] should be logical, according to the logic of the game's universe. In a fantasy game, a puzzle can rely on magic, but the magic must be consistent throughout the game. A puzzle should be original in some way, not just a rehash of an earlier puzzle with different objects." (Steve Meretzky). "My basic principle of designing puzzles is that the player should always know what he's trying to accomplish. Metaphorically, a player should always be able to find a locked door before he finds the key" (Mike Roberts in the *TADS* manual). "In all cases, after a particularly arduous puzzle, reward the player with a few simpler ones" (C. E. Forman, *XYZZYnews* 1). "Err on the side of easy. (He said, waiting to be struck dead for hypocrisy.)" (Andrew Plotkin). "There's definitely a difference between 'satisfying' and 'pertinent'." (Lucian Smith. These last quotations from the round-table discussion on puzzles in *XYZZYnews* 14.)   ●For more on the invented language in 'Edifice', see 'Parlez-Vous Nalian' in *XYZZYnews* 16.

§51   The room description

When beginning to code a design, it is tempting to give rooms temporary descriptions ("Slab room." "Cloister."), and leave the writing for later. There is no more depressing point than facing a pile of 50 room descriptions to write, all at once, and feeling that one's enthusiasm has altogether gone. (The same applies to making an over-detailed design before doing any coding.) Besides, when testing the rooms concerned, one has no feeling of what the game will look like except tatty, and this is also depressing. Also, writing room descriptions forces the designer to think about what the room is ultimately for. So most designers like to write a few at a time, as coding goes on, but to write them properly: and edit later for consistency and second thoughts.

In any room description there are usually one to three essentials to get across, and the rest is better cut or relegated to text appearing only if the player chooses to examine something in particular. Even the most tedious junctions deserve description, however, and description is more than a list of exits. Here is 'Advent' at its most graceful:

Shell Room
You're in a large room carved out of sedimentary rock. The floor and walls are littered with bits of shells embedded in the stone. A shallow passage proceeds downward, and a somewhat steeper one leads up. A low hands and knees passage enters from the south.
In Limestone Passage
You are walking along a gently sloping north/south passage lined with oddly shaped limestone formations.

Note the geology, the slight unevenness of the ground and the variation in the size of the tunnels. Nothing happens here, but it seems a real place.

Flippant room descriptions are best avoided if they will be often revisited. Subtler humour is more durable:

On the wall by the bed is a slightly curved, full-length mirror. You reflect upon this for a while.

(From the Cambridge University game 'Xenophobia' (Jonathan Mestel, 1989). This wording is also neat in that it applies equally well on the tenth visit to a location as on the first, whereas text like "Astonished to see a mirror, you leap back..." would not.) About once in a game an author can get away with something like this:

Observation Room
Calvin Coolidge once described windows as "rectangles of glass." If so, he may have been thinking about the window which fills the western wall of this room. A tiny closet lies to the north. A sign is posted next to the stairs which lead both upwards and downwards.

A characteristic piece of Steve Meretzky† from 'Leather Goddesses of Phobos', demonstrating the lengths one has to go to when faced with a relentlessly ordinary junction-with-window. The sentence Meretzky is at pains to avoid is "You can go up, down or north." With care it is even possible to remove mention of a room's exits altogether, but only if the information is presented in some other way. For instance:

Dark Cave
Little light seeps into this muddy, bone-scattered cave and always you long for fresh air. Strange bubbles, pulsing and shifting as if alive, hang upon the rock at crazy, irregular angles.
Black crabs scuttle about your feet.
>south
The only exit is back out north to the sea-shore.

Here, the "You can't go that way" message for the room has taken up the slack.

Experienced players know all of the various formulae used in room descriptions by heart: "You're in", "You are in", "This is", "You have come to" and so forth. This, perhaps, is why some designers prefer impersonal room descriptions, not mentioning "you" unless to say something other than the obvious fact of being present. Once into the text then, as in all writing, vocabulary counts. If there is a tree, of what species? If a chair, of what style? ('Cutthroats' (Mike Berlyn and Jerry Wolper, 1984) describes a cupboard of no particular interest as a "lopsided wooden dresser" for the sake of painting the scene.) Room descriptions should not always describe static, fixed things, should bring in senses other than sight and should not always be monochrome. Plainness and repetition are to be avoided at almost any cost:

You're on a winding drive outside a magnificent door. Exits are west to a woodshed, upwards to a vine and in through a door. You can see a vine.
>west

---

† But Meretzky was not always as corny as his reputation. Influenced by 'Suspended', which he had play-tested and later called "probably the most interesting and daringly different game Infocom ever did", he used a virtual reality theme to construct almost the only work of early IF to contain serious political themes: 'A Mind Forever Voyaging' (1985).

> You're in a woodshed in the swamp. Exits are east to a winding drive and
> west to a herb garden. You can see a candle and a woodpile.

('The Price of Magik', BBC Micro version – in the Amiga version of the later
'Time and Magik Trilogy' re-release, the winding drive description ran to
an eighty-word essay, and did away entirely with the mechanically-generated
"exits are" sentence.) So much for what is bad. The following, from 'Advent'
again, is something much more dangerous: the mediocre room description.

> *Whirlpool Room*
> You are in a magnificent cavern with a rushing stream, which cascades over a
> sparkling waterfall into a roaring whirlpool which disappears through a hole
> in the floor. Passages exit to the south and west.

This seems a decent enough try, but no novelist would write like this. Each
important noun – "cavern", "stream", "waterfall", "whirlpool" – has its
own adjective – "magnificent", "rushing", "sparkling", "roaring". The two
"which" clauses in a row are a little unhappy. "Cascades" is good, but does
a stream cascade "over" a waterfall? Does a whirlpool itself disappear? The
"hole in the floor" seems incongruous. Surely it must be underwater, indeed
deep underwater? Come to that, the geography could be better used, which
would also help to place the whirlpool within the cave (is it in the middle? on
one edge?). And why "Whirlpool Room", which sounds like one of the perks
of a health club? Here is a second draft:

> *Whirlpool Ledge*
> The path runs a quarter-circle from south to west around a broken ledge
> of this funnel cavern. A waterfall drops out of the darkness, catching the
> lamplight as it cascades into the basin. Rapid currents whip into a roaring
> whirlpool below.

Even so, there is nothing man-made, nothing alive, no colour and besides it
seems to miss the essential feature of all the mountain water-caves I've ever
been to, so let us add a second paragraph (with a line break, which is easier on
the eye):

> Blue-green algae hangs in clusters from the old guard-railing, which has
> almost rusted clean through in the frigid, soaking air.

The algae and the guard-rail offer possibilities. Perhaps there are frogs who
could eat insect-eggs in the algae, or perhaps the player might find a use for
iron oxide, and could scrape rust from the railing. Certainly the railing should
break if a rope is tied to it. Is it safe to dive in? Does the water have a hypnotic
effect on someone staring into it? Is there anything dry which would become
damp if the player brought it through here? Might there be a second ledge
higher up where the stream falls into the cave?

△ Lack of variety comes in many forms. Brian Howarth's eleven "Mysterious Adventures" games written for the Scott Adams game engine invent some interesting milieux ('Feasibility Experiment' (1982), with objects like "Vague Shapes", is worth a look) but they are highly repetitive and difficult to tell apart. The main weakness of 'Enchanter' is a sparse, location-heavy map, especially in the prologue, where many rooms over-describe their neighbours. Slightly at odds with the traditional dungeon elsewhere, 'Enchanter' blends in horror tableaux: dead grass "seems to grip at your feet", a demon statue "seems to reach towards you". There's a lot of "seeming" motion, because the deserted, blasted landscape is largely static: "listless waves barely stir the flotsam and jetsam" sums it up only too well. The outcome would have been mediocre had the puzzles in the game not been exceptionally good, and a few of the interior locations appealing. Here is a fine example of the interior room as vista, overlooking a landscape and drawing together the whole game's map:

Map Room
This room in the high tower appears to be a map room, with hundreds of ancient maps covering the walls. A huge globe, made of gold, sits on a pedestal in the center of the room. Through the tower windows can be seen a vast forest stretching out to the northeast and the sea, covered in fog, to the east and south. Stairs to the south lead to the bottom of the tower.

. . . . .

It is a vexed question just how much land occupies a single location. Usually a location represents a single room, perhaps ten yards across at the most. Really large chambers are usually given several locations, so that a ballroom might be divided into corners with names like "Ballroom Northwest" and "Ballroom Southwest". The "huge cave about 3,000 feet across" of 'Acheton' occupies no less than 16 locations, which although it conveys a sense of space can also seem repetitious and wasteful.

At the other extreme it is sometimes necessary for a single location to do duty for a great swathe of ground, especially out of doors, where drawing the map can leave one with the same frustration as the set-designer for a Wagnerian opera: everything indistinct and without edges. 'Spellbreaker', under tight constraints on locations, includes one-location meadows and volcanos. The reverse position is taken by the distinctive and plausible 'Gateway to Karos' (Derek Haslam, 1984). Locations are superimposed in a square map-like grid onto the rivers, cliffs, forest and so forth of the island of Karos, so that each location represents perhaps one square kilometer:

Eastlands
You are in a cluster of roofless, abandoned buildings, apparently part of an ore-washing mill. A dry water-channel runs northward, and a path leads west.

399

A garden spade, well used but still strong and sharp, lies abandoned here.

(About a dozen neighbouring locations share the short name "Eastlands".) A middle position between 'Spellbreaker' and 'Gateway to Karos' is taken by 'She's Got a Thing For a Spring' (1997), an evocation by the nature photographer Brent VanFossen of the mountains of northwest America. Almost an interactive postcard, this thoroughly appealing game features elks, mooses, eagles and so forth, but is equally vivid with terrain and vegetation:

> *Granite Canyon*
> You're on a shelf overlooking a small canyon, apparently carved by the nearby stream and 20 or 30 feet deep. A rocky path enters from the west beside a tangle of blackberries, and dead ends at a ledge overlooking the stream below. Above you, granite walls continue to rise, the pink stones a beautiful contrast to the clear blue sky. An animal trail leads up, too steep to walk, but you might be able to make it in a scramble.
> Beside you stands a small tower supporting one end of a steel cable.
> The end of a spruce branch is just barely visible deep inside the blackberries.

A single location can also substitute for an infinite expanse, such as the Neverending Lane of 'Jinxter'.

Another consideration in outdoor locations is that the slow process of sunrise and sunset ought to affect room descriptions. 'Christminster' organises time so as to keep the player indoors between seven and ten p.m. so that only two states are needed, full day and full night. 'A Mind Forever Voyaging' derives most of its impact from its depiction of the same city decaying in ten-year stages, as it rolls forward in history like H. G. Wells's classic (and classically filmed) novel *Things To Come*. The definitive shifting-description game of recent years is Andrew Plotkin's 'A Change in the Weather' (1995):

> You're standing on a ledge, on a rather steep, overgrown hillface. Greenery hides the stream below and the hilltop above, and the meadows and sky beyond sweep away into the incandescent west.

> You're standing on a ledge, on a rather steep, overgrown hillface. Rain hides the stream below and the hilltop above, and to the west is only dark.

Descriptions alter not just through time passing, but also because of differences in perspective. Still the most remarkable example is the 'Suspended' complex, which a player in suspended animation controls through robots with different sensory perceptions. Here is the same place from four points of view:

> I'm in a large room which looks like the inside of a globe. The walls seem sculptured with wiring, swirling around the room's perimeter, leading into a tall column. The column itself has a door on its face. Doorways lead to the west, south, east and northeast.

Sonar indicates a large, spherical open area with a hollow column running from floor to ceiling. The column reflects sonar evenly indicating no distinguishing external characteristics.

All around me charges flow, shaped by the very nature of this room. The electrons are being channeled into an electrical column, central to this environment.

A small humming can be detected from a column which extends from floor to ceiling.

Another device, used in the spy thriller 'Border Zone' (Marc Blank, 1987), is to respond to directions not with a description of the new location but with a response about how you got there:

>east
You open the door and walk out into the passageway. You scan the passageway, noting guards at either end, machine guns poised at their sides. You don't remember them from the beginning of the trip, so you can only suppose that security has been tightened in the search for the American agent.

>look
Outside Your Compartment
You are standing in the passageway that runs along the length of the car. At either end of the passageway, a guard is standing, machine gun poised at his side. Right now, you're standing outside your own compartment.

● **REFERENCES**
Mike Berlyn (*XYZZYnews* 17) groups the issues here under the headings Size/Scope, Ceilings, Floor/Ground, Walls, Lighting and Mood ("a depressed person is not likely to have yellow-and-red throw pillows": oh?).   ●Gerry Kevin Wilson offers three don'ts for room descriptions: "1. Don't mention a player's actions in a description. 2. Don't mention moveable objects in a description. 3. Don't exceed one screenful of text in a description."   ●"Very often, a map or the plan of a building can suggest a plot element that no amount of abstract thought could generate." (Gil and Beryl Williamson, in *Computer Adventures – The Secret Art.*)   ●Wisest of all, perhaps: "It's awful to sit down and think, 'I've got to write fifty room descriptions today, and each one of them has to be clear, crisp and vivid while conveying exactly the information I want it to convey' " (Gareth Rees, Usenet posting, 7/6/94). Don't write them all at once.

§52 Finishing

"[A game in alpha-testing has] on the order of 4,000 bugs. Maybe fifty percent are spelling and punctuation errors, extra spaces, missing blank lines, and so on. Maybe one percent are crashes."

"I try to make sure that the sun is in the right position, or if you're in outer space the sun and moon are where they're supposed to be – stuff like that... The wooden beam [in 'Infidel'] is described as being a certain length and width, and I calculated that it would have to weigh 500 pounds."

— Max Buxton and Gary Brennan (Infocom play-testers), 1987

 So the game is built: the wood is rough and splintered, but it's recognisably a game. There is still a good month's work to do, easier work if less creative, and beyond that a good deal of drudgery to fix bug after bug after bug.† The first post-design task is to sort out the scoring system, usually awarding points out of some pleasingly round number and dividing them into rankings. Here is 'Zork II':

Beginner (0), Amateur Adventurer (40), Novice Adventurer (80), Junior Adventurer (160), Adventurer (240), Master (320), Wizard (360), Master Adventurer (400)

This is disappointingly bland, and a more pleasing tradition is to name ranks for the player's profession in the game – so that an orchestral musician might begin as Triangle and rise through Second Violinist to Conductor. (In 'Sherlock', the lowest rank – corresponding to zero achievement – is Chief Superintendent of Scotland Yard.) Among the questions to ask are: will every winner of the game necessarily score exactly 400 out of 400? (This can be difficult to arrange if even small acts are scored.) Will everyone entering the end game already

---

† Dave Lebling starts work in the morning: "Even a cup of yummy coffee won't improve things when you see 'page 1 of 12' on the first bug report form." Many good-natured pieces about testing appear in Infocom's publicity newspapers. At best, it was enormous fun, and Liz Cyr-Jones's testing department made a lively and exhilarating summer job. But there were also tensions. The tester who wrote that 12-page form saw it not as dismaying but as the proud result of a job well done. It could be frustrating that the bugs would be fixed at random intervals, or not at all, while revised versions of the game would sometimes arrive without any clear indication of what had altered. Brian Moriarty redesigned great swathes of game at the last minute, and the fact that he had always said he would did not make this any less maddening.

have a score of 360, and so have earned the title "Wizard"? Will the rank "Amateur" correspond exactly to having got out of the prologue and into the middle game?

Unless the scoring system is worked out and the game can pass its entire transcript of the "winning" solution without crashing or giving absurd replies, it is too soon to go into play-testing.

△ Scoring systems vary greatly. 'Adventure Quest' is scored "out of about 6,000", and exemplifies the pinball-machine-like tendency to offer points by 5s, 10s or 100s. Other games feel that one puzzle is one point, or award percentages, and still others frown on score altogether because "that's not how life works". In 'Moonmist', scores are described thus: "[Well, so far you've met Lord Jack and all of the guests, washed up from your trip... but you haven't found the hidden treasure nor enough evidence nor identified the ghost!]". In 'Zork III', the player's "potential" is given out of 7, corresponding to which of seven challenges have been encountered (so that a score of 7 does not mean the game is over). In 'The Lurking Horror', 20 major puzzles are awarded 5 points apiece for a maximum of 100: the 20th puzzle is to win the game. In some ports of 'Advent' 1 point is awarded for each room visited for the first time, and 1 for never having saved the game, a mean trick, plus the infamous "Last Lousy Point", awarded without any clue for dropping a particular object in a particular place, an irrelevant act achieving nothing. (People used to have to disassemble the mainframe game to discover this.)

. . . . .

During the writing and maintenance of 'Christminster', Gareth Rees kept a log of all 475 modifications prompted by play-testers and players. This log is archived with the game's source code at ftp.gmd.de and makes an interesting case study. 224 reports requested additional interactivity and responses, often to reasonable but wrong guesses made by the player. A further 86 arose from incorrect responses or inconsistencies, 32 from typographical errors and 79 from mistakes in computer programming, for instance in the game's complicated algorithms to handle telephony and the mixing of liquids.

At every stage in writing an interactive fiction it is easy to lapse into the habit of writing an uninteractive one. A designer who has written a linear story and then introduced some puzzles may imagine that the literary style and effect of the game comes from the text originally written, but that isn't altogether true: most of the player's time at the keyboard is spent trying the wrong thing, so most of the player's experience of the game lies in how it deals with wrong guesses. This means that it's essential to respond to as many of attempts as possible, acknowledging that the player has made honest attempts, and so helping to form a sort of relationship:

In the aquarium is a baby sea-serpent who eyes you suspiciously. His scaly
body writhes about in the huge tank.
>take serpent
He takes you instead. *Uurrp!*

This is from 'Zork II', a program which is at least twice the size of 'Advent'
in spite of implementing a much smaller design. Almost all of that disparity is
due to its generous stock of responses. Similarly, 'Zork I' contains possibly the
first examples of alternative solutions to puzzles (the cyclops can be defeated
in two different ways, as can the Loud Room). If a play-tester can think of a
reasonable solution to which the game does not respond, it is worth considering
a redesign of the puzzle to allow both solutions. Even if not, a response should
be made which acknowledges that the player has made a good guess.

. . . . .

Bugs in interactive fiction are individually puny, yet daunting by their number,
like a column of army ants. Just as the 'Christminster' log (see above) gives an
idea of routine testing, so Graeme Cree's catalogue of bugs in released Infocom
games (at www.xyzzynews.com) shows what can slip through the most rigorous
testing regime. Here are some common types of bug:

- Slips of punctuation, spelling or grammar: for instance, "a orange". Infocom's
  games are quite clean in this respect, in part because an experienced editor of
  books, John Prince, proof-read their text. (The Inform compiler allows a designer
  to extract all the text of a game for spell-checking.)
- Rooms being dark when they ought to be light (which tends not to show if the
  designer habitually carries a lamp when testing), or not changing their state of
  light/darkness when they should: as for instance when a skylight opens, or when the
  sun sets, or when the candles in 'Zork I' are blown out. In 'Sherlock' (21/871214)
  an expert player can cross fog-bound London without a lamp, exploiting various
  items and places which turn out to have (undescribed) light.
- Secondary properties of an object neglected: such as a fish being marked as edible,
  or a door as fixed in place.† 'Starcross' (15/820901) neglected to mark a light
  beam as being inanimate, so that the player could get rid of it by typing "beam,
  go west".
- Map connections missed or mismatching. In 'Suspended' (8/840521), the corridor
  northeast from East End to Alpha FC has no connection back southwest: the
  designer simply forgot to make one.
- Something which ought to happen only once being possible more than once: such
  as the breaking of a window, or a character greeting the player as a stranger. The
  only known bug in any release of 'Wishbringer' (68/850501) allowed the player

---

† It wasn't until the fifth proofs of §12 of this manual that any of us noticed that the
"great stone slab" altar of 'Ruins' had never been made static.

to take back a spent gold coin and spend it again, gaining ever more points *ad infinitum.*

- Failing to properly revise the state of the game after a major event. In 'Deadline' (18/820311), Ms Dunbar was sometimes able to appear even after her death and, indeed, to be present in the same room as her dead body.
- Small illogicalities: messages such as "The ball bounces on the ground and returns to your hand." in mid-air or while wading through a ford; or being able to swim with a suit of armour on, or wave the coat you're wearing, or eat while wearing a gas mask. In 'Hollywood Hijinx' (37/861215), you can empty a bucket of water while swimming underwater.
- Failing to check that necessary objects are actually present when the player tries by implication to use them. In 'The Witness' (22/840924), you can "get a drink" anywhere in the game.
- Containers with surreal abilities: such as a purse which can hold a stepladder, or a candle whose flame remains lit, or a book which can still be read even when stowed away inside a rucksack. Infocom's struggle with the 'Zork' container bug has passed into legend. Numerous cases were attended to, but in all eleven releases of 'Zork I' you can still put the raft in the coffin, and then the coffin in the raft, causing both to vanish.
- Forgotten names: for instance 'Planetfall' (20/830708) forgot to allow the player to call the microbe monster "microbe".
- Inadequate namings: in 'Deadline' (19/820427) the bathroom door on the first floor was impossible to open because the game called it simply "door", but with a closet door in the same location, an ambiguity arose which nothing the player could type would resolve.
- Actual bugs in code intended to extend the game's simulation of the world, and especially with ropes and liquids: in 'Infidel' (22/830916) filling the chalice when it is already full results in the text "The silver chalice is filled with water. The silver chalice is empty."

. . . . .

The days of play-testing are harrowing. Dave Lebling again, on 'Suspect':

>bartender, give me a drink
"Sorry, I've been hired to mix drinks and that's all."

>dance with alicia
Which Alicia do you mean, Alicia or the overcoat?

Veronica's body is slumped behind the desk, strangled with a lariat.
>talk to veronica
Veronica's body is listening.

("Little bugs, you know? Things no one would notice. At this point the tester's job is fairly easy. The story is like a house of cards – it looks pretty solid but the slightest touch collapses it.")

Good play-testers are worth their weight in gold. Their first contribution is to try things in a systematically perverse way. To quote Michael Kinyon, whose effect may be felt almost everywhere in the present author's games,

> A tester with a new verb is like a kid with a hammer; every problem seems like a nail.

And here is Neil deMause, on one of his play-testers:

> He has an odd compulsion, when he plays IF games, to close doors behind him. It's a bizarre fastidiousness, not even remotely useful for an IF player, but I love him for it, because he has uncovered bugs in this way that I never would have found.

Games substantially grow in play-testing, and come alive. Irene Callaci's acknowledgements could speak for all designers:

> I thought perhaps beta testing might reveal a couple of odd, off-the-wall commands that weren't implemented, or maybe a typo here and there, or possibly an adjective or two I had forgotten. Not! I wasn't even close to being finished, and I didn't even know it. 'Mother Loose' grew from 151K to 199K during the beta testing period alone. Looking back now, if I had released 'Mother Loose' when I thought it was ready, I would have crawled under a rock from embarrassment. Thank you, thank you, thank you to all my beta testers.

More is true even than this: the play-tester is to interactive fiction as the editor is to the novel, and should be credited and acknowledged as such. Major regions of 'Curses' and 'Jigsaw' were thrown out politely but firmly by my own play-testers as being substandard or unsuitable.† A radical response to the play-tester's doubts is almost always better than papering over cracks.

After a first pass by one or two play-testers, and a consequent redrafting exercise, the game can go to beta testing at the hands of perhaps six or seven volunteers, who come to it fresh and treat it more as an entertainment and less as an unexploded bomb. (At one time Infocom used two phases of beta-testing, sometimes involving as many as 200 volunteers, even after pre-alpha and alpha-testing in house.) It is wise to insist on reports in writing or email, or some concrete form, and to ask for a series of reports, one at a time, rather than waiting a month for an epic list of bugs. It can be useful for play-testers to keep transcripts of their sessions with the game, and send them verbatim, because these transcripts are eloquent of how difficult or easy the puzzles are and which wrong guesses are tried. In its debugging version, 'Jigsaw' provided a verb called "bug" purely to help players type comments into such a transcript:

---

† Similarly, the published source code to 'Christminster' contains "offcuts" such as a pulley-and-rope puzzle in the clock tower.

```
>bug Miss Shutes is known as he
Oh dear.
>bug The corn bread isn't edible
Is that so?
```

It is worth keeping in touch with play-testers to ensure that they are not utterly stuck because of a bug or an unreasonable puzzle, but it's important to give no hints unless they are asked for.

.   .   .   .   .

A game is never finished, only abandoned. There is always one more bug, or one more message which could be improved, or one more wry response to drop in. Debugging is a creative process, even beyond the initial release, and games commonly have four to ten revisions in their first couple of years in play.

In the end, of course, the designer walks away. Almost all the pre-1990 designers cited in the bibliography are still alive, but few are still designing, and they often speak of their games as something fun but belonging to another time in their lives: something they feel faintly self-conscious about, perhaps, something that they did years ago: when they were in high school, when their kids were young, when they did a little testing for Infocom, when computers were less visual, when it was the state of the art, when the Ph.D. was at an impasse. But if twenty-five years is an epoch in computing, it is not a long time in the history of art, and the early designers remain a presence in a genre which is younger and less settled than sometimes appears. Once in a while Scott Adams causes a *frisson* by throwing a remark into a newsgroup mostly read by designers to whom he seems a historical figure coeval with Scott of the Antarctic. Can such a man really have an email address?

In a recent radio broadcast (1999), Douglas Adams said that the great enjoyability of working on his games with Infocom was having fun with a new medium before it became an art form and had serious articles written about it. (Which pretty much puts this chapter in its place.) But that original fascination dies hard, and the first and happiest discovery of anyone researching into interactive fiction is that designers past are only too pleased to be rediscovered, and willing to go to great trouble – hunting through archives, attics and obsolete equipment – to see that their games can be trodden again.

An adventure game can be one of the most satisfying of works to have written: perhaps because one can always polish it a little further, perhaps because it has hidden and secret possibilities. But perhaps too because something is made as well as written: and once made can never be unmade, so that there will always be a small brick building by the end of the road, and in it there will always be keys, food, a bottle and the lamp.

Appendices

§A1 Library attributes

absent	A 'floating object' (one with a found_in property, which can appear in many different rooms) which is absent will in future no longer appear in the game. Note that you cannot make a floating object disappear merely by giving it absent, but must explicitly remove it as well.
animate	"Is alive (human or animal)." Can be spoken to in "richard, hello" style; matches the creature token in grammar; picks up "him" or "her" (according to gender) rather than "it", likewise "his"; an object the player is changed into becomes animate; some messages read "on whom", etc., instead of "on which"; can't be taken; its subobjects "belong to" it rather than "are part of" it; messages don't assume it can be "touched" or "squeezed" as an ordinary object can; the actions Attack, ThrowAt are diverted to life rather than rejected as being 'futile violence'.
clothing	"Can be worn."
concealed	"Concealed from view but present." The player object has this; an object which was the player until ChangePlayer happened loses this property; a concealed door can't be entered; does not appear in room descriptions.
container	Affects scope and light; object lists recurse through it if open (or transparent); may be described as closed, open, locked, empty; a possession will give it a LetGo action if the player tries to remove it, or a Receive if something is put in; things can be taken or removed from it, or inserted into it, but only if it is open; likewise for "transfer" and "empty"; room descriptions describe using when_open or when_closed if given; if there is no defined description, an Examine causes the contents to be searched (i.e. written out) rather than a message "You see nothing special about..."; Search only reveals the contents of containers, otherwise saying "You find nothing". *Note:* an object cannot be both a container and a supporter.
door	"Is a door or bridge." Room descriptions describe using when_open or when_closed if given; and an Enter action becomes a Go action. If a Go has to go through this object, then: if concealed, the player "can't go that way"; if not open, then the player is told either that this cannot be ascended or descended (if the player tried "up" or "down"), or that it is in the way (otherwise); but if neither, then its door_to property is

408

consulted to see where it leads; finally, if this is zero, then it is said to "lead nowhere" and otherwise the player actually moves to the location.

edible
"Can be eaten" (and thus removed from game).

enterable
Affects scope and light; only an enterable on the floor can be entered. If an enterable is also a container then it can only be entered or exited if it is open.

female
This object has a feminine name. In games written in English, this makes her a female person, though in other languages it might be inanimate. The parser uses this information when considering pronouns like "her". (In English, anything animate is assumed to be male unless female or neuter is set.)

general
A general-purpose attribute, defined by the library but never looked at or altered by it. Available for designers to use if they choose to do so.

light
"Is giving off light." (See §19.) Also: the parser understands "lit", "lighted", "unlit" using this; inventories will say "(providing light)" of it, and so will room descriptions if the current location is ordinarily dark; it will never be automatically put away into the player's SACK_OBJECT, as it might plausibly be inflammable or the main light source.

lockable
Can be locked or unlocked by a player holding its key object, which is given by the property with_key; if a container and also locked, may be called "locked" in inventories.

locked
Can't be opened. If a container and also lockable, may be called "locked" in inventories.

male
This object has a masculine name. In games written in English, this makes him a male person, though in other languages it might be inanimate. The parser uses this information when considering pronouns like "him". (In English, anything animate is assumed to be male unless female or neuter is set.)

moved
"Has been or is being held by the player." Objects (immediately) owned by the player after Initialise has run are given it; at the end of each turn, if an item is newly held by the player and is scored, it is given moved and OBJECT_SCORE points are awarded; an object's initial message only appears in room descriptions if it is unmoved.

neuter
This object's name is neither masculine nor feminine. (In English, anything without animate is assumed neuter, because only people and higher animals have gender. Anything animate is assumed male unless female or neuter is set. A robot, for instance, might be an animate object worth making neuter.)

on
"Switched on." A switchable object with on is described by with_on in room descriptions; it will be called "switched on" by Examine.

open
"Open door or container." Affects scope and light; lists (such as inventories) recurse through an open container; if a container, called

"open" by some descriptions; things can be taken or removed from an open container; similarly inserted, transferred or emptied. A container can only be entered or exited if it is both enterable and open. An open door can be entered. Described by when_open in room descriptions.

openable   Can be opened or closed, unless locked.

pluralname   This single object's name is in the plural. For instance, an object called "seedless grapes" should have pluralname set. The library will then use the pronoun "them" and the indefinite article "some" automatically.

proper   Its short name is a proper noun, and never preceded by "the" or "The". The player's object must have this (so something changed into will be given it).

scenery   Not listed by the library in room descriptions; "not portable" to be taken; "you are unable to" pull, push, or turn it.

scored   The player gets OBJECT_SCORE points for picking it up for the first time; or, if a room, ROOM_SCORE points for visiting it for the first time.

static   "Fixed in place" if player tries to take, remove, pull, push or turn it.

supporter   "Things can be put on top of it." Affects scope and light; object lists recurse through it; a possession will give it a LetGo action if the player tries to remove it, or a Receive if something is put in; things can be taken or removed from it, or put on it; likewise for transfers; a player inside it is said to be "on" rather than "in" it; room descriptions list its contents in separate paragraphs if it is itself listed. *Note:* an object cannot be both a container and a supporter.

switchable   Can be switched on or off; listed as such by Examine; described using when_on or when_off in room descriptions.

talkable   Player can talk to this object in "thing, do this" style. This is useful for microphones and the like, when animate is inappropriate.

transparent   "Contents are visible." Affects scope and light; a transparent container is treated as if it were open for printing of contents.

visited   "Has been or is being visited by the player." Given to a room immediately after a Look first happens there: if this room is scored then ROOM_SCORE points are awarded. Affects whether room descriptions are abbreviated or not.

workflag   Temporary flag used by Inform internals, also available to outside routines; can be used to select items for some lists printed by WriteList-From.

worn   "Item of clothing being worn." Should only be an object being immediately carried by player. Affects inventories; doesn't count towards the limit of MAX_CARRIED; won't be automatically put away into the SACK_OBJECT; a Drop action will cause a Disrobe action first; so will PutOn or Insert.

Note. The only library attributes which it's useful to apply to locations are `light`, `scored` and `visited`.

§A2 Library properties

The following table lists every library-defined property. The banner headings give the name, what type of value makes sense and the default value (if other than 0). The symbol ⊕ means "this property is additive" so that inherited values from class definitions pile up into a list, rather than wipe each other out. Recall that `false` is the value 0 and `true` the value 1.

`n_to, s_to, e_to, w_to, ...` *Room, object or routine*

For rooms These twelve properties (there are also `ne_to`, `nw_to`, `se_to`, `sw_to`, `in_to`, `out_to`, `u_to` and `d_to`) are the map connections for the room. A value of 0 means "can't go this way". Otherwise, the value should either be a room or a door object: thus, `e_to` might be set to `crystal_bridge` if the direction "east" means "over the crystal bridge".

Routine returns The room or object the map connects to; or 0 for "can't go this way"; or 1 for "can't go this way; stop and print nothing further".

Warning Do not confuse the direction properties `n_to` and so on with the twelve direction objects, `n_obj` et al.

`add_to_scope` *List of objects or routine*

For objects When this object is in scope (unless it was itself only placed in scope by `PlaceInScope`) so are all those listed, or all those nominated by the routine. A routine given here should call `PlaceInScope(obj)` to put `obj` in scope.

No return value

`after` *Routine* NULL ⊕

Receives actions after they have happened, but before the player has been told of them.

For rooms All actions taking place in this room.

For objects All actions for which this object is noun (the first object specified in the command); and all fake actions for it.

Routine returns `false` to continue (and tell the player what has happened), `true` to stop here (printing nothing).

The `Search` action is a slightly special case. Here, `after` is called when it is clear that it would be sensible to look inside the object (e.g., it's an open container in a light room) but before the contents are described.

`article` *String or routine* `"a"`

For objects Indefinite article for object or routine to print one.

No return value

`articles` *Array of strings*

For objects: If given, these are the articles used with the object's name. (Provided for non-English languages where irregular nouns may have unusual vowel-contraction rules with articles: e.g., with French non-mute 'H'.)

before	*Routine* NULL ⊕

Receives advance warning of actions (or fake actions) about to happen.

For rooms All actions taking place in this room.

For objects All actions for which this object is noun (the first object specified in the command); and all fake actions, such as Receive and LetGo if this object is the container or supporter concerned.

Routine returns false to continue with the action, true to stop here (printing nothing). First special case: A vehicle object receives the Go action if the player is trying to drive around in it. In this case:

Routine returns 0 to disallow as usual; 1 to allow as usual, moving vehicle and player; 2 to disallow but do (and print) nothing; 3 to allow but do (and print) nothing. If you want to move the vehicle in your own code, return 3, not 2: otherwise the old location may be restored by subsequent workings.

Second special case: in a PushDir action, the before routine must call AllowPushDir() and then return true in order to allow the attempt (to push an object from one room to another) to succeed.

cant_go	*String or routine* "You can't go that way."

For rooms Message, or routine to print one, when a player tries to go in an impossible direction from this room.

No return value

capacity	*Number or routine* 100

For objects Number of objects a container or supporter can hold.

For the player-object Number of things the player can carry (when the player is this object); the default player object (selfobj) has capacity initially set to the constant MAX_CARRIED.

daemon	*Routine*

This routine is run each turn, once it has been activated by a call to StartDaemon, and until stopped by a call to StopDaemon.

describe	*Routine* NULL ⊕

For objects Called when the object is to be described in a room description, before any paragraph break (i.e., skipped line) has been printed. A sometimes useful trick is to print nothing in this routine and return true, which makes an object 'invisible'.

For rooms Called before a room's long ("look") description is printed.

Routine returns false to describe in the usual way, true to stop printing here.

description	*String or routine*

For objects The Examine message, or a routine to print one out.

For rooms The long ("look") description, or a routine to print one out.

No return value

413

---

door_dir   *Direction property or routine*

For compass objects   When the player tries to go in this direction, e.g., by typing the name of this object, then the map connection tried is the value of this direction property for the current room. For example, the n_obj "north" object normally has door_dir set to n_to.

For objects   The direction that this door object goes via (for instance, a bridge might run east, in which case this would be set to e_to).

Routine returns   The direction property to try.

---

door_to   *Room or routine*

For objects   The place this door object leads to. A value of 0 means "leads nowhere".

Routine returns   The room. Again, 0 (or false) means "leads nowhere". Further, 1 (or true) means "stop the movement action immediately and print nothing further".

---

each_turn   *String or routine*   NULL   ⊕

String to print, or routine to run, at the end of each turn in which the object is in scope (after all timers and daemons for that turn have been run).

No return value

---

found_in   *List of rooms or routine*

This object will be found in all of the listed rooms, or if the routine says so, unless it has the attribute absent. If an object in the list is not a room, it means "present in the same room as this object".

Routine returns   true to be present, otherwise false. The routine can look at the current location in order to decide.

Warning   This property is only looked at when the player changes rooms.

---

grammar   *Routine*

For animate *or* talkable *objects*   This is called when the parser has worked out that the object in question is being spoken to, and has decided the verb_word and verb_wordnum (the position of the verb word in the word stream) but hasn't yet tried any grammar. The routine can, if it wishes, parse past some words (provided it moves verb_wordnum on by the number of words it wants to eat up).

Routine returns   false to carry on as usual; true to indicate that the routine has parsed the entire command itself, and set up action, noun and second to the appropriate order; or a dictionary value for a verb, such as 'take', to indicate "parse the command from this verb's grammar instead"; or minus such a value, e.g. -'take', to indicate "parse from this verb and then parse the usual grammar as well".

`initial`	*String or routine*

For objects   The description of an object not yet picked up, used when a room is described; or a routine to print one out.

For rooms   Printed or run when the room is arrived in, either by ordinary movement or by PlayerTo.

Warning   If the object is a door, or a container, or is switchable, then use one of the when_ properties rather than initial.

No return value

`inside_description`	*String or routine*

For objects   Printed as part or all of a room description when the player is inside the given object, which must be enterable.

`invent`	*Routine*

This routine is for changing an object's inventory listing. If provided, it's called twice, first with the variable inventory_stage set to 1, second with it set to 2. At stage 1, you have an entirely free hand to print a different inventory listing.

Routine returns   Stage 1: false to continue; true to stop here, printing nothing further about the object or its contents.

At stage 2, the object's indefinite article and short name have already been printed, but messages like " (providing light)" haven't. This is an opportunity to add something like " (almost empty)".

Routine returns   Stage 2: false to continue; true to stop here, printing nothing further about the object or its contents.

`life`	*Routine* NULL ⊕

This routine holds rules about animate objects, behaving much like before and after but only handling the person-to-person events:

    Attack Kiss WakeOther ThrowAt Give Show Ask Tell Answer Order

See §17, §18 and the properties orders and grammar.

Routine returns   true to stop and print nothing, false to resume as usual (for example, printing "Miss Gatsby has better things to do.").

`list_together`	*Number, string or routine*

For objects   Objects with the same list_together value are grouped together in object lists (such as inventories, or the miscellany at the end of a room description). If a string such as "fish" is given, then such a group will be headed with text such as "five fish".

A routine, if given, is called at two stages in the process (once with the variable inventory_stage set to 1, once with it set to 2). These stages occur before and after the group is printed; thus, a preamble or postscript can be printed. Also, such a routine may change the variable c_style (which holds the current list style). On entry, the variable parser_one holds the first object in the group, and parser_two the current depth of recursion in the list. Applying x=NextEntry(x,parser_two); moves x on from parser_one to the next item in the group. Another helpful variable is listing_together, set up to the first object of a group being listed (or to 0 whenever no group is being listed).

Routine returns   Stage 1: false to continue, true not to print the group's list at all.
Routine returns   Stage 2: No return value.

---

name   *List of dictionary words*   ⊕

For objects   A list of dictionary words referring to this object.

Warning   The parse_name property of an object may take precedence over this, if present.

For rooms   A list of words which the room understands but which refer to things which "do not need to be referred to in this game"; these are only looked at if all other attempts to understand the player's command have failed.

Warning   Uniquely in Inform syntax, these dictionary words are given in double quotes "thus", whereas in all other circumstances they would be 'thus'. This means they can safely be only one letter long without ambiguity.

---

number   *Any value*

A general purpose property left free: conventionally holding a number like "number of turns' battery power left". (Now unnecessary, number is a feature left over from earlier versions of Inform where it was less easy to make new properties.)

For compass objects   Note that the standard compass objects defined by the library all provide a number property, in case this might be useful to the designer.

---

orders   *Routine*

For animate *or* talkable *objects*   This carries out the player's orders (or doesn't, as it sees fit): it looks at actor, action, noun and second to do so. Unless this object is the current player, actor is irrelevant (it is always the player) and the object is the person being ordered about.

If the player typed an incomprehensible command, like "robot, og sthou", then the action is NotUnderstood and the variable etype holds the parser's error number.

If this object is the current player then actor is the person being ordered about. actor can either be this object -- in which case an action is being processed, because the player has typed an ordinary command -- or can be some other object, in which case the player has typed an order. See §18 for how to write orders routines in these cases.

Routine returns   true to stop and print nothing further; false to continue. (Unless the object is the current player, the life routine's Order section gets an opportunity to meddle next; after that, Inform gives up.)

parse_name	*Routine*

For objects   To parse an object's name (this overrides the name but is also used in determining if two objects are describably identical). This routine should try to match as many words as possible in sequence, reading them one at a time by calling NextWord(). (It can leave the "word marker" variable wn anywhere it likes).

Routine returns   0 if the text didn't make any sense at all, −1 to make the parser resume its usual course (looking at the name), or the number of words in a row which successfully matched.

In addition to this, if the text matched seems to be in the plural (for instance, a blind mouse object reading blind mice), the routine can set the variable parser_action to the value ##PluralFound. The parser will then match with all of the different objects understood, rather than ask a player which of them is meant.

A parse_name routine may also (voluntarily) assist the parser by telling it whether or not two objects which share the same parse_name routine are identical. (They may share the same routine if they both inherit it from a class.) If, when it is called, the variable parser_action is set to ##TheSame then this is the reason. It can then decide whether or not the objects parser_one and parser_two are indistinguishable.

Routine returns   −1 if the objects are indistinguishable, −2 if not.

plural	*String or routine*

For objects   The plural name of an object (when in the presence of others like it), or routine to print one; for instance, a wax candle might have plural set to "wax candles".

No return value

react_after	*Routine*

For objects   Acts like an after rule, but detects any actions in the vicinity (any actions which take place when this object is in scope).

Routine returns   true to print nothing further; false to carry on.

react_before	*Routine*

For objects   Acts like a before rule, but detects any actions in the vicinity (any actions which take place when this object is in scope).

Routine returns   true to stop the action, printing nothing; false to carry on.

short_name	*Routine*

For objects   The short name of an object (like "brass lamp"), or a routine to print it.

Routine returns   true to stop here, false to carry on by printing the object's 'real' short name (the string given at the head of the object's definition). It's sometimes useful to print text like "half-empty " and then return false.

---

short_name_indef   *Routine*

For objects If set, this form of the short name is used when the name is prefaced by an indefinite article. (This is not useful in English-language games, but in other languages adjectival parts of names agree with the definiteness of the article.)

---

time_left   *Number*

Number of turns left until the timer for this object (if set, which must be done using StartTimer) goes off. Its initial value is of no significance, as StartTimer will write over this, but a timer object must provide the property. If the timer is currently set, the value 0 means "will go off at the end of the current turn", the value 1 means ". . . at the end of next turn" and so on.

---

time_out   *Routine*   NULL   ⊕

Routine to run when the timer for this object goes off (having been set by StartTimer and not in the mean time stopped by StopTimer).
Warning A timer object must also provide a time_left property.

---

when_closed   *String or routine*

For objects Description, or routine to print one, of something closed (a door or container) in a room's long description.
No return value

---

when_open   *String or routine*

For objects Description, or routine to print one, of something open (a door or container) in a room's long description.
No return value

---

when_on   *String or routine*

For objects Description, or routine to print one, of a switchable object which is currently switched on, in a room's long description.
No return value

---

when_off   *String or routine*

For objects Description, or routine to print one, of a switchable object which is currently switched off, in a room's long description.
No return value

---

with_key   *Object*   nothing

The key object needed to lock or unlock this lockable object. A player must explicitly name it as the key being used and be holding it at the time. The value nothing, or 0, means that no key fits (though this is not made clear to the player, who can try as many as he likes).

---

§A3 Library routines

The Inform library files contain about three hundred routines, almost all of which are "private" in the sense that they are difficult for designers to use, not useful anyway, and subject to change without notice as the library is maintained and rewritten. The routines in this appendix are those which are "open to the public". Designers are encouraged to make use of them.

`Achieved(tasknum)` *see* §22

Signals to the library that task number `tasknum` has been achieved, so that points may be awarded if it has not been achieved before.
No return value

`AfterRoutines()` *see* §6

This should be called in the action routine, such as `TakeSub`, of a group 2 action, such as `Take`, once the action has taken place but before anything is printed. It runs through the `after` rules as laid out in §6.
Routine returns `true` if the action has been interrupted by some other rule, `false` if not.

`AllowPushDir()` *see* §15

Used only inside the `before` rule for a `PushDir` action, this routine signals to the library that the attempt to push an object from one place to another should be allowed.
No return value

`Banner()` *see* §21

Prints the game banner. Normally unnecessary, but should be used soon after if your game suppresses the banner at the `Initialise` stage.
No return value

`ChangePlayer(obj,flag)` *see* §21

Cause the player at the keyboard to play as the given object `obj`, which must provide a number property. If the `flag` is `true`, then subsequently print messages like "(as Ford Prefect)" in room description headers. This routine, however, prints nothing itself.
No return value

`CommonAncestor(obj1,obj2)` *see* §3

A routine used internally by the library when working out visibilities, and which might as well be available for public use. Returns the nearest object in the object tree which (directly or indirectly) contains both `obj1` and `obj2`, or else returns `nothing` if no such object exists. For instance if `Bedquilt` contains `bottle` and the `player` carrying a `lamp`, the common ancestor of lamp and bottle is Bedquilt.
Routine returns The common ancestor or `nothing`.

`DictionaryLookup(word,length)` *see §34*

Takes the word stored character by character in the array `word->0`, `word->1`, ...,
`word->(length-1)` and looks it up in the story file's dictionary.
Routine returns The dictionary value (e.g., `'t'`, `'a'`, `'k'`, `'e'` will return `'take'`) or
zero if the word isn't in the dictionary.

`GetGNAOfObject(obj)` *see §37*

Determines the gender-number-animation of the short name of the given object `obj`.
Routine returns The GNA, which is a number between 0 and 11: see table of GNA
values in §34.

`HasLightSource(obj)` *see §19*

Determines whether or not `obj` "has light", i.e., casts light outward to objects containing
`obj`: see §19 for a more exact definition.
Routine returns `true` or `false`.

`IndirectlyContains(obj1,obj2)` *see §3*

The condition `obj2 in obj1` only tests whether `obj2` is directly contained in `obj1`, so
that `lamp in player` would fail if the lamp were in a rucksack carried by the player.
`IndirectlyContains(player,lamp)` would return true. Formally, the test is whether
`obj2` is a child of `obj1`, or is a child of a child of `obj1`, or ... and so on. See also the
library routine `CommonAncestor` above.
Routine returns `true` or `false`.

`IsSeeThrough(obj)` *see §19*

Determines whether or not `obj` "is see-through", i.e., allows light to pass through it.
An object is see-through if it has `transparent`, or `supporter`, or `enterable` (unless it
is also a closed `container`).
Routine returns `true` or `false`.

`Locale(obj,tx1,tx2)` *see §26*

Prints out the paragraphs of room description which would appear if `obj` were the
room: i.e., prints out descriptions of objects in `obj` according to the usual rules. After
describing the objects which have their own paragraphs, a list is given of the remaining
ones. The string `tx1` is printed if there were no previous paragraphs, and the string `tx2`
otherwise. (For instance, you might want "On the ledge you can see" and "On the
ledge you can also see".) After the list, nothing else is printed, not even a full stop.
Routine returns The number of objects printed in the list, possibly zero.

LoopOverScope(R,actor)   *see §32*

Calls routine R(obj) for each object obj in scope for the given actor. If no actor is given, the actor is assumed to be the player.
No return value

LTI_Insert(position,character)   *see §36*

Inserts the given character at the given position in the standard library array buffer used to hold the text typed by the player, moving subsequent text along to make room. (This is protected against overflowing the buffer.)
No return value

MoveFloatingObjects()   *see §8*

"Floating objects" is Inform library jargon for "objects which use found_in to be present in several locations at once". This routine adjusts the positions of objects across the whole game, ensuring that they are consistent with the current states of the property found_in and the attribute absent, and should be called after any game event which has changed these states.
No return value

NextWord()   *see §28*

Finds the next dictionary word in the player's input, that is, the word at position wn in the input, moving the word number wn on by one. (The first word is at position 1.)
Routine returns   The dictionary value, or 0 if the word is not in the dictionary or if the word stream has run out, or the constant THEN1__WD if the "word" was a full stop, or the constant COMMA_WORD if it was a comma.

NextWordStopped()   *see §28*

Finds the next dictionary word in the player's input, that is, the word at position wn in the input, moving the word number wn on by one. (The first word is at position 1.)
Routine returns   The dictionary value, or 0 if the word is not in the dictionary, or the constant THEN1__WD if the "word" was a full stop, or the constant COMMA_WORD if it was a comma, or −1 if the word stream has run out.

NounDomain(o1,o2,type)

This routine is one of the keystones of the parser, but see also ParseToken below: the objects given are the domains to search through when parsing, almost always the location and the actor, and the type indicates a token. The only tokens safely usable are: NOUN_TOKEN, for ⌐noun⌐, HELD_TOKEN, for ⌐held⌐ and CREATURE_TOKEN, for ⌐creature⌐. The routine parses the best single object name it can from the current position of wn.
Routine returns   nothing for "no match", or the object matched for a success, or the constant REPARSE_CODE to indicate that it had to ask a clarifying question: this

reconstructed the input drastically and the parser must begin all over again. NounDomain should only be used by general parsing routines and these should always return GPR_REPARSE if NounDomain returned REPARSE_CODE, thus passing the buck upwards.

ObjectIsUntouchable(obj,flag)   *see §32*

Determines whether any solid barrier, that is, any container that is not open, lies between the player and obj. If flag is true, this routine never prints anything; otherwise it prints a message like "You can't, because ... is in the way." if any barrier is found.
Routine returns   true if a barrier is found, false if not.

OffersLight(obj)   *see §19*

Determines whether or not obj "offers light", i.e., contains light so that its contents are visible to each other: see §19 for a more exact definition.
Routine returns   true or false.

ParseToken(tokentype,tokendata)   *see §31*

This is the library's own "general parsing routine", and parses the word stream against the specified token. Because some of these tokens require too much setting-up work to parse, and anyway are not very useful, only two token types are open to the public. If tokentype is ELEMENTARY_TT, then tokendata must have one of the following values: NOUN_TOKEN, HELD_TOKEN, MULTI_TOKEN, MULTIHELD_TOKEN, MULTIEXCEPT_TOKEN, MULTIINSIDE_TOKEN, CREATURE_TOKEN and NUMBER_TOKEN. Alternatively, tokentype can be SCOPE_TT and tokendata must then be a "scope routine".
Routine returns   GPR_FAIL if parsing fails; GPR_PREPOSITION if a match is made but results in no data; GPR_NUMBER if a match is made, resulting in a number; GPR_MULTIPLE if a match is made, resulting in a multiple object; GPR_REPARSE if the parser has had to rewrite the text being parsed and would now like parsing to begin again from scratch; otherwise, an object which the parser has matched against the text.

PlaceInScope(obj)   *see §32*

Used in "scope routines" (only) when scope_stage is set to 2 (only). Places obj in scope for the token currently being parsed. No other objects are placed in scope as a result of this, unlike the case of ScopeWithin.
No return value

PlayerTo(obj,flag)   *see §21*

Moves the player to obj, which can either be a location or something enterable. If flag is false, then run a Look action to print out a room description: but if flag is true, print nothing, and if flag is 2, print a room description but abbreviate it if the room has been visited before.
No return value

PronounNotice(obj)   see §33

Resets the pronouns to the object obj. This means that all pronouns which can match against the object are set equal to it: for instance, "Aunt Jemima" would match 'her' but not 'it', "the grapes" would match 'them' and so on.
No return value

PronounValue(pronoun)   see §33

Finds the current setting of pronoun, which has to be the dictionary value of a legal pronoun in the current language: in the case of English, that means 'it', 'him', 'her' or 'them'.
Routine returns   The setting, or nothing if it is unset.

ScopeWithin(obj)   see §32

Used in "scope routines" (only) when scope_stage is set to 2 (only). Places the contents of obj in scope for the token currently being parsed, and applies the rules of scope recursively so that contents of see-through objects are also in scope, as is anything added to scope.
No return value

SetPronoun(pronoun,obj)   see §33

Changes the current setting of pronoun, which has to be the dictionary value of a legal pronoun in the current language: in the case of English, that means 'it', 'him', 'her' or 'them'.
No return value

SetTime(time,rate)   see §20

Set the game clock (a 24-hour clock) to the given time (in seconds since the start of the day), to run at the given rate r: $r = 0$ means it does not run, if $r > 0$ then r seconds pass every turn, if $r < 0$ then $-r$ turns pass every second.
No return value

StartDaemon(obj)   see §20

Makes the daemon of the object obj active, so that its daemon routine will be called at the end of every turn.
No return value

StartTimer(obj,period)   see §20

Makes the timer of the object obj active. Its time_left property is set initially to period, then decreased by 1 at the end of every turn in which it was positive. At the end of the turn when it was zero, the timer is stopped and the object's time_out property is called.
No return value

`StopDaemon(obj)`   *see §20*

Makes the daemon of the object `obj` no longer active, so that its `daemon` routine will no longer be called at the end of every turn.
No return value

`StopTimer(obj)`   *see §20*

Makes the timer of the object `obj` no longer active, so that its `time_left` routine will no longer be decreased and `time_out` will not be called as originally scheduled.
No return value

`TestScope(obj,actor)`   *see §32*

Tests whether the object `obj` is in scope to the given `actor`. If no actor is given, the actor is assumed to be the player.
Routine returns   `true` or `false`.

`TryNumber(wordnum)`   *see §28*

Tries to parse the word at `wordnum` as a non-negative number, recognising decimal numbers and English ones from "one" to "twenty".
Routine returns -1000 if it fails altogether, or the number, except that values exceeding 10000 are rounded down to 10000.

`UnsignedCompare(a,b)`

The usual > condition performs a signed comparison, and occasionally, usually when comparing addresses in memory of routines or strings, you need an unsigned comparison.
Routine returns   Returns 1 if $a > b$, 0 if $a = b$ and -1 if $a < b$, regarding a and b as unsigned numbers between 0 and 65535. (That is, regarding -1 as 65535, -2 as 65534, ..., -32768 as 32768.)

`WordAddress(wordnum)`   *see §28*

Find where word number `wordnum` from what the player typed is stored.
Routine returns   The `->` array holding the text of the word.

`WordInProperty(word,obj,prop)`   *see §34*

Tests whether `word` is one of the dictionary values listed in the array given as the property `prop` of object `obj`. (Most often used to see if a given dictionary word is one of the name values.)
Routine returns   `true` or `false`.

`WordLength(wordnum)`   *see §28*

Find the length (number of letters) of the word numbered `wordnum` from what the
player typed.
Routine returns   The length.

`WriteListFrom(obj,st)`   *see §27*

Write a list of `obj` and its siblings, with the style being `st`. To list all the objects inside
`X`, list from `child(X)`. The style is made up by adding together some of the following
constants:

`NEWLINE_BIT`	New-line after each entry
`INDENT_BIT`	Indent each entry according to depth
`FULLINV_BIT`	Full inventory information after entry
`ENGLISH_BIT`	English sentence style, with commas and 'and'
`RECURSE_BIT`	Recurse downwards with usual rules
`ALWAYS_BIT`	Always recurse downwards
`TERSE_BIT`	More terse English style
`PARTINV_BIT`	Only brief inventory information after entry
`DEFART_BIT`	Use the definite article in list
`WORKFLAG_BIT`	At top level (only), only list objects which have the `workflag` attribute
`ISARE_BIT`	Prints " is " or " are " before list
`CONCEAL_BIT`	Misses out `concealed` or `scenery` objects

`YesOrNo()`

Assuming that a question has already been printed, wait for the player to type "yes",
"y", "no" or "n".
Routine returns   `true` for "yes" or "y", `false` for "no" or "n".

§A4   Library message numbers

Answer: "There is no reply."
Ask: "There is no reply."
Attack: "Violence isn't the answer to this one."
Blow: "You can't usefully blow that/those."
Burn: "This dangerous act would achieve little."
Buy: "Nothing is on sale."
Climb: "I don't think much is to be achieved by that."
Close: 1. "That's/They're not something you can close." 2. "That's/They're already closed." 3. "You close ⟨x1⟩."
Consult: "You discover nothing of interest in ⟨x1⟩."
Cut: "Cutting that/those up would achieve little."
Dig: "Digging would achieve nothing here."
Disrobe: 1. "You're not wearing that/those." 2. "You take off ⟨x1⟩."
Drink: "There's nothing suitable to drink here."
Drop: 1. "The ⟨x1⟩ is/are already here." 2. "You haven't got that/those." 3. "(first taking ⟨x1⟩ off)" 4. "Dropped."
Eat: 1. "That's/They're plainly inedible." 2. "You eat ⟨x1⟩. Not bad."
EmptyT: 1. ⟨x1⟩ " can't contain things." 2. ⟨x1⟩ " is/are closed." 3. ⟨x1⟩ " is/are empty already." 4. "That would scarcely empty anything."
Enter: 1. "But you're already on/in ⟨x1⟩." 2. "That's/They're not something you can enter." 3. "You can't get into the closed ⟨x1⟩." 4. "You can only get into something freestanding." 5. "You get onto/into ⟨x1⟩."
Examine: 1. "Darkness, noun. An absence of light to see by." 2. "You see nothing special about ⟨x1⟩." 3. "⟨x1⟩ is/are currently switched on/off."
Exit: 1. "But you aren't in anything at the moment." 2. "You can't get out of the closed ⟨x1⟩." 3. "You get off/out of ⟨x1⟩."
Fill: "But there's no water here to carry."
FullScore: 1. "The score is/was made up as follows:^" 2. "finding sundry items" 3. "visiting various places" 4. "total (out of MAX_SCORE)"
GetOff: "But you aren't on ⟨x1⟩ at the moment."
Give: 1. "You aren't holding ⟨x1⟩." 2. "You juggle ⟨x1⟩ for a while, but don't achieve much." 3. "⟨x1⟩ doesn't/don't seem interested."
Go: 1. "You'll have to get off/out of ⟨x1⟩ first." 2. "You can't go that way." 3. "You are unable to climb ⟨x1⟩." 4. "You are unable to descend ⟨x1⟩." 5. "You can't, since ⟨x1⟩ is/are in the way." 6. "You can't, since ⟨x1⟩ leads nowhere."
Insert: 1. "You need to be holding ⟨x1⟩ before you can put it/them into something else." 2. "That/Those can't contain things." 3. "⟨x1⟩ is/are closed." 4. "You'll need to take it/them off first." 5. "You can't put something inside itself." 6. "(first taking it/them off)^" 7. "There is no more room in ⟨x1⟩." 8. "Done." 9. "You put ⟨x1⟩ into ⟨second⟩."

Inv: 1. "You are carrying nothing."   2. "You are carrying"

Jump: "You jump on the spot, fruitlessly."

JumpOver: "You would achieve nothing by this."

Kiss: "Keep your mind on the game."

Listen: "You hear nothing unexpected."

LMode1:   " is now in its normal brief printing mode, which gives long descriptions of places never before visited and short descriptions otherwise."

LMode2:   " is now in its verbose mode, which always gives long descriptions of locations (even if you've been there before)."

LMode3:   " is now in its superbrief mode, which always gives short descriptions of locations (even if you haven't been there before)."

Lock: 1. "That doesn't/They don't seem to be something you can lock."   2. "That's/They're locked at the moment."   3. "First you'll have to close ⟨x1⟩."   4. "That doesn't/Those don't seem to fit the lock."   5. "You lock ⟨x1⟩."

Look: 1. " (on ⟨x1⟩)"   2. " (in ⟨x1⟩)"   3. " (as ⟨x1⟩)"   4. "^On ⟨x1⟩ is/are ⟨list⟩"   5. "[On/In ⟨x1⟩] you/You can also see ⟨list⟩ [here]."   6. "[On/In ⟨x1⟩] you/You can see ⟨list⟩ [here]."

LookUnder: 1. "But it's dark."   "You find nothing of interest."

Mild: "Quite."

ListMiscellany: 1. " (providing light)"   2. " (which is/are closed)"   3. " (closed and providing light)"   4. " (which is/are empty)"   5. " (empty and providing light)"   6. " (which is/are closed and empty)"   7. " (closed, empty and providing light)"   8. " (providing light and being worn"   9. " (providing light"   10. " (being worn"   11. " (which is/are "   12. "open"   13. "open but empty"   14. "closed"   15. "closed and locked"   16. " and empty"   17. " (which is/are empty)"   18. " containing "   19. " (on "   20. ", on top of "   21. " (in "   22. ", inside "

Miscellany: 1. "(considering the first sixteen objects only)^"   2. "Nothing to do!"   3. " You have died "   4. " You have won "   5. (The RESTART, RESTORE, QUIT and possibly FULL and AMUSING query, printed after the game is over.)   6. "[Your interpreter does not provide undo. Sorry!]"   7. "Undo failed. [Not all interpreters provide it.]"   8. "Please give one of the answers above."   9. "^It is now pitch dark in here!"   10. "I beg your pardon?"   11. "[You can't "undo" what hasn't been done!]"   12. "[Can't "undo" twice in succession. Sorry!]"   13. "[Previous turn undone.]"   14. "Sorry, that can't be corrected."   15. "Think nothing of it."   16. ""Oops" can only correct a single word."   17. "It is pitch dark, and you can't see a thing."   18. "yourself" (the short name of the selfobj object)   19. "As good-looking as ever."   20. "To repeat a command like "frog, jump", just say "again", not "frog, again"."   21. "You can hardly repeat that."   22. "You can't begin with a comma."   23. "You seem to want to talk to someone, but I can't see whom."   24. "You can't talk to ⟨x1⟩."   25. "To talk to someone, try "someone, hello" or some such."   26. "(first taking not_holding)"   27. "I didn't understand that sentence."   28. "I only

understood you as far as wanting to "   29. "I didn't understand that number."
30. "You can't see any such thing."   31. "You seem to have said too little!"
32. "You aren't holding that!"   33. "You can't use multiple objects with that
verb."   34. "You can only use multiple objects once on a line."   35. "I'm not
sure what "⟨pronoun⟩" refers to."   36. "You excepted something not included
anyway!"   37. "You can only do that to something animate."   38. "That's not
a verb I recognise."   39. "That's not something you need to refer to in the course
of this game."   40. "You can't see "⟨pronoun⟩" (⟨value⟩) at the moment."
41. "I didn't understand the way that finished."   42. "None/only ⟨x1⟩ of those
is/are available."   43. "Nothing to do!"   44. "There are none at all available!"
45. "Who do you mean, "   46. "Which do you mean, "   47. "Sorry, you can
only have one item here. Which exactly?"   48. "Whom do you want [⟨actor⟩] to
⟨command⟩?"   49. "What do you want [⟨actor⟩] to ⟨command⟩?"   50. "Your
score has just gone up/down by ⟨x1⟩ point/points."   51. "(Since something
dramatic has happened, your list of commands has been cut short.)"   52. "Type
a number from 1 to ⟨x1⟩, 0 to redisplay or press ENTER."   53. "[Please press
SPACE.]"

No: see **Yes**

NotifyOff: "Score notification off."

NotifyOn: "Score notification on."

Objects: 1. "Objects you have handled:^"   2. "None."   3. " (worn)"   4. "
(held)"   5. " (given away)"   6. " (in ⟨x1⟩)" [without article]   7. " (in ⟨x1⟩)"
[with article]   8. " (inside ⟨x1⟩)"   9. " (on ⟨x1⟩)"   10. " (lost)"

Open: 1. "That's/They're not something you can open."   2. "It seems/They
seem to be locked."   3. "That's/They're already open."   4. "You open ⟨x1⟩,
revealing ⟨children⟩"   5. "You open ⟨x1⟩."

Order: "⟨x1⟩ has/have better things to do."

Places: "You have visited: "

Pray: "Nothing practical results from your prayer."

Prompt: 1. "^>"

Pronouns: 1. "At the moment, "   2. "means "   3. "is unset "   4. "no pronouns
are known to the game."

Pull: 1. "It is/Those are fixed in place."   2. "You are unable to."   3. "Nothing
obvious happens."   4. "That would be less than courteous."

Push: see **Pull**

PushDir: 1. "Is that the best you can think of?"   2. "That's not a direction."   3.
"Not that way you can't."

PutOn: 1. "You need to be holding ⟨x1⟩ before you can put it/them on top of
something else."   2. "You can't put something on top of itself."   3. "Putting
things on ⟨x1⟩ would achieve nothing."   4. "You lack the dexterity."   5. "(first
taking it/them off)^"   6. "There is no more room on ⟨x1⟩."   7. "Done."   8.
"You put ⟨x1⟩ on <second>."

Quit: 1. "Please answer yes or no."   2. "Are you sure you want to quit? "

Remove: 1. "It is/They are unfortunately closed."   2. "But it isn't/they aren't there now."   3. "Removed."

Restart: 1. "Are you sure you want to restart? "   2. "Failed."

Restore: 1. "Restore failed."   2. "Ok."

Rub: "You achieve nothing by this."

Save: 1. "Save failed."   2. "Ok."

Score: "You have so far/In that game you scored ⟨score⟩ out of a possible MAX_SCORE, in ⟨turns⟩ turn/turns"

ScriptOn: 1. "Transcripting is already on."   2. "Start of a transcript of"

ScriptOff: 1. "Transcripting is already off."   2. "^End of transcript."

Search: 1. "But it's dark."   2. "There is nothing on ⟨x1⟩."   3. "On ⟨x1⟩ is/are ⟨list of children⟩."   4. "You find nothing of interest."   5. "You can't see inside, since ⟨x1⟩ is/are closed."   6. "⟨x1⟩ is/are empty."   7. "In ⟨x1⟩ is/are ⟨list of children⟩."

Set: "No, you can't set that/those."

SetTo: "No, you can't set that/those to anything."

Show: 1. "You aren't holding ⟨x1⟩."   2. "⟨x1⟩ is/are unimpressed."

Sing: "Your singing is abominable."

Sleep: "You aren't feeling especially drowsy."

Smell: "You smell nothing unexpected."

Sorry: "Oh, don't apologise."

Squeeze: 1. "Keep your hands to yourself."   2. "You achieve nothing by this."

Strong: "Real adventurers do not use such language."

Swim: "There's not enough water to swim in."

Swing: "There's nothing sensible to swing here."

SwitchOff: 1. "That's/They're not something you can switch."   2. "That's/ They're already off."   3. "You switch ⟨x1⟩ off."

SwitchOn: 1. "That's/They're not something you can switch."   2. "That's/ They're already on."   3. "You switch ⟨x1⟩ on."

Take: 1. "Taken."   2. "You are always self-possessed."   3. "I don't suppose ⟨x1⟩ would care for that."   4. "You'd have to get off/out of ⟨x1⟩ first."   5. "You already have that/those."   6. "That seems/Those seem to belong to ⟨x1⟩."   7. "That seems/Those seem to be a part of ⟨x1⟩."   8. "That isn't/Those aren't available."   9. "⟨x1⟩ isn't/aren't open."   10. "That's/They're hardly portable."   11. "That's/They're fixed in place."   12. "You're carrying too many things already."   13. "(putting ⟨x1⟩ into SACK_OBJECT to make room)"

Taste: "You taste nothing unexpected."

Tell: 1. "You talk to yourself a while."   2. "This provokes no reaction."

Touch: 1. "Keep your hands to yourself!"   2. "You feel nothing unexpected."   3. "If you think that'll help."

Think: "What a good idea."

Tie: "You would achieve nothing by this."

429

ThrowAt: 1. "Futile."   2. "You lack the nerve when it comes to the crucial moment."

Turn: see **Pull**

Unlock: 1. "That doesn't seem to be something you can unlock."   2. "It's/ They're unlocked at the moment."   3. "That doesn't/Those don't seem to fit the lock." 4. "You unlock ⟨x1⟩."

VagueGo: "You'll have to say which compass direction to go in."

Verify: 1. "The game file has verified as intact."   2. "The game file did not verify properly, and may be corrupted (or you may be running it on a very primitive interpreter which is unable properly to perform the test)."

Wait: "Time passes."

Wake: "The dreadful truth is, this is not a dream."

WakeOther: "That seems unnecessary."

Wave: 1. "But you aren't holding that/those."   2. "You look ridiculous waving ⟨x1⟩."

WaveHands: "You wave, feeling foolish."

Wear: 1. "You can't wear that/those!"   2. "You're not holding that/those!"   3. "You're already wearing that/those!"   4. "You put on ⟨x1⟩."

Yes: "That was a rhetorical question."

§A5   Entry point routines

By definition, an "entry point routine" is a routine which you can choose whether or not to define in your source code. If you do, the library will make calls to it from time to time, allowing it to change the way the game rules are administered. The exception is `Initialise`, which is compulsory.

`AfterLife()`   *see §21*

When the player has died (a condition signalled by the variable `deadflag` being set to a non-zero value other than 2, which indicates winning), this routine is called: by setting `deadflag` to be `false` again it can resurrect the player.
No return value

`AfterPrompt()`   *see §22*

Called just after the prompt is printed: therefore, called after all the printing for this turn is definitely over. A useful opportunity to use box to display quotations without them scrolling away.
No return value

`Amusing()`   *see §21*

Called to provide an "afterword" for players who have won: for instance, it might advertise some features which a successful player might never have noticed. This will only be called if you have also defined the constant `AMUSING_PROVIDED` in your own code.
No return value

`BeforeParsing()`   *see §30*

Called after the parser has read in some text and set up the `buffer` and `parse` tables, but has done nothing else yet except to set the word marker `wn` to 1. The routine can do anything it likes to these tables provided they remain consistent with each other, and can leave the word marker anywhere.
No return value

`ChooseObjects(obj,c)`   *see §33*

When `c` is `false`, the parser is processing an "all" and has decided to exclude `obj` from it; when `c` is `true`, it has decided to include it. When `c` is 2, the parser wants help in resolving an ambiguity: perhaps using the `action_to_be` variable the routine must decide how appropriate `obj` is for the given action.
Routine returns   When `c` is `false` or `true`, return `false` to accept the parser's decision, 1 to force inclusion of `obj`, 2 to force exclusion. When `c` is 2, return a numerical score between 0 and 9, with 0 being "inappropriate" and 9 "very appropriate".

DarkToDark()   *see §19*

Called when a player goes from one dark room into another one, which is a splendid excuse to kill the player off.

DeathMessage()   *see §21*

If the player's death occurs because you have set deadflag to a value of 3 or more, this entry point is called to print up a suitable "You have died"-style message.
No return value

GamePostRoutine()   *see §6*

A kind of super-after rule, which applies to all actions in the game, whatever they are: use this only in the last resort.
Routine returns   false to allow the action to continue as usual, true to stop the action and print nothing further.

GamePreRoutine()   *see §6*

A kind of super-before rule, which applies to all actions in the game, whatever they are: use this only in the last resort.
Routine returns   false to allow the action to continue as usual, true to stop the action and print nothing further.

Initialise()   *see §21*

An opportunity to set up the initial state of the game. This routine is compulsory and has one compulsory task: to set location to the place where the player begins, or to the enterable object in or on which the player begins. It's usual to print a welcoming message as well.
Routine returns   true or false to continue as usual; 2 to suppress the game banner, which would otherwise be printed immediately after this routine is called.

InScope()   *see §32*

An opportunity to change the library's definition of what is in scope. This acts as a sort of global version of a scope token routine: it should use the library routines ScopeWithin and PlaceInScope to define what scope should be. It may want to look at the library variable et_flag. If this is true, the scope is being worked out in order to run through each_turn. If it's false, then the scope is being worked out for everyday parsing.
Routine returns   false to tell the parser to add all the usual objects in scope as well, or true to tell the parser that nothing further is in scope.

`LookRoutine()`   *see §26*

Called at the end of every Look action, that is, room description.
No return value

`NewRoom()`   *see §21*

Called when the room changes, before any description of it is printed. This happens in the course of any movements or uses of `PlayerTo`.
No return value

`ParseNoun(obj)`   *see §28*

To do the job of parsing the `name` property (if `parse_name` hasn't done it already). This takes one argument, the object in question, and returns a value as if it were a `parse_name` routine.
Routine returns   The number of words matched, or 0 if there is no match, or −1 to decline to make a decision and give the job back to the parser. Note that if −1 is returned, the word number variable `wn` must be left set to the first word the parser should look at -- probably the same value it had when `ParseNoun` was called, but not necessarily.

`ParseNumber(text,n)`   *see §28*

An opportunity to parse numbers in a different, or additional, way. The text to be parsed is a byte array of length n starting at `text`.
Routine returns   0 to signal "no match", 1 to 10000 to signal "this number has been matched".

`ParserError(pe)`   *see §33*

The chance to print different parser error messages such as "I don't understand that sentence". pe is the parser error number and the table of possible values is given in §33.
Routine returns   `true` to tell the parser that the error message has now been printed, or `false` to allow it to carry on and print the usual one.

`PrintRank()`   *see §22*

Completes the printing of the score. Traditionally, many games have awarded the player a rank based on the current value of the variable `score`.
No return value

`PrintTaskName(n)`   *see §22*

Prints the name of task n, which lies between 0 and NUMBER_TASKS minus 1.
No return value

`PrintVerb(v)`   *see §30*

A chance to change the verb printed out in a parser question (like "What do you want
to (whatever)?") in case an unusual verb via UnknownVerb has been constructed. v is
the dictionary address of the verb.
Routine returns   true to tell the parser that the verb has now been printed, or false to
allow it to carry on and print the usual one.

`TimePasses()`   *see §20*

Called after every game turn, which is to say, not after a group 1 action such as "score"
or "save", but after any other activity. Use this entry point only as a last resort, as it's
almost certainly easier and tidier to use timers and daemons.
No return value

`UnknownVerb(word)`   *see §30*

Called by the parser when it hits an unknown verb, so that you can transform it into a
known one. word is the dictionary value of this unknown verb.
Routine returns   false to allow the parser to carry on and print an error message, or
the dictionary value of a verb to use instead.

§A6   Answers to all the exercises

> World is crazier and more of it than we think,
> Incorrigibly plural. I peel and portion
> A tangerine and spit the pips and feel
> The drunkenness of things being various.
>
> — Louis MacNeice (1907–1963), *Snow*

Exercises in Chapter II

• 1 (p. 80)   Here's one way: attach a property to the mushroom which records whether or not it has been picked.

```
mushroom_picked,
after [;
    Take: if (self.mushroom_picked)
            "You pick up the slowly-disintegrating mushroom.";
          self.mushroom_picked = true;
          "You pick the mushroom, neatly cleaving its thin stalk.";
    Drop: "The mushroom drops to the ground, battered slightly.";
],
```

Note that the mushroom is allowed to call itself self instead of mushroom, though it doesn't have to.

• 2 (p. 81)   Here is one possibility. Don't forget the light, or the player will find only darkness at the foot of the steps and won't ever be able to read the description.

```
Object Square_Chamber "Square Chamber"
  with description
            "A sunken, gloomy stone chamber, ten yards across. A shaft
            of sunlight cuts in from the steps above, giving the chamber
            a diffuse light, but in the shadows low lintelled doorways
            lead east and south into the deeper darkness of the
            Temple.",
  has  light;
```

The map connections east, south and back up will be added in §9.

• 3 (p. 90)   The neatest way is to make the door react to movement through it:

```
Class ObligingDoor
  with name 'door',
      react_before [;
          Go: if (noun.door_dir == self.door_dir)
                  return self.open_by_myself();
          Enter: if (noun == self) return self.open_by_myself();
      ],
      open_by_myself [ ks;
          if (self has open) rfalse;
          print "(first opening ", (the) self, ")^";
          ks = keep_silent; keep_silent = true;
          <Open self>; keep_silent = ks;
          if (self hasnt open) rtrue;
      ],
  has door openable lockable static;
```

Here react_before picks up any action in the same location as the door, whether or not it directly involves the door. So if the door is the east connection out of this location, it reacts to the action Go e_obj action (because e_obj.door_dir is e_to, which is the door's door_dir as well). Another point to notice is that it reacts to Enter as well. Normally, if the player types "go through oaken door", then the action Enter oaken_door is generated, and the library checks that the door is open before generating Go e_obj. Here, of course, the whole point is that the door is closed, so we have to intercept the Enter action as early as possible. (A caveat: if door_dir values are to be routines, the above needs to be complicated slightly to call these routines and compare the return values.)

• 4 (p. 90)   The following assumes that all the keys in the game belong to a class called Key, and that there are no more than 16 of them. This allows the set of keys tried so far to be stored (as a bit vector) in a 16-bit Inform integer, and as games with many keys and many doors are exceptionally irritating, the limit is a blessing in disguise. Add the following to the ObligingDoor class:

```
has_been_unlocked,
which_keys_tried,
before [ key_to_try j bit ks;
    Open:
        if (self has locked) {
            if (self.has_been_unlocked) {
                key_to_try = self.with_key;
                if (key_to_try notin player)
                    "You have mislaid ", (the) key_to_try,
```

```
                         " and so cannot unlock ", (the) self, ".";
                    print "(first unlocking ";
                }
                else {
                    bit=1;
                    objectloop (j ofclass Key)
                    {   if (self.which_keys_tried & bit == 0
                            && j in player) key_to_try = j;
                        bit = bit*2;
                    }
                    if (key_to_try == nothing) rfalse;
                    print "(first trying to unlock ";
                }
                print (the) self, " with ", (the) key_to_try, ")^";
                ks = keep_silent; keep_silent = true;
                <Unlock self key_to_try>; keep_silent = ks;
                if (self has locked) rtrue;
            }
    Lock: if (self has open) {
                print "(first closing ", (the) self, ")^";
                ks = keep_silent; keep_silent = true;
                <Close self>; keep_silent = ks;
                if (self has open) rtrue;
            }
    Unlock:
        bit=1;
        objectloop (j ofclass Key) {
            if (second == j)
                self.which_keys_tried = self.which_keys_tried + bit;
            bit = bit*2;
        }
],
after [;
    Unlock: self.has_been_unlocked = true;
],
```

• 5 (p. 91)   Briefly: provide a GamePreRoutine which tests to see if second is an object, rather than nothing or a number. If it is, check whether the object has a second_before rule (i.e. test the condition (object provides second_before)). If it has, send the second_before message to it, and return the reply as the return value from GamePreRoutine. If second isn't an object, be sure to explicitly return false from GamePreRoutine, or you might inadvertently run into the] at the end, have true returned and find lots of actions mysteriously stopped.

Exercises in Chapter III

• 6 (p. 109)   At the key moment, `move orange_cloud to location`, where the orange cloud is defined as follows:

```
Object orange_cloud "orange cloud"
  with name 'orange' 'cloud',
       react_before [;
           Look: "You can't see for the orange cloud surrounding you.";
           Go, Exit: "You wander round in circles, choking.";
           Smell: if (noun == nothing or self) "Cinnamon? No, nutmeg.";
       ],
  has  scenery;
```

• 7 (p. 110)   It's essential here to return `true`, to prevent the library from saying "Dropped." as it otherwise would. Fortunately `print_ret` causes a return value of `true`:

```
after [;
    Drop: move noun to Square_Chamber;
          print_ret (The) noun, " slips through one of the burrows
              and is quickly lost from sight.";
],
```

(The rest of the Wormcast's definition is left until §9 below.) This is fine for 'Ruins', but in a more complicated game it's possible that other events besides a Drop might move items to the floor. If so, the Wormcast could be given an `each_turn` (see §20) to watch for items on the floor and slip them into the burrows.

• 8 (p. 113)   The Wormcast has one orthodox exit (west) and three confused ones:

```
Object Wormcast "Wormcast"
  with description
              "A disturbed place of hollows carved like a spider's web,
              strands of empty space hanging in stone. The only burrows
              wide enough to crawl through begin by running northeast,
              south and upwards.",
       w_to Square_Chamber,
       ne_to [; return self.s_to(); ],
       u_to [; return self.s_to(); ],
       s_to [;
           print "The wormcast becomes slippery around you, as though
               your body-heat is melting long hardened resins, and
               you shut your eyes tightly as you burrow through
               darkness.^";
```

```
        if (eggsac in player) return Square_Chamber;
        return random(Square_Chamber, Corridor, Forest);
    ],
    cant_go "Though you feel certain that something lies behind
        the wormcast, this way is impossible.",
  has  light;
```

This is a tease, as it stands, and is in need of a solution to the puzzle and a reward for solving it.

• 9 (p. 113)   Define four objects along the lines of:

```
CompassDirection white_obj "white wall" compass
  with name 'white' 'sac' 'wall', door_dir n_to;
```

This means there are now sixteen direction objects, some of which refer to the same actual direction: the player can type "white" or "north" with the same effect. If you would like to take away the player's ability to use the ordinary English nouns, add the following line to Initialise:

```
remove n_obj; remove e_obj; remove w_obj; remove s_obj;
```

('Curses' does a similar trick when the player boards a ship, taking away the normal directions in favour of "port", "starboard", "fore" and "aft".) As a fine point of style, turquoise (*yax*) is the world colour for 'here', so add a grammar line to make this cause a "look":

```
Verb 'turquoise' 'yax' * -> Look;
```

• 10 (p. 114)   This time it's not enough to define a new way of saying an old direction: "xyzzy" is an entirely new direction. It needs a direction property, say xyzzy_to, and this property needs to be declared as a "common property", partly for efficiency reasons, partly because that's just how the library works. (Common properties are those declared in advance of use with Property. See §3 for further details.) So:

```
Property xyzzy_to;
CompassDirection xyzzy_obj "magic word" compass
  with name 'xyzzy', door_dir xyzzy_to;
```

• 11 (p. 114)   We exchange the east and west direction references:

```
[ SwapDirs o1 o2 x;
  x = o1.door_dir; o1.door_dir = o2.door_dir; o2.door_dir = x;
];
[ ReflectWorld;
  SwapDirs(e_obj, w_obj);
```

439

```
    SwapDirs(ne_obj, nw_obj);
    SwapDirs(se_obj, sw_obj);
];
```

• 12 (p. 114)   This is a prime candidate for using variable strings (see §1.11):

```
[ NormalWorld; string 0 "east"; string 1 "west"; ];
[ ReversedWorld; string 0 "west"; string 1 "east"; ];
```

where NormalWorld is called in Initialise and ReversedWorld when the reflection happens. Write @00 in place of "east" in any double-quoted printable string, and similarly @01 for "west". It will be printed as whichever is currently set.

• 13 (p. 114)   Make all the location objects members of a class called:

```
Class Room
  with n_to, e_to, w_to, s_to, ne_to, nw_to, se_to, sw_to,
       in_to, out_to, u_to, d_to;
```

These properties are needed to make sure we can always write any map connection value to any room. Now define a routine which works on two opposite direction properties at a time:

```
[ TwoWay x dp1 dp2 y;
    y = x.dp1; if (metaclass(y) == Object && y ofclass Room) y.dp2 = x;
    y = x.dp2; if (metaclass(y) == Object && y ofclass Room) y.dp1 = x;
];
```

Note that some map connections run to doors (see §13) and not locations, and any such map connections need special handling which this solution can't provide: so we check that y ofclass Room before setting any direction properties for it. The actual code to go into Initialise is now simple:

```
objectloop (x ofclass Room) {
    TwoWay(x, n_to, s_to);    TwoWay(x, e_to, w_to);
    TwoWay(x, ne_to, sw_to);  TwoWay(x, nw_to, se_to);
    TwoWay(x, u_to, d_to);    TwoWay(x, in_to, out_to);
}
```

• 14 (p. 117)   The following code only works because react_before happens in advance of before. It uses react_before (rather than each_turn, say, or a daemon) to see if the gloves can be joined, in order to get in ahead of any Look, Search or Inv action which might want to talk about the gloves; whereas the before routine applies only if the player specifically refers to one of the gloves by name:

```
Class Glove
```

```
 with name 'white' 'glove' 'silk',
       article "the",
       react_before [;
           if (self in gloves) rfalse;
           if (parent(right_glove) ~= parent(left_glove)) rfalse;
           if (left_glove has worn && right_glove hasnt worn) rfalse;
           if (left_glove hasnt worn && right_glove has worn) rfalse;
           if (left_glove has worn) give gloves worn;
               else give gloves ~worn;
           move gloves to parent(right_glove);
           move right_glove to gloves; move left_glove to gloves;
           give right_glove ~worn; give left_glove ~worn;
       ],
       before [;
           if (self notin gloves) rfalse;
           move left_glove to parent(gloves);
           move right_glove to parent(gloves);
           if (gloves has worn) {
               give left_glove worn; give right_glove worn;
           }
           remove gloves;
       ],
   has clothing;
Object -> gloves "white gloves"
   with name 'white' 'gloves' 'pair' 'of',
        article "a pair of",
   has  clothing transparent;
Glove -> -> left_glove "left glove"
   with description "White silk, monogrammed with a scarlet R.",
        name 'left';
Glove -> -> right_glove "right glove"
   with description "White silk, monogrammed with a scarlet T.",
        name 'right';
```

• **15** (p. 119) "That was an unaccompanied bass pedal solo by Michael Rutherford... this is *The Musical Box*." (Announcement following tuning-up in a Genesis concert, Peter Gabriel, February 1973.) The easy thing to forget here is to make the container openable, because all the keys in the world won't help the player if the box hasn't got that.

```
Object -> "musical box",
  with name 'musical' 'box',
       with_key silver_key,
```

```
        capacity 1,
   has  lockable locked openable container;
Object -> -> "score of a song" with name 'score' 'music' 'song',
        article "the",
        description "~The Return of Giant Hogweed~.";
Object -> silver_key "silver key"
   with name 'silver' 'key';
```

• 16 (p. 120)

```
Object -> bag "toothed bag"
   with name 'toothed' 'bag',
        description "A capacious bag with a toothed mouth.",
        before [;
            LetGo: "The bag defiantly bites itself
                    shut on your hand until you desist.";
            Close: "The bag resists all attempts to close it.";
        ],
        after [;
            Receive:
                "The bag wriggles hideously as it swallows ",
                (the) noun, ".";
        ],
   has  container open openable;
```

• 17 (p. 121)

```
Object -> glass_box "glass box with a lid"
   with name 'glass' 'box' 'with' 'lid'
   has  container transparent openable open;
Object -> steel_box "steel box with a lid"
   with name 'steel' 'box' 'with' 'lid'
   has  container openable open;
```

• 18 (p. 121)   See §14 for switchable, used below to make the power button actually do something.

```
Object television "portable television set"
   with name 'tv' 'television' 'set' 'portable',
        before [;
            SwitchOn: <<SwitchOn power_button>>;
            SwitchOff: <<SwitchOff power_button>>;
            Examine: <<Examine screen>>;
        ],
```

```
   has  transparent;
Object -> power_button "power button"
   with name 'power' 'button' 'switch',
        after [;
            SwitchOn, SwitchOff: <<Examine screen>>;
        ],
   has  switchable;
Object -> screen "television screen"
   with name 'screen',
        before [;
            Examine: if (power_button hasnt on) "The screen is black.";
                "The screen writhes with a strange Japanese cartoon.";
        ];
```

• 19 (p. 121)   The describe part of this answer is only decoration. Note the careful use of inp1 and inp2 rather than noun or second, just in case an action involves a number or some text instead of an object. (See the note at the end of §6.)

```
Object -> macrame_bag "macrame bag"
   with name 'macrame' 'bag' 'string' 'net' 'sack',
        react_before [;
            Examine, Search, Listen, Smell: ;
            default:
                if (inp1 > 1 && noun in self)
                    print_ret (The) noun, " is inside the bag.";
                if (inp2 > 1 && second in self)
                    print_ret (The) second, " is inside the bag.";
        ],
        before [;
            Open: "The woollen twine is knotted hopelessly tight.";
        ],
        describe [;
            print "^A macrame bag hangs from the ceiling, shut tight";
            if (child(self)) {
                print ". Inside you can make out ";
                WriteListFrom(child(self), ENGLISH_BIT);
            }
            ".";
        ],
   has  container transparent openable;
Object -> -> "gold watch"
   with name 'gold' 'watch',
        description "The watch has no hands, oddly.",
```

```
      react_before [;
          Listen:
               if (noun == nothing or self) "The watch ticks loudly.";
      ];
```

For WriteListFrom, see §27.

• 20 (p. 124)   The "plank breaking" rule is implemented here in its door_to routine.
Note that this returns true after killing the player.

```
Object -> PlankBridge "plank bridge"
   with description "Extremely fragile and precarious.",
        name 'precarious' 'fragile' 'wooden' 'plank' 'bridge',
        when_open "A precarious plank bridge spans the chasm.",
        door_to [;
            if (children(player) > 0) {
                deadflag = true;
                "You step gingerly across the plank, which bows under
                your weight. But your meagre possessions are the straw
                which breaks the camel's back!";
            }
            print "You step gingerly across the plank, grateful that
                you're not burdened.^";
            if (self in NearSide) return FarSide; return NearSide;
        ],
        door_dir [;
            if (self in NearSide) return s_to; return n_to;
        ],
        found_in NearSide FarSide,
   has   static door open;
```

There might be a problem with this solution if your game also contained a character
who wandered about, and whose code was clever enough to run door_to routines for
any doors it ran into. If so, door_to could perhaps be modified to check that the actor
is the player.

• 21 (p. 124)

```
Object -> illusory_door "ironbound door",
   with name 'iron' 'ironbound' 'door',
        door_dir e_to, door_to Armoury,
        before [;
            Enter: return self.vanish();
        ],
        react_before [;
```

```
        Go: if (noun == e_obj) return self.vanish();
    ],
    vanish [;
        location.(self.door_dir) = self.door_to; remove self;
        print "The door vanishes, shown for the illusion it is!^";
        <<Go e_obj>>;
    ],
  has  locked lockable door openable;
```

We need to trap both the Go e_obj *and* Enter illusory_door actions and can't just wait for the latter to be converted into the former, because the door's locked, so it never gets as far as that.

• 22 (p. 128)

```
Object -> cage "iron cage"
  with name 'iron' 'cage' 'bars' 'barred' 'iron-barred',
       when_open
           "An iron-barred cage, large enough to stoop over inside,
           looms ominously here.",
       when_closed "The iron cage is closed.",
       inside_description "You stare out through the bars.",
  has  enterable container openable open transparent static;
```

• 23 (p. 129)   First define a class Road:

```
Class Road has light;
```

Every road-like location should belong to this class, so for instance:

```
Road Trafalgar_Square "Trafalgar Square"
with n_to National_Gallery, e_to Strand,
     w_to Pall_Mall, s_to Whitehall,
     description "The Square is overlooked by a pillared statue
         of Admiral Lord Horatio Nelson (no relation), naval hero
         and convenience to pigeons since 1812.";
```

Now change the car's before as follows:

```
    before [ way;
        Go: way = location.(noun.door_dir)();
            if (~~(way ofclass Road)) {
                print "You can't drive the car off-road.^";
                return 2;
            }
            if (car has on) "Brmm! Brmm!";
```

445

```
                print "(The ignition is off at the moment.)^";
        ],
```

The first line of the Go clause works out what the game's map places in the given direction. For instance, noun is e_obj, so that its direction property is held in noun.door_dir, whose value is e_to. Sending Trafalgar_Square.e_to(), we finally set way to Strand. This turns out to be of class Road, so the movement is permitted. As complicated as this seems, getting a car across the real Trafalgar Square is substantially more convoluted.

• 24 (p. 130)   We can't push up or down, but the ball lives on a north to south slope, so we'll just convert pushing up into pushing north, and down into south. Inserting these lines into the before rule for PushDir does the trick:

```
if (second == u_obj) <<PushDir self n_obj>>;
if (second == d_obj) <<PushDir self s_obj>>;
```

• 25 (p. 132)   The following involves more parsing expertise than is strictly needed, partly because it's a good opportunity to show off a routine called ParseToken. First we define:

```
Class Biblical with name 'book' 'of';
Class Gospel class Biblical with name 'gospel' 'saint' 'st';
Gospel "Gospel of St Matthew" with name 'matthew', chapters 28;
Gospel "Gospel of St Mark" with name 'mark', chapters 16;
Gospel "Gospel of St Luke" with name 'luke', chapters 24;
Gospel "Gospel of St John" with name 'john', chapters 21;
...
Biblical "Book of Revelation" with name 'revelation', chapters 22;
```

And here is the Bible itself:

```
Object -> "black Tyndale Bible"
  with name 'bible' 'black' 'book',
        initial "A black Bible rests on a spread-eagle lectern.",
        description "A splendid foot-high Bible, which must have
            survived the burnings of 1520.",
        before [ bk ch_num;
            Consult:
                do {
                    wn = consult_from;
                    bk = ParseToken(SCOPE_TT, BiblicalScope);
                } until (bk ~= GPR_REPARSE);
                if (bk == GPR_FAIL) "That's not a book in this Bible.";
                if (NextWord() ~= 'chapter') wn--;
                ch_num = TryNumber(wn);
```

```
            if (ch_num == -1000)
                "You read ", (the) bk, " right through.";
            if (ch_num > bk.chapters) "There are only ", †
                (number) bk.chapters," chapters in ",(the) bk,".";
            "Chapter ", (number) ch_num, " of ", (the) bk,
                " is too sacred for you to understand now.";
    ];
```

The first six lines under Consult look at what the player typed from word consult_from onwards, and set bk to be the Book which best matches. The call to ParseToken makes the parser behave as if matching $\boxed{\texttt{scope=BiblicalScope}}$, which means that we need to define a scope routine:

```
[ BiblicalScope bk;
  switch (scope_stage) {
      1: rfalse;
      2: objectloop (bk ofclass Biblical) PlaceInScope(bk); rtrue;
  }
];
```

See §32 for more, but this tells the parser to accept only the name of a single, specific object of class Biblical. The effect of all of this fuss is to allow the following dialogue:

> >look up gospel in bible
> Which do you mean, the Gospel of St Matthew, the Gospel of St Mark, the Gospel of St Luke or the Gospel of St John?
> >mark
> You read the Gospel of St Mark right through.
> >look up St John chapter 17 in bible
> Chapter seventeen of the Gospel of St John is too sacred for you to understand now.

For a simpler solution, Consult could instead begin like this:

```
wn = consult_from;
switch (NextWord()) {
    'matthew': bk = St_Matthew;
    'mark': bk = St_Mark;
...
    default: "That's not a book in this Bible.";
}
```

---

† Actually, Philemon, II. John, III. John and Jude have only one chapter apiece, so we ought to take more care over grammar here.

• 26 (p. 137)   Note that whether reacting before or after, the psychiatrist does not cut any actions short, because his `react_before` and `react_after` both return `false`.

```
Object -> psychiatrist "bearded psychiatrist"
  with name 'bearded' 'doctor' 'psychiatrist' 'psychologist' 'shrink',
      initial "A bearded psychiatrist has you under observation.",
      life [;
          "He is fascinated by your behaviour, but makes no attempt
          to interfere with it.";
      ],
      react_after [;
          Insert: print "~Subject associates ", (name) noun, " with ",
              (name) second, ". Interesting.~^^";
          PutOn: print "~Subject puts ", (name) noun, " on ",
              (name) second, ". Interesting.~^^";
          Look: print "^~Pretend I'm not here.~^^";
      ],
      react_before [;
          Take, Remove: print "~Subject feels lack of ", (the) noun,
              ". Suppressed Oedipal complex? Hmm.~^^";
      ],
  has  animate;
```

• 27 (p. 139)   There are several ways to do this. The easiest is to add more grammar to the parser and let it do the hard work:

```
Object -> computer "computer"
  with name 'computer',
      theta_setting,
      orders [;
          Theta: if (noun < 0 || noun >= 360)
                      "~That value of theta is out of range.~";
              self.theta_setting = noun;
                  "~Theta set. Waiting for additional values.~";
          default: "~Please rephrase.~";
      ],
  has  talkable;
...
[ ThetaSub; "You must tell your computer so."; ];
Verb 'theta' * 'is' number -> Theta;
```

• 28 (p. 139)   Add the following lines, after the inclusion of Grammar:

```
[ SayInsteadSub; "[To talk to someone, please type ~someone, something~
```

```
        or else ~ask someone about something~.]"; ];
Extend 'answer' replace * topic -> SayInstead;
Extend 'tell'   replace * topic -> SayInstead;
```

A slight snag is that this will throw out "nigel, tell me about the grunfeld defence" (which the library will normally convert to an Ask action, but can't if the grammar for "tell" is missing). To avoid this, you could instead of making the above directives Replace the TellSub routine (see §25) by the SayInsteadSub one.

• **29 (p. 140)** Obviously, a slightly wider repertoire of actions might be a good idea, but:

```
Object -> Charlotte "Charlotte"
  with name 'charlotte' 'charlie' 'chas',
       simon_said,
       grammar [;
            self.simon_said = false;
            wn = verb_wordnum;
            if (NextWord() == 'simon' && NextWord() == 'says') {
                if (wn > num_words) print "Simon says nothing, so ";
                else {
                    self.simon_said = true;
                    verb_wordnum = wn;
                }
            }
       ],
       orders [ i;
            if (self.simon_said == false)
                "Charlotte sticks her tongue out.";
            WaveHands: "Charlotte waves energetically.";
            default: "~Don't know how,~ says Charlotte.";
       ],
       initial "Charlotte wants to play Simon Says.",
  has  animate female proper;
```

(The variable i isn't needed yet, but will be used by the code added in the answer to the next exercise.) The test to see if wn has become larger than num_words prevents Charlotte from setting verb_wordnum to a non-existent word, which could only happen if the player typed just "charlotte, simon says". If so, the game will reply "Simon says nothing, so Charlotte sticks her tongue out."

• **30 (p. 140)** First add a Clap verb (this is easy). Then give Charlotte a number property (initially 0, say) and add these three lines to the end of Charlotte's grammar routine:

```
    self.number = TryNumber(verb_wordnum);
```

```
    if (self.number ~= -1000) {
        action = ##Clap; noun = 0; second = 0; rtrue;
    }
```

Her orders routine now needs the new clause:

```
Clap: if (self.number == 0) "Charlotte folds her arms.";
      for (i=0: i<self.number: i++) {
          print "Clap! ";
          if (i == 100)
              print "(You must be regretting this by now.) ";
          if (i == 200)
              print "(What a determined person she is.) ";
      }
      if (self.number > 100)
          "^^Charlotte is a bit out of breath now.";
      "^^~Easy!~ says Charlotte.";
```

• 31 (p. 140)   The interesting point here is that when the grammar property finds the word "take", it accepts it and has to move verb_wordnum on by one to signal that a word has been parsed succesfully.

```
Object -> Dan "Dyslexic Dan"
  with name 'dan' 'dyslexic',
      grammar [;
          if (verb_word == 'take') { verb_wordnum++; return 'drop'; }
          if (verb_word == 'drop') { verb_wordnum++; return 'take'; }
      ],
      orders [;
          Take: "~What,~ says Dan, ~you want me to take ",
                  (the) noun, "?~";
          Drop: "~What,~ says Dan, ~you want me to drop ",
                  (the) noun, "?~";
          Inv: "~That I can do,~ says Dan. ~I'm empty-handed.~";
          No: "~Right you be then.~";
          Yes: "~I'll be having to think about that.~";
          default: "~Don't know how,~ says Dan.";
      ],
      initial "Dyslexic Dan is here.",
  has  animate proper;
```

Since the words have been exchanged before any parsing takes place, Dan even responds to "drop inventory" and "take coin into slot".

• 32 (p. 141)   Suppose Dan's grammar (but nobody else's) for the "examine" verb is to be extended. His grammar routine should also contain:

```
if (verb_word == 'examine' or 'x//') {
    verb_wordnum++; return -'danx,';
}
```

(Note the crudity of this: it looks at the actual verb word, so you have to check any synonyms yourself.) The verb "danx," must be declared later:

```
Verb 'danx,' * 'conscience' -> Inv;
```

and now "Dan, examine conscience" will send him an Inv order: but "Dan, examine cow pie" will still send Examine cow_pie as usual.

• 33 (p. 141)   See §20 for the_time and other chronological matters. In particular, note that the game will need to call the library's SetTime routine to decide on a time of day.

```
[ AlTime x; print (x/60), ":", (x%60)/10, x%10; ];
Object -> alarm_clock "alarm clock"
  with name 'alarm' 'clock',
       alarm_time 480, ! 08:00
       description [;
           print "The alarm is ";
           if (self has on) print "on, "; else print "off, but ";
           "the clock reads ", (AlTime) the_time,
           " and the alarm is set for ", (AlTime) self.alarm_time, ".";
       ],
       react_after [;
           Inv: if (self in player) { new_line; <<Examine self>>; }
           Look: if (self in location) { new_line; <<Examine self>>; }
       ],
       daemon [ td;
           td = (1440 + the_time - self.alarm_time) % 1440;
           if (td >= 0 && td <= 3 && self has on)
               "^Beep! Beep! The alarm goes off.";
       ],
       grammar [; return 'alarm,'; ],
       orders [;
           SwitchOn: give self on; StartDaemon(self);
               "~Alarm set.~";
           SwitchOff: give self ~on; StopDaemon(self);
               "~Alarm off.~";
           SetTo: self.alarm_time=noun; <<Examine self>>;
```

451

```
              default: "~On, off or a time of day, pliz.~";
          ],
          life [;
              "[Try ~clock, something~ to address the clock.]";
          ],
      has  talkable;
```

(So the alarm sounds for three minutes after its setting, then gives in.) Next, add a new verb to the grammar:

```
Verb 'alarm,'
    * 'on'  -> SwitchOn
    * 'off' -> SwitchOff
    * TimeOfDay -> SetTo;
```

using a token for parsing times of day called ⟨TimeOfDay⟩: as this is one of the exercises in §31, it won't be given here. Note that since the word "alarm," can't be matched by anything the player types, this verb is concealed from ordinary grammar. The orders we produce here are not used in the ordinary way (for instance, the action SwitchOn with no noun or second would never ordinarily be produced by the parser) but this doesn't matter: it only matters that the grammar and the orders property agree with each other.

● 34 (p. 141)

```
Object -> tricorder "tricorder"
    with name 'tricorder',
         grammar [; return 'tc,'; ],
         orders [;
             Examine: if (noun == player) "~You radiate life signs.~";
                  print "~", (The) noun, " radiates ";
                  if (noun hasnt animate) print "no ";
                  "life signs.~";
             default: "The tricorder bleeps.";
         ],
         life [;
             "The tricorder is too simple.";
         ],
    has  talkable;
 ...
Verb 'tc,' * noun -> Examine;
```

● 35 (p. 141)

```
Object replicator "replicator"
    with name 'replicator',
```

```
        grammar [;  return 'rc,'; ],
        orders [;
            Give:
                if (noun in self)
                    "The replicator serves up a cup of ",
                    (name) noun, " which you drink eagerly.";
                "~That is not something I can replicate.~";
            default: "The replicator is unable to oblige.";
        ],
        life [;
            "The replicator has no conversational skill.";
        ],
   has  talkable;
Object -> "Earl Grey tea" with name 'earl' 'grey' 'tea';
Object -> "Aldebaran brandy" with name 'aldebaran' 'brandy';
Object -> "distilled water" with name 'distilled' 'water';
...
Verb 'rc,' * held -> Give;
```

The point to note here is that the ⌷held⌷ token means 'held by the replicator' here,
as the actor is the replicator, so this is a neat way of getting a 'one of the following
phrases' token into the grammar.

• 36 (p. 141)   This is similar to the previous exercises. Suppose that the crew are all
members of the class StarFleetOfficer. The orders property for the badge is then:

```
orders [;
    Examine:
        if (parent(noun))
            "~", (name) noun, " is in ", (name) parent(noun), ".~";
        "~", (name) noun, " is no longer aboard this demonstration
        game.~";
    default: "The computer's only really good for locating the crew.";
],
```

and the grammar simply returns 'stc,' which is defined as:

```
[ Crew i;
  switch(scope_stage)
  { 1: rfalse;
    2: objectloop (i ofclass StarFleetOfficer) PlaceInScope(i); rtrue;
  }
];
Verb 'stc,' * 'where' 'is' scope=Crew -> Examine;
```

An interesting point is that the scope routine scope=Crew doesn't need to do anything at scope stage 3 (usually used for printing out errors) because the normal error-message printing system is never reached. Something like "computer, where is Comminder Doto" causes a ##NotUnderstood order.

• 37 (p. 142)

```
Object -> Zen "Zen"
  with name 'zen' 'flight' 'computer',
        initial "Square lights flicker unpredictably across a hexagonal
            fascia on one wall, indicating that Zen is on-line.",
        grammar [; return 'zen,'; ],
        orders [;
            ZenScan: "The main screen shows a starfield,
                turning through ", noun, " degrees.";
            Go: "~Confirmed.~ The ship turns to a new bearing.";
            SetTo: if (noun > 12) "~Standard by ", (number) noun,
                    " exceeds design tolerances.~";
                if (noun == 0) "~Confirmed.~ The ship's engines stop.";
                "~Confirmed.~ The ship's engines step to
                standard by ", (number) noun, ".";
            Take: if (noun ~= force_wall) "~Please clarify.~";
                "~Force wall raised.~";
            Drop: if (noun ~= blasters)   "~Please clarify.~";
                "~Battle-computers on line.
                Neutron blasters cleared for firing.~";
            NotUnderstood: "~Language banks unable to decode.~";
            default: "~Information. That function is unavailable.~";
        ],
  has   talkable proper static;
Object -> -> force_wall "force wall"
  with name 'force' 'wall' 'shields';
Object -> -> blasters "neutron blasters"
  with name 'neutron' 'blasters';
...
[ ZenScanSub; "This is never called but makes the action exist."; ];
Verb 'zen,'
    * 'scan' number 'orbital' -> ZenScan
    * 'set' 'course' 'for' scope=Planet -> Go
    * 'speed' 'standard' 'by' number -> SetTo
    * 'raise' held -> Take
    * 'clear' held 'for' 'firing' -> Drop;
```

Dealing with Ask, Answer and Tell are left to the reader. As for planetary parsing:

```
[ Planet;
  switch (scope_stage) {
      1: rfalse; ! Disallow multiple planets
      2: ScopeWithin(galaxy); rtrue; ! Scope set to contents of galaxy
  }
];
Object galaxy;
Object -> "Earth" with name 'earth' 'terra';
Object -> "Centauro" with name 'centauro';
Object -> "Destiny" with name 'destiny';
```

and so on for numerous other worlds of the oppressive if somewhat cheaply decorated Federation.

• 38 (p. 142)   This is a typical bit of "scope hacking", in this case done with the InScope entry point, though providing the viewscreen with a similar add_to_scope routine would have done equally well. See §32.

```
[ InScope;
    if (action_to_be == ##Examine or ##Show && location == Bridge)
        PlaceInScope(noslen_maharg);
    if (scope_reason == TALKING_REASON)
        PlaceInScope(noslen_maharg);
    rfalse;
];
```

The variable scope_reason is always set to the constant value TALKING_REASON when the game is trying to work out who you wish to talk to: so it's quite easy to make the scope different for conversational purposes.

• 39 (p. 142)   Martha and the sealed room are defined as follows:

```
Object sealed_room "Sealed Room"
  with description
          "I'm in a sealed room, like a squash court without a door,
          maybe six or seven yards across",
  has  light;
Object -> ball "red ball" with name 'red' 'ball';
Object -> martha "Martha"
  with name 'martha',
      orders [ r;
          r = parent(self);
          Give:
```

```
            if (noun notin r) "~That's beyond my telekinesis.~";
            if (noun == self) "~Teleportation's too hard for me.~";
            move noun to player;
            "~Here goes...~ and Martha's telekinetic talents
                magically bring ", (the) noun, " to your hands.";
        Look:
            print "~", (string) r.description;
            if (children(r) == 1) ". There's nothing here but me.~";
            print ". I can see ";
            WriteListFrom(child(r), CONCEAL_BIT + ENGLISH_BIT);
            ".~";
        default: "~Afraid I can't help you there.~";
    ],
    life [;
        Ask: "~You're on your own this time.~";
        Tell: "Martha clucks sympathetically.";
        Answer: "~I'll be darned,~ Martha replies.";
    ],
  has animate female concealed proper;
```

but the really interesting part is the InScope routine to fix things up:

```
[ InScope actor;
   if (actor == martha) PlaceInScope(player);
   if (actor == player && scope_reason == TALKING_REASON)
       PlaceInScope(martha);
   rfalse;
];
```

Note that since we want two-way communication, the player has to be in scope to Martha too: otherwise Martha won't be able to follow the command "martha, give me the fish", because "me" will refer to something beyond her scope.

• 40 (p. 145)   In an outdoor game on a summer's day, one way would be to make a scenery object for the Sun which is found_in every location and has light. A sneakier method is to put the line

```
    give player light;
```

in Initialise. Now there's never darkness near the player. Unless there are wrangles involving giving instructions to people in different locations (where it's still dark), or the player having an out-of-body experience (see §21), this will work perfectly well. The player is never told "You are giving off light", so nothing seems incongruous in play.

• 41 (p. 146)   Just test if HasLightSource(gift) == true.

• **42** (p. 148)   This is a crude implementation, for brevity (the real 'Zork' thief has an enormous stock of attached messages). It does no more than choose a random exit and move through it on roughly one turn in three. A `life` routine is omitted, and of course this particular thief steals nothing. See 'The Thief' for a much fuller, annotated implementation.

```
Object -> thief "thief"
  with name 'thief' 'gentleman' 'mahu' 'modo',
       each_turn "^The thief growls menacingly.",
       daemon [ direction thief_at way exit_count exit_chosen;
           if (random(3) ~= 1) rfalse;
           thief_at = parent(thief);
           objectloop (direction in compass) {
               way = thief_at.(direction.door_dir);
               if (way ofclass Object && way hasnt door) exit_count++;
           }
           if (exit_count == 0) rfalse;
           exit_chosen = random(exit_count); exit_count = 0;
           objectloop (direction in compass) {
               way = thief_at.(direction.door_dir);
               if (way ofclass Object && way hasnt door) exit_count++;
               if (exit_count == exit_chosen) {
                   move self to way;
                   if (thief_at == location) "^The thief stalks away!";
                   if (way == location) "^The thief stalks in!";
                   rfalse;
               }
           }
       ],
  has  animate;
```

(Not forgetting to `StartDaemon(thief)` at some point, for instance in the game's `Initialise` routine.) So the thief walks at random but never via doors, bridges and the like, because these may be locked or have rules attached. This is only a first try, and in a good game one would occasionally see the thief do something surprising, such as open a secret door. As for the name, "The Prince of Darkness is a gentleman. Modo he's called, and Mahu" (William Shakespeare, *King Lear* III iv).

• **43** (p. 148)   We shall use a new property called `weight` and decide that any object which doesn't provide any particular weight will weigh 10 units. Clearly, an object which contains other objects will carry their weight too, so:

```
[ WeightOf obj t i;
   if (obj provides weight) t = obj.weight; else t = 10;
```

```
    objectloop (i in obj) t = t + WeightOf(i);
    return t;
];
```

Once every turn we shall check how much the player is carrying and adjust a measure of the player's fatigue accordingly. There are many ways we could choose to calculate this: for the sake of example we'll define two constants:

```
Constant FULL_STRENGTH = 500;
Constant HEAVINESS_THRESHOLD = 100;
```

Initially the player's strength will be the maximum possible, which we'll set to 500. Each turn the amount of weight being carried is subtracted from this, but 100 is also added on (without exceeding the maximum value). So if the player carries more than 100 units then strength declines, but if the weight carried falls below 100 then strength recovers. If the player drops absolutely everything, the entire original strength will recuperate in at most 5 turns. Exhaustion sets in if strength reaches 0, and at this point the player is forced to drop something, giving strength a slight boost. Anyway, here's an implementation of all this:

```
Object WeightMonitor
  with players_strength,
       warning_level 5,
       activate [;
           self.players_strength = FULL_STRENGTH;
           StartDaemon(self);
       ],
       daemon [ warn strength item heaviest_weight heaviest_item;
           strength = self.players_strength
               - WeightOf(player) + HEAVINESS_THRESHOLD;
           if (strength < 0) strength = 0;
           if (strength > FULL_STRENGTH) strength = FULL_STRENGTH;
           self.players_strength = strength;
           if (strength == 0) {
               heaviest_weight = -1;
               objectloop(item in player)
                   if (WeightOf(item) > heaviest_weight) {
                       heaviest_weight = WeightOf(item);
                       heaviest_item = item;
                   }
               if (heaviest_item == nothing) return;
               print "^Exhausted with carrying so much, you decide
                   to discard ", (the) heaviest_item, ": ";
               <Drop heaviest_item>;
               if (heaviest_item in player) {
```

```
                        deadflag = true;
                        "^Unprepared for this, you collapse.";
                    }
                    self.players_strength =
                        self.players_strength + heaviest_weight;
                }
                warn = strength/100; if (warn == self.warning_level) return;
                self.warning_level = warn;
                switch (warn) {
                    3: "^You are feeling a little tired.";
                    2: "^Your possessions are weighing you down.";
                    1: "^Carrying so much weight is wearing you out.";
                    0: "^You're nearly exhausted enough to drop everything
                        at an inconvenient moment.";
                }
            ];
```

When exhaustion sets in, this daemon tries to drop the heaviest item. (The actual dropping is done with Drop actions: in case the item is, say, a wild boar, which would bolt away into the forest when released. Also, after the attempt to Drop, we check to see if the drop has succeeded, because the heaviest item might be a cannonball superglued to one's hands, or a boomerang, or some such.) Finally, of course, at some point – probably in Initialise – the game needs to send the message WeightMonitor.activate() to get things going.

• 44 (p. 148)   Note that we use StopTimer before StartTimer in case the egg timer is already running. (StopTimer does nothing if the timer isn't running, while StartTimer does nothing if it is.)

```
Object -> "egg timer in the shape of a chicken"
  with name 'egg' 'timer' 'egg-timer' 'eggtimer' 'chicken' 'dial',
       description
           "Turn the dial on the side of the chicken to set this
           egg timer.",
       before [;
           Turn: StopTimer(self); StartTimer(self, 3);
               "You turn the dial to its three-minute mark, and the
               chicken begins a sort of clockwork clucking.";
       ],
       time_left,
       time_out [;
           "^~Cock-a-doodle-doo!~ says the egg-timer, in defiance of
           its supposedly chicken nature.";
       ];
```

459

• **45** (p. 149)   See the next answer.

• **46** (p. 149)

```
Object tiny_claws "sound of tiny claws" thedark
  with article "the",
       name 'tiny' 'claws' 'sound' 'of' 'scuttling' 'scuttle'
            'things' 'creatures' 'monsters' 'insects',
       initial "Somewhere, tiny claws are scuttling.",
       before [;
           Listen: "How intelligent they sound, for mere insects.";
           Touch, Taste: "You wouldn't want to. Really.";
           Smell: "You can only smell your own fear.";
           Attack: "They easily evade your flailing about.";
           default: "The creatures evade you, chittering.";
       ],
       each_turn [; StartDaemon(self); ],
       turns_active,
       daemon [;
           if (location ~= thedark) {
               self.turns_active = 0; StopDaemon(self); rtrue;
           }
           switch (++(self.turns_active)) {
               1: "^The scuttling draws a little nearer, and your
                   breathing grows loud and hoarse.";
               2: "^The perspiration of terror runs off your brow.
                   The creatures are almost here!";
               3: "^You feel a tickling at your extremities and kick
                   outward, shaking something chitinous off. Their
                   sound alone is a menacing rasp.";
               4: deadflag = true;
                   "^Suddenly there is a tiny pain, of a
                   hypodermic-sharp fang at your calf. Almost at once
                   your limbs go into spasm, your shoulders and
                   knee-joints lock, your tongue swells...";
           }
       ];
```

• **47** (p. 150)   Either set a daemon to watch for the_time suddenly dropping, or put such a watch in the game's TimePasses routine.

• 48 (p. 150)   A minimal solution is as follows. Firstly, we'll define a class of outdoor locations, and make two constant definitions:

```
Constant SUNRISE = 360;  ! i.e., 6 am
Constant SUNSET = 1140;  ! i.e., 7 pm
Class OutdoorLocation;
```

We handle night and day by having a light-giving scenery object present in outdoor locations during the day: we shall call this object "the sun":

```
Object Sun "sun"
  with name 'sun',
       found_in [;
           if (real_location ofclass OutdoorLocation) rtrue;
       ],
       before [;
           Examine: ;
           default: "The sun is too far away.";
       ],
       daemon [;
           if (the_time >= SUNRISE && the_time < SUNSET) {
               if (self has absent) {
                   give self ~absent;
                   if (real_location ofclass OutdoorLocation) {
                       move self to place;
                       "^The sun rises, illuminating the landscape!";
                   }
               }
           } else {
               if (self hasnt absent) {
                   give self absent; remove self;
                   if (real_location ofclass OutdoorLocation)
                       "^As the sun sets, the landscape is plunged
                       into darkness.";
               }
           }
       ],
  has light scenery;
```

In the Initialise routine, you need to call StartDaemon(Sun);. If the game starts in the hours of darkness, you should also give the Sun absent. Daybreak and nightfall will be automatic from there on.

● 49 (p. 150)   Because you don't know what order daemons will run in. A 'fatigue' daemon which makes the player drop something might come after the 'mid-air' daemon has run for this turn. Whereas each_turn happens after daemons and timers have run their course, and can fairly assume no further movements will take place this turn.

● 50 (p. 150)   It would have to provide its own code to keep track of time, and it can do this by providing a TimePasses() routine. Providing "time" or even "date" verbs to tell the player would also be a good idea.

● 51 (p. 156)   Two reasons. Firstly, sometimes you need to trap orders to other people, which react_before doesn't. Secondly, the player's react_before rule is not necessarily the first to react. Suppose in the deafness example that a cuckoo also has a react_before rule covering Listen, printing a message about birdsong. If this happens before the player object is reached, the deafness rule never applies.

● 52 (p. 156)

```
orders [;
    if (gasmask hasnt worn) rfalse;
    if (actor == self && action ~= ##Answer or ##Tell or ##Ask) rfalse;
    "Your speech is muffled into silence by the gas mask.";
],
```

● 53 (p. 157)   The common man's *wayhel* was a lowly mouse. Since we think much more highly of the player:

```
Object warthog "Warthog"
  with name 'wart' 'hog' 'warthog', description "Muddy and grunting.",
      initial "A warthog snuffles and grunts about in the ashes.",
      orders [;
          Go, Look, Examine, Smell, Taste, Touch, Search,
              Jump, Enter: rfalse;
          Eat: "You haven't the knack of snuffling up to food yet.";
          default: "Warthogs can't do anything so involved. If it
              weren't for the nocturnal eyesight and the lost weight,
              they'd be worse off all round than people.";
      ],
  has  animate proper;
```

Using ChangePlayer(warthog); will then bring about the transformation, though we must also move the warthog to some suitable location. The promised nocturnal eyesight will be brought about by giving the warthog light for the period when the player is changed to it.

• 54 (p. 157)   Change the `cant_go` message of the wormcast, dropping an even larger hint on the way:

```
cant_go [;
    if (player ~= warthog)
        "Though you begin to feel certain that something lies
        behind and through the wormcast, this way must be an
        animal-run at best: it's far too narrow for your
        armchair-archaeologist's paunch.";
    print "The wormcast becomes slippery around your warthog
        body, and you squeal involuntarily as you burrow
        through the darkness, falling finally southwards to...^";
    PlayerTo(Burial_Shaft); rtrue;
],
```

• 55 (p. 157)   This is more straightforward than it sounds. The most interesting point is that the map connection isn't between two rooms: it's between an enterable object, the cage, and a room, the burial chamber.

```
Object -> cage "iron cage"
    with name 'iron' 'cage' 'bars' 'barred' 'frame' 'glyphs',
        description "The glyphs read: Bird Arrow Warthog.",
        when_open
            "An iron-barred cage, large enough to stoop over inside,
            looms ominously here, its door open.  There are some glyphs
            on the frame.",
        when_closed "The iron cage is closed.",
        after [;
            Enter:
                print "The skeletons inhabiting the cage come alive,
                    locking bony hands about you, crushing and
                    pummelling. You lose consciousness, and when you
                    recover something grotesque and impossible has
                    occurred...^";
                move warthog to Antechamber; remove skeletons;
                give self ~open; give warthog light;
                self.after = 0;
                ChangePlayer(warthog, 1); <<Look>>;
        ],
        floor_open false,
        inside_description [;
            if (self.floor_open)
                "From the floor of the cage, an open earthen pit cuts
                down into the burial chamber.";
```

```
                "The bars of the cage surround you.";
        ],
        react_before [;
            Go: if (noun == d_obj && self.floor_open) {
                    PlayerTo(Burial_Shaft); rtrue;
                }
        ],
    has  enterable transparent container openable open static;
Object -> -> skeletons "skeletons"
    with name 'skeletons' 'skeleton' 'bone' 'skull' 'bones' 'skulls',
        article "deranged",
     has pluralname static;
Object Burial_Shaft "Burial Shaft"
    with description
                "In your eventual field notes, this will read:
                ~A corbel-vaulted crypt with an impacted earthen plug
                as seal above, and painted figures conjecturally
                representing the Nine Lords of the Night. Dispersed
                bones appear to be those of one elderly man and
                several child sacrifices, while other funerary remains
                include jaguar paws.~ (In field notes, it is essential
                not to give any sense of when you are scared witless.)",
        cant_go
                "The architects of this chamber were less than generous in
                providing exits. Some warthog seems to have burrowed in
                from the north, though.",
        n_to Wormcast,
        u_to [;
            cage.floor_open = true;
            self.u_to = self.opened_u_to;
            move selfobj to self;
            print "Making a mighty warthog-leap, you butt at the
                earthen-plug seal above the chamber, collapsing your
                world in ashes and earth. Something lifeless and
                terribly heavy falls on top of you: you lose
                consciousness, and when you recover, something
                impossible and grotesque has happened...^";
            ChangePlayer(selfobj); give warthog ~light; <<Look>>;
        ],
        before [;
            Jump: <<Go u_obj>>;
        ],
        opened_u_to [;
```

```
            PlayerTo(cage); rtrue;
        ],
    has   light;
```

• 56 (p. 158)

```
        orders [;
            if (player == self) {
                if (actor ~= self)
                    "You only become tongue-tied and gabble.";
                rfalse;
            }
            Attack: "The Giant looks at you with doleful eyes.
                ~Me not be so bad!~";
            default: "The Giant cannot comprehend your instructions.";
        ],
```

• 57 (p. 164)   Give the "chessboard" room a short_name routine (it probably already has one, to print names like "Chessboard d6") and make it change the short name to "the gigantic Chessboard" if and only if action is currently set to ##Places.

• 58 (p. 165)

```
Class Quotation;
Object PendingQuote; Object SeenQuote;
[ QuoteFrom q;
  if (~~(q ofclass Quotation)) "*** Oops! Not a quotation. ***";
  if (q notin PendingQuote or SeenQuote) move q to PendingQuote;
];
[ AfterPrompt q;
  q = child(PendingQuote);
  if (q) {
    move q to SeenQuote;
    q.show_quote();
  }
];
Quotation AhPeru
  with show_quote [;
            box "Brother of Ingots -- Ah, Peru --"
                "Empty the Hearts that purchased you --"
                ""
                "-- Emily Dickinson";
        ];
```

QuoteFrom(AhPeru) will now do as it is supposed to. The children of the object PendingQuote act as a last in, first out queue, so if several quotations are pending in the same turn, this system will show them in successive turns, most recently requested first.

• 59 (p. 191)   Place the following definition in between the inclusion of "Parser.h" and of "Verblib.h":

```
Object LibraryMessages
   with before [;
           Prompt: switch (turns) {
               1: print "^What should you, the detective, do now?^>";
               2 to 9: print "^What next?^>";
               10: print "^(Aren't you getting tired of seeing ~What
                   next?~ From here on, the prompt will be much
                   shorter.)^^>";
               default: print "^>";
           }
           rtrue;
       ];
```

• 60 (p. 191)   Looking in §A4, we find that the offending message is Go, number 1, but that this message appears in two cases: when the player is on a supporter, which we want to deal with, and when the player is in a container, which we want to leave alone.

```
Object LibraryMessages
   with before [ previous_parent;
           Go: if (lm_n == 1 && lm_o has supporter) {
                   print "(first getting off ", (the) lm_o, ")^";
                   previous_parent = parent(player);
                   keep_silent = true; <Exit>; keep_silent = false;
                   if (player in parent(previous_parent)) <<Go noun>>;
                   rtrue;
               }
       ];
```

Note that after we've tried to perform an Exit action, either we've made some progress (in that the player is no longer in the same parent) and can try the Go action again, or else we've failed, in which case something has been printed to that effect. Either way, we return true.

• 61 (p. 191)

```
Object LibraryMessages
```

```
with before [;
          Push: if (lm_n == 3 && noun has switchable) {
                   if (noun has on) <<SwitchOff noun>>;
                   <<SwitchOn noun>>;
                }
      ];
```

Exercises in Chapter IV

• 62 (p. 194)   Simply define the following, for accusative, nominative and capitalised nominative pronouns, respectively.

```
[ PronounAcc i;
    if (i hasnt animate || i has neuter) print "it";
    else { if (i has female) print "her"; else print "him"; } ];
[ PronounNom i;
    if (i hasnt animate || i has neuter) print "it";
    else { if (i has female) print "she"; else print "he"; } ];
[ CPronounNom i;
    if (i hasnt animate || i has neuter) print "It";
    else { if (i has female) print "She"; else print "He"; } ];
```

• 63 (p. 196)   We first set up the pieces. Bobby Fischer (Black, lower case, vs D. Byrne, Rosenwald Tournament, New York, 1956), aged thirteen and with queen *en prise*, is about to play Be6! and will win.

```
Array Position ->
    "r...r.k.\
    pp...pbp\
    .qp...p.\
    ..B.....\
    ..BP..b.\
    Q.n..N..\
    P....PPP\
    ...R.K.R";
```

(The backslashes \ remove spacing, so that this array contains just 64 entries.) Now for the objects. It will only be an illusion that there are sixty-four different locations, so we make sure the player drops nothing onto the board's surface.

```
Object Chessboard
  with description [;
          print "A square expanse of finest ";
```

```
        if ((self.rank + self.file - 'a') % 2 == 1)
            print "mahogany"; else print "cedarwood"; ".";
    ],
    short_name [;
        if (action==##Places) { print "the Chessboard"; rtrue; }
        print "Square ", (char) self.file, self.rank; rtrue;
    ],
    rank 1, file 'a',
    n_to  [; return self.try_move_to(self.rank+1,self.file);   ],
    ne_to [; return self.try_move_to(self.rank+1,self.file+1); ],
    e_to  [; return self.try_move_to(self.rank,  self.file+1); ],
    se_to [; return self.try_move_to(self.rank-1,self.file+1); ],
    s_to  [; return self.try_move_to(self.rank-1,self.file);   ],
    sw_to [; return self.try_move_to(self.rank-1,self.file-1); ],
    w_to  [; return self.try_move_to(self.rank,  self.file-1); ],
    nw_to [; return self.try_move_to(self.rank+1,self.file-1); ],
    try_move_to [ r f na p;
        if (~~(r >= 1 && r <= 8 && f >= 'a' && f <= 'h'))
            "That would be to step off the chessboard.";
        move Piece to self; na = Piece.&name; na-->1 = 'white';
        give Piece ~proper ~female;
        p = Position->((8-r)*8 + f - 'a');
        switch (p) {
            '.': remove Piece;
            'p', 'r', 'n', 'b', 'q', 'k': na-->1 = 'black';
        }
        switch (p) {
            'p', 'P': na-->0 = 'pawn';
            'r', 'R': na-->0 = 'rook';
            'n', 'N': na-->0 = 'knight';
            'b', 'B': na-->0 = 'bishop';
            'q', 'Q': na-->0 = 'queen'; give Piece female;
            'k', 'K': na-->0 = 'king'; give Piece proper;
        }
        switch (p) {
            'p': Piece.short_name = "Black Pawn";
            ...
            'K': Piece.short_name = "The White King";
        }
        self.rank = r; self.file = f; give self ~visited;
        return self;
    ],
    after [;
```

```
Drop: move noun to player;
        "From high above, a ghostly voice whispers ~J'adoube~,
        and ", (the) noun, " springs back into your hands.";
    ],
  has  light;
Object Piece
  with name '(kind)' '(colour)' 'piece' 'chess',
      short_name "(A short name filled in by Chessboard)",
      initial [; "This square is occupied by ", (a) self, "."; ],
  has  static;
```

And to get the player onto the board in the first place,

```
        PlayerTo(Chessboard.try_move_to(1,'a'));
```

● 64 (p. 197)   Use the invent routine to signal to short_name and article routines to change their usual habits:

```
Object "ornate box"
  with name 'ornate' 'box' 'troublesome',
      altering_short_name,
      invent [;
          self.altering_short_name = (inventory_stage == 1);
      ],
      short_name [;
          if (self.altering_short_name) { print "box"; rtrue; }
      ],
      article [;
          if (self.altering_short_name) print "that troublesome";
          else print "an";
      ],
  has  container open openable;
```

Thus the usual short name and article "an ornate box" becomes "that troublesome box" in inventory listings, but nowhere else.

● 65 (p. 200)   This answer is cheating, as it needs to know about the library's lookmode variable (set to 1 for normal, 2 for verbose or 3 for superbrief, according to the player's most recent choice). Simply include:

```
[ TimePasses;
  if (action ~= ##Look && lookmode == 2) <Look>;
];
```

• 66 (p. 203)

```
[ DoubleInvSub item number_carried number_worn;
  print "You are carrying ";
  objectloop (item in player) {
      if (item hasnt worn) { give item workflag; number_carried++; }
      else { give item ~workflag; number_worn++; }
  }
  if (number_carried == 0) print "nothing";
  else WriteListFrom(child(player),
          FULLINV_BIT + ENGLISH_BIT + RECURSE_BIT + WORKFLAG_BIT);
  if (number_worn == 0) ".";
  if (number_carried == 0) print ", but"; else print ". In addition,";
  print " you are wearing ";
  objectloop (item in player)
      if (item hasnt worn) give item ~workflag;
      else give item workflag;
  WriteListFrom(child(player),
      ENGLISH_BIT + RECURSE_BIT + WORKFLAG_BIT);
  ".";
];
```

• 67 (p. 204)

```
Class Letter
  with name 'letter' 'scrabble' 'piece' 'letters//p' 'pieces//p',
      list_together [;
          if (inventory_stage == 1) {
              print "the letters ";
              c_style = c_style | (ENGLISH_BIT + NOARTICLE_BIT);
              c_style = c_style &~ (NEWLINE_BIT + INDENT_BIT);
          }
          else print " from a Scrabble set";
      ],
      short_name [;
          if (listing_together ofclass Letter) rfalse;
          print "letter ", (object) self, " from a Scrabble set";
          rtrue;
      ],
      article "the";
```

The bitwise operation c = c | ENGLISH_BIT sets the given bit (i.e., adds it on to c) if it wasn't already set (i.e., if it hadn't already been added to c). The operation &~, which is actually two operators & (and) and ~ (not) put together, takes away something if it's present and otherwise does nothing. As many letters as desired can now be created, along the lines of

```
Letter -> "X" with name 'x//';
```

• 68 (p. 204)

```
Class Coin
  with name 'coin' 'coins//p',
       description "A round unstamped disc, presumably local currency.",
       list_together "coins",
       plural [;
           print (address) self.&name-->0;
           if (~~(listing_together ofclass Coin)) print " coins";
       ],
       short_name [;
           print (address) self.&name-->0;
           if (~~(listing_together ofclass Coin)) print " coin";
           rtrue;
       ],
       article [;
           if (listing_together ofclass Coin) print "one";
           else print "a";
       ];
Class GoldCoin   class Coin with name 'gold';
Class SilverCoin class Coin with name 'silver';
Class BronzeCoin class Coin with name 'bronze';
SilverCoin ->;
```

The trickiest lines here are the print (address) ones. This is the least commonly used printing-rule built into Inform, and is only really used to print out the text of a dictionary word: whereas

```
    print (string) 'gold';
```

is likely to print garbled and nonsensical text, because 'gold' is a dictionary word not a string. Anyway, these lines print out the first entry in the name list for the coin, so they rely on the fact that name words accumulate in the front of the list. The class Coin starts the list as ("coin", "coins"), whereupon SilverCoin augments it to ("silver", "coin", "coins"). Finally, because a dictionary word only stores up to nine letters, a different solution would be needed to cope with molybdenum coins.

• 69 (p. 205)   Firstly, a printing rule to print the state of coins. Coin-objects will have a property called heads_up which is always either true or false:

```
[ Face x; if (x.heads_up) print "Heads"; else print "Tails"; ];
```

471

There are two kinds of coin but we'll implement them with three classes: Coin and two sub-categories, GoldCoin and SilverCoin. Since the coins only join up into trigrams when present in groups of three, we need a routine to detect this:

```
[ CoinsTogether cla member p common_parent;
  objectloop (member ofclass cla) {
      p = parent(member);
      if (common_parent == nothing) common_parent = p;
      else if (common_parent ~= p) return nothing;
  }
  return common_parent;
];
```

Thus CoinsTogether(GoldCoin) decides whether all objects of class GoldCoin have the same parent, returning either that parent or else nothing, and likewise for SilverCoin. Now the class definitions:

```
Class Coin
  with name 'coin' 'coins//p',
       heads_up true, article "the", metal "steel",
       after [;
           Drop, PutOn:
               self.heads_up = (random(2) == 1); print (Face) self;
               if (CoinsTogether(self.which_class)) {
                   print ". The ", (string) self.metal,
                       " trigram is now ", (Trigram) self;
               }
               ".";
       ];
[ CoinLT common_parent member count;
  if (inventory_stage == 1) {
      print "the ", (string) self.metal, " coins ";
      common_parent = CoinsTogether(self.which_class);
      if (common_parent &&
          (common_parent == location || common_parent has supporter)) {
          objectloop (member ofclass self.which_class) {
              print (name) member;
              switch (++count) {
                  1: print ", "; 2: print " and ";
                  3: print " (showing the trigram ",
                     (Trigram) self, ")";
              }
          }
      }
      rtrue;
  }
```

```
            c_style = c_style | (ENGLISH_BIT + NOARTICLE_BIT);
            c_style = c_style &~ (NEWLINE_BIT + INDENT_BIT);
       }
       rfalse;
];
Class GoldCoin class Coin
 with name 'gold', metal "gold", interpretation gold_trigrams,
       which_class GoldCoin,
       list_together [; return CoinLT(); ];
Class SilverCoin class Coin
 with name 'silver', metal "silver", interpretation silver_trigrams,
       which_class SilverCoin,
       list_together [; return CoinLT(); ];
Array gold_trigrams -->    "fortune" "change" "river flowing" "chance"
                           "immutability" "six stones in a circle"
                           "grace" "divine assistance";
Array silver_trigrams --> "happiness" "sadness" "ambition" "grief"
                           "glory" "charm" "sweetness of nature"
                           "the countenance of the Hooded Man";
```

(There are two unusual points here. Firstly, the CoinsLT routine is not simply given as the common list_together value in the coin class since, if it were, all six coins would be grouped together: we want two groups of three, so the gold and silver coins have to have different list_together values. Secondly, if a trigram is together and on the floor, it is not good enough to simply append text like "showing Tails, Heads, Heads (change)" at inventory_stage 2 since the coins may be listed in a funny order. In that event, the order the coins are listed in doesn't correspond to the order their values are listed in, which is misleading. So instead CoinsLT takes over entirely at inventory_stage 1 and prints out the list of three itself, returning true to stop the list from being printed out by the library as well.) To resume: whenever coins are listed together, they are grouped into gold and silver. Whenever trigrams are visible they are to be described by either Trigram(GoldClass) or Trigram(SilverClass):

```
[ Trigram acoin cla member count state;
  cla = acoin.which_class;
  objectloop (member ofclass cla) {
      print (Face) member;
      if (count++ < 2) print ","; print " ";
      state = state*2 + member.heads_up;
  }
  print "(", (string) (acoin.interpretation)-->state, ")";
];
```

Note that the class definitions refer to their arrays, but do not actually include the arrays themselves – this saves each coin carrying a copy of the whole array around with it, which would be wasteful. It's a marginal point, though, as there are only six actual coins:

```
GoldCoin -> "goat" with name 'goat';
GoldCoin -> "deer" with name 'deer';
GoldCoin -> "chicken" with name 'chicken';
SilverCoin -> "robin" with name 'robin';
SilverCoin -> "snake" with name 'snake';
SilverCoin -> "bison" with name 'bison';
```

If these were found in (say) a barn, we might have to take more care not to let them be called "goat" and so on, but let us assume not.

• 70 (p. 205)   There are innumerable methods for sorting, and an extensive research literature can advise on which method is likely to perform fastest in which circumstances. Here matters are complicated by the fact that it is not easy to exchange two objects in the tree without shuffling many other objects backwards and forwards to do so. The solution below is concise rather than efficient. Briefly, if there are N members of the AlphaSorted class then the game pauses before play begins to make N^2 comparisons of strings (this could easily be made faster but only happens once anyway): it then numbers off the members 1, 2, 3, ... in their correct alphabetical order, and subsequently uses this list to check only those objects which have moved since they were last checked.

```
Object heap1; Object heap2; Object heap3; Object heap4;
Class AlphaSorted
   with last_parent, last_sibling, sort_ordering,
       react_before [ t u v;
           Look, Search, Open, Inv:
               if (parent(self) == self.last_parent
                   && sibling(self) == self.last_sibling) rfalse;
               if (self.sort_ordering == 0)
                   objectloop (t ofclass AlphaSorted)
                       t.order_yourself();
               t = parent(self);
               while ((u = child(t)) ~= 0) {
                   if (u ofclass AlphaSorted) {
                       v = self.sort_ordering - u.sort_ordering;
                       if (v < 0) move u to heap1;
                       if (v == 0) move u to heap2;
                       if (v > 0) move u to heap3;
                   }
                   else move u to heap4;
               }
```

```
            while ((u = child(heap1)) ~= 0) move u to t;
            while ((u = child(heap2)) ~= 0) move u to t;
            while ((u = child(heap3)) ~= 0) move u to t;
            while ((u = child(heap4)) ~= 0) move u to t;
            self.last_parent = parent(self);
            self.last_sibling = sibling(self);
    ],
    order_yourself [ y val;
        objectloop (y ofclass AlphaSorted
                    && CompareObjects(self, y) > 0) val++;
        self.sort_ordering = val + 1;
    ];
```

The above code assumes that a routine called CompareObjects(a,b) exists, and returns a positive number, zero or a negative number according to whether a should come after, with or before b in lists. You could substitute any sorting rule here, but here as promised is the rule "in alphabetical order of the object's short name":

```
Array sortname1 -> 128;
Array sortname2 -> 128;
[ CompareObjects obj1 obj2 i d l1 l2;
  sortname1 --> 0 = 125; sortname2 --> 0 = 125;
  for (i = 2: i < 128: i++) { sortname1->i = 0; sortname2->i = 0; }
  @output_stream 3 sortname1; print (name) obj1; @output_stream -3;
  @output_stream 3 sortname2; print (name) obj2; @output_stream -3;
  for (i = 2: : i++) {
      l1 = sortname1->i; l2 = sortname2->i;
      d = l1 - l2; if (d) return d;
      if (l1 == 0) return 0;
  }
];
```

• 71 (p. 210)

```
parse_name [ n w colour;
    if (self.ripe) colour = 'red'; else colour = 'green';
    do { w = NextWord(); n++; } until (w ~= colour or 'fried');
    if (w == 'tomato') return n;
    return 0;
],
```

• 72 (p. 210)

```
Object -> "/?%?/ (the artiste formally known as Princess)"
  with name 'princess' 'artiste' 'formally' 'known' 'as',
```

475

```
kissed false,
short_name [;
    if (~~(self.kissed)) { print "Princess"; rtrue; }
],
react_before [;
    Listen: print_ret (name) self, " sings a soft siren song.";
],
initial [;
    print_ret (name) self, " is singing softly.";
],
parse_name [ x n;
        if (~~(self.kissed)) {
            if (NextWord() == 'princess') return 1;
            return 0;
        }
        x = WordAddress(wn);
        if (x->0 == '/' && x->1 == '?' && x->2 == '%'
            && x->3 == '?' && x->4 == '/') {
            ! See notes below for what this next line is for:
            while (wn <= parse->1 && WordAddress(wn++) < x+5) n++;
            return n;
        }
        return -1;
],
life [;
    Kiss: self.kissed = true; self.life = NULL;
        "In a fairy-tale transformation, the Princess
        steps back and astonishes the world by announcing
        that she will henceforth be known as ~/?%?/~.";
],
has   animate proper female;
```

The line commented on above needs some explanation. What it does is to count up the number of "words" making up the five characters in x->0 to x->4. This isn't really needed in the example above, but it would be if (say) the text to be matched was a.,.a because the full stops and comma would make the parser consider this text as five separate words, so that n should be set to 5.

• 73 (p. 210)   Something to note here is that the button can't be called just "coffee" when the player's holding a cup of coffee: this means the game responds sensibly to the sequence "press coffee" and "drink coffee". Also note the call to PronounNotice(drink), which tells the Inform parser that the pronouns (in English, "it", "him", "her", "them") to reset themselves to the drink where appropriate.

```
Object -> drinksmat "drinks machine",
```

```
    with name 'drinks' 'machine',
         initial
             "A drinks machine has buttons for Cola, Coffee and Tea.",
    has  static transparent;
Object -> -> thebutton "drinks machine button"
  with button_pushed,
       parse_name [ w n flag drinkword;
           for (: flag == false: n++) {
               switch (w = NextWord()) {
                   'button', 'for':
                   'coffee', 'tea', 'cola':
                       if (drinkword == 0) drinkword = w;
                   default: flag = true; n--;
               }
           }
           if (drinkword == drink.&name-->0 && n==1 && drink in player)
               return 0;
           self.button_pushed = drinkword; return n;
       ],
       before [;
           Push, SwitchOn:
               if (self.button_pushed == 0)
                   "You'll have to say which button to press.";
               if (parent(drink) ~= 0) "The machine's broken down.";
               drink.&name-->0 = self.button_pushed;
               move drink to player;
               PronounNotice(drink);
               "Whirr! The machine puts ", (a) drink,
                   " into your glad hands.";
           Attack: "The machine shudders and squirts cola at you.";
           Drink: "You can't drink until you've worked the machine.";
       ];
Object drink
  with name 'liquid' 'cup' 'of' 'drink',
       short_name [;
           print "cup of ", (address) self.&name-->0;
           rtrue;
       ],
       before [;
           Drink: remove self;
               "Ugh, that was awful. You crumple the cup and
               responsibly dispose of it.";
       ];
```

• 74 (p. 210)   Most of the work is handed over to WordInProperty(w,obj,prop), a
routine in the library which checks to see if w is one of the entries in the word array
obj.&prop, returning true or false as appropriate:

```
parse_name [ n;
    while (WordInProperty(NextWord(), self, name)) n++;
    return n;
],
```

• 75 (p. 210)   Create a new property adjective, and move names which are adjectives
to it: for instance,

```
name 'tomato' 'vegetable', adjective 'fried' 'green' 'cooked',
```

Then, again using WordInProperty routine as in the previous answer,

```
[ ParseNoun obj n m;
    while (WordInProperty(NextWord(),obj,adjective) == 1) n++; wn--;
    while (WordInProperty(NextWord(),obj,name) == 1) m++;
    if (m == 0) return 0; return n+m;
];
```

• 76 (p. 210)

```
[ ParseNoun obj;
    if (NextWord() == 'object' && TryNumber(wn) == obj) return 2;
    wn--; return -1;
];
```

• 77 (p. 210)   Since this affects the parsing of all nouns, not just a single object, we
need to set the entry point routine:

```
[ ParseNoun;
    if (NextWord() == '#//') return 1;
    wn--; return -1;
];
```

• 78 (p. 210)

```
[ ParseNoun;
    switch (NextWord()) {
        '#//': return 1;
        '*//': parser_action = ##PluralFound; return 1;
    }
```

```
    wn--; return -1;
];
```

• 79 (p. 213)   This solution is a little simplified, as it only allows the player to write single words on cubes. Notice that if two cubes have the same text written on them, then they become indistinguishable from each other again.

```
Class FeaturelessCube
  with description "A perfect white cube, four inches on a side.",
       text_written_on 0 0 0 0 0 0 0 0, ! Room for 16 characters of text
       text_length,
       article "a",
       parse_name [ i j flag;
           if (parser_action == ##TheSame) {
               if (parser_one.text_length ~= parser_two.text_length)
                   return -2;
               for (i = 0: i < parser_one.text_length: i++)
                   if (parser_one.&text_written_on->i
                       ~= parser_two.&text_written_on->i) return -2;
               return -1;
           }
           for (:: i++, flag = false) {
               switch (NextWordStopped()) {
                   'cube', 'white': flag = true;
                   'featureless', 'blank':
                       flag = (self.text_length == 0);
                   'cubes': flag = true; parser_action = ##PluralFound;
                   -1: return i;
                   default:
                       if (self.text_length == WordLength(wn-1))
                           for (j=0, flag=true: j<self.text_length: j++)
                               flag = flag && (self.&text_written_on->j
                                   == WordAddress(wn-1)->j);
               }
               if (flag == false) return i;
           }
       ],
       short_name [ i;
           if (self.text_length == 0) print "featureless white cube";
           else {
               print "~";
               for (i = 0: i<self.text_length: i++)
                   print (char) self.&text_written_on->i;
```

```
                    print "~ cube";
              }
              rtrue;
       ],
       plural [;
              self.short_name(); print "s";
       ];
Object -> burin "magic burin"
   with name 'magic' 'magical' 'burin' 'pen',
         description
              "This is a magical burin, used for inscribing objects with
              words or runes of magical import.",
         the_naming_word,
         before [ i;
              WriteOn:
                   if (~~(second ofclass FeaturelessCube)) rfalse;
                   if (second notin player)
                        "Writing on a cube is such a fiddly process that
                        you need to be holding it in your hand first.";
                   if (burin notin player)
                        "You would need some powerful implement for that.";
                   second.text_length = WordLength(self.the_naming_word);
                   if (second.text_length > 16) second.text_length = 16;
                   for (i=0: i<second.text_length: i++)
                        second.&text_written_on->i
                             = WordAddress(self.the_naming_word)->i;
                   second.article="the";
                   "It is now called ", (the) second, ".";
         ];
```

And this needs just a little grammar, to define the "write ... on ..." command:

```
[ AnyWord; burin.the_naming_word=wn++; return burin; ]
[ WriteOnSub; "Casual graffiti is beneath an enchanter's dignity."; ];
Verb 'write' 'scribe'
    * AnyWord 'on' held -> WriteOn
    * AnyWord 'on' noun -> WriteOn;
```

AnyWord is a simple example of a general parsing routine (see §31) which accepts any single word, recording its position in what the player typed and telling the parser that it refers to the burin object. Thus, text like "write pdl on cube" is parsed into the action <WriteOn burin cube> while burin.the_naming_word is set to 2.

• 80 (p. 214)   This is a little more subtle than first appears, because while the warning must be printed only once, the rule allowing "cherubs" to be recognised might need to be applied many times during the same turn – for instance, if the player types "get cherubs" where there are twelve plaster cherubs, the rule must allow "cherubs" twelve times over.

```
Global cherubim_warning_turn = -1;
Class Cherub
  with parse_name [ n w this_word_ok;
          for (::) {
              w = NextWord();
              this_word_ok = false;
              if (WordInProperty(w, self, name)) this_word_ok = true;
              switch (w) {
                  'cherub': this_word_ok = true;
                  'cherubim': parser_action = ##PluralFound;
                      this_word_ok = true;
                  'cherubs':
                      if (cherubim_warning_turn == -1) {
                          cherubim_warning_turn = turns;
                          print "(I'll let this go once, but the
                              plural of cherub is cherubim.)^";
                      }
                      if (cherubim_warning_turn == turns) {
                          this_word_ok = true;
                          parser_action = ##PluralFound;
                      }
              }
              if (this_word_ok == false) return n;
              n++;
          }
      ];
```

Then again, Shakespeare wrote "cherubins" (in 'Twelfth Night'), so who are we to censure?

• 81 (p. 215)   This makes use of the entry point routine, to meddle directly with the parsing table produced by the text. (See §2.4 for details of the format of this table.) Note that BeforeParsing is called *after* this table has been constructed.

```
Object -> genies_lamp "brass lamp"
  with name 'brass' 'lamp',
      colours_inverted false,
      before [;
          Rub: self.colours_inverted = ~~self.colours_inverted;
```

```
                  "A genie appears from the lamp, declaring:^^
                  ~Mischief is my sole delight:^
                  If white means black, black means white!~^^
                  She vanishes away with a vulgar wink.";
        ];
Object -> white_stone "white stone" with name 'white' 'stone';
Object -> black_stone "black stone" with name 'black' 'stone';
...
[ BeforeParsing;
    if (genies_lamp.colours_inverted)
        for (wn = 1 ::)
            switch (NextWordStopped()) {
                'white': parse-->(wn*2-3) = 'black';
                'black': parse-->(wn*2-3) = 'white';
                -1: return;
            }
];
```

• 82 (p. 221) You can fix this using the PrintVerb entry point routine:

```
[ PrintVerb word;
    if (word == 'go.verb') {
        if (go_verb_direction ofclass String) print "go somewhere";
        else {
            print "go to ",
                (name) real_location.(go_verb_direction.door_dir);
        }
        rtrue;
    }
    rfalse;
];
```

• 83 (p. 225) The puckish comedy of the footnote was introduced into adventure games by 'The Hitchhiker's Guide To The Galaxy'.†

```
Class Footnote with number 0, text "Text of the note.";
Footnote coinage
    with text "D.G.REG.F.D is inscribed around English coins.";
...
[ Note f fn;
```

---

† Not even the present author can bear to compare Douglas Adams to Edward Gibbon, so the reader is referred to Anthony Grafton's historiography *The Footnote: A Curious History* (1997).

```
    if (f.number == 0)
        objectloop (fn ofclass Footnote && fn ~= f)
            if (fn.number >= f.number)
                f.number = fn.number + 1;
    print "[", f.number, "]";
];
[ FootnoteSub fn;
    if (noun <= 0) "Footnotes count upward from 1.";
    objectloop (fn ofclass Footnote)
        if (fn.number == noun) {
            print "[", noun, "]. "; fn.text(); return;
        }
    "You haven't seen a footnote with that number.";
];
Verb meta 'footnote' 'note' * number -> Footnote;
```

And then you can code, for instance,

```
    print "Her claim to the throne is in every pocket ",
        (Note) coinage, ", her portrait in every wallet.";
```

• 84 (p. 228)

```
[ FrenchNumber n;
    switch (NextWord()) {
        'un', 'une': n=1;
        'deux': n=2;
        'trois': n=3;
        'quatre': n=4;
        'cinq': n=5;
        default: return GPR_FAIL;
    }
    parsed_number = n; return GPR_NUMBER;
];
```

• 85 (p. 228)   The token is demonstrated here with a command "status team", which lists off the team members and their current locations.

```
[ StatusSub; print "is in ", (name) parent(noun), "^"; ];
[ Team x y;
    if (NextWord() ~= 'team') return GPR_FAIL;
    objectloop (y ofclass Adventurer) multiple_object-->(++x) = y;
    multiple_object-->0 = x;
    return GPR_MULTIPLE;
];
```

```
Verb 'status' * Team -> Status;
```

• 86 (p. 228)   First we must decide how to store floating-point numbers internally: in this case we'll simply store $100x$ to represent x, so that "5.46" will be parsed as 546. This means that we can't parse numbers larger than $327.6749999\ldots$ but it would be easy to store numbers differently to make room for larger ones, if we needed to.

```
[ FloatingPoint i start digits integer fraction stop n;
  integer = TryNumber(wn++);
  if (integer == -1000) return GPR_FAIL;
  switch (NextWordStopped()) {
      THEN1__WD: if (NextWordStopped() == -1) return GPR_FAIL;
          start = WordAddress(wn-1); digits = WordLength(wn-1);
          for (i = 0: i < digits: i++) {
              if (start->i < '0' || start->i > '9') return GPR_FAIL;
              if (i<3) fraction = fraction*10 + start->i - '0';
          }
      'point':
          do {
              digits++;
              switch (NextWordStopped()) {
                  -1: stop = true;
                  'nought', 'oh', 'zero': n = 0;
                  default: n = TryNumber(wn-1);
                      if (n < 0 || n > 9) { wn--; stop = true; }
              }
              if ((~~stop) && digits <= 3) fraction = fraction*10 + n;
          } until (stop);
          digits--;
          if (digits == 0) return GPR_FAIL;
      -1: ;
      default: wn--;
  }
  for (: digits < 3: digits++) fraction = fraction*10;
  parsed_number = integer*100 + (fraction+5)/10;
  return GPR_NUMBER;
];
```

Here the local variables `integer` and `fraction` hold the integer and fractional part of the number being parsed, and the last calculation performs the rounding-off to the nearest 0.01. Note that `NextWord` and `NextWordStopped` return a full stop as the constant `THEN1__WD`, since it usually plays the same grammatical role as the word "then": "east then south" and "east. south" are understood as meaning the same thing. Further exercise: with a little more code, make "oh point oh one" also work.

• 87 (p. 228)   Again, the first question is how to store the number dialled: in this case, into a string array, and we store only the digits, stripping out spaces and hyphens. The token is:

```
Constant MAX_PHONE_LENGTH = 30;
Array dialled_number -> MAX_PHONE_LENGTH + 1;
[ PhoneNumber at length dialled dialled_already i;
  do {
      if (wn > num_words) jump number_ended;
      at = WordAddress(wn); length = WordLength(wn);
      for (i=0: i<length: i++) {
          switch (at->i) {
              '0', '1', '2', '3', '4', '5', '6', '7', '8', '9':
                  if (dialled < MAX_PHONE_LENGTH)
                      dialled_number -> (++dialled) = at->i - '0';
              '-': ;
              default: jump number_ended;
          }
      }
      wn++;
      dialled_already = dialled;
  } until (false);
 .number_ended;
  if (dialled_already == 0) return GPR_FAIL;
  dialled_number->0 = dialled_already;
  return GPR_PREPOSITION;
];
```

To demonstrate this in use,

```
[ DialPhoneSub i;
  print "You dialled <";
  for (i=1: i<=dialled_number->0: i++) print dialled_number->i;
  ">";
];
Verb 'dial' * PhoneNumber -> DialPhone;
```

• 88 (p. 228)   The time of day will be returned as a number in the usual Inform time format, as hours times 60 plus minutes, where the 'hours' part is between 0 and 23. Which gives a value between 0 and 1439: and here is a routine to convert an hours value, a minutes value and a dictionary word which can be either 'am' or 'pm' into an Inform time.

```
Constant TWELVE_HOURS = 720;
```

485

```
[ HoursMinsWordToTime hour minute word x;
  if (hour >= 24) return -1;
  if (minute >= 60) return -1;
  x = hour*60 + minute; if (hour >= 13) return x;
  x = x%TWELVE_HOURS; if (word == 'pm') x = x + TWELVE_HOURS;
  if (word ~= 'am' or 'pm' && hour == 12) x = x + TWELVE_HOURS;
  return x;
];
```

For instance, HoursMinsWordToTime(4,20,'pm') returns 980, the Inform time value for twenty past four in the afternoon. The return value is −1 if the hours and minutes make no sense. Next, because the regular TryNumber library routine only recognises textual numbers up to 'twenty', we need a modest extension:

```
[ ExtendedTryNumber wordnum i j;
  i = wn; wn = wordnum; j = NextWordStopped(); wn = i;
  switch (j) {
      'twenty-one': return 21;
      ...
      'thirty': return 30;
      default: return TryNumber(wordnum);
  }
];
```

Finally the time of day token itself, which is really three separate parsing tokens in a row, trying three possible time formats:

```
[ TimeOfDay first_word second_word at length flag illegal_char
      offhour hr mn i;
  first_word = NextWordStopped();
  if (first_word == -1) return GPR_FAIL;
  switch (first_word) {
      'midnight': parsed_number = 0; return GPR_NUMBER;
      'midday', 'noon': parsed_number = TWELVE_HOURS;
          return GPR_NUMBER;
  }
  !   Next try the format 12:02
  at = WordAddress(wn-1); length = WordLength(wn-1);
  for (i=0: i<length: i++) {
      switch (at->i) {
          ':': if (flag == false && i>0 && i<length-1) flag = true;
              else illegal_char = true;
          '0', '1', '2', '3', '4', '5', '6', '7', '8', '9': ;
          default: illegal_char = true;
      }
```

```
}
if (length < 3 || length > 5 || illegal_char) flag = false;
if (flag) {
    for (i=0: at->i~=':': i++, hr=hr*10) hr = hr + at->i - '0';
    hr = hr/10;
    for (i++: i<length: i++, mn=mn*10) mn = mn + at->i - '0';
    mn = mn/10;
    second_word = NextWordStopped();
    parsed_number = HoursMinsWordToTime(hr, mn, second_word);
    if (parsed_number == -1) return GPR_FAIL;
    if (second_word ~= 'pm' or 'am') wn--;
    return GPR_NUMBER;
}
!   Lastly the wordy format
offhour = -1;
if (first_word == 'half') offhour = 30;
if (first_word == 'quarter') offhour = 15;
if (offhour < 0) offhour = ExtendedTryNumber(wn-1);
if (offhour < 0 || offhour >= 60) return GPR_FAIL;
second_word = NextWordStopped();
switch (second_word) {
    ! "six o'clock", "six"
    'o^clock', 'am', 'pm', -1:
        hr = offhour; if (hr > 12) return GPR_FAIL;
    ! "quarter to six", "twenty past midnight"
    'to', 'past':
        mn = offhour; hr = ExtendedTryNumber(wn);
        if (hr <= 0) {
            switch (NextWordStopped()) {
                'noon', 'midday': hr = 12;
                'midnight': hr = 0;
                default: return GPR_FAIL;
            }
        } else wn++;
        if (hr >= 13) return GPR_FAIL;
        if (second_word == 'to') {
            mn = 60-mn; hr--; if (hr<0) hr=23;
        }
        second_word = NextWordStopped();
    ! "six thirty"
    default:
        hr = offhour; mn = ExtendedTryNumber(--wn);
        if (mn < 0 || mn >= 60) return GPR_FAIL;
```

487

```
            wn++; second_word = NextWordStopped();
    }
    parsed_number = HoursMinsWordToTime(hr, mn, second_word);
    if (parsed_number < 0) return GPR_FAIL;
    if (second_word ~= 'pm' or 'am' or 'o^clock') wn--;
    return GPR_NUMBER;
];
```

True to the spirit of the Inform parser, this will also parse oddities like "quarter thirty o'clock", and we don't care.

• 89 (p. 229)   Here goes: we could implement the buttons with five separate objects, essentially duplicates of each other. (And by using a class definition, this wouldn't look too bad.) But if there were 500 slides this would be less reasonable.

```
[ ASlide w n;
    if (location ~= Machine_Room) return GPR_FAIL;
    w = NextWord(); if (w == 'the' or 'slide') w = NextWord();
    switch (w) {
        'first', 'one':   n = 1;
        'second', 'two':  n = 2;
        'third', 'three': n = 3;
        'fourth', 'four': n = 4;
        'fifth', 'five':  n = 5;
        default: return GPR_FAIL;
    }
    if (NextWord() ~= 'slide') wn--;
    parsed_number = n;
    return GPR_NUMBER;
];
Array slide_settings --> 5;
[ SetSlideSub;
    slide_settings-->(noun-1) = second;
    "You set slide ", (number) noun, " to the value ", second, ".";
];
[ XSlideSub;
    "Slide ", (number) noun, " currently stands at ",
        slide_settings-->(noun-1), ".";
];
Extend 'set' first * ASlide 'to' number -> SetSlide;
Extend 'push' first * ASlide 'to' number -> SetSlide;
Extend 'examine' first * ASlide -> XSlide;
Extend 'look' first * 'at' ASlide -> XSlide;
```

• 90 (p. 229)

```
Global from_char; Global to_char;
[ QuotedText start_wn;
   start_wn = wn;
   from_char = WordAddress(start_wn);
   if (from_char->0 ~= '"') return GPR_FAIL;
   from_char++;
   do {
       if (NextWordStopped() == -1) return GPR_FAIL;
       to_char = WordAddress(wn-1) + WordLength(wn-1) - 1;
   } until (to_char >= from_char && to_char->0 == '"');
   to_char--;
   return GPR_PREPOSITION;
];
```

(The code above won't work if the user types "foo"bar", though, because " is a word separator to Inform. It would be easy enough to compensate for this if we had to.) The text is treated as though it were a preposition, and the positions where the quoted text starts and finishes are recorded, so that an action routine can easily extract the text and use it later.

```
[ WriteOnSub i;
   print "You write ~";
   for (i = from_char: i <= to_char: i++) print (char) i->0;
   "~ on ", (the) noun, ".";
];
Verb 'write' * QuotedText 'on' noun -> WriteOn;
```

• 91 (p. 229)   (See the NounDomain specification in §A3.) This routine passes on any GPR_REPARSE request, as it must, but keeps a matched object in its own third variable, returning the 'skip this text' code to the parser. Thus the parser never sees any third parameter.

```
Global third;
[ ThirdNoun x;
   x = ParseToken(ELEMENTARY_TT, NOUN_TOKEN);
   if (x == GPR_FAIL or GPR_REPARSE) return x;
   third = x; return GPR_PREPOSITION;
];
```

The values GPR_MULTIPLE and GPR_NUMBER can't be returned, since a noun token – which is what the call to ParseToken asked for – cannot result in them.

•92 (p. 229)

```
[ InformNumberToken n wa wl sign base digit digit_count;
  wa = WordAddress(wn);
  wl = WordLength(wn); sign = 1; base = 10; digit_count = 0;
  if (wa->0 ~= '-' or '$' or '0' or '1' or '2' or '3' or '4'
                       or '5' or '6' or '7' or '8' or '9')
        return GPR_FAIL;
  if (wa->0 == '-') { sign = -1; wl--; wa++; }
  else {
        if (wa->0 == '$') { base = 16; wl--; wa++; }
        if (wa->0 == '$') { base = 2; wl--; wa++; }
  }
  if (wl == 0) return GPR_FAIL;
  n = 0;
  while (wl > 0) {
        if (wa->0 >= 'a') digit = wa->0 - 'a' + 10;
        else digit = wa->0 - '0';
        digit_count++;
        switch (base) {
            2: if (digit_count == 17) return GPR_FAIL;
           10: if (digit_count == 6) return GPR_FAIL;
               if (digit_count == 5) {
                   if (n > 3276) return GPR_FAIL;
                   if (n == 3276) {
                       if (sign == 1 && digit > 7) return GPR_FAIL;
                       if (sign == -1 && digit > 8) return GPR_FAIL;
                   }
               }
           16: if (digit_count == 5) return GPR_FAIL;
        }
        if (digit >= 0 && digit < base) n = base*n + digit;
        else return GPR_FAIL;
        wl--; wa++;
  }
  parsed_number = n*sign; wn++; return GPR_NUMBER;
];
```

•93 (p. 229)   Add the following, as the opening lines of the InformNumberToken routine, which also needs a new local variable w:

```
w = NextWordStopped(); if (w == -1) return GPR_FAIL;
switch (w) {
    'true':   parsed_number = true; return GPR_NUMBER;
```

```
    'false':    parsed_number = false; return GPR_NUMBER;
    'nothing': parsed_number = nothing; return GPR_NUMBER;
    'null':     parsed_number = NULL; return GPR_NUMBER;
}
wn--;
```

• 94 (p. 229)   Insert the following just after wa and wl have been set:

```
if (wl == 3 && wa->0 == ''' && wa->2 == ''') {
    parsed_number = wa->1; wn++; return GPR_NUMBER;
}
```

• 95 (p. 229)   First a tricky little routine which takes as its arguments a printing rule Rule and a value v, and compares the current word against the text that would result from the statement print (Rule) v; (assuming that this does not exceed 126 characters). Not only that, but lower and upper case letters are allowed to match each other. The routine either sets parsed_number to v and returns true, if there's a match, or returns false if there isn't.

```
Array tolowercase -> 256;
Array attr_text -> 128;
[ TestPrintedText Rule value j k at length f addto;
  if (tolowercase->255 == 0) {
      for (j=0: j<256: j++) tolowercase->j = j;
      for (j='A',k='a': j<='Z': j++,k++) tolowercase->j = k;
  }
  attr_text-->0 = 62; @output_stream 3 attr_text;
  Rule(value);
  @output_stream -3;
  k = attr_text-->0; addto = 0;
  at = WordAddress(wn);
  length = WordLength(wn);
  if (Rule == DebugAttribute && at->0 == '~') {
      length--; at++; addto = 100;
  }
  if (k == length) {
      f = true;
      for (j=0: j<k: j++)
          if (tolowercase->(attr_text->(j+2)) ~= at->j)
              f = false;
      if (f) { parsed_number = value + addto; rtrue; }
  }
  rfalse;
];
```

Note that the special rule about ˜ (which adds 100 to the value in parsed_number) is set up only to apply if attributes are being looked at. Now simply add the lines:

```
for (n=0: n<48: n++)
    if (TestPrintedText(DebugAttribute, n)) {
        wn++; return GPR_NUMBER;
    }
```

as the first lines of InformNumberToken. The routine DebugAttribute is only present if the game has been compiled with Debug mode on, but it seems very unlikely that the above code would be needed except for debugging anyway.

● 96 (p. 229)   Properties are numbered from 1 (which is always name) up to some highest one, P, and the trickiest thing in answering this exercise is to find out what P is. One devious way would be to define the following object right at the very end of your source code:

```
Object with zwissler;
```

Being the final new property to be created, the value of zwissler (named after A. M. F. Zwissler, the last person in the Oxford and District telephone directory for 1998) will be P. A tidier approach is to have read, or if possible written, the *Inform Technical Manual*, which reveals that the value #identifiers_table-->0 is exactly P+1. Anyway, the actual parsing is quite like the corresponding case for attributes. Define a suitable printing rule:

```
[ PrintProperty n; print (property) n; ];
```

and then add the next round of comparisons to InformNumberToken:

```
for (n=1: n<#identifiers_table-->0: n++)
    if (TestPrintedText(PrintProperty, n)) { wn++; return GPR_NUMBER; }
```

This and the preceding five exercises, put together, are most of the way to a token which would parse any Inform expression. For a full definition of this, see the InfixRvalueTerm token in the Infix debugger's library file "Infix.h". ("Rvalue" is compiler slang for a value which can appear on the right-hand side of an = assignment.)

● 97 (p. 232)   (Note that when a game is compiled with Debug mode, it already has this verb provided.) The following is slightly more useful than what the exercise asked for: it omits to mention the compass directions, making the output much less verbose. (The reason it does so is that compass directions are, for efficiency reasons, only in scope when the current reason for scope checking is PARSING_REASON, whereas because ScopeSub carries out a LoopOverScope the reason here will be LOOPOVERSCOPE_REASON.)

```
Global scope_count;
[ PrintIt obj;
   print_ret ++scope_count, ": ", (a) obj, " (", obj, ")";
```

```
];
[ ScopeSub; scope_count = 0; LoopOverScope(PrintIt);
  if (scope_count == 0) "Nothing is in scope.";
];
Verb meta 'scope' * -> Scope;
```

Under normal circumstances, "Nothing is in scope" will never be printed, as – at the very least – an actor is always in scope to himself, but since it's possible for designers to alter the definition of scope, this routine has been written to be cautious.

• 98 (p. 232)   As in the previous answer, the compass directions do not appear in the loop over scope, which neatly excludes walls, floor and ceiling:

```
[ MegaExam obj; print "^", (a) obj, ": "; <Examine obj>; ];
[ MegaLookSub; <Look>; LoopOverScope(MegaExam); ];
Verb meta 'megalook' * -> MegaLook;
```

• 99 (p. 234)   A slight refinement of such a "purloin" verb is already defined in the library (if the constant DEBUG is defined), so there's no need. But here's how it could be done:

```
[ Anything i;
  if (scope_stage == 1) rfalse;
  if (scope_stage == 2) {
      objectloop (i ofclass Object) PlaceInScope(i); rtrue;
  }
  "No such in game.";
];
```

(This disallows multiple matches for efficiency reasons – the parser has enough work to do with such a huge scope definition as it is.) Now the token scope=Anything will match anything at all, even things like the abstract concept of 'east'. The restriction to i ofclass Object excludes picking up classes.

• 100 (p. 235)   For brevity, the following solution assumes that both sides of the window are lit, and that any objects with descriptions as separate paragraphs (for instance the initial descriptions for objects not yet moved) already describe clearly which side of the window they are on. We are only worrying about the piles of items in the "You can also see…" part of the room description. Note the sneaky way looking through the window is implemented, and that the 'on the other side' part of the room description isn't printed in that case.

```
Global just_looking_through;
Class Window_Room
 with description
```

```
            "This is one end of a long east/west room.",
    before [;
        Examine, Search: ;
        default:
            if (inp1 ~= 1 && noun ~= 0 && noun in self.far_side)
                print_ret (The) noun, " is on the far side of
                    the glass.";
            if (inp2 ~= 1 && second ~= 0 && second in self.far_side)
                print_ret (The) second, " is on the far side of
                    the glass.";
    ],
    after [;
        Look:
            if (just_looking_through) rfalse;
            print "^The room is divided by a great glass window,
                stretching from floor to ceiling.^";
            if (Locale(location.far_side,
                    "Beyond the glass you can see",
                    "Beyond the glass you can also see")) ".";
    ],
  has light;
Window_Room window_w "West of Window"
  with far_side window_e;
Window_Room window_e "East of Window"
  with far_side window_w;
Object "great glass window"
  with name 'great' 'glass' 'window',
      before [ place;
          Examine, Search: place = location;
              just_looking_through = true;
              PlayerTo(place.far_side,1); <Look>; PlayerTo(place,1);
              just_looking_through = false;
              give place.far_side ~visited; rtrue;
      ],
      found_in window_w window_e,
  has  scenery;
```

A few words about inp1 and inp2 are in order. noun and second can hold either objects or numbers, and it's sometimes useful to know which. inp1 is equal to noun if that's an object, or 1 if that's a number; likewise for inp2 and second. (In this case we're just being careful that the action SetTo eggtimer 35 wouldn't be stopped if object 35 happened to be on the other side of the glass.) We also need:

```
[ InScope actor;
```

```
    if (parent(actor) ofclass Window_Room)
        ScopeWithin(parent(actor).far_side);
    rfalse;
];
```

• 101 (p. 235)   For good measure, we'll combine this with the previous rule about moved objects being in scope in the dark:

```
Object Dark_Room "Dark Room"
  with description "A disused broom cupboard.";
Object -> light_switch "light switch"
  with name 'light' 'switch',
       player_knows,
       initial "On one wall is the light switch.",
       after [;
           SwitchOn: give Dark_Room light;
           SwitchOff: give Dark_Room ~light;
       ],
  has  switchable static;
Object -> diamond "shiny diamond"
  with name 'shiny' 'diamond'
  has  scored;
Object -> dwarf "dwarf"
  with name 'voice' 'dwarf' 'breathing',
       life [;
           Order:
               if (action == ##SwitchOn && noun == light_switch) {
                   give Dark_Room light;
                   light_switch.player_knows = true;
                   StopDaemon(self);
                   if (light_switch has on) "~Typical human.~";
                   give light_switch on; "~Right you are, squire.~";
               }
       ],
       daemon [;
           if (location == thedark && real_location == Dark_Room)
               "~You hear the breathing of a dwarf.";
       ],
  has  animate;
[ InScope person i;
  if (person in Dark_Room)
      if (person == dwarf || light_switch.player_knows)
          PlaceInScope(light_switch);
```

```
   if (person == player && location == thedark)
       objectloop (i in parent(player))
           if (i has moved || i==dwarf)
               PlaceInScope(i);
   rfalse;
];
```

And in the game's Initialise routine, call StartDaemon(dwarf) to get respiration under way. Note that the routine puts the light switch in scope for the dwarf – if it didn't, the dwarf would not be able to understand "dwarf, turn light on", and that was the whole point. Note also that the dwarf can't hear the player in darkness, no doubt because of all the heavy breathing.

• 102 (p. 236) In the Initialise routine, move newplayer somewhere and Change-Player to it, where:

```
Object newplayer "yourself"
  with description "As good-looking as ever.",
       add_to_scope nose,
       capacity 5,
       orders [;
           Inv: if (nose.being_held)
                   print "You're holding your nose. ";
           Smell: if (nose.being_held)
                   "You can't smell a thing with your nose held.";
       ],
  has  concealed animate proper transparent;
Object nose "nose"
  with name 'nose', article "your",
       being_held,
       before [ possessed nonclothing;
           Take: if (self.being_held)
                   "You're already holding your nose.";
               objectloop (possessed in player)
                   if (possessed hasnt worn) nonclothing++;
               if (nonclothing > 1) "You haven't a free hand.";
               self.being_held = true; player.capacity = 1;
               "You hold your nose with your spare hand.";
           Drop: if (~~(self.being_held))
                   "But you weren't holding it!";
               self.being_held = false; player.capacity = 5;
               print "You release your nose and inhale again.  ";
               <<Smell>>;
       ],
```

```
    has  scenery;


• 103 (p. 236)

  Object steriliser "sterilising machine"
    with name 'washing' 'sterilising' 'machine',
         add_to_scope top_of_wm go_button,
         before [;
             PushDir: AllowPushDir(); rtrue;
             Receive:
                 if (receive_action == ##PutOn)
                     <<PutOn noun top_of_wm>>;
             SwitchOn: <<Push go_button>>;
         ],
         after [;
             PushDir: "It's hard work, but the steriliser does roll.";
         ],
         initial [;
             print "There is a sterilising machine on casters here
                 (a kind of chemist's washing machine) with a ~go~
                 button. ";
             if (children(top_of_wm) > 0) {
                 print "On top";
                 WriteListFrom(child(top_of_wm),
                     ISARE_BIT + ENGLISH_BIT);
                 print ". ";
             }
             if (children(self) > 0) {
                 print "Inside";
                 WriteListFrom(child(self), ISARE_BIT + ENGLISH_BIT);
                 print ". ";
             }
             print "^";
         ],
    has  static container open openable;
  Object top_of_wm "top of the sterilising machine",
    with article "the",
    has  static supporter;
  Object go_button "~go~ button"
    with name 'go' 'button',
         before [; Push, SwitchOn: "The power is off."; ],
    has  static;
```

• **104** (p. 236)   The label object itself is not too bad:

```
Object -> label "red sticky label"
  with name 'red' 'sticky' 'label',
       stuck_onto nothing,
       unstick [;
           print "(first removing the label from ",
               (the) self.stuck_onto, ")^";
           self.stuck_onto = nothing;
           move self to player;
       ],
       saystuck [;
           print "^The red sticky label is stuck to ",
               (the) self.stuck_onto, ".^";
       ],
       before [;
           Take, Remove:
               if (self.stuck_onto) {
                   self.unstick(); "Taken.";
               }
           PutOn, Insert:
               if (second == self.stuck_onto)
                   "It's already stuck there.";
               if (self.stuck_onto) self.unstick();
               if (second == self) "That would only make a red mess.";
               self.stuck_onto = second; remove self;
               "You affix the label to ", (the) second, ".";
       ],
       react_before [;
           Examine: if (self.stuck_onto == noun) self.saystuck();
       ],
       react_after [ x;
           x = self.stuck_onto; if (x == nothing) rfalse;
           Look: if (IndirectlyContains(location, x) &&
                   ~~IndirectlyContains(player, x)) self.saystuck();
           Inv:  if (IndirectlyContains(player, x)) self.saystuck();
       ],
       each_turn [;
           if (parent(self)) self.stuck_onto = nothing;
       ];
```

Note that label.stuck_onto holds the object the label is stuck to, or nothing if it's unstuck: and that when it is stuck, it is removed from the object tree. It therefore has to be moved into scope, so we need the rule: if the labelled object is in scope, then so is the label.

```
Global disable_self = false;
[ InScope actor i1 i2;
  if (disable_self || label.stuck_onto == nothing) rfalse;
  disable_self = true;
  i1 = TestScope(label, actor);
  i2 = TestScope(label.stuck_onto, actor);
  disable_self = false;
  if (i1 ~= 0) rfalse;
  if (i2 ~= 0) PlaceInScope(label);
  rfalse;
];
```

This routine has two interesting points: firstly, it disables itself while testing scope (since otherwise the game would go into an endless recursion), and secondly it only puts the label in scope if it isn't already there. This is just a safety precaution to prevent the label reacting twice to actions, and isn't really necessary since the label can't already be in scope, but is included for the sake of example.

• 105 (p. 239)   Firstly, create a class Key of which all the keys in the game are members. Then:

```
Global assumed_key;
[ DefaultLockSub;
  print "(with ", (the) assumed_key, ")^"; <<Lock noun assumed_key>>;
];
[ DefaultLockTest i count;
  if (noun hasnt lockable) rfalse;
  objectloop (i in player && i ofclass Key) {
      count++; assumed_key = i;
  }
  if (count == 1) rtrue; rfalse;
];
Extend 'lock' first * noun=DefaultLockTest -> DefaultLock;
```

(and similar code for "unlock"). Note that "lock strongbox" is matched by this new grammar line only if the player only has one key: the <DefaultLock strongbox> action is generated: which is converted to, say, <Lock strongbox brass_key>.

• 106 (p. 240)   A neat combination of the two entry points described in this section:

```
[ ChooseObjects obj code;
  obj = obj; ! To stop Inform pointing out that obj was unused
  if (code == 1) {
```

```
        ! If the parser wants to include this object in an "all"
        ! in a faintly lit room, force it to be excluded:
        if (action_to_be == ##Take or ##Remove
            && location ofclass FaintlyLitRoom) return 2;
  }
  return 0; ! Carry on, applying normal parser rules
];
```

Since that excludes everything from an "all", the result will be the error message "Nothing to do!". As this is not very descriptive:

```
[ ParserError error_code;
  if (error_code == NOTHING_PE)
      ! The error message printed if an "all" turned out empty
      if (action_to_be == ##Take or ##Remove
          && location ofclass FaintlyLitRoom)
          "In this faint light, it's not so easy.";
  rfalse; ! Print standard parser error message
];
```

All this makes a room so dark that even carrying a lamp will not illuminate it fully. If this is undesirable, add the following to the start of ChooseObjects:

```
    objectloop (whatever in location)
        if (HasLightSource(whatever)) return 0;
```

Exercises in Chapter V

• 107 (p. 255)   After checking for any irregular forms, which take precedence, the dative routine looks to see if the last letter is "e", as in this case it is, and then checks to see if the first six, "cyning", form a word in the dictionary:

```
Object -> "searo"
  with name 'searo', dativename 'searwe';
Object -> "Cyning"
  with name 'cyning';
[ dative obj word a l;
  ! Irregular dative endings
  if (obj provides dativename)
      return WordInProperty(word, obj, dativename);
  ! Regular dative endings
  a = WordAddress(wn-1);
  l = WordLength(wn-1);
  if (l >= 2 && a->(l-1) == 'e') {
```

```
        word = DictionaryLookup(a, l-1);
        if (WordInProperty(word, obj, name)) rtrue;
    }
    rfalse;
];
[ dativenoun;
    if (NextWord() == 'to') return ParseToken(ELEMENTARY_TT, NOUN_TOKEN);
    wn--;
    parser_inflection = dative;
    return ParseToken(ELEMENTARY_TT, NOUN_TOKEN);
];
```

The upshot is that the game designer only has to give names in the dativename property if they are irregular.

• 108 (p. 255)   The easiest way is to further elaborate dativenoun:

```
[ dativenoun it;
    switch (NextWord()) {
        'toit': it = PronounValue('it');
            if (it == NULL) return GPR_FAIL;
            if (TestScope(it, actor)) return it;
            return GPR_FAIL;
        'to': ;
        default: wn--; parser_inflection = dative;
    }
    return ParseToken(ELEMENTARY_TT, NOUN_TOKEN);
];
```

Note that it isn't safe to always allow "it" to be referred to, as "it" might be an object in another room and now out of scope. (We might want to use ParserError to give a better error message in this case, since at the moment we'll just get the generic "I didn't understand that sentence" message.) Another possible way for a pronoun to fail is if it remains unset. In the case of English "it", this is unlikely, but a pronoun applying only to "a group of two or more women" might well remain unset for hundreds of turns.

• 109 (p. 255)   Actually one simple solution avoids fussing with tokens altogether and just adds all the possible variant forms to the names of the objects:

```
Object ... with name 'brun' 'bruna' 'hund' 'hunden';
Object ... with name 'brunt' 'bruna' 'hus' 'huset';
```

A better way is to switch between two different inflections, one for indefinite and the other for definite noun phrases. The catch is that until you start parsing, you don't know whether it will be definite or not. But you can always take a quick look ahead:

```
[ swedishnoun;
```

```
    parser_inflection = swedish_indefinite_form;
    if (NextWord() == 'den' or 'det')
        parser_inflection = swedish_definite_form;
    else wn--;
    return ParseToken(ELEMENTARY_TT, NOUN_TOKEN);
];
```

Now either write

```
Object ... with swedish_indefinite_form 'brun' 'hund',
    swedish_definite_form 'bruna' 'hunden';
```

or else swedish_definite_form and swedish_indefinite_form routines to work out the required forms automatically. (Still another way is to rewrite all indefinite forms as definite within LanguageToInformese.)

● 110 (p. 268)

```
[ LanguageToInformese x;
  ! Insert a space before each hyphen and after each apostrophe.
  for (x=2: x<2+buffer->1: x++) {
      if (buffer->x == '-') LTI_Insert(x++, ' ');
      if (buffer->x == ''') LTI_Insert(++x, ' ');
  }
  #ifdef DEBUG;
  if (parser_trace >= 1) {
      print "[ After LTI: '";
      for (x=2: x<2+buffer->1: x++) print (char) buffer->x;
      print "']^";
  }
  #endif;
];
```

● 111 (p. 268)   Insert the following code:

```
for (x=1: x<=parse->1: x++) {
    wn = x; word = NextWord();
    at = WordAddress(x);
    if (word == 'dessus') {
      LTI_Insert(at - buffer, ' ');
      buffer->at     = 's'; buffer->(at+1) = 'u'; buffer->(at+2) = 'r';
      buffer->(at+3) = ' '; buffer->(at+4) = 'l'; buffer->(at+5) = 'u';
      buffer->(at+6) = 'i';
      break;
    }
```

502

```
      if (word == 'dedans') {
        LTI_Insert(at - buffer, ' ');
        LTI_Insert(at - buffer, ' ');
        buffer->at     = 'd'; buffer->(at+1) = 'a'; buffer->(at+2) = 'n';
        buffer->(at+3) = 's'; buffer->(at+4) = ' '; buffer->(at+5) = 'l';
        buffer->(at+6) = 'u'; buffer->(at+7) = 'i';
        break;
      }
  }
```

Actually, this assumes that only one of the two words will be used, and only once in the command. Which is almost certainly good enough, but if not we could replace both occurrences of break with the code:

```
    @tokenise buffer parse;
    x = 0; continue;
```

so catching even multiple usages.

• 112 (p. 268)   (This solution by Gareth Rees.)

```
[ LTI_Shift from chars i
   start    ! Where in buffer to start copying (inclusive)
   end      ! Where in buffer to stop copying (exclusive)
   dir;     ! Direction to move (1 for left, -1 for right)
   if (chars < 0) {
       start = from; end = buffer->1 + chars + 3; dir = 1;
       if (end <= start) return;
       buffer->1 = buffer->1 + chars;
   } else {
       start = buffer->1 + chars + 2; end = from + chars - 1; dir = -1;
       if (start <= end) return;
       if (start > buffer->0 + 2) start = buffer->0 + 2;
       buffer->1 = start - 2;
   }
   for (i=start: i~=end: i=i+dir) buffer->i = buffer->(i - chars);
];
```

• 113 (p. 268)   The "beware" part is handled by never breaking any word which is already within the dictionary, together with only allowing "da" and "dar" to be broken away from a dictionary word. Thus no break occurs in "davon" if there's a person in the game called "Davon", while no break occurs in "dartmouth" because there's no word "tmouth" in the dictionary.

```
[ LanguageToInformese x c word at len;
```

```
    for (x=0: x<parse->1: x++) {
        word = parse-->(x*2 + 1);
        len = parse->(x*4 + 4);
        at = parse->(x*4 + 5);
        if (word == 0 && buffer->at == 'd' && buffer->(at+1) == 'a') {
            c = 2; if (buffer->(at+2) == 'r') c = 3;
            ! Is the rest of the word, after "da" or "dar", in dict?
            if (DictionaryLookup(buffer+at+c, len-c)) {
                buffer->at = ' '; buffer->(at+1) = ' ';
                if (c == 3) buffer->(at+2) = ' ';
                LTI_Insert(at+len, 's');
                LTI_Insert(at+len, 'e');
                LTI_Insert(at+len, ' ');
                break;
            }
        }
    }
];
```

Note that the text " es" is appended by inserting 's', then 'e', then a space. The routine will only make one amendment on the input line, but then only one such preposition is likely to occur on any input line, so that's all right then.

• 114 (p. 270)   Most of the work goes into the printing rule for GNAs:

```
[ GNA g;
  g = GetGNAOfObject(noun);
  switch (g) {
      0,1,2,3,4,5: print "animate ";
      default: print "inanimate ";
  }
  switch (g) {
      0,1,2,6,7,8: print "singular ";
      default: print "plural ";
  }
  switch (g) {
      0,3,6,9: print "masculine";
      1,4,7,10: print "feminine";
      default: print "neuter";
  }
  print " (GNA ", g, ")";
];
[ GNASub;
  print "GNA ", (GNA) noun, "^",
```

```
          (The) noun, " / ", (the) noun, " / ", (a) noun, "^";
    ];
    Verb meta 'gna' * multi -> GNA;
```

• **115** (p. 271)

```
    Constant LanguageContractionForms = 3;
    [ LanguageContraction text;
      if (text->0 == 'a' or 'e' or 'i' or 'o' or 'u'
                    or 'A' or 'E' or 'I' or 'O' or 'U') return 2;
      if (text->0 == 'z' or 'Z') return 1;
      if (text->0 ~= 's' or 'S') return 0;
      if (text->1 == 'a' or 'e' or 'i' or 'o' or 'u'
                    or 'A' or 'E' or 'I' or 'O' or 'U') return 1;
      return 0;
    ];
```

• **116** (p. 272)

```
    Array LanguageArticles -->
     !    Contraction form 0:     Contraction form 1:
     !    Cdef   Def    Indef     Cdef   Def    Indef
          "Le "  "le "  "un "     "L'"   "l'"   "un "      ! 0: masc sing
          "La "  "la "  "une "    "L'"   "l'"   "une "     ! 1: fem sing
          "Les " "les " "des "    "Les " "les " "des ";    ! 2: plural
                                !        a         i
                                !        s    p    s    p
                                !        m f  n m  f n  m f  n m f n
    Array LanguageGNAsToArticles --> 0 1 0 2 2 2 0 1 0 2 2 2;
```

• **117** (p. 272)

```
    Array LanguageArticles -->
     ! Contraction form 0:   Contraction form 1:   Contraction form 2:
     ! Cdef   Def    Indef   Cdef   Def    Indef   Cdef   Def    Indef
       "Il "  "il "  "un "   "Lo "  "lo "  "uno "  "L'"   "l'"   "un "
       "La "  "la "  "una "  "Lo "  "lo "  "una "  "L'"   "l'"   "un'"
       "I "   "i "   "un "   "Gli " "gli " "uno "  "Gli " "gli " "un "
       "Le "  "le "  "una "  "Gli " "gli " "una "  "Le "  "le "  "un'";
                            !        a         i
                            !        s    p    s    p
                            !        m f  n m  f n  m f  n m f n
    Array LanguageGNAsToArticles --> 0 1 0 2 3 0 0 1 0 2 3 0;
```

• 118 (p. 272)   One contraction form, and one article set (numbered 0), in which all
three articles are blank:

```
Constant LanguageContractionForms = 1;
[ LanguageContraction text; return 0; ];
Array LanguageArticles --> "" "" "";
                          !            a            i
                          !            s    p       s    p
                          !            m f n m f n m f n m f n
Array LanguageGNAsToArticles --> 0 0 0 0 0 0 0 0 0 0 0 0;
```

• 119 (p. 273)

```
Array SmallNumbersInFrench -->
   "un" "deux" "trois" "quatre" "cinq" "six" "sept" "huit"
   "neuf" "dix" "onze" "douze" "treize" "quatorze" "quinze"
   "seize" "dix-sept" "dix-huit" "dix-neuf";
[ LanguageNumber n f;
   if (n == 0)    { print "z@'ero"; rfalse; }
   if (n < 0)     { print "moins "; n = -n; }
   if (n >= 1000) { if (n/1000 ~= 1) print (LanguageNumber) n/1000, " ";
                    print "mille"; n = n%1000; f = true; }
   if (n >= 100)  { if (f) print " ";
                    if (n/100 ~= 1) print (LanguageNumber) n/100, " ";
                    print "cent"; n = n%100; f = true; }
   if (n == 0) rfalse;
   if (f) { print " "; if (n == 1) print "et "; }
   switch (n) {
       1 to 19: print (string) SmallNumbersInFrench-->(n-1);
       20 to 99:
         switch (n/10) {
             2: print "vingt";
                if (n%10 == 1) { print " et un"; return; }
             3: print "trente";
                if (n%10 == 1) { print " et un"; return; }
             4: print "quarante";
                if (n%10 == 1) { print " et un"; return; }
             5: print "cinquante";
                if (n%10 == 1) { print " et un"; return; }
             6: print "soixante";
                if (n%10 == 1) { print " et un"; return; }
             7: print "soixante";
                if (n%10 == 1) { print " et onze"; return; }
                print "-"; LanguageNumber(10 + n%10); return;
```

```
         8: if (n%10 == 0) { print "quatre vingts"; return; }
            print "quatre-vingt";
         9: print "quatre-vingt-"; LanguageNumber(10 + n%10);
            return;
      }
      if (n%10 ~= 0) { print "-"; LanguageNumber(n%10); }
   }
];
```

• 120 (p. 273)

```
[ LanguageTimeOfDay hours mins i;
  i = hours%12;
  if (i == 0) i = 12;
  if (i < 10) print " ";
  print i, ":", mins/10, mins%10;
  if (hours>= 12) print " pm"; else print " am";
];
```

• 121 (p. 277)

```
[ FrenchNominativePronoun obj;
  switch (GetGNAOfObject(obj)) {
      0, 6: print "il";  1, 7: print "elle";
      3, 9: print "ils"; 4, 10: print "elles";
  }
];
```

Exercises in Chapter VII

• 122 (p. 310) The following implementation is limited to a format string $2 \times 64 = 128$ characters long, and six subsequent arguments. %d becomes a decimal number, %e an English one; %c a character, %% a (single) percentage sign and %s a string.

```
Array printed_text --> 65;
Array printf_vals --> 6;
[ Printf format p1 p2 p3 p4 p5 p6   pc j k;
  printf_vals-->0 = p1; printf_vals-->1 = p2; printf_vals-->2 = p3;
  printf_vals-->3 = p4; printf_vals-->4 = p5; printf_vals-->5 = p6;
  printed_text-->0 = 64; @output_stream 3 printed_text;
  print (string) format; @output_stream -3;
  j = printed_text-->0;
```

```
for (k=2: k<j+2: k++) {
    if (printed_text->k == '%' && k<j+2) {
        switch (printed_text->(++k)) {
            '%': print "%";
            'c': print (char) printf_vals-->pc++;
            'd': print printf_vals-->pc++;
            'e': print (number) printf_vals-->pc++;
            's': print (string) printf_vals-->pc++;
            default: print "<** Unknown printf escape **>";
        }
    }
    else print (char) printed_text->k;
}
];
```

• 123 (p. 311)   The is from the *Popol Vuh*, the source of Maya mythology.

```
[ TitlePage i;
    @erase_window -1; print "^^^^^^^^^^^^^^^";
    i = 0->33; if (i > 30) i = (i-30)/2;
    style bold; font off; spaces(i);
    print "            RUINS^";
    style roman; print "^^"; spaces(i);
    print "[Please press SPACE to begin.]^";
    font on;
    box "But Alligator was not digging the bottom of the hole"
        "Which was to be his grave,"
        "But rather he was digging his own hole"
        "As a shelter for himself."
        ""
        "-- from the Popol Vuh";
    @read_char 1 -> i;
    @erase_window -1;
];
```

• 124 (p. 311)   First put the directive Replace DrawStatusLine; before including the library; define the global variable invisible_status somewhere. Then give the following redefinition:

```
[ DrawStatusLine width posa posb;
    if (invisible_status) { @split_window 0; return; }
    @split_window 1; @set_window 1; @set_cursor 1 1; style reverse;
    width = 0->33; posa = width-26; posb = width-13;
    spaces (width);
```

```
   @set_cursor 1 2;  PrintShortName(location);
   if (width > 76) {
       @set_cursor 1 posa; print "Score: ", sline1;
       @set_cursor 1 posb; print "Moves: ", sline2;
   }
   if (width > 63 && width <= 76) {
       @set_cursor 1 posb; print sline1, "/", sline2;
   }
   @set_cursor 1 1; style roman; @set_window 0;
];
```

For simplicity this and the following answers assume that the player's visibility ceiling is always either darkness or the location: imitate the real DrawStatusLine in "parserm.h" if you need situations when the player is sealed into an opaque container.

• 125 (p. 311)   First put the directive Replace DrawStatusLine; before including the library. Then add the following routine anywhere after treasures_found, an 'Advent' variable, is defined:

```
[ DrawStatusLine;
   @split_window 1; @set_window 1; @set_cursor 1 1; style reverse;
   spaces (0->33);
   @set_cursor 1 2;  PrintShortName(location);
   if (treasures_found > 0) {
       @set_cursor 1 50; print "Treasure: ", treasures_found;
   }
   @set_cursor 1 1; style roman; @set_window 0;
];
```

• 126 (p. 312)   Replace with the following. (Note the use of @@92 as a string escape, to include a literal backslash character.) This could be made more sophisticated by looking at the metaclass of location.u_to and so forth, but let's not complicate things:

```
Constant U_POS 28; Constant W_POS 30; Constant C_POS 31;
Constant E_POS 32; Constant I_POS 34;
[ DrawStatusLine;
   @split_window 3; @set_window 1; style reverse; font off;
   @set_cursor 1 1; spaces (0->33);
   @set_cursor 2 1; spaces (0->33);
   @set_cursor 3 1; spaces (0->33);
   @set_cursor 1 2;  print (name) location;
   @set_cursor 1 51; print "Score: ", sline1;
   @set_cursor 1 64; print "Moves: ", sline2;
```

```
  if (location ~= thedark) {
    ! First line
    if (location.u_to)   { @set_cursor 1 U_POS; print "U"; }
    if (location.nw_to)  { @set_cursor 1 W_POS; print "@@92"; }
    if (location.n_to)   { @set_cursor 1 C_POS; print "|"; }
    if (location.ne_to)  { @set_cursor 1 E_POS; print "/"; }
    if (location.in_to)  { @set_cursor 1 I_POS; print "I"; }
    ! Second line
    if (location.w_to)   { @set_cursor 2 W_POS; print "-"; }
                           @set_cursor 2 C_POS; print "o";
    if (location.e_to)   { @set_cursor 2 E_POS; print "-"; }
    ! Third line
    if (location.d_to)   { @set_cursor 3 U_POS; print "D"; }
    if (location.sw_to)  { @set_cursor 3 W_POS; print "/"; }
    if (location.s_to)   { @set_cursor 3 C_POS; print "|"; }
    if (location.se_to)  { @set_cursor 3 E_POS; print "@@92"; }
    if (location.out_to) { @set_cursor 3 I_POS; print "O"; }
  }
  @set_cursor 1 1; style roman; @set_window 0; font on;
];
```

• 127 (p. 312) The tricky part is working out the number of characters in the location name, and this is where @output_stream is so useful. This time Replace with:

```
Array printed_text --> 64;
[ DrawStatusLine i j;
  i = 0->33;
  font off;
  @split_window 1; @buffer_mode 0; @set_window 1;
  style reverse; @set_cursor 1 1; spaces(i);
  @output_stream 3 printed_text;
  print (name) location;
  @output_stream -3;
  j = (i-(printed_text-->0))/2;
  @set_cursor 1 j; print (name) location; spaces(j-1);
  style roman;
  @buffer_mode 1; @set_window 0; font on;
];
```

Note that the table can hold 128 characters (plenty for this purpose), and that these are stored in printed_text->2 to printed_text->129; the length printed is held in printed_text-->0. ('Trinity' actually does this more crudely, storing away the width of each location name.)

• 128 (p. 314)

```
Global indent; Global d_indent = 1;
[ StartWavyMargins;
  @put_wind_prop 0 8 WavyMargins; @put_wind_prop 0 9 1;
];
[ StopWavyMargins;
  @put_wind_prop 0 8 0; @put_wind_prop 0 9 0; @set_margins 0 0 0;
];
[ WavyMargins;
  indent = indent + d_indent*10;
  if (indent == 0 or 80) d_indent = -d_indent;
  @set_margins indent indent 0;
  StartWavyMargins();
];
```

• 129 (p. 317)   The following routine returns the ZSCII code of the key pressed, for good measure:

```
[ PressAnyKey k; @read_char 1 -> k; return k; ];
```

• 130 (p. 317)   The keyboard is allowed only one tenth of a second to respond before an interrupt takes place, which is set to stop waiting:

```
[ KeyHeldDown k;
  @read_char 1 1 Interrupt -> k; return k;
];
[ Interrupt; rtrue; ];
```

The second 1 in the @read_char is the time delay: 1 tenth of a second.

• 131 (p. 317)   Place the directive Replace KeyboardPrimitive; somewhere before any library files are included. At the end of the file, add these lines:

```
[ KeyboardPrimitive b p k;
  b->1 = 0; p->1 = 0; @aread b p 100 Hurryup -> k;
];
[ Hurryup; print "^Hurry up, please, it's time.^"; rfalse; ];
```

The number 100 represents one hundred tenths of a second, i.e., ten seconds of real time.

• 132 (p. 317)   This time, we need to make use of the "terminating character", the value stored by the @aread opcode, which is 0 if and only if the reading was halted by an interrupt routine. If so, the command is written by hand and then tokenised using the @tokenise opcode.

```
Global reminders; Global response;
[ KeyboardPrimitive b p k;
  reminders = 0; response = b;
  response->1 = 0; p->1 = 0;
  @aread response p 50 Hurry -> k;
  if (k ~= 0) return;
  response->1 = 4; response->2 = 'l'; response->3 = 'o';
  response->4 = 'o'; response->5 = 'k';
  @tokenise b p;
];
[ Hurry;
  switch (++reminders) {
      1: print "^(Please decide quickly.)^";
      2: print "^(Further delay would be unfortunate.)^";
      3: print "^(I really must insist on a response.)^";
      4: print "^(In ten seconds I'll make your mind up for you.)^";
      6: print "^(~look~ it is, then.)^"; rtrue;
  }
  rfalse;
];
```

Note that Hurry is called every five seconds.

• 133 (p. 317)   The timing is the easy part. We shall send the message run_sand to the hourglass every time the game asks the player for a command, and then every second thereafter:

```
[ KeyboardPrimitive b p k;
  hourglass.run_sand(); b->1 = 0; p->1 = 0;
  @aread b p 10 OneSecond -> k;
];
[ OneSecond; hourglass.run_sand(); rfalse; ];
```

The catch is that time spent looking at menus, or waiting to press the space bar after the interpreter prints "[MORE]", isn't registered, and besides that a turn may take more or less than 1 second to parse. So you wouldn't want to set your watch by this hourglass, but on the author's machine it keeps reasonable enough time. Here's the object:

```
Object -> hourglass "hourglass"
  with name 'hourglass',
       sand_in_top,
       when_on [;
```

```
        print "An hourglass is fixed to a pivot on the wall. ";
        switch (self.sand_in_top/10) {
            0: "The sand is almost all run through to a neat pyramid
               in the lower bulb.";
            1: "About a quarter of the sand is left in the upper
               bulb.";
            2: "The upper and lower bulbs contain roughly equal
               amounts of sand.";
            3: "About three-quarters of the sand is still to run.";
            4: "Almost all of the sand is in the upper bulb.";
        }
    ],
    when_off
        "An hourglass fixed to a pivot on the wall is turned
        sideways, so that no sand moves.",
    before [;
        Turn: if (self hasnt on) <<SwitchOn self>>;
            self.sand_in_top = 40 - self.sand_in_top;
            "You turn the hourglass the other way up.";
    ],
    after [;
        SwitchOn:
            if (self.sand_in_top < 20)
                self.sand_in_top = 40 - self.sand_in_top;
            "You turn the hourglass so that the bulb with most sand
            is uppermost, and the grains begin to pour through.";
        SwitchOff:
            "You turn the hourglass sideways.";
    ],
    run_sand [;
        if (self has on && (--(self.sand_in_top) < 0)) {
            self.sand_in_top = 40 - self.sand_in_top;
            if (self in location)
                "^The hourglass elegantly turns itself to begin
                again, all of the sand now in the uppermost bulb.";
        }
    ],
  has  static switchable;
```

● 134 (p. 318)

```
 Array mouse_array --> 4;
 [ Main k;
```

```
@mouse_window 0;
for (::) {
    @read_char 1 -> k;
    @read_mouse mouse_array;
    switch(k) {
        253, 254: if (k == 253) print "Double-";
            print "Click at (", mouse_array-->0, ",",
                mouse_array-->1, ") buttons ",
                mouse_array-->2, "^";
    }
}
];
```

• **135** (p. 318)   This needs another replacement of `KeyboardPrimitive`:

```
Zcharacter terminating 252;
Array mouse_array --> 4;
[ KeyboardPrimitive b p k s i;
  b->1 = 0; p->1 = 0;
  @aread b p -> k;
  if (k ~= 252) return;
  @read_mouse mouse_array;
  s = Do_M-->(1 + mouse_array->7);
  for (i=1: i<=s->0: i++) { b->(i+1) = s->i; print (char) s->i; }
  new_line; b->1=s->0; @tokenise b p;
];
```

And the menu itself must be created:

```
Array D1 string "Do";
Array D2 string "look";
Array D3 string "wait";
Array D4 string "inventory";
Array Do_M table D1 D2 D3 D4;
[ Initialise;
  ...
  @mouse_window 0;
  @make_menu 3 Do_M ?Able;
  "*** Unable to generate menu. ***";
  .Able;
  ...
];
```

• 136 (p. 319)   By encoding one or more "characters" into an array and using @save and @restore. The numbers in this array might contain the character's name, rank and abilities, together with some coding system to show what possessions the character has (a brass lamp, 50 feet of rope, etc.)

• 137 (p. 319)   This means using a "bones file" like those generated by the game 'Hack'. To begin with, two arrays. The array bones_file will hold a number from 0 to 9 (the number of ghosts currently present), followed by the locations of these ghosts.

```
Array bones_filename string "catacomb.bns";
Array bones_file --> 10;
Class Ghost(10)
  with short_name "ghost", plural "ghosts", name 'ghost' 'ghosts//p',
  has  animate;
```

The game's Initialise routine should do the following:

```
  @restore bones_file 20 bones_filename -> k;
  if (k == 0) bones_file-->0 = 0;
  for (k=1: k<=bones_file-->0: k++) {
      g = Ghost.create(); move g to bones_file-->k;
  }
```

This only leaves updating the bones file in the event of death, using the entry point AfterLife:

```
[ AfterLife k;
  if (bones_file-->0 == 9) {
      for (k=2: k<=9: k++) bones_file-->(k-1) = bones_file-->k;
      bones_file-->9 = real_location;
  }
  else bones_file-->(++(bones_file-->0)) = real_location;
  @save bones_file 20 bones_filename -> k;
];
```

This code doesn't trouble to check that the save worked properly, because it doesn't much matter if the feature goes awry: the spirit world is not a reliable place. However, if the restore fails, the game empties the bones_file array just in case some file-handling accident on the host machine had loaded only half of the array, leaving the rest corrupt.

• 138 (p. 320)   First, Replace a routine in the library called ActionPrimitive. This little routine calls all action subroutines, such as TakeSub, as and when needed. Its new version pauses to catch a stack frame:

```
[ ActionPrimitive x;
  if ((x = ExceptionHandler()) ~= 0)
```

```
        "^*** Exception: ", (string) x, " ***";
];
Global exception;
[ ExceptionHandler;
  @catch -> exception;
  indirect(#actions_table-->action);
  rfalse;
];
```

Then an action getting in trouble can simply execute a statement like:

```
@throw "Numeric overflow" exception;
```

TABLE 1A: GENERAL OPERATORS

Lvl	Operator	Placed	Asc	Purpose
0	,	between	left	separating values to work out
1	=	between	right	set equal to
5	+	between	left	16-bit signed addition
	–	between	left	16-bit signed subtraction
6	*	between	left	16-bit signed multiplication
	/	between	left	16-bit signed integer division
	%	between	left	16-bit signed remainder
	&	between	left	bitwise AND
			between	left	bitwise OR
	~	before		bitwise NOT
7	->	between	left	byte array entry
	-->	between	left	word array entry
8	–	before		16-bit signed negation
9	++	before		add 1 to then read
	++	after		read then add 1 to
	--	before		subtract 1 from then read
	--	after		read then subtract 1 from
10	.&	between	left	property array
	.#	between	left	property array size
11	(...)	after		routine call
12	.	between	left	property value
13	::	between	left	"superclass" operator

- "Lvl" refers to precedence level: thus *, on level 6, binds more tightly than +, down on level 5, so that 1+2*3 means 1+(2*3).

- – is "left associative", so a-b-c means (a-b)-c. = is "right associative", so v1=v2=7 means v1=(v2=7), setting both variables equal to 7.

- Although the table of operators has been divided over two pages, conditions and expressions can be freely mixed. When a condition is used as a value, it is always true (1) or false (0). When a value is used as a condition, any non-zero value is considered true, and only zero is considered false.

TABLE 1B: CONDITION OPERATORS

Lvl	Operator	Placed	Asc	Purpose
2	&&	between	left	one condition AND another
	||	between	left	one condition OR another
	~~	before		this condition NOT true
3	==	between	none	equal to?
	~=	between	none	not equal to?
	>	between	none	greater than?
	>=	between	none	greater than or equal to?
	<	between	none	less than?
	<=	between	none	less than or equal to?
	has	between	none	object has this attribute?
	hasnt	between	none	object hasn't this attribute?
	in	between	none	first obj a child of second?
	notin	between	none	first obj not a child of second?
	ofclass	between	none	obj inherits from class?
	provides	between	none	obj provides this property?
4	or	between	left	separating alternative values

- Conditions have no associativity and if you type a==b==c then Inform will ask you to add brackets for clarity.

- In the condition (C1 && C2), Inform decides on C1 first: if C1 is false then C2 is never considered at all. Similarly, if C1 is true then (C1 || C2) must be true and C2 is never considered.

TABLE 2A: LOWER ZSCII CHARACTER SET

	+0	+1	+2	+3	+4	+5	+6	+7
0								
8	*del*	tab		em		new		
16								
24								*esc*
32	sp	!	"	#	$	%	&	'
40	(	)	⋆	+	,	-	.	/
48	0	1	2	3	4	5	6	7
56	8	9	:	;	<	=	>	?
64	@	A	B	C	D	E	F	G
72	H	I	J	K	L	M	N	O
80	P	Q	R	S	T	U	V	W
88	X	Y	Z	[	\	]	^	_
96	`	a	b	c	d	e	f	g
104	h	i	j	k	l	m	n	o
112	p	q	r	s	t	u	v	w
120	x	y	z	{	|	}	~	

- To convert a character to a ZSCII value, add the numbers in the same row and column. For instance, the Inform constant 'J' is 72 plus 2 equals 74.

- Blank boxes indicate that no character exists with that value. The value will never be read from the keyboard and it is an error to try to print (char) it.

- Italicised entries can be read from the keyboard but not printed.

- "em" (an em-space) and "tab" (a tab-skip) are print-only, and only available if Inform is compiling a Version 6 game.

- ZSCII does not (normally) have "smart quotes", that is, different characters for opening and closing quotations " and ". Some interpreters automatically smarten them when printed, though. And ZSCII does have ≪French≫ and ≫German≪ quotation marks (see table 2B).

TABLE 2B: HIGHER ZSCII CHARACTER SET

	+0	+1	+2	+3	+4	+5	+6	+7
128		↑	↓	←	→	*f1*	*f2*	*f3*
136	*f4*	*f5*	*f6*	*f7*	*f8*	*f9*	*f10*	*f11*
144	*f12*	*k0*	*k1*	*k2*	*k3*	*k4*	*k5*	*k6*
152	*k7*	*k8*	*k9*	ä @:a	ö @:o	ü @:u	Ä @:A	Ö @:O
160	Ü @:U	ß @ss	» @>>	« @<<	ë @:e	ï @:i	ÿ @:y	Ë @:E
168	Ï @:I	á @'a	é @'e	í @'i	ó @'o	ú @'u	ý @'y	Á @'A
176	É @'E	Í @'I	Ó @'O	Ú @'U	Ý @'Y	à @`a	è @`e	ì @`i
184	ò @`o	ù @`u	À @`A	È @`E	Ì @`I	Ò @`O	Ù @`U	â @^a
192	ê @^e	î @^i	ô @^o	û @^u	Â @^A	Ê @^E	Î @^I	Ô @^O
200	Û @^U	å @oa	Å @oA	ø @\o	Ø @\O	ã @~a	ñ @~n	õ @~o
208	Ã @~A	Ñ @~N	Õ @~O	æ @ae	Æ @AE	ç @,c	C @,C	th @th
216	eth @et	Th @Th	Eth @Et	£ @LL	œ @oe	Œ @OE	¡ @!!	¿ @??
224								
232								
240								
248						*men*	*dbl*	*clk*

- The cursor keys, function keys, numeric keypad keys and mouse clicks (menu click, double click, single click) are read-only. Mouse support is available only to a Version 6 game.

- The given escape-character sequences can be typed into source code. For instance print "@AEsop"; prints "Æsop".

- "Eth" and "Th(orn)" are Icelandic characters.

- Characters 155 to 251 are configurable using the directive Zcharacter, which can in principle move any Unicode character in. See §36.

TABLE 3: COMMAND LINE SWITCHES

Sw	To	Meaning
-d*	0 to 2	contract double spaces: never (0), after full stops (1) after full stops, exclamation and question marks (2)
-e	off/on	economise by using the declared abbreviations
-g*	0 to 2	traces calls: none (0), all outside libraries (1), all (2)
-i	off/on	ignore default switches set within the file
-k	off/on	output Infix debugging information (and switch -D on)
-r	off/on	record all the text to a transcript file
-v*	3 to 8	compile to this Version of story file (default 5)
-C*	0 to 9	source is ASCII (0), or ISO 8859-1 to -9 (default 1)
-D	off/on	automatically include library's debugging features
-F*	0 or 1	use temporary files to reduce memory consumption
-M	off/on	compile as a Module for future linking
-S	on/off	compile strict error-checking at run-time (on by default)
-U	off/on	link in precompiled library modules
-X	off/on	include the Infix debugger
-a	off/on	trace assembly-language (without hex dumps; see -t)
-c	off/on	more concise error messages
-f	off/on	frequencies mode: show how useful abbreviations are
-h*	on/1/2	print help information: on filenaming (1), switches (2)
-j	off/on	list objects as constructed
-l	off/on	list every statement run through Inform
-m	off/on	say how much memory has been allocated
-n	off/on	print numbers of properties, attributes and actions
-o	off/on	print offset addresses
-p	off/on	give percentage breakdown of story file
-q	off/on	keep quiet about obsolete usages
-s	off/on	give statistics
-t	off/on	trace assembly-language (with full hex dumps; see -a)
-u	off/on	work out most useful abbreviations (very very slowly)
-w	off/on	disable warning messages
-x	off/on	print a hash # for every 100 lines compiled
-y	off/on	trace linking system
-z	off/on	print memory map of the Z-machine
-E*	0, 1, 2	errors in Acorn (0), Microsoft (1) or Mac (2) style

- The lower group has no effect except on what is printed out.
- The * stands for a decimal digit, 0 to 9. You can also clear any switch with a tilde, so -~x turns -x off.

TABLE 4: STATEMENTS

```
box ⟨line-1⟩ ⟨line-2⟩ ... ⟨line-n⟩
break
continue
do ⟨code block⟩ until ⟨condition⟩
font on or off
for (⟨initial code⟩:⟨condition to carry on⟩:⟨update code⟩) ⟨code block⟩
give ⟨object⟩ ⟨attribute-1⟩ ... ⟨attribute-n⟩
if ⟨condition⟩ ⟨code block⟩
if ⟨condition⟩ ⟨code block⟩ else ⟨code-block⟩
jump ⟨label⟩
move ⟨object⟩ to ⟨destination⟩
new_line
objectloop ⟨condition choosing objects⟩ ⟨code block⟩
print ⟨list of printing specifications⟩
print_ret ⟨list of printing specifications⟩
remove ⟨object⟩
return ⟨optional value⟩
rfalse
rtrue
spaces ⟨number of spaces to print⟩
string ⟨number⟩ ⟨text⟩
style roman or bold or underline or reverse or fixed
switch (⟨value⟩) ⟨block of cases ... default: ...⟩
while ⟨condition⟩ ⟨code-block⟩
```

- Statements must be given in lower case.

- A statement beginning with a double-quoted string instead of a keyword like if is taken as a print_ret statement.

- Code blocks consist of either a single statement or a group of statements enclosed in braces { and }.

- The following low-level statements should not be used for Inform games:

```
inversion
quit
read ⟨text-buffer⟩ ⟨parsing-buffer⟩
restore ⟨label⟩
save ⟨label⟩
```

TABLE 5: DIRECTIVES

```
Abbreviate ⟨word-1⟩ ... ⟨word-n⟩
Array ⟨new-name⟩ ⟨type⟩ ⟨initial values⟩
Attribute ⟨new-name⟩
Class ⟨new-name⟩ ⟨body of definition⟩
Constant ⟨new-name⟩ = ⟨value⟩
Default ⟨possibly-new-name⟩
End
Endif
Extend ⟨grammar extension⟩
Global ⟨new-name⟩ = ⟨value⟩
Ifdef ⟨symbol-name⟩
Ifndef ⟨symbol-name⟩
Ifnot
Iftrue ⟨condition⟩
Iffalse ⟨condition⟩
Import ⟨list of imported goods⟩
Include ⟨source code filename⟩
Link ⟨module filename⟩
Lowstring ⟨text⟩
Message ⟨message-type⟩ ⟨diagnostic-message⟩
Object ⟨header⟩ ⟨body of definition⟩
Property ⟨new-name⟩
Release ⟨number⟩
Replace ⟨routine-name⟩
Serial "⟨serial number⟩"
Switches ⟨list of switches⟩
Statusline score or time
System_file
Verb ⟨verb-definition⟩
Zcharacter etc.
```

• Nearby is an obsolete abbreviation for Object ->, now deprecated. A few other directives, Dictionary, Fake_action, Ifv3, Ifv5, Stub, Trace and Version, are either also obsolete or for compiler maintenance only.

TABLE 6A: ACTIONS PROVIDED BY THE LIBRARY: GROUP 1

Action	Typically produced by	Notes
Pronouns	"pronouns"	lists settings of "it" and so on
Quit	"quit"	
Restart	"restart"	
Restore	"restore"	
Save	"save"	
Verify	"verify"	checks story file integrity
ScriptOn	"script on"	
ScriptOff	"script off"	
NotifyOn	"notify on"	score change notification on
NotifyOff	"notify off"	and off
Places	"places"	list places visited
Objects	"objects"	list objects moved
Score	"score"	
FullScore	"fullscore"	full breakdown of score
Version	"version"	prints version numbers
LMode1	"brief"	normal room descriptions
LMode2	"verbose"	always full room descriptions
LMode3	"superbrief"	always abbreviated

- A number of other group 1 actions are present in a game compiled with the -D "Debugging" switch. These actions come and go with different library releases and their presence shouldn't be relied on. See the library's "Grammar" file to see the current set.

- The library also defines four fake actions which have nothing to do with the world model. TheSame and PluralFound are defined by the parser as ways for the program to communicate with it. Miscellany and Prompt are defined as slots for LibraryMessages.

TABLE 6B: ACTIONS PROVIDED BY THE LIBRARY: GROUP 2

Action	Typically produced by	Notes
Look	"look"	
Examine	"examine fish"	
Search	"look inside cup"	
Inv	"inventory"	
InvTall	"inventory tall"	*becomes* Inv
InvWide	"inventory wide"	*becomes* Inv
Take	"take fish"	*KS*
Drop	"drop fish"	*KS*
Remove	"take dice from cup"	*KS*
PutOn	"put cup on board"	*KS*
Insert	"put dice in cup"	*KS*
LetGo	*fake*	*caused by* Remove
Receive	*fake*	*caused by* PutOn *and* Insert
Empty	"empty sack"	*becomes* EmptyT d_obj
EmptyT	"empty bag on box"	*for each item inside, becomes* Remove *then* Drop/PutOn/Insert
Transfer	"transfer egg to box"	*becomes* Drop/PutOn/Insert
Go	"north"	*KS special rules apply: see* §15
Enter	"enter cage"	*KS can become* Go *if into a* door
GetOff	"get off table"	*KS*
GoIn	"enter"	*becomes* Go in_obj
Exit	"exit"	*KS can become* Go out_obj
Unlock	"unlock door"	*KS*
Lock	"lock door"	*KS*
SwitchOn	"switch radio on"	*KS*
SwitchOff	"switch radio off"	*KS*
Open	"open door"	*KS*
Close	"close door"	*KS*
Disrobe	"take hat off"	*KS*
Wear	"wear hat"	*KS*
Eat	"eat fish"	*KS*
Wait	"wait"	

• Actions marked *KS* run "silently" when the library's variable keep_silent is set true. This means that if successful they print nothing: if unsuccessful, however, they print text as normal.

• Look and Examine actions send after messages after printing descriptions. Search sends after when the search is known to be possible but before the result is printed.

525

TABLE 6C: ACTIONS PROVIDED BY THE LIBRARY: GROUP 3

Action	Typically produced by	Notes
LookUnder	"look under doormat"	
Listen	"listen [to tape]"	noun *can be* nothing
Taste	"taste marinade"	
Touch	"touch paint"	
Pull	"pull trolley"	
Push	"push trolley"	
Wave	"wave wand"	
Turn	"turn dial"	
PushDir	"push trolley north"	*special rules apply: see §15*
ThrowAt	"throw dart at board"	
ThrownAt	*fake*	*caused by* ThrowAt
JumpOver	"jump over fence"	
Tie	"tie rope [to hook]"	second *can be* nothing
Drink	"drink absinthe"	
Fill	"fill bottle"	
Attack	"fight soldiers"	
Swing	"swing on rope"	
Blow	"blow pipe"	
Rub	"clean table"	
Set	"set trap"	
SetTo	"set timer to 10"	second *not an object*
Buy	"buy ice cream"	
Climb	"climb ladder"	
Squeeze	"squash tomato"	
Burn	"burn papers [with match]"	second *can be* nothing
Dig	"dig lawn [with spade]"	second *can be* nothing
Cut	"cut paper"	
Consult	"look up fish in book"	sets noun and the topic
Tell	"tell jemima about austin"	sets noun and the topic
Answer	"say confirmed to avon"	sets noun and the topic
Ask	"ask jemima about isaac"	sets noun and the topic
Give	"give coin to troll"	
Show	"show pass to guard"	
AskFor	"ask jemima for daisies"	
WakeOther	"wake sleeper"	
Kiss	"kiss jemima"	

526

Action	Typically produced by	Notes
Sleep	"sleep"	
Sing	"sing"	
WaveHands	"wave"	*see also* Wave
Swim	"swim", "dive"	
Sorry	"sorry"	
Strong	*very rude words*	
Mild	*fairly rude words*	
Jump	"jump"	*see also* JumpOver
Think	"think"	
Smell	"smell coffee"	noun *can be* nothing
Pray	"pray"	
VagueGo	"go"	
Yes	"yes"	
No	"no"	
Wake	"wake up"	*see also* WakeOther

TABLE 6D: ACTIONS SENT TO LIFE RULES

Action	Typically produced by
Answer	"say yes to cashier"
Ask	"ask woman about plutonium"
Attack	"fight soldiers"
Give	"give coin to charon"
Kiss	"kiss jemima"
Order	"thorin, go west"
Show	"show pass to benton"
Tell	"tell paris about helen"
ThrowAt	"throw axe at dwarf"
WakeOther	"wake beauty up"

Cited Works of Interactive Fiction

 The following bibliography includes only those works cited in the text of this book: it makes no claim to completeness or even balance. An index entry is followed by designer's name, publisher or organisation (if any) and date of first substantial version. The following denote formats: *ZM* for Z-Machine, *L9* for Level 9's A-code, *AGT* for the Adventure Game Toolkit run-time, *TADS* for TADS run-time and *SA* for Scott Adams's format. Games in each of these formats can be played on most modern computers. Scott Adams, "Quill"-written and Cambridge University games can all be mechanically translated to Inform and then recompiled as *ZM*. The symbol ◇ marks that the game can be downloaded from ftp.gmd.de, though for early games sometimes only in source code format. *Sa1* and *Sa2* indicate that a playable demonstration can be found on Infocom's first or second sampler game, each of which is ◇. Most Infocom games are widely available in remarkably inexpensive packages marketed by Activision. The 'Zork' trilogy has often been freely downloadable from Activision web sites to promote the "Infocom" brand, as has 'Zork: The Undiscovered Underground'.

'Abenteuer', 264. German translation of 'Advent' by Toni Arnold (1998). *ZM* ◇

'Acheton', 3, 113 ex*8*, 348, 353, 399. David Seal, Jonathan Thackray with Jonathan Partington, Cambridge University and later Acornsoft, Topologika (1978--9).

'Advent', 2, 47, 48, 62, 75, 86, 95, 99, 102, 105, 113 ex*8*, 114, 121, 124, 126, 142, 146, 147, 151, 159, 159, 179, 220, 221, 243, 264, 312 ex*125*, 344, 370, 377, 385, 386, 390, 393, 394, 396, 398, 403, 404, 509 an*125*. Will Crowther (c. 1975) and Don Woods (1976). Ported to many formats, including *L9*, *TADS* and *ZM*. ◇

'Advent (430-point version)', 349. Extension by Don Woods (1978). ◇

'Advent (501-point version)', 349. Extension by David Long (1978). ◇ Also available in a *TADS* version (albeit out of 551 points) by David Picton. ◇

'Advent (550-point version)', 349. Extension by David Platt (1979). ◇

'Adventure Quest', 370, 389, 403. Mike, Nick and Pete Austin, Level 9 (1983). *L9*

'Adventureland', 2, 121, 151, 200, 200, 348, 349, 358, 393. Scott Adams, Adventure International (1978). *SA* ◇. Also an Inform version (1994). *ZM* ◇

'Alice Through the Looking-Glass', 2, 86, 121, 130, 142, 210, 221. Gareth Rees, Inform tutorial example, from the opening scenes of the novel by Lewis Carroll. *ZM* ◇

'Amnesia', 352, 378. Thomas M. Disch, Electronic Arts (1986).

'Asylum', 352. William Denman, Med Systems Software (1985).

'Aventura', 243, 264. Spanish translation of 'Advent' by Jose Luiz Diaz (1997). *ZM* ◇

'Avon', 367, 392. Jonathan Partington, Cambridge University (1982), Topologika.

'Balances', 2, 86, 121, 130, 135, 142, 151, 159, 193, 200, 210, 214, 221, 234, 236, 242. Graham Nelson (1994). *ZM* ◊

'Ballyhoo', 354, 372, 378, 383. Jeff O'Neill, Infocom (1985). *ZM*

'Beyond Zork', 42, 317, 371, 392. Brian Moriarty, Infocom (1987). *ZM*

'BJ Drifter', 374. Big Al (1998). *ZM* ◊

'Border Zone', 401. Marc Blank, Infocom (1987). *ZM*

'Brand X', 364, 392. Peter Killworth and Jonathan Mestel, Cambridge University (1983). Also *ZM* ◊. Evolved into 'Philosopher's Quest', *q.v.*

'Breakers', 355. Rod Smith, Joe Vierra and William Mataga, Synapse Software (1986).

'Brimstone: The Dream of Gawain', 356. James Paul, David Bunch and Bill Darrah, Synapse Software (1985).

'Castle of Riddles', 352. Peter Killworth, Acornsoft (1984).

'A Change in the Weather', 400. Andrew Plotkin (1995). *ZM* ◊

'Christminster', 115, 361, 372, 375, 377, 378, 381, 386, 387, 391, 400. Gareth Rees (1995). *ZM* ◊

'Coke Is It', 115. Lucian Smith, J. Robinson Wheeler, Michael Fessler, Adam Cadre, Dan Shiovitz and David Dyte (1999). *ZM* ◊

'Colossal Adventure', 349. Pete Austin's port of 'Advent' for Level 9 (1983). *L9*

'Colossal Cave', 75. Pete Austin's port of 'Advent' for Level 9 (1983). *L9*

'Cosmic Capers', 366. *See* 'HitchHiker-64'.

'CosmoServe', 360. Judith Pintar (1991). *AGT* ◊

'Countdown to Doom', 353. Peter Killworth, Acornsoft (1984) and subsequently Topologika.

'The Cove', 362. Kathleen M. Fischer (2000). *ZM* ◊

'The Crack of Doom', 380. Norton Truter, John Haward and Philip Mitchell, Melbourne House (1989), from *The Lord of the Rings* by J. R. R. Tolkien.

'The Creation', 144. Suggested but never-written Infocom game by Marc Blank.

'Crobe', 377, 385. Jonathan Partington, Cambridge University (1986). Also *ZM* ◊

'Curses', 38, 89, 105, 156 ex52, 187, 188, 203, 285, 334, 336, 361, 370, 370, 373, 375, 380, 394, 406, 439 an9, 462 an52. Graham Nelson (1993). *ZM* ◊

'Cutthroats', 397. Mike Berlyn and Jerry Wolper, Infocom (1984). *ZM*

'Dallas Quest', 351. James Garon, Datasoft (1984), from the television soap opera.

'Dog Star Adventure', 358. Lance Micklus (1979). ◊

'Dungeon Adventure', 370, 393. Mike, Nick and Pete Austin, Level 9 (1984). *L9*

'Edifice', 392, 395. Lucian Smith (1997). *ZM* ◊

'Enchanter', 35, 193, 349, 370, 371, 375, 381, 386, 394, 399. Marc Blank and Dave Lebling, Infocom (1983). *ZM*

'Essex', 356. Bill Darrah, Synapse Software (1985).

'Essex MUD', 346. Roy Trubshaw and Richard Bartle (1979).

'Fahrenheit 451', 351. Len Neufeld and Byron Preiss, Spinnaker/Telarium (1984), from the novel by Ray Bradbury.

'Feasibility Experiment', 399. Brian Howarth, Mysterious Adventures (1982). *SA* ◊

'Trinity', 114 ex*11*, 304, 312 ex*127*, 339, 354, 371, 375, 376, 379, 383, 389, 390, 391, 510 an*127*. Brian Moriarty, Infocom (1986). *ZM Sa2*

'Varicella', 391. Adam Cadre (1999). *ZM* ◇

'Winchester's Nightmare', 362. Nick Montfort (1999). *ZM* ◇

'Wishbringer', 354, 375, 394. Brian Moriarty, Infocom (1985). *ZM Sa2*

'Witness', 191 ex*59*, 466 an*59*. Stu Galley, Infocom (1983). *ZM*

'The Witness', 191 ex*59*, 366, 368, 369, 375, 376. Stu Galley, Infocom (1983). *ZM*

'Wonderland', 367. David Bishop, Magnetic Scrolls (1990), from the novel by Lewis Carroll.

'Yellow Peril', 363. Dorothy Millard (1994). ◇

'Zazie – Una lettura interattiva', 344. Luca Melchionna, from a novel by Raymond Queneau (1999). *ZM* ◇

'Zork', 149, 179, 193, 249, 339, 379. Timothy Anderson, Marc Blank, Bruce Daniels, Dave Lebling and others, MIT (1977--9). A public-domain version called 'Dungeon' (a name later regretted) was circulated to universities world-wide in 1978 and much imitated. Divided into three parts for a commercial release 1980--2, with final fragments appearing in 'Enchanter' and 'Sorcerer'. ◇

'Zork I', 142, 148 ex*42*, 149, 188, 233, 326, 385, 389, 390, 393, 404, 405. Subtitle 'The Great Underground Empire'. Marc Blank and Dave Lebling, Infocom (1980). *ZM Sa1 Sa2* (and a further version, the 'Mini-Zork I' file, is also ◇)

'Zork I: Das Große Unterweltreich', 243. Never-released German translation of 'Zork I' by Jeff O'Neill, Infocom (1989). *ZM*

'Zork II', 113 ex*8*, 364, 378, 383, 393, 393, 404. Subtitle 'The Wizard of Frobozz'. Marc Blank and Dave Lebling, Infocom (1981). *ZM*

'Zork III', 380, 386, 387, 403. Subtitle 'The Dungeon Master'. Marc Blank and Dave Lebling, Infocom (1982). *ZM*

'Zork: The Undiscovered Underground', 1. Mike Berlyn and Marc Blank, Activision under the Infocom label (1997), written to accompany the graphical game 'Zork: Grand Inquisitor'. *ZM*

'Zugzwang', 320. Magnus Olsson (1998). *ZM* ◇

Index of Exercises

The first page reference given is to the exercise and the second to the solution.

General Index

See also the index of exercises, the index of works of interactive fiction (except for 'Ruins' which has its entry in this index), and the appendices and tables. For detailed definitions of library rules, see the entry here on 'rules given in full'.

Statements, directives and names of things built-in to the Inform language are in typewriter font: thus `for` (statement), `Object` (directive), `random` (built-in function). Typewriter is also used for identifier names defined in the library, such as `score` (library variable) and `NextWord` (library routine). For such names, the page reference in bold face is to the detailed description in the Appendix. Verbs are double-quoted: thus "inventory" (library verb). Library files are written thus: `"linklpa.h"` (library file), ending ".h" even though on some operating systems the filenames omit these endings. Grammatical structures used by the parser are in angle brackets: ⟨noun phrase⟩.

A page reference in the form "123 ex7" means exercise number 7 on page 123. Similarly, "298 an7" means "answer to exercise 7 on page 298".

:: (superclass operator), 64.
' (character constants), 10.
' (dictionary words), 10.
" (double-quotation mark), 7.
@ (for assembly opcodes), 306.
! (comment character), 6.
! (ICL comment character), 287.
* (marking a routine to watch), 104.
* (multiplication operator), 13.
+ (addition operator), 13.
+ (setting pathnames in ICL), 288.
++ (increment operator), 15.
, (join assignments operator), 26.
- (subtraction operator), 13.
- (unary minus operator), 14.
-- (decrement operator), 15.
--> (array operator), 40.
-> (byte array operator), 42.
-> (in grammar lines), 217.

-> (indicating object parentage), 51.
-> (store result of opcode), 306.
-D (Debugging switch), 95, 96.
-e (economy mode switch), 334.
-i (ignore `Switches` switch), 287.
-k (debugging info switch), 105.
-M (module switch), 281.
-s (statistics switch), 285.
-S (Strict mode switch), 6, 96, 100.
-U (use modules switch), 281.
-v (story file version switch), 305.
-X (Infix switch), 96.
-x (row of hashes switch), 285.
. (label marker), 36.
. (property operator), 56.
.# (property array size operator), 58.
.& (property array operator), 57.
/ (dividing prepositions), 223.
/ (division operator), 13.

characters legal in unquoted Inform
  source code, 294.
Charlotte's game, 140 ex*29*, 449 an*29*.
Chaucer, Geoffrey, 348.
`child` (built-in function), 50.
`children` (built-in function), 50.
`ChooseObjects` (entry point routine),
  239, **431**.
circumflex accents, 29.
Clarke, Amanda, 174.
Clarke, Arthur C., 351.
`Class` (built-in metaclass), 49, 65.
`Class` (directive), 60.
`class` (part of `Object` statement), 61.
classes:
  and additive properties, 86.
  defined, 48.
  example of, 84.
  inheritance rules, 86.
Clavell, James, 366.
clearing the screen, 311.
Cleese, John, 326.
Clinton, William J., 30.
`clothing` (library attribute), 116, **408**.
`"clothing.h"` (library extension), 117.
Clover, Andrew, 143, 151, 230.
clues, 392.
`"cmap.h"` (library extension), 114.
Coconut of Quendor, 371.
code blocks, 21.
Coe, Michael D., 174.
Collatz, Lothar, 27.
colours, 311.
⟨command⟩, 245.
command line syntax, 286.
comments, 6.
common properties, 56, 70.
`CommonAncestor` (library routine), **419**.
`Compass` (library object), 261.
compass rose, 312 ex*126*, 509 an*126*.
`CompassDirection` (library class), 113,
  261.
compilation, 5.

`compile` (ICL command), 288.
compiler error, 290.
component parts of objects, 236.
CompuServe, 360.
Conan Doyle, Sir Arthur, 367, 368,
  390.
"conan, put every sword into the box"
  (parsing example), 250.
`concealed` (library attribute), 108, **408**.
conditional compilation, 278.
conditions, 18.
conjunction (in parsing), 246.
connection of possessive adjectives to
  pronouns, 265.
⟨connective⟩, 246.
constant, 10.
`Constant` (directive), 39.
`consult_from` (library variable), 131.
`##Consult` (library action), 131.
`consult_words` (library variable), 131.
`container` (library attribute), 118, **408**.
Contention of Ajax and Ulysses, The, 87.
continents, 43.
`continue` (statement), 26.
contraction forms, 271.
`"converse.h"` (library extension), 333.
Coolidge, Calvin, 397.
`copy` (built-in message), 66.
copyright message (of a game), 75.
copyright on Inform, ii.
copyright symbol, 261.
Cornelson, David, 4, 236, 362.
Covington, Alan, 346.
`create` (built-in message), 66.
creating data structures, 38.
creating objects during play, 65.
`creature` (grammar token), 222.
Cree, Graeme, 366, 368.
Crimes Against Mimesis, 365.
Croft, Lara, 157 ex*55*.
Cross, Duncan, 4.
Crowther, Patricia, 343.
Crowther, Will, 3, 4, 75, 343, 393.

Mayan, 114 ex*9*.
Nalian, 392.
Norwegian, 267, 269.
Norwegian, rural dialects of, 269.
of the Pacific rim, 30.
Old English, 254, 254.
Russian, 266.
Spanish, 243, 248, 252, 264, 267, 269.
Swedish, 255 ex*109*, 501 an*109*.
Swiss French (dialect of French), 258.
Tagalog, 248.
Lanz, Volker, 143.
Laskey, Mike, 360.
Last Lousy Point, 403.
last (part of Extend directive), 219.
Latin, 246, 252, 253, 267, 269, 272 ex*118*, 506 an*118*.
Leary, Dave, 361.
Lebling, P. David, 3, 249, 305, 321, 339, 376, 378, 380, 383, 390, 392, 402, 405.
Legend Entertainment, 357.
LeGuin, Ursula K., 370.
Les plaisirs de la porte, 122.
##LetGo (library fake action), 119.
Letwin, Gordon, 349.
Level 9, 114 ex*10*, 351.
Lewis, C. S., 106, 147, 369, 376.
Lewis, Tony, 105.
Leyendas de Guatemala, 167.
library, 5.
library messages, 190.
 catalogued, 426.
library routines, 419.
LibraryMessages (library object), 190.
life (library property), 134, **415**.
ligatures, 29.
light, 144.
 daylight, 150 ex*48*, 461 an*48*.
light (library attribute), 78, 145, **409**.
light source puzzles, 386.

line break (white space), 6.
Link (directive), 281.
linking, 281.
"linklpa.h" (library file), 282.
"linklv.h" (library file), 283.
"links.h" (library extension), 126.
list style, 201.
list_together (library property), 203, **415**.
"Lister.h" (library extension), 205, 277.
listing_together (library variable), 204.
Little Women, 215.
Liz Cyr-Jones, 350.
lm_n (library variable), 190.
lm_o (library variable), 191.
local variables, 11.
Locale (library routine), 200, **420**.
location (library variable), 75.
lockable (library attribute), **409**.
locked (library attribute), 119, **409**.
Long Count of Mayan time, 233.
long jump, 319.
Long, David, 349.
"longint.h" (function library), 36.
Look, 198.
"look inside", 120.
lookmode (library variable), 469 an*65*.
LookRoutine (entry point routine), 199, **433**.
LoopOverScope (library routine), 232, **421**.
LOOPOVERSCOPE_REASON (library constant), 235.
loops, in object tree, 52.
Lovecraft, H. P., 354.
LTI_Insert (library routine), 268, **421**.
luck, 393.

McCaffrey, Anne, 366.
McCarthy, C. A., 376.
McLean, Don, 342.

Mac OS, 286.

Macbeth, 152.

machinery puzzles, 387.

MacNeice, Louis, 435.

magic, 369.

Magnetic Scrolls, 351.

Maharg, Noslen, 142 ex*38*.

Main (compulsory routine), 7.

@make_menu (assembly opcode), 318.

"makemaze.inf" (example game), 114.

making grammar, 92.

male (library attribute), 195, 269, **409**.

Malmberg, David R., 359, 360.

Mammoth Cave, 75, 342.

"manual.h" (library extension), 333.

map connections, 112.

Master Game, 379.

master-list of commands, 97.

Mataga, William, 355, 356.

MAX_CARRIED (library constant), 160.

MAX_SCORE (library constant), 162.

MAX_TIMERS (library constant), 148.

Maya directions, 439 an*9*.

Mayan dictionary, 132.

mazes, 385.

⟨me-word⟩, 249, 262.

"megalook" verb, 232 ex*98*, 493 an*98*.

Meier, Stefan, 363.

Melbourne House, 249, 351, 380.

Melchionna, Luca, 344.

members, 60.

memory, 288.

 compiler settings, 288.

 maximum size of game, 334.

 needed by compiler, 288.

 small, large or huge, 288.

memory settings, 286.

Menick, Jim, 363.

Menu (library class), 327.

menu of text options, 326.

"Menus.h" (optional library file), 326.

Merchant of Venice, The, 367.

Meretzky, Steve, 357, 370, 379, 395, 397.

Merical, Joe, 193.

Merry Wives of Windsor, The, 367.

Message (directive), 280.

messages, 62.

 macaw example, 84.

 maximum parameters, 338.

 to routines, strings and classes, 69.

 tracing all messages sent, 99.

"messages" (library verb), 62, 99.

Mestel, Jonathan, 364, 396.

'meta' actions, 90.

meta (part of Verb directive), 217.

metaclass (built-in function), 49.

Metaclass (imaginary directive), 72.

metaclass, definition of, 49.

Micklus, Lance, 358.

Micro Adventurer, 350.

mid-air location, 150 ex*49*.

middle game, 377.

midnight, 150 ex*47*.

Mikado, The, 201.

Milton, Marcus, 358.

MIT Dynamic Modelling Group, 350.

Mitchell, Philip, 380.

MMULTI_PE (library constant), 237.

MOD file, 324.

modular extensions, 190.

modules, 281.

"money.h" (library extension), 193.

Montaigne, Michel de, 134.

Montfort, Nick, 4, 362.

Monty Python's Flying Circus, 118.

mood mazes, 391.

moon rainbow, 364.

Moriarty, Brian, 349, 354, 371, 376, 394, 402.

Moskowitz, Denis, 117.

mouse clicks, 520.

@mouse_window (assembly opcode), 318.

move (statement), 51.

@move_window (assembly opcode), 313.
"MoveClass.h" (library extension),
    143.
moved (library attribute), **409**.
MoveFloatingObjects (library
    routine), 109, **421**.
"movie.h" (library extension), 193.
moving all objects in one place to
    another, 54.
MULTI_PE (library constant), 237.
multiexcept (grammar token), 222.
multiheld (grammar token), 222.
Murie, Andrew C., 236.
Murphy, Jamie, 244.

n_to (library property), **412**.
nagual, 157 ex*53*.
⟨name⟩, 248.
name (library property), 106, 206, 248,
    416.
(name) (built-in printing rule), 31.
names per object (limit), 338.
Naming of Cats, The, 206.
Nardinocchi, Ilario, 243.
narrator, 368.
Nation, Terry, 140.
ne_to (library property), **412**.
Nelson, Admiral Lord Horatio, 445
    an*23*.
Nelson, Graham, ii, 4, 359, 361.
Nelson, Toby, 4.
neuter (library attribute), 195, 269,
    409.
neutral form (German), 257.
new_line (statement), 33.
New Testament, 132 ex*25*, 446 an*25*.
New York Times, The, 1.
Newell, Bob, 4, 243.
NewRoom (entry point routine), 155,
    433.
Newton, Isaac, 67.
NextWord (library routine), 207, **421**.

NextWordStopped (library routine),
    227, **421**.
Nilsson, Thomas, 359, 364, 372.
Niven, Larry, 353.
NO_PLACES (library constant), 164.
⟨no-word⟩, 262.
nominative pronouns, 277 ex*121*, 467
    an*62*.
Norwegian, 267, 269.
    rural dialects of, 269.
nose, 236 ex*102*, 497 an*102*.
NOTHELD_PE (library constant), 237.
nothing (built-in constant), 49.
NOTHING_PE (library constant), 237.
notify_mode (library variable), 163.
"notify" verb, 163.
notin (object not in this? operator),
    53.
##NotUnderstood (library fake action),
    138.
⟨noun⟩, 248.
noun (library variable), 89, 225.
⟨noun phrase⟩, 246.
noun phrases:
    animation, 247.
    definite and indefinite, 247.
    gender, 247.
    GNA, 247.
    number, 247.
    quantity, 247.
NounDomain (library routine), **421**.
"NPCEngine" (library extension), 143.
⟨number⟩, 246.
number base, 9.
number (library property), **416**.
NUMBER_PE (library constant), 237.
NUMBER_TASKS (library constant), 162.
number (grammar token), 222.
numbers, 9.
nw_to (library property), **412**.

object 31, 210 ex*76*.
Object (built-in metaclass), 49.

animals, 390.
capacity and exhaustion, 386.
clues to, 392.
conversation, 391.
decipherment, 392.
earth and digging, 389.
fire, 388.
keys and doors, 387.
light source, 386.
luck and randomness, 393.
machinery, 387.
mazes, 385.
monsters, 390.
optional puzzles, 394.
people, 390.
plants, 390.
rewards for solving, 394.
riddles, 392.
ropes and chains, 392.
timed, 386.
utility objects, 387.
vehicles, 388.
water, 388.

Queneau, Raymond, 344.
questions, asking yes or no, 164.
questions, parsing the player's, 233.
Quill, The, 358.
Quirie, Duncan, 358.
quit (statement), 36.
quotation marks (European), 29.
quotations beautiful, 165.
quoted text, 489 an*90*.

radix, 9.
Raleigh, Sir Walter, 364.
random (built-in function), 35, 295.
"random" (library verb), 97.
random numbers, 34.
Raszewski, L. Ross, 37, 46, 73, 95,
    124, 193, 230, 236, 320, 333, 337.
Ravenous Bugblatter Beast of Traal,
    366.

Ravipinto, Daniel, 380.
reached, statement which cannot be,
    31.
react_after (library property), 94,
    137, **417**.
REACT_AFTER_REASON (library
    constant), 235.
react_before (library property), 93,
    109, 137, **417**, 436 an*3*.
REACT_BEFORE_REASON (library
    constant), 235.
@read_char (assembly opcode), 316.
@read_mouse (assembly opcode), 318.
read (statement), 44.
"read" versus "examine", 133.
reading books, 131.
real_location (library variable), 145.
reasons for scope searching, 235.
receive_action (library variable),
    120.
##Receive (library fake action), 119.
"recording" (library verb), 97.
recreate (built-in message), 66.
recursion, 18, 21.
    limit to extent of, 338.
Redrup, Bob, 385.
Reed, Ken, 358.
Rees, Gareth, 2, 4, 78, 142, 143, 205,
    361, 372, 378, 381, 383.
Release (directive), 283.
remainder, 13.
remaining (built-in message), 66.
##Remove (library action), 89.
remove (statement), 52.
Rendezvous with Rama, 353.
Rennie, John, 389.
Replace (directive), 191, 280.
replace (part of Extend directive),
    219.
replacing grammar, 219.
"replay" (library verb), 97.
resolution of dictionary, 207, 259, 337.
resolving ambiguity, 239.

@restore (assembly opcode), 319.
restore (statement), 36.
resurrection, 159.
return (statement), 18.
return values, 16.
reverse (part of Verb directive), 218.
rewards for solving puzzles, 394.
rfalse (statement), 18.
Rian, Jørund, 4.
Riccardi, Giovanni, 243.
Rice, Grantland, 160.
Richard Dyer, 350.
Richards, Matthew, 3.
Richie, Stuart, 352.
riddles, 392.
ring accents, 29.
Ritchie, Dennis, 22.
Rivals, The, 188.
Roberts, Mike, 1, 359, 361, 367, 386,
    388, 395.
Robertson, Evin, 46.
Rodgers, Steve, 358.
Romeo and Juliet, 28.
room descriptions, 198.
ROOM_SCORE (library constant), 162.
"room", etymology of, 76.
ropes and chains, 392.
Rothstein, Edward, 1.
Routine (built-in metaclass), 49, 69.
routines, 16.
    as property values, 57, 83.
    marking to be watched, without Infix
        (trace routines switch), 104.
    maximum depth of recursion, 338.
    simple example of, 79.
    see also interrupt routines.
*Royal Society For Putting Things On Top
    Of Other Things, The*, 118.
rtrue (statement), 18.
'Ruins', 74, 369.
    DeathMessage entry point, 158.
    Initialise entry point, 153.
    PhotographSub action routine, 92.

PrintRank entry point, 163.
Treasure class, 84.
Antechamber, 171.
    iron cage, 463 an55.
    skeletons, 463 an55.
Burial Shaft, 463 an55.
    ancient honeycomb, 85.
ending, 174.
Forest, 74.
    month-old newspaper, 166.
    mushroom, 77, 435 an1.
    packing case, 118.
    red-tailed macaw, 83.
    speckled mushroom, 167.
    stone-cut steps, 80, 83.
    wet-plate camera, 92.
iron cage, 445 an22.
lattice diagram, 381.
low mist, 108.
Lower End of Canyon, 172.
    horrifying chasm, 119, 158.
map of game, 168.
player's initial possessions, 153.
    Mayan dictionary, 131.
    sketch map of Quintana Roo, 166.
    sodium lamp, 125.
Pumice-Stone Ledge, 173.
    incised bone, 173.
scoring system, 84.
Shrine, 170.
    mummified priest, 135, 138.
    paintings, 170.
    slab altar, 127.
sound of scuttling claws, 149 ex45.
Square Chamber, 81 ex2, 106.
    carved inscriptions, 107.
    shaft of sunlight, 107.
Stooped Corridor, 123.
    pygmy statuette, 85.
    stone door, 122.
title page, 508 an123.
transformed to *wayhel*, 157 ex53.
Upper End of Canyon, 172.

Wuthering Heights, 167.
Wyber, Brendon, 361.

Xarfaggio's Physical Malepsy, 370.
XYZZY, nothing happens.
XYZZYnews, 1.

Y2, 393.
Yans, Cynthia, 360.
Yeandle, Graeme, 358.
⟨yes-word⟩, 262.
"yesno.h" (library extension), 95.
YesOrNo, 164.
YesOrNo (library routine), 425.
"you don't need to refer to", 106.

Z-machine:
    assembly language, 306.
    encoding text for dictionary, 317.

introduction to, 304.
limitations of, 334.
memory architecture of, 307.
stack, 307.
versions of, 305, 334.
Z-characters, 259.
Z-machine standard, 5.
    testing adherence to, 308.
Z-Machine Standard Code for
    Information Interchange, *see* ZSCII.
Z-Machine Standards Document, The, 2.
Zazie dans le métro, 344.
Zcharacter (directive), 260, 317.
ZIL, 304.
"znsi.h", 46.
Zork Implementation Language, 304.
ZSCII, 10, 260.
ZSCII value, 519.
Zwissler, A. M. F., 492 an96.

Colophon

This edition was begun on a beige Acorn Risc PC700 in 1999 and finished on a lime green Apple iMac DV in 2001, in the attic of a North Oxford town house (just across the road from the one in which Tolkien wrote *The Lord of the Rings*). The text was set in Monotype Plantin, a font based on designs by Christophe Plantin of Antwerp (1514–89), augmented by Computer Modern Roman typewriter by Donald Knuth (1938–). The printer's ornaments are with one exception detailed from works of Albrecht Dürer (1471–1528): Chapter I, *Melancholia I* (engraving, 1514); Chapter II, *The Wire-Drawing Mill* (watercolour and gouache on paper, 1489); Chapter III, *St Jerome in his Study* (engraving, 1514); Chapter IV, *Portrait of a Young Venetian Woman* (oils on wood panel, 1505); Chapter V, *Traumgesicht* (ink on paper, 1525); Chapter VI, *The Large Turf* (watercolour and gouache on paper, 1503); Chapter VII, *The Knight, Death and the Devil* (engraving, 1513); Chapter VIII, *Wing of a Roller* (watercolour and gouache on vellum, 1512). The ornament to §23 is believed to be *tzutz*, the Mayan verb for completion. Type was set using CMacTEX3.6, Tom Kiffe's port of Knuth's program (1983), employing macros adapted from those used to typeset *The TEXbook* (though sadly not the \plugh macro in that work's Appendix D). Indices and bibliography were prepared automatically by scripts written in MacPerl 5, Matthias Neeracher's port of Larry Wall's formatting language. Final PDF was distilled using dvipdfm by Mark A. Wicks, and the book was printed from PDF by DeHARTs Printing of Silicon Valley.

facilis descensus Averno
noctes atque dies patet atri ianua Ditis
sed revocare gradum superasque evadere ad auras
hoc opus, hic labor est... latet arbore opaca
aureus et foliis et lento vimine ramus...